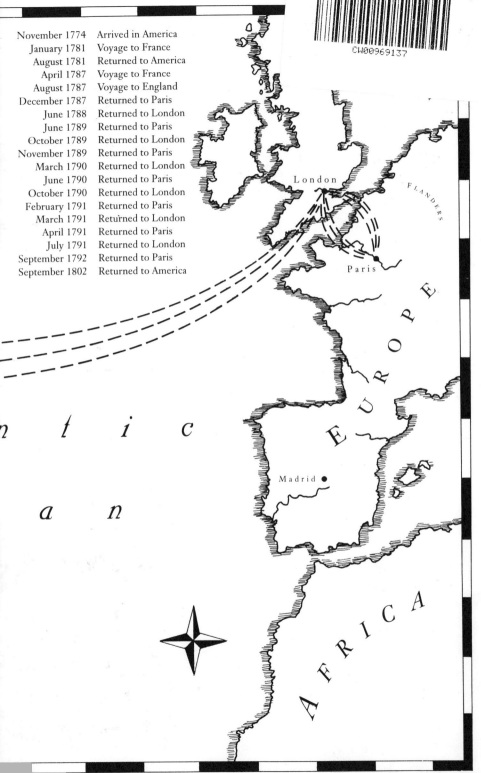

London

Paris

FLANDERS

EUROPE

Madrid

AFRICA

n t i c

a n

Map by Christopher Brunt

Born: 1737

THOMAS PAINE
Apostle of Freedom

THOMAS PAINE
Apostle of Freedom

By Jack Fruchtman, Jr.

Four Walls Eight Windows, New York/London

Published in the United States by:
Four Walls Eight Windows
39 West 14th Street, room 503
New York, N.Y., 10011

U.K. offices:
Four Walls Eight Windows/Turnaround
27 Horsell Road
London, N51 XL, England

First printing November 1994.

Library of Congress Cataloging-in-Publication Data:
Fruchtman, Jack.
Thomas Paine: apostle of freedom/ by Jack Fruchtman, Jr.
p.   cm.
Includes bibliographical references and index.
ISBN: 0-941423-94-8
1. Paine, Thomas, 1737-1809. 2. Political scientists—United States—Biography. 3.
Revolutionaries—United States—Biography.
I. Title.
JC178.V2F78 1994
320.5'1'092—dc20
[B]
94-22790
CIP

Printed in the United States

10 9 8 7 6 5 4 3 2 1

Text design by HelioTrope

To my father and in memory of my mother

"Thomas Paine, one of the founders of American Independence, whose extraordinary genius must ever command attention and whose writings have summoned to action the minds of the most enlightened politicians of Europe! How different this Apostle of Freedom from those gorgeous mansions tenanted by the founders of the French Republic!"

—Henry Redhead Yorke, 1802

Table of Contents

Abbreviations

AJ   *Agrarian Justice* (1795-96), in *CW*, vol. 1.

AR   *The Age of Reason*, Part One (1794); Part Two (1796), edited by Philip S. Foner (New York: Citadel Press, 1974), also in *CW*, vol. 1.

CS   *Common Sense* (1776), edited by Isaac Kramnick (Harmondsworth: Penguin, 1976), also in *CW*, vol. 1.

CW   *The Complete Writings of Thomas Paine*, edited by Philip S. Foner, Two Vols. (New York: Citadel Press, 1945). Unless otherwise noted, this collection was used for this study.

DF   *Decline and Fall of the English System of Finance* (1796), in *CW*, vol. 2.

GW   *Letter to George Washington* (1796), in *CW*, vol. 2.

RM   *Rights of Man*, Part One, 1791; Part Two, 1792, edited by Henry Collins, with an introduction by Eric Foner (Harmondsworth: Penguin, 1984), also in *CW*, vol 1.

Note: the grammar and spelling have all been modernized in the quotations, with the exception of the poetry.

List of Illustrations

Thomas Paine, engraving by William Sharp after a portrait in oil by George Romney, 1792. (Courtesy of the Collection of The New-York Historical Society)

John Locke (1632-1704). (Courtesy of The Mansell Collection, London)

Augustus Henry, the Duke of Grafton (1735-1811). (Williamson, *Thomas Paine: His Life, Work and Times*, 1973)

Privateer advertisement from the *New York Mercury*, December 4, 1758, during the Seven Years War. (Courtesy of the Collection of the New-York Historical Society)

Philadelphia in the late eighteenth century by W. Birch, 1799. (Courtesy of the Collection The New-York Historical Society)

First edition of *Common Sense*, 1776. (Courtesy of The American Philosophical Society)

Benjamin Franklin (1706-1790) by Joseph Siffred Duplessis, 1778. (Courtesy of The Fogg Museum, Harvard University Art Museums)

Gouverneur Morris (1752-1816) and Robert Morris (1734-1806) by Charles Willson Peale. (Courtesy of The Pennsylvania Academy of Fine Arts, Philadelphia. Bequest of Richard Ashhurst.)

The Marquis de Lafayette (1757-1834) during the American Revolution. (Courtesy of The Collection of The New-York Historical Society)

George Washington (1732-1799) by Charles Willson Peale. (Courtesy of the Collection of The New-York Historical Society)

John Adams (1735-1826). (Courtesy of the Collection of The New-York Historical Society)

Thomas Jefferson (1743-1826) by Rembrandt Peale. (Courtesy of the Collection of The New-York Historical Society)

Bridge, modeled on Paine's design, over the Wear River in Sutherland, England. (Williamson, *Thomas Paine: His Life, Work and Times*, 1973)

"Arrest of Louis XVI and Marie Antoinette at Varennes," June 1791. (Courtesy of the Musée Carnavalet)

"A Democrat" with Paine's Rights of Man in his pocket. (Courtesy of The British Museum)

Calendrier Perpétuel, designed by Philippe François Fabre D'Eglantine (1755-1794). (Courtesy of the Musée Carnavalet)

"The Rights of Man, or Tommy Paine, the little American tailor, taking the measure of the crown for a new pair of revolution breeches" by James Gillray, 1791. (Courtesy of The British Museum)

"Sedition, Levelling, and Plundering;" or, the pretended friends of the people in council," depicting a conspiring Joseph Priestley (1733-1804) and Paine, by Isaac Cruikshank, 1792. (Courtesy of The British Museum)

Last portrait of Louis XVI by Ducreux, 1793. (Courtesy of the Musée Carnavalet)

Execution of Louis XVI, January 21, 1793. (Courtesy of the Musée Carnavalet)

"Fashion Before Ease" by James Gillray, 1793. (Courtesy of The American Philosophical Society)

Georges Jacques Danton (1759-1794) on his way to execution, by Wille, 1794. (Courtesy of the Musée Carnavalet)

"Cool Arguments!!!" depicting defense counsel Thomas Erskine. (1750-1823), by Isaac Cruikshank, 1794. (Courtesy of The British Museum)

"Tom Paine's Nightly Pest" by James Gillray. (Courtesy of The British Museum)

"Mad Tom's first practical essay on the rights of man," by Isaac Cruikshank, 1797. (Courtesy of The British Museum)

"The Repeal of the Test Act" with Paine, in profile, standing on the right, Richard Price (1723-1791), above him on the pulpit, with his hand held up, and Joseph Priestley immediately on Price's right breathing fire and smoke. (Courtesy of The British Museum)

"Who Wants Me", depicting the radical Paine writing titles that allude to his works, by Isaac Cruikshank. (Courtesy of The American Philosophical Society)

Part 1, *Rights of Man*, 1792. (Courtesy of The American Philosophical Society)

Thomas Paine by John Wesley Jarvis, 1806. (Courtesy of the Collection of The New-York Historical Society)

Paine's New Rochelle cottage, c. 1812. (Courtesy of the Collection of The New-York Historical Society)

293 Bleecker Street, New York, Paine's residence Winter 1808-09, photograph from 1903. (Courtesy of the Collection of The New-York Historical Society)

"Paine, Sin and the Devil," a letter from Satan to Paine with an allusion to Joseph Priestley. (Courtesy of The British Museum)

"The political champion turned resurrection man," depicting William Cobbett (1763?-1835) with Paine's bones. (Courtesy of The British Museum)

Author's Note and Acknowledgements

My interest in Thomas Paine dates back nearly thirty-five years to my freshman year in college, when I first encountered the small but powerful volume *Common Sense*. This work comprised Paine's brilliant argument of why America had to separate from Great Britain. Interest in eighteenth-century studies as the central focus of my scholarly research dates from a later moment, most particularly when I fell under the influence of the remarkable J.G.A. Pocock at Johns Hopkins University, who has been for more than fifteen years a model, a mentor and a friend. My first published works on the eighteenth century stemmed from the interest John Pocock took in my earliest explorations into the relationship between religion and politics of the period. The fruits of this investigation became the subject of several articles on late-eighteenth century radicalism as well as two book-length scholarly studies, one on Paine himself: *Thomas Paine and the Religion of Nature*.

In writing this book, I have had the support and encouragement of several people. Whatever shortcomings exist here are my own responsibility. Above all, I wish to acknowledge the distinguished contributions of Moncure Daniel Conway, A.Owen Aldridge, David Freeman Hawke, Bernard Vincent, and especially Eric Foner. They, more than anyone, have allowed those of us who followed to carry Paine studies onward, seeking an understanding of more complex patterns in his life and thought. In addition, I wish to thank Mary Gallagher and Elizabeth Nuxoll, editors of *The Papers of*

Robert Morris, who have focused my attention on heretofore unrecognized Paine materials and helped me understand eighteenth century monetary equivalents in the late twentieth-century.   Isaac Kramnick of Cornell, Wilson Carey McWilliams of Rutgers, and James R. Stoner of Louisiana State have been supporters of my work on Paine, and for that I am deeply grateful. H. George Hahn, my colleague at Towson State, was especially helpful in suggesting several works about the British Navy. I appreciate Bill Jordan's introduction to my editor, John Oakes, at Four Walls Eight Windows, who, with the most sympathetic pen, understood my goals in writing this new biography of an extraordinary figure and devoted generous amounts of time to seeing it completed. I also appreciate the support of Dan Simon at Four Walls as well as JillEllyn Riley, who worked indefatigably to accomplish so many tasks associated with the production of this book. Herbert Goldman has provided me over the years with the most constant support and wise counsel.

JoAnn Fruchtman, my best friend and best critic, helped in innumerable ways, including reading the manuscript at various stages of development, but most of all by just being there. Our daughters, Liana, Shira, and Hannah, were always patient with me as I worked on my Paine projects for what to them must have seemed like a millennium. Finally, a special note of gratitude to all the folks at Gay Head, who indulged my incessant preoccupation with the charms and frustrations of writing a second book on Thomas Paine.

Jack Fruchtman, Jr.
Gay Head, Massachusetts
July 1994

1 · Introduction

Thomas Paine has long been a controversial figure. He has attracted both scholarly and popular interest and will continue to do so, thanks to his spirited involvement in the major social and political issues of the late eighteenth and early nineteenth centuries. He wrote and said things that distinguished him as one of the great original thinkers, whose observations seem intensely relevant even today. But Thomas Paine was not a political philosopher. He was a progressive journalist and statesman who thought that his duty was to expose wrongs as well as all the stupidities and frailties of his fellow human beings. As he once wrote, in defense of his life's work: "My motive and object in all my political works . . . have been to rescue man from tyranny and false systems and false principles of government, and enable him to be free." He said the same about his writings on religion. He undertook them "to bring man to a right reason that God has given him [and] to impress on him the great principles of divine morality, justice, mercy, and a benevolent disposition to all men and to all creatures."[1]

Paine's political and religious tracts and pamphlets never fell into the category of pure objective journalism. They were incisive, though biting, commentaries and criticism. He attacked anything that seemed to him to sidetrack humanity's long struggle for the common good, liberty and rights of all people, especially those who were the victims of tyranny and terror, slavery and poverty. Most of the time he wrote simply because he was moved; at other times, because he was paid. In either case, he claimed that he always wrote from deep personal conviction and belief, and this was surely true. A man of compassion, he never capitalized on the marvelous success of his principal works. As a result, he received very little money for the work he did on behalf of American, British, or French liberty. He wrote because he thought he had to do his part, no matter how small, to serve the cause of human progress in the world.

To ascribe the word "apostle" to Thomas Paine, even when it is linked to freedom, is to emphasize the essentially religious character of his work. Beneath his criticisms of organized religion lay an abounding faith and belief in the wonders of God's universal creation. He truly thought he was undertaking God's work on earth: to better the condition of human beings everywhere. Paine held that a person could believe in God, could believe that the spirit of the divine permeated every aspect of the universe, and at the same time deny that the teachings of organized religion possessed more than a particle of truth. As he once put it: "The great Father of all is pleased with variety of devotion, and that the greatest offense we can act is that by which we seek to torment and render each other miserable. For my own part, I am fully satisfied that what I am now doing, with an endeavor to conciliate mankind, to render their condition happy, to unite nations that have hitherto been enemies, and to extirpate the horrid practice of war, and break the chains of slavery and oppression, is acceptable in His sight, and being the best service I can perform, I act it cheerfully." (*RM* 271) Paine's task, as he saw it, was to spread not a divine message revealed specially to him, but the political and social message that human beings could improve their living conditions when they acknowledged the godliness of life itself and their own creative abilities to transform political and social evils into liberty, equality, and justice.

Throughout his long life (he lived to be seventy-two), Paine had several careers, but it was as a journalist that he became an international figure both deeply admired and just as deeply despised. He made his debut on the political scene in 1776, with the appearance of his first influential work, *Common Sense*. The range of Paine's interests and activities became so great it is no wonder that in recent years scholars have paid increased attention to his political thought. Beginning in 1976, with the appearance of a major re-evaluation of his revolutionary ideas by Eric Foner, there have been five recent studies which analyze his political thought from varying perspectives.[2] These works, each with their own individual virtues, are hardly biographical.[3] His life, as opposed to his work, has not been the central focus of intellectual historians and political theorists.[4]

But Paine's life and work were inseparable. He was no armchair critic, because he was as much a political actor as he was writer and critic. He often suffered for his involvement: his enemies viciously attacked or ridiculed him or tried to ignore him; worst of all, for ten months, he was imprisoned in France under horrible and frightening conditions.

The approach taken here is to fill a void in Painite studies. The critical analyses of Paine seem to isolate one particular aspect of his thinking during a given period of his life. Foner, for example, whose work on Paine is splendid, chose to focus on the man as a radical thinker engaged in the social and political context of revolutionary America. A. Owen Aldridge, perhaps the most persistent Paine scholar ever, has provided us with a general description of the influences on Paine's thinking in America before the Revolution. David Wilson has prepared a comparative study of Paine and Cobbett, who was at first an enemy of Paine, later his disciple, and Gregory Claeys has primarily centered his attention on Paine's *Rights of Man*. In my own earlier work I, too, explored a single theme, Paine's religion of nature, which I believe figured pivotally and significantly throughout his work. As for the biographies in print, they present an account of Paine's life with little or no interpretation of how his thinking evolved over time, or especially of how his views evolved in France before and after his imprisonment.

Historians and commentators have failed to determine how Paine's ideas fit ideologically with the radicalism of the late eighteenth century. John Pocock has summarized the frustration of several of his colleagues when he wrote that Paine

> remains difficult to fit into any kind of category. *Common Sense* breathes an extraordinary hatred of English governing institutions, but it does not consistently echo any established radical vocabulary; Paine had no real place in the club of Honest Whigs to which Franklin had introduced him in London, and his use

of anti-Normanism to insist that Britain did not have a constitution but rather a tyranny does not permit us to think of him (as contemporaries might have) as a New Model soldier risen from the grave. Moreover, when the Revolutionary War was over Paine returned to live under "the royal brute of Britain" as if nothing had happened, nor was he pursued by the authorities until the very different circumstances of 1791.[5]

My intention is to show why this assessment, which others have reflected in their work on Paine, is misleading and how it misses the point of Paine's life and work.

There are no disparities between Paine's daily activities and his political and religious principles. This was what made him a true "apostle of freedom." The overall theme here is that Paine's life as a journalist, which was something he came to quite by accident in 1775, imparted to him much of his character and style. His approach to journalism was far from scholarly. He deliberately used his pen as a weapon to tear away the fabric of tyranny wherever he saw it: monarchy, when he argued that kings were no better than the lowliest of God's creatures; religious superstition, when he examined how the Church tried to control the mind with fantasies and falsehoods; and slavery, when he saw how it flourished even in America. He attacked when he felt he needed to, and when that failed, he worked with those whom he thought made a difference—but always according to the principles he held.

One result of his journalism and his political action was that he was constantly on the move. From England, where he was born, he moved to America, then to France, followed by a trip to England, then he shuttled back and forth between England and France several times before he settled for ten years in France, before his final return to America 1802, where he died seven years later. He himself once said that he was a wanderer, and indeed he was. The very idea of wandering was emblematic of his lifestyle, his quest for what he thought was right. But Paine was a wanderer in another sense. His political and social ideas also developed in ways that mirrored a wandering lifestyle. From his arrival in Philadelphia in 1774 until his death in New York thirty-five years later, we can detect four stages of development in his political and social ideas. He began with the perspective of Lockean liberal ideas and classical republican thought. In France, he was led to appreciate Rousseau's ideas of community and virtue. His third phase came at the end of the Reign of Terror, when he found a new spirituality where he sought God's wholeness and oneness in the universe.[6] Unfortunately this spirituality did not last during his final years in America, when he fell into the fourth and the darkest, unhappiest phase of his life and thought.

And yet, there is a constant thread through all of these stages: Paine's underlying faith that God's spirit and vitality permeated the universe. In this context, the stage I refer to as the spiritual explains in far more penetrating ways Paine's French experience, especially that period from 1793 to 1802, when he returned to America. These years saw Paine's well-known attacks on the Bible, and the established Church, and all of organized religion, as well as his encounters and friendships with radical journalists and his association with the members of a group called the Social Circle, which dabbled in spiritualism and Illuminism.[7]

I use the term *spirituality* here for lack of a better term. Even in Paine's earliest published works, such as *Common Sense* in 1776, he used Biblical and prophetic imagery to distinguish the natural inclinations of human beings from the evils of monarchy and aristocracy. But his views were never religious in the traditional meaning of that word. If anything, he was not merely a deist, one who believed that God had created the universe and then left it to humanity to better it or destroy it, but a pantheist, someone who believed that the spirit of God, a power beyond human capacity to comprehend fully, was present in every aspect of life on earth.[8] This belief became most clearly focused in the late 1790s, with Paine's association with members of the Social Club, who thought they could open the farthest reaches of the mind and soul to the goodness of God. Through them, Paine entered into Freemasonry and Theophilanthropism, a curious mixture, but they took his thinking to new dimensions, beyond Rousseau's concepts of the corporate nation and social responsibility.

The first stage of Paine's intellectual development, Lockean liberalism and classical republicanism, unfolded in America in the mid-1770s. At that time, Paine's ideas about American separation from Britain were considered radical. He had the courage to advocate American independence openly when others were only thinking about it or discussing it in private. He set forth these ideas principally, though not exclusively, in the context of the ideas of John Locke, the great English philosopher of the previous century. It was Locke who influenced the American leaders of the Revolution in 1776, as well as the framers of the American Constitution eleven years later. From Locke, whose ideas were in the air at the end of the eighteenth century, the Americans gained the language and theory of liberal democracy. Despite Paine's later claim that "I never read Locke, nor ever had the work in my hand," he was, as were all Americans, well-acquainted with Lockean concepts of human rights and liberties and especially the obligation to resist tyranny.[9] Lockean ideas permeated his thinking, especially in *Common Sense*, Paine's great call for America to separate from Britain. Paine carefully framed these ideas in a religious context, how and why it was the Americans' duty to demand and win independence from the empire.

Paine spoke the language of virtue and corruption, the distinctive vocabulary of classical republicanism.[10] His contemporary, Edmund Burke, regarded today as the founder of modern conservative thought, also spoke that language, although quite differently from Paine. At one time Paine's friend, Burke later became his opponent in the debate over the French Revolution. The classical republicans searched for a virtuous citizenry to overcome corrupt governors. Often it was the virtuous who sought to achieve public goals that were in everyone's interest, as opposed to corrupt politicians who sought only to achieve their own ends, their own interests. Their corruption came in several forms and was criticized most vociferously by radical Whigs, like Paine, and less energetically by more establishment Whigs, like Burke.

Classical republican writers perceived several problems plaguing English politics. The traditions of historic English liberty supposedly had been preserved in the Glorious Revolution of 1688 when James II, absolute in religion (Catholic) and in politics (absolute monarchy), was forced from the throne in a virtually bloodless revolution. At the time, the ancient English constitution, consisting of the balanced divisions of king, lords, and commons, had been saved in the nick of time after the leaders of the Lords and Commons had decided together to invite James' daughter, Mary, and her Dutch husband, William, the Prince of Orange, to take the English throne.[11] However, new corruptions (evils, the work of the devil, to Paine) set in, and one of the most obvious and critical of these was the increase in conflicts of interest. Eighteenth-century conflicts seem obvious and grotesque to our contemporary eyes. A member of the Commons (the legislature) often held a place in the king's court (the executive). It would be as if a member of the U.S. House of Representatives held a cabinet-level post in the White House. Opposition Whigs referred to these people as "placemen," because they held places in the court as well as a place in the Commons.

In addition, Parliament met infrequently, and, worse yet, its members held seven-year terms, which meant that they were open to greater temptations to accept those places in the court. At the same time, representation in Parliament was uneven and spotty, often controlled by the wealthy landowners. In some cases, representation was non-existent: when, for example, the major cities sent no representatives to Parliament. As a member of the Commons, Edmund Burke was part of the Rockingham faction, controlled by Charles Watson-Wentworth (the second Marquis of Rockingham). A man claiming to seek virtue in government, Burke forcefully attacked places and pensions, introducing several bills in Parliament to end this corrupt system, but to no avail.

When Paine used the language of classical republicanism, he argued for the creation of an appropriate structure of good government, the republic. The republic guaranteed that government sought the common good of all rather than the individual interests of a corrupt few. This could supposedly be done by insuring that a virtuous citizenry participated in governmental decision-making. Elections were of particular importance. When the people elected their representatives, then the governing institutions were based on the balance of the one (executive), the few (the upper house of government), and the many (the lower house). This model was an effective system of checks and balances, and in 1789 the new American government took on this structure with its President, Senate, and House of

Representatives.[12] Paine himself pointed out in the second part of
the *Rights of Man* that the "public good" was the essential meaning of
the term "republic," which derived from the Latin *res publica*, the
public thing or good.

Paine often drew upon the traditions of both liberalism and
republicanism. But after his move to France, he also incorporated the
concept of social democracy, which laid the foundation for the most
radical social and economic proposals in eighteenth-century England
and America. In the second part of the *Rights of Man*, especially, and
later in *Agrarian Justice*, both of which he wrote in France, Paine
came under the influence of the great Swiss philosopher Jean-Jacques
Rousseau.

In these tracts, Paine's assault on Burke's reaction to the
French Revolution was absent. Paine's goal was to consider how to
help the less fortunate members of society, especially the working
poor. That he was familiar with Rousseau's works is undeniable.
Paine cited them throughout his own writings. Whether he read
them thoroughly is another matter. And yet, in revolutionary France,
Rousseau's idea of the achievement of community and virtue was
expounded by all leaders (and followers) of French liberty. For Paine,
political leaders acquired social virtue only when all people were
properly cared for, when the needs of the poor became the responsibility of government to alleviate, when everyone participated in creating the community's good health. In these writings, Paine argued
for many of the policies which twentieth-century moderns have associated with the liberal welfare state: free public education, public
assistance, old-age benefits, and inheritance taxes on the wealthy. The
astonishing fact is that Paine argued for these policies two hundred
years before the rise of the social welfare state.

During Paine's last years in Paris, he expanded his intellectual horizons but nonetheless fell into a final period of bitterness,
despair, and frustration. Beginning in the early 1790s with his association with the Social Circle, but especially toward the end of that
decade when he had become disillusioned with the French
Revolution and was quite ill, Paine developed a new spirituality as a
result of his relationship with several radical French writers. Through
them and their spiritualist ideas, he found new meaning in seeking a

higher spiritual consciousness. He was the friend of several people who, on the European continent, were known as the Illuminati—who saw God dwelling in all His creation throughout the universe and who believed that everything in life was touched by the divine. In 1802, Paine finally decided to return to America, his adopted home, where the loneliness and bitterness that had been masked by his spiritualism began to reemerge. He had some friends left in America, it was true, who warmly welcomed him, but more often he was greeted by the unremitting slurs of his former enemies. In his last years, his writings only occasionally achieved their former biting power and penetrating deftness.

The years of Paine's wandering from England to America to Europe and back to America were filled with great turmoil and unrest. They contrasted sharply with his first thirty-seven years, when English society was calm and quiescent, a period still in the shadow of an age of stability.[13] England's first real prime minister, Robert Walpole, though corrupt, had created an aura of political and social equilibrium in the third and fourth decades of the century. This balance continued into the 1750s, as Paine wandered throughout England. When George III ascended the throne in 1760, religious controversy was still confined to books and pamphlets, but it soon boiled over into demands for greater freedom for those who refused to adhere to the official Church of England. Members of the dissenting sects—the Quakers, Presbyterians, Methodists, Congregationalists, or Unitarians—possessed neither the right to vote nor the right to hold public office. Citizenship was defined by how much property a man (not a woman) owned and whether he belonged to the Anglican establishment, the official state church of the nation. At the same time, after 1760, disenchantment with the established order developed into ever-louder demands for the people's greater involvement in the political process: the widening of the franchise, the end of the system of "rotten boroughs" (which were usually controlled by the local gentry) and bribery, equal election districts, and frequent parliaments. One borough was so rotten that although it elected two members to Parliament, it had no inhabitants. Another example was two representatives for a borough which had been under water for a generation. In yet another, while everyone was "theoretically" qualified to vote, in reality there were only six houses with a total of one voter.

Through periods of stability or turmoil, Thomas Paine was never content to simply meditate on the corruptions. He was always searching and challenging, often frustrated with his life, looking for ways to uncover the injustices encountered by ordinary people. Strong political and religious views often arouse admiration or hatred, and this was certainly the case throughout Paine's career as a journalist. His views of George III and Britain before, during, and immediately after the American Revolution were the cause of some of the most scurrilous writings about him, mostly by Loyalists. This was to be expected. Even a great patriot like John Adams not only disliked but misunderstood Paine. The two men had great personal conflicts, especially toward the end of Paine's life. But while Adams was far more conservative than Paine on most political, economic, and religious issues, Adams clearly went to the extreme when he agreed with the assessment of Paine he heard by John Witherspoon, the president of the College of New Jersey (later Princeton). Paine was "intemperate and could not write until he had quickened his thoughts with large draughts of rum and water. . . he was in short a bad character . . . soon obnoxious by his manners."[14]

Paine's French revolutionary activities were another source of controversy. At times, even his closest friends wondered why Paine was so heavily involved in every political and social cause. After he was elected an honorary member of the United Irishmen, this ditty was soon passed around to sing his "praises" and his drinking:

> The mighty Thomas Paine
> Who freedom did maintain,
> With energy of reason and sense,
> Was stupid as an ass
> Till first he took a glass,
> Then truth sprung from his cruskeen lan.

More laudable of Paine and his work were these verses, sung by the ardent Irish patriot Arthur O'Connor, who reputedly distributed them on his way to prison in 1798. At first blush the verse seems to endorse monarchy and denounce Paine:

> The pomp of courts and pride of kings,
> I prize above all earthly things;
> I love my country; the king,
> Above all men his praise I sing:
> The royal banners are displayed,
> And may success the standard aid.
>
> I fain would banish far from hence,
> The Rights of Man and Common Sense;
> Confusion to his odious reign,
> That foe to princes, Thomas Paine!
> Defeat and ruin seize the cause
> Of France, its liberties, and laws!

The poem is not what it seems. Finding himself in enough trouble without adding to it by condemning the crown, O'Connor had hidden his republican sentiments in a most clever manner: when properly read, the poem carries the opposite sentiment when the first line of the first verse is immediately followed by the first line of the second verse, and so on. Thus,

> The pomp of courts and pride of kings,
> I fain would banish far from hence;
> I prize above all earthly things
> The Rights of Man and Common Sense.[15]

On his return to the United States in 1802 after fifteen years' absence, Paine was greeted simultaneously with applause and disdain. Toasts welcomed him back to America. One of them hailed him as "Thomas Paine—the bold advocate of rational liberty—the People's Friend." But his opponents were ready for him, too. A New York newspaper, the *Saturday Evening Post*, in its September 24, 1803 edition, urged him to do the following:

> And having spent a lengthy life in evil,
> Return again unto thy parent Devil.[16]

Throughout his long life, Thomas Paine irritated many and inspired others. The target of scorn and the object of veneration, in life and in thought, Paine was always a democratic, though acerbic, journalist: an apostle of freedom.

Part One

Beginnings

2 • Thetford and Beyond

In the late summer of 1792, Thomas Paine had two contrasting experiences which give us important insights into his character. The first was in England, the second in France, just a few days later. He was fifty-five years old and at the pinnacle of his career as a radical journalist and political activist. Known on both sides of the Atlantic as one of the most advanced thinkers in the world, Thomas Paine had received acclaim for his lucid works on American independence and the rights of man. On September 13, 1792, along with John Frost, an English lawyer friend and fellow radical, and Achille Audibert, a leader in the French Revolution and "one of the municipal officers of Calais," Paine left England for the very last time. In hot pursuit was a team of British agents, convinced that he was carrying radical tracts which he had written, tracts which the king had recently proclaimed to be not only wicked but treasonable. If the agents found such tracts on his person, they intended to seize them. The agents caught up with the trio in Dover, detained them for a while, searched their belongings, found nothing of great importance, and let them all go.[1] The three men boarded a boat for France.

Paine was leaving England not because he feared the threats of the government, but because in 1792 he had a higher calling: he had just been elected to the French National Convention and was on his way to do what he could to help France write a new constitution. He and his companions crossed the Channel and arrived in Calais, the very jurisdiction that had elected Paine, where they were greeted by a vast crowd of onlookers and well-wishers. A greater contrast to his exit from England could hardly have been imagined. Paine's accompanying friend Frost noted that

> all the soldiers on duty were drawn up; the officer of the guard
> embraced him on landing, and presented him with the national
> cockade, which a handsome young woman, who was standing
> by, begged the honor of fixing in his hat, and returned it to him,
> expressing a hope that he would continue his exertions in the
> behalf of Liberty, France, and the rights of man. A salute was
> then fired from the battery to announce to the people of Calais
> the arrival of their new representative.

With cheers of greeting and shouts of "Vive Thomas Paine!" the
entourage met town officials, who offered an official welcome "with
the greatest affection." Audibert translated for Paine, who responded that he would devote his life "to their cause." That evening, at a
special reception, the mayor of Calais officially announced Paine's
election as the town's representative and once again a huge crowd of
people shouted their robust greetings and applause, "Vive la nation!"
"Vive Thomas Paine!" The trip to Paris took three days. Through
the towns of Abbeville, Clermont, and Amiens, huge throngs of people shouted to them along the highway. Walking into the convention
hall where the Legislative Assembly was just finishing its work in
preparation for the National Convention to begin, Paine was again
greeted with loud and long cheers.[2]

But life had not always been so thrilling for Thomas Paine.
In fact, his life had a rather dismal beginning. For his first thirty-
seven years there was nothing that forecasted his future successes and
triumphs or which gave a clue that he would be known as the writer
of some of the most moving and memorable phrases in history. One
word describes those early years: failure. Just about everything he
tried to do until he left for America in 1774 went awry. Several times
he tried his hand as a maker of stays for women's corsets, the craft of
his father, and failed. He tried twice to be a government tax collector, and for very different reasons was twice dismissed. He could not
hold his job as a teacher. He tried to run a tobacco-goods store. It
went bankrupt. He married twice: his first wife died only a few
months after their marriage; he and his second wife separated after
three years. It is difficult to assess how Paine felt during these years,

to determine whether he was happy, whether he enjoyed life, whether he planned to wander as often as he did. His only real success was to be well-informed. He loved to read the newspapers, but most likely read little else.[3] He loved to engage in conversation, to argue points of politics, science, and even philosophical principle. When he lived for awhile in Lewes, for example, he often went to the local tavern to drink wine, eat oysters, and pass away the evening in heated debates over the issues of the day. One thing is certain: there is not a speck of evidence in his first thirty-seven years to indicate that he would become a world-shaking, though rootless, journalist.

Thomas Paine was born on January 29, 1737 into a lower-middle class family in the small Norfolk town of Thetford, some seventy-five miles northeast of London. At the time, Thetford had a mere two thousand inhabitants. Only thirty-one of them were eligible to vote for the two representatives to Parliament, a fact that was consistent with the rest of England's five million residents. Only some six thousand people voted for half of Parliament. Like many rural towns in eighteenth-century England, Thetford was controlled by a wealthy Whig magnate, the Duke of Grafton, who along with most of his fellow aristocrats decided which of his supporters was to represent his district in Parliament.

The Whig ascendancy, as it is known, had occurred after the defeat of absolutism in the Glorious Revolution of 1688. A combination of leaders from the Lords and Commons forced the Catholic Stuart king, James II, to flee the throne. By the time of Paine's birth, a new era opened in politics with the end of the threat of absolutism in religion and government. And yet the reality of a constitutional monarchy did not guarantee the participation of everyone in the political process. The foundation of a person's social and political standing was still based on the amount of property owned. The landed gentry—like the Graftons—did very well, because they owned vast amounts of land. With their huge mansions and fine horse-drawn carriages, they lived grandly. People without property or with an income of less than forty pounds a year were, simply put, disenfranchised: they neither voted nor held office.[4]

Thetford itself was a pleasant enough little market town in

comparison to other areas of the nation. Very much a part of its sur-
rounding countryside, it did not experience the same economic fluctuations as did its more industrially-developed neighbors like
Liverpool or Manchester. While the slightest rise in prices, fall in
wages, or poor harvests set off unrest and food riots in other areas of
England, Thetford was still immune to such tumult. The countryside there was rich and fertile and the harvests strong. The fields were
still open; enclosure would not take place on a grand scale until the
second half of the century. A young boy could run freely and cavort
through the meadowlands. There, wild animals, thousands of wild-
flowers, and hundreds of birds greeted the early-morning riser.
When young Thomas walked to school, he crossed over the river
Thet on the town bridge, built in 1697, and passed the stagecoach
stop, where he might have watched the drivers change horses or the
passengers disembark for the night at a small lodge known as the Bell,
built around the sixteenth century. While the town was not particularly well-known, Thetford did claim some famous folk. Thetford's
Guildhall was built by Sir Joseph Williamson, the founder and editor
of England's first newspaper, the *London Gazette*, a propaganda sheet
for the government. The Norfolk historian, the Reverend Francis
Blomefield, lived there, and Paine often later commented that they
attended the same grammar school.

Towns like Thetford had their wide ranges of social classes,
from wealthy aristocrats who had substantial annual incomes to the
casual poor who possessed nothing or virtually nothing.
Amusements were few. For the ladies of the middle class, there were
teas and picnics. For the men, drinking, gambling, cock-fighting
(which Paine detested), and other distractions were usually available
for members of all social classes. If an inn, tavern, or even an assembly room large enough were available, there might be dances for the
townspeople or even a presentation of a play by a travelling theater
company. But the Thetfords of England were growing steadily
throughout the eighteenth century, although it was not until the following century, when industrialization was rapidly spreading, that
they experienced staggering growth rates. In the 1740s and 1750s,
they typically numbered only a few thousand souls, where everyone
knew one another. Agriculture dominated the economy, but the

trades among the skilled craftsmen flourished in several areas: textiles (encompassing weavers, linenmakers, drapers, and clothiers), leather-goods (cordwainers, saddlers, tanners), metals (tinners, farriers), builders (carpenters, joiners, masons), and several more. Retailers and shopkeepers were to be found in every market town because it was the focal point of the rural region: there, bakers, grocers, apothe-caries, barber-surgeons, and other craftsmen kept neatly maintained shops for the convenience of the local community, and they could do quite well.

Thomas Paine's father, Joseph Pain (Thomas added the *e* only after he came to America), was such a craftsman: he was a maker of stays for women's corsets. Stays, usually made of whalebone or steel, were designed as part of waistcoats to give an hourglass shape to dresses. Each town had at least one staymaker, because he provid-ed such an important service to high-born ladies. As artisans, stay-makers were members of the lower sort, as they were then called, or the lower-middle class. Pain's annual income was around some t h i r ty pounds, fairly decent especially when compared to that of a ploughman, who earned only eight pounds a year, or a day laborer, who earned but one pound a year. A schoolmaster could count on an annual stipend of only between ten and twenty pounds. Of course, members of the landed gentry, men like the Dukes of Bedford and Northumberland, pulled in as much as 50,000 pounds per annum (nearly $500,000 in contemporary terms), in the last half of the cen-tury although Grafton, the Thetford duke, probably saw far less, more like the conventional 10,000 pounds per year.

Still, the Paine family was financially secure as part of the middle-class artisans of the community, and historical evidence shows the increasing enrichment of the middle class, especially after 1750, when the economy began to strengthen with strong harvests and stable wages and prices.[5] Paine's first biographer, writing in 1791, Francis Oldys (the pen name for George Chalmers, who hated Paine) called Joseph Pain "a reputable citizen and though poor an honest man."[6] In 1737, the same year as Thomas's birth, Joseph Pain was made a freeman, which gave him the right of pasturage. He owned a small farm in the country.[7] In town, the Pains lived in a middle-class section on Bridge Street (near the town bridge) in a small brick house. The family later moved, somewhat ironically, to Heathenstreet, originally called Paien Street, the name from which the family's own quite possibly derived.

Thomas' mother, Frances Cocke, was eleven years older than her husband. According to Oldys, whose biography of Paine was deeply hostile and no doubt sponsored by Paine's government enemies, Frances was "a woman of sour temper and an eccentric character." She was nearly forty when Thomas was born. A daughter, Elizabeth, born on August 29, 1738, died soon after birth. There were no other children. A member of the established Church of England, Frances Cocke's father was a middle-class lawyer, possibly tracing his lineage back to the legal scholar Richard Cocke, who wrote *English Law, or a Summary Survey of the Household of God Upon Earth in 1651.* At thirty-seven, late in life for the time, she married the artisan Pain, who was beneath her social station.

In marked contrast to Frances' Anglicanism, Joseph was a Quaker who tried to instill in his young son the virtues of the faith. Founded in the seventeenth century by George Fox, Quakerism began as an organization of fervent evangelists who dissented from the Church of England's doctrine. Like other religious sects which refused to accept the official liturgy of the Church's Thirty-Nine Articles of Faith, the Quakers were known as dissenters, or non-conformists. The Act of Toleration in 1689 had allowed dissenters to worship freely, but, like those with no property, they were second-class citizens without voting privileges or the right to hold public office. Nor could they attend the state universities in Oxford or Cambridge. Quakers were often suspicious of religious and governmental authority, which after all had long discriminated against them, and Joseph Pain was no exception: he passed along his mistrust of authority to his son, a current of which ran throughout Paine's writings. Just as important, he transmitted to the boy the sense of inner-light spiritualism that was part of Quaker doctrine: that all people carry within themselves a spark of light lit by the divine to drive them to do good. By the time of Thomas' birth in 1737, Quakers were widely known as a fairly conventional, mild, and peaceful folk, famous for their pacifism. Like Joseph Pain, many Quakers were lower-middle class artisans, tradesmen, or craftsmen.

Despite young Thomas' immersion in Quaker principles, his mother initially prevailed over Joseph in impressing her own religious beliefs on Thomas. While this was not to last, she had come from the more socially prominent family, after all, and the couple had been married in the Church in 1734. Frances sent Thomas off to live with her sister, who probably had him baptized (though no baptismal records survive) and taught him the Anglican catechism. He learned the Bible well, and all through his life he could recite long passages from memory. (He later wrote Part One of *The Age of Reason*, where he quoted extensively from the Bible, without the Scriptures before him.) His aunt made certain that he was confirmed in the Church by the Bishop of Norfolk.

The resulting tension between Anglicanism and Quakerism—two very different, contrasting religions—had to have been a source of serious confusion to the boy. In the end, his Quaker background dominated, and for most of his life, Paine regarded himself as a Quaker. He even hoped to be buried in a Quaker cemetery.[8] Only once did he claim to be a member of the Church of England. Even if he often identified himself as a Quaker, however, Paine hardly seemed satisfied with all Quaker principles, once remarking that "though I reverence their philanthropy, I cannot help smiling at the conceit that if the taste of a Quaker could have been consulted at the Creation what a silent and drab-colored Creation it would have been! Not a flower would have blossomed its gaieties, nor a bird been permitted to sing." He attributed his "exceedingly good moral education and a tolerable stock of useful learning" to his father's Quaker background. In Thetford, he attended a "free" school until he was thirteen (it was free because the Graftons had endowed it). There, he learned to read and write, but he never learned Latin, which could have helped him escape from rural England to a city and to one of the professions in law, medicine, theology. Latin, however, was an anathema to the Quakers. It smacked of popery, he said in *The Age of Reason*, in an unveiled reference to the dangers of Catholicism. (*AR* 84, 82)

Paine did, on the other hand, learn the subjects contained in the Latin books of the school. His earliest interests were in science and poetry, and he dabbled in both of them later in life. As an adult, he engaged in scientific invention, from his famous iron bridge to smokeless candles, from gunboats to flaming arrows. He seemed to have loved writing poetry (admittedly not very good poetry), and he always sang songs, when asked and even when asked not to. At age eight, he is reputed to have sung of the loss of a crow which he buried in the garden in his yard:

> Here lies the body of John Crow,
> Who once was high, but now is low;
> Ye brother crows take warning all,
> For as you rise, so must you fall.

At thirteen, with no hope of advancement to the universities or even the dissenting academies, he left school to become an apprentice staymaker in his father's shop. Apparently a spunky lad, he sought adventure, especially after his schoolmaster, the Reverend William Knowles, told him about his own escapades as a naval chaplain on a man-o'-war roaming from India, the Indies, and Africa to North America.[9] Paine read a history of Virginia that belonged to Knowles, and America must have seemed not only distant, but marvelous and attractive. He no doubt learned that the French tried to secure their Canadian fortresses against the British by pushing them right up against the seacoast of North America and, if possible, into the Atlantic. Paine read about the defeat of French forces in western Virginia by British soldiers under the command of a young colonel named George Washington. Soon, however, Washington was forced to surrender to a larger French force on the Virginia frontier. When the Seven Years War (1756-1763) broke out, as England and France vied for empire in India and America, Paine's dream for a more exciting life suddenly became a real possibility.

In 1756, he left his father's shop for London to become a journeyman (a day worker for a master craftsman), most likely through a connection of his father's, to master staymaker John Morris. One day, feeling, as he said, "raw and adventurous," and probably thinking of Knowles' stories, he became "heated with the false heroism of a [ship's] master." The youth signed on to a privateer called the *Terrible*, skippered, strangely enough, by a Captain

William Death. Paine's father got wind of his intentions and stopped him before the ship disembarked, using "affectionate and moral remonstrance."[10] (*RM* 218-19) Paine had no way of knowing that ten years earlier, in 1746, a man who would be most influential in his life had experienced the same problem with his own son. William Franklin, Benjamin's son, ran away from home at age sixteen to join a privateer during King George's War. His father, too, stopped him before the ship sailed. Curiously, the elder Franklin himself had tried to join a privateer during Queen Anne's War against France (it began a few months after she ascended the throne in 1702 and did not end until after her death in 1714). Young Franklin was persuaded against joining by his own father and uncle.

Having missed sailing on the *Terrible*, Paine read in the newspapers of the ship's battle against a French privateer, the *Vengeance*. The *Terrible*, he later recalled, "stood the hottest engagement of any ship," and he was right (*CS* 104). It sustained huge losses: the ship was heavily damaged. Over one hundred fifty men died, including Captain Death, as well as all the other officers, except one. Their French enemies left the wounded and dying below deck to perish. In all, just seventeen crewmen of the *Terrible* survived the battle. The *Vengeance*, to the credit of the *Terrible*, also lost her captain, several officers, and at least two-thirds of her crew.[11] The ongoing clash of British and French interests in the Indies and North America convinced Paine again to join a ship's crew.

Paine was soon off, this time to do a tour just as the memory of his father's admonitions "began to wear away." In 1756, still the first year of the Seven Years War, he sailed on the *King of Prussia*, skippered, he later reported, by a "Capt. Mendez."[12] (*RM* 219)

Eighteenth-century English privateers were, as the name suggests, privately-owned merchant ships or man-o'-wars officially commissioned by the High Court of the Admiralty in times of war. The government granted their owners licenses, or letters of marque and reprisal, which distinguished these seamen from ordinary pirates, although they were often regarded as such anyway. Indeed, the privateer on which Paine eventually served, the *King of Prussia*, had a crew with two known pirates on board.[13] Without the letter of marque and reprisal, the captain and his entire crew, if captured, would be treated as pirates and simply hanged. Otherwise, they were considered prisoners of war.

Privateers were empowered by the crown to attack enemy merchant ships and seize their cargo for their own profit. The booty was split between the captain, his officers, and the men. The vast majority of the prize went first to the captain, then to the officers. The average take of the captain for a nine to twelve month voyage could have been as high as three hundred pounds. The remainder was divided evenly among the crew. These ships often had an easy time when going after merchant vessels. Some were quite large man-o'-wars, with crews up to two hundred and fifty or more men, and carrying as many as thirty-two twelve-pound cannons, as large as a naval frigate, the standard ship in the eighteenth-century British navy during the Seven Years War and for thirty years afterward.[14] Other ships were small, though very fast, which allowed them to prey on merchant ships. The smaller ones usually had around 120 men in the crew and some less than fifty men. More modest ships had as few as ten. A schooner, for example, might have carried just ten men and four four-pound guns. Small maybe, but large enough to win the prize. Given the number of officers and sailors killed on the *Terrible*, the ship Paine was prevented from joining, it must have been a fairly large vessel. The *King of Prussia*, the boat on which he did go to sea, was a large man-o'-war carrying a crew of about two hundred fifty men with two gundecks, giving it a distinct five times advantage over any merchant ship.

Despite the size of their ships, however, privateer captains usually tried to avoid battles, if only to preserve the merchant ships' cargoes and to protect the safety of their men. A shot across the bow or through the sails was often enough for a merchant captain to surrender his ship. He was simply not equipped with weaponry and manpower to resist a privateer. Besides, he knew that privateer skippers were under orders to treat all prisoners fairly and well, to feed and shelter them, and to bring them safely into port. The problem was when two enemy privateers confronted one another. Then a true sea battle exploded into action, as happened with the *Terrible* and the *Vengeance*. Paine never indicated how he liked life on board ship, but it was brutal at best: the most misery came from days of boredom on the high seas while the crew awaited action. In addition, all sailors on the privateers and warships suffered long, cold nights on watch with clothes permanently damp since the salt in the water attracted moisture, and there was never enough fresh water to rinse them. Sailors endured days without landing, at times bad food (though in comparison to what the poor ate, the food was generally ample), vermin such as rats, cockroaches, and weevils, exhaustion, alcoholism, and diseases like pneumonia and scurvy.

The pay appeared to be low (about one to five pounds per month), but Paine actually earned about thirty pounds a year, because the *King of Prussia* was quite successful. Indeed, in the service of the British navy during the Seven Years War, the pay for ordinary seamen was just short of abysmal: nineteen shillings a month with one shilling going to the Chatham Chest (a hospital) and six pence to the Greenwich Hospital. Compared to a ploughman who earned only about eight pounds an entire year, however, this wage was undoubtedly attractive.[15] Generally, sickness was endemic on these ships: more men died of disease during the Seven Years War than in battle. Harsh discipline was often enforced by an efficient officer corps, the members of which knew that many seamen had been forcibly impressed into service. Paine's situation was different since he had chosen to sign on. In all, his journey, which took him from England and lasted about a year and a half, allowed him to see action several times. The *King of Prussia* recorded the successful seizure of nine ships and their cargo.[16]

When Paine finally ended his tour of duty, he did not sign on with another ship, although the war lasted until 1763. He had witnessed a great deal of killing and disease, and also the terrible price that commerce paid when privateers voraciously preyed on innocent merchant ships. Years later, he looked back and condemned privateering: in war, "the regular markets [are] destroyed, the channels of trade broken up, the high road of the seas infested with robbers of every nation." (*RM* 214) Still, the impressionable young man of nineteen could not help but be staggered by the sights and sounds of the sea and the deep, dark, starry nights. His later interests in science, astronomy, and inventions all may have had their origins in his life on board a privateer, coupled with the dexterity that he learned as a staymaker in his father's shop. He later wrote about the importance of navies for defense and commerce. He devised a plan for small gunboats and argued on behalf of the rights of neutral ships in wartime. Above all, he learned by experience that Quaker pacifism was irrelevant in the heat of battle, and that combat was often necessary for a good cause (though the captains and owners of privateers might have had self-serving causes which excluded God, king, and country). In 1756, Paine physically left his father's house. Within three years, his spiritual separation from that house, his father's "moral remonstrance," and Quaker authority was complete.

Soon after leaving the *King of Prussia*, Paine tried his hand again as a journeyman staymaker first briefly in London, then Dover. In April of 1759, he opened his own shop as a master staymaker in Sandwich (Kent). At twenty-two, according to his friend and later biographer, Clio Rickman, Paine was a man with broad shoulders who stood five feet, ten inches tall. He was of medium, though athletic, build, but his intense blue eyes, "full of fire, the eyes of an apostle," as one historian has remarked, attracted the most attention. [17] Rickman was drawn to them: "His eye, of which the painter could not convey the exquisite meaning, was full, brilliant, and singularly piercing. He had in it the 'muse of fire.' " [18] Portraits of him, especially one of him at fifty-five by George Romney from which an engraving was taken, show those eyes to be penetrating as they stare out at the observer through two hundred years of time.[19] In the Romney work, not a hint of a smile crosses Paine's mouth, the source of his stories, his wit, his opinions, and his laughter. Next to him lies a quill in an inkstand separated by his two most acclaimed works, *Common Sense* and the *Rights of Man*. His dress is that of a well-to-do merchant or banker. He wears no powdered wig, but then again, he considered himself in 1792 to be an American (despite his constant plea that he wished to be remembered as a citizen of the world). He is shown erect and confident, maybe standing. As he grew older, he tended to stoop a bit. He had a rather long nose, which became pendulous and drooped with age. Those who knew him late in life often commented on its redness, which they associated with heavy drinking. Paine did in fact drink alcoholic beverages, wine and brandy mostly, though moderately.[20] Only in his last years, when he

was old, tired, and ill, occasionally absent-minded, rejected by friends X
and ignored by foes, did he drink heavily. Until then, he was self-
confident, with a bounce in his step, his conversation and even in his
signature, especially the "T" of his Thomas with its very masculine
upwards swinging double swirl and upright vectors.

In September of 1759, he married the young Mary Lambert,
who worked as a maid in the homes of wealthy merchants. Nothing
much is known about Mary Lambert. According to Paine's earliest
biographer Chalmers, she was a pretty young woman who died a few
months after the marriage in 1760, possibly in childbirth.[21] Paine
never said what became of Mary, and there has been a great deal of
speculation, by Paine's enemies and partisans alike, that he had little
sexual interest in women, although he often flirted with them and
enjoyed their company. Whether his marriage to Mary was ever
consummated is not known. To assert she died in childbirth remains
pure conjecture.

His staymaking shop in Sandwich soon had serious financial
problems. One night, as the creditors were literally breaking down
the door, Mary and Thomas snuck out of town for Margate. Mary's
father, a customs officer, soon convinced Paine to join the customs
service as an excise taxman. Paine applied for a position. To enter
the excise, a candidate had to have the support of a local aristocrat
before he could even take the entrance examination. Paine was supported by Lord Falkland. Mary's father, who had once served as a
collector, either knew Falkland from his earlier experience or Paine
simply applied to him through the agency of intermediary aristocrats.
Paine spent a year at home in Thetford studying for the written
examination. On December 1, 1762, he was accepted as a supernumerary or unattached officer, meaning that he had to wait for an
opening. In August 1764, he was appointed to the Alford Out-Ride
in Lincolnshire in northern England along the Northern Sea.

The job of excise taxmen was to collect an internal customs
duty, mainly on alcoholic beverages (principally beer and ale), but also
on salt, soap, tobacco, and other goods as well. Excise officers spent
long hours on the road and were often the victims of smugglers and
thieves. They had to file written reports to London and, of course,
collect the tax. Notoriously poorly paid members of a bureaucracy,

their work was often shoddy and disorganized. Many of them allowed goods, which should have been taxed, to pass through without assessment. This meant that they accepted whatever the owner of the merchandise told them the goods were worth and then applied the excise stamp without ever having examined them firsthand. In other words, many collectors issued reports that were simply wrong. Thomas Paine soon fell into this slipshod practice. He allowed some goods to pass through without collecting the tax, and his supervisors dismissed him from the service on August 29, 1765, just one year after his appointment. His notice read as follows:

> Thomas Pain, Officer of Alford (Lincolnshire), Grantham collection, having on July 11th stamped the whole ride, as appears by the specimens not being signed in any part thereof, though proper entry was shown in journal and the victualler's stocks drawn down in his books as if the same had been surveyed that day, as by William Swallow, Supervisor's letter of 3rd instant, and the collector's report thereon, also by said Pain's own confession of the 13th instant, ordered to be discharged.[22]

Out of the need to earn a living, Paine returned to staymaking, this time again as a journeyman to a man named Gudgeon in the town of Diss, near his original home in Norfolk. Paine was fired or he hated the job, because after a few months in 1766, he went to Lincolnshire, also as a staymaker. Years later, Paine recalled a strange incident that happened one summer evening in Lincolnshire, when he and a widow he was visiting went for a walk in a garden. They suddenly saw the outline of what he called "a white shapeless figure, without head or arms, moving along one of the walks at some distance from us." He left the lady and tracked the object, which seemed to disappear every time a bush got between them. Paine did not believe in the supernatural, in ghosts or spirits of any kind. Being uncertain whether what he saw was real, he finally caught up to it, reached out to touch it, and wondered whether "my hand will pass through the air, or shall I feel anything?"

He soon found that the object was real—in fact, a woman. She had been at dinner with Paine and the widow and had, he thought, retired to bed feeling ill. All she said that evening was,

"'Life has no pleasure for me.'" She was engaged to marry a man who married someone else. She had gone out after dinner with her apron tied over her head so no one would know who she was. Her intention, said Paine, was "to drown herself in a pond at the bottom of the garden," but he had stopped her in time. Paine and his companion got the woman home and into bed. Gradually, her sadness dissipated because he led "her into subjects that might, without doing violence to her feelings, and without letting her see the direct intention of it, steal her as it were from the horror she was in." [23] Paine seemed delighted to report that she later married happily and had a family.

Paine soon gave up staymaking for good. In 1766, he moved back to London, where he taught English at an academy maintained by Daniel Noble, who was an elder and preacher at the Sabbath-Keeping Baptist Church in Goodman's Field.[24] No record exists of how Paine's students responded to his teaching. He stayed only until Christmas that year. Years later, Mr. Darby, one of his former students, visited him in Philadelphia, Paine recommended him to George Washington: "it is his intention to visit camp," he told the General, "and wait on your Excellency." Darby wanted to see "the great world of America," and Paine was pleased to see him.[25]

London was the center of political opposition in England. In the period just before Paine's arrival, the political radical John Wilkes had openly criticized and attacked the government in his paper, the *North Briton*. He ridiculed George III and his principal advisor, Lord Bute, whom he accused of having an illicit affair with the Queen Mother. The paper was shut down, and Wilkes, having been found guilty of seditious libel, was exiled. He returned in 1768 and ran for a seat in Parliament three times, each time being denied his place because of his previous conviction. He eventually became the mayor of London. Paine knew of Wilkes' activities and the opposition movement in London. They were often the centerpiece of the discussions in the great London taverns and public houses where the debate centered on the nature of a free press and parliamentary reform. Within a decade, with the spectacle of American independence from the British crown, the subject of discussion moved to the more radical arena of ending the monarchy and creating extra-parliamentary organizations and associations. Both topics, the government thought, were among the most subversive of the day. Paine's political education no doubt began with the encounters he made in London in the late 1760s and the ongoing news of the Wilkes affair.

At Christmas, Paine left Noble's academy in London and moved to another school in Kensington, and taught there for only three months. He wanted to return to the customs service, despite the low pay in the excise. Perhaps he liked the security of working as a government collector, or perhaps he thought it gave him status as a government bureaucrat, something he lacked as a tradesman or schoolmaster. At any rate, in July of 1767, he filed a petition to be reinstated and was soon promised the next vacancy. He declined the job, because it was in Cornwall, and he did not want to move that far from home.

In February of 1768, he accepted a job as exciseman in Lewes, the county seat of Sussex where the courts, the annual Assizes, heard civil and criminal complaints for the region. His London political education now turned to political action in Lewes. For the first time, Paine became directly involved in the practical affairs of politics at a moment when there was a shift in English political practice. Until the middle of the eighteenth century, the parish was the foundation of local government. Here the local electorate voted for their unpaid officials: constables, churchwardens, overseers of the highways, and others. Elections in Lewes were confirmed at the White Hart Tavern, where Paine served on a committee known as the Society of Twelve, a kind of town council. This group validated the election and presented the new town officers with the insignia and other manifestations of their offices.[26]

Lewes had been a virtual hotbed of opposition politics all through the seventeenth and into the eighteenth centuries. During the English Civil War, it had been the seat of radical organizations, which longed for the creation of true English republicanism (without king). It was known as an "anti-popery" town, with its huge Guy Fawkes Day celebration on November 5 each year. On that date in 1605, several English Roman Catholics, including Fawkes, a soldier recently returned from Flanders, had plotted to blow up King James I and both houses of Parliament. The conspirators, in what came to be known as the Gunpowder Plot, rented a cellar underneath the House of Lords, but unfortunately for Fawkes, the authorities caught wind of their scheme. Fawkes was arrested the morning of the fifth when he went into the cellar, and the arrest, imprisonment, and execution of his co-conspirators quickly followed. Thereafter, several cities, and none more than Lewes, celebrated with pomp and grandeur the demise of this popish plot. Echoing just this sentiment, Paine later used the theme of "popery" in government to underscore his distaste for the English monarchy and its corruption. Radical Londoner John Wilkes and his call for liberty were well known in Lewes, and Wilkes visited there in the 1770s.[27]

Once in town, Paine took lodgings with the owner of a tobacco/grocery store, Samuel Ollive. Ollive was a prominent citizen of the town, which, though small and rural, was twice the size of Thetford. Samuel Ollive and Henry Verral, former owners of the White Hart, had both been constables, making the tavern the center of politics and social life. In the following year, 1769, when Ollive died, leaving behind a widow and daughter, Paine moved out, apparently for propriety's sake. But he was soon helping the widow run the store, or, rather, run it into the ground, given Paine's lack of expertise and experience in business. Mrs. Ollive might have brought Paine in as a partner, although the records are not clear on that point. He very likely received no income from the store. On March 26, 1771, at age thirty-four, Paine married Mrs. Ollive's daughter, Elizabeth, in his second marriage. One of the witnesses was Henry Verral, Ollive's old friend and former colleague in the constabulary. Paine's second marriage was also doomed to failure, lasting only three years.

Paine appeared to be happy in Lewes, so involved was he in its politics and society. He stayed there for some six years, a long time for the wandering Paine. While in Lewes, Paine wrote a campaign song for a Whig candidate to Parliament by the name of Rumbold, for which he received three guineas. He also met a young boy, Thomas Clio Rickman, who became a poet and printer. He and Paine later became lifelong friends, and Rickman was to be one of his first favorable biographers.[28] He engaged in long, usually convivial discussions while drinking wine and brandy and eating oysters at the White Hart, where he was a member of the Headstrong Club.

The tradition of the club was that at the end of each evening's discussion, the most obdurate participant was awarded a prize, the so-called Headstrong Book. Paine, it was said, received the prize more often than anyone else. Rickman described the Book, the same one passed around each time, as "no other than an old Greek Homer, which was sent the morning after a debate vehemently maintained, to the most obstinate haranguer of the club. This book had the following title, as implying that Mr. Paine the best deserved and the most frequently obtained it:

THE HEADSTRONG BOOK;

or;

THE ORIGINAL BOOK OF OBSTINACY,

written by

****** ****, OF LEWES, IN SUSSEX,

and revised and corrected by

THOMAS PAIN." [29]

In Lewes, he wrote (and undoubtedly sang) one of his first poems (or songs), an elegy on the death of General James Wolfe, who was killed in the Battle of Quebec during the French and Indian Wars. The poem first appeared in print in 1775 in the *Pennsylvania Magazine*, which Paine edited in Philadelphia, but he wrote it in Lewes. In fairly primitive verse, the poem told of Wolfe's heroic efforts (ironically, given Paine's later views of the king of England) to defend the empire:[30]

> In a mouldering cave where the wretched retreat,
> Britannia sat wasted with care;
> She mourned for her Wolfe, and exclaim'd against fate
> And gave herself up to despair.
> The walls of her cell she had sculptured around
> With the feats of her favorite son;
> And even the dust, as it lay on the ground,
> Was engraved with the deeds he had done.

As the poem continued, Jove sent Mercury to tell Britannia that Wolfe was not dead but only removed to a loftier state. Jove's council decreed that he "be called to the armies above."[31] This song was very popular in America, and its inclusion helped to increase sales of the *Pennsylvania Magazine* in its first months of operation.

In Lewes, Paine also wrote a longer, humorous poem, "Farmer Short's Dog Porter: A Tale," which told the story of a farmer who voted in an election for candidates who were not to the liking of the local justices of the peace. Because they could not indict the farmer for anything, they charged his dog, Porter, as follows:

> That he, this dog, did then and there
> Pursue, and take, and kill a hare;
> Which treason was, or some such thing,
> Against our Sovereign Lord the King.

The judges immediately sent the local sheriff to deliver the proper papers, but not to arrest the miscreant pup.

> The Constable was bid to job,
> And bring the farmer—not the dog.

Perhaps the judges were too drunk to notice, but it was poor Porter who appeared before the bench.

> The justices received the felon,
> With greater form than I can tell on.
> And quitting now their wine and punch,
> Began upon him all at once.

Evidence indicated that Porter had in fact picked up the scent of the hare and chased it. There was, however, no indication that he had killed the bunny. In fact, in trying to outdistance Porter, she (the bunny) had run headlong into a lake and drowned. The justices decided that Porter might not have killed her directly, but that his actions were a contributing factor in her demise.

> So had the dog not chased the hare,
> She never had been drown'd—that's clear!

The end, and English justice, came quickly. Poor Porter was taken out and hanged.

> This logic, rhetoric, and wit,
> So nicely did the matter hit,
> That Porter, though unheard, was cast,
> And in a halter breathed his last.
> And the justices? Why, they
> adjourned to dine
> And whet their logic up with wine.[32]

As happy as Paine might have been in Lewes, he was also quite destitute. The customs service, as was usual for the profession, paid him only fifty pounds a year, which was more than his father had earned as a staymaker. But after expenses for his horse and lodging when he was on the road as an outrider, he and his wife barely had enough to live on, only one shilling and ninepence farthing a day. After four years of Paine's work in the service, in April of 1772, the couple had to sell everything they owned just to survive. Paine was well aware that his financial plight was not unique, that all families of excise taxmen suffered under the same problems. After some urging from his co-workers, who apparently knew he had some talent in writing, he decided to prepare a petition outlining the struggle of these families and to present it in person to every member of Parliament. This was to be his first attempt at prose and his first defense of the underclass.

3 · "Poverty begets meanness"

For Paine's first political experience, he had to go to London. Because he had no money, his fellow excisemen heavily subsidized him. Each of nearly three thousand officers in the service donated three shillings for a total of five hundred pounds to cover the costs of printing four thousand copies of the document and sending Paine to Parliament. The pamphlet demanded higher wages, and Paine lobbied for this cause in London throughout the winter of 1772-73. In his first political argument, Paine showed promise that he could write an engagingly eloquent tract, though his writing was often marred by decorous overstatement. Poverty, he wrote, "begets a degree of meanness that will stoop to almost anything. . . . [P]overty, like grief, has an incurable deafness, which never hears; the oration loses all its edge, and '*To be, or not to be*' becomes the only question." The impact of poverty on the soul bred frustration, complacency, and even hopelessness:

> Persons first coming into the excise form very different notions of it, to what they have afterwards. The gay ideas of promotion soon expire. The continuance of work, the strictness of the duty, and the poverty of the salary, soon beget negligence and indifference: the course continues for a while, the revenue suffers, and the officer is discharged; the vacancy is soon filled up, new ones arise to produce the same mischief and share the same fate.[1]

The best qualified were treated this way and ruined, and it was for them that he asked Parliament to improve conditions. Paine was justly proud of this first effort, despite the fact that Parliament never responded to it. He courageously left his post to work on behalf of his fellows. He even sent Oliver Goldsmith, the Anglo-Irish author, a copy of the pamphlet, hoping to engage his literary reputation in the cause.[2] There was no response.

On his return to Lewes in April of 1774, Paine was once again dismissed from the service. He had abandoned his post without permission.

> Thomas Pain, Officer of Lewes, 4th O. Ride Sussex Collection having quitted his business, without obtaining the Board's leave for so doing, and being gone off on account of the debts which he hath contracted, as by letter of the 6th instant from Edward Clifford, Supervisor, and the said Pain having been once before discharged, Ordered that he be again discharged.[3]

Poverty no doubt contributed to his separation from Elizabeth just two months later. (He never saw her again. She died in 1808, just eight months before his own death.) There has been some speculation about the failure of Paine's second marriage. Chalmers claimed that it failed because Paine was impotent. But this claim is without evidence, and Paine's long-time friend and biographer, Clio Rickman, said that "no physical defect on the part of Mr. Paine can be adduced as a reason for such conduct."[4] Ironically, James Cheetham, as unfriendly a biographer as Chalmers, claimed that when Paine lived with the Bonneville family in Paris in the late 1790s, he entered into an illicit affair with Marguerite de Bonneville, the wife of his friend, Nicolas de Bonneville.[5] Cheetham also claimed that Paine was the father of Marguerite's son, who was named Thomas Paine Bonneville. Conway suggested that Elizabeth, who was an orthodox member of the Church, found Paine's developing liberal religious views incompatible with her own and wanted to end the relationship for that reason alone. Perhaps the true reason for their separation lies in a comment Paine made to Rickman: "it is nobody's business but my own; I had cause for it, but I will name it to no one."[6]

The marriage and separation bothered Paine, at least for a while. Several years later, he wrote to Kitty Nicholson Few (the daughter of the leader of the New York republican faction) about marriage and why it was not for all people. He might well have been in platonic love with this young, beautiful woman. "The married state," he told her, "has not a sincerer friend than I am," though clearly it was not for everyone. "It is," he went on, "the harbor of human life."

> For a few years we may glide along the tide of youthful single life and be wonderfully delighted; but it is a tide that flows but once, and what is still worse, it ebbs faster than it flows, and leaves many a hapless voyager aground. I am one, you see, that have experienced the fate I am describing. I have lost my tide.[7]

He seemed clearly puzzled by his failure to develop a strong relationship with a woman.

In the year after he settled in America, as editor of the *Pennsylvania Magazine*, Paine wrote about unhappy marriages. He said that

> as ecstasy abates, coolness succeeds, which often makes way for indifference, and that for neglect: sure of each other by the nuptial band, they no longer take any pains to be mutually agreeable; careless if they displease; and yet angry if reproached; with so little relish for each other's company that anybody else's is welcome, and more entertaining. Their union thus broke, they pursue separate pleasures; never meet but to wrangle, or part but to find comfort in other society."[8]

Was Paine talking about himself, about Elizabeth? He later corresponded with his friend, Lady Smyth, when he was imprisoned in Paris during the Terror, and wrote her love poems. But were these more than platonic? It is difficult, if not impossible, to say.

What is known is that from Lewes and Elizabeth, Paine set off once again for London. He had no visible source of income during this period. Some of his former excise colleagues accused him of keeping up to thirty pounds from the collection taken to support his appeal to Parliament on their behalf. No evidence supports the charge, but he apparently did no work in London. Instead, he attended scientific lectures there and later wrote about hearing Benjamin Martin and James Ferguson, two important scientists and instrument makers of the day. He especially admired Dr. John Bevis, a famous astronomer. Through his connections in the excise and while lobbying in Parliament, he had met a commissioner of the Board of Excise, George Lewis Scott, who was, Paine said, "one of the most amiable characters I know of." Scott introduced Paine to Benjamin Franklin, the Philadelphia printer and publisher, inventor and scientist, now turned diplomat as Pennsylvania's agent in London.[9]

Paine was clearly out of his element in these circles. All of these men, with the exception of Franklin who left school at age ten, were highly educated, and all were certainly well-read. Paine was still something of a country bumpkin. Even later, in the 1780s when he met Edmund Burke, Paine's manner contrasted with this worldly graduate of Dublin's Trinity College, member of Parliament from Bristol, and leading Whig spokesman for the Rockingham faction. The advantage Paine always had, however, was his innate charm and disposition, his matter-of-fact manner of speaking, his ability to make a point in a clear and concise way, and his easy conversational style. Franklin, for one, was almost immediately taken with him: as a result of their discussions, Paine decided to abandon England altogether and wander off to America. Franklin wrote him a letter of introduction, which Paine was to give to Franklin's son-in-law, Richard Bache, and his son, William Franklin, then royal governor of New Jersey. The letter described Paine as a worthy young man (of thirty-seven!), who might make a fine schoolmaster or tutor.

> The bearer, Mr. Thomas Pain, is very well recommended to me as an ingenious worthy young man. He goes to Pennsylvania with a view of settling there. I request you to give him your best advice and countenance, as he is quite a stranger there. If you can put him in a way of obtaining employment as a clerk, or assistant tutor in a school, or assistant surveyor (of all which I think him very capable) so that he may procure a subsistence at

least, till he can make acquaintance and obtain a knowledge of the country, you will do well, and much oblige your affectionate father.[10]

    Paine left England on the *London Packet* in October of 1774. Most of the one hundred twenty passengers on board became ill with typhus ("dismal and dangerous"), including Paine himself. Only seven did not become sick, and five died, their bodies cast into the sea. Paine was so ill with this "putrid fever" that he had to be carried off the ship when he arrived in Philadelphia on November 30. Dr. John Kearsley cared for him because he had received word that the "young" Paine was Franklin's friend. Paine was in bed for six weeks before he was able to see Bache and give him the letter from his father-in-law.[11] Bache immediately engaged him as a tutor for the sons of several of his friends.

    Robert Aitken was a Philadelphia printer who, along with the president of the College of New Jersey, Dr. John Witherspoon, decided to start a magazine the following year. Aitken asked Paine to write for the journal and soon hired him as the editor. Paine entered the inner circle of Philadelphia society and became friends, sometimes close friends, with many of the articulate advocates of the American cause. The *Pennsylvania Magazine: or, American Monthly Museum*, already had a ready-made list of six hundred subscribers. Despite Witherspoon's initial support of Paine, he later turned against him when he thought Paine edited his pieces too heavily. He later accused him of being opportunistic in supporting American independence, because in England Paine had written in support of Britain. According to John Adams, Witherspoon also claimed that Paine "could not write until he had quickened his thoughts with large draughts of rum and water."[12] For these reasons, Witherspoon opposed Paine's appointment the following year to a position in the new American government.

    The America Paine saw on his arrival at the end of 1774 was in the midst of a colony-wide debate over British imperial policy. Most Americans considered themselves Englishmen, and they demanded the same rights that they believed Englishmen in the British Isles enjoyed.[13] In the meantime, the crown did whatever it could to subject the colonies to its will, to force them to behave as it deemed proper. They were English, of course, the British ministry said, and they already possessed the same rights and liberties that all Englishmen had. A people did not lose their political personality just because they stepped away from their native soil. But they also had the same responsibilities. They had to be loyal to the Church and king, and as colonists they were required to provide to the crown those things that England herself was unable to produce. While some Americans-qua-Englishmen demanded direct participation in the political decisions being made in Westminster, the crown responded that the colonists already participated, as they had always, in decision-making through a political concept known as "virtual representation."[14]

Virtual representation meant participation that did not necessarily include direct involvement. According to the crown, it did not matter whether every eligible person was permitted to vote in a particular election. What mattered was that some people of all social standings must be able to vote. This meant that even though Americans did not have an opportunity to send representatives to Parliament, there were people in England just like them who did. As a result, Americans were virtually, if not directly, represented.

Some Americans rejected this theory outright. Perhaps the British ministry, particularly under George Grenville, the king's chief minister, could have explained more fully and in greater detail the nature of the financial crisis facing England as a result of the Seven Years War. Revenues ran far short, and as a result the British debt had jumped from seventy-five million to one hundred forty-five million pounds during the war. Besides, Grenville was mindful that he had to finance over ten thousand British troops in North America, whose job it was to police the Canadian and western frontiers (if not to remind the Americans continually that they were still part of the empire). But even if his willful American subjects had had representatives in Parliament, they still would never have voted in favor of any of the acts that required them to send their revenues to England. A whole series of British legislation, they thought, threatened their identity as part of the empire: the Stamp Act (1765), which required them to have revenue stamps placed on a large array of commodities, ranging from newspapers, pamphlets, and almanacs to legal documents and liquor licenses (even dice and playing cards); the Declaratory Act (1766), which said that Parliament could enact laws for the colonies in all cases; or the Townshend Duties (1767), which placed duties on paper, lead, painters' colors, and of course tea.

When faced with great unrest and opposition in the colonies as these laws reached American shores, Parliament repealed many, but not all, of the measures. In 1770, the Townshend duties were ended, but the tea tax remained, for example. By then, Grenville had been replaced by Lord North, who wanted to retain some symbolic control over the colonies by keeping the duty on tea. One immediate result of this was the infamous Boston Massacre in March of that year, when a group of Bostonians heckled and threw snowballs at several British troops who quickly grew tired of the scene and fired into the crowd. When the smoke cleared, five Bostonians lay dead, several wounded. Although things settled down for awhile, the British were not through: in early 1773, Parliament passed the Tea Act, which gave the East India Company a monopoly on the importation of tea into the colonies.

In the short run, this act precipitated the Boston Tea Party in December of 1773, when several hundred people, dressed as Indians, stormed the ships in the Boston harbor and threw ten thousand pounds' worth of tea into the water. The British immediately set forth a series of laws, known in England as the Coercive Acts, in America as the Intolerable Acts. These pieces of legislation, in the long run, led directly to Paine's call for separation and independence. They accomplished several goals that Lord North (and George III) wanted to achieve: the Boston harbor was closed; all town meetings were prohibited; British troops became immune from local laws and courts (they could do whatever they had to do to maintain the peace); and perhaps worst of all, from the colonists' perspectives, the Massachusetts upper house was transformed from a representative body to one appointed by the newly-appointed royal governor, General Thomas Gage, commander-in-chief of British troops in America. Gage had replaced Thomas Hutchinson, whom the British ministry thought was too weak to control the unruly citizens of Boston. This was the last in a series of acts the Americans regarded as being designed to force them to do whatever king and Parliament demanded.

The Americans and the English obviously did not agree on these issues. Indeed, the Americans had no say in any of them. They had to consider other alternatives. One result was the meeting in the summer of 1774 of the First Continental Congress, an illegal undertaking because it did precisely what the crown and Parliament were doing: it engaged in the making of laws, treaties, and even a naval force. Such things, the colonists decided, the Americans themselves had to do on their own. They believed they had to reaffirm their inherent right to make these decisions themselves. Moreover, they thought they might need to gain the requisite political experience and, at the same time, form an armed force in case they were unable to resolve their difficulties with the crown. The prevailing attitude was that reconciliation was still possible, if not probable, but they shared a constant, underlying fear that armed struggle might be the result of these disputes. By April of 1775, the first major clash between Americans and British forces took place at Lexington and Concord in Massachusetts.

Thomas Paine's arrival in November of 1774 had no impact on any of this. It is not even clear that he was fully aware of the significance of these events. When he first came to America, he even thought reconciliation was possible, but he soon realized that it was not. In any case, one of the first things he did when he recovered from his illness was to remember his manners: he thanked Benjamin Franklin for his letter of introduction, especially after Aitken hired him, first as a principal writer, then as editor, of the *Pennsylvania Magazine*.[15]

Philadelphia in 1774 was the virtual capital of America, and within three years it was the official capital of the United States. The seat of the recently formed Continental Congress, the population of the City of Brotherly Love included some 30,000 souls, the largest among the thirteen colonies. Founded by Quaker William Penn in 1682, it was still less than a mile square when Paine arrived there. The city retained its Quaker heritage, although by the mid-eighteenth century it had become a mishmash of religions and nationalities.[16] As the commercial center of British America, there were s e v eral wealthy merchants and manufacturers, of building materials and textiles in particular, as well as thousands of successful artisans, craftsmen, and mechanics: from carpenters to bakers to tailors and weavers. Paine, as a staymaker and a man with broad, liberal-minded views, fitted perfectly into his newly-adopted community. Its port was the largest, most active one in America, accommodating as many as 100 ships at one time at high tide. There was little poverty, little unemployment, and a good deal of prosperity. "Nothing there recalled the miserable London hovels and the other abominations of the English capital."[17]

With a high rate of literacy in the colonies, even the artisans and craftsmen read the newspapers and pamphlets of the day. Their interests, and their discussions, ranged from science to politics. Philadelphia was a lively place for Paine to reside. A sense of equality between the classes existed. In America, there were no hereditary titles or privileges, but there were some very wealthy men. Despite the proclaimed equality between the merchant, on the one hand, and the cordwainer, bricklayer, or hatter, on the other, the former often held the latter in disdain. At the same time, Philadelphia was the cultural capital of America with its theater, music, arts, and of course journalism, a field that Paine entered. His writing for the *Pennsylvania Magazine,* a number of essays and poems, some quite thoughtful and lyrical, gives some indication of his frame of mind.

Authors commonly used pseudonyms in England and Europe throughout this period, and Paine was no exception. He often signed his work anonymously with names taken or simply sounding like they were derived from antiquity, like "Comus," "Atlanticus," or "Amicus." On other occasions, he might use a descriptive English appellation, like "A Lover of Peace" or, after 1776, "Common Sense." Since these writings of 1775 constituted his first published literary and political works, it has become difficult to determine which of them may be attributed to Paine. The historical debate about which essays of the mid-1770s may be correctly attributed to Paine, especially since several of them were unsigned, centers primarily on the work of Moncure Daniel Conway, Philip S. Foner, A. Owen Aldridge, and most recently Isaac Kramnick and Michael Foot. Conway and Foner, though separated by a half century, seem to have the same ideas about what Paine might or might not have written. Aldridge doubts Paine's authorship of many of the essays in the Foner collection, noting that "some pieces can be positively identified, but there are problems with others which seem in one way or another to be linked to Paine, but lack conclusive ties."[18]

Following the publication of *Common Sense* in January of 1776, when Paine's style became more clearly recognizable and the themes he wished to pursue more clearly focused, the task of identification becomes notably less complicated. Also after that time, Paine himself began to identify in his correspondence the essays and pamphlets that he was about to write or indeed had already published. Because his interests were so wide-ranging and because he was so engaged in discovering his own style and his own voice, following his texts as they have appeared in his collected works is the most logical strategy. It also does the greatest justice to his life and writings. Discrepancies and disagreements among historians and commentators appear in the notes to the chapters.

Paine first wrote two introductory pieces for the inaugural issue of the *Pennsylvania Magazine*, an essay entitled "To The Public" and one called "The Magazine in America." In the first, he hailed the progress that humanity had made, making modern times so far advanced from the past. He also focused on the strengths of the New World, particularly as opposed to those of the Old. As an early environmentalist, he was convinced that Americans, because they were far healthier than their European counterparts, escaped the pollution of Europe. "Those who are conversant with Europe would be tempted to believe that even the air of the Atlantic disagrees with the constitution of foreign vices; if they survive the voyage, they either expire on their arrival or linger away in an incurable condition. There is a happy something in the climate of America which disarms them of all their power both of infection and attraction."[19] This was the beginning of Paine's long love affair with America. In his second essay, he argued that "a magazine," unlike the newspapers, "is the nursery of genius."[20] It was certainly the nursery of his genius, for within two months of his editorship, the magazine had attracted fifteen hundred subscribers—a significant number—thanks in large part to Paine's newly found journalistic skills.[21]

Indeed, he seemed surprised by the changed direction in his life. He later wrote that he had never contemplated becoming a journalist. He never knew he had the talent for it. It was impossible for him to have known. Aside from a few poems and songs he had composed, all Paine had really written before 1775 was his treatise on the excisemen.[22] His new career was now set, and something he hardly knew until now, success itself, was in the wind. His tide had indeed changed.

One of his most discursive essays was his uncharacteristic reflection on Alexander the Great, a parable about kings. Paine wrote that he left town one day to walk in the country. Crossing the Schuylkill, which he likened to the river Styx, "everything conspired to hush me into a pleasing kind of melancholy—the trees seemed to sleep—and the air hung round me with such unbreathing silence, as if listening to my very thoughts." His reverie took him to the real Styx, and there he asked Charon where Alexander was. Told he was approaching, Paine looked up and saw two people in a grand chariot roar past him. He asked Charon which one was Alexander the Conqueror. Charon's reply was as amusing as it was condemnatory. Why, Alexander was the horse in front,

> for whatever he was on the other side of the water is nothing now, he is a horse here; and not always that, for when he is apprehensive that a good licking is intended for him, he watches his opportunity to roll out of the stable in the shape of a piece of dung, or in any other disguise he can escape by.

Paine rushed off to the stable to find Alexander the Horse, who ran away as soon as Paine drew near. Paine then returned to the Styx with a bug that he had inadvertently picked up, only to find it was in fact Alexander himself. "[H]olding up the emperor between my finger and thumb, he exhibited a most contemptible figure of the downfall of tyrant greatness. . . . I suffered him to nibble on a pimple that was newly risen on my hand, in order to refresh him; after which I placed him on a tree to hide him, but a Tom Tit coming by, chopped him up with as little ceremony as he put whole kingdoms to the sword. On which I took my flight, reflecting with pleasure that I was not Alexander the Great."[23]

In the next issue of the magazine, he addressed class distinctions again—this time the subordination of a shepherd to an aristocrat who had stolen the shepherd's love and was about to marry her. Cupid threw the lord, whom Paine named Gothic, and the young damsel, Ruralinda, into a strange, deep sleep just at the moment of the wedding ceremony. They appeared to be awake, but truly they were not. Gothic imagined that his new wife, so much younger than he, engaged in countless affairs, which she perhaps did. Ruralinda dreamed that her old husband was dead. He cried out, she rejoiced. The wedding party thought them both mad and conveyed them away, she to her cottage, he to the manor. On awakening, the couple decided to go no further, and the shepherd was restored to his love, who was given "a handsome dowry" by Lord Gothic.[24] This was one of the most positive accounts Paine ever gave of an aristocrat but perhaps only because Paine was able to reform him in the end. More characteristic was his sharp, deafening criticism of both kings and aristocrats, as in the dialogue he attributed to General Thomas Gage, the British governor of Massachusetts, and General Wolfe, who was killed in 1759 at the Battle of Quebec.

In this piece, Wolfe, whom Paine had earlier heralded as a hero, returned to earth to scold Gage, who had been depriving his fellow British subjects of liberty. As governor, Gage had enforced the hated Intolerable Acts in Massachusetts and done whatever he could to quell dissident attacks against the crown. He ordered the arrests of leaders like John Hancock and Samuel Adams. Defending himself in Paine's essay, Gage told Wolfe that he was only carrying out the orders of his king, George III, orders which had been "sanctified by the Parliament of Great Britain. All the wisdom and liberty of the whole empire were collected in that august assembly." But Wolfe was unpersuaded: "The American colonies are entitled to all the privileges of British subjects. Equality of liberty is the glory of every Briton." Gage demurred. No, he said, the people of Massachusetts Bay were in rebellion against him, and as they were against him, they stood against England as well. Wolfe would have none of this. Heaven knew about the corruption of crown, Parliament, and Gage. Wolfe demanded that Gage immediately resign and return to England to "restore the perpetual harmony between Britain and her colonies." Unamused early on by the relationship between the imperial government and the Americans, Paine was already moving toward the principles he soon championed in *Common Sense.*

For example, he vigorously attacked the aristocracy, which he deemed totally unreformable. He roundly assailed the sad and cruel rule of Lord Robert Clive in India. Clive's troops, in the service of the East India Company, consolidated control in the Bengal and other parts of India. His efficient, often ruthless, administration, ferreted out corruption but he overreached his own resources. By the early 1770s, Britain took control and India became part of the empire. Recalled to London, his political enemies charged him with embezzlement, and though acquitted in 1773, he committed suicide the following year.

Stories of his mistreatment of the Indian population were legion, and Paine repeated them, no doubt because he wanted to show the extreme measures that aristocracy took to protect its interests. "The wailing widow, the crying orphan, and the childless parent remember and lament; the rival nabobs court his favor; the rich dread his power, and the poor his severity. Fear and terror march like pioneers before his camp, murder and rapine accompany it, famine and wretchedness follow in the rear." But Clive was now dead, Paine continued, and he had Clive regret his oppressive practices. Clive wailed, " 'Could I unlearn what I've already learned—unact what I've already acted—or would some sacred power convey me back to youth and innocence, I'd act another part—I'd keep within the value of humble life, nor wish for what the world calls pomp.' " But it was too late. He was condemned forever to hold onto his memory and his fate. Paine also attacked what he considered to be the primitive aristocratic practice of duelling. Along with Jefferson, he thought that duelling was ritualistic and a vestige of feudalism, unfit for a democratic-republican society. "Gothic and absurd," he called it, it should be outlawed, but Paine rightly figured that it was not to be any time soon.

In a similar manner, he attacked the whole idea of titles, claiming that people ought to get only those they deserve. In this way, a king was given the title, the *"Honorable* plunderer of his country, or the *Right Honorable* murderer of mankind." Kings and such become nothing more than "glowworms" which "extinguish themselves into common reptiles." Already Paine showed his facility to create images that riveted, even profoundly disturbed, his audience. In an anticlerical poem, often dismissed by many Paine biographers, "The Tale of the Monk and the Jew Versified," published in March 1775, he foreshadowed his later abhorrence (especially in *The Age of Reason*) for the mythologies created by priests to blind mankind of the true nature of religious faith and belief. An "unbelieving Jew" named Mordecai, while skating on some pretty thin ice, fell into the freezing water and couldn't get out. His head stuck out through the hole because his chin caught the lip of the ice. He pleaded with a monk, a "Papist," who was skating by, to give him a hand. But the monk considered it heresy to help a Jew. Before he offered his hand, therefore, the monk demanded that the poor man renounce his Judaism and declare himself a true Christian believer. Here Paine got the Jew's Eastern European accent just right:

> "Forswear mine fait? No! Got forbid!
> Dat would be fery base indeed,
> Come, never mind such tings as deeze,
> Tink, tink, how fery hard it freeze.
> More coot you do, more coot you be,
> Vat signifies your fait to me?
> Come, tink agen, how cold and vet,
> And help me out von little bit."

The monk of course refused, unable to give up a chance to convert the Jew to the true faith. When the Jew saw that he had no choice, he agreed to convert, but only if first the monk pulled him out of his waiting icy grave. And here the duplicity of both of them sprang forth. The monk naturally wanted to hear an "Amen" before he yanked Mordecai up. So the Jew repented and condemned his co-religionists as cheaters and liars all. Hearing such a strong attack on Jews, the monk began to wonder whether this one was cheating and lying, too. No, replied the Jew, he would be as Christian as this monk, who of course was hardly practicing Christian charity by blackmailing him. In the end, Mordecai is thrust to his icy death, a

Christian the monk believed, a Jew in fact.

> The bigot Papist, joyful hearted,
> To hear the heretic converted,
> Replied to the *designing Jew*,
> This was a happy fall for you;
> You'd die a Christian now,
> For if you live, you'll break your vow.
> Then said no more, but in a trice
> Popp'd Mordecai beneath the ice.[29]

Paine's attack on organized religion, especially the Judeo-Christian tradition, was the keystone of his own religious belief. Hebrew scripture and Christian theology as set forth in the Bible were nothing but lies and fables designed to blind all people to the truth of God's creation. The goal of all organized religion, Judaism or Christianity or Islam, was to control as many people as possible, to keep them enslaved to the theology of a particular group for its own enrichment.

This theme of slavery spilled over into some of his earliest pieces in the *Magazine,* which focused on the horrors of slavery and the slave trade. In Philadelphia, he lived across the street from a place where newly arrived slaves were sold to the highest bidders. He found the trade in human cargo particularly abhorrent and disgusting. These people had committed no crimes and were not the conquered victims in war, but for over three hundred years Europeans had been capturing young Africans and sending them into slavery.[30] The numbers concerning the American trade, which officially began in 1619 when a Dutch sea captain sold twenty Africans to colonists in Jamestown, are staggering. Best estimates have it that nearly twelve million human beings were enslaved from Africa. Although the vast majority of Black slaves worked the tobacco fields and plantations in the southern colonies, the northern and middle colonies also participated in the slave trade and slavery. Between 1728 and 1790 more than thirteen hundred advertisements seeking information on the whereabouts of runaway slaves in the Philadelphia/New Jersey/Baltimore area appeared in the *Philadelphia Gazette,* a newspaper for which Paine soon wrote. Rewards for returned "property" ranged anywhere from five to sixteen dollars, depending on the sex, age, and work capability of the individual slave. The very month that Paine arrived in Philadelphia, the following advertisement appeared in the *Gazette*. Note that the reward is higher for the perpetrator of the escape than it is for the slave himself.

> Five Pounds for the Negro, with reasonable charges, on delivering him at Philadelphia, and Ten Pounds for the person who took him away, if convicted of the crime. Ran away, about the 24th of June, 1774, from the subscriber, living in Philadelphia, a Negro man, named Caesar, of a middling black color, about 22 years of age, 5 feet 3 or 4 inches high, well made, with a long neck and falling shoulders, walks very upright, has bandy well made legs, with thick muscular calves, a large mouth and lips, is much inclined to laugh, and when he laughs shows much of his gums and teeth, is talkative and impertinent, with often an elevated voice, where he dares to make free, is insolent, and ready to box amongst his companions, and is fond of playing scraps of tunes on the fife. He having taken a Bristol pipe box, about two feet and a half long, with sundry clothes, may change his dress, but may have on either a mended cloth color, or an old dark blue superfine cloth coat, a blue nap round about or sea jacket, lined with white flannel, and a red and white narrow striped ditto, green plush or black stocking breeches, remarkably narrow striped Irish ticken breeches and trousers, thread stockings, &c. The above reward of five pounds, and charges, on delivering the Negro at Philadelphia, and also the ten pounds, on proving and prosecuting to conviction the person, who aided, assisted, or carried him off, will be punctually paid by
>
> Philip Wilson[31]

Paine's friend and mentor Benjamin Franklin has long been credited with launching the first American critical assault on slavery in his 1751 *Observations Concerning the Increase of Mankind*. In Pennsylvania, the Quaker influences worked profusely against the institution, and Paine, with his own Quaker background, was a perfect anchor to the movement. For Paine, these enslaved Black people had the same right to freedom as any person. Like several men in Philadelphia such as David Rittenhouse and Benjamin Rush, he vehemently attacked slavery and the slave trade. Rush once told James Cheetham, who was at first an admirer, then later a severe critic of Paine, that Paine had sent him a letter attacking the slave trade, and "an extract from it was published in the *Columbia Magazine*."[32] In one of his first essays, Paine wrote that slavery was a "monstrous" outrage, a "barbarous usage." There were "many evils attending the practice; as selling husbands away from wives, children from parents, and from each other, in violation of sacred and natural ties."

Americans now ought to give serious consideration to ending both slavery and the trade in human lives altogether. "But what singular obligations are we under to these injured people!" he exclaimed.[33] Just a few weeks later, Franklin returned from Britain and established the first anti-slavery organization in America. Its first president was Benjamin Rush, and Paine was among its first members. A few months later, Paine was back on the subject, looking toward the day when a dual freedom will prevail: America from Britain, Black slaves from their white masters. Along with these freedoms will come the end of "the horrid cruelties" the British caused to be suffered by the inhabitants of India. Even the American Indians will be freed from the "treachery and murder" of the white man.[34] It was a brief essay but full of broad-based themes encompassing all the entrapped people known to him, including women.[35] His concern for the poor and downtrodden was also in evidence in a short piece in which he advocated public assistance for young people just starting out in life and social security for the elderly, a theme he would not return to until 1792 and then again in 1797.[36] Eventually Pennsylvania became the first state in the union to abolish slavery, which it did by an act of the Assembly in 1780.[37]

All this demonstrated that in 1775 Paine was thinking in terms of freedom, which to him ultimately meant American separation from Britain. He wrote about a dream of a beautiful countryside abundant with delicious fruit and lovely flowing streams, thousands of flowers, and hundreds of beautiful songbirds. It "seemed as if they were the threshold of the celestial region," it was so enchanting. Suddenly the sun grew ever hotter, and everything rapidly dried up. He began to suffocate in the heat, as "the fountains dried away; and the atmosphere became a motionless lake of air, loaded with pestilence and death." Huge, dark clouds rolled in, and a heavy silence fell over the parched land.

After a while, thunder began to roar in the distance, and the heavens opened up in a furious storm so mighty that he had to take cover or be in danger of losing his life. Another deluge from the biblical ages had come. But then everything was restored, and Paine's lyricism rose to its highest pitch.

> The air, purged of its poisonous vapors, was fresh and healthy. The dried fountains were replenished, the waters sweet and wholesome. The sickly earth, recovered to new life, abounded with vegetation. The groves were musical with innumerable songsters, and the long-deserted fields echoed with the joyous sound of the husbandman. All, all was felicity.

Awakening from the dream and continuing on his way, he came upon a companion who interpreted his dream as Joseph did for Pharaoh.

The country he had dreamed of was America, a beautiful, uncorrupted land with endless promise. But the stifling heat and the dark clouds, the thunder, lightning, and murderous storm were the forces of the beast which was trying to destroy her. It was Britain, which had caused a tempest in America. Everything that America had tried to do to quench the hunger and thirst of "the beast" had failed. So now, "the cause is before a higher court, the court of providence, before whom the arrogance of kings, the infidelity of ministers, the general corruption of government, and all the cobweb artifice of courts, will fall confounded and ashamed."[38] The message was clear: America will have to fight the beast, for, as Paine said just two months later, "the reign of Satan is not ended."

At this time, perhaps drawing on the Protestant historical tradition, Paine frequently used the image of Britain as Satan, the Devil, or sometimes using a well-known pagan figure, the Roman god, Saturn, who was so bestial he devoured his own children. Mother Britain was devouring her child, America. "The portrait of a parent red with the blood of her children is a picture fit only for the galleries of the infernals," he told his fellow Quakers, who failed to perceive the severity of the oppressive British regime.[39]   Later, in

Common Sense, he revived this horrible image, no doubt to bewilder and frighten his readers. America's people have fled, not as children from the soft embrace of their mother, but from "the cruelty of the monster." (*CS* 84) The answer was armed struggle to protect the guardian, Liberty herself:

> But hear, O ye swains ('tis a tale most profane),
> How all the tyrannical powers,
> Kings, Commons, and Lords, are uniting amain
> To cut down this guardian of ours.
> From East to the West blow the trumpet to arms,
> Thro' the land let the sound of it flee:
> Let the far and the near all unite with a cheer,
> In defense of our Liberty Tree.[40]

This poem exuded juvenile rhyme and technique, but it clearly set forth Paine's developing sentiments about Britain. He also approached the problems between Britain and America from another direction. He joined with a young scientist, Captain Thomas Pryor, in developing a technique to produce saltpeter, a key component in the manufacture of gunpowder, in people's homes. They could then supply the saltpeter to the nation's military magazines for storage and use whenever it was needed. In November in the *Pennsylvania Journal*, he announced their experiments, which appeared to lay the foundations for a true armed struggle against Britain.[41]

By this time, in the fall of 1775, Paine was working on the early drafts of *Common Sense*, his eloquent argument for American separation from Britain. He took time from it to comment on something that the Pennsylvania Assembly had recently done, namely instruct its delegates to the Continental Congress about what they should do if a vote on separation from England arose. They were directed to vote against independence. As delegates to Congress elected directly by the state Assembly, they were to do as the Assembly wanted. In the same issue of the *Journal* in which his piece on saltpeter appeared, Paine severely castigated the Pennsylvania Assembly for binding the minds and hands of its delegates.

This argument raised a much larger question about representation which Edmund Burke dealt with just a year earlier when he was elected to Parliament as a member from Bristol: just what is the proper role of a representative? To represent one's constituency only (to follow its instructions) or the nation (to achieve the good of people)? Burke's answer was that a deputy represented the national interest, not the narrower interest of a particular constituency. So wrote Burke to his electors:

> Certainly, gentlemen, it ought to be the happiness and glory of a representative to live in the strictest union, the closest correspondence, and the most unreserved communication with his constituents. Their wishes ought to have great weight with him; their opinions high respect; their business unremitted attention. It is his duty to sacrifice his repose, his pleasure, his satisfactions, to theirs—and above all, ever, and in all cases, to prefer their interest to his own.
> But his unbiased opinion, his mature judgment, his enlightened conscience, he ought not to sacrifice to you, to any man, or to any set of men living. These he does not derive from your pleasure—no, nor from the law and the constitution. They are a trust from Providence, for the abuse of which he is deeply answerable. Your representative owes you, not his industry, but his judgment; and he betrays, instead of serving you, if he sacrifices it to your opinion.[42]

Agreeing here with Burke, who would become his ideological nemesis during the French Revolution, Paine argued that instructions from constituents were faulty, misguided, and just plain wrong. At the same moment, Paine was working on the pamphlet that he hoped would influence the congressional decision on independence by voting for separation.

But Paine's arguments went deeper than a mere disagreement over separation. He was revolted by the idea that an Assembly should have the right to bind the will of its delegates with a set of instructions. The delegates had minds of their own, and because they were involved in the debates in Congress directly on a national level (and the members of the Assembly were not), they should vote their own minds.

Paine wrote:

> When I voted at the last Election for a representative in the
> House in which you now sit, I never meant to invest any of you
> with such a power, and I protest against your assuming it. The
> delegates in Congress are not the delegates of the Assembly but
> of the People—of the Body at large. For convenience sake only,
> we at present consent to your nominating them; but we may as
> well be without delegates if they must act solely under your
> influence, and thus circumstanced they can only set there as
> ciphers.

Even in Britain, he said, despite the depth of corruption, the houses
of Parliament did not instruct each other what to do. America as a
nation was united in its efforts to achieve the rights and liberties due
her from Britain. The delegates to Congress, instead of being given
instructions from their states, must meet in unity and strength for the
good of all American citizens, and not only for the good of
Pennsylvania.

   The opponents of separation immediately censured Paine's
ideas in the same newspaper when a writer identifying himself as a
"Pennsylvania Associator" called Paine's desire of seeing America and
Britain separate a "pernicious hope."[43] In an early indication of his
tenacity and vigor when he was under attack, just one month before
the appearance of *Common Sense*, Paine retorted that instructions like
this had only unwanted effects. Besides, the assemblymen were not
involved in all the discussions and debate, which were to follow when
the question of separation came up, so how could they make a judgment in advance of a "fair hearing" on all sides of the issue? To make
a judgment now was to forestall just what was needed — a decision
that was based on continental, not provincial, interests. "I despise the
narrow idea of acting provincially," he exclaimed, "and reprobate the
little unworthy principle, conveyed in the following words, 'In behalf
of this colony,' and the more so, because by a late resolve, all colony
distinctions are to be laid aside. `Tis the American cause," he virtu-
ally shouted in all capital letters, "the American Congress, the
American army, &c. &c. whom God preserve."[44] Thomas Paine was
undoubtedly moving faster than any other citizen in America toward

the concept of national unity.

Paine remained the editor of the *Pennsylvania Magazine* only until the fall of 1775 when he had a financial dispute with Aitken, the publisher. Paine apparently wanted more money, and Aitken refused. Paine left the magazine and worked on the pamphlet that soon awakened Americans to the true nature of their condition. Having come to America at a time when his political consciousness was just beginning to unfurl, he later told Franklin that he "thought it very hard to have the country set on fire about my ears almost the moment I got into it."[45] But he was soon responsible for some of the sparks that set that fire, as he admonished his fellow Americans to use their "common sense" and make the final break with Britain.

Part Two

Liberty and the Republic

4 · "Common sense will tell us"

Throughout 1775, the Americans had ambivalent feelings about their relationship with Britain. Their uncertainty seems peculiar from the vantage point of the late-twentieth century, because actual fighting had already occurred in Lexington and Concord that April. Eight Americans had died when a force of some twelve hundred Redcoats marched from Boston to seize a cache of arms the rebels had stored in Concord. Paul Revere and others had warned of the approaching British troops, and skirmishing had continued all day as the British forces were pushed back to Boston, leaving some two hundred and seventy-three of them dead.[1] Despite actual combat, however, most Americans believed that the proper end of the tensions between the colonists and the monarchy was through a negotiated settlement. After all, the Americans thought of themselves as English first and American merely as a circumstance of residence. For most of them, separation from the empire was unthinkable. They were only a small number of people, under two million in all the colonies, spread out over the eastern coast of America. They believed, as their English cousins did, that life was in fact hierarchical by rank and position and that some people were dependent on others because that was the way it had always been. So the Second Continental Congress drafted and then dispatched to George III the Olive Branch Petition outlining the Americans' desire for reconciliation.

At the same time, Congress authorized the formation of a Continental Army, under the command of Virginian George Washington, planter-turned-military commander, because relations were deteriorating rapidly. War preparations increased on both sides. Militias drilled on village greens, production of musketry and cannon increased, and the tavern talk over rum and beer was whether peace or war would prevail. On the British side, the administration of Lord North, the Prime Minister, hoped for a settlement. The king, too, wished to end the tensions that had developed over legislation Parliament had passed the year before to subordinate the colonies, especially the five Intolerable Acts.

In the fall and early winter of 1775-76, Paine listened to and participated in the debates over America's relationship with Britain. He later acknowledged that he was initially reluctant to participate as deeply as he eventually did in the drive for American independence. "All the plans or prospects of private life (for I am not by nature fond of, or fitted for a public one and feel all occasions of it where I must act personally a burden) all these plans, I say, were immediately disconcerted, and I was at once involved in all the troubles of the country."[2] Paine did not act from the basis of wealth or property, for he had neither. His decision to become involved was based purely on principle. To him, there was no natural linkage between America and Britain. America's future was not contingent on what happened in Westminster. Moreover, the idea that Americans possessed the so-called rights of Englishmen was fraught with error, even danger. There was nothing particularly civilized about rights that king and Parliament could obliterate with the stroke of a pen and the fire of a musket. For Paine, it made no sense to continue the relationship with the English. It only made sense, common sense, to separate. The result was his great pamphlet of January 1776.

The idea for writing such a pamphlet likely came from Benjamin Rush, the physician-writer of Philadelphia, who later signed the Declaration of Independence. In 1776, Rush was only thirty-one years old, but he already enjoyed a wide reputation as a popular physician and polemicist for the American cause. Rush was baptized into the Church of England. His father died when he was five, and though he received a great deal of care and love from his mother, he soon came under the influence of Presbyterian ministers Samuel Finley and Samuel Davies, who were proponents of the religious revival movement in mid-century known as the Great

Awakening. Rush spent his life thereafter as a proponent of Presbyterianism, more pointedly Calvinism, though by 1782 he believed in universal salvation. Educated in science and medicine at Edinburgh, Rush inquired throughout his life into the nature of the physical world, learning how to heal the ill, while at the same time seeking the philosophical order of things, as time brought mankind spiritually and practically to the millennium. He saw the struggle between Britain and America on a grand historical scale: America's mistreatment by British tyrants only proved that the forces of evil were pitted against the forces of right and virtue, and right and progress would eventually win out as a sign of the millennium's approach.

Rush had often spoken to his friends about why it was right for America to separate from Britain. Among these friends were astronomer and instrument maker David Rittenhouse and George Clymer, the latter also a signer of the Declaration of Independence. Rittenhouse, the inventor of the "Orrery," a famous planetarium in America, was initially trained to make mathematical instruments, and attempted to perfect the telescope, but his interest and involvement in politics soon led him to the cause of independence.[3] Clymer, two years younger than Paine, was a successful Philadelphia merchant, who later became the first president of the Bank of Philadelphia and a participant, along with financier Robert Morris, in the formation of the Bank of North America. Later a delegate to the Constitutional Convention in 1787, Clymer served in the House of Representatives in the first Federal Congress.[4]

Paine met these men through his association with Aitken's *Pennsylvania Magazine.* Aitken's bookshop also provided a meeting place for people like Paine to air their anti-British feelings. In his autobiography, Rush noted that as soon as he was introduced to Paine by Aitken at the bookshop one day, he felt a kinship with the immigrant. Rush was pleased to learn that Paine "had realized the independence of the colonies upon Great Britain, and that he considered the measure as necessary to bring the war to a speedy and successful issue."[5] Rush wrote in his *Autobiography* that he had been giving some thought to publishing an essay on American independence, since no one had forcefully argued in print why America ought to separate from Britain. He had some second thoughts about writing it himself, however, because his medical practice had somewhat declined after he published an antislavery tract. He was more than happy to suggest that Paine do it. Paine agreed and probably began writing around the first of November, especially since he had before him several American newspaper commentaries outlining the British side.[6] It was time for the Americans themselves to present the public argument for separation.

Despite Paine's often brilliant and eminently quotable words, he found writing a difficult task. He wrote slowly, frequently agonizing over phrases and sentences. (This problem remained with him throughout his life.) He showed various parts of the essay to Rush during the drafting, gaining advice along the way, and when he had completed it, at Rush's suggestion, he took it to Franklin, Rittenhouse, and Samuel Adams (a brewer and the radical cousin of John Adams) for all of them to review and edit. They made few changes. When Paine requested title proposals, Rush recommended "common sense."

Paine's pamphlet of this name was both an extraordinary achievement and overnight success. In spite of his lack of a formal education (or maybe because of it), he demonstrated an ability to write clearly and succinctly. The work was not very long; it conformed to the conventional length of political pamphlets in eighteenth century discourse. But in its glistening words of hope and enthusiasm, it shook America and England. It was certainly more impressive than anything Paine had written to date—longer, more expansive, more cogent, more powerful. Until 1776, he had written only a few journal essays and his plea to Parliament on behalf of the excise tax collectors. In *Common Sense*, he wrote as if he had spent a lifetime composing discourses.

No one has ever satisfactorily explained Paine's achievement. Perhaps it is simply that like a cat enraged by a dog, he struck out at the powerful oppressor. *Common Sense* was also successful because it was physically accessible. Printed cheaply, it was sold at the very low price of two shillings a copy. Paine later estimated to his friend Henry Laurens that it probably sold well over one hundred fifty thousand copies in 1776 in America, "exclusive of the great run it had in

England and Ireland." It was, he exclaimed, "the greatest sale that any performance ever had since the use of letters." An exaggeration, certainly, but Paine's work was no doubt an immense financial success, though Paine never realized a penny's profit from it. He turned his share, which would have numbered in the thousands of pounds, over to the American cause. In all, more than one-fifth of all the colonists read the pamphlet, or had it read to them.[7]

The pamphlet was also written in a language that any person could easily understand. The language was simple and straightforward. Unlike many of his contemporary pamphleteers, Paine avoided long, convoluted sentences and classical references and used instead the familiar vocabulary and word patterns of everyday street discourse. This rhetoric was characteristic of his style for the rest of his career. Historians have debated whether this style was new or old, or perhaps neither.[8] The pamphlet appealed to a cross-section of people: to artisans, craftsmen, and tradesmen as well as to bankers, manufacturers, and industrialists. Finally, Paine's use of imagery made the pamphlet an extraordinary work. Not only did he write well; he did so grippingly, using images and metaphors of a high, sophisticated caliber, but which never alienated his readers. His images, lively and sharp, were profoundly meaningful to his readers who understood exactly what he meant when he not merely belittled the king of England but turned him into a monster. Even God hated kings: "'Tis a form of government which the word of God bears testimony against, and blood will attest to it." (*CS* 80) His stylistic qualities more than anything else made *Common Sense* one of the truly great bestsellers of the century.[9]

Paine's pamphlet is still today his best known, most often quoted work. It was a powerful piece, containing some of the most memorable lines in American history. "The sun never shined on a cause of greater worth." "Now is the seed-time of continental union, faith and honor." "A new era for politics is struck; and a new method of thinking hath arisen." "The present winter is worth an age if rightly employed, if lost or neglected, the whole continent will partake of the misfortune." "When we are planning for posterity, we ought to remember that virtue is not hereditary." "We have every opportunity and every encouragement before us to form the noblest, purest constitution on the face of the earth." "We have it in our power to begin the world over again." "A situation similar to the present hath not happened since the days of Noah until now." "The birthday of a new world is at hand." (*CS* 82, 89, 110, 120) The examples never seem to end. These phrases, as persuasive as they were individually, were not, however, meant to stand alone. They were inter-related: Paine developed them into a powerful, imaginative, imagery-filled, cohesive and irrefutable case for the colonies to separate from Britain. After *Common Sense* it was very difficult, if not impossible, for the colonists not to be convinced that separation from the empire was correct. The Continental Congress' Declaration of Independence just five months later on July 4, 1776, came as almost an inevitability after Paine's little essay.

Nothing Paine said in the pamphlet was understated. On the contrary, for the Americans to understand the full significance of continuing their relationship with the British, they had to see the complete picture, because what was happening in America had an impact on the entire world. Paine announced at the outset that "the cause of America is in a great measure the cause of all mankind." (*CS* 63) The British were already at war with America, but this war had a universal quality. Liberty was at stake everywhere, should the ministry successfully subjugate the Americans. With this warning as a foundation, Paine attacked the shibboleths of British politics, such as the division of power among king, lords, and commons. The pamphlet debunked everything British: the system of government, the so-called rights of Englishmen, the very idea of monarchy itself, and ultimately the relationship between England and America.

To forge a powerful argument to convince his still-relatively new American audience, Paine made use of two ideologies well known in the colonies: the principles of classical republicanism with its focus on the republic, virtue, and corruption; and the ideas of the great English political philosopher and activist, John Locke, who had written the central document on rights and liberties, *The Second Treatise of Civil Government*, one hundred years earlier at the time of the Glorious Revolution of 1688. In essence, these two potent ideologies turned Paine into the model "thinking" revolutionary.[10]

Locke's ideas were well-known in the colonies, as they were

in England. His defense of the essential rights and liberties of all human beings, including the right to resist tyrannical authority, were discussed practically on a daily basis in the inns and taverns of America. In effect, they were immediately familiar and identifiable by most informed Americans.

Locke, like Paine, was no mere armchair theorist of government. An associate of the Earl of Shaftesbury (Anthony Ashley Cooper), Locke was also a political activist. As one of the founders of the Whig party, which stood in opposition to court and crown, Locke's patron Lord Shaftesbury had objected to the rule of the Stuart king, Charles II, who along with his courtiers tried to increase the power of the king at the expense of Parliament. Even before the death of Charles II, Shaftesbury joined the attempt to exclude from the throne Charles' brother James II, a decided Roman Catholic and monarchical absolutist. For his efforts, Shaftesbury was forced to flee to Holland in 1681. Locke was exiled two years later and joined Shaftesbury. Together they conspired with other Whig leaders to plot the overthrow of James. Having ruled for only three years (1685-88), James fled to France after his forces under John Churchill (later the duke of Marlborough) deserted him in the virtually bloodless Glorious Revolution in December of 1688.

Like many of his contemporaries, Thomas Paine understood the nature of Lockean political theory, even if he never read Locke, as he later claimed. Locke's ideas virtually saturated the air of Philadelphia in 1776. In *Common Sense*, Paine made direct use of Locke's distinction between society and government, holding, as had Locke, that society (which was natural) preceded government, which men had to consciously (and artificially) create. People in a pre-political condition of life had originally lived together, said Locke, without government. Because they naturally understood the laws of nature through their reason, they soon learned that it was as incumbent on each of them to take care of their fellows as it was to protect their own good. When a person saw someone steal something from a neighbor, therefore, that person was, under the law of nature, required to be police, prosecutor, judge, jury, and even executioner of the law. This state of affairs, Locke had said, was inconvenient. The people soon learned that when they entered into a social contract with one another, they gave up some of their natural rights in exchange for greater security and safety. Government took care of protecting their interests, on the one hand, and the people, on the other, agreed to obey the laws that their government enacted for their benefit. In his pamphlet, Paine clearly used Lockean terms and Lockean ideas. As Locke had asserted that human beings possessed a faculty to reason, of understanding things, so Paine agreed. In fact, the very title of his work indicated that, as he himself said, when faced with a particularly difficult problem, a person ultimately found the answer because "common sense will tell us." (*CS* 105) Common sense allows us to develop solutions to intricate problems, social, economic, or political.

In addition, Paine agreed with Locke when he said that his subject was government, something categorically different from society. Paine had nothing positive to say about government. In a famous passage, he said that while society was good, government was evil, though necessary. "Government, like dress, is the badge of lost innocence." (*CS* 65) Like Adam and Eve, who needed no clothes in the Garden of Eden but found shame after their expulsion, so too men had lost their political innocence. They needed government to protect their freedom and security. Otherwise the few, who destroyed both of those things, triumphed. Accordingly, the people joined together to form the first true direct democracy in history: there were no representatives, who acted as the intermediaries between the citizen and his government. Every person represented himself.[11] "Some convenient tree will afford them a State House, under the branches of which, the whole colony may assemble to deliberate on public matters. It is more than probably that their first laws will have the title only of Regulations, and be enforced by no other penalty than public disesteem. In this first parliament every man, by natural right will have a seat." (*CS* 67) Shortly thereafter, as more and more people understood the convenience of government protecting their rights and liberties and providing greater security for their property and persons, a representative system evolved, because it was no longer practical for all those people to travel great distances to represent themselves. Elections must have taken place often just to insure that government followed the will of the people, and not its own inclinations.

This was precisely the problem of the English system of government: it followed the inclinations of court and crown and not of the people. That system was based on good republican principles which had become corrupted and debased because of the overweening power of the king and the aristocracy. The English had historically claimed that their government represented all the people of the nation, because power was divided into three major branches, which Paine termed "two ancient tyrannies, compounded with some new republican materials." Here Paine reflected, very clearly, classical republican values with their emphasis on structure. The English government was not, however, a true republic. Its composition of a balanced, or mixed, regime was faulty, even corrupt. It consisted of:

> First. The remains of monarchical tyranny in the person of the king.
> Secondly. The remains of aristocratical tyranny in the persons of the peers.
> Thirdly. The new republican materials, in the persons of the commons, on whose virtue depends the freedom of England. (*CS* 68-69)

Only the last of these, as Paine himself pointed out, was "virtuous," a key term in classical republican thought. Virtue was the highest value, and it meant that there was a commitment to achieve the public good, the common interest, through widespread citizen participation in decision-making. And in England, only the House of Commons qualified. The other two institutions sought only to aggrandize their own class (royal or aristocratic) with additional power and wealth.

English government therefore had failed to distribute power equitably among its branches—king, lords, and commons (the one, the few, and the many). It had in reality reserved power only for the first two, crown and nobility. Those two ancient tyrannies, monarchy and aristocracy, rode roughshod over the common people. "The plain truth is that it is wholly owing to the constitution of the people, and not to the constitution of the government that the crown is not as oppressive in England as in Turkey." (*CS* 71) So while the English people did not face the same problems as those who lived in the most tyrannical states, they were still in danger of being totally subjugated, and the Americans along with them. God himself rejected monarchical forms, which were "ranked in scripture as one of the sins of the Jews, for which a curse in reserve is denounced against them."[12] (*CS* 73)

To persuade his audience, whom he must have thought mainly believers, Paine described the scriptural foundation of monarchy and concluded that it was nothing more than "popery in government." (*CS* 76) This term had a rhetorical effect. Paine knew full well the potentially negative impact of the term "popery." It was in use throughout the seventeenth and eighteenth centuries to evoke the anti-Catholic sentiments which infected the English countryside. It stimulated memories of England's most horrifying Catholic monarchs: Bloody Queen Mary; the father of James II, Charles I, beheaded in 1649; and worst of all, James II himself, forced to flee the throne in 1688 because of shared fears among Whig and Tory leaders that he sought to establish "popery" in both religion (Catholicism) and government (absolutism). What Paine suggested was deeply alarming to every Protestant American: If England was once more veering toward popery, what then of America's future?

Again, Paine turned to Locke. Only this time, instead of focusing on Locke and the origins of government and society, he looked to what Locke had said about resistance, even revolution. Locke indicated the appropriate moment for revolutionary action in words that Jefferson incorporated into the Declaration of Independence a scant few months after the spectacular appearance of Thomas Paine's pamphlet.

> Whenever the legislators endeavor to take away and destroy the property of the people or to reduce them to slavery under arbitrary power, they put themselves into a state of war with the people, who are thereupon absolved from any further obedience and are left to the common refuge. . . [I]f a long train of abuses, prevarications and artifices, all tending the same way, make the design visible to the people, and they cannot feel what they lie under and see whither they are going, it is not to be wondered that they should then rouse themselves and endeavor to put the

rule into such hands which may secure to them the ends for which government was at first erected.[13]

In effect, resistance to a constituted authority was a last resort, undertaken only after the people had exhausted all other avenues of resolution.[14] Paine understood this and agreed. Americans struggled long, hard, and unsuccessfully with the British, who had imposed on them greater and greater economic burdens. Everything that the Americans had tried in peace had "been ineffectual, and the period of debate is closed." Paraphrasing Locke's caution that the turn to force was reserved as the final step, Paine wrote: "Arms, as the last resource, decide the contest; the appeal was the choice of the king, and the continent hath accepted the challenge."

Because it was now "the seed time of continental union, faith, and honor," there could be only one thing to do: " 'TIS TIME TO PART," all in capital letters, Paine literally bellowed to his readers from the written page. If Americans did not understand this now, they would see that if they waited any longer, it would be too late. Not only would a greater tyranny expand over the continent, but the nation would soon go bankrupt paying the expenses of this tyranny, all on American soil, and the people enslaved forever. God himself had never meant for one distant people to control another: "Even the distance at which the Almighty hath placed England and America is a strong and natural proof that the authority of the one over the other was never the design of Heaven." (*CS* 82, 87)

Paine couched his argument in a language designed to inflame, to convince his readers that there were no alternatives to separation from England and in effect to get them to go to war against the English government. He offered a good deal of his message consequently in extreme terms. Monarchy was always evil, kings eternally animalistic, noblemen invariably voracious, the people consistently virtuous. At the same time, he less ardently addressed problems of the economy, commerce, and trade in the America he hoped to see soon free and independent. Here Paine was cool-tempered, and not at all at his rhetorical best. Even so, he knew that a solid economic foundation with good trade relations was necessary for the maintenance of the republic. A strong economy was the handmaiden of political organization laid out in the republic. For purposes of the pamphlet, however, economic issues were secondary. Only on the major question—independence—did Paine embark on a quest for the most persuasive argument possible. Here his use of language was replete with imagery that burned in the minds of his readers.

At times Paine's colorful images became too blindingly bright. He mixed and confused them, but this probably mattered little to his readers. America was, he said, "an infant state," and this was an appropriate time for her to seek independence. "We are sufficiently numerous and, were we more so, we might be less united." After all, once a child has been weaned from its mother, it is ready to have meat. It was ready to take its place in the world. (*CS* 107, 83) On another occasion, he claimed that Americans were "parents," who knew that the British rule over America must end. The Americans had "no joy, knowing that this government was not sufficiently lasting to ensure anything which we may bequeath to posterity." Their children would be lost, if strong, forthright action were not taken and taken now. Besides, America was greater in size than Britain. "In no instance hath nature made the satellite larger than its primary planet." If America did not separate now, then "it is leaving the sword to our children, and shrinking back at a time, when a little more, a little farther, would have rendered this continent the glory of the earth." (*CS* 87, 91)

In these more passionate moments, Paine used strong, unforgettable language to awaken Americans to the reality that faced them. First, his goal was to convince them that they could indeed achieve the goal of separation. We see that, for example, in his famous phrase, "We have it in our power to begin the world over again." (*CS* 120) All the people must become aware of that power. What Americans needed, he said, was objectivity, the ability to stand back and view the situation as it really was. Paine himself had not an objective bone in his body. He had opinions on everything, whether he was informed or not.[15] But it was critical, he said, for Americans to see where they stood, to see how the English government was smothering them. Unfortunately, it was impossible to be part of something and have an objective view of it at the same time, just as it was impossible for "a man, who is attached to a prostitute . . . to choose or judge of a wife."[16] (*CS* 71) Still, the effort must be made. His task was to demonstrate, by using common sense, the true nature of the British government and why the Americans must move now to escape its grasp.

The first thing to note about monarchs was that they were the most vicious brutes on earth. They ruled illegitimately (indeed, they held their positions unlawfully), and they were cannibals. The ancients idolized dead monarchs, but moderns have improved on this by worshiping live ones. In reality, monarchs are worms of the earth: "How impious is the title of *sacred majesty* applied to a worm, who in the midst of his splendor is crumbling into dust." (*CS* 72) Incredibly, the people of England have fallen into worship of these king-worms with great reverence. George III, whose name he refused to write out, has "sunk himself beneath the rank of animals, and contemptibly crawl[s] through the world like a worm." He was not a human being anymore, but "an apostate from the order of mankind." (*CS* 114)

At times Paine described the king as lower than the lowest creatures on earth; at other times he described him as the "beast of Britain" or the "Royal Brute of Britain." Like the Roman god Saturn (a conventional eighteenth-century image), who destroyed his own children, the king was murdering and gobbling up his subjects. After the massacre at Lexington in April of 1775, Paine had no doubt that this "Pharaoh," this "wretch," could "unfeelingly" hear of the slaughter of his own people and "composedly sleep with their blood upon his soul." (*CS* 92) This pharaoh was worse than the most horrid creature in the animal world. "Even brutes do not devour their young, nor savages make war upon their families." (*CS* 84) The king was the pimp who had prostituted his own children. "Can ye give to prostitution its former innocence?" he demanded to know. Just as that was impossible so was any tendency or desire to restore harmony and reconciliation with the "robber and murderer," who now "provoke us into justice." (*CS* 114, 92, 95, 98, 99, 100)

This language made the "killing of the king," as historian Winthrop Jordan has shown, a less painful experience for those who were reticent about a break from Britain.[17] How the figurative cannibalism by monarchs came about generally was not difficult to fathom: the strongest among a group seized control and refused to give it up for himself or his progeny. This "ruffian of some restless gang" threatened the others with harm or worse, and forever after the world was stuck with kings, "the chief among plunderers." (*CS* 77)

England, he admitted, had had some good kings, though the opposite kind are more typical. The English monarchy arose because "a French bastard landing with an armed banditti" made himself king against the wishes of the native inhabitants. But this illegitimate scoundrel, this "usurper," possessed sufficient military power to seize control and then force the local population to do his will. (*CS* 79) This development, like others before and after it in history, was a crime, a criminal act against an essentially free people who were never asked whether they wanted this villain for their king. He drew a parallel to this incident from the Bible, the original sin of Adam and Eve. Just as all men were indicted as a result of Adam's sin, so all Englishmen were doomed to acknowledge the heirs of William the Conqueror as monarch. "It unanswerably follows that original sin and hereditary succession are parallels," he concluded. "Dishonorable rank! Inglorious connection! Yet the most subtle sophist cannot produce a juster simile." (*CS* 78)

The time had come, after a century-long struggle, to rid the world of monarchy and of the senseless and automatic succession of monarchs' children and their children's children to the throne. Why at that moment? Because America was a new nation, a new world where everything was possible; a world as different from the old as was imaginable, as virtuous as the old was corrupt, as innocent as the old was decrepit. "Time hath found us," he said, because America is the place where "we have every opportunity, and every encouragement before us, to form the noblest, purest constitution on the face of the earth." And then in words which have been echoed and re-echoed a thousand times, Paine set forth the theme of beginning the world over again, to move literally back in time beyond the hereditary succession of illegitimate, bestial, criminal monarchs and beyond the original sin of Adam to the moment when the world first began.[18] "The birthday of a new world is at hand, and a race of men perhaps as numerous as all Europe contains, are to receive their portion of freedom from the event of a few months." (*CS* 100, 120)

America was the only place in the world where human beings could achieve true freedom. "A new era for politics is struck; a new method of thinking hath arisen." (*CS* 82) No place in the world held open such an opportunity. "Freedom hath been hunted around the globe," he says, "Asia, and Africa, have long expelled her. Europe regards her like a stranger, and England hath given her warning to depart. O! receive the fugitive, and prepare in time an asylum for mankind." (*CS* 100) Building on his religious theme, Paine proclaimed that God himself had ordained that America move away from British control. God sent the navigators to discover America, "as if the Almighty graciously meant to open a sanctuary to the persecuted in future years, when home should afford neither friendship nor safety." (*CS* 87) Once separate, Americans could create the best form of government, though it would not be perfect, since there is no such thing as a perfect government.

Law, not tyranny, would reign supreme, because "in America the law is king," whereas in countries with tyrants "the King is law." He described in vivid terms how after the bonds with England had been thrown off, a ceremonial purification rite would take place with the high point being the smashing of the crown, its pieces "scattered among the people whose right it is." (*CS* 98) This symbolic ceremony became a part of the *fêtes révolutionnaires* in France after the fall of the monarchy, which Paine at times witnessed when he resided in France from 1787 to 1802. The crown demolished, Paine foresaw the calling of a constitutional convention. To advocate such a thing was the most radical idea that a person could have in the late eighteenth century. For the British monarchy, a convention represented a direct threat to its legitimacy (and longevity), and anyone who recommended such action was immediately suspected of treason. From this moment on, Paine was under the eye of governmental officials in America and England. Later, when he advocated the same thing in the *Rights of Man*, he provided some additional prosecutorial grist for the government's subsequent case against him.

Paine's ideas about a constitutional convention clearly presaged the convention that eventually met in Philadelphia in 1787 and decided on a future government for America. The convention's duty, wrote Paine, was to devise a constitutional structure to guarantee the freedom of the American people. This constitution, or "Charter," as Paine called it, echoing the English aristocracy's own "Declaration of Independence," the Magna Carta of 1215, must set "the number and manner of choosing members of Congress, members of Assembly, with their date of sitting, and drawing the line of business and jurisdiction between them." (*CS* 97)

Paine, like James Madison, understood that the national government might potentially conflict with the states. The science of federalism was just developing. Jurisdiction thus became a fascinating issue, one which is not yet resolved in our own time. Along with the stabilization of government comes the security of property and freedom, especially religious liberty, because many people were in America to escape the grip of the English Church.

Here Paine's writing once again reflected classical republican principles: a republic without king, with an executive separated from the legislature that balanced the disparate elements of society. Once the charter established a political structure, the convention must dissolve itself, and the new government convene to represent the interests of the American people. The assembly, which was later bicameral and known as the United States Senate and the House of Representatives, was to have annual elections. Each colony was to have several districts from which a certain number of delegates would be sent to Congress. There was to be broad representation with at least thirty delegates from each colony. The total number of delegates would be, at a minimum, three hundred ninety (eerily close to today's four hundred thirty five representatives). Congress would legislate, but a super-majority (three-fifths) would be needed to enact laws.

Moreover, the government would have a president, elected by the Congress on a rotating basis. Each colony would have an opportunity to have one of their number elected president so that no one colony predominated. Twelve years later, in 1788, in the *Federalist Paper*, Number 10, Madison wrote about the declining danger of factions in a broadly-based republic like the United States. This idea directly opposed classical republican theory, which for centuries had presumed that a republic could only exist in small states where everyone knew everybody else. Paine's concept of a limited presidency was a solution to the problems posed by a large-scale republic like that he recommended for America. In his proposal, Paine had included the major ingredients of a true republic as he knew it: the one, represented by a President, though controlled by the few, the Senate, and the many, the House of Representatives. Thereafter, the constitutional convention would have to decide the following items, which he curiously and uncharacteristically ended with a prayer:

> drawing the line of business and jurisdiction between [the Senate and House]: (Always remembering that our strength is continental, not provincial;) Securing freedom and property to all men, and above all things the free exercise of religion, according to the dictates of conscience; with such other matter as is necessary for a charter to contain. Immediately after which, the said conference to dissolve, and the bodies which shall be chosen conformable to the said charter to be the legislators and governors of this continent for the time being: Whose peace and happiness, may God preserve, Amen. (*CS* 97)

The Americans could form a republic, one independent of British tyranny, if they had the backbone to do it.

Paine knew that the separation he advocated meant war, that an American declaration of independence from Britain was in effect a declaration of war on Britain. He felt compelled in the second edition of *Common Sense* to address his own people, the Quakers, who believed that bearing arms and going to war were unconscionable. Indeed, they had formally pledged their loyalty to George III. Paine was incensed. He argued that while he himself was a Quaker, he could not argue against war, because the alternative was sinister. In fact, his goal was not war. He wanted only to defend the American people against horrid tyranny and its corruption. "Kings are not taken away by miracles, neither are changes in government brought about by any other means than such as are common and human." (*CS* 127) Despite his rationale, Paine's *Common Sense* was truly a declaration of war against the Beast of Britain, the brute he denounced with all the passion of his soul.

Finally, the new American republic was to have a sound economy, a firm financial base, and trade arrangements with all the important powers of the world. He lashed out against those nations,

England being foremost in his mind, which had debased their economies by high national indebtedness. In America, in contrast, "debts we have none; and whatever we may contract on this account will serve as a glorious memento of our virtue." (*CS* 101) America might contract a debt, but it would be a result of having to borrow money from other nations in order to prosecute the war against England. It was not a debt on the same level as that of England, which had developed its debt from specious acts of war against other nations for its aggrandizement. America's debt in this struggle "is a national bond." (*CS* 102) It held the states together for a virtuous cause against a corrupt regime. When the war ended, the debt would shrink as American resources, including its navy, were turned to commercial expansion and trade. "We ought to view the building a fleet as an article of commerce, it being the natural manufactory of this country. It is the best money we can lay out. A navy when finished is worth more than it cost. And is that nice point in national policy, in which commerce and protection are united." (*CS* 103)

Paine's rhetorical style, using both the ideas of Lockean liberalism and classical republicanism, was a summons to the Americans, a call to arms for them to renew themselves by separating from Britain and by creating a form of government that the world had never before seen or experienced. The Americans' duty was to act in the way in which God had originally created them: not to destroy others through the enslavement of their minds and hearts, but to sustain complete freedom and security in an environment of mutual respect without fear and intimidation. Surely man was imperfect. God did not intend to make a perfect human being: that was as if God had recreated himself.

Common Sense appeared anonymously on January 10, 1776. Paine's deal with his publisher, Robert Bell, was to-the-point. If the pamphlet lost money, Paine personally promised to cover the costs. If it earned anything, half the profits would go to the publisher, the other half to buy mittens for American troops stationed in Canada. Bell set the price at two shillings, which Paine thought too high. He wanted the message to have a wide audience. Despite the price, people bought the pamphlet. The author was variously thought to be John Adams, Benjamin Rush, Benjamin Franklin, or even the young

Thomas Jefferson, who was thirty-three in 1776. Only in the third edition did Paine's name appear on the cover, although Franklin early on told his friends that it was Paine.[19] Until then, the pamphlet was anonymous with only the words "By an Englishman" on the cover. Many suspected it was an attempt to fool people into thinking that the writer was not an American.

Bell, a transplanted Scot, was not satisfied with his deal with the author. As a result, he submitted a bill to Paine for payment of nearly thirty pounds for the costs of publishing the pamphlet. Paine wanted to wait for sales to cover those costs, but Bell insisted on payment, and Paine eventually complied. The relationship with Bell was all but destroyed because of this incident. Paine found another publisher, and subsequently a second edition was produced by two different publishers: a scavenged one by Bell, and a new (now official) one by the brothers William and Thomas Bradford. The Bradford version, with Paine's additions, was longer by about a third. They lowered the price of the pamphlet to just one shilling.

Paine paid for the printing of six thousand copies from his own pocket, and another six thousand were printed by the Bradfords. Bell complained that the Bradford edition was printed on poor paper and in small type. Paine had had enough of Bell, however, and eventually let anyone publish the pamphlet at their own cost. Pirated editions appeared almost immediately. Bell published several of these, including additional unauthorized materials purportedly written by Paine. But Paine never added a thing after the third edition with his address to the Quakers. Bell earned a small fortune with his counterfeit work, and Paine never received a penny for his most famous writing. By Paine's own estimation, the pamphlet sold some one hundred twenty thousand in the first three months, and about five hundred thousand in all.[20]

The pamphlet was wildly heralded as a courageous statement concerning the direction that the Americans now had to take. Washington remarked that "a few more of such flaming arguments as were exhibited at Falmouth and Norfolk, added to the sound doctrine and unanswerable reasoning in the pamphlet *Common Sense* will not leave members [of Congress] at a loss to decide upon the propriety of separation."[21] Charles Lee, originally an English military officer, who had fought in the French and Indian Wars but now lived in Virginia, was convinced that American independence was a necessity. Paine's pamphlet, he said, was "a masterly, irresistible performance."[22]   Samuel Cooper, the famous Boston preacher, asked Franklin, "How is *Common Sense* relished among you? It is eagerly read and greatly admired here. The inability of our enemies to subdue us by force is more and more apparent."[23] Indeed, the impact of the pamphlet had been immediate in that it created "a powerful change" in the mind and spirit of Virginians who now knew what must be done. Even John Adams, who detested the radical tone of the pamphlet, claimed that "without the pen of the author of *Common Sense*, the sword of Washington would have been raised in vain."[24]

While Paine was immersed in his pamphlet, the British ministry enhanced its military operations in the colonies. Norfolk was shelled and, like Falmouth (now Portland) in New England, was burned just a week before *Common Sense* appeared. It became increasingly clear that George III meant to hold on to his American possessions. After all, he was recruiting hired troops in Germany (at thirty crowns per soldier) and was already moving them across the Atlantic. *Common Sense* intensified the debate over reconciliation. By the spring of 1776, while British forces in America grew rapidly, the French, whose hatred of the British was historically rooted in several wars between England and France, sought ways to help the new nation by secretly supplying arms and munitions. The French Finance Minister, the Comte de Vergennes, Charles Gravier, a seasoned diplomat who had held posts in Trier, Constantinople, and Stockholm, dispatched the dramatist and secret agent Caron de Beaumarchais to determine how to help. Beaumarchais (the author of "The Barber of Seville" and "The Marriage of Figaro") established a phony company called Rodérigue Hortalez and Co. to import arms privately to America. The outcome was potentially good for the Americans, who were to have French armaments, and for the French, who would sell arms and at the same time see their British enemy beaten. Unfortunately for Paine, the transactions set off a series of events known as the Silas Deane affair, which eventually led to Paine's disgrace and his forced resignation from government service.

In Philadelphia, Paine met Thomas Jefferson, who had arrived for the Continental Congress. Unlike his lifelong rival, John Adams, who was often coarse despite his education and upbringing, Jefferson was polished and sophisticated. A master of law, classical literature, and politics, he had studied architecture, history, and science. He had a supple, inquiring mind, though he was never a systematic thinker. He was a true representative of the American enlightenment.[25] Educated at William and Mary College, he had studied law in Williamsburg with George Wythe, one of the most well-versed men in the law and classics in Virginia, with whom he soon served in the Congress. Jefferson was elected to the House of Burgesses in 1769, despite his mere twenty-six years. As a well-known, popular young man in Virginian politics, he was therefore a natural candidate for the Continental Congress. Jefferson, who was to become a close friend and later supporter of Paine's in France and afterwards in America again, now told Paine that the Virginians, like the people of New Hampshire, wanted to draw up their own constitution. He informed Paine when they first met that Virginia had already drafted a Declaration of Rights. The Continental Congress was readying itself to debate separation. Its members agreed to meet in the summer of 1776.

5 · No Summer Soldiers and Sunshine Patriots

Not everyone who read Paine's small pamphlet advocating separation agreed with it. Indeed, as with new proposals in any time, there were several responses. Loyalists believed that America was and ought always be part of the British empire. Others thought that separation was unrealistic, that America could not go it alone in the world, and that English-Americans always needed their British brethren to support them in trade and commercial activities. John Adams, later an adversary, agreed with Paine's arguments for independence, which Adams himself and several members of Congress "had been repeating again and again." Adams, cool and aloof most of the time, was a man of deep principle, who was not particularly sociable and found it difficult to take criticism from either friend or foe. "He can't dance, drink, game, flatter, promise, dress, swear with gentlemen, and small talk and flirt with the ladies," an admirer once said of him.[1]

Adams was Paine's contemporary, born just two years before him in 1735. He was thirteen years younger than his cousin Samuel, who was a close friend of Paine. John Adams and Paine, however, had little in common. Adams, Harvard-educated and a lawyer, was willing to risk defending British soldiers in a sensational trial. He defended Captain Thomas Preston, the officer in charge during the infamous Boston Massacre in 1770, claiming that every Englishman deserved legal representation in a court of law. Several days of demonstrations and unrest throughout Boston preceded the Massacre as hundreds protested the Townshend duties and the presence of the royal guards. On the evening of March 5, Preston took several soldiers to rescue a young private surrounded by a mob, only to find himself and his men equally in trouble. With snow and ice balls flying, one soldier fired a lone shot that ended in a volley, killing five and wounding six. Adams' decision to defend Preston revealed his own sense of justice, engraved in his soul by his Puritan upbringing. He had always coveted fame, and received it in 1770 by representing Preston, but he could have just as easily refused because he despised British misrule in America and its oppressive duties. Even Adams, however, was not prepared for the radical tones of *Common Sense*.

A true patriot, who deeply believed in the American cause, Adams often spoke openly of his admiration of the British constitution with its historic sense of balance between king, lords, and commons. Because of that equilibrium, he believed in English liberty and the rights of Englishmen, often claiming that the English were the freest people in the world. As an American, however, he repudiated the British treatment of its American possessions. Adams agreed, therefore, with Paine's overall points about the need for America to separate from Britain, but Paine's language annoyed him. In fact, he was stunned by Paine's strong rhetoric and imagery and especially his appeal to democracy, which in the eighteenth century was always equated with radicalism, even anarchy. Adams refused to believe, for example, that Britain had no constitution. It did, and while it was grounded firmly in good republican principles, Paine declined to see the balance between king, lords, and commons that Adams had found.

Adams engaged in ad hominem attacks. He claimed that Paine, "an emigrant from New Gate" (emphasizing his country of origin), was only an opportunist, "a star of disaster." Paine had after all written his pamphlet only after receiving the principal arguments from Rush. Adams also hated Paine's references to the Bible, saying they were based on either "honest ignorance or foolish superstition, on one hand, or . . . willful sophistry and knavish hypocrisy, on the other." Even worse, Paine's arguments concerning the right form of government flowed "from simple ignorance and a mere desire to please the democratic party in Philadelphia." Adams clearly was frightened by Paine's "democratical" outlook, which was "without any restraint or even an attempt at any equilibrium or counterpoise, that it must produce confusion and every evil work."

In response, Adams published his own views, which contained the "counterpoise," the balanced government he thought Paine's recommendations had lacked.[2] While Adams, like Paine, wanted to see in America a republic with a freely-elected Congress, a strong presidency, and an independent judiciary, he thought the pamphlet had been overrated. "It has been a general opinion that this pamphlet was of great importance in the revolution," he later recalled. "I doubted it at the time and have doubted it to this day. It probably converted some to the doctrine of independence and gave others an excuse for declaring in favor of it. But these would all have followed Congress with zeal."[3] Adams conveniently overlooked the impact that Paine's writing had on those very members of Congress who would not have necessarily voted for separation.

Paine's views were not so very different from the views of others in his circle, except perhaps in degree. David Rittenhouse, George Clymer, Benjamin Rush, Charles Willson Peale, and several others agreed with him. Rush, for example, approvingly commented that "its effects were sudden and extensive upon the American mind."[4] Paine had first wanted to give the pamphlet the title "plain truth" but was dissuaded when he saw that the title, *Common Sense*, was more appropriate. Indeed, he even explicitly used the theme of common sense in the text.[5] However, the motif, "plain truth," ironically soon became the title of one of the better known attacks on *Common Sense*. Appearing in March of 1776, shortly after the publication of Paine's tract, *Plain Truth* was published anonymously by an Eastern Shore of Maryland Loyalist named James Chalmers, who was unknown until the middle of the twentieth century.[6] The work was not a particularly important response to Paine's call for independence. Paine himself largely ignored it: "a performance which hath withered away like a sickly unnoticed weed, and which even its advocates are displeased at, and the author ashamed to own."[7]

A far more important and critical attack came in a series of letters written by William Smith, provost of the College of Philadelphia. Smith was a wealthy leader of the Loyalist faction in that city. His letters against *Common Sense*, all signed "Cato," appeared in the *Pennsylvania Gazette* in April of 1776. They tore into Paine's call for independence and a republic. Americans must resist, he fumed, Paine's trek down "the dark and untrodden way of independence and republicanism."[8] While Paine ignored Chalmers's attack, he assailed Smith's criticism in a series of letters, which appeared the same month in a rival newspaper, the *Pennsylvania Journal.* As was the convention of the time, Paine used a pen name: the letters bore the signature, "The Forester."

Paine's Forester was more earthy than "Old Common Sense," as Paine was soon to be called during the war against Britain. He continued to use the themes first set forth in his celebrated pamphlet, adding only one major point. He took issue with Cato's decision to address his remarks to "the people of Pennsylvania." Paine argued that the struggle ought not to be won or lost on a local but on a continental basis. "[T]he great business of the day is Continental. And he who dares to endeavor to withdraw this province from the glorious union by which all are supported, deserves the reprobation of all men." One other significant aspect of Paine's retort to Cato was his increasing impatience with an adversary.

Paine often took attacks personally and, like a frightened animal, lashed out at his opponent with all the venom and vituperation he could muster. He gradually developed the use of invective and censure and often dismissed his opponents' most serious objections. He dismissed Cato out of hand with the words, "the first of Cato's letters is insipid in its style, language and substance. . . . There is nothing in [it] worthy of notice but the following insinuating falsehood."

The personal rebuke was never beneath Paine. He used the technique best in the first part of the *Rights of Man* in a celebrated attack on Edmund Burke. Later, when he returned to America in 1802, his verbal assaults on the Federalists, especially John Adams, were masterful. For Cato, he snarled: "Until you clear up this, Sir, you must content yourself with being ranked among the rankest of the writing Tories." Turning to Cato's adulation of George III, Paine moaned, "It suits not Cato to speak the truth. It is his interest to dress up the sceptered savage in the mildest colors."[9] "Sceptered savage" seems to have been an invention of Paine's, one that never really caught on as it might have had he used it in a widely circulated work like *Common Sense*. Paine had the audacity to assert that he was actually avoiding a personal censure. This, of course, was an outright lie. Paine sometimes said that he was not doing the very thing he was in fact doing. Here we have a perfect example of just that: "I think it necessary, once for all," he claimed, "to endeavor to settle as clearly as I can, the following point, viz: How far personality is concerned in any political debate. The general maxim is that measures and not men are the thing." The reality was that both the principle and the man were the thing, and he never tired of assailing both of them, simultaneously and at will. After all, for Paine, it was important to know the man behind the opinion, for "could the wolf bleat like the lamb, the flock would soon be enticed into ruin; wherefore to prevent the mischief, he ought to be *seen* as well as *heard*."

Paine did not stop at attacking Cato. He used the Forester letters to get at what he saw as the real target, the king and Parliament of England. Cato had argued that the king wanted to reconcile England and the American colonies. Paine would have none of it. "Were even the king of England here in person, he could not ratify the terms or conditions of reconciliation," because the acts which oppressed the Americans were acts of Parliament, not of the king, and "There is no body of men more jealous of their privileges than the Commons: Because they sell them. Mark that, Cato. I have not the least doubt upon me but that their business . . . is downright bribery and corruption. It is the machine by which they effect all their plans."[11] Later, he barked that Cato's "Jesuitical cunning" tried to turn the dispute between the Americans and British into a quarrel between lovers. Paine asked, "What comparison is there . . . between the silent tears of pensive sorrow, and rivers of blood—between sweet strife of affection, and bitter strife of death—between the curable calamities of pettish lovers, and the sad sight of a thousand slain!"[12] Paine's preference was republican government, where "the power of kings is shut out." He found it laughable that there could ever be kingship in any case, because "nature seems sometimes to laugh at mankind by giving them so many fools for kings; at other times, she punishes their folly by giving them tyrants."

Paine ended the third letter with an address "To the People," in contradistinction to Cato, who had the provincial temerity to send his letters to the people of Pennsylvania alone. For Paine, all Americans, and not only Pennsylvanians, faced the issues of independence, war, trade, indeed survival. "To live beneath the authority of those whom we cannot love, is misery, slavery, or what name you please. In that case, there would never be peace," he instructed his readers, his American compatriots.[13]

Paine devoted his final letter to wondering why the people of Pennsylvania had failed to elect candidates who supported independence rather than reconciliation. He was astonished to see that three of four candidates who advocated independence had lost. This was due to the political clout of the back-county farmers, who had a conservative outlook, and the strength of the Loyalist factions of Philadelphia. Paine was disappointed. He attributed the power of these two groups to a single factor: Pennsylvania lacked a written constitution, and because it did, it had "a temporary form of government." The same was true of Britain. It, too, lacked a constitution, which was always prior to government, a distinction he laid out in a pamphlet later in the spring, *Four Letters on Interesting Subjects*.[14] Paine's pamphlet added a new dimension to the debate. It was a panegyric to republican government, protected by a constitutional arrangement that only the people could achieve. He even cited Niccolo Machiavelli, the great Renaissance proponent of classical republicanism.[15]

Paine had devoted parts of *Common Sense* to castigating the English government for asserting that it was a true republic. It was not, so long as the king and lords dominated the commons, the sole repository of the public good. In his four letters, he went further: the sole safeguard of the people's liberty was a written constitution that the people themselves had designed in convention, an idea that he later developed to great, sophisticated heights in the *Rights of Man*. "If you ask an Englishman what he means when he speaks of the English constitution, he is unable to give you any answer. The truth is," he proclaimed, "the English have no fixed constitution."[16]

Now, the whole idea of holding a convention to create a constitution was radical enough, and English authorities certainly regarded it as dangerous. It suggested that the people should move outside of the parliamentary structure that had existed for hundreds of years to create a new form of government. Paine had that goal in mind precisely, and this frightened the moderate factions of Philadelphia, just as it horrified George III and the Parliament. Accordingly, in each of his letters, Paine provided strong arguments to support American independence, as he had in *Common Sense* and the "Forester's Letters." He also put forth the arguments, as he did later in a *Pennsylvania Gazette* essay, his *Crisis* papers, *Public Good*, and elsewhere, that Americans must look upon themselves as a single people united for a common cause, and not provincially connected to individual states.[17] In addition, he vigorously advocated that Pennsylvania design for itself a new, written constitution, something that began shortly after independence was declared.

Most importantly, Paine argued that England had never had a constitution and never would. The Parliament could change the constitutional structure of England by a simple enactment: it could "do anything but make a man a woman," he said. The primary purpose of a constitution was to do two things: first, to set forth in some detail the form a government was to take, and then, more critically, to set limits on that government's power. In terms of the first, as a good believer in Lockean theory, Paine felt "the simplest is the best," and forecast his support of the soon-to-be-formed Pennsylvania constitution with its unicameral legislature. "The more houses the more parties; and perhaps the ill consequence to this country would be that the landed interest would get into one house and the commercial interest in the other." Dangerously opposed to one another, the government would face gridlock. Better there should be one house.

As for the second issue, the limits that a constitution placed on government, Paine laid out an array of ideas from the English legal tradition later integrated into the American Constitution in 1787. He mentioned the historic right of habeas corpus and the revered legal practice of trial by jury, both of which directly protected the rights of the accused. Like his radical compatriots in America and England, he opposed the conflicts of interest that arose when a member of the legislature also held a seat in Congress. In addition, he thought frequent elections, annually in this case, created an important check on members of Congress. He also believed that there must be a limitation on the terms of the executive, something the American Constitution did not address until the twenty-second amendment was ratified in 1951. He did not think members of the military ought to be excluded from government, for otherwise they would "form a distinct party of their own." He concluded with a citation of Machiavelli, the Florentine republican theorist, who counseled that the constitution should occasionally be examined and reexamined "at certain periods according to its first principles. This would correct abuses."[18]

After the failure of the Pennsylvania elections in 1776 to support separation from England, Paine was certain that the states themselves, working individually, could not provide the leadership necessary to bring about American independence. He now counted on Congress to act, and the session in which independence was discussed was soon to begin.

By the time the Declaration of Independence was published in July, most Americans expected it. Times had changed in the six months since *Common Sense* had appeared. Certainly the British were preparing for war, though they were still speaking of peace and reconciliation. On the morning of July 12, General William Howe and his brother, Admiral Richard Howe, arrived in New York's harbor with one hundred thirty-eight and one hundred fifty ships, respectively, and nearly thirty thousand troops, not for purposes of war, of course, but to speak to General Washington, who had set up headquarters in New York. Both the Howes and Washington thought New York/New Jersey represented a strategic midpoint of America, and they were preparing for the worst. In the meantime, a smaller British force, about ten thousand men, disembarked in Canada under the command of General Guy Carleton. Another three thousand or so entered the Carolinas.

A few days after the Declaration was distributed, Paine joined a group of volunteers, called Associators, and went to Perth Amboy in New Jersey to serve in General Daniel Roberdeau's flying camp—a military unit established to move quickly (or "fly") to an emergency, get the job done, and then disband. Paine spent the next two months in Perth Amboy, hearing that talks between the

Americans and British had failed (they had hardly started). This news was followed by the rush of General Howe's troops through Long Island and a string of retreats by General Washington across the Hudson and eventually across the Delaware as well. In September, as *Common Sense* was being translated for a French edition, Paine was posted to Fort Lee to serve as aide-de-camp to General Nathanael Greene.[19] Greene was, like Paine, a Quaker, and also essentially a self-made man. At one time an ironsmith, Greene was rejected by the guard in Rhode Island for a physical disability (he had a gimpy right leg). He nonetheless rose very quickly through the ranks as an enlisted man. By 1774 he attained the rank of general. Later in the war, he reorganized the Continental Army in the south and eventually defeated the British at Charleston in 1781, just one year after an American defeat there. Late in life, Paine declared Greene to have been "the best general in the American army."[20]

Despite his rhetoric in *Common Sense*, Paine, and everyone else for that matter, knew the condition of the Continental Army. In the pamphlet, he had boasted that "our present numbers are sufficient to repel the force of all the world. The Continent [by which he clearly meant settled America] hath, at this time, the largest body of armed and disciplined men of any power under Heaven." (*CS* 100, 101) Still, he was aware that the colonies looked upon themselves as independent units and not part of a united nation. The United States of America was no more than a concept. Colonial soldiers fought for their states, not for the nation.[21] At the same time, Paine knew the condition of the armed forces that General Washington led. Unlike the crack troops from Britain and their brutal Hessian mercenaries, of whom there were more than seventeen thousand five hundred, the Americans were a shoddy bunch. The American soldiers served typically only for a year, earned seven dollars a month, and had to buy their own uniforms. They were a true citizen army. They were also ill-trained, and they woefully lacked discipline. Sometimes their muskets even failed to fire properly. Washington's retreat from New York proved that it was a difficult, if not impossible, task to move beyond the Painite polemic of *Common Sense* or the Jeffersonian rhetoric of the Declaration to actually win the war, and with it independence.

On November 16, while serving with General Greene, Paine

watched from a high New Jersey hilltop as Fort Washington on the Hudson, under the command of Colonel Robert Magaw, was taken by the enemy. It was a devastating event. The grand concepts embedded in July's Declaration came crashing down in the reality of military defeat. At Fort Washington, General Washington lost nearly half his troops from the New York area. The new nation was in danger of being abruptly cut in half with the British having a clear road to Philadelphia. They and their Hessian hired hands knew the pitiful condition of the American troops, who were often shoeless, without food and other provisions, without ammunition.

The winter was coming fast. It began to rain a few days after Magaw's surrender. In order to avoid another direct confrontation with the British, Washington ordered the evacuation of Fort Lee, which Greene had tried to hold. Greene and his men fled on November 20, leaving the cooking pots simmering on the fires. Shadowed by Cornwallis and always in danger of a complete rout by Howe's victorious forces, Washington and Greene moved their men toward Hackensack through a muddy, cold mire. While the British never attacked, the Americans were demoralized, broken, cold, sick, and hungry. What was worse, many troops' volunteer tours of duty were nearly up. Reinforcements from the north were not arriving as quickly as Washington had hoped. Probably because he was under orders to press for negotiation, not unconditional surrender, Howe did not attack to destroy the remnants of Washington's bedraggled army. He could have given the knockout blow to the American cause then and there.

In the retreat with Greene and Washington, Paine too was demoralized. Legend has it that he wrote out his thoughts every night on a drumhead before a campfire. He himself later recounted that a day or so after he arrived in Philadelphia on December 8, 1776, "in what I may call a passion of patriotism [I] wrote the first number of the *Crisis*. It was published on the 19th of December, which was the very blackest of times."[22]   Several years later, he turned Washington's retreat into a work of military genius. "This retreat is one of those extraordinary circumstances, that in future ages may probably pass for fable."[23]   But now, the moment was not one for which fable was appropriate. The Americans had to be given straight information, the facts as they were. He began to publish the series *The American Crisis,* which he hoped would inspire Americans to renew their struggle for rights and liberty, for the liberal democratic republic.

This series of papers, which appeared in Philadelphia and other newspapers across the country from 1776 to 1783, was Paine's major writing effort for the rest of the war. Most of the essays were printed at his own expense. In all, there were at least eighteen, including "The Crisis Extraordinary" and two called "A Supernumerary Crisis." In each of them, Paine is concerned with either a military or a diplomatic issue, which came before the new nation each year of the war.[24] Little of what he had to say was theoretical, because his concern was the American war against Britain. Unlike *Common Sense,* which often fell into the ethereal realm of political principles, *The American Crisis* focused on the very tangible problems of war and peace, combat and negotiation, victory and defeat. He did, however, couch all his language in the vocabulary of Lockean and republican principles. He never lost sight of his overall general political beliefs.

The opening lines of "Crisis One" are the most dramatic, most memorable that Paine ever wrote, surpassing even any of those in *Common Sense.* There are few passages in the modern English language more powerful than the sentiments he expressed that day. Paine skillfully captured the despondency and the gloom of a moment when things looked so lost, so bleak, and at the same time retained the hope and optimism that the Americans could achieve independence and create a new republic. Before crossing the Delaware to attack the sleeping Hessians on Christmas Day, Washington read Paine's pamphlet to his troops:

> These are the times that try men's souls. The summer soldier
> and the sunshine patriot will, in this crisis, shrink from the ser-
> vice of their country; but he that stands it now, deserves the love
> and thanks of man and woman. Tyranny, like hell, is not easily
> conquered; yet we have this consolation with us, that the harder
> the conflict, the more glorious the triumph. What we obtain
> too cheap, we esteem too lightly: it is dearness only that gives

everything its value. Heaven knows how to put a proper price upon its goods; and it would be strange indeed if so celestial an article as Freedom should not be highly rated. Britain, with an army to enforce her tyranny, has declared that she has a right (not only to tax) but "to bind us in all cases whatsoever," and if being bound in that manner is not slavery, then is there not such a thing as slavery upon earth. Even the expression is impious; for so unlimited a power can only belong to God.[25]

It was said these words were read aloud in every American military encampment, and while Washington's victory in Trenton on Christmas Day, 1776, was probably attributable to the Hessians' excessive celebration of the holiday, some said that Paine's invigorating words carried the day. Paine paid for the cost of publication and distribution, and once again, he lost an opportunity to capitalize on the power of his pen: he had covered the cost of the original printing, two coppers, and once the essay was published, other printers reprinted it.[26] Whatever profits were due him, he again turned over to the American cause.

The essay accomplished its intended purpose. It restored sufficient confidence that even Paine's future enemy, James Cheetham, wrote that its appearance meant that now "militiamen who, already tired of the war, were straggling from the army, returned. Hope succeeded to despair, cheerfulness to gloom, and firmness to irresolution."[27] Paine described the events at Forts Washington and Lee and the subsequent retreat of the Americans, saying they "bore it with a manly and martial spirit. All their wishes centered in one, which was, that the country would turn out and help them to drive the enemy back." He speculated that the British had attacked the middle states first rather than New England because there were more Loyalists (whom he called Tories) there than in the north. The middle states were infested with them. A Tory, he said, was nothing more than "a coward; for servile, slavish, self-interested fear is the foundation of Toryism; and a man under such influence, though he may be cruel, never can be brave." If the Tory should win, Americans would be forced to swear "allegiance to one whose character is that of a sottish, stupid, stubborn, worthless, brutish man."

That, Paine said, was to "make a whore of my soul."[28]

Washington's attack on the Hessians in Trenton was successful, because it revitalized his men's confidence and will. This was the
goal of the entire *Crisis* series. Washington's victory at Trenton, and
then later at Princeton, coupled with a few strategic mistakes the
British command made, worked hand in hand with Paine's stimulating writings.

As Paine published his *Crisis* papers during the rest of the
war, he took an active part in discussions of the proposed, very radical Pennsylvania constitution, which allowed for only one legislative
body and gave the vote to all able-bodied men, including tradesmen,
artisans, and craftsmen. The English model was a bicameral legislature elected only by property owners. The idea of one assembly acting to check the possibility of domination by the other assembly was
attractive to most Americans. It did not take very long for a stormy
debate to erupt. Those who wanted the vote to stay only with the
middle class—people like the great financier Robert Morris and
Matthew Slough, a wealthy manufacturer and businessman—were
pitted against the "Constitutionalists"—people like Paine and his
friends Timothy Matlack (a former brewer), Charles Willson Peale
(the artist), and other tradesmen and artisans, who believed in universal manhood suffrage. These issues all came together in the Silas
Deane affair, which broke out nearly two years later, when the problem of war profiteering became a very controversial issue of public
debate. Now, after the initial British victories, America's difficulties
only deepened as the British, in the full fury of their resolve to retain
the colonies as part of the empire, sent thousands more soldiers.

In January, Paine heard that William Howe, commander-in-
chief of the British forces in America, had offered to pardon all
Americans who stopped fighting and declared their loyalty to the
king of England. Paine thought that instead of fighting, he could
perform greater service to the American cause by continuing to write.
With Howe's offer before him, he dashed off "Crisis Two," which
roundly rejected any thought of reconciliation with Britain. Writing
from Philadelphia, Paine said that when Howe was a soldier-in-arms,
he had only armies to contend with, but now he had an army and an
entire country to defeat. "It has been the folly of Britain to suppose

herself more powerful than she really is, and by that means has arro-
gated to herself a rank in the world she is not entitled to."

In truth, Britain had often had to ally itself with other
armies: in the present case it was the Germans, the Hessians. The
British and the Germans might be successful in taking Philadelphia,
but they could not quash American determination to be free from
British control. No simple offer of pardon would lead to what Howe
wanted. "It is surprising to what a pitch of infatuation, blind folly
and obstinacy will carry mankind, and your lordship's drowsy proclamation," Paine taunted the Viscount, "is a proof that it does not even
quit them in their sleep. Perhaps you thought America too was taking a nap, and therefore chose, like Satan to Eve, to whisper the delu-
sion softly, lest you should awaken her." No, America would not stop
because of a stupid offer made by a man, who was merely "proud to
lick the dust that kings have trod upon." And these kings, as he had
emphasized in *Common Sense*, were not even human:

> If you mean the power of pardoning, it is an oblique proof that
> your master was determined to sacrifice all before him; and that
> you were two months in dissuading him from his purpose.
> Another evidence of his savage obstinacy! From your own
> account of the matter we may justly draw these two conclusions:
> 1st, that you serve a monster; and 2d, that never was a messen-
> ger sent to a more foolish errand than yourself. . . . [As for the
> Tories in America] tell them to take their leave of America, and
> all that once was theirs. Recommend them for consolation to
> your master's court; there perhaps they may make a shift to live
> on the scraps of some dangling parasite, and choose companions
> among thousands like themselves. A traitor is the foulest fiend
> on earth.

It was in "Crisis Two" that Paine wrote the phrase "the United States
of America," the first time it was ever used in history. It quickly
caught on.[29]

Congress was apparently impressed with Paine's ease and
agility with words. It appointed him secretary for a commission
which was negotiating treaties with the Indian tribes in Easton
(Pennsylvania). The effort was successful, largely because of Indian

antipathy toward British rule. On his return, at the suggestion of John Adams, Paine was named, on April 17, Secretary of the Committee for Foreign Affairs for the Congress. Adams had thought that since Paine was poor and desperate, but "a ready writer and an industrious man," he "might be useful and earn a living." Witherspoon, the only member of Congress to object to the nomination, claimed that when Paine was in England, he "was very intemperate" and had written "against the American cause." Witherspoon thought Paine was "a bad character and not fit to be placed in a situation" such as this one.[30]

Paine had been ambivalent about American independence when he first came to America, and even said so in "Crisis Seven" and elsewhere. His ambivalence quickly converted into fervent American patriotism.

> I happened to come to America a few months before the breaking out of hostilities. I found the disposition of the people such that they might have been led by a thread and governed by a reed. Their suspicion was quick and penetrating, but their attachment to Britain was obstinate, and it was at that time a kind of treason to speak against it. They disliked the ministry, but they esteemed the nation. Their idea of grievance operated without resentment, and their single object was reconciliation. Bad as I believed the ministry to be, I never conceived them capable of a measure so rash and wicked as the commencing of hostilities; much less did I imagine the nation would encourage it. I viewed the dispute as a kind of lawsuit in which I supposed the parties would find a way either to decide or settle it. I had no thoughts of independence or of arms. The world could not then have persuaded me that I should be either a soldier or an author. If I had any talents for either, they were buried in me.

And then he uttered one of his often-repeated formulas. "But when the country into which I had just set foot was set on fire about my ears, it was time to stir. It was time for every man to stir."[31] His new position as Secretary of the Committee for Foreign Affairs had little power, but Paine thought it carried great prestige.[32] He had the gall to elevate his position, styling himself at times the Foreign Affairs

Minister of the United States. One thing was certain: it was a position that gave him access to information on which to build a complete picture of American policy. He was delighted and surprised, and besides that, it provided him a small income. He told Franklin, who had just been sent to France to negotiate military assistance for the American cause, that he thought "the honor to be the greater as the appointment was [not] only unsolicited on my part but made unknown to me."[33]

For the time being, Paine continued to worry about British Loyalists. He was not certain he had fully responded to Howe's offer of pardon. He tried again in "Crisis Three," which was published two days after his appointment. He suggested that all Americans take a loyalty oath to the cause of liberty, something which the Pennsylvania Council accepted for that its citizens in June. Anyone who refused should pay an annual property tax of between ten and twenty percent. With typical venom, he attacked the very idea of what a Tory was. Since many Tories were Quakers, he attacked his co-religionists and especially the alleged mistress of George III, who reputedly was a Quaker herself. "It is remarkable that the whole race of prostitutes in New York were Tories," he said, "and the schemes for supporting the Tory cause in this city, for which several are now in jail, and one hanged, were concerted and carried on in common bawdy-houses, assisted by those who kept them."[34] Again, the British could never defeat the Americans, whose resolve was too great. The road to peace, honor, and commerce was paved with *independence*.

But the British made a good run at it. Two months later in July 1777, it appeared that they would try to take Philadelphia. Paine had warned Richard Henry Lee about this prospect. A member of the Continental Congress, Lee had introduced the motion that led to independence. He soon advocated making Washington commander-in-chief, and he was right from Paine's perspective.[35] After the devastating defeat of American forces at the battle of Brandywine in September, Congress was forced to flee westward to Lancaster, where its members reconvened. Paine devoted "Crisis Four" to Congress's flight from Philadelphia. Things were beginning to go quite badly for the Americans. They were only to become increasingly worse as Washington prepared to hole up in Valley Forge for the winter, which turned out to be unusually harsh and bitter.

The times that had tried men's souls seemed to overwhelm them now. Paine exhorted the defeated army to continue. He wrote to Franklin that he and David Rittenhouse were experimenting with an arrow with a head of fire which could be shot across the Delaware, presumably to burn up the stores of ammunition that the British had there. "I have made a draft of a bow, something on the plan of the Steel Cross by which I think [it] will [be possible] to throw an iron arrow across the Delaware. I purpose enclosing the fire in a bulb near the top," and here Paine drew Franklin a picture of the burning arrow, hoping it had some practical application in the war.[36] He knew that things did not look bright. Nonetheless, in "Crisis Four," the last of the series Paine wrote in Philadelphia, he again mustered his rhetoric: "We are not moved by the gloomy smile of a worthless king, but by the ardent glow of generous patriotism. We fight not to enslave, but to set a country free, and to make room upon the earth for honest men to live in. In such a case we are sure that we are right; and we leave to you the despairing reflection of being the tool of a miserable tyrant."[37]

Washington's troops were readying for a British assault when a tremendous rainstorm came upon them, so fierce in its fury that it nearly destroyed all the Americans' ammunition and powder. They had to wait for new supplies. Meanwhile, the British were aligned along the Schuylkill awaiting the moment to take Philadelphia. Paine later wrote to Franklin: "It was a beautiful still moonlight morning and the streets as full of men, women and children as on a market day. On the evening before I was fully persuaded that unless something done the city would be lost."

Paine went to see John Bayard, a Philadelphia merchant who had been elected Speaker of the Pennsylvania Assembly, to tell him that something must be done while Washington waited for his new supply of ammunition. He suggested a ploy to confuse and distract the British, hoping that in their caution to avoid defeat, they might withdraw from the area of the city. "If only an appearance of defense be made in the city by throwing up works at the heads of the streets, it will make the enemy very suspicious how they threw themselves between the city and General Washington, and between two rivers, which must have been the case." Bayard and William Bradford, then a colonel in the Continental Army and Paine's second printer of *Common Sense*, agreed it was a good idea, but when they took it to General Thomas Mifflin, he seemed uninterested. The city soon fell, and Paine blamed the disaster on Mifflin's inaction.

Paine now thought he should go to Trenton, where he had sent his chest full of official documents. Instead, he spent time with his friend Colonel Joseph Kirkbride in Bordentown (until the British burned his house down) and then at Washington's camp, although for awhile he had difficulty locating it. He later told Franklin of his distress and fear. "I kept pretty high up the country, and being unwilling to ask questions, not knowing what company I might be in, I was there three days before I fell in with [the camp]." There, he was again with General Greene, who asked him to stay until the morning of September 30, while the Americans tried to trick the British into believing that rebel forces were bivouacking just three miles from the city. In reality, they were moving to Germantown for a counterattack. At 5:00 a.m., Paine too set off for Germantown. "I met no person for several miles riding, which I concluded to be a good sign." His optimism was soon crushed when he began to encounter several retreating American troops wounded and frightened, including General Nash, who was so battered that Paine did not recognize him. There was chaos and confusion everywhere. The counterattack had failed dismally. Paine was warned that if he continued on, the British certainly would capture him. Paine never exactly understood the true "cause of that day's miscarriage."

Paine returned to Washington's headquarters, where the General was totally perplexed over how everything had gone awry so quickly. "A new army," Paine reasoned, "once disordered is difficult to manage, the attempt dangerous. To this may be added a prudence in not putting matters to too hazardous a trial the first time. Men must be taught *regular* fighting by practice and degrees, and though the expedition failed, it had this good effect—that they seemed to feel themselves more important *after* it than *before*, as it was the first general attack they had ever made." For the next several days, Paine was involved in action along what came to be the frontlines between the Americans and British positions. As aide-de-camp to General

Greene, once again Paine was engaged in an expedition to try to pass through enemy lines in an effort to retake the city. They were repulsed, and then confronted with "a cannonade, by far the most furious I ever heard."

For two weeks, Paine was with the Kirkbrides yet again but soon returned to camp in the midst of battle until he went off to visit Washington at Valley Forge, where the army "began to build huts; they appeared to me like a family of beavers: everyone busy; some carrying logs, others mud, and the rest fastening them together. The whole was raised in a few days, and is a curious collection of buildings in the true rustic order."[38] There was some good news, though, despite the loss of Philadelphia and the crushing defeat of the counterattack. The defeat of the forces of General John ("Gentleman Johnny") Burgoyne in the Saratoga campaign in the fall was a major turning point in the war. Burgoyne and other British generals had thought to end the revolution quickly by invading from Canada, joining Sir William Howe coming up the Hudson from New York, and meeting with another British army under Barry St. Leger hooking in from the Mohawk Valley. St. Leger was to meet Burgoyne's forces in Albany, but when his Indian troops deserted, he was forced to retreat to Montreal. Burgoyne was left open to severe pressure from American militiamen, including the famous Green Mountain Boys, who badly chewed up his forces in August near Bennington. Although they were able to take Fort Ticonderoga, Burgoyne's troops, now too few in number, were ill-equipped to fight on the frontier. Surrounded near present-day Saratoga Springs, Burgoyne surrendered on October 17, 1777. It was the first important major victory of American forces over Britain in the war.

Paine was ecstatic. He told Richard Henry Lee that Burgoyne's surrender "has the air of a national treaty; it is binding, not only on Burgoyne as a general, but on England as a nation." He was wrong, of course, but even so the defeat had two immediate consequences. First, it inspired the French to give serious consideration to supporting the American cause against their enemy, England, because it appeared as though the Americans had a chance for success. Second, it inspired the American troops themselves, giving them pause, really for the first time, to think that their independence from Britain might be more than a mere dream. America could be a nation in its own right.

Still, Paine was worried. Recruitment was going poorly, and he wondered whether an army of draftees chosen by lottery might work. Men who were not drawn would have to pay one or two dollars as compensation for not serving, and that seemed to be quite fair to him.[39]

Toward the end of the severe winter of 1777-78, Paine lived in the Lancaster home of William Henry, a scientist, gunsmith, and member of the Lancaster municipal government. The two men talked, among other things about powering boats by steam, anticipating Robert Fulton's invention. There was not much to do, officially at least. The government again came under siege and was forced to move from Lancaster to York, but Paine remained in Lancaster.

According to one of William Henry's sons, John Joseph, Paine did relatively little there. He ate a great deal and slept most of the day. The boy contrasted Paine's habits with those of David Rittenhouse, who apparently lived in the same house. By then, Rittenhouse was head of the treasury for the state of Pennsylvania. He was at his desk every day, reviewing the details of all the written reports he received on the costs of the war and the affairs of his state. While Rittenhouse "was employing his hours in the duties of his office . . . Paine would be a snoring away his precious time in his easy chair, regardless of those injunctions imposed upon by Congress, in relation to his political compositions. His remissness, indolence, or vacuity of thought caused great heart-burning among many primary characters in those days."[40] It is difficult to determine the accuracy of this account. Paine was obviously actively writing his *Crisis* papers and determined at the same time to carry on his official duties as Secretary of the Committee for Foreign Affairs. He could have been exhausted—both physically and mentally. He had been on the road until his arrival at the Henry home, and he often felt he had to carry the burden of America's war effort on his shoulders, if only to summon the energy and spirit to write about it.

In any case, by spring 1778, his worst fears became reality. The American army was in total disarray. Despite the victories of the fall, the long winter had worn down the volunteers. They missed their shops or farms, their families. The soldiers' mood was at the lowest point in the war. In glaring contrast, British troops were warm and comfortable in Philadelphia, virtually living in luxury compared-to the American troops at Valley Forge. In March Paine surveyed the situation from Lancaster. He addressed the first part of "Crisis Five" to General Howe: it was "like administering medicine to the dead, or endeavoring to convert an atheist by scripture." But he said nothing of the horrid impact of the severe winter on Washington's troops, nor did he mention the constant talk of replacing Washington with General Horatio Gates, who had been successful the previous fall in Saratoga against the British forces under the command of General John Burgoyne. Instead, he undertook a frontal assault against Howe, who had just been granted a peerage. "As a proper prelimi-nary towards the arrangement of your funeral honors, we readily admit of your new rank of *knighthood*," he told Howe. "The title is perfect in character and is your own more by merit than creation. There are knights of various orders, from the knight of the windmill to the knight of the post. The former is your patron for exploits, and the latter will assist you in settling your accounts."

As usual, Paine was on target with his sniping rhetoric. He took up with Howe a complaint he had about the secret issuance of counterfeit money into the American economy by British spies. This was an issue that Paine returned to the following month in a letter to Henry Laurens: the distribution of counterfeit cash amounted to "a conduct so basely mean in a public character [it] is without precedent or pretence." Could Paine have really meant "without precedent?" Surely the distribution of counterfeit currency, while it might have potentially somewhat weakened the American economy, was not as horrible as the war itself. But Paine launched his verbal foray against Howe with all the bitterness he could muster. As he had compared the king of England to a snake in *Common Sense*, he now did the same with Lord Howe. The General's actions demonstrated "an inbred wretchedness of heart made up between the venomous malignity of a serpent and the spiteful imbecility of an inferior reptile." Forgerers faced the gallows, he said, and Howe ought to be taken to the gibbet. Paine had no proof that Howe was behind the scheme, but then that factor did not matter much, either, from his point of view. Within two months, Howe resigned his command and returned to England to explain (and defend) his military leadership before Parliament. His replacement was Sir Henry Clinton, who three years later, in 1781, remained in New York, expecting an attack by Washington's forces that never came. It was his delay in sending reinforcements to help General Cornwallis in the Yorktown campaign which effectively ended the war.

Paine devoted the second part of "Crisis Five" to the American people. In many respects, it was a panegyric to General Washington, who was under increasing pressure from his American opponents for having suffered terrible defeats and undertaken embarrassing withdrawals almost since the beginning of the war. In the course of his unrelenting attack on Howe, he had already cited Washington's "unabated fortitude," which had "saved the spark that has since blazed in the north with unrivalled lustre." Paine now argued that the loss of Philadelphia did not have as great an impact on the war as the British expected. They had thought that "the soul of all America was centered there and would be conquered there." In fact, the city was hardly any of the things the British thought. Its loss to the British actually had more advantages to it "than injuries." It had not been used as a port for at least a year, it had no shipbuilding capacity, and it was not a center of manufacturing. Whether any of this were true or not did not matter; Paine said it with the authority of truth. Besides the fortitude of the nation was much too great. "America is her own mistress and can do what she pleases," he asserted. He could have added that Paine was his own master and could say whatever pleased him.

Paine ended the piece with a plan for the government to increase the size of the Continental Army and to acquire more funding for it. He adopted a confident and optimistic tone, when the facts seemed to weigh against such hopefulness. Was he trying to rally the troops at a moment of despair, when Washington was defeated in Philadelphia and his army lying in shreds at Valley Forge? Or was he attempting something more? His language mirrored the images and metaphors of *Common Sense*, as he defended the integrity and honor of the high command of the American forces.

Vigor and determination will do anything and everything. We began the war with this kind of spirit, why not end it with the same? . . . The present spring, if rightly improved, will free us from our troubles and save us the expense of millions. We have now only one army to cope with. No opportunity can be fairer; no prospect more promising. . . .

I would wish to revive something of that virtuous ambition which first called America into the field. Then every man was eager to do his part and perhaps the principal reason why we have in any degree fallen therefrom is because we did not set a right value by it at first, but left it to blaze out of itself, instead of regulation and preserving it by just proportions of rest and service. . . .

The men are ready for the field with the greatest possible expedition, because it becomes the duty of the inhabitants themselves in every part of the country to find their proportion of men instead of leaving it to a recruiting sergeant, who, be he ever so industrious, cannot know always where to apply.[41]

Paine wrote a few years later that he had wanted to protect Washington against the onslaught of those, especially John Adams, who wanted to see him replaced him as commander-in-chief. "When a party was forming, in the latter end of 1777, and beginning of 1778, of which John Adams was one, to remove Mr. Washington from the command of the army on the complaint that *he did nothing,* I wrote the fifth number of the 'Crisis,' and published it at Lancaster . . . to ward off that meditated blow."[42] Adams resented the accusation, and denied he had sought Washington's removal and replacement. "That insolent blasphemer of things sacred and transcendent libeller of all that is good Tom Paine. . . [asserts] the scandalous lie that I was one of a faction in the fall of the year 1777 against General Washington. It is indeed a disgrace to the moral character and the understanding of this age that this worthless fellow should be believed in anything. But impudence and malice will always find admirers."[43] In any case, if Paine's goal in "Crisis Five" was to defend Washington, he was successful. Washington stayed on.

6 · Financial Plagues and Silas Deane

I n the spring of 1778, Paine revisited the issue of counterfeit
money with his friend Henry Laurens, the same issue he had
written of in "Crisis Five." By then, this problem had taken on
exaggerated significance both in terms of Paine's worries over it and
its overall impact on the war effort. Laurens was then serving as the
president of the Continental Congress, having succeeded John
Hancock the previous November 1st. American troops were in
appalling condition, and Paine thought that part of the problem was
bogus money. American authorities had arrested several Loyalists in
Lancaster and charged them with attempting to issue "counterfeit
Continental money" in an effort to bankrupt the American economy.
Paine was concerned that the law passed by the Congress against the
production and distribution of fake currency was unclear. The law
stated that it was a felony to produce and distribute counterfeit
money "emitted" by Congress. The word "emitted" might have had
"only a retrospect meaning by supplying the idea of 'which have been'
'emitted by Congress.'" The defense counsel argued at trial that the
law was worded in such a way as not to cover counterfeit currency
issued *after* the law was passed. Paine specifically wanted Laurens and
the Congress to point out what their intentions were when the law
passed. Paine hated to see a fight lost over the American currency
system as much as he did on the battlefield.

In any case, as it turned out, the court soon acquitted one of
the suspects, and the other was found guilty "only of a fraud," because
he was convicted of the distribution rather than the production of the
bad money. The whole affair was a waste of time. Paine should have

spent his hours thinking about the dismal condition of American troops and what might be done about it. But he did not.[1] In May 1778, Paine moved to Yorktown when he heard of two conflicting events: the British had offered the Americans a peace proposal and the French were in the process of forming an alliance with the Americans. The previous February, Lord North had offered the Americans just about everything they had wanted, short of independence. Apparently this offer occurred after one of the commissioners sent by North, George Johnstone, the former Royal Governor of Georgia, attempted to bribe a number of American leaders, including Joseph Reed, the president of the Pennsylvania Supreme Executive Council. His exposure tainted the commissioners' plan, and Congress rejected the offer in June. In a scathing attack on the bribery attempt, Paine wrote a poem "To Governor Johnstone" under his famous pseudonym of "Common Sense." There, with his usual bluster, the poet sneered at the low "mongrel arts of sap and fraud" perpetrated on the Americans.

> Must Johnstone be the man? Must he, whose tongue
> Such able peals of elocution rung,
> Whose tow'ring genius seem'd at times to rise,
> And mix a kindred fervor with the skies,
> Whose pointed judgment, and connected sense,
> Gave weight to wit, and worth to eloquence;
> Must he, Oh shame to genius! be the first
> To practice acts himself so loudly curst?
> Must he exhibit to a laughing mob,
> A turncoat patriot conquer'd by a job;
> And prove from under his adult'rous pen
> How few are just of all the sons of men?

He praised the genius of the man, but condemned the meanness of his actions, comparing him to the recently-dead, former first minister of the king: "Of Pitt and you this contrast may be said,/The dead is living, and the living dead."[2] "Common Sense" could hardly have been more cutting in his attack on Johnstone.

In contrast to this bungled scheme stood the French, steadfast in their support of the American cause. With that support, Paine

was optimistic. He now claimed to believe the Americans were finally in a military position to win the war. At the same time, he still
hoped that in the end England would declare war on France, because
France supported the Americans. The result might well be an internal revolution, which would bring down the British monarchy. "The
danger arising to Britain by the mean policy which I suppose she will
adopt is that by sending her forces to America and failing at the same
time in making fair weather with France, she will expose herself to be
conquered at home."[3] As for the French, no example was better than
the young, valiant Marquis de Lafayette, wounded at Brandywine,
who returned to Paris to recover. "His amiable and benevolent manners have been a living contradiction to the narrow spirited declara-
tions of the British Commissioners," Paine bitterly commented. "He
happily returns in safety."[4] The two men—Lafayette and Paine—
met again, in Paris: once in the spring of 1781, and then again after
the next great revolution of the eighteenth century.

The British commissioners now issued a Manifesto and
Proclamation that all Americans must remain subjects of the British
empire. Paine's response to the peace proposal, addressed directly to
the commissioners, appeared as "Crisis Six," written in Philadelphia
shortly after the British withdrawal from the city. The paper was an
effort grounded in Paine's belief in national unity. Paine, buoyed by
news of a formal alliance with France, now argued that America
could not lose the war: Britain "cannot refuse to acknowledge our
independence with greater obstinacy than she before refused to repeal
her laws [specifically, the Intolerable Acts]; and if America alone
could bring her to the one, united with France she will reduce her to
the other."

For the first time in a long time, he was probably realistical-
ly optimistic that America's separation from Britain might well be
successful. After the terrible defeats and retreat of the winters of
1776-77 and 1777-78 and the disarray of American troops, he now
thought victory was possible over the British empire, or at least in
print he thought so: "You are prosecuting a war," he wrote to the
British in "Crisis Six," "in which you confess you have neither object
nor hope, and that conquest, could it be effected, would not repay the
charges. In the meanwhile, the rest of your affairs are running to ruin,

and a European war kindling against you. In such a situation, there is neither doubt nor difficulty, the first rudiments of reason will determine the choice, for if peace can be procured with more advantages than even a conquest can be obtained, he must be an idiot indeed that hesitates."[5] A liberal, democratic republic in America, he argued, would soon be a reality. Besides, America continued to enjoy "the interposition of Providence," who showered "her blessings on our endeavors." America could not possibly lose with Providence on America's side. Four days later Paine told Franklin that the British goal of subjecting America to the empire was a long way off.[6] He was convinced that the British were so confused that they did not know what to do with their troops currently occupying New York. Although they had withdrawn from Philadelphia, and Paine was preparing to return there, his comments were, as usual, highly speculative. He had no inside knowledge of the plans of the British command, even though he might have thought that he did by virtue of his lofty position as Secretary of the Committee for Foreign Affairs. He probably did have access to information from the American perspective, but to assert special knowledge about British activities was purely Painite presumption.

A month later, in November, he renewed his attack on Britain with an address directed to the people of England. He told them that they would never defeat America, and had no business trying. Britain was a trading country, and to go to war was the total opposite of commerce. It was "like setting a bulldog upon a customer at the shop door. The least degree of common sense shows the madness" of such an act. The English people's interest was simply not served by the prosecution of this war. They only suffered financial hardships. Paine at this point claimed, as he did in later pieces, that his interests were not parochial just because he was an American. His interests, on the contrary, were "universal. My attachment is to all the world, and not to any particular part." Britain was far better off to end the hostilities and let America go free. He attacked George III in a poem citing his horrid treatment of the Americans.

In language designed to place the king in the worst of all possible lights, he compared him to bloodstained Cain:

> From flight to flight the mental path appears
> Worn with the steps of near six thousand years,
> And fill'd throughout with ev'ry scene of pain,
> From Cain to George, and back from George to Cain.
> Alike in cruelty, alike in hate,
> In guilt alike, and more alike in fate;
> Both curs'd supremely (for the blood they drew)
> Each from the rising world while each was new.

George, the "second Cain" who was a "true likeness of the first," tortured the Americans because of their desire to be free. Americans have tried their best to convince him to let them go but he ignored all their entreaties. Only "one prayer is left, which dreads no proud reply,/That He who made you breathe, would bid you die."[7] By this time, the commissioners sent by England were now on their way home, hopefully with a copy of "Crisis Six," which Paine had addressed to them. "In so doing they carry back more *Common Sense* than they brought."[8]

Just as things were beginning to look a bit better on the military front, the worries of Pennsylvanians were deepening about the constitution they had adopted two years earlier shortly after the colonies separated from England. At that time, all the colonies, with the exception of Connecticut, immediately drafted new constitutions, given the fact that the old colonial charters were suddenly made null and void by the Declaration of Independence. Pennsylvania's was a radical document, providing for a weak executive and unitary legislature with voting based on male citizenship, not a minimal property qualification, which was the prevalent principle in the English system. Paine entered the debate in a four-part "Serious Address to the People of Pennsylvania," which appeared in December in the *Packet*. He had never before addressed this subject nor had he even voted in the 1776 election of the members of the constitutional convention, but he was very much in favor of Pennsylvanians allowing more time to see whether their constitution would work. He was impressed by the risks the people of Pennsylvania had taken by adopting such a radical document, especially with its broad suffrage (although it did not provide women the vote). "We are a people upon experiments," he explained, and although we were "under one continental government [we] have the happy opportunity of trying variety in order to discover the best."

The novelty of the Pennsylvania government was what made it significant and important, especially the electoral provisions giving every man the right to vote. If voting were limited, the people might as well "live in a land of mutes." If the state constitution failed to work precisely as its framers intended, they, or others, should change it. Besides, because other states had their own political make-up, which most likely would be dissimilar to Pennsylvania's, each of them could learn from the others what might work well: "Out of many posterity may choose a model, and while the diversity lasts all men may be pleased by residing in that which they like best." The Pennsylvania constitution guaranteed freedom, "the associate of innocence, not the companion of suspicion." A constitution could never be too free, as some disparagers have asserted about Pennsylvania's. For Paine, it was the equality of voters that insured freedom for all, that made it "a generous constitution." This broad freedom insured that the civil rights of man and his religious liberty were secured. It was not a matter of government's "toleration" of these rights. On the contrary, toleration is a *"grant"* of liberty, whereas true freedom is a *"confirmation"* of it. Government could only recognize and protect rights that the people already possessed. It had no authority to bestow rights on them as a gift. This was because Paine considered "freedom as personal property," and for that reason alone the constitution in its present state ought to be "confirmed in preference to why it ought to be altered."9

Such was his faith in human beings at the moment that the Silas Deane affair grew from a whisper to a roar.

Although the issues involved in the Silas Deane affair are easily stated, what actually happened is not clear even today. America needed outside assistance to prosecute the war against England, and France was amenable to supplying munitions and arms. Anglo-French relations were particularly poor in these years, due to France's humiliating defeat in the Seven Years War, which had ended in 1763.

She lost almost all of her American possessions, including Canada, to the English. Thirteen years later, in 1776, Foreign Minister Charles Gravier Vergennes and other leading Frenchmen supported the idea of helping America against their old enemy. Their goals were not, like Paine's and his American compatriots, liberty, justice, rights, and the republic. The French lent their assistance to the Americans with the hope they would regain some of their North American possessions, especially Canada. The problem was how to work out a secret arms deal between France and America—secret because France did not want to fight another war against England. The French wanted to punish the English, with whom they had signed a peace treaty in 1763, enter into a commercial treaty with the Americans, and at the same time reestablish themselves firmly in the Western Hemisphere.

The Continental Congress was vitally interested in French arms throughout 1776 and 1777. The war was then proceeding badly for the Americans, the soldiers ill-equipped (especially as far as gunpowder was concerned). The idea of aiding the American cause may have actually first come from the French crown. As early as 1775, Vergennes directed an envoy by the name of Achard de Bonvouloir to find out whether the Americans might be interested in French support. De Bonvouloir initially made contact with Arthur Lee, younger brother of the Congressman from Virginia, Richard Henry Lee, and then Congress' secret agent in London. Eight years younger than his brother, Arthur Lee had first practiced medicine after receiving a medical degree from the University of Edinburgh. Soon, his interest turned to law, and he traveled to London where he became a radical pamphleteer. The Americans were very interested in pursuing aid from France. Lee wrote to Vergennes, "We offer to France, in return for her secret assistance, a secret treaty of commerce, by which she will secure for a certain number of years after peace is declared all the advantages with which we have enriched England for the past century, with, additionally, a guarantee of her possessions according to our forces."[10] There is nothing in this letter about payment for goods supplied. Generally the Americans thought France was offering a gift. Certainly Lee did.

Congress secretly commissioned Silas Deane, then a delegate from Connecticut, to go to France in April of 1776 to meet several times with his French counterpart in Paris, Caron de Beaumarchais, playwright and the friend of Louis XVI, and Foreign Minister Vergennes. Born the same year as Paine, Silas Deane was raised in Connecticut where he graduated from Yale. He was soon a successful lawyer and merchant, and served in the Connecticut Assembly. By 1776, he represented his state in the Continental Congress. Deane seemed to be a likely candidate, because in fact he was already going to Europe on business on behalf of his commercial partners, one of whom was Robert Morris.

Accordingly, in March of 1776 a Committee of Secret Correspondence, consisting of Robert Morris, Benjamin Franklin, John Jay, and two others, authorized Deane to "go into France, there to transact such business, commercial and political, as we have committed to his care, in behalf and by authority of the Congress of the thirteen united colonies."[11] This dual role never appeared to the members of the Committee as being a conflict of interest because they wanted him to appear as a private merchant who would work openly in France but then deal secretly on behalf of the United States. To maintain strict confidentiality, the Committee never revealed to Congress just what Deane's instructions were.[12] Through his connections there, he agreed to serve as the American agent to seek military supplies and clothing from France and a treaty of alliance between France and the new nation. The American government agreed to cover all of his expenses and pay him a five percent commission on the value of all concessions he obtained. Deane was to secure gunpowder and arms for America as a gift or at a cost which was reasonable for both countries. In addition, if it were possible, he was to try to secure French recognition of the new American republic and even sign a treaty of friendship and mutual aid with France. On Deane's arrival in France in the summer of 1776, Vergennes put him in touch with Beaumarchais, whom the government had placed at the head of the bogus firm, Roderigue Hortalez and Co., specifically to channel arms and munitions secretly to the Americans. The French and the Spanish governments together (the Spanish king was Louis XVI's uncle) funded the operation with two million livres in gold. Another million was to come from French financiers.[13]

In the next year, twelve ships carried military cargo to the

United States, including, in the very first shipment, enough supplies to equip 25,000 men, precisely what the Americans had requested. French equipment and supplies became a critical factor in the American victory at Saratoga and set the foundation for an open Franco-American alliance. Congress sent three envoys (Benjamin Franklin, Arthur Lee, and again Deane) to France to continue the discussions. It soon became clear, to Lee at least, that most likely Beaumarchais and probably also Deane were playing some financial games. Gunpowder was arriving in America with invoices at five times the original cost. Muskets, which the French government had turned over to Hortalez for nothing, came in marked at half their original cost with the specific indication on the invoices that they were not gifts of the French crown.

When Congress was handed a bill for four and one half million livres in late 1777, Deane was recalled from Paris. He did not appear immediately, as requested, but waited until the French had established diplomatic relations with the Americans and returned with the new French ambassador, Conrad Alexandre Gérard de Rayneval, the first official emissary to the new United States.[14] Conveniently and no doubt on purpose, Deane left his papers behind in Paris. He appeared twice before a secret congressional committee and was apparently unable to convince the members that French intentions had changed or that he had not benefitted personally from any of the transactions. As Secretary of the Committee for Foreign Affairs, Paine knew all of this: he was in charge of holding all the papers having to do with the incident.

When Deane defended himself in the press in early December, Paine was furious. He responded by revealing the secret information he had been gathering. In essence, he went public about America's dealings with the French, a move he later deeply regretted. The charge of war profiteering was not unique to Deane. Others had been accused of it, including General Nathanael Greene and Robert Morris. Morris had channeled government contracts to his own firm, Willing, Morris, and Company when he served as chairman of a congressional committee seeking supplies for the United States.[15] In Congress, Richard Henry Lee of Virginia and Henry Laurens of South Carolina roundly criticized the actions of these people.

Laurens had served in the Continental Congress since 1777 and was its president in 1777-78. What was unsettling in the matter was Paine's timing of his announcement of the American-French relationship. He embarrassed both nations, just as the French ambassador arrived with Deane on these shores.

Was Deane working for the United States or for himself? Did he inflate prices to rake off profits for himself and later split them with Beaumarchais? There were some who believed that Silas Deane was doing all he could for the American cause. He could not be at fault for wanting to earn some money on the deals he was making with the French because he was, in the end, accomplishing the ultimate goal of arming the Americans against the British. Deane's supporters in the Continental Congress included the great financiers like Robert Morris, Gouverneur Morris (who, while no relation to Robert, was a signer and principal stylist of the American Constitution), Matthew Clarkson, and Paine's namesake but no relation, Robert Treat Paine, a signer of the Declaration of Independence, who had prosecuted the British soldiers after the Boston Massacre.

Paine's relationship with Robert Morris and Gouverneur Morris throughout his life was tempestuous, to say the least. The former, for whom Paine later wrote as a hired pen in the mid-1780s, is known today as "the financier of the American revolution," a statement that is true, but fogged by questions of how much self-interest he invested in the cause, how much patriotism. A signer of the Declaration, Robert Morris had come with his family from London to Philadelphia where he was apprenticed to the merchant firm of Charles Willing. So successful was he that by 1757 he was a partner with Willing's son, Thomas, after the elder Willing died. Although he opposed British financial restrictions on the Americans, he thought the initiation of the Declaration in July of 1776 was premature. Within a month, he had changed his mind, and as a member of the Continental Congress, he signed it. With the war on, Robert Morris invested in various ventures independent of Willing and became the wealthiest, most successful merchant in America.

For his part, Gouverneur Morris, a graduate of King's (now Columbia) University, practiced law and served in the Continental

Congress, devoting his legal expertise to assisting Robert Morris with the financial affairs of the new nation. Like Robert, he too served in the Constitutional Convention of 1787, and later, to Paine's regret, as the American Minister to France in 1792. Though outwardly in favor of American independence and a strong, central government, he opposed any concessions to end slavery in America. Later, in France, Morris, who harbored positive feelings regarding aristocratic rule and who was always skeptical of democracy, was openly hostile to Paine, whom he rightly considered to be a supporter of the radical revolutionary ideas, which Morris rejected. It was no wonder he was one of Deane's most able partisans. After his confrontation with the two Morrises over the affair, Paine reconciled a bit with Robert, but never again did he have a satisfactory relationship with Gouverneur. The tensions between them boiled over again after the French Revolution when Paine was imprisoned and Morris, by then American Minister to France, did nothing to help free him.

It is easy to suggest that the dispute was a matter of good combatting evil, truth and virtue battling deception and self-interest. This is not, however, the case, and history is not yet clear about the relative weight of either side. What is clear is that the real loser was Thomas Paine. It was Paine who revealed to the public, and hence to the international community, that America was involved with the French before the Treaty of Alliance between the United States and France was signed in 1778. Because this revelation violated U.S. policy at the time, Paine was soon forced to resign his position as Secretary of the Committee for Foreign Affairs in the Continental Congress (which was tantamount to dismissal). Were the French arms, then, a gift or were they to be paid for later? Was Beaumarchais involved in war profiteering, as Paine charged, or was he only carrying out his duty to the best of his abilities? What was Robert Morris' part in the affair? Gouverneur's role? Were they intimately involved in American diplomatic and military affairs because they believed in the cause or because they wanted to enrich themselves at the expense of America? Paine thought these men were all war profiteers, and he said so.

One historian has unearthed several documents in British archives which prove that Deane was both self-interested and a monarchist—in fact, a traitor to the American cause.[17] This conclusion is supported by a letter Deane wrote from Paris to Robert Morris, in which he strongly argued that it was in America's best interest to maintain commercial relations with England. "Thus in Europe, we shall be either excluded from our ancient and certain markets, or at least rivalled in them, and we shall have no certainty of new ones, nor any security against heavy duties and impositions." He presumed that America would face an "immense" national debt (visionary that he was). America was at a critical moment in her history, Deane wrote, and her future lay with Great Britain.[18]

There can be no doubt about Paine's intentions. He had no financial or other private interest at stake. This is clear in his first salvo, an open letter to Silas Deane, which was in response to a December 5, 1778 apologia from Deane himself, who had complained that Congress had shut its ears against his defense.[19] Paine's letter, signed by "Common Sense," appeared in the *Pennsylvania Packet* on December 15, 1778, ten days after Deane's was printed. Paine's was an uncharacteristic piece with no personal invective or venom aimed at Deane. He basically accused him of some indiscretions and a lack of candor. "The convulsion which the public were thrown into by his address will, I hope, justify my taking up a matter in which I should otherwise have been perfectly silent; and whatever may be its fate my intention is a good one."[20] Paine should have kept his silence because tempers soon flared, including his own. As was customary with him, once involved in the altercation, he allowed passion to overcome reason. He revealed too much about the secret negotiations between the Americans and the French. The French, for their part, certainly wanted to see the British defeated, but they did not want war with Britain. The Americans appreciated this sentiment. While they welcomed French assistance, they were not prepared to announce the consummation of the treaty of friendship with France until France was ready to do so.

Several replies supporting Deane immediately emerged, especially one by Paine's old adversary, William Smith, writing once again as "Plain Truth," as he had two years earlier in replying to *Common Sense*. Smith claimed that Deane was a public official who "had formed and cultivated the esteem of a valuable political and commercial connection, not only in France but in other parts of Europe." Paine would have none of this. Perhaps it was the specter of William Smith once again rising against him. Perhaps he learned additional secrets about Deane that he now wished to reveal. Or perhaps he just decided that Deane was a scoundrel, which was what he conveyed in a long, open letter, which appeared in five installments in the *Pennsylvania Packet* from the end of December 1778 into January 1779. Paine was aware that Deane was a private citizen—not a "public Minister"—who was engaged by the United States to act on its behalf to secure needed supplies for the war effort.[21] A few days after writing this letter, Paine's embitterment deepened when Robert Morris answered Paine's charges by defending Deane. Paine immediately extended his attack to Morris, who, he said, had earned too much money too fast by dispensing government contracts to himself and his friends, including Deane. Paine asked whether it was "right that Mr. Deane, a servant of Congress, should sit as a member of that House, when his own conduct was before the House of judgment? Certainly not. But the *interest* of Mr. Deane has sat there in the person of his partner, Mr. Robert Morris, who, at the same time that he represented this State, represented likewise the partnership in trade." This was corruption, pure and simple. "Why not as well go halves with every Quartermaster and Commissary in the army? No wonder if our Congress should lose its vigor, or that the remains of public spirit should struggle without effect."[22]

The most damaging remarks, those which proved fatal to Paine's position with the American government, came in installment three of his long, open letter in the *Pennsylvania Packet*. On January 5th, Paine openly revealed the new Franco-American link. He wanted to expose everything as a

> principle of public justice. It shows, in the first instance, that
> the greatness of the American cause drew, at its first begin
> ning, the attention of Europe, and that the justness of
> it was such as appeared to merit support; and in the second
> instance, that those who are now her allies, *prefaced that
> alliance by an early and generous friendship*; yet, that we
> might not attribute too much to human or auxiliary aid, so
> unfortunate were those supplies, that only one ship out of the

three arrived. The Mercury and Seine fell into the hands of the enemy.[23]

The link between the French and the Americans was now set forth for everyone to see, including the embarrassed French Minister Gérard, who was rightfully shocked. He appealed directly to the new president of the Congress, John Jay, a Deane supporter, to take action. On January 6, Jay, who had been Chief Justice of the New York Supreme Court, summoned Paine to a session of the Congress that Moncure Daniel Conway calls a "serio-comical performance," one that foreshadowed the Red Scares of two centuries later.[24]

Paine was asked whether he was the author of the pieces signed "Common Sense." He answered that indeed he was. This sparked strong words the following day from Gouverneur Morris, who was not only a strong Deane supporter but also appalled by the premature revelation "Common Sense" had made about the new Franco-American alliance. Morris wanted Paine removed, and had he been discharged (instead of agreeing to resign), he would have been the first person ever to have been fired by the American government. Instead, the very next day, he voluntarily resigned his office as Secretary of the Committee for Foreign Affairs. "My wish and my intentions in all my late publications," he wrote, "were to preserve the public from error and imposition, to support as far as laid in my power the just authority of the representatives of the people, and to cordialize and cement the union that has so happily taken place between this country and France."[25]

Freed from his responsibilities as a public official, Paine now allowed his full fury and ridicule to pour from his pen. He was hesitant only insofar as he used a pseudonym, only this time instead of "Common Sense," he signed his pieces "Comus," a figure traditionally linked in classical antiquity with satire and mockery. He attacked not only Silas Deane and the two Morrises, but also Representative William Henry Drayton of South Carolina, whom he had once praised in "Crisis Three" as a strong supporter of the American cause. (Drayton's was one of the first voices of praise for Paine's *Common Sense*.) Now, events had changed all that. Paine saw that "the devil backs the king of England, and S. Deane backs W.H.D. because he has good 'ears,' and they are not 'shut,' " a direct reference to Deane's own complaint from the previous December that Congress had shut its ears when it came to his defense. Having finished with Drayton, Comus took on Paine's more serious rival, Gouverneur Morris, yet again, only to damage further an already strained relationship.[26] A few days after this piece, Paine attacked a joint effort by Drayton and Morris, their *Observations of the American Revolution,* when they failed to take into consideration America's military efforts at the beginning of the war. Paine's enemies, the Deane supporters, of course did not let him get away with such a vociferous assault on Drayton and Morris. In July, an anonymously published, shortened ode appeared in the *Evening Post,* attacking him with the same ridicule he had poured on his enemies:

> Hail mighty Thomas! In whose works are seen
> A mangled Morris and distorted Deane;
> Whose splendid periods flash for Lees defense,
> Replete with everything but common sense.
> In pity tell, by what exalted name
> Thou would'st be damned to eternal fame.
> Shall Common Sense, or Comus, greet thine ear,
> A piddling poet, or puft pamphleteer.
> And eager to traduce the worthiest men,
> Despise the energy of Drayton's pen.[27]

Paine's attempts to justify his revelations, which he considered part of his support of the American cause against those in Congress (including Deane) who sought only to aggrandize themselves, were all in vain. Congress made no mention of them in its records. Nearly four months later, he wondered why he had received no responses to any of his inquiries. "I am unable to account for the seeming inattention of Congress in collecting information at this particular time, from whatever quarter it may come," he wrote.[28] The French government was delighted to sell the arms to the Americans, but quite apprehensive about Paine's revelations concerning Deane and the public involvement of France in American affairs. Gérard had offered to pay Paine seven hundred pounds per year to write essays placing France in a favorable light in an attempt to sway American public opinion. The Minister found that because of his delicate position as ambassador, he could not possibly submit commentary to the press in his own name. He had already been annually paying a clergyman, Dr. Samuel Cooper, the pastor of Boston's Brattle Square Church, some two hundred pounds sterling, and Rep. Hugh Henry Brackenridge somewhat less, four hundred continental dollars.[29] But Paine's voice was better known and respected, and his pen was the most powerful in the new nation. Besides, Gérard knew that Paine had reaped no benefits from the sales of *Common Sense* or the papers in *The American Crisis*. He was, the diplomat wrote to Vergennes, a "starving author" ["un auteur affamé"]. The deal was that he was to receive $1,000 a year.[30]

After several attempts by Gérard to hire Paine, he finally had to give up. Paine just could not accept the offer. He later recalled that "as I considered myself standing on a nice and critical ground [having lost his position as Secretary], and lest my reputation should be afterwards called in question, I judged it best to communicate the whole matter to an honorable friend."[31] The friend he wrote to on January 14, 1779 was Henry Laurens. Paine seemed genuinely embarrassed. "I certainly have some awkward natural feeling, which I never shall get rid of," he sighed. "I was sensible of a kind of shame at the Minister's door today, lest anyone should think I was going to solicit a pardon or a pension. . . . I shall never make a courtier, I see that."[32] Interestingly, Gérard claimed that he was successful in getting Paine to accept, but he was wrong. Earlier that same month when he defended the Pennsylvania constitution, Paine had added his thoughts about paid authors, which clearly gave his position on writing for the French government: "the wretch who will write on any subject for bread, or in any service for pay . . . stands equally in rank with the prostitute who lets out her person."[33]

Did Gérard lie to his superiors, desiring them to think that he had secured the services of a popular propagandist in America? The answer may never be known. What is certain is that although Paine did not agree to this deal, he soon accepted an offer from Robert Morris himself to become his hireling, this time for the Americans, and from 1781 to 1783, he wrote on behalf of French interests when he entered into an agreement with La Luzerne, Gérard's successor. By then, the Deane episode was history.

But in 1779, it was the current, burning issue of the day, and Paine did not let up in his attacks on Deane and his allies. He felt humiliated, especially after Gérard, now apparently angry at Paine's refusal, wrote to Congress, implying that there were some (unnamed) persons who were spreading "false and dangerous insinuations" about recent transactions between the United States and France. Such talk "might mislead ignorant people," he said, "and put arms into the hands of the enemy." Paine immediately felt that the persons Gérard had not named was none other than Thomas Paine. "I feel myself exceedingly hurt by some expressions in Mr. Gérard's letter to Congress," and he intended to give the Minister "a most polite opportunity of doing me justice."[34] When Gérard stuck to his story, Paine, now embarrassed more than ever, stayed by himself for several weeks, telling General Greene that "the roguery will soon come out." He also wrote General Washington that day, telling him the same thing: "That there has been foul play somewhere is clear to everyone—and where it lies will, I believe, soon come out."[35]

It did come out: Paine soon took a job as a clerk in the office of his friend, Owen Biddle, a fellow Quaker, who had fervently favored American independence. Biddle, a lawyer by training, was the head of the Pennsylvania Board of War. There, Paine continued to attack Deane's wrongdoing, and indirectly Gérard's charges, throughout 1779. By March, Paine could tell Franklin that he was recovering, for "the scale of affairs is now entirely turned as to the public sentiment," although Deane and his supporters were fighting back.[36] As a result, the issue became one of social and economic class as much as political principle. On one side were the radicals, the so-called constitutionalists in Philadelphia such as Paine, who wanted to prove that what he said was totally selfless, inspired by love for his adopted country, support for its independence, and belief in its future. On the other side were people like Deane and Gouverneur and Robert Morris, who, according to Paine, wanted to maintain the status quo and enrich themselves. Paine attacked his social betters, in other words, and suffered for it. He had become a social and political outcast. After all, had not Gouverneur Morris, at the height of the Deane affair, complained in Congress that any gentleman from Europe would have thought Paine to be "a mere adventurer from England, without fortune, without family or connections, ignorant even of grammar. . . . This is the man whom we would remove the office, and this is the man, who has been just now puffed as of great importance."[37]   Congress never took action against Deane. Eventually the affair was dropped from the public press, and Dean went to Europe, never to return, dying in poverty.[38]

Paine also continued to attack Robert and Gouverneur Morris and others whom he believed profited from their commercial interests in the war effort. He was particularly anxious when the freighter the *Victorious* showed up at the Philadelphia port with its entire cargo addressed to Robert Morris, who Paine thought was selling at prices far above a profit margin. In May, Paine's friends elected him to serve on two committees to investigate such activity, one specifically to investigate the *Victorious* cargo, another to look into Morris's purchase of flour for the French navy at a cost lower than a committee of citizens had advocated. As inflation was rapidly rising, especially in Philadelphia, the wealthy folk did not seem affected by it. It appeared that their engagement in war profiteering held them harmless from price increases. During the summer, Paine involved himself in the debate over price controls, but to no effect, because the issue once again entangled him with Robert Morris, who argued that price controls would not work. Merchants, Morris said, would be forced to sell their goods at cost or even below cost. Besides, the government was not strong enough to enforce such controls.[39] Although Paine and the Morrises in the middle of the next decade agreed about the financial future of America, especially about the Bank of North America, tensions between them were never overcome.

Paine was now viciously attacked in the press, first anonymously by yet another self-ascribed "Cato," who turned out to be a dealer in iron and steel, Whitehead Humphreys. Humphreys was later joined by "A Friend to Cato and to Truth." Supported by artist Charles Willson Peale and other republican friends, Paine was lauded as a great advocate of American liberty. This alliance helped him neither economically nor politically. He had lost his job as Secretary of the Committee for Foreign Affairs with the new American government and was not to get it back, and his work for Biddle brought in little money. He continued to suffer financially, though he had some money saved in reserve. He told Henry Laurens in September that he had "a right to ride a horse of my own, but I cannot now even afford to hire one, which is a situation I never was in before, and I begin to know that a sedentary life cannot be supported without jolting exercise." As a consequence of his strapped financial condition, he thought he might collect all of his writings, including *Common Sense*, into a large edition and sell them by what he hoped would be a large subscription. He also planned to write a history of the American Revolution, which clearly would have been a vast new undertaking for him. He would write it objectively, he said, but it would have moral content so that when school children read his abridgement, they would learn the true lessons of the war and the evils of the British empire. Unlike "The Beggar's Opera," he said, he would not render "the villain pleasing in the hero."[40] He even asked the Pennsylvania Supreme Executive Council to grant him a literary pension, a request it never granted.

Paine, of course, had never written a work of history. His writings had been journalistic, covering only current events, and while he could accumulate enough information to set forth his political position, he had no experience at all in collecting, organizing, and documenting a major historical study. He knew that he could only undertake his history if he had access to British documents. In any case, he never wrote the history nor published a collection of his work.

In 1779-80, the financial condition of the states was bleak, matching Paine's own mood and finances. Hungry, increasingly radicalized townsfolk in Philadelphia resented the war profiteering they perceived among merchants and manufacturers. In October 1779, in what came to be known as the Fort Wilson Riot, several hundred citizens gathered in the common to complain about monopolists and profiteers. Their target was the house of James Wilson, a legal theorist (and later Supreme Court justice) who had defended several Loyalists in American courts. The rioters stormed his house, in which several gunmen were waiting, and a good deal of blood was shed.[41] Several people were killed or wounded, and the battle might have continued had not Joseph Reed, chairman of the Executive Council (an office like mayor in modern times), arrived with members of the Philadelphia Light Horse to break it up. Paine was not involved in this fracas but condemned the actions of both the armed men in Wilson's house and the rioters outside in what he called "a tragedy of errors." Clearly worried the British would think that the Americans were divided about their commitment to continue the war, Paine wrote in the *Pennsylvania Packet* that the riot was not a protest against the war but was the result of a misunderstanding about who was in the house at the time. It was "the unfortunate blunder of friends."[42]

In November, Paine was named clerk of the Pennsylvania Assembly. There, he immediately helped draft an anti-slavery act. As Paine had long opposed both the slave trade and the institution of slavery, he now had an opportunity to participate in the creation of a legislative measure calling for gradual abolition of the practice. Soon the war re-entered the picture, this time with a vengeance. The financial problems of the United States were worsening. Taxes were not being collected to fund the war effort, and American currency was constantly being devalued. Congress seemed to have no credit to borrow against. In addition, recruiting for the military was often a slow, tedious affair. Who wanted to join the cause when there was no guarantee of clothing, food, ammunition, or pay? The Americans suffered severe losses in the south as Georgia fell, and Charleston, South Carolina, was on the verge of defeat. In March of 1780 in "Crisis Eight," the first addition to this series he had written in over a year and a half, Paine ignored these losses and spoke optimistically to the English people. He told them that "every campaign, by a gradual decay, has lessened your ability to conquer."[43] The Americans were intent on winning this war because they would never submit to England. In fact, the war was once again collapsing around Paine.

Paine was fully aware of the critical financial condition of the army and the government. He had read to the Pennsylvania Assembly a letter from General Washington about the devastating morale among American troops. Washington had written that there was "in every line of the army the most serious features of mutiny and sedition."[44] Paine donated $500, practically all of his savings, to the

American cause and asked that others do the same. He stood ready to give yet another $500, which was all the money he had in reserve. He apparently was willing to go absolutely penniless to help the war effort. "How then is the army to be recruited, clothed, fed, and paid?" he asked a Philadelphia merchant, Hugh McClenaghan.[45] Robert Morris followed suit and got other merchants to contribute to the private collection. Paine's donation stimulated additional contributions, leading to the accumulation of more than three hundred thousand pounds for the army, which would have been well over $25 million in 1991 dollars.[46] This sum was the impetus for the creation of the Bank of North America, the institution which soon successfully funded the war effort to the end.

With the fall of Charleston and the surrender of some three thousand American soldiers there, Paine wrote in "Crisis Nine," published in June 1780, that the Americans were now reinvigorated in their struggle against the British. In defeat he wanted to see reasons for optimism. A new flame has broken forth, "like the blaze of 1776," which "will kindle into action the scattered sparks throughout America," he wrote.[47] His optimism was a few weeks later magnified when he was awarded, quite by surprise to him, an honorary master's degree from the University of Pennsylvania for his efforts on behalf of the American cause. Not all was so pleasing, however. News from West Point had it that the American garrison there had been betrayed by its commanding officer, General Benedict Arnold. Arnold had served well in the Continental Army, taking Fort Ticonderoga with Ethan Allen, and he pushed into Canada in the Quebec campaign, though he failed to capture Montreal. His troops were exhausted by the time they reached there. He served with distinction in Connecticut, and for his efforts was promoted from Brigadier to Major General. Afterwards his troubles with his military superiors began. As commander of Philadelphia, he actually faced a court martial following several disputes over the disposition of supplies for the army. He was cleared of these charges, though embittered. In 1780 he obtained his command of West Point and shortly thereafter entered into correspondence with Sir Henry Clinton, the commander-in-chief of British forces in America. In exchange for a high rank in the British army and a sum of money,

Arnold agreed to turn over West Point to the British. The plan was frustrated at the last minute when Major John André, aide to General Clinton, was captured in New York with all the documents on his person. Arnold escaped to England only to lead British troops into battle against his former countrymen.

Paine was furious. He recounted the whole business, including Arnold's flight from America aboard the ship, the *Vulture*, "on which it might be truly said that one vulture was receiving another." For Paine, Arnold was "a desperado," the only military officer in America's short history to have betrayed his country. Here Paine uncharacteristically turned to divine authority for an answer to the betrayal, turning his Providence into a watchful lady-protectorate. "But why if Providence had the management of the whole [affair], did she let Arnold escape? Perhaps to be hung afterwards by the enemy for some act of traitorship against them. In this case, he will have no apology left and all parties will call him what they now think, a villain." If there were a good side to this business, it was this: that having to bribe an American military officer proved that Britain was almost defeated, "a confession of inability to conquer."[48] America now survived as England became the pariah of the world.

Paine continued to worry over the fragmentation of the American states. At the present moment, they were united only by the war effort and little else. Such a thought caused him to consider how to effect a more effective bond. He immediately set to work on a pamphlet, *Public Good*, in which, presaging the Constitutional Convention seven years later, he appealed for a convention to be called to create a stronger central government. It was the first such appeal to be made and it went directly against the thinking of several of his radical republican friends, who still saw a strong central government as the great engine of tyranny. Paine soon had some difficulties explaining himself to his colleagues.

A year earlier, representatives from the Indiana Company had asked Paine to write a pamphlet denouncing Virginia's claim to lands in the West which Indians had granted to them. Paine had initially refused. But when he saw documents that refuted Virginia's claim, he wrote the pamphlet, *Public Good*, hoping that the stronger central government he called for would overcome the financial problems America experienced in the war effort as well as any arguments about the disposition of western lands. The pamphlet focused on the future disposition of the western lands. States on the western border of the United States could conceivably expand to the western edge of the continent. Who knew how far that might be? States with western limits, such as Maryland or Delaware, had no place to expand. Serious tensions were created between the border states and those "landlocked" to the west. Paine argued that all land not yet incorporated as part of a state should belong to the nation as a whole. This could only be done if the United States had a stronger central government.[49] The Indiana Company officials were so pleased with *Public Good* that they granted Paine title to twelve thousand acres of land, a grant Paine apparently neglected to apply for until two years later. When he finally did so, he was accused of being a hired pen for the company, but vehemently denied the charge.

In any case, Paine thought the financial problems of America were great enough to cause a danger of losing everything to the British. And he apparently thought it was time to end the war through a settlement. Accordingly, he asked Joseph Reed, the Executive Council chairman, to send him to England to negotiate a peace with the English ministry. He told Nathanael Greene, "I see my way so clearly before me in this opinion, that I must be more mistaken than I ever yet was on any political measure, if it fails of its end. I take it for granted that the whole country, ministry, minority, and all, are tired of the war . . . and accommodate their feelings to a treaty for peace."[50] Reed did not think it a good idea for a state representative to negotiate on behalf of the nation. The idea was dropped. But financial problems deepened. General Washington had written that while one state raised revenue for Congress, another did not and a third paid only one-third its requested share. "All differ either in the manner, the matter, or so much in point of time," Washington wrote, "that we are always working up hill, and ever shall be; and, while such a system as the present one or rather want of one prevails, we shall ever be unable to apply our strength or our resources to any advantage. . . . The crisis, in every point of view, is extraordinary."[51] Paine responded with his own "Crisis Extraordinary," which echoed Washington's sentiment: it was now time for Congress to have the power to levy taxes directly.

This was not to be. The states were not interested in giving up any of their newly-won sovereignty to some national entity, not even for the greater good, the public good. Paine contacted the French once again. By now, Paris had recalled Gérard, perhaps in part because the government learned that he had never signed Paine to any agreement, and Paine was unstoppable in his attacks on Deane. Anne-César de La Luzerne, who soon had more success with Paine than Gérard, was sent to replace him. Paine approached the new ambassador, who in turn thought it was in his interest to talk to Paine. He too figured that Paine could enhance France's image in the eyes of the American public.

At the same time, Congress was looking for ways to improve its treasury. The two paths converged: John Laurens, the son of Paine's friend Henry, was commissioned to go to France to try to secure more financial assistance. Young Laurens, who the year before had been captured by the British at Charleston but quickly exchanged for a British officer, asked Paine to accompany him as his secretary. But nourishing remnants of bad feelings over the Silas Deane affair, some members of Congress did not want Paine to have an official position. While this point of contention was under discussion, young Laurens introduced Paine to two French noblemen, both of whom Paine deeply admired and with whom he later had much contact: the Marquis de Lafayette, who had returned to America, though briefly, and the Chevalier Chastellux. The friendship was almost immediate. The two French aristocrats later reported to La Luzerne—who passed on the information to Foreign Minister Vergennes—that Paine was such a good friend to France, his pen could write on behalf of French causes.

Some ten years later, Paine and Lafayette dined frequently together when Paine moved more or less permanently to France. For now, he decided to go with young Laurens, but only as his companion, a decision that was bolstered by his rejection as a member into the American Philosophical Society. In January, one month before their departure, Dr. James Hutchinson, a friend of Paine and a surgeon in the army, nominated Paine's name to the Society, but on the 19th, the Society refused to accept him. While no official reason was given, Paine's argumentative style likely sparked resentment against him, especially when nomination practically meant automatic admission. So now he wanted to go to France, at least for awhile. William Jackson acted as the official secretary. The three men left together in February of 1781.

7 · A Hired Pen

With this first trip to France in 1781, a five-year period began in which Thomas Paine used his skills to work more openly on behalf of the United States to insure that his liberal-republican ideals were implemented. He wanted very badly to go to France, because he thought he could help young Laurens and Benjamin Franklin, the latter who was already there as the American Minister, convince authorities there that it was in their practical interests to support American independence. While Arthur Lee and John Adams, along with Franklin, had earlier been commissioned to discuss France's ongoing commitment to the American cause, it was up to Laurens and Paine to highlight the extreme urgency of the moment. They knew better than anyone the condition of the American armed forces, and a loss to Britain could severely hurt French interests.

In transmitting Congress' written request to Louis XVI, Franklin wrote to Vergennes, the Foreign Minister, just as Laurens, Paine, and Jackson were departing.

> The present conjuncture is critical; that there is some danger lest the Congress should lose its influence over the people, if it is found unable to procure the aids that are wanted; and that the whole system of the new government in America may thereby be shaken; that, if the English are suffered once to recover that country, such an opportunity of effectual separation as the present may not occur again in the course of ages; and that the possession of those fertile and extensive regions, and that vast sea-

coast will afford them so broad a basis for future greatness by
the rapid growth of their commerce and breed of seamen and
solders as will enable them to become the *Terror of Europe*, and
to exercise with impunity that insolence, which is so natural to
their nation, and which will increase enormously with the
increase of their power.[1]

England, France's traditional enemy, would be weaker without the
North American colonies. Without French financial and military
assistance, the American cause might well be lost, and the potential
gains the British would achieve would be immense, politically and
militarily.

The crossing was not without some excitement. In a letter to
James Hutchinson, who had nominated him to the American
Philosophical Society, Paine later recounted that at one point, it
appeared as though the ship, the *Alliance*, had run aground and was
sinking. Soon the crew found that the vessel had smashed into some
huge ice floes. Tension and fear rose among the passengers; the danger literally escalated by the minute. "The wind increased to a severe
gale," he recalled, "and before we could take in the sails one of them
was torn in two. Nothing could now be done but to lay the ship to
and let her take her chance. The ice became every moment more formidable, and we began to apprehend much danger from it as when
we first supposed ourselves on ground." Huge chunks of ice came
crashing into the sides of the wooden ship and parts of the craft were
torn apart, just missing by seconds sweeping young Laurens into the
sea. For more than seven hours in a black night, the ship heaved and
yawed in the thundering seas, buffeted by a never-ending cascade of
ice.

Only at dawn did the seas settle. The rest of the passage was
safe. A few days after their horrifying nighttime experience, "we had
a glorious breeze." The ship gave chase to the British ships they saw
under sail but could not catch them. The crew did, however, free a
Venetian ship that had been captured as the prize of a Scottish vessel, the *Russel*, for what Paine considered to have been no good reason. The Venetian ship was under a neutral command, though its
cargo of pepper, indigo, glass bottles, and the like was certainly valu-

able. The captain and his son did not speak English, but through a kind of sign language, the son made it known that his captors had locked him in irons. The captain of the *Alliance*, having examined the Venetian's papers, ruled that the actions of the skipper of the *Russel* were acts of piracy. "The justice of America and the honor of her flag made it a duty incumbent on her officers to put the much injured Venetian in possession of his property and restore him to the command of his vessel without accepting either recompense or salvage." For Paine this was an act of humanity.

Within a few days they were near their destination. Finally, Laurens, Paine, and Jackson arrived at L'Orient on March 9, 1781, where crowds of local citizens and officials warmly greeted them. "I find myself no stranger in France," Paine commented. "People know me almost as generally here as in America. The commandant of L'Orient paid me very high compliments on what he called the great success and spirit of my publications."[2] In the crowd was Franklin's grandnephew, who found Paine exceedingly interesting and good-natured. He only wished the writer had been less opposed to Silas Deane (the elder Franklin as well had found Deane a trustworthy sort while the profiteer was in France).

Laurens, Jackson, and Paine then set off for Nantes. There, a Philadelphian named Elkanah Watson introduced them to the mayor and other town officials and spent some time with Paine, interpreting for him. Watson's reminiscences about Paine are full of great detail about why he loathed the man but loved his ideas. He wrote in his diary that Paine was "coarse and uncouth in his manners, loathsome in his appearance, and a disgusting egotist." Many people, on first encountering Paine, came away with a negative impression, and Watson was no exception. This was, after all, the only time he seemed to have met him. Paine's friends, those few men and women with whom he drew close, understood him and appreciated his often gratuitous display of his knowledge and interpretation of political events. They easily forgave his eccentricities, especially his talkative personal style, his singing, his occasional uncouthness.

But not Watson: Watson had no appreciation for the man, and besides, he wrote his memoirs, after Paine's final return to America in 1802, when Paine was in ill repute across much of the country. Watson claimed that Paine loved nothing more than constantly "rejoicing most in talking of himself and reading the effusions of his own mind." Moreover, claimed Watson, no one could stand to be in the same room with Paine for very long, including French officials, because of the odor exuded from his filthy body, "the brimstone odor," Watson called it.

Watson wrote that after Paine asked to borrow a clean shirt, Watson was able to convince him to take a bath. Paine insisted on reading some English newspapers because he wanted to catch up on the news he had missed while sailing to France. He became so involved in reading in his bath that Watson told his servant in French, so Paine could not understand, to increase the temperature of the bathwater so much that "le Monsieur serait bien bouilli" [the gentleman would be well boiled]. By the time the bath ended, Watson described Paine as practically being "parboiled . . . much to his improvement and my satisfaction."

Despite Paine's physical rankness, Watson clearly understood the contribution he had made to the American cause, and indeed was indebted to him for stimulating American independence with the publication of *Common Sense*. Watson recalled that in 1775 or 1776, he heard a group of prominent leaders in Providence express "abhorrence" at the idea of independence from the crown, but that when Paine's pamphlet finally appeared, it "passed through the continent like an electric spark," leading directly to the congressional announcement of independence on July 4, 1776. "The name of Paine was," Watson recalled, "precious to every whig heart and had resounded throughout Europe."[3]

Laurens was successful in negotiating with the French, thanks largely to Franklin, who took him from agency to agency and even to the king, Louis XVI. Inexperienced in diplomatic affairs as he was, Laurens, who was only twenty-six at the time, at one point was a bit overzealous in his efforts to obtain French agreement to help the Americans. Vergennes, the Foreign Minister, complained about the super-eagerness of the young diplomat, who had been educated in France and fluently spoke the language. Trained as a lawyer in London's Middle Temple, young Laurens was a brash, often impulsive member of Washington's staff. His devotion to Washington was unshakable (and Washington to him), especially when the Americans sustained early losses in the war and some wanted to replace Washington with Horatio Gates. For Franklin, Laurens had been the right choice. It "was a wise measure to send" him because he "could speak knowingly of the state of the army." The young man was to return to America thoroughly possessed of my esteem."[4] Washington overlooked the young man's faults: "no man possessed more amor patrioe [love of country], in a word, he had not a fault that I ever could discover, unless intrepidity bordering upon rashness could come under that denomination, and to this he was incited by the purest motives."[5]

The more mature Paine and the seasoned Franklin, then seventy-five years old, were more composed in presenting their arguments, although there was some disgruntlement among some Americans who felt that Franklin had long been neglecting his duties and was instead enjoying Parisian life too much in his advanced years. Others thought he had begun to lose his intellectual capabilities. (Franklin wrote at the time that "I do not know that my mental faculties are impaired; perhaps I shall be the last to discover that."[6]) They were eventually able to arrange for an extraordinary grant of six million livres and loans worth ten million.[7] This was the first major foreign aid grant that the United States received, and it cemented the first major alliance of the new nation. France clearly understood how necessary it was to assist America defeat her historic enemy, Great Britain, and she was willing to pay the costs.

Paine spent most of his time in Paris visiting Benjamin Franklin and a few other Americans, like Adams and Lee. He stayed with Franklin, along with Jackson and Laurens, in Passy (today in the sixteenth arrondissement), then a suburb of the city, drafting major portions of the documents that bound France closer to the Americans. While Louis XVI admired Paine, he apparently never received him. Paine had few French contacts mainly because he did not speak French (and never learned). While he later attributed much of the success of the trip to young Laurens, Franklin was the true darling of the French court. Paine spent his time pulling together the financial and military statistics, literally sending in reams of reports, memoranda, letters, and other correspondence, to convince Vergennes and the Foreign Ministry of the gravity of the American position.

In the end, the statistics won, because the French by the end of May were well-acquainted with the American's vital need of more military assistance. Paine wrote much, perhaps all, of Laurens' report to Congress on the success of the mission. After more than two months in France, one ship with the Marquis de Lafayette on board as a personal escort embarked for America, loaded with "clothing for nearly 20,000 men, with arms, ammunition, etc., which will supply some of your wants."[8] A few weeks later on June 1st, Paine and Laurens left for America via Boston, carrying with them two and a half million livres in silver and accompanied by two ships loaded with military supplies and clothing. When Paine, along with the French supplies and funds, returned to America via Boston at the end of August (it took them nearly three months because of the circuitous route they had to take to avoid British warships), he was again virtually penniless. He had spent his savings on the trip because Congress had not covered his expenses. He had no job. He even had to borrow a dollar, he said, "at Bordentown to pass the ferry with."[9] In the meantime, the supplies were carted southward from Boston, and delivered to General Washington. He soon distributed the hard cash to his troops and clothed them properly, in anticipation of the final assault against Cornwallis in the effort which virtually ended the war.

Paine was desperate financially. Laurens was paid $200 for his contribution to secure French aid for America. Paine received nothing. He had written one of the century's greatest bestsellers, *Common Sense*, and had not earned a single penny from it. His other writings like *The American Crisis* were no less selflessly done on behalf of the American cause. He never profited from them, either. He had even paid for his own trip to France in order to help increase French financial support, and he had worked hard to persuade France. At one point, though without money himself, he had selflessly obliged a group of army officers who asked him to petition General Washington for their pay.[10] Washington and Robert Morris, now Superintendent of Finance, soon saw this "memorial" Paine had written on behalf of the soldiers.[11]

John Laurens returned to his duties, basically forgetting

about his friend. Before they parted, he had asked Paine, however, to do him a favor, as if he thought Paine were truly his private secretary: pick up his boots which were being made for him. In October, Paine wrote Laurens to tell him that he had gone for the boots the day after John left Philadelphia to return to Virginia, "but they were not done, and I directed the man to bring them to me as soon as finished." Paine quickly added that he was glad they were not ready because he did not have the cash anyway. "I must be obliged to borrow the money to pay for them." Paine was obviously annoyed with young Laurens. He wished Laurens "had thought of me a little before you went away," he complained.[12]

The very next month Paine appealed on his own behalf to George Washington, who as commander-in-chief, he thought, was in the best position to help him financially. The British were well ensconced in New York, leaving the General, then in Philadelphia, little to do for the moment in terms of the war effort. Paine seemed to trust him implicitly: "as there is satisfaction in speaking where one can be conceived and understood, I divulge to you the secret of my own situation, because I would wish to tell it to somebody, and as I do not want to make it public, I may not have a fairer opportunity." Ever since he had first come to the colonies seven years earlier, Paine had without hesitation supported the American cause. At the same time, he had also "declined the customary profits which authors are entitled to, and I have always continued to do so."

He did not want to appear ungrateful. He simply had no money and did not know whom else he could petition. He had been fair with America, and he expected America to be fair with him. He was now hurt to see America "so cold and inattentive to matters which affect her reputation." He related that he had served in official and unofficial capacities for the American cause. In exchange, he had received nothing. At one point, he had even had to find work "as a common clerk to Owen Biddle," but this he kept secret because news of it was bad for America's name. It would have caused the people of the world to have "an ill opinion of her honor and generosity." In contrast, wherever he went, he found that people respected and admired him. They were grateful for his work on behalf of the Revolution. But no one had helped him, and he could not continue in his present financial penury. His intention was eventually to settle in France or Holland to continue his work on behalf of liberty and justice. "There is something peculiarly hard that the country which ought to have been to me a home has scarcely afforded me an asylum."[13] He hoped that the gentleman plantation owner-turned-general would help him.

Washington soon responded that he promised to do what he could. As Paine later wrote, Washington "became affectionately interested in the account I gave him, and concerted with a friend or two to make my continuance in America convenient to myself until a proper time might offer to do it more permanently."[14] A little money was raised and forwarded to Paine, who now hoped that the United States government itself would investigate the matter and come up with a way to reward him for his past efforts. In his letter to Washington, Paine also mentioned that he planned to respond to Abbé Guillaume Thomas François Raynal's interpretation of the American Revolution. This popular French theologian had written a philosophical interpretation of the history of the Indies, which was translated into a pirated English version and published in America in 1776. In his view, a people had the right to revolt against their oppressors and the right to decide when they would or would not pay taxes. These ideas had led to his condemnation by the Parlement of Paris in 1781.

Paine had received his copy of Raynal's history from Robert Morris, to whom he commented, "there are several mistakes in it, and his opinions are often [in] contradiction to one another."[15] What had especially upset him was the final volume of Raynal's history, entitled *The Revolution of America*, where he argued that the American separation from Britain basically followed the same pattern that all revolutions did with but one essential exception: the main reason for the American desire for independence was not that principles of democratic-republicanism had stimulated revolution; taxation alone had. Paine thought Raynal's views had placed the United States in a rather bad light in terms of its alliance with France. He set the record straight in a response, which he wrote six months later in the summer of 1782.

For now, in very short order, Washington thought that

Paine's pen would be a useful addition to stimulate American public opinion in favor of the government's actions during the war. In the fall of 1781 he asked Morris to hire Paine as a writer and pamphleteer. Morris agreed. But to reinforce his opinion, Morris asked both Gouverneur Morris and Robert Livingston, then Secretary for Foreign Affairs, what they thought about the idea. They concurred: Livingston was to channel information to Paine, who was then to write newspaper articles in support of (or in opposition to) whatever the issues demanded. In September, Morris wrote to Paine, suggesting that he might work for him as a writer. Paine thought this quite a good idea, but to protect himself, he wrote in turn to Washington and then to La Luzerne, the French Minister in America, suggesting he might write for them, too (La Luzerne apparently was interested in countering the anti-French material that Deane was now writing in England). He wanted to have a more or less official position with both governments.

The agreement between Paine, on the one side, and Morris, Washington, and Livingston, on the other, was formally entered into on February 10, 1782.

> The subscribers, taking into consideration the important situation of affairs at the present moment, and the propriety and even necessity of informing the people and rousing them into action; considering also the abilities of Mr. Thomas Paine as a writer, and that he has been of considerable utility to the common cause by several of his publications: They are agreed that it will be much for the interest of the United States that Mr. Paine be engaged in their service of the purpose above mentioned.

Paine's task was to write newspaper columns in support of American commerce, legislation, and whatever official action the American government was taking. His only caveat was that he would never write anything with which he personally disagreed. He was to be paid $800 per year for his "secret services." No news of Paine's hiring was ever released, because, they decided, public notice would "injure the effect of Mr. Paine's publications and subject him to injurious personal reflections."[16] Paine could hardly wait for the arrangement to begin. He wrote to Morris that he was "under no difficulty of accepting the proposal, because I will know that it is not only out of friendship to me but out of justice to me." Without his new "job," he thought about leaving journalism and contemplated "getting a [real?] livelihood."[17] For now, since he had no money at all, he asked Morris for an advance.

The first piece Paine wrote in his new position was "Crisis Ten," published the very next month. Paine was now the hired pen for both the American and the French governments. Three months earlier, on October 19, 1781, seven thousand British soldiers surrendered at Yorktown after General Cornwallis was virtually cut off from all supplies by sea and outnumbered on land. Even so, the British Parliament, after a speech by George III, decided to continue the war. "Crisis Ten" focused on the reasons why it was necessary for the Americans to bring the English to total defeat. Paine believed that enthusiasm for the war was seriously flagging as the economic condition of the country worsened. The real threat behind all of this, as in *Common Sense*, was George himself. "Like Pharaoh on the edge of the Red Sea, he sees not the plunge he is making, and precipitately drives across the flood that is closing over his head." America could, and would, defeat Britain, but it would need strong national unity, the leadership of a robust central government. In 1776, Paine had been the first to go before the public to advocate American independence. He now was among the first to champion national unity. Every state must raise taxes for a common cause: to continue the progress of the war. "Our taxes are our insurance money; they are what we pay to be made safe, and, in strict policy, are the best money we can lay out."[18] Paine's piece convinced few, however, of the necessity of supporting the national cause through the national government. Most people's allegiance was still to their individual state.

Paine pursued the theme of national unity and national resolve against the British, which he had already addressed in *Public Good* a year and a half earlier.[19] He wanted American loyalty to be redirected through the leaders in Philadelphia. At the same time, he wrote newspaper articles about raising taxes. Plaudits were insufficient. Only money could feed, clothe, and pay the soldiers. "Government and the people do not in America constitute distinct bodies," he wrote in an April "Crisis" paper.

> They are one, and their interest the same. Members of
> Congress, members of Assembly, or Council, or by any other
> name they may be called, are only a selected part of the people.
> They are the representatives of majesty, but not majesty itself.
> That dignity exists inherently in the universal multitude and,
> though it may be delegated, cannot be alienated. Their estates
> and property are subject to the same taxation with those they
> represent, and there is nothing they can do that will not equally
> affect themselves as well as others. If they call for supplies, they
> call on themselves in common with the country. Their situation
> enables them to know the more secret circumstances of things,
> and that such or such revenues are necessary for the security and
> defense of their constituents, and the accomplishment of the
> great object for which they are chosen. And here the distinction
> ends.[20]

The people must learn that they were one people, united in the cause
of war, and pay taxes to the national government as a show of that
unity. Those who objected to higher taxes were mean-spirited. They
did not understand that taxes paid for the liberty and the republic the
nation was fighting to achieve and that taxes preserved the safety of
young and old alike.

In the meantime, the British tried a new tactic by attempting
to interpose themselves between the Americans and the French. A
possibly stronger Franco-American alliance was too dangerous for
Britain to ignore. Paine asked Washington to join him and Robert
Morris as "part of an evening at my apartment [to] eat a few oysters
or a crust of bread and cheese" and to talk about a proper response.[21]
Paine's answer came, in part because of his arrangement with
Washington and Morris in part because of a request from La
Luzerne, in "Crisis Eleven," which appeared in May of 1782. Paine's
language was as colorful as ever, mixing metaphor after metaphor in
a glorious attack on his favorite current enemy. No matter how hard
Lady Britain tried, she could not seduce her American victims into
her boudoir.

It is now the hurricane months of British politics. Every day seems to have a storm of its own, and they are scudding under the bare poles of hope. Beaten, but not humble; condemned, but not penitent; they act like men trembling at fate and catching at a straw. From this convulsion, in the entrails of their politics, it is more than probable, that the mountain groaning in labor will bring forth a mouse, as to its size, and a monster in its make. They will try on America the same insidious arts they tried on France and Spain.

We sometimes experience sensations to which language is not equal. The conception is too bulky to be born alive, and in the torture of thinking, we stand dumb. Our feelings, imprisoned by their magnitude, find no way out—and in the struggle of expression every finger tries to be a tongue. The machinery of the body seems too little for the mind, and we look about for help to show our thoughts by. Such must be the sensation of America whenever Britain, teeming with corruption, shall propose to her to sacrifice her faith.

But, exclusive of the wickedness, there is a personal offense contained in every such attempt. It is calling us villains: for no man asks the other to act the villain unless he believes him inclined to be one. No man attempts to seduce the truly honest woman. It is the supposed looseness of her mind that starts the thoughts of seduction, and he who offers it calls her a prostitute. Our pride is always hurt by the same propositions which offend our principles; for when we are shocked at the crime, we are wounded by the suspicion of our compliance.[22]

The Americans continued their effort against Britain with vigor and determination. So far as Paine was concerned, the British ministry was already drowning in the war effort.

An embarrassing situation now arose, which Paine, as the hired pen of Livingston and Washington, had to help resolve. Washington considered the event a British atrocity. An American officer, a Captain Huddy of the Jersey militia, was hanged without trial after being captured in a skirmish with the British. General Clinton angered by what he considered a violation of military justice, demanded that the British hand over the officer responsible for the summary execution. When the British predictably refused this request, Washington threatened to execute a nineteen-year-old British officer, Captain Charles Asgill, in exchange. Asgill's name had been drawn by lot from the names of British prisoners of war.

Livingston asked Paine to set forth the facts underlying the case and to condemn the British execution. The result was "A Supernumerary Crisis" in which Paine wrote, "The history of the most savage Indians does not produce instances exactly of this kind. They, at least, have a formality in their punishments. With them it is the horridness of revenge, but with your army it is a still greater crime, the horridness of diversion."[23] In the fall, he asked Washington for "a suspension of [Asgill's] fate."[24] Paine's humanitarian impulse led him consistently to oppose the "death penalty"—a few years later, he admired Robespierre's speech against capital punishment, and he bravely defied his fellow legislators in Paris in calling for exile, not death, for Louis XVI. He never changed his mind about this, though Robespierre certainly did. Asgill was eventually released, but only after the French government, Vergennes to be specific, interceded on his behalf. Huddy's executioner was never brought to justice.

Paine spent part of the summer of 1782 in Bordentown in the pleasant company of the Kirkbrides, with whom he stayed, and the Bordens.[25] (Colonel Kirkbride had lived in Bordentown since the British burned down his Bucks County, Pennsylvania, home.) Paine now tried to work seriously on his history of the American Revolution, an enterprise which he never completed. In fact, what he did write was his response to Raynal's interpretation of the Revolution. Raynal's view that the Americans had declared independence only because they objected to paying British taxes was dead wrong. Moreover, Raynal had gone even farther and declared that the British had offered peace terms as early as 1778 but the Americans had refused them, because they had already entered into an alliance with the French.

Paine disagreed with both of these assertions. The war against Britain was in truth based on the eternal moral principles of democracy, and the alliance with France was formed after, not before, the British offered peace terms. The cause of America was more than taxation.

In short, other revolutions may have originated in caprice or generated in ambition; but here, the most unoffending humility was tortured into rage, and the infancy of existence made to weep.

A union so extensive, continued and determined, suffering with patience and never in despair, could not have been produced by common causes. It must be something capable of reaching the whole soul of man and arming it with perpetual energy. It is in vain to look for precedents among the revolutions of former ages, to find out by comparison the causes of this.

The spring, the progress, the object, the consequences, nay, the men, their habits of thinking, and all the circumstances of the country are different. Those of other nations are, in general, little more than the history of their quarrels. They are marked by no important character in the annals of past events; mixed in the mass of general matters, they occupy but a common page, and while the chief of the successful partisans stepped into power, the plundered multitude sat down and sorrowed. Few, very few of them are accompanied with reformation, either in government or manners; many of them with the most consummate profligacy. Triumph on the one side, miser on the other were the only events. Pains, punishments, torture, and death were made the business of mankind, until compassion, the fairest associate of the heart, was driven from its place, and the eye, accustomed to continual cruelty, could behold it without offense.

But as the principles of the present Revolution differed from those which preceded it, so likewise did the conduct of America both in government and war.

Indeed, the American war against Britain was the first war to be based on principle in the history of the world. "War, so much the trade of the world, has here been only the business of necessity; and when the necessity shall cease, [America's] very enemies must confess, that as she drew the sword in her just defense, she used it without cruelty, and sheathed it without revenge." As for the alliance with the French, "the signing the Treaty of Paris, the sixth of February, 1778, could have no effect on the mind or politics of America, until it was *known in America*." The American government had not entered into its new relationship with France until after it had rejected the British peace offer.

Paine went to great lengths to sound reasonable. He set forth one of the most important principles a journalist must bear in mind when refuting an argument. Never write in the white heat of anger, or as he put it more elegantly, try always to respond by combining "warm passions with a cool temper" (which must have been hard for him, given his previous dealings with the Silas Deane affair when he could hardly control his fury). Paine the journalist tried to do just that here. He decried what he considered Raynal's ignorance of the American Revolution. But he subdued his anger sufficiently to put forth an image of America that he wanted the world to see. He knew that this work would appear in France, and he knew that he had to couch his language in painfully logical terms. Because he believed (and wanted the world to believe) that the American cause was based on universally-held principles, he ended his rejoinder with the argument that the principles of this revolution encompassed all people everywhere. The result was to be the development of a "universal society, whose mind rises above the atmosphere of local thoughts, and considers mankind, of whatever nation or profession they may be, as the work of one Creator."[26] This was one of the earliest examples in American history of the discussion of a world federation of nations.

Paine sent his pamphlet to his American and French patrons. His essay delighted La Luzerne, who sent it to Paris, where it was immensely successful. Vergennes had his government grant Paine fifty guineas for writing the work. Being a hired pen suited Paine: he was now a journalist who shaped events to the liking of his bosses. He apparently enjoyed serving the French in this way. Over the next year, he received a total of $300 from them, which included payment for his response to a pamphlet encouraging Americans to buy British-made goods. The pamphlet had been republished in *Rivington's New York Gazette*. Paine's answer, which he again called "A Supernumerary Crisis," argued that "America is now sovereign," and she can trade with whomever she pleased, even if she chose not to deal with the British. "Our national honor must unite with our interest to prevent injury."[27]

While all this was happening, Paine sent a copy of his *Letter to Raynal* pamphlet to the Earl of Shelburne, a Whig magnate who had become the king's first minister. Curiously, within a very few years, Paine for a short time became the Earl's friend. For now, however, Shelburne continued to oppose American separation. Paine in a moment of pique addressed "Crisis Twelve" to him, a copy of which he also mailed to him. Paine wrote in polite terms, but often couched his language in condescension and ridicule. He argued that it was impossible to reconcile the differences between the two nations. The Earl had offered to come before the Congress to present the reasons why the war must end and America remain part of the empire.

> That the country which for more than seven years has sought our destruction should not cringe to solicit our protection is adding the wretchedness of disgrace to the misery of disappointment; and if England has the least spark of supposed honor left, that spark must be darkened by asking and extinguished by receiving the smallest favor from America; for the criminal who owes his life to the grace and mercy of the injured is more executed by the living than he who dies.

No, reconciliation will not work. "As America is gone, the only act of manhood is to *let her go*."[28] The war must continue to the bitter end.

Paine now turned his attention to the nation's terrible financial condition. The states simply were not volunteering their share to help pay for the war. Paine's agreement with Morris and Livingston meant that he would write on behalf of the government to convince the states to raise funds through taxes, especially so the American government could pay the interest on loans, which the Dutch had granted. Congress levied a five percent duty on all imported goods, which each state was to collect and forward to Philadelphia. Under the Articles of Confederation, all states had to accept the imposition of such a duty if a total of nine states agreed, and indeed all except Rhode Island did.[29] For a variety of reasons (its tiny size, its inability to expand westward), in 1776 Rhode Island hesitated to ratify the Articles, and a few years later it had the dubious distinction of being the last state to ratify the Constitution, which actually became effective in 1788 without Rhode Island's vote. Now, the smallest state refused to pay the taxes levied.

The opposition in Rhode Island was led by David Howell, a state delegate to Congress, who sent letters and articles, some anonymous, to the *Providence Gazette*. He apparently encouraged several others, including his co-delegate Jonathan Arnold and Providence town clerk Theodore Foster, to join him in trying to convince the Rhode Island Assembly not to pay the tax. They relied on an economic argument: the impost was unnecessary to pay the Dutch loan interest. They even tried to stir the fires by associating the United States government with tyranny. They lambasted nationalists like Robert Morris and others who were intent on creating a centralized government mirroring English political corruption with placemen and pensioners, that is, people who took their "places" in government or received a pension from the court in exchange for adhering to the crown's policies, no matter what they were. Soon, they were forwarding copies of their Rhode Island pieces to Philadelphia newspapers, and Paine was anxious to respond to these articles.[30]

Paine reported to Morris in November of 1782 that he had begun to work on his arguments in favor of the tax. Adopting a theme he later used in his letters to the citizens of Rhode Island, he explained that "as a republic, there are matters Continental, others which are *Statacal*," clearly meaning having to do with the states. Now was the time for citizens to come to the support of the continent, and not merely their own individual states.[31] Once again, Paine was an advocate of national unity over parochial interests. It took the Americans another five years to realize that the loose Articles of Confederation just were not workable and that if the country were to hold together, they had to craft a stronger national government.

For several months, Paine wrote on behalf of the United States to encourage Rhode Island officials to accept the new duty. Signed "a friend to Rhode-Island and the Union," Paine's letters appeared from December 1782 to February 1783. He thought that because the citizens of Providence had warmly welcomed him home from France with Laurens, he was well-liked and admired there. So he traveled to Providence to make his case in person. He hoped to contain arguments against the tax in Rhode Island and keep them out of the Philadelphia newspapers.

Howell was now taking his opposition to a higher plane. He

suggested that American national debt was increasing rapidly enough
to threaten financial decay and he announced, anonymously, that
American officials had long been working on a new secret loan from
the Dutch and a commercial treaty with the Swedes. If this were so,
Howell argued, there was no need for the states to supply additional
revenue, and in any case a tax imposed by Congress on a state was not
related in any way to the success of obtaining a foreign loan or a commercial treaty. In an "Extract of a Letter from A gentleman in
Philadelphia to his Friend in this Town," Howell argued that

> the national importance of the United States is constantly rising
> in the estimation of European powers, and the civilized world.
> Such is their credit that they have of late failed in no applica
> tion for foreign loans—and the only danger on that score is that
> of contracting too large a debt. Instead of regretting that our
> credit was no better established by an impost or permanent rev
> enue to be mortgaged for thepurpose, posterity, when they fell
> the weight of debt thereby transmitted on them, will
> admire at its extent and rejoice it went not further.

Howell's letter appeared in newspapers in both Philadelphia and
Boston. Members of Congress were infuriated by what they considered Howell's breach of trust. The talks with the Swedes, in particular, had been secret, and to announce them now in the press, before
the deal was consummated, endangered American foreign policy.
Moreover, Sweden was the first nation to make overtures to the new
United States for a commercial treaty, and to make this prospective
relationship public now could seriously compromise negotiations.
Besides, the argument that the United States could fulfill all of its
financial needs through dealings from abroad threatened Congress'
ability to raise sufficient revenue from the states to pay for the war
effort.[32]

Although Paine also worried about a growing debt, he
thought the main principle involved was the defeat of British tyranny in America, and the tax, to be paid by all states, was critical if the
war were to be properly funded. Paine, at the urging of Robert
Morris, went to Rhode Island to help settle the matter. He argued

that every citizen of the United States possessed two "personalities," a dual citizenship, just as he had told Morris—a state "personality" and a national "personality." Rhode Islanders must exercise their national citizenship and support the country as a whole. His views met with both strong opposition and strong support. In the end, Rhode Islanders refused to accept the new tax. Many of them claimed that Paine was the hired pen of the merchant interests of Philadelphia, which of course he was, though he vehemently denied it. "I am no sycophant to Congress, I write for no pension from them. It is absurd for me to conceive that at this time, when they are laboring by every method to procure money to recompense the virtue of the army, who have saved the country, that they should give me a reward."[33]

When Paine later applied for the position of archivist of the United States, members of the Rhode Island delegation accused him of having been a hired pen. Paine hotly countered that his principles had not been compromised, that he never wrote anything for anyone if he disagreed with its premises and principles. In fact, Morris, Livingston, and Washington had subsidized his writing for a very short period of time, from February 10, 1782 (the date of the agreement) until April 18, 1783 (the end of the war), and he never wrote anything he did not firmly believe.

On April 18, 1783, Washington announced that hostilities between England and America had ceased. The next day, having returned to Philadelphia, Paine printed his penultimate "Crisis" paper, at a moment when "the times that tried men's souls are over—and the greatest and completest revolution the world ever knew, gloriously and happily accomplished."[34] There was to be one final paper in December, but this one in April was the last to be numbered: it was "Crisis Thirteen," named in honor of the newly independent thirteen states. The themes again were a centralized government, national unity, and the opportunity "to form the noblest, purest constitution on the face of the earth." (*CS* 120) Other states were following Rhode Island and rescinding their acquiescence to the national tax—first, Maryland, then Massachusetts, then North and South Carolina. The spectacle of a Congress hamstrung by its inability to raise revenue directly from the states only strengthened the resolve of those who believed that America had to have a stronger, more centralized government. This was the only way in which the democratic republic, with its emphasis on the participation of a virtuous citizenry protecting their rights and liberties, could ever come into existence.

These arguments were not played out until the American Constitutional Convention some four years later in Philadelphia, but already the drive toward centralization of authority, the "Federalist" position, could be seen in the struggle with Rhode Island over the tax. Paine had already been rapidly moving in that direction. Years later, he recounted that "*when the states saw themselves wrong enough to be put right,*" then the time would arrive for a wholesale renovation of government.[35] (*GW* 2:692)

In this "Crisis" paper, he gratuitously announced to his readers that he himself had played a peculiarly important and "selfless" role in the business of the tax. He did not mention he had been paid by Morris, Livingston, and Washington (or the French) to back their arguments. He had acted, he said, "to conciliate the affections, unite the interests, and draw and keep the mind of the country together; and the better to assist in this foundation work of the revolution, I have avoided all places of profit or office, either in the state I live in, or in the United States; kept myself at a *distance from all parties and party connections, and even disregarded all private and inferior concerns.*"[36] The end of the war effectively ended his relationship with Morris and Livingston. In the last three years before he wandered from the United States in 1787, he stabilized his financial situation and worked on an invention, an iron bridge without piers. No longer in the employ of Morris, Livingston, and Washington, he had to find some way to obtain some ready cash. Two months after the war ended, he approached Congress on June 7, 1783 and detailed the services he had performed for the government over the past seven years.

Paine said that he had been suffering in poverty for a long time but was loath to reveal his condition to the public, except to a very few close friends. He had accepted subsidies from top American leaders and the French, but that was all a private, secret affair. Now, however, he could go on no longer. Many Americans had "estates and fortunes to defend." He had none. In serving his country, he had "neither sought, received, nor stipulated for any honors, advantages, or emoluments for myself."[37]   (One might wonder whether this included his relationship with Morris, Livingston, and Washington.) There was no president of the United States under the Articles of Confederation because the framers of that document had feared a strong executive. There was, however, a president of the Congress who acted as a kind of chief executive of the United States, when Congress was not in session. At the time, the president of Congress was Elias Boudinot from New Jersey. Congress, then sitting in Princeton, took the matter under consideration. And consideration. And consideration.

A few weeks later, Paine was still at it, this time writing to a congressional committee, hoping that its members would agree that he had performed a worthy service to the United States. "It is the practice of monarchies in general to show their countenance to flatterers and partisans," he told them, "but the principle on which republics are founded supposes them to be the patrons of virtue and public spirit, and where this is wanting the principle of a republic is not there. . . . This much I may venture to say, that I have the honor of being ranked among the founders of an empire, which does not afford me a home."[38]

The problem was in large measure complicated by the manner in which the Articles of Confederation, which the states had ratified back on November 15, 1777, had prescribed the constitutional structure of the American government. The United States was in effect a creation of its individual states. Having declared themselves free and independent of Britain the previous July, they also had declared themselves virtually free and independent of each other as well. Paine had had a good taste of this arrangement in his arguments in Rhode Island. He faced it once again, this time in making a case on his own behalf. Under the Articles, the Congress was the central feature of the government. Because there was no independent president, there was no chief executive who acted as a counterbalance to the will of the legislature. There was, in effect, no union. There was simply a confederation of states, and Article II made that clear when it asserted that "each state retains it sovereignty, freedom and independence, and every power, jurisdiction and right, which is not by this confederation expressly delegated to the United States, in

Congress assembled."

This language actually diminished the entire idea of a "United States of America." It suggested that the United States as an autonomous and separate entity existed *only* when Congress was in session ("in assembly"), and that most of the time the states were still pretty much on their own. All states had one vote in Congress (though they had the authority to send as many as seven delegates, but a majority among them had to agree if the vote of their state were to count). For a bill to pass, at least nine of the thirteen states had to vote in its favor. In 1787, the Preamble to the American Constitution, largely drafted and refined by Gouverneur Morris, moved away from the concept of a government by the states to one formed by "We the People of the United States." It was the "People" who now sought "to form a more perfect Union." But in 1783, it was virtually impossible to get nine states to agree on anything, as Paine unfortunately discovered.[39] It was no wonder he advocated stronger, national unity.

Peace finally came on September 3, 1783. Washington traveled to Princeton where Congress was then sitting, and the General was given a house, under congressional authority, in Rocky Hill. There was a good deal of celebrating, including a grand dinner to celebrate the American victory over Britain. In attendance were the General, of course, the French Minister to the United States, many members of Congress, including its president, Elias Boudinot. Paine was not invited. He was down the road in Bordentown, suffering from a bout of scarlet fever. He was laid up for about a month. He wrote to Washington, then the most esteemed man in America, asking for his support. Washington invited him to his new home near Princeton, where together they participated in scientific experiments. Apparently the water in a nearby creek could be set ablaze because of its chemical composition, and he and Washington stirred up some bottom mud and ignited a fire over the water.[40]

While there, Washington promised to address Congress on Paine's behalf, and he even suggested that Paine himself come to Congress to make his case: "your presence may remind Congress of your past services to this country; and if it is in my power to impress them, command my best exertions with freedom, as they will be ren-

dered cheerfully by one who entertains a lively sense of the importance of your works, and who with much pleasure subscribes himself
your sincere friend."[41] Robert Morris also suggested that Paine write
directly to Congress, which he did. When Congress referred Paine's
request to one of its committees, he addressed a long, drawn-out letter to that committee. For one of the first (and only times) in his life,
he seemed embarrassed about having to write about himself. He told
Washington about his letter with some uncharacteristic humility. "A
man's judgment in his own behalf, situated as I am, is very likely to
be wrong, and between the apprehensions of saying too little, or too
much, he probably errs in both." But Paine was not deterred, despite
the "awkwardness in information coming from me."[42] He mailed his
letter, which he hoped at long last would lead to some personal good.

Paine would have been delighted if Congress had appointed
him official historiographer of the United States, something that
Washington himself had suggested. He would finally be able to write
his long-anticipated (by no one but himself, of course) history of the
American Revolution. In his lengthy letter to the committee, he
went into great detail about how he thought the United States had
mistreated him financially on a plane in reverse to how well he had
treated America ideologically. His letter read almost like a legal brief,
outlining all the previous events and his accomplishments over the
past nine years, from the time he arrived in America in November of
1774 until October of 1783. All he wanted from Congress was compensation for his past services, and nothing for anything in the future.
In fact, he even offered to become the historiographer without recompense. "If after this I undertake a history of the revolution it will
be perfectly voluntary and with freedom to myself, and if Congress
pleases to give me the appointment of historiographer as honorary
and without salary or conditions, it will facilitate the collections of
materials and give the work the foundation of impartiality and clear
it of all appearance or suspicion of influence."[43] Working without
congressional pay meant to Paine that the historian had to be totally
dedicated to objectivity and truth. The letter was remarkably candid.

The committee and then Congress actually deliberated the
matter. The committee thought it was a good idea, but the Congress
itself never put it to a vote. With what resources he had left at his

disposal, Paine now purchased a house and five acres of land in Bordentown. (Rumor had it that toward the end of 1783 he had received 2,400 livres, or $6,000 in 1991 dollars, from the French for his services.) He spent the autumn in quiet seclusion, often visiting his friends the Kirkbrides, waiting to hear from the Congress. Finally, it appeared that some of the states would act, but individually, not together through Congress. In December, while visiting New York, he confided in James Duane, the Mayor of New York, his desire to live in that state. He also told him that "I have but two resources left, the one is to apply to the states individually, the other is to go to Europe."[44] He soon undertook the former, but within three years decided the latter course was correct.

Before he left to return to Philadelphia and eventually his farm in Bordentown, he wrote his final "Crisis" paper, which appeared in December 1783. Britain was convinced that the newly independent states of America would never be united into a nation. Paine feared that this prediction might turn out to be accurate. Signing himself as "Common Sense," he alluded to the footdragging "by sundry persons in a certain state," by which he meant Rhode Island, who refused to act as if they were part of a larger entity than their own small state. "United, she [America] is formidable, and that with the least possible charge a nation can be so; separated, she is a medley of individual nothings, subject to the sport of foreign nations."[45] It was time for America to act like the United States it claimed to be, and not like thirteen separate and distinct nations. If the states failed to unite, the political experiment on these shores was doomed to failure.

In the spring of 1784, the New York Assembly voted to offer Paine his choice of two farms that the state had seized from British Loyalists, and he made plans to travel to New York as soon as the ice melted. He chose one with two hundred seventy-seven acres in New Rochelle, which had been owned by Frederick Devoe, who had stuck by the British during the war. Paine kept the farm until his death in 1809.[46] Washington attempted to accomplish a similar goal in Virginia. Working with James Madison, Richard Henry Lee, and John Marshall, Washington tried to persuade the Virginia Assembly to donate land worth four thousand pounds to Paine.[47] In June he wrote Madison, asking "Can nothing be done in our Assembly for poor Paine? Must the merits and services of *Common Sense* continue to glide down the stream of time, unrewarded by this country?" The same day, he wrote Patrick Henry, asking that something be done for Paine. "Convinced as I am of the efficacy of his publications, and of the little attention shown him for them, I could not withhold this attempt to serve him."[48]

The effort failed, no doubt because of Paine's anti-Virginian stance in *Public Good* when he decried Virginia's western land claims. Those who remembered and resented Paine's position voted against offering him anything. A final proposal was made to sell the land and give half the proceeds to Paine. That too failed. In Pennsylvania, John Dickinson, the President of Pennsylvania (as the chief executive of the commonwealth was then called), worked with the Supreme Executive Council to get land or cash for Paine. In March of 1785, the council voted what Paine thought was a measly sum of five hundred pounds. He thought the amount was low because he had supported the Bank of North America, which so many people in the western part of the state had opposed because they thought it was controlled by the eastern merchants and manufacturers. Five hundred pounds was, however, as Conway put it, "a snug little fortune in those days."[49]

Finally, in September of 1785, Paine specifically asked Congress for a grant of $6,000. This amount of money covered only his minimal expenses during the war when he worked without compensation. He did not include in this request expenses incurred during the year he served as Secretary of the Committee for Foreign Affairs during the Silas Deane imbroglio. "If Congress will please to order my private expenses to be reimbursed me, which I have naturally incurred by my service to the States, I desire no more." Congress finally granted him an allowance of $3,000. This amount made Thomas Paine as wealthy as he would ever be.[50] He would never again see so much money all at once. It allowed him to devote his attention, at least for the moment, to other matters, especially the design and construction of his iron bridge.

8 · Invention and Finance

I n the winter of 1784, Paine waited for good weather so he could travel from Bordentown to New York to see the farm that the New York legislature had given him. He told his good friend Lewis Morris (Gouverneur's half brother) that there was just too much ice, so he stayed put for the time being. In the meantime, he told Morris of his idea of establishing a philosophical society in New York, one to parallel the American Philosophical Society in Philadelphia. Except Franklin and Rittenhouse, he thought there were no others undertaking scientific or mechanical experimentation in the latter city, although he himself was about to embark on his bridge design.

So Paine considered going to New York with the thought of creating a new association to draw people's "attention to objects of public and agreeable utility and to introduce as many subjects of easy and popular conversation as possible." Paine, who had been rejected by the American Philosophical Society in 1781, now hoped to capitalize on a new institution, which would no doubt grant him membership and from which he might launch his bridge design. Paine told Morris he was ready to live in any place other than his current state. Pennsylvania "is a place neither of science nor society and the most country retreat is to me preferable to Philadelphia. As I have yet my place of citizenship to fix, I had much rather it were in the state of New York than Pennsylvania, and if it can be ordered so, I should like to have a residence amongst you in preference to any place I have yet been in America." He was sick of Philadelphia, even though nearly a year later, on January 22, 1785, he was finally admitted into the American Philosophical Society. Because he advocated a stronger central government and closer union of states, his more radical friends, whom he called "the hot-headed whigs of Pennsylvania," could not understand why he seemed to have abandoned his earlier views in support of a confederacy of states. He closed his letter to Morris on a touching note. He that Morris' "old friend, Button," Paine's little horse which was a gift from Morris, "sends as many compliments as can be expected from a horse."[1] Years later, writing from Paris, he wrote referred wistfully to Button in his letters to his caretaker and others in America.

By springtime, Paine finally made it to New Rochelle to see his farm. Not surprisingly, he was just delighted. He told Washington, anticipating the award of the farm, that he hoped other states would follow suit. They did not. He also congratulated the General on his position with the new Society of the Cincinnati, founded to celebrate the end of the war and the disbanding of the Continental Army. Washington, who was almost universally regarded as a national hero, became its first president. The Society was named for the fifth century B. C. Roman general, Cincinnatus, who, having led his troops into victory, retired to private life to his farm rather than continue to rule as dictator. Many republicans objected to the Society. Because its membership was limited to former military officers of the Army, the republicans believed it was the foundation of a military aristocracy.

But not Paine. He believed that even if "every part of the institution" was not quite consistent with republican principles, "it is material to the future freedom of the country that the example of the late army retiring to private life, on the principles of Cincinnatus, should be commemorated, that in future ages it may be imitated." He also wrote Washington that he had written "a new song for the Cincinnati."[2] Although it is not clear which of the several patriotic songs he wrote during the American Revolution was this panegyric to Cincinnati, one thing is certain: Paine deeply hoped that American victory assured the long existence of American rights and liberties. In "Hail Great Republic," which might well have been his new song for the Cincinnati, the poet intoned phrases highly reminiscent of the language of *Common Sense*.

> Let laureates make their birthdays known,
>> Or how war's thunderbolts are hurl'd;
> Tis ours the charter, ours alone,
>> To sing the birthday of a world!
>>> Be thou forever great and free,
>>> The land of Love and Liberty![3]

The patriotic and republican Tammany Society of New York was soon founded as a counterweight to combat the influence of the clearly patrician Society of Cincinnatus with its military overtones.[4] At first mainly social and ceremonial, Tammany's name was derived from the Delaware Indian Chief Tamenend who supposedly greeted William Penn. The Society did not become a major political force until the 1800 presidential election when it fell under the obdurate control of Aaron Burr. For the time being, it was mainly a social club.

Now in New York for the next several months (he rented out his Bordentown and New Rochelle farms and grazing land), Paine became a sought-after guest. He spent a great deal of time with the Commodore James Nicholson and his family, especially his daughters Hannah and Catherine ("Kitty"). Kitty and Paine later corresponded when Paine lived in France, and she would be one of the last to see him alive in 1809. Commodore Nicholson had served in the Continental Navy, seeing action against the British from 1778 until his capture by superior naval forces in 1781. He was now a leader among the republicans in New York City, and was soon to become a follower of Jefferson. Thanks largely to his association with Nicholson and Lewis Morris, who lived in Morrisania just north of the city, Paine's social circle was exceedingly wide among the republican leaders of the city. Paine often dined with the Clintons. George Clinton had fought valiantly in the Revolution, although his defense of the Hudson failed with the fall of Forts Clinton and Montgomery. He helped draft New York's new constitution and became the first governor of New York, a post he held for six consecutive terms from 1777 to 1795. He later served as Vice-President of the United States in the second Jefferson and first Madison Administrations.[5] Paine also enjoyed the company of Aaron Burr, who, like Clinton, had a distinguished military career during the war, although he had to leave military service in 1779 because of ill health. A lawyer by training and profession, he was a well-known spokesman for republican causes.

In the fall, having enough of New York and desiring to check on his New Jersey farm, Paine returned home to Bordentown to work on his bridge design.

For a while now, Paine escaped the whirlwind of politics and journalism. Once victory over the British was assured, except for the emerging controversy over the Bank of North America, Paine's interest in political and social issues faded for the time being. Perhaps he was enervated by the dizzying experience of war and advocacy. Certainly, there was plenty to do to move the country along the democratic lines he had suggested in Common Sense and the Crisis papers. He could have been in the very center of several reform movements in education, abolitionism, women's rights. But he chose to go home and engage in scientific and mechanical invention. The Pennsylvania Assembly had given him five hundred pounds and Congress $3,000 "for my service to the States during the war and the progress of the revolution."[6] Why should he continue to think about politics when he had his own particular projects to engage his time and attention?

Most journalists find that they need to practice their craft all the time. If they spend too much time away from writing, their skills become tarnished and dulled. Thomas Paine did not have this need. He was often inclined, content, and able to put down his pen and turn his attention to something besides writing and politics and then return to writing whenever he felt the urge to do so. Perhaps this was a result of his late arrival to journalism. He had, after all, spent his first thirty-seven years doing a variety of things other than writing. Paine for now kept pretty much to himself on his farm in Bordentown, where he occupied himself with inventions. The eighteenth century was a time of great inventiveness, especially by laymen—those who were not scientists or mechanics. Benjamin Franklin was typical with his inquiries into all kinds of new, handy things. His experiments on everything from electricity and lightning to home medical remedies are well known, and Paine too engaged in experimentation. He felt that America was a peculiarly provocative place for the imagination, and the war with Britain was a powerful stimulant: "It energized invention and lessened the catalogue of impossibilities."[7] Paine's problem sometimes was that he left projects, other than his writings, unfinished. This was true of his mechanical inventions. He worked tirelessly for a while to develop a new product or mechanical device, but often when achievement was in view, his interest flagged, and he moved to something else.

In September of 1785, writing from New York, he welcomed Franklin home from France "to a land of peace." Franklin had completed his tour as the first American Minister to Paris. (His replacement was Thomas Jefferson.) Paine was delighted at the thought of working with his good friend and former mentor once again. "I have the additional pleasure in reflecting that so far as I have hitherto gone I am not conscious of any circumstance in my own conduct that should give you one repentant thought for being my patron and introducer to America."[8] The next week, he wrote that he was interested in developing a new candle that smoked less than an ordinary one. The flame, he said, came from one end and the smoke from the opposite end; as "a quantity of air enters into the candle between the tallow and the flame . . . in its passage downwards [it] takes the smoke with it."[9] According to one of Paine's friends, John Hall, who was a mechanic and neighbor in Bordentown, recently arrived from Leicester with letters of introduction, and who worked with him on these inventions, his candles "greatly improved the light." In fact, Paine's invention was partially successful. There was less smoke from his candles, but he never bothered to market them.

When nothing came of this enterprise, he began another project. He talked to John Fitch, who stayed with him in Bordentown in March 1786, of boats moving upstream under steampower. Hall said that Paine gave Fitch some ideas about improving his steam engines, which never really panned out. He later met Robert Fulton, gave him some suggestions too, but of course Fulton had his own ideas about steamboats. Most important of all of his enterprises was his attention to bridge construction. He soon began to conduct experiments with John Hall.[10] Hall and Paine worked together on a new design for a long, pierless iron bridge over water.

In an age like the late-twentieth century, when work is so

highly fragmented, the thought of a smooth transition from activist politician and political commentator to inventor/engineer is jarring and difficult to understand. We are unaccustomed to the spectacle of scientists and engineers writing on politics or political commentators designing bridges. We have become used to the compartmentalization of labor and the professions. It is insufficient to say merely that because technical knowledge was so primitive two hundred years ago, anyone could improve existing techniques. Nor is it sufficient to argue that the eighteenth century, the Age of the Enlightenment, created an atmosphere for those with unusually fertile minds to do many things well. Surely, those times were different, but there is more. The vast majority of people in eighteenth-century Europe and America were barely educated, and illiteracy was high among the classes termed "the lesser sort," which included the working poor, the rural laborer, and the unemployed. Only a very few people, those like Franklin and Paine, Rittenhouse and Rush, moved freely from one profession to another, and this speaks more of them as individuals than of the "period." For Paine to feel comfortable in both political commentary and engineering attests to his genius and talent. So if today the two seem at odds with one another, they melded together quite nicely when Paine decided to devote himself to bridge design and construction and to put aside for awhile his concerns about the economy and politics.

In the fall of 1785, when Paine returned from New York to Bordentown, to visit the Kirkbrides, he had asked John Hall to assist him on his bridge project. He told Hall that he was confident that "we can make a beginning here."[11] Paine then began the project that took him from America to England and to France over the next several years. Within two months, he read that a new bridge over the Schuylkill River was planned, and he told George Clymer, now a member of Congress, that he was interested in applying for the rights to build it. He did not think that a bridge with piers would work in the Schuylkill, because piers could not tolerate the ice that built up in winter. Paine's idea was a bridge without piers with a tremendous arch to withstand the rigors of the cold and ice.[12] Moreover, since it was to be of iron, not wood, it would supposedly last "four times as long or much longer," so the costs of building it would be covered by the tolls in no time at all.[13]

Paine later revealed that he got this idea from nature: the bridge was built in sections, like a spider's web. "I naturally supposed that when nature enabled that insect to make a web she taught it the best method of putting it together."[14] Paine started out with great enthusiasm and energy. Within a few months, he was sending Hall to Franklin with two models: one in wood, one in metal. But his work with Hall did not always go smoothly. At one point, for example, when they thought they had the model erected, it was apparently lopsided. The recriminations flew back and forth. When Hall complained that he was blamed for the problem, Paine, he recalled, "denied that and words rose high. I at length swore by God that it was straight when I left it; he [Paine] replied as positively the contrary, and I think myself ill used in this affair." Hall was apparently as mad as Paine. By the end of the year, a wrought iron model of the bridge was erected for a viewing by Franklin and Rittenhouse. Both were impressed. They encouraged Paine to solicit the state Assembly for a subsidy to build it, although Rittenhouse thought it was probably too expensive. By January 1, 1787, the model was on display in the Pennsylvania State House. Paine was depending on the state to cover the cost of construction, which he estimated at around $33,000.[15]

The bridge now occupied a great deal of Paine's time. It was the main reason he eventually decided to leave America and wander off to France and then England. Unable to sell his design to a Philadelphia investor to span the Schuylkill River, he asked Franklin what he should do. Franklin suggested that if he had the endorsement of both the Royal Society of London and the French Academy of Sciences, perhaps he would have more luck. Indeed, he might even build his bridge across the Thames or the Seine.

Bridge or no bridge, politics was once again entering into Paine's life, beginning in the fall of 1785, though Paine would not return to the political arena until early in 1786. What drew him out was the controversy concerning the Bank of North America. Paine for the first time found himself opposing the progressives, called Constitutionalists, for whom he had once served as mouthpiece. They took their name from their support of the radical, unicameral Pennsylvania constitution of 1776. They were certain that the divisions they perceived in Philadelphia, especially in the assembly, were class-based with the wealthy and ambitious trying to hold down the workingmen, the artisans, and tradesmen.

While it may be impossible to determine with any certainty what precisely caused this change in his attitude, some of it was probably due to the continuing influence of Lockean economic theory, especially Locke's ideas of property and money. In his *Second Treatise of Civil Government*, Locke had argued that God had originally given to man the earth to hold in common. It was a gift to all men, who were entitled, indeed obligated to use it for their benefit and improvement. God was also a conservationist in his creation. His desire was that human beings should cultivate the land, but not waste it. Therefore no one person should accumulate more land than he needed. Otherwise the crops that grew on his land were surplus and suitable only for the trash heap. To avoid this problem, God had instilled in all human beings the understanding that once they had reached the limits of the land that they could use, they should stop at that point and go no farther.

This admonition concerning land limitation existed, however, only in the state of nature, in the pre-political condition of life. Once men had entered into civil society with a government making laws for them to obey, another economic set of conditions came into being. For along with civil society came the invention of money, which took exchange from goods and services to hard species (or in Locke's, as in Paine's, time, paper currency). Money had in effect transformed the earlier set of rules that God had laid out to natural man. Money was an artificial means of exchange, and a single person was under no obligation to limit his accumulation of it, his access to wealth. Accordingly, Locke had been quite active in the creation of the Bank of England in 1694 and in fostering the wholesale development of English commerce and trade. It was his goal, in the last years of his life (Locke died in 1704) to advocate the economic betterment of his country just as he had worked for its political improvement twenty years earlier.

Paine's support of the Bank of North America was motivated by his continuing adherence to the theories of Lockean economics and classical republican principles, which must first be examined if the politics of the controversy are to make sense. Throughout this period, therefore, Paine used the vocabulary of the Lockean and classical-republican languages—of rights (especially property rights) as well as a civic virtue and the achievement of the common good. He believed that a sound financial base was necessary for a stable republic. Paine, too, wanted to see America progress commercially and financially. He had already said as much with his famous statement in *Common Sense* some ten years earlier: "Our plan is commerce, and that, well attended to, will secure us the peace and friendship of all Europe." (*CS* 86) Now, for perhaps the first time since independence, America had the opportunity to enrich itself if the bank were to remain a viable part of the nation's financial base. Paine was certain that it benefited not only the few (the Morrises, Wilson, and the other shareholders alone), but everyone. A nation's wealth redounded to the lowest depths of society, he thought, and did not remain only for the well-to-do. The bank, he thought, was a democratizing institution with vast economic possibilities.

Unlike in 1776, however, Thomas Paine was now no longer the spokesman for the Constitutionalists. Writing for Morris and Livingston had already proven that he could be a voice for conservative mercantile and commercial interests. And now, ten years later, in his 1786 principal defense of the bank, *Dissertations on Government; The Affairs of the Bank; and Paper Money*, Paine outlined his theories about the future financial stability of America in terms of money, property, and the bank. The goal of the republic, Paine said, was to achieve the public good (the res publica), "the good of every individual collected. It is the good of all, because it is the good of everyone: for as the public body is every individual collected, so the public good is the collected good of those individuals." All well and good and certainly understandable to his American readers, who accepted these ideas as readily as he had. But Paine went farther. First, he reminded his readers that civil society, as Locke had said, came into existence through a social contract, or what Paine called a mutual compact. Government, once created through the mechanism of this contract, had the responsibility to insure the continuing search for justice and right for all citizens. The role of the legislator became particularly critical in seeing that these ends were met.

The second manifestation of Lockean ideas appeared at this point. Legislators obviously had as their primary task the responsibility to make law for the good of the republic. These laws applied to all persons in the commonwealth. They related to, among other things, the familiar areas of the administration of justice, the preservation of the peace, the security of property, and raising the necessary revenues for the functioning of government. But legislators also had yet another responsibility: rather than only make laws, they sometimes created "acts of agency or negotiations." These are not general laws specifically for the entire community to obey but "are acts of contract and agreement on the part of the state with certain persons therein mentioned and for certain purposes therein recited." When this occurred, the state was, in law, defined as a person and was bound by the contract just as an individual was in a similar arrangement.

What sorts of acts of agency were these? Unlike the arena of law enumerated above, these acts had to do with "transactions of business" in which the government might engage, such as selling land which is publicly owned, borrowing money on behalf of the government, acquiring the services of an individual or a group to perform certain tasks on behalf of the people (constructing a public building, for example). These acts were, "in short, every act in which two parties, the state being one, are particularly mentioned or described and in which the form and nature of a bargain or contract is comprehended." The main difference between private and governmental contracts was that the latter, though they named the specific individuals involved, must be made for the public good in precisely the same way that the laws of the state were intended to advance the good of all. This after all was the nature of the republic, and the government could not enter into a contract to enrich only a few, but it must see to the welfare of everyone.

The bank, in this instance, was such an act of agency, designed to support and enhance "the finances of the country." As a contract between the commonwealth of Pennsylvania and the stockholders of the bank, the terms were binding on both parties and could not be breached by the act of either one without the other. This was precisely how contracts were to be performed. A court of law convened and a trial by jury took place in case of a breach of contract by either party. In other words, the state alone was incapable of dissolving the bank charter unless the stockholders of the bank first agreed. It did not take the simple passage of a bill of repeal like ordinary legislation. This was the same with the bank, which came into existence at a time when a tremendous shortage of money and credit made it very difficult for the government to pay and equip soldiers during a critical period of the war. In other words, the bank had originally been designed to help the American cause against Britain, and now it was to help all Americans create a future of financial prosperity and stability. Paine recounted how this had worked during the war.

> The spring of 1780 was marked with an accumulation of misfortunes. The reliance placed on the defense of Charleston failed and exceedingly lowered or depressed the spirits of the country. The measures of the government, from the want of money, means and credit, dragged on like a heavy loaded carriage without wheels, and were nearly got to what a countryman would understand by a dead pull.
>
> The Assembly of that year met, by adjournment, at an unusual time, the tenth of May, and what particularly added to the affliction was that so many of the members, instead of spiriting up their constituents to the most nervous exertions, came to the Assembly furnished with petitions to be exempt from paying taxes. How the public measures were to be carried on, the country defended, and the army recruited, clothed, fed, and paid, when the only resource, and that not half sufficient, that of taxes, should be relaxed to almost nothing, was a matter too gloomy to look at.

Much better than these petitions for tax exemptions, would have been said Paine, a reiteration of Jefferson's Declaration of Independence when Americans had pledged "our lives, our fortunes, and our sacred honor."

So much for the fortunes and sacred honor. Now they wanted a tax break. At that dismal moment in 1780, a letter from General Washington in the field came in, and Paine, as the clerk of the Assembly, read it aloud. It was full of despair and disconsolation.

The troops were demoralized, unpaid, and threatened mutiny unless quick action were taken. "There was now no time to lose. . . . What with the depreciation of the currency and slow operation of taxes and the petitions to be exempted therefrom, the treasury was moneyless and the government creditless."[16] The only hope was private credit and the voluntary aid of private individuals. With that, Paine had sent his $500 to Blair M'Clenaghan, a prominent Philadelphia merchant, who he hoped would add more to it and start a "society" for this public purpose, a financial institution, to hold contributions from other individuals. M'Clenaghan joined with Robert Morris with a deposit of two hundred pounds each.[17] Within a week or so, the contributions totaled four hundred pounds in hard species and over one hundred thousand in Continental dollars. Shortly thereafter, the fund was open to the entire community, and the initial merchant subscribers collected upwards of three hundred thousand pounds.

The bank was on the way: Morris became the Superintendent of Finances and within a year the organization, started by Paine, Morris and M'Clenaghan, became the Bank of North America, incorporated under the laws of United States in December 1781 and then Pennsylvania in April 1782.

> The establishment of the bank in one of the most trying vicissitudes of the war, its zealous services in the public cause, its influence in restoring and supporting credit, and the punctuality with which all its business has been transacted, are matters that so far from meriting the treatment it met with from the late Assembly are an honor the State and what the body of her citizens may be proud to own.

The bank, even after the war, continued to promote the financial prosperity and well-being of the commonwealth. Accordingly, Paine rejected the Constitutionalist position that the bank served only the interests of the few.

Now the bank was embroiled in controversy, because the nation was in an economic depression. Most people found it difficult to satisfy their basic needs: food, clothing, and shelter. The price of agricultural goods from the farms was very low. Many debtors, again particularly farmers, found themselves owing great sums of money. If the bank refused to issue more paper money to cover their debts, then the bank was worthless to them, because they already had no specie, no gold or silver.   When the bank did not issue the paper currency they thought they deserved, they decided it was time to kill the bank. These debtors supported the Constitutionalists, who virtually controlled the Pennsylvania Assembly, who also wanted to repeal the bank's charter. The debtors started a petition drive against the bank, and their cause quickly gained support in the Assembly. It began to look very bad for the future of the bank.

On the other side were those who, along with Paine, found the bank an important resource for continuing the financial development and progress of the United States. Like the Bank of England and the Banque de France, the Bank of North America was an institution which potentially placed its country's finances on a stable economic footing. More important, however, the bankers themselves and the manufacturers, the new industrialists, and the merchants of Philadelphia, people like Morris and Livingston, saw the bank as a mechanism to enhance their own wealth. They were right, of course, because they controlled the operation of the bank, especially in terms of lending money and setting interest rates. They became the most important and influential creditors in the country.

All this had the makings of a class conflict on two fronts. First, there was the obvious quarrel between between wealthy creditors and poor debtors. The creditors owned a significant portion of the bank and wanted to keep it going for their own good. The debtors viewed the bank as an impediment, because its operators refused to issue new paper currency at the same rate as hard specie. The bank was therefore useless to them, and in fact stood in the way of the state of Pennsylvania issuing more currency on its own. Some of their fears were baseless. There were no guarantees that without the bank, the state would create more paper currency. But no matter how irrational they may have been, it was clear that the struggle quickly became one between rich and poor. This was not a new conflict, but it was significant for this new nation just acquiring a sense of its own national character and its own financial structure.

In the eyes of the Constitutionalists, Robert Morris (known as "Robert the Cofferer" for his great support of the bank) and his co-

conspirators, who included James Wilson and Gouverneur Morris, were interested only in economic gain—for themselves. To the radical townsfolk, Wilson, the lawyer whose house had been the scene in 1779 of the "Fort Wilson" riot and who defended Loyalists in court, was as suspect as Robert and Gouverneur. If Morris was the "Cofferer," they called Wilson "James the Caledonian" and Gouverneur "Gouverno the cunning man." These three, selfish as they were, sought only to "mill the corn," that is, seize the money, for themselves at the expense of the farmer, the artisans, the craftsmen of Philadelphia and all of America.[18]

In addition to pitting rich against poor, the bank struggle also divided urban from rural folk. The manufacturers and merchants were all citified people, residents of Philadelphia, whereas the debtors were primarily back-county farmers who lived on the edge of what was thought of as the civilized world. These country folk were on the frontier, subject to isolation and Indian attacks. They believed that Philadelphia had basically deserted them personally and economically.

Creditors countered the debtors' arguments with a spate of pamphlets which were so highly technical that they were nearly incomprehensible to the layman. Thomas Paine, who hated the very idea of paper money, wrote the first clearly expressed opinion on the bank, just as John Locke had done nearly one hundred years earlier in England. In *Common Sense*, he had alluded to his aversion to paper money, suggesting at one point that if America had no need for its ships at the end of the war, they could be sold, "and by that means replace our paper currency with ready gold and silver." (*CS* 103) His antagonism was not based on mere rhetoric. He had both personal and ideological reasons for opposing paper money. First of all, he had had bad experience with the near-worthless American continental money, the Continentals. When Congress issued this currency, it appeared that the right decision had been made. "It was easy times while Continental money lasted. The dream of wealth supplied the reality of it; but when the dream vanished, the government did not awake."[19] Paine had told Henry Laurens in 1778 that when counterfeit money began to circulate in Philadelphia, he saw how easy it was to abuse paper currency, which he saw as having "a tendency to invite and encourage a species of treason, the most prejudicial to us of any or all the other kinds."[20]

Secondly, as part of a longer ideological dispute between those who supported and those who opposed paper currency, Paine was now a participant in a historic struggle which had roots in the seventeenth century. The debate over the relative value of paper money and specie was first fought in England nearly one hundred years before the crisis over the Bank of North America. In the 1690s, there had been a "paper war" over this very issue, so-named because so much paper and ink were consumed by both sides.[21] It had pitted the new, monied interests (the rising class of financiers) against the old, landed interests, who did not fully understand the emerging financial and economic arrangements.[22] Money, capital, interest rates, size of principal, all these were new ideas which in another century would become an essential part of the British and American economies.

In that paper war of the 1690s, the classical republican writers often supported the use of gold or silver against those who wanted to exchange goods with paper money. Paine, as a radical writer who virulently opposed king and court, might well have sided with the opponents of the bank, those whom he now regarded as "crazy brained politicians." In fact, he sometimes felt some pangs of conscience about opposing his usual allies. He saw this personal dilemma coming in the spring of 1785: "It is not an agreeable thing for a man to stand in opposition to his friends, especially circumstanced with them as I was."[23] But the bank was important for the future economic and financial stability and prosperity of not only Pennsylvania but the United States itself. The future of America looked bright to Paine, despite the angry divisions caused by the debate over the future of the bank. "I am certain of the approbation of every serious thinking man who wishes to see the country in prosperous circumstances." So he argued against those "crazy brained politicians"—the progressives (the Constitutionalists)—who at one time had thought that he was on their side.[24] He now appeared to them very much the conservative spokesman for the merchants and manufacturers, indeed for Robert Morris himself.[25] They thought he had in fact sold out to the monied interests of Philadelphia. But

Paine argued that for the government to issue paper as money was like "putting an apparition in the place of a man; it vanishes with looking at it, and nothing remains but the air."[26]

Now the paper war of the 1690s was virtually repeated in Philadelphia in 1785 and 1786. As early as April 1785, Paine was involved in the battle over the bank when an open letter he wrote to Thomas Fitzsimmons appeared in the *Pennyslvania Gazette*. Fitzsimmons, born in Ireland, had served as an officer in the American Revolution, then later as a member of Congress under the Articles of Confederation (he later took part in the Constitutional Convention in 1787 and was elected to the new Federal Congress in 1789). Fitzsimmons, one of the original organizers of the Bank of North America, now opposed the issuance of paper money. On April 19th, Paine's letter to Fitzsimmons assailed the Pennsylvania Assembly's attack on the bank. The Assembly's action was, he said, "an ill-digested, precipitate, impolitic, faithless piece of business, in which party and prejudice is put for patriotism." This was a somewhat ironic observation in that the Assembly had just voted to give Paine five hundred pounds for his services on behalf of the American cause. "The House appears to me so exceedingly wrong in this business, both as to the matter and manner of it, that my private judgment on the case cannot go with them and must go against them, disregarding consequences to myself." The repeal of the bank's charter would have serious repercussions for the future finances of Pennsylvania and the nation.

Paine was more frightened by the role of "party" in this affair than by anything else. He believed that party, or special interests, tried to seize control of the Assembly and dominate it to its own liking, leaving everyone else to suffer for themselves. By creating a charter and then revoking it with so much ease, the Assembly exercised "a power that in the change and fluctuations of party might be dangerous to the rights and property of every man." The citizens would lose faith in their government's ability to govern, and the whole constitutional enterprise stood in danger of being destroyed: "acts, when so easily and frequently changed, lost the force and dignity of laws, and ceased to command respect." The attack on the bank was nothing more nor less than a frontal assault on the constitutional structure that Pennsylvanians had set up in 1776. Concerned as he was with the financial stability that the bank provided, Paine also framed the issue in terms of the political consequences which devolved from any attempt to repeal the bank's charter.[27]

The problem was exacerbated when Pennsylvania repealed the charter in September of 1785 just as Paine and Hall were getting started on the bridge. While he worked on his model, Paine funneled his anger into drafting his pro-bank pamphlet (the *Dissertations on Government*) and a series of "Letters on the Bank," which appeared in Philadelphia newspapers, both of which appeared in the spring of 1786. Tensions over the issue were intensified by generally bleak economic conditions and price fixing in Philadelphia. Paine was once again accused of being Morris' hired pen. The first accusation came in a speech in the Pennsylvania Assembly by John Smilie from Fayette County, who opposed the bank and who had once been Paine's friend. He called Paine "an unprincipled author whose pen is let out for hire."[28] But Smilie, retorted Paine, "loves to talk about what he does not understand." He was "always exposing his want of knowledge in haranguing about the balance of trade."[29] The fact was that people like Smilie and his anti-bank associate, George Emlen, failed to understand the nature of an institution like the bank, because they were back-county farmers. Paine did not hesitate to launch personal attacks. "The frontier parts of the state are called settlements," he wrote, and these chaps were settlers. "A settler is not yet a farmer; he is only in the way of being so." Commerce (and the bank) seemed distant and incomprehensible to such a person. "He cries out that a bank is of no use. But the case is he is not yet in a condition to participate of its usefulness. When he is, he will think otherwise."[30]

Paine was at his usual sarcastic best in deprecating the idea of printed currency. "Paper money is like dram-drinking, it relieves for a moment by deceitful sensation, but gradually diminishes the natural heat, and leaves the body worse than it found it. Were not this the case, and could money be made of paper at pleasure, every sovereign in Europe would be as rich as he pleased. But the truth is, that it is a bubble and the attempt vanity." In a more serious vein, he explained why paper money was a terrible idea.

> Paper money appears at first sight, to be a great saving, or rather that it costs nothing; but it is the dearest money there is. The ease with which it is emitted by an assembly at first, serves as a trap to catch people in at last. It operates as an anticipation of the next year's taxes. If the money depreciates, after it is out, it then, as I have already remarked, has the effect of fluctuation stock, and the people become stockjobbers to throw the loss on each other.
>
> If it does not depreciate, it is then to be sunk by taxes at the price of *hard money*; because the same quantity of produce, or goods, that would procure a paper dollar to pay taxes with, would procure a silver one for the same purpose. Therefore, in any case of paper money it is dearer to the country than hard money, by all the expense which the paper, printing, signing, and other attendant charges come to, and at last goes into the fire.[31]

Nothing took the place of gold and silver. Paine was convinced that the bank was needed to maintain hard specie as the sole means of monetary exchange.

In his *Dissertations*, Paine argued that the repeal of the charter made no economic sense. As he himself had helped start the bank in 1780 with his own $500, so even now he continued to keep his money there: "Between eight and nine hundred pounds . . . money which I brought from New York, and deposited there ever since last September, for which I do not receive a single farthing interest. This money the country has had the use of, and I think it safer under the care of the bank, until I have occasion to call for it, than in my own custody." More than helping an individual depositor like Thomas Paine, the bank promoted the interests and welfare of the nation. He tried to show that even the deep-woods farmer was the beneficiary of the institution. It prevented the development of monopolies, where very few men were able to dominate the market at the expense of the rest.

> The whole community derives benefit from the operation of the bank. It facilitates the commerce of the country. It quickens the means of purchasing and paying for country produce and

hastens on the exportation of it. The emolument, therefore, being to the community, it is the office and duty of government to give protection to the bank. . . . If a farmer or a miller comes to the city with produce, there are but few merchants that can individually purchase it with ready money of their own; and those few would command nearly the whole market for country produce; but by means of the bank this monopoly is prevented, and the chance of the market enlarged.[32]

To promote the dissolution of the bank was to promote monopolies.

Paine's support for the bank as an institution which was useful and beneficial to all Americans stimulated his vehement opposition to paper money. He had witnessed the devaluation of the Continental and never wished to see that again. His hostility toward paper money pitted him even more against the debtors, whom, as underdogs, he normally supported. His position on this subject was consistent on two counts. First, he claimed that the bank ultimately helped the debtors, if they could only understand its significance in the larger economy of America. Second, throughout his life, he argued on behalf of the usefulness of gold and silver, hard or natural specie, which always retained its value, and not paper money, which lost its value as people lost faith in it. For Paine, even "a hobnail or a piece of wampum far exceeds" the value of paper money. "The alchemist may cease his labors and the hunter after the philosopher's stone go to rest, if paper can be metamorphosed into gold and silver, or made to answer the same purpose in all cases." But this was impossible. Paine was convinced that the bank served as a mechanism to keep hard specie in the country, which once again was in the financial interests of the entire nation. The enemies of the bank accused it of "banishing the specie," but in fact that action would have violated all principles of the bank or the merchants, who needed hard specie to carry on their commercial affairs.[33]

Paine's participation in the debate continued throughout 1786. He certainly thought about it one evening while he was with Franklin in Philadelphia around Christmas time. His friend and associate John Hall related a story about him one evening at dinner when Paine had harsh words with an old friend, a Captain Coltman.

Paine and Coltman had sailed together from England more than ten years earlier, and Paine often stayed in the Coltman house when he was in town. Coltman attacked Paine's position on the bank, claiming it had caused him to lose a considerable amount of money. Paine took it personally and "swore by God, let who would, it was a lie. . . . They quarrelled a considerable time, but at length they parted tolerably cooly." Later when it was time to eat, the Captain, upset by the argument, "said he knew now he could not eat his dinner."[34]

With the bank's charter repealed, Paine fought long and hard to have it restored. For his efforts he was viciously attacked in the press as a sot and a traitor to progressive politics. This was the beginning of the stories about his sordid drinking habits, stories which followed him throughout his life. The venom in these tales would remain unmatched until the appearance of Cheetham's malicious biography in 1809, the year of Paine's death.

Paine hated to be viewed as a party man, although he supported the Republicans, or Anti-Constitutionalists (Morris' party), as they were also called. The latter name was a result of the party's opposition to the radical Pennsylvania Constitution of 1776. The Anti-Constitutionalists believed that the 1776 instrument, with its single house and weak executive, was a potentially dangerous force in politics. If one party gained control of the Assembly, say a party of elites, the common people would be totally forgotten because invariably the party in power worked for the interests of its own people, its own members. By the end of the year, having carried the Pennsylvania election of 1786, the Republicans had achieved both a bicameral legislature and a restored bank, now newly strengthened.

Paine saw that the old Pennsylvania constitution was unable to fulfill his own expectations, and at year's end, before he retired once again to his farm in Bordentown, he announced his support for a two-house legislature: a government with only one house meant "perpetual convulsions of imperfect measures and rash proceedings" in government.[35] A bicameral legislature for Pennsylvania avoided this problem, because one house would counteract the power of the other. This position represented a big change in Paine's thinking from 1776, when he had given the unicameral structure of the Pennsylvania Constitution his full support. By then, Paine was once again tiring of the political scene.

Just at this time Paine was having difficulty finding financial support for his bridge. He hoped Hall would soon return to Bordentown with some iron so that they could continue their work. In the meantime, however, the Pennsylvania Assembly refused to endorse it. It appeared that the legislators wanted to erect a bridge with piers across the Schuylkill, which for Paine was the wrong bridge design for that river. "They may sink money," he told George Clymer, "but they never will sink piers that will stand." He was sorely disappointed. He appealed to Thomas Fitzsimmons, a member of Congress, suggesting that if a bridge with piers were erected over the river, it would "cause such an alteration in the bed and channel of the river that there is no saying what course it may take, or whether it will not force a new channel somewhere else."[36]

He began to think that Franklin was right about securing the support of the Royal Society of London and the French Academy. He considered a return to England to look for backers there. The trip would give him an opportunity to visit his aging parents at his home in Thetford. He told Franklin in March 1787, "My father and mother are yet living whom I am very anxious to see, and have informed them of my coming in the ensuing summer."[37] He had, after all, been away for thirteen years.

If his plans for the bridge did not work out in England, then perhaps he could try them out in Paris, where bridges seemed to be going up all the time. Besides, he knew Lafayette there, and he was certain the Marquis could help him. Otherwise, he would go immediately to see Jefferson, the American Minister in France, who no doubt would introduce him to several more individuals in high places with influence.

Paine was not timid about asking Franklin for yet another letter of recommendation, as he had done in 1774 when he left England for America. Franklin, who considered him "his adopted political son," was glad to comply and immediately sent off letters to a host of important French scientists and politicians, among them La Rochefoucauld d'Enville (the translator of the *Constitutions of the Thirteen States of America*), Jean Baptiste Le Roy of the French Academy, Louis Le Veillard, and the Comte d'Estaing. Franklin's letter to Rochefoucauld was typical:

> The bearer of this is Mr. Paine, the author of a famous piece
> entitled *Common Sense*, published here with great effect on the
> minds of the people at the beginning of the Revolution. He is
> an ingenious, honest man, and as such I beg leave to recom-
> mend him to your civilities. He carries with him the model of a
> bridge of a new construction, his own invention, concerning
> which I intended to have recommended him to M. Peyronnet
> [sic], but I hear he is no more. You can easily procure Mr. Paine
> a sight of the models and drawings of the collection appertain-
> ing to the *Ponts et Chaussées*. They must afford him useful lights
> on the subject. We want a bridge over our river Schuylkill, and
> have no artist here regularly bred to that kind of architecture.[38]

Franklin was wrong about the early death of French architect, Jean
Perronet (1708-94), whom Paine met almost as soon as he arrived.
"Your old friend Perronet, the bridge architect, is yet living," he said,
"I was introduced to him by M. Le Roy. He has taken a residence in
the Elysian Fields for the purpose of being near the works. He has
invited me to see his house at Paris where all his drawings and models are."[39] In addition, Franklin also wrote to Jefferson, telling him
that "you are well acquainted with Mr. Paine's merit, and need no
request of mine to serve him in his views, and introduce him where it
may be proper and of advantage to him."[40]

    With Franklin's generous letters, Paine decided he should
first go to Paris, then onto England in the summer to see his parents.
How long did he plan to be away? Although the answer is not clear,
he did mention that he needed more time than he had had on his earlier visit to France six years before. He wanted to meet the Comte de
Vergennes, the Foreign Minister, who knew him by reputation and
who had paid him for writing on behalf of French interests. Paine
said that he was "personally unknown" to Vergennes, so he asked
Franklin to send the Minister a letter of introduction, because, as he
said in a moment of unexpected modesty "it so often happens that
men live to forfeit the reputation at one time they gained at another
that it is prudent not to presume too much in one's self." In any case,
Paine thought that he would return sometime "next winter," in

1788.[41] He did not come back to America for fifteen years.

So Thomas Paine left for France on April 26, 1787. Within a month after his departure, a gathering of delegates from all but one of the states took place in Philadelphia to review the defects of the Articles of Confederation. Their charge was to propose amendments to strengthen that document. Did Paine believe this effort would be worthwhile? If party politics were involved, it would not. "A man under the tyranny of party spirit," he wrote just before he left for Le Havre, "is the greatest slave upon earth, for none but himself can deprive him of the freedom of thought."[42] The results of their labor in Philadelphia was not a revision of the Articles. Instead, they drafted the American Constitution.

But Paine was on his way out of town, out of his adopted country, and did not have politics, party, or otherwise on his mind. He left America owning a farm in New Rochelle and a house in Bordentown, and both were rented to tenants. He had money in the bank. He had come to America in 1774, impoverished and in obscurity. He left celebrated and well-situated. America had been good to him, and he to it. He could not have projected that within just over two years, a new revolution would consume his passion, and that of the world, for a generation.

9 · France

or the next four years, Paine wandered back and forth between
England and France like a traveling salesman. He kept saying
his intention was to return to America, but he would not do so
until 1802.[1] In 1787 and 1788, his attention was divided between
two attractions: his bridge, for which he obsessively sought construction money, and politics. Arriving in Le Havre on May 26, 1787, he
traveled overland to Paris, apparently enjoying the sights along the
way. He seemed especially taken with the luxuriant countryside. He
told Franklin that "the country from Havre to Rouen is the richest I
ever saw. The crops are abundant, and the cultivation in nice and
beautiful order. Everything appeared to be in fullness; the people are
very stout, the women exceedingly fair, and the horses of a vast size
and very fat."

The letters of introduction that Benjamin Franklin, long a
favorite in Paris social circles, had written for Paine had an immediate positive impact. He wrote Franklin in June of 1787 that "my
reception here, in consequence of them, has been abundantly cordial
and friendly. I have received visits and invitations from all who were
in town. The Duc de Rochefoucauld and General Chastellux are in
the country. I dined yesterday with an old friend of yours, M.
Malesherbes, who is of the new Council of Finances, and who
received me with a heartiness of friendship."[2] He was soon welcomed
into Lafayette's circle. Lafayette was a hero and friend to many
Americans, including Thomas Paine. As a young man of twenty, he
evaded official French neutrality during the Revolution to join
Washington's troops as a major general against British forces.

Wounded at Brandywine and having suffered through the harsh winter at Valley Forge, he later distinguished himself during the
Yorktown campaign. Paine had met Lafayette in Philadelphia, just
before he left for Paris with John Laurens to obtain French aid for the
American cause. Equally popular in France, Lafayette now served in
the Assembly of Notables and the Estates General. He was to be an
important centrist figure during the Revolution in France, first as the
head of the National Guard and then as commander-in-chief of
French forces against Austria. The Marquis remembered Paine and
his work during the American Revolution. *Common Sense*, in French
translation, was especially admired in France. Lafayette was not surprised when the American Minister to France, Thomas Jefferson,
guided Paine to Lafayette's group with a request to help fund Paine's
bridge.

That summer, Paine dined with Jefferson and the Comte de
Moustier (who soon replaced La Luzerne as the French Minister to
the United States) and later (thanks to Franklin) with the famous scientist Jean-Baptiste Le Roy, who spoke fluent English. Le Roy
introduced him to other scientists and inventors, including the aged
bridge architect, Terenet, an old friend of Franklin's. "He has invited me," Paine wrote, "to see his house at Paris, where all his drawings
and models are."[3] Paine was immediately invited to display his
bridge to the French Academy in July, at which time a committee, led
by eminent mathematicians Jean Charles de Borda, Abbé Charles
Bossut, and Le Roy, all reviewed its structure and aesthetics. They
approved it without reservation, a significant step in Paine's long
quest. They concluded "that Mr. Paine's plan of an iron bridge is
ingeniously imagined, that the construction of it is simple, solid and
proper . . . and that it is deserving of a trial." Paine of course thought
a bridge, designed by himself, across the Seine was most appropriate.
This never happened. He sent a copy of the report to Franklin via
George Clymer in August, hoping perhaps that the Pennsylvania
Assembly would see the virtues of his design.[4] With the French
Academy's decision in hand, he now turned his attention to the sights
and sounds of France.

Paine enjoyed Parisian life immensely. He was luxuriating in
a style to which he was quite unaccustomed. Despite his artisan's

background and lack of formal education, he had no contact with the lower orders of French society. He was constantly in aristocratic company, eating well, and undoubtedly pushing his democratic ideas on some of the most important noblemen of the realm. He dined often with Lafayette, who during the French revolutionary years became Paine's very close friend. In 1788, during one of his trips to England, Paine wrote to Jefferson and pointedly asked him to "remember me with much affection to the Marquis de Lafayette."[5]

In addition, a letter from Franklin to the Duc de la Rochefoucauld d'Enville gave Paine the opportunity to spend time with this famous moderate politician. La Rochefoucauld did not survive beyond the September Massacres of 1792, when he was murdered by a mob that attacked him and other aristocrats after the fall of the monarchy. Another of Paine's aristocratic acquaintances was the Marquis de Chastellux, who had been elected a member of the American Philosophical Society in 1781, the same year Paine's membership was rejected. Paine considered himself a friend of Chastellux having first met him in Philadelphia when Chastellux was visiting Lafayette.

Lafayette also introduced Paine to the Marquis de Condorcet, the famous French mathematician and member of the French Academy of Sciences, who was to be Paine's close friend until the Terror.[6] Like most men of the French Enlightenment, Condorcet believed in the ultimate perfectibility of society, a man thoroughly convinced that life moved ineluctably toward improvement. As a mathematician, he even calculated that throughout all of history, human development had advanced through nine epochs, which ended with the French Revolution. The tenth epoch was the highest stage, with man's perfection realized. In the 1790s, he and Paine collaborated on republican tracts and educational reform.

With these august friendships and acquaintances, it was a wonder that Paine could maintain his democratic-republican, much less his revolutionary, ideals. But he did, and he did so quite easily, because he was certain that he could convince these moderate-thinking men of the righteousness of his social and political beliefs. He was nearly right. All of them were persuaded that the revolutionary forces unleashed by the revolution after July of 1789 were unstoppable, and most tried to cope with the stormy flow of events. Lafayette managed to survive, though only in Austrian prisons. Unfortunately, La Rochefoucauld did not, and Chastellux died before the revolution was truly underway.

By 1787, France, like England and the Dutch Republic, was near bankruptcy. To help resolve the country's financial problems, the king had summoned a group of prominent aristocrats and churchmen called the Assembly of Notables to find a means to raise revenues. The Assembly failed (it was an Assembly of "No-ability," Paine later said) because of Lafayette's opposition to its tax reform proposals. (*RM* 106) The cause of the government's financial problems, the Assembly asserted, was that taxes were not levied equally on all three estates: the clergy, the aristocracy, and everyone else. Indeed, this assessment was right, but only in part. Aristocrats and clergy lived basically tax-free in France. But Lafayette went further, to argue that France's financial problems were due to the excesses of the crown. The king dismissed the Assembly on May 25, 1787, and in an effort to raise taxes, sent his reform package directly to the regional parlements, including the powerful Parlement de Paris. The response of these institutions was that only the Estates General, which the king had not called for one hundred fifty years (since 1614), could undertake tax reform, thereby producing new taxes.

At the same time, during the summer of 1787, tensions between the British and the French increased over a rebellion in the Netherlands. It appeared that, just as there was unrest in France over the monarchy and aristocracy, there was discontent in Holland with rule by the Stadtholder, William V, the Prince of Orange. As the leader of the republic, he had alienated the middle class, which now wished for a true republican government. The French government supported these people, known as Patriots, while the English championed the Stadtholder. To make matters worse, the Prussians, who supported the Stadtholder because he was married to a Prussian princess, sent troops into the Netherlands. All-out war was now possible, because the French, in their support of the Patriots, contemplated sending in their own troops, while England appeared ready to step in on the side of the Prussians and the Stadtholder. It appeared as though a general European war was brewing.

With tensions quickly rising between the English and the French, Paine, unable to contain himself in a dispute, wrote the *Prospects on the Rubicon*. Here he argued that peace was better than war, because the cost of the war fell on those least able to fund it: the poor, including the working poor. In this respect, he made one of his most sweeping, extraordinary, humanistic statements. "I defend the cause of the poor, of the manufacturers, of the tradesmen, of the farmers, and of all those on whom the real burden of taxes falls—but above all, I defend the cause of humanity." He had, at one point in 1776, supported a war against tyranny, but in the present circumstances he advocated peace. Too many people profited by "a rumor of war," he wrote. "There are thousands who live by it; it is their harvest, and the clamor which those people keep up in newspapers and conversations passes unsuspiciously for the voice of the people, and it is not till after the mischief is done that the deception is discovered."[7] Do not be misled into a war that would only lead to the financial advantage of a few, he warned.

Having written his pamphlet in August, impatient of waiting for progress regarding his bridge, Paine wandered off to England on August 30, 1787, principally to see his father and mother. His stay lasted three months, equal to the time he had spent in Paris. One of the things he hoped to determine was whether the Marquis of Lansdowne (William Petty Fitzmaurice, the Earl of Shelburne until 1784) was interested in investing in his bridge. He was not. He wrote Lansdowne from Thetford, asking if he could see him when he was in London, but it did no good. In fact, Paine had more serious matters to attend to, for he learned on his arrival that his father had died some five months earlier. He had to spend most of his time in England arranging his mother's financial affairs with an English investor named Peter Whiteside. After establishing a program by which she received nine shillings a month for the rest of her life, he planned to return to France.

Paine's social life when in London was obviously far better than it was those several weeks in Thetford. First, despite his well-known radical stance against the British government's American policy before and during the Revolution, the English ministry never bothered him. He was not yet regarded as seditious in the same way he would be after he insulted George III in the second part of the *Rights of Man*. In the capital, he met Edmund Burke, thanks to a letter of introduction from Henry Laurens. His hopes with Burke, like those with Lansdowne, was to find suitable financing for his bridge. Paine had admired Burke since his support of the American cause against England in the 1760s and 1770s. Burke had denounced the Stamp Act, and while he never actually supported separation, he did not think maintenance of English control was worth a war. In any case, the two men seemed to like one another immediately, and spent a good deal of time together.

At one point, Burke reported to John Wilkes, the radical pamphleteer and journalist and Mayor of London, that he seemed to be in constant contact with Paine. He told Wilkes that he was going to dine "with the duke of Portland, in company with the great American Paine."[8] Once again, however, Paine was unsuccessful in promoting his bridge, but he again met Burke in 1788 and the two of them traveled together with Peter Whiteside throughout the Midland ironworks to search for materials for Paine's bridge.

In England, Paine also met John Trumbull (a painter of miniatures) and Benjamin West (the great American historical painter). Trumbull, like Paine, had served in the Continental Army during the Revolution as an aide to General Gates, although their tours of duty seemed not to have coincided. Trumbull retired from the army a colonel, to devote himself fulltime to painting. West, in contrast, had become a painter at eighteen. At twenty-two, he went to Europe to study in Italy, eventually settled in London, and became the king's historical painter in 1772. One of his students in London, who returned to agitate on behalf of the American cause, was Charles Willson Peale, a close friend of Paine's in Philadelphia. After the revolutionary war, Trumbull left America to study under West in London, although he was at first imprisoned and then deported when the government suspected him of spying for the Americans (his father was the governor of Massachusetts). He was able to return to London in 1784.

West and Trumbull's circle included a lively and enthusiastic crowd of people. Through them, Paine met Joel Barlow, the Connecticut writer and radical, who was already known for his satirical poem, *The Anarchiad*. In the late 1780s, Barlow worked for the Scioto Company, an American corporation which sold land in the western parts of the United States. Barlow had just finished *The Vision of Columbus* (revised in 1807 as *The Columbiad*), a panegyric to America. Paine and Barlow became lifelong friends. Two other men involved in land deals with whom Paine associated were Daniel Parker and Peter Whiteside, who were in business with Robert Morris. Whiteside was the same person who had helped Paine with his mother's finances, and later both Parker and Whiteside helped him to find financing for his bridge. After Paine received word that the bridge model had been approved by the French Academy, he sent it to Sir Joseph Banks, the famous naturalist, who some fifteen years earlier had gone to Tahiti with Captain James Cook. Banks was the president of the Royal Society of London. Naturally, Paine was hopeful that he could locate funding in England to build the structure across the Thames. Two rivers, the Thames and the Seine, with Paine's bridge spanning both would have been a great triumph for the inventor. He even dreamed of designing a structure that crossed the English Channel.

In December, Paine hurried back to France after he heard that Beaumarchais, who years earlier had been involved on the French side with Silas Deane, was now interested in erecting a span across the Seine, clearly in direct competition to Paine's efforts. Before he left London, he sent a letter to an unnamed French official, urging him to do whatever he could to bind England and France closer together. "I consider the English very much in the dark with respect to the temper and disposition of France," he told the official, who was most likely the secretary of the Archbishop of Toulouse, the Cardinal de Brienne.[9] "They live on an island, and are wrong in all their ideas of this country. As I was born in England and lived several years in that country as well as in America, I am acquainted with their errors and prejudices and can judge better of them than they can judge themselves." He asked his correspondent to convey to the French government that "there is no disposition of the French ministry to break terms with England, if England gives no cause of a rupture."[10] England had "no business" in continental affairs, and he particularly cited the growing unrest in Holland and the potential intervention by European powers there. Paine's point was that England should just stay out of this problem. If England did, a closer relationship between the English and the French could then grow and develop.

Paine obviously saw himself not only as an inventor of bridges, but as a flowering American diplomat, no matter how unofficial he might have been in representing the United States. He was soon sending dispatches filled with information on British affairs to Jefferson, first in Paris, and then in the United States, after Jefferson returned to America from his tour of duty. Paine sent Jefferson's views about a closer French-British relationship to Edmund Burke. He hoped these views might entice Burke to engage the English ministry in drawing closer to France. This was the moment, he later wrote Burke, when there was "such a fair opportunity to bring England and France into a better understanding with each other than had formally been the case, and as a man always feels a happy consolation with any attempt to do good, that I wrote to the Abbé Morellet on this subject, knowing that he was in the confidence of the Archbishop of Toulouse. . . . I mentioned to him that if I found anything of the same disposition in England towards a better understanding with France which I saw in France towards England that I would, so far as lay in my power, endeavor to influence it." All this was to no avail. Burke did nothing.[11]

Paine next set off for Paris to engage Lafayette and Jefferson to drum up finances for his bridge. He remained there until June of 1788. Jefferson soon told Paine that he had better come up with his own means to fund the construction if he ever wanted to see his bridge built. Paine had at one point actually hoped to convince Robert Morris to build it for him, but he told Jefferson that he had heard Morris' business affairs were "deranged." He was right. Morris had become involved in land speculation, was soon bankrupt, and then later spent time in debtor's prison. He eventually died penniless. Paine therefore planned to return once again to England to search for money. He was very pessimistic. He told Jefferson that he was miserably "casting about to find some way to accomplish this point."[12]

By this time, Paine, Jefferson, and Lafayette had heard that the Americans had drafted a new Constitution which had been submitted to the states for ratification. They were all delighted with it. Probably in the spring of 1788, Paine read the record of the constitutional debates, which had arrived in Paris. He had heard stories, true or not, about John Adams' desire for America to have a monarchy. Adams, he said, "who has some strange ideas," must be quite upset with the idea that the president served only for four years, instead of for life, and that "the presidency does not devolve by hereditary succession."[13] His suspicions about Adams' desire for a monarchy never left Paine's mind, and it was something he constantly returned to. When Paine eventually came back to America in 1802, he was convinced that the Federalists in general, and Adams in particular, wanted to destroy the new American Constitution and replace it with a monarchy.

He, Jefferson, and Lafayette discussed the operation of the Constitutional Convention and the ratification process. The three had learned of James Wilson's arguments in favor of ratification in Pennsylvania, and Paine took exception to Wilson's distinction between natural and civil rights. Wilson, he said, had "confounded the terms" liberty and security. Human beings, on entering into the social contract to form civil society, did not give up all of their natural rights in exchange for security, as Wilson had suggested. On the contrary, Paine wrote to Jefferson in the spring, the individual always retained some natural rights. In making his argument, Paine used the ideas of the social contract that John Locke had explained. At a point long ago, before there was government, men lived in a "state of nature," which they soon found inconvenient. And yet while in the state of nature, they were totally free and independent. The problem was that they soon realized they would be better off if they collectively joined forces to stave off attacks by others on their rights and liberties. This was precisely what had happened in the United States.

> Suppose twenty persons, strangers to each other, to meet in a country not before inhabited. Each would be a sovereign in his own natural right. His will would be his law, but his power, in many cases, inadequate to his right; and the consequences would be that each might be exposed, not only to each other, but to the

other nineteen. It would then occur to them that their condition would be much improved if a way could be devised to exchange that quantity of danger into so much protection so that each individual should possess the strength of the whole number.

In this way, those twenty men exchanged their natural rights for civil rights. They gave up complete and total freedom for the security they now enjoyed in the greater society. They were now obliged to obey the laws of the government, which they themselves had consented to form. This obedience provided them with greater security than ever before.

     The crux of the matter was that, despite their entrance into civil society, they still retained some natural rights: "the rights of thinking, speaking, forming and giving opinions." These are "rights of personal competency." They had in fact given up some rights, the rights of "personal protection," because they had handed those rights to the government as the caretaker for the good of all.[14] These included the right of an individual to do anything within his power to acquire and protect his property. This distinction between rights of personal competency and rights of personal protection was quite advanced for the late-eighteenth century. Many of the states in America had specifically included those rights of personal competency in their state constitutions. Several Americans opposed the inclusion of these bills of rights in the new Constitution because they thought the laws undermined the authority of the document. And yet, just three years later, the ninth amendment was ratified along with the Bill of Rights. That amendment echoed Paine's arguments: it specifically mentioned those natural rights which were "retained by the people."

     In June of 1788, Paine again returned to London. For the next two years, he was in frequent contact with Jefferson who was serving in Paris for another year, as if the two of them were on equal terms. Jefferson had as much as told Paine that he needed to know what was going on in England. "I must beg a continuance of your correspondence, because I have great confidence in your communications, and since Mr. Adams' departure am in need of authentic information from that country."[15] Paine deeply relished his quasi-ambassadorial status and the quasi-endorsement that Jefferson gave him. In his letters to Jefferson, Paine passed on whatever inside information he picked up in conversations with Burke as well as the Duke of Portland, Charles James Fox, the Marquis of Lansdowne, and other Whig leaders. He spent a week, he told Jefferson, at Portland's estate in Buckinghamshire seeking information about the Whig opposition. Portland (William Henry Cavendish-Bentnick), who had once held the post of First Lord of the Treasury in the king's cabinet, was now the head of the Whig opposition against William Pitt. As he had earlier shown, Paine was never beneath dining with a nobleman, no matter how conservative he might be, whether French or British, and his dinners with Portland proved that point beyond question. Portland, in 1792, became a great supporter of legislation proscribing seditious writings, which was specifically aimed at the writings of Thomas Paine. This law was the foundation of the case that year to prosecute Paine for printing the *Rights of Man*. For now, as a pragmatist when it came to eating and relaxing with the upper crust, Paine welcomed all opportunities.

In addition to Portland, Paine spent a great deal of time with Charles James Fox. A long-time friend and ally of Edmund Burke until their break over the French Revolution, Fox had been an outspoken critic of Lord North's American policy before the war broke out in 1776. Known as a proponent of liberal reform, Fox, like Burke, was one of Parliament's outstanding orators. Also like Burke, he had become attached to the Whig opposition to the ministry through Lord Rockingham (Charles Watson-Wentworth), Burke's patron. With the fall of Lord North in 1782, Fox served in the shortlived Rockingham ministry in 1782 as Foreign Minister. He and Burke were delighted to serve together in the ministry that year, but it was only a brief tenure. Rockingham died suddenly that year at age fifty-two, and his Whig rival, the Earl of Shelburne, was appointed the king's First Minister. To Burke's dismay, Fox at that point joined his former Tory rival, Lord North, to oppose Shelburne, and when Shelburne's ministry ended, the famous Fox-North coalition came to power. That linkage lasted an even shorter time, however, because George III appointed William Pitt (the Younger) his First Minister in 1783. Now five years later, Fox stood in vehement opposition to the Pitt administration's anti-French policies. Paine reported all of this to Jefferson.

Paine also visited Shelburne, now the Marquis of Lansdowne. He had been the subject of one of Paine's barbs in *Crisis Twelve*, which Paine dedicated to him, and like his predecessor, Lord North, Shelburne had opposed American independence. In the fall of 1782, Paine had called his opposition "a perfidy so notorious cannot be hid."[16] For awhile now, the two seemed to enjoy each other's confidence, or at least Paine thought so. Lansdowne told him in September of 1788 that British attitudes toward France were all wrong, and that the English ministry will surely "'cut the throat of confidence'" between England and France.[17] Soon thereafter, Paine had a falling out with Lansdowne over whether the United States and England ought to draw closer in their relationship. Paine thought not, that in fact England and France ought to have closer ties, despite their historic antagonisms toward one another. He even suggested that Lansdowne become the Minister for England in Paris. Lansdowne disagreed, and their relationship cooled, or as Paine told Jefferson in February of 1789, "I am not so much in the good graces of the Marquis of Lansdowne."[18]

With all of these contacts, Paine now thought of himself as a quasi-official United States minister to England in these years. He hoped that this status could be transformed into something more formal, but that was not to be. That position soon belonged to his old nemesis Gouverneur Morris, who resented the interference from the upstart Paine, who, he said, "talks a great deal upon subjects of little moment." How and why Paine never realized the enmity Gouverneur Morris had for him is astounding. In his diary, for example, Morris could have hardly have been more direct (though it was of course a private entry). His disdain for Paine was crystal clear. He wrote that he went to see Lafayette, who told him that "he wishes to have a meeting of Mr. Short, Mr. Paine, and myself, to consider their judiciary, because his place imposes on him the necessity of being in the right. I tell him that Paine can do him no good for that altho he has an excellent pen to write, he has but an indifferent head to think."[19] (The "Mr. Short" to whom Morris referred was William

Short, Jefferson's young secretary and Chargé d'Affaires.) Moncure
Conway, Paine's first serious biographer, believes that Morris was
irresistible to Paine. "His cordial manners disarm suspicion, and we
presently find the author pouring into the ear of his secret detractor
what state secrets he learns in London."[20]

Paine's activities in London—in fact just about everything
about Paine—irked Gouverneur Morris no end. Morris had arrived
first in France on personal business for himself, Robert Morris, and
others. They were interested in buying the war debt that the
Americans had owed the French (some $34 million) for their help
during the Revolution. They planned to pay fifty cents on the dollar,
and then to demand a lucrative return on their investment from the
American government.[21] Almost exactly a year later, President
Washington sent Morris to London as the informal American
ambassador to England, before officially assigning him to France in
mid-1791. Morris' primary task in England was to negotiate the
final removal of English troops from American soil in exchange for a
commercial treaty with the United States.

Morris thought Paine was clearly out of his element in
England when he spoke to English officials and politicians.
Consistently patrician in his views, Morris thought of Thomas Paine
as a low-class, brash, unfortunate rogue. He hated radical republican
ideas. Paine's views were exactly radical, precisely republican. Even
before the Revolution in France broke out in the summer of 1789,
Morris announced that the republicanism which he already saw blos-
soming throughout Paris was "a moral influenza."[22]

Throughout this time, Paine continued his efforts to erect his
bridge somewhere. He eventually acquired a patent for his design,
which was valid in England, Ireland, and Scotland. Paine now grew
professionally close to Whiteside, who went with him to register the
bridge design at the Royal Society. He told Jefferson that should he
send Paine any letters, they should be addressed to him at Whiteside's
lodgings on Broad Street in London.[23]

By the fall, near Sheffield (in Rotherham), things began to
look quite good. There, Paine met the Walker brothers, who operated an iron foundry, "the most eminent in England in point of establishment and property," he told Jefferson. The Walkers were inter-

ested in Paine's bridge design. "Their opinion is very decided that it can be executed either in wrought or cast iron, and I am to go down to their works next week to erect an experiment[al] arch."[24] Paine worked with the Walkers throughout the winter of 1788-89 and into the spring. He spent time with the Walkers' foreman, William Yates, making arrangements to erect a model of his bridge, which he hoped to materialize by the fall of 1789.

In January, he wrote a long letter to Catherine "Kitty" Nicholson Few, the daughter of Commodore James Nicholson, the New York republican leader. Kitty had just been married to Colonel William Few, a senator from Georgia, and Paine wrote to congratulate her. It was a deeply affectionate letter of pure wistful poetry, a bit sad and melancholic, even a bit romantic. There, he commented on happy marriages, something he obviously never had had occasion to experience fully. He himself was "a sort of wanderer," not made to fit into the married state. Still, he hoped that his lady acquaintances accepted him as "not the churlish enemy of their sex, not the inaccessible coldhearted mortal nor the capricious tempered oddity, but one of the best and most affectionate of their friends." Paine's ambiguous attitudes toward women permeated his letter. Always at arm's length, he claimed to desire their company and attention—but never too intimately.[25] He asked that she send his regards to her parents as well as to Lewis Morris who was holding some of Paine's funds and was also looking after his New Rochelle caretaker, Mr. Constable.

In addition to his work at the ironworks, in the winter of 1788-89 and the following spring, Paine continued to hunt for money for the construction of his bridge model. He received reports on how fine a design he had crafted, but still there were no takers. He wrote to Thomas Walker that a project in Dublin now looked promising, although he was uncertain whether he could convince anyone to accept his design. He also told Walker, as he had mentioned to Kitty Few earlier, that the king had again gone mad (George III suffered occasional bouts of insanity, "porphyria" it was diagnosed as, beginning in 1780, and effectively gave up direct control of the government to Pitt after 1784). This time the king had become insane in November of 1788. "How far the nation may be safe with a man of a deranged mind at the head of it" was anyone's guess.

As far as Paine was concerned, it was time to convene an English national convention, as the Americans had done in the summer of 1787. England needed to create a new constitution. To propose a convention raised the specter of extra-parliamentary, and hence illegal, organizations, and this was tantamount to treason, because it would undermine the privileged position of king and lords. Paine knew this suggestion could have easily caused him trouble with the authorities, but he was undaunted. A month later, he again mentioned the idea to Jefferson. "Had Mr. Pitt proposed a national convention at the time of the king's insanity, he had done right. But instead of this he has absorbed the right of the nation in a right of Parliament," namely the House of Lords, "over which the people have no control." Paine thought it was clear that the power abdicated by the deranged king had fallen to Pitt, as his First Minister, and in this he was right. Pitt, who almost singlehandedly revived the moderate Whig faction in England at the end of the century, was until his removal in 1801 in control of the government. The Prince of Wales (also George), who served as regent, was only sixteen years old. Pitt had achieved his goal, which was "to take power from one part of the government [the Commons] to add it to another, for he has increased the power of the Peers [the Lords], not the rights of the people." The situation in England appeared dismal.

In contrast to English politics, the French political situation was more attractive. Louis XVI's convening of the Estates General was a brilliant decision. "An internal alliance" between the king and his people made a formidable relationship, and England ought well to be worried. Little did Paine know that that alliance would in short order came crashing down in revolutionary violence, and then terror. It was England that Paine saw in serious trouble, especially with its growing indebtedness. "The money is all in paper," he told Jefferson, "and the quantity is greater than the object to circulate it upon and therefore shows that the market is glutted, and consequently the ability for farther paper exertions is lessened."[26] England was surely soon to be bankrupt.

In April Paine was off again to visit his ironworks in

Rotherham, looking after his bridge. A model was being constructed, and in the next month, he wrote that he and the Walkers had
erected an "experiment rib." Paine took the opportunity to send Sir
Joseph Banks, the president of the Royal Society of London, a full
analysis of the model structure. Banks informed Paine that he had
forwarded the account to the Society, which had taken quite an interest in it. Banks thought that as a result of the Society's review, he
could send Paine a number of suggestions about improving his
design. At the same time, Paine asked the Walker brothers to manufacture a full scale-sized bridge so it could be set up in London. He
hoped to find a purchaser to erect it "over the Thames—which
appears to me the most advantageous of all objects." He thought this
scheme would work because the owner of a private bridge could
charge a toll for users, and a span over the Thames would be lucrative. By summer, Paine and the Walkers had agreed on a plan to
build the bridge and transport it to London. Paine's job, more difficult since he now had little money with him, was to finance the
expenses from the time the bridge arrived in London to its erection.
Then, they would sell the project, if possible, and divide the proceeds
from the sale equally.

Paine was forced to draw on some funds he had in America:
some of it was in stock and some in cash (Lewis Morris held some to
pay whatever expenses there were on Paine's New Rochelle farm).
He also had his properties in Bordentown and New Rochelle from
which he received rent. In any event, he did not want to borrow any
money. He wanted to draw on his own resources, because he was certain that he would sell the bridge and have an immediate return on
the investment. He asked Jefferson to help him, because he was leaving his post in Paris. Since Jefferson was to be in America in the fall,
Paine wrote on July 13, "I am not acquainted with the method of
negotiating money matter, but if you can accommodate me in his and
will direct me how the transfer is to be made I shall be much obliged
to you."[27] Paine wrote these words from London the day before Paris
crowds stormed the Bastille, the inauguration of the French
Revolution.

By September, Paine's work was going swimmingly well, and
he was content. He wrote Jefferson that "though I have a slender

opinion of myself for executive business, I think, upon the whole, that I have managed this matter tolerably well." He asked Jefferson to extend his regards to all his friends, including "our beloved General Washington," back home.[28] This sentiment was to prove ironic, for within a very short period of time Paine grew furious with Washington. Jefferson, now having returned to America, left William Short behind to run the embassy. Paine's hope to succeed Jefferson as the American Minister to France, since he had not been appointed to the post in England (he never even raised that subject with the Americans), floundered when he once again lost out to Gouverneur Morris, who soon arrived from London to take the posting.

Jefferson, unlike Morris, was exceedingly optimistic about the prospects for France's future, especially if France based its new government on rights and liberties. "These are the materials of a superb edifice," he wrote Paine before he left Paris, commenting on several suggestions of the Estates General regarding a declaration of rights and liberties. "The hands which have prepared them are perfectly capable of putting them together, and of filling up the work of which these are only the outlines. While there are some men among them of very superior abilities, the mass possess such a degree of good sense as enables them to decide well."[29] Paine passed this letter on to Edmund Burke and unwittingly added to Burke's building arsenal of invective that he soon launched against the Revolution.

Despite Paine's hope for speedy proof of his engineering skills, it was not until the spring of 1790 that the model was actually ready. At that time, Paine wrote to Benjamin Rush in Philadelphia that his bridge was finally ready to be erected. "It is an arch of one hundred and ten feet span, and five feet high, from the chord line. It is as portable as common bars of iron, and can be put up and taken down at pleasure, and is, in fact, rendering bridges a portable manufacture."[30] He also told Rush that Lafayette had given him a key to the Bastille to send to George Washington because of his great leadership in the American cause some thirteen years before. Except for an abortive attempt to erect a model of his bridge in 1790 in Paddington, this episode sparked the beginning of the end of Paine's obsession with bridge design and construction.

The model of Paine's bridge actually stayed up for a year. When it was finally dismantled, some 620 pounds was owed on its construction, and although Peter Whiteside, the chief investor, probably ought to have paid it, he could not because by then he, like Robert Morris, was bankrupt. Paine was stuck with the bill, and no money. Two American merchants, Cleggett and Murdoch, obviously Paine admirers, bailed him out. The next year, while Paine was still in France, the Walker brothers erected a bridge based on his design over the Wear River near Sunderland. It was financed by two men, Milbanke and Burdon, who profited quite well from it. While Paine was acknowledged as the principal designer, he never received a penny from the bridge. Regarding any payment to Paine, Milbanke wrote that "with respect . . . to any gratuity to Mr. Paine, though ever so desirous of rewarding the labors of an ingenious man, I do not feel how . . . I have it in my power."[31] Once again, the wandering journalist, now inventor, departed, unpaid for his efforts. His attention now focused on the events in France.

Meantime, in the days after July 14, 1789, the Revolution brewed in the Paris summer. News of the Revolution had taken some time to make its way through the French countryside to the provinces. When it did, two things simultaneously occurred: the remarkable events of the "night of August 4" and the Great Fear, as it is now known. Three weeks after the fall of the royal prison, the Bastille, on July 14, the French National Assembly made monumental changes in the country's social structure. In July, peasant uprisings and unrest began to take place throughout the countryside, only to become increasingly violent and vicious, sparking the great panic of the summer of 1789.[32] The peasants attacked the chateaux, where they destroyed the feudal records citing the "dues" that they owed their landlords. The dues, significant portions of their crops—in cash or in kind—were what peasants had to turn over to their landlords in exchange for their "protection." The mass attack by the peasants provoked the beginning of the Great Fear, and contributed to the Assembly's decision on August 4, 1789 to end the feudal system entirely. Property ownership was no longer based on the medieval traditions but on a modern monied basis, something French liberal economists, known as the "physiocrats," had been advocating throughout the end of the century. A strong economic base for a modern economic system, they held, was land, and wealth was produced through agricultural production. Abundance generated through high prices, hence a monied economy, led to a healthy economy. Property now was to be exchanged for bourgeois currency, and those dues were ended. This social and economic revolution was as important as the storming of the Bastille. Even the Church was vulnerable: the tithes, the fundamental monetary resource of the clergy, were ended.[33]

When Paine left London in November of 1789, he returned to a France that, with the termination of the feudal structure and its dues, was quite different from the one he had left. There was an air of change in the atmosphere everywhere he went. He was delighted that Lafayette, Condorcet, and other revolutionary leaders had invited him to return, and Paine's life was, as usual, active on a social as well as an intellectual level. Through Lafayette, Paine was introduced to an English-speaking Belgian baroness, Cornélie de Vasse, who apparently wanted a closer relationship than Paine was willing to offer.[34] She invited him to her apartment, but something made him keep his distance. Paine clearly was not an amorous man. His two marriages had failed miserably and he was not about to embark on another relationship, at least not yet and not with the baronness. She had written two works that Paine undoubtedly found offputting: *The Confessions of a Intrepid Woman* and *The Art of Reforming Men and Making them Constant*. She wrote Paine letters, requesting his replies to her desire to see him, but he apparently never bothered to respond.

In Paris, Paine also ran into Thomas Christie, a young Scot who was a nephew of scientist and radical dissenter Joseph Priestley. Christie's political views mirrored those of Thomas Paine, and from the time the two had earlier met in London, they quickly hit it off. In May of 1788, at age twenty-seven, Christie had founded *The Analytical Review*, a radical journal published in London by Joseph Johnson, who over the years printed several radical tracts and pamphlets, including Paine's *Rights of Man*. Christie's journal lasted until 1799. In it, he proclaimed that the events in France would stimulate world revolution, an idea that Paine had used in 1776 in *Common Sense* and soon repeated in the *Rights of Man*. "The emancipation of

France may be followed by a restoration of their ancient rights to the Austrian Netherlands, and in time by the emancipation of Spain and other countries of Europe," Christie proclaimed. "We seem to be advancing to a great era in the history of human affairs."[35]

Twenty-four years his senior, Paine became the mentor of the young Christie, who in January of 1792 was a founding member of the radical London Corresponding Society. The Society, the brain-child of Thomas Hardy, a Scottish shoemaker with little formal education, was designed to appeal directly to the lower orders of English society to spread reformist social and political ideas throughout the nation. It was a "corresponding" society because its counterparts in other urban areas, such as Birmingham, Sheffield, and Manchester, were in constant contact with each other, exchanging ideas, plans, and strategies for the future. With its appeal to the working class, it was one of the most advanced English political organizations of its time.

Christie, a former medical student, had decided to make banking his career, as his father had done. In Paris, however, he became Paine's constant companion, and like Paine, was to respond to Burke's attack on the revolution in his own *Letters on the Revolution in France*. Together, Christie and Paine joined the Paris-based British Club, whose members included several Scottish and English citizens, most of whom were sympathetic to the French revolutionary cause.[36]

Paine once again returned to London in March of 1790 "expressly for the purpose of erecting an iron bridge, which Messrs. Walkers of Rotherham, Yorkshire, and I have constructed and is now ready for putting together." The day before his departure, he wrote to Rush to keep him up to date on the events in Paris. "Be assured," Paine wrote him, "everything is going on right." There were a few "inconveniences," but with individuals as great as George Washington and Lafayette acting as models, the future for France was bright. In England, however, the political situation was rapidly deteriorating, because the adherents of church and state protested bitterly, "and all those who were interested in the remains of the feudal system join in the clamor." But Paine remained convinced that the prospects for a future republican England were quite good, given the model of France. He closed the letter with the wish of once again seeing "my much beloved America," but immediately added even America needed reform, especially by abolishing "the infernal traffic in Negroes. We must push that matter further on your side of the water. I wish that a few well instructed could be sent among their brethren in bondage; for until they are enabled to take their own part, nothing will be done." Paine continued his denunciation of slavery and the slave trade which he had begun from the time he first came to America. He had hoped that the bill ending the slave trade would pass Parliament after William Wilberforce had introduced it in 1789.[37] It failed, and it would not be until 1807 that the slave trade would be abolished from the British empire.

When Paine returned to London, he had with him the key to the Bastille that Lafayette had given him for George Washington. He dispatched it to Washington with the words, "I feel myself happy in being the person through whom the Marquis has conveyed this early trophy of the spoils of despotism, and the first ripe fruits of American principles transplanted into Europe, to his master and patron." He told the President that he planned to return to Paris in time for a parade in honor of the new French constitution, a parade in which, he said, he had the privilege of carrying the American flag. "I have not the least doubt of the final and complete success of the French Revolution. Little ebbings and flowings, for and against, the natural companions of revolutions, sometimes appear, but the full current of it is, in my opinion, as fixed as the Gulf Stream."[38] He was delighted that the king and queen of France thought of themselves as the leaders of the revolutionary changes. The king had after all verbally accepted all of the changes the National Assembly had made. By the end of the month, he told Washington that "the French Revolution is not only complete, but triumphant."[39] He was wrong, of course. He soon realized that the Revolution would only succeed without king or queen.

Paine now learned two important pieces of information. First of all, his mother, whom he briefly visited when she became quite ill, had died in Thetford at the age of ninety-four. Secondly, Edmund Burke, his one-time friend and companion, was writing a very critical tract on the French Revolution. Paine immediately set about framing a response to Burke's pamphlet, which he had not yet seen. In fact, Paine had already begun writing his own version of the events of July 1789, and he planned to incorporate much of this work into a response to Burke. He saw quite a bit of Burke socially, although they apparently never discussed the events in France. At about this time, he heard some unsettling news from Paris. In the Faubourg St. Antoine district, turbulent riots had been crushed by the Marquis de Lafayette, the head of the National Guard. Paine did not think the riots very important, although they clearly indicated that the Revolution was not "as fixed as the Gulf Stream." Paine thought them to be just some of the "ebbings and flowings." The American Chargé d'Affaires William Short, who in Jefferson's absence represented American interests in France, thought otherwise. And so did Burke, who was busily writing his *Reflections on the Revolution in France.*[40]

All of that would have to wait for the appearance of Burke's grand critique. For now, Paine turned to an incident in the Nootka Sound where the Spanish had seized a number of English ships off of British Columbia. These ships, part of the English East India Company fleet, were engaged in trade between China and North America, but the Spanish were convinced that the British intended to settle Nootka Sound, which Spain claimed as part of its territory. The Pitt ministry refused to recognize Spanish rights, and it looked as though war might break out over the incident. Pitt believed the British navy with its one hundred fifteen ships was strong enough to repel a Spanish attack and figured on the support of both the Netherlands and Prussia. The Spanish relied on the backing of the French. Combined, their total warships equaled the one hundred fifteen vessels of the English fleet. Pitt met with his Interior Minister Grenville and General Francisco del Miranda, who dreamed of liberating Spanish America, to plan for war. The French were irrevocably split, because while Louis supported the Spanish claim (there was an alliance, the Family Compact), the Assembly did not. Ultimately the dispute was settled (especially when Spain realized it could not rely on French support). From London, Paine wrote a series of letters to Short, all the time believing that in fact France would eventually help its Spanish allies. He apparently wished to see the demise of monarchical England, even by means of a Franco-Spanish alliance. He was, of course, not only wrong but self-deluded about a potential French/Spanish coalition.[41] The affair ended peacefully in October when Spain finally recognized British control of the western territories of North America.

Paine worked throughout the summer of 1790 to get his bridge erected at Leasing-Green in Paddington. A quick trip to Paris, where he marched in the Federation Festival parade on July 14, 1790 commemorating the first anniversary of the seizure of the Bastille, was followed by his return to London in October. And then on November 1, 1790, Burke's great pamphlet appeared.

10 · Burke's Response: "The Swinish Multitude"

Edmund Burke was Irish-born (1729), and, although nominally a Protestant (his father had converted for reasons of political and social advancement as a lawyer in Dublin), he was undoubtedly at heart an Irish nationalist and a Catholic sympathizer. Educated at Protestant-bound Trinity College in Dublin, he attended the Inns of Court, the great English law schools in London. By profession he was a writer, philosopher, orator, politician, and not a lawyer. At age thirty, he attached himself to the Secretary to Ireland William Hamilton as his private secretary. By that time, Burke was already the author of two influential works of philosophy. The first of these, a work on aesthetics, had appeared four years earlier. In *A Philosophical Enquiry into the Origin of Our Ideas of the Sublime and the Beautiful*, Burke argued that emotional responses to works of art and nature were based on human experiences. A year later, *A Vindication of Natural Society* appeared as an inquiry into the moral basis of society. He was for many years the editor of the *Annual Register*, a notable political journal of its day, and he was a loyal member of Dr. Samuel Johnson's social club. His political career began seriously in 1765 when the Earl of Rockingham, the great Whig magnate who was First Lord of the Treasury, appointed him his private secretary. The following year, through his Rockingham connections, Burke was elected to Parliament, first from Wendover, then Bristol and Malton. For many years, Burke was a spokesman for the Rockingham Whigs, holding the position at one point in 1770 of parliamentary agent for the New York Assembly. After Rockingham's early death in 1782, Burke became associated with his longtime friend and parliamentary colleague, Charles James Fox. By 1789 both of them were in opposition to the king's First Minister, William Pitt.

Burke's pursuits were a mixture of reform politics firmly rooted in the history of British social and political institutions. He opposed a wide array of official British activities, including English policy toward the American colonies. In addition, he was against the use of English troops to quell riots brought about by economic difficulties. He favored the broadening of the rights of English (and of course Irish) Roman Catholics. Perhaps most importantly, he devoted his career to maintaining his concept of English rights and liberties, which meant primarily forestalling the encroachments made by the English crown against the Parliament. He fought a long losing battle over ending, or at least limiting, the king's patronage system, which often led to conflicts of interest when members of Parliament were given financial incentives to serve in the king's court. Appalled by the ill treatment of Asiatic Indians by the British, he led the failed impeachment of Warren Hastings, the Governor General of India, in a trial which lasted nearly seven years.

Despite these reformist efforts and despite a distinguished career in letters, Burke is generally regarded in history as one of the founders of modern conservative thought. Conservatism must be carefully defined, however, in its eighteenth-century context, not in its late twentieth-century "blend of American patriotism, evangelical religion and free-enterprise values," as John Pocock has pointed out. Burke's conservatism was rooted in the idea that the past must be valued for providing a workable and stable framework for all future progress.[1] Without this linkage to the past, to history and historical development, human beings run the risk of not being firmly anchored in place and time: they would not know who they were or where they were headed. The events in France stimulated him to think more deeply than ever before about such matters. Thomas Paine had been delighted ten years earlier when Burke suggested that England could do quite well without the American colonies. Burke did not frame the issue in the context of rights and liberties, as had Paine in *Common Sense*. In fact, his position was essentially pitched from an economic perspective: Britain did not gain enough from the colonies financially to mandate that she keep them. Hence, if reconciliation failed, he proposed they be let loose.[2]

Burke and Paine had been friends from the moment they met in England in 1787. Their trip through northern England in search of a proper ironworks to make a model of Paine's bridge had solidified their relationship. Where they came to differ was over the meaning, nature, significance, and future of the French Revolution, an event which split them so far apart that they never again discussed politics with each other.[3]

Burke's initial view of the Revolution was, like most Britons, truly ambivalent.[4] He really did not know how to react, for example, to the spectacle at the Bastille on July 14, 1789. Just three weeks after that event, in a letter to his friend, Lord Charlemont in Ireland, he used words which clearly relayed his confusion and dismay.

> As to us here our thoughts of everything at home are suspended by our astonishment at the wonderful spectacle which is exhibited in a neighboring and rival country. What spectators and what actors! England gazing with astonishment at a French struggle for liberty, and not knowing whether to blame or to applaud!

"To blame or to applaud": Burke would soon decide to attack what he considered the degeneration of that "struggle for liberty" into chaos and terror. Even in that summer of 1789, he displayed a deep skepticism about France's future. He went on to tell Charlemont that

> the spirit [there] it is impossible not to admire, but the old Parisian ferocity has broken out in a startling manner. It is true that this may be no more than a sudden explosion. If so, no indication can be taken from it. But if it should be character rather than accident, then that people are not fit for liberty and must have a strong hand like that of their former masters to coerce them. Men must have a certain fund of natural moderation to qualify them for freedom, else it become noxious to themselves and a perfect nuisance to everybody else. What will be the event, it is hard, I think, still to say. To form a solid constitution requires wisdom as well as spirit, and whether the

French have wise heads among them, or if they possess such
whether they have authority equal to their wisdom, is to be seen.
In the meantime the progress of this whole affair is one of the
most curious matters of speculation that ever was exhibited.[5]

Burke soon concluded that even if there were "wise heads" among the
French, they would never be in a position to set the course of the
Revolution in a way that would preserve liberty and order. Whatever
moderation that was there, he saw dissolving into a muddled mess.

As it turned out, within a month of writing this, he had
changed his mind. His friend, William Windham, had recently
returned from France, joyous over the events unfolding there. Burke
was unpersuaded that the new National Assembly could do anything
at all. "I very much question whether they are in a condition to exercise any function of decided authority, or even whether they are possessed of any real deliberative capacity, or the exercise of free judgment in any point whatsoever, as there is a mob of their constituents
ready to hang them if they should deviate into moderation or in the
least depart from the spirit of those they represent. What has happened puts all speculation to the blush, but still I should doubt
whether in the end France is susceptible of the democracy that is the
spirit, and in a good measure to the form, of the constitution they
have in hand."[6]

If he had remaining doubts, a few weeks later he was no
longer ambivalent about the monumental events in France. On
October 5 and 6, a large mob marched on Versailles, forcing the king
and queen to return to Paris. Burke was as appalled, as he later wrote
about this event in the *Reflections*, as he was angered by the scene.
Burke told a young family friend (Charles-Jean-François Depont, to
whom he addressed his pamphlet) in November that while he loved
liberty as much as the next man, liberty devoid of authority based in
historical foundations was empty and void of meaning. Burke predicted that the French (and all lovers of liberty), until they acquired
this firm grounding, would pass through great and horrible periods of
"chaos and darkness."[7]

Burke soon not only learned of the "shameful" spectacle of
the return of the king and queen to Paris, but by the beginning of the

new year, he also had before him in pamphlet form the inflammatory sermon that the Rev. Richard Price had delivered before the Revolution Society (a society formed to commemorate the anniversary of the Glorious Revolution) on November 4, 1789. A well-known and popular Unitarian minister, Price taught at Hackney College, one of the great dissenting academies of the century. There were several of these institutions where the children of non-Anglican believers (such as Unitarians and Presbyterians) could obtain a higher education. Those who refused to accept the liturgy and faith of the Church of England were denied admission to either Oxford or Cambridge. Moral philosophy, theology, political economy and mathematics were the staple of the curriculum in these academies so that graduates either entered the non-subscribing (non-Anglican) ministry or commerce.

A gentle, soft-spoken man, it was said that when Price walked down the street, even the little children cried out, "Make way, make way, make way for the good Dr. Price!" By 1789 he had for nearly thirty years been a distinguished philosopher and political theorist. Although by profession a clergyman, like his good friend and close associate Joseph Priestley (also a Unitarian minister with far-reaching interests in chemistry and politics), Price had devoted his life to his faith. He had also written several tracts on demography and life insurance. For that reason, even today Price is known as a founder of actuarial science. Like many Enlightenment figures, Price was a feisty promoter of rights and liberties. An early supporter of the American and French Revolutions, he and Priestley believed that the French Revolution heralded the end of tyranny throughout Europe.[8]

In his sermon, the *Discourse on the Love of Our Country*, which Price had delivered that day to the members of the Revolution Society, he had based his arguments on an appeal to human reason and human rights. People, he said, possessed certain inalienable or inherent rights of which no one could deprive them. They were the creators of their government, and they had the right to "cashier" their leaders when they deprived the people of those rights. Price's inflammatory words were obviously employed to rouse his listening audience at the Old Jewry (the chapel where he preached which was on the site of a former Jewish ghetto):

> We shall enjoy the transporting hope of soon becom-
> ing members of a perfect community. . . . What an eventful
> period is this! I am thankful that I have lived to see it; and I
> could almost say, Lord now lettest thou servant depart in peace
> for mine eyes have seen thy salvation. . . . I have lived to see
> Thirty Millions of People, indignant and resolute, spurning at
> slavery and demanding liberty with an irresistible voice. Their
> king led in triumph and an arbitrary monarch surrendering him-
> self to his subjects. . . . Tremble all ye oppressors of the world!
> Take warning all ye supporters of slavish governments and slav-
> ish hierarchies![9]

The entire spectacle at the Old Jewry had appalled Burke. Lord
Charles Stanhope sometimes known as "Citizen Stanhope" for his
liberal views and long an admirer of Paine, had chaired that meeting.
The first time he had met Paine, he asked him, "have I the pleasure
of shaking hands with the author of *Common Sense?*"[10] Stanhope was
obviously a strong supporter of the Revolution in France. As he later
told Burke, "the Revolution in France is one of the most striking and
memorable pages in history; and no political event was, perhaps, ever
more pregnant with good consequences to future ages. That great
and glorious Revolution will in time disseminate throughout Europe,
liberality of sentiment and a just regard for political, civil, and religious liberty. It will in all probability make the world for centuries
prosperous, free, and happy."[11]

A month and a half after Price delivered his sermon, Paine,
perhaps unwittingly, was supplying Burke with information about
French affairs, information that Burke eventually used to fill his
response to Price and all those who supported the Revolution. On
January 17, 1790, Paine wrote Burke from Paris primarily about his
bridge. He also told him how ecstatic he was about the progress of
the Revolution. The Revolution, he went on, was now all but complete, and the prospects were good for finishing the new constitution
as well. French finances, unlike those of England, were on a sound
financial footing, and the people seemed content to see a stable
republic formed for their own benefit. Paine then reviewed in some

detail the events which transpired from the seizure of the Bastille to the time that he wrote his letter in January. The king, he argued, was safe (little could he project the trial and execution in exactly three years). He even surmised that Louis XVI "should feel himself tranquil" at the moment. Paine was so pleased with the unfolding history in France that it was at this point that he wrote lines which clearly frightened Burke and perhaps even motivated him to complete his pamphlet. Paine wrote:

> The Revolution in France is certainly a forerunner to other revolutions in Europe. Politically considered it is a new mode of forming alliances affirmatively with countries and negatively with courts. There is no foreign court, not even Prussia, that could now be fond of attacking France; they are afraid of their armies and their subjects catching the contagion. Here are reports of matters beginning to work in Bohemia and in Rome. In Spain the Inquisition has condemned thirty-nine French works among which is the French declaration of rights. But the condemnation by reciting the heads of each work appear to me to have the effect of spreading the doctrines, at least it makes it known that there are such works and such doctrines in places where otherways it would not be known, and even that knowledge will have some effect.

Nothing could be of greater import to Paine than this prospect. He even sent Burke several letters he had received from Jefferson, including the one from July 11, 1789, which focused on the abstract principles of rights and liberties that Burke soon condemned. Surely nothing could have horrified Burke more than receiving all of this information from Thomas Paine.[12]

And yet, just a few months later in April, Paine, curiously, seemed confused about whether Burke would actually publish his thoughts about the Revolution. "I am now inclined to think that after all this vaporing of Mr. B., he will not publish his pamphlet." Why he said this is unclear, but however skeptical Paine was about Burke's desire to write on the Revolution, he soon realized that something would probably be forthcoming. Paine told Thomas Christie that he had visited an opposition bookseller, John Debrett, who sold anti-government materials. Debrett informed him that "Mr. Burke's pamphlet was in the press." (It was not quite yet.) Charles James Fox and Lord Stanhope also told him they thought the pamphlet was due out soon. Both men were champions of parliamentary reform and supporters of America and France. To advocate reform in the Parliament essentially meant opposition to the so-called corrupt boroughs, which were controlled by the great landed aristocrats, and it meant support of annually elected parliaments, equal electoral districts, and the end to the king's ability to appoint members of Parliament to lucrative places in his court.

At the same time, Paine reported that he also ran into a mutual friend of his and Burke's, a Dr. Lawrence. He told Dr. Lawrence that " 'I am exceedingly sorry to see a friend of ours so exceedingly wrong.' 'Time,' says he, 'will show if he is.' 'He is,' said I, 'already wrong with respect to time past.' "[13] Paine now told Christie that if Burke's pamphlet should appear, he definitely planned to respond to it. He hoped to see it soon because he had other matters, mainly his bridge model, to settle.

Just a few days after going to Debrett's publishing house, Paine dined with Price. As it turned out, Burke's pamphlet would be as much an attack on Price as it was on the Revolution in France. Burke argued that it was men who thought like Price who destroyed the political and social stability that it had taken centuries to develop. Price's support of the Revolution in France was based on moral and political abstractions: on a theory of rights which had no grounding in the historical experience of mankind. With few modifications, these were ideas that Jefferson, Paine, and every revolutionary writer easily approved of. Burke vehemently disagreed. Such abstractions caused chaos and destruction. The royal family had been publicly humiliated by being returned so horridly from Versailles, and all of them were now in danger for their lives, all for so-called rational, abstract rights. Even worse, the threat of world revolution was, to him, a horrifying thought.

As early as February 9, nine months before his pamphlet appeared, Burke denounced the spectacle of the French Revolution as an act of barbarism and setting forth a future chaos that would last for a long, long time.

The French had shown themselves the ablest architects of ruin that had hitherto existed in the world. In that very short space of time they had completely pulled down to the ground, their monarchy, their church, their nobility, their law, their revenue, their army, their navy, their commerce, their arts, and their manufactures. Our friendship and our intercourse with that nation had once been, and might again become, more dangerous to us than their worst hostility.[14]

Burke argued that if people based their ideas about human beings and their government on abstract rights, they would be forever threatened with anarchy and chaos. Why was this so? Burke's historical and organic theory (although he did not call it that) of human development maintained that human beings had developed political and social institutions over thousands of years. They could not simply cast these institutions from the face of the earth. His brand of conservatism was "based on the claim that human beings acting in politics always start from within a historically determined context, and that it is morally as well as practically important to remember that they are not absolutely free to wipe away this context and reconstruct human society as they wish."[15] At one time, slaves were ruled by tyrants, but now—with the progress that had taken place in time— slavery was ending, and people were much better off than ever before. The institutions which had lasted had done so essentially because they had worked. The ones which did not work had been lost to history, or simply scuttled.

This was Burke's famous argument from historical prescription: if institutions, such as monarchy and aristocracy, lasted over time and they worked, they were therefore "prescribed" for men's use until such a time as they simply withered away. He had an inkling of this happening as early as 1773 when he took one of his few trips to France, this time to spend a few weeks with the *philosophes*, radical philosophers like Voltaire and Diderot, who provided the theoretical foundation for the termination of the French monarchy, aristocracy, and clergy. Burke did not trust them. They had no sense of what the historical roots of France, especially in religious matters, meant for its future development and eventual reform. Burke told the Commons that "under the systematic attacks of these people, I see some of the props of good government already beginning to fail."[16] Revolution, if it blew away institutions wholesale without regard to their historical grounding, was a direct denial of prescription.

Now, the French had undertaken a revolution without "wisdom," without "moderation" (as he told Charlemont), a revolution which tore people from their institutional grounding in politics and society. Such a state of affairs worked against the human development which had taken place over eons of time. To believe otherwise was not to rest human political and social institutions on the slowly shifting waves of history but on rapid, revolutionary abstractions. Price's sermon, Burke wrote, was metaphysical speculation, with all its appeal to abstractions such as rights and liberties and reason. It was nothing more than "the public declaration of a man much connected with literary caballers and intriguing philosophers, with political theologians and theological politicians both at home and abroad. I know they set him up as a sort of oracle, because, with the best intentions in the world, he naturally *philippizes* and chants his prophetic song in exact unison with their designs." Burke clearly wanted his accusation to make Price look like a French agent!

The claim that a literary or philosophical "cabal" (a term Burke loved to use to describe those who fomented a French-variety revolution in England) existed in London was ridiculous. Price might have thought he and his friends at the Old Jewry and the London Tavern (the famous meeting place of Whig opponents) were "philosophic," but they were not. In the past some writers, Burke said, had "made some noise in their day," but no more. "At present they repose in lasting oblivion. Who, born within the last forty years, has read one word of Collins, and Toland, and Tindal, and Chubb, and Morgan, and that whole race who called themselves Freethinkers [all deists, like Paine]? Who now reads Bolingbroke? Who ever read him through?"[17]

Henry St. John, Viscount Bolingbroke, who was also a deist and a Tory opponent of Robert Walpole, had written *The Idea of a Patriot King* in 1749. As an attack on arguments for divine right, his work appealed to Whig opposition leaders. Bolingbroke, like Price, attacked the overweening power of the crown, situating appropriate political authority in the people who possessed the right to choose their kings (Bolingbroke knowing of no king appointed by God).[18] Burke demurred. No king should offer his crown to the people to legitimize his rule. Every English king governed by what Burke called "a fixed rule of succession, according to the laws of his country." Price and his friends in the Revolution Society wanted to establish an electoral college, as the Americans had, to determine who should and should not be king. Such was not the way that history had developed the institutional arrangements of Great Britain. No "political Divine" like Price could change that. The British people denied him the opportunity. They had established (or better, reestablished) their rights of legal sovereignty and the ancient rights of Englishmen in 1688 when they seized the throne from the Catholic king and absolutist, James II, who had denied them their rights as participants, through law and Parliament, in decision-making and as members of the established Church of England. Now, according to Price and his cohorts, Englishmen had acquired some new rights: to elect their governors, to throw them out of office, and even to form a new government whenever they wanted. "This new, and hitherto unheard-of bill of rights, though made in the name of the whole people," Burke wrote, "belongs to those gentlemen and their faction only. The body of the people of England have no share in it. They utterly disclaim it."

The Glorious Revolution of 1688 had achieved the goal that its supporters at the time sought: it had successfully preserved the ancient heritage, laws, and principles of English historical development. Now the Revolution in France, in a single effort, destroyed a thousand years of French history and tradition. Burke was still most horrified by the spectacle of the king and queen's forced march from Versailles to Paris on October 6, 1789, at which time they were confined to the Tuileries Palace, making Louis and his bride virtual prisoners of the Revolution. The famous passage in the *Reflections* is remarkable, not only for Burke's rhetoric, but for his emotional agony:

> It is now sixteen or seventeen years since I saw the queen of
> France, then the dauphiness, at Versailles, and surely never

lighted on this orb, which she hardly seemed to touch, a more delightful vision. I saw her just above the horizon, decorating and cheering the elevated sphere she just began to move in— glittering like the morning star, full of life and splendor and joy. Oh! what a revolution! and what a heart must I have to contemplate without emotion that elevation and that fall! Little did I dream when she added titles of veneration to those of enthusiastic, distant, respectful love, that she should ever be obliged to carry that sharp antidote against disgrace concealed in that bosom; little did I dream that I should have lived to see such disasters fallen upon her in a nation of gallant men, in a nation of men of honor and of cavaliers. I thought ten thousand swords must have leaped from their scabbards to avenge even a look that threatened her with insult. But the age of chivalry is gone. That of sophisters, economists, and calculators has succeeded; and the glory of Europe is extinguished forever.[19]

Many things angered Paine about Burke's pamphlet. He was especially appalled at this very passage, which induced him to write one of his most quoted remarks. He simply dismissed what Burke had said. Burke, he fumed, was "not affected by the reality of distress touching his heart, but by the showy resemblance of it striking his imagination. He pities the plumage, but forgets the dying bird." (RM 51) In trying to explain what Burke was getting at, "'chivalry' was not a mere emotive term. It was the name of a complex historical phenomenon."[20] Europe had emerged from barbaric ages largely as a result of the rise of the chivalric codes. Europe had discovered, in fact, the rights of man.

For Burke, Price and his ilk might have discovered rights, but that was all that they had done. Their so-called rights were not rights in the way Burke meant that term. Their rights were not prescribed by history. They were not bound in law or history but only in the say-so of people like Richard Price. These "metaphysic rights," these "pretended rights," were false, both morally and politically. Supposedly discovered by human reason, they were even less real. Man's rational sense was a computing scale. It allowed him to do mathematical problems of addition and subtraction, not to discover new moral principles like rights and liberties.

But the real England and true Englishmen were not like this. Men such as Price might make the most clamor and attract the most attention in asserting their so-called rights of man. They were not, however, like the stalwart men of good faith who understood what it meant to be English. Burke explained this in a wonderfully imaginative (and amusing) famous portrait drawn from the field of nature.

> Because half a dozen grasshoppers under a fern make the field ring with their importunate chink, whilst thousands of great cattle, reposed beneath the shadow of the British oak, chew the cud and are silent, pray do not imagine that those who make the noise are the only inhabitants of the field; that of course they are many in number, or that after all they are other than the little, shrivelled, meager, hopping, though loud and troublesome, insects of the hour.

An image not to be forgotten: the great, strong British oak, the tree of life and knowledge, protecting the intrepid and valiant people, who quietly withstood the verbal assaults of the raucous radicals who thought they had discovered this new thing, these rights of men. Well, Burke had something to teach here: if there were no such things as natural rights, Englishmen did indeed have something called rights, "the *real* rights of men." They had the right to obey the laws of their government. They had a right to justice, to earn a profit, to inheritance. They could have their day in court if they were charged with crimes. "They have a right to the fruits of their industry, and to the means of making their industry fruitful. They have a right to the acquisitions of their parents, to the nourishment of their offspring, to instruction in life, and to consolation in death." But an Englishmen, much less an Englishwoman, has no right to participate in the management of government. History has not decreed it. And yet, history has shown that Englishmen in Burke's time were far more advanced socially and politically than any other people in the world.

In other words, there had indeed been progress, though incremental and gradual. Institutions must not be uprooted wholesale and disposed of, which is precisely what had happened in France: the economists with their theories, calculators who knew nothing of chivalry, and sophists who spoke words without content had all taken over. The result, Burke predicted, was a tyranny the likes of which the world had never seen, a dictator who would rule over men without the benefit of the prescriptive institutions of stability and order. This was what would happen if the common people tried to rule themselves, and here Burke used one of his most unfortunate phrases, quoted in ridicule by his enemies for over two hundred years, from 1790 until our own time. Let the rights of man take effect, and "learning will be cast into the mire, and trodden down under the hoofs of the swinish multitude." Burke predicted no less than the entire degeneration of the Revolution into anarchy and tyranny to be followed by dictatorship, disorder, and severe harm to just about every citizen of France.

Without its deep-rooted historical moorings, which had kept government and society firmly fastened on a slow, gradual course toward improvement and progress, the foundations of life would be grounded in loose loamy soil. The institutions which the people had become used to and on which they relied were now constantly shifting and tilting until, with the slightest rupture or bit of unrest, they would all just collapse. Government did not change like fashion, or as Burke put it, radicals like Price believed that "government may vary like modes of dress and with as little ill effect."

In fact, Burke's anticipation of the inevitable decline of the Revolution appeared at the very moment when so many citizens still believed that they could build a new democratic republic on the ruins of the old regime. For a two year period, from the fall of the Bastille on July 14, 1789 to the arrest of the king and queen after they escaped and were captured in Varennes on June 25, 1791, the Revolution progressed on fairly democratic terms. A new political system, clearly a constitutional monarchy, was erected with a much reduced executive role, a unicameral legislature (the new National Assembly) elected by voters with property qualifications. It all appeared, at least for a while, to be stable and secure. There was no bloodbath, no butchery, no carnage. But "that Assembly, since the destruction of the orders, has no fundamental law, no strict convention, no respected usage to restrain it. Instead of finding themselves obliged to conform to a fixed constitution, they have a power to make a constitution which shall conform to their designs."

The European powers, especially Austria, Prussia, and soon England, were terrified that the events in France could (and indeed would) happen in their countries. Their goal to destroy revolutionary ideas by crushing the Revolution itself, coupled with the desire among some of the most radical of the French revolutionaries themselves, led to war between the new France and the old regime states in a general European conflagration in the spring of 1792. With the flight of the king to Austrian lines, his capture and return to Paris meant only one thing: the radicalization of the Revolution to heights few could have predicted.

In the fall of 1792, the horrible September Massacres broke out with the murder of hundreds of political prisoners in the French jails. This was soon followed, almost inevitably, with dictatorship of Robespierre and St. Just and then the execution of the king in January 1793. In addition, there was the brutal suppression of counter-rebellion in the French provinces. France was fighting all of Europe and itself at the same time. The church was on the way to being subdued: the revolutionary government had nationalized its lands in 1789, and as of July 1791 the priests had to swear obedience to the Revolution under the new Civil Constitution of the Clergy. All that was left was the coming Reign of Terror in 1793. But who could have predicted such a turn of events? Edmund Burke had in 1790. While he did not identify their names, he was not surprised by the rise of Robespierre and his colleagues or the eventual one-man rule of Napoleon Bonaparte: "the person who really commands the army is your master—the master . . . of your king, the master of your Assembly; the master of your whole republic."[21]

The awful years between 1792 and 1794 partially vindicated Burke's predictions of the demise of the Revolution. And yet, Burke never considered the bald fact that, during the monarchy, peasants and quite often the middle class as well had suffered under the camouflage of the pretty filigrees of Versailles and Paris salons. Nor did he ever see that the Revolution's mitigating effects did exist: it set forth the conditions for a meritocracy rather than the continuation of the corrupt aristocracy of the old regime. Of course, in 1790, when Paine read Burke's *Reflections*, he had no knowledge of the direction of the Revolution. For him, as for Price, Priestley, and other opposition thinkers of the age, the Revolution was the most momentous, the most positive event in the progressive history of the world. It would inaugurate an era of peace, freedom, and human rights. This is exactly what Paine said in his response, which was published the next year as Part One of the *Rights of Man*.

11 · The "inherent, indefeasible" Rights of Man

One thing is certain about Thomas Paine: friendship never impeded his engagement in an argument. The publication of Burke's *Reflections* was a case in point. Paine had admired Burke's bold stance against British policy regarding America in 1776, and he and Burke had personally gotten along quite well, especially when Paine was trying to sell his bridge. He had often visited Burke on his estate in Beaconsfield, and they spoke about reconciliation between England and France. Burke was Paine's senior by almost ten years, but they were fast becoming close friends when, in 1789, the French Revolution virtually ended that relationship. Indeed, after reading Burke's attack on the Revolution, Paine was convinced that Burke had written it in the service of the British crown. While there is no evidence to support Paine's claim, soon after the appearance of his *Reflections* Burke was awarded an annual pension by the court of George III. Paine smugly looked upon this stipend as a direct connection to Burke's service to king, country, and religion. (*RM* 119)

But that was later. Now Paine had to concentrate on what Burke had said, as did several others. In fact, Paine's published reaction to Burke's *Reflections* was one of nearly forty-five major ones which appeared over the course of the next several years.[1] Joseph Priestley wrote a response, as did Paine's close friend Thomas Christie, although other than the *Rights of Man*, perhaps the most well-known attacks on Burke were those by Mary Wollstonecraft (*A Vindication of the Rights of Man*, which she shortly followed up with her feminist *A Vindication of the Rights of Woman*) and by James Mackintosh (*Vindiciae Gallicae*). Even the poets were attracted to comment on Burke's themes, especially his use of the unfortunate term "the swinish multitude." In Ireland, a songbook entitled *A Tribute to the Swinish Multitude* appeared and included several songs, some parodying Burke:

> Ye vile Swinish herd, in the stye of taxation,
> What would ye be after disturbing the nation?
> Give over your grunting—be off—to your stye!
> Nor dare to look out, if a King passes by:
> Get ye down, down—down, keep ye down!
>
> Do you know what a king is? By Patrick I'll tell ye;
> He has power in his pocket to buy you and sell you;
> To make you his soldiers or keep you at work;
> To hang you, and cure you, for ham or salt pork!
>
> Do you think that a king is nor more than a man?
> Ye Irish, ye swinish ironical clan!
> I swear by his office, his right is divine,
> To flog you and feed you and treat you like swine.[2]

Of these responses, Paine's was (and still is) the most famous. More than anything else, he was furious with his old friend, Edmund Burke. He told Thomas Walker that he was "so out of humor with Burke with respect to the French Revolution" that he intended to set the record straight. Burke had provided an argument which set forth the reasons to protect the rights only of the privileged, of nobility, and of men like Burke attached to that nobility. "My idea of supporting liberty of conscience and the rights of citizens is that of supporting those rights in *other people*, for if a man supports only his *own* rights for his *own* sake, he does no moral duty."[3]

   The arguments of the *Rights of Man*, Part One, are fresh and clear with each reading, as is evident from the abundant commentary on the work.[4] Paine's attack on monarchy went farther than he had attempted in *Common Sense* or the *Crisis* series. His denunciation of the aristocracy was as biting as it ever was to be, and his assault on

Burke's love of tradition as a fixation which missed the main point—the rights of all human beings—was a powerful rebuke of Burkean arguments. Burke did not understand that he was living in a time of extraordinary and rapid change, that this was, as he put it, "an age of Revolutions, in which everything may be looked for." (*RM* 146) Burke's arguments for historical continuity, for gradual progress, for prescriptive constancy, had no place in contemporary times. The world was changing rapidly, "rendering modes of government obsolete," and it was time for people like Burke to realize that the era of despotism had ended and could not be reborn.

Much of Paine's attack was directed against Burke himself, not only at what Burke said. This was, again, typical of Paine's journalistic style. Burke labored "in vain to stop the progress of knowledge." (*RM* 118) His language was "gay and flowery," full of "theatrical representations" and "manufactured for the sake of show." It was like a point of land Paine claimed to know in America called "Point-no-Point," because "as you proceed along the shore . . . it continually recedes and presents itself at a distance before you; but when you have got as far as you can go, there is no point at all." (*RM* 49) Burke ought to have remembered, Paine rebuked, that he was not writing drama. He was supposed to be writing political analysis. "In the rhapsody of his imagination, he has discovered a world of windmills, and his sorrows are, that there are no Quixotes to attack them." (*RM* 50)

The ideas that Burke attacked were only figments of his imagination. Paine could not "consider Mr. Burke's book in scarcely any other light than a dramatic performance," pure fiction, made up from nothing more than what Burke himself had created in his own mind. (*RM* 59) How was it possible for anyone to respond to Burke's assault on human rights? It was nearly impossible, unless he followed "Mr. Burke through a pathless wilderness of rhapsodies, and a sort of descant on governments, in which he asserts whatever he pleases, on the presumption of its being believed, without offering either evidence or reasons for so doing." (*RM* 64) Burke had made groundless statements: he decried the loss of power of the king; he wept over the decline of the aristocracy; he wailed at the thought of the loss of those institutions which made government in France what it once was, an oppressive, tyrannical regime.

Paine attacked Burke's portrayal of the downfall of the authority of the king and the nobility in words which were as disparaging as they were damning. Again, in his famous passage, he claimed that Burke "pities the plumage, and forgets the dying bird. . . . His hero or his heroine [the king and the queen] must be a tragedy-victim expiring in show, and not the real prisoner of misery, sliding into death in the silence of a dungeon." (*RM* 51) The people of France themselves were sacrificial victims of their government. Under the old regime, the people had no opportunity to improve their lives. The government had ruthlessly brutalized them, tearing out their very soul.

In *Common Sense*, Paine had reserved his greatest venom for George III, but here the nobility, or as he wrote, the "No-ability," took the brunt of his censure. Paine saw in Louis XVI a man who was himself a victim of history. For now, he wrote that Louis XVI was a king who was "very different from the general class called by that name." He was "a man of a good heart," someone who under other circumstances, at a different time, would have been an ordinary person had he not been born to be king. It was the aristocracy who, in defying its own laws of moral behavior, exploited the people.

> The more aristocracy appeared, the more it was despised; there was a visible imbecility and want of intellects in the majority, a sort of je ne sais quoi, that while it affected to be more than citizen, was less than man. It lost ground from contempt more than from hatred; and was rather jeered at as an ass, than dreaded as a lion. (*RM* 106)

Aristocrats were nothing more than "a band of interested men . . . Lords of the bed-chamber, Lords of the kitchen, Lords of the necessary-house, and the Lord knows what besides." They were hopelessly worthless. They were thieving scoundrels and parasitic boors. These men more than anyone else were the causes of most of France's sordid history of oppression and horror.

The only possible resolution of this problem was for the people to realize that human beings possessed something called rights, natural and civil. To overcome their victimization, the French people must assert these rights. To answer Burke properly, Paine provided his own history of the events which led to the eruptions in France, especially the moment the Bastille was seized in July of 1789. He then offered his response to Burke's assault on human rights. Its argument was grounded in Lockean and republican ideas about the origin and nature of man.

Paine's *Rights of Man* was one of the most ardent and clear defenses of human rights, liberty, and equality in any language. So enthralled was Paine with the French Declaration of the Rights of Man and Citizen that he even included it in his work with a few comments of his own. (*RM* 110-12) Human beings, wrote Paine, were born with certain inalienable rights, which were "neither devisable, nor transferable, nor annihilable, but are descendible only." (*RM* 124) For Paine, human rights were part of life itself. With the creation of man came the rights of man. They were God's gift (they came into being "under the auspices of [their] Creator"), and no one could deprive a person of them. (*RM* 114) They permeated the universe, because they were "the illuminating and divine principle of the equal rights of man." The very existence of these rights proved that the divine was present in everything in life. "Every generation is equal in rights to the generations which preceded it," he said, "by the same rule that every individual is born equal in rights with his contemporary." (*RM* 66) The rights of man were inherent in all men, and they were the same in every person, regardless of economic or social status.

Like Locke, Paine wrote that people have rights naturally, and as they joined together to form society and then government, they transformed a number of their natural rights into civil rights, that is, rights protected by government against encroachments by other individuals as well as by government itself. Hence, government existed to protect the security of the people and, at the same time, to ensure that people are able to enjoy their rights in civil society. Rights of free speech, opinion, conscience, association (in America those rights became embodied in the first amendment to the Constitution in the same year the first part of the *Rights of Man* appeared) were all part of the natural rights which a properly constituted government must protect. In every country with a monarchy and aristocracy, government robbed the people of the very rights it was supposed to protect. Kings and nobles had usurped the rights which God had given to all people everywhere. This is why, Paine wrote, echoing Locke once again, "a Nation has at all times an inherent indefeasible right to abolish any form of government it finds inconvenient, and establish such as accords with its interest, disposition, and happiness." (*RM* 143)

This statement seems to imply that the people can choose a new form of government any time and for any reason. Paine was interested in polemic here, obviously, and not reality. Even in the eighteenth century, it was very difficult to overturn a government whenever the people (or some segment thereof) simply found it time to do so. To protect the right of citizens to a government of their own choosing, Paine believed there must be a strong constitution that was easily accessible to the public. "The American [state] constitutions were to liberty, what a grammar is to language: they define its parts of speech, and practically construct them into syntax." (*RM* 95) Just as the people had to be protected against those individuals who infringed upon their rights and liberties, so must the people be wary of a government which itself might deny their rights. Necessarily, then, the government must be a republican one in which political power is protected by a balance of power among its various branches.

Paine, like Madison, knew that human beings left to their own devices would try to dominate each other. Madison had written in *Federalist Paper*, Number 51, that because men were not angels, "ambition must be made to counteract ambition."[5] The only form of government that came close to protecting human rights was a republic, so long as the representation was equal:

> The representation being equal throughout the country, and complete in itself, however it may be arranged into legislative and executive. They have all one and the same natural source. The parts are not foreigners to each other, like democracy, aristocracy, and monarchy. As there are no discordant distinctions, there is nothing to corrupt by compromise, nor confound by contrivance. Public measures appeal of themselves to the under-

standing of the Nation, and, resting on their own merits, disown any flattering application to vanity. (*RM* 142)

Men's aggressive behavior towards fellow human beings must be checked by institutional safeguards, and this the republic could achieve.

Paine used the opportunity here to comment on the English government, which he said had no constitution and was no republic, themes he had originally addressed in *Common Sense*. "The continual use of the word *Constitution* in the English Parliament, shows there is none, and that the whole is merely a form of government without a constitution, and constituting itself with what powers it pleases." (*RM* 131) There was an appearance of a constitutional government, but since the document itself was unwritten no one had ever seen it. In a famous passage, Paine challenged Burke to exhibit one if he could. "Can then Mr. Burke produce the English Constitution? If he cannot, we may fairly conclude, that though it has been so much talked about, no such thing as a constitution exists, or ever did exist, and consequently that the people have yet a constitution to form." (*RM* 71-72)

In contrast was the constitutional structure France was fashioning under the National Assembly. France now had a new social contract under which the constitution was to be formed, and from that point on future assemblies were to meet to set forth the laws of the republic "according to the principles and forms prescribed in that constitution," with amendments and alterations added whenever necessary. (*RM* 72-73) In addition, France had the opportunity to create a solid financial footing for the new republic. Already, "the National Assembly is paying off the capital of its debt; and while taxes have increased near a million a year in England, they have lowered several millions a year in France." (*RM* 138) This constitutionality was what differentiated the new, progressive institutions from those of England, and this was why Burke was dead wrong in his assessment of the circumstances in France.

The first part of the *Rights of Man* was, then, a classic statement of the importance of rights and liberties. It was radical only insofar as the principles stated were dissonant with the manner in which most countries were governed. Most Americans accepted these principles. The framers of the American Constitution and Thomas Jefferson (who was still the American envoy to France during the drafting of that document) believed in them. These assertions of the political rights and liberties of people vis-à-vis their government are what have been the framework of revolutions throughout the world since Paine first articulated them when this first part appeared on February 22, 1791. Much of what he argued for here, however, was derived from the generally accepted string of ideas that have their roots in John Locke's principles of government. A year later, Paine added Part Two to the *Rights of Man*, this time presenting social and economic ideas which were very progressive in terms of the late eighteenth century. Paine was to go so far as to suggest the contemporary social welfare state, nearly one hundred fifty years ahead of its time.

Part One was initially published by Joseph Johnson in London, but Paine moved the work almost immediately to J. S. Jordan, a radical printer and bookseller, after Johnson lost courage and refused to continue with the effort. So anxious was he to return to Paris that Paine left the actual publication in the hands of his friends, William Godwin, Thomas Holcroft, and Brand Hollis. This time he was gone only a few weeks.

Each of these men were prominent radicals in their own right. Godwin, husband of Mary Wollstonecraft (and the father of Mary Godwin Shelley, who wrote *Frankenstein*) was the author of several works. Among his most famous works were his novel *The Adventures of Caleb Williams*, which appeared in 1794, and his 1793 anarchist tract *Enquiry Concerning Political Justice*. In the latter, he argued that since human beings were naturally rational creatures, they lived in harmony with no need of government, laws, or institutions of any sort. Holcroft, an author and playwright, wrote two novels inspired by his friend Godwin, *Anna St. Ives* in 1792 and *Hugh Trevor*, which was published over a three year period from 1794 to 1797. Finally, Thomas Brand Hollis, an urban radical activist in London, had been a strong supporter of the association movement in the 1780s, which spawned the Society for Constitutional Information. He had once served in Parliament, although in 1774, he was jailed for bribery in his attempt to be reelected. At any rate, Paine's work was in good hands, and in February of 1791 the *Rights of Man* appeared, selling for a mere three shillings a copy.

Within three months of its appearance in England, a French translation by François Soulès was published in Paris, to be followed by a second translation the following year, this time by Paine's friend, François Xavier Lanthenas, who later translated many of Paine's works into French. Along with Nicolas de Bonneville, Lanthenas later worked with Paine in the Social Circle, a radical organization in Paris which attempted to spread ideas of revolution and spiritualism throughout France in the 1790s.

As for the *Rights of Man* in America, after several newspapers in the U.S. carried portions of the pamphlet, a full-blown American edition appeared with an unauthorized preface by Thomas Jefferson, then serving as Secretary of State in the first Washington administration. Jefferson had received a copy of the work from James Madison, who had himself borrowed what was perhaps the only copy in the country from the clerk of the House of Representatives, John Beckley. Beckley intended to have the work printed by an American publisher, so he told Jefferson that after he read the pamphlet to forward it to the printer.

Jefferson sent the work to Jonathan Bayard Smith, a prominent Philadelphia merchant, a trustee of the University of Pennsylvania and the College of New Jersey. Smith, like Jefferson, had supported American independence from Britain and, also like Jefferson, was a member of the American Philosophical Society. He also was a great admirer and friend of Thomas Paine. Jefferson thought that Smith was the printer's brother. He sent along with the pamphlet a note that clearly showed his elation that the work was to be available in the United States. "Something is at length to be said against the political heresies which have sprung up amongst us. [I have] no doubt our citizens will rally for a second time around the standard of Common Sense." Jonathan Smith was in fact not the printer's brother, but his father: nineteen-year old Samuel Harrison Smith, who although quite green as a printer later moved to Washington to found the *National Intelligencer*, one of the great republican newspapers of the era, for which Paine later wrote after his return to America in 1802.

Now, Jefferson, who claimed he did not know the elder Smith personally, made clear in his note that he was acting on Beckley's wishes. When the *Rights of Man* appeared a week later (Jefferson sent the note on April 26, and the work was published on May 3), to Jefferson's great dismay, the following appeared as the preface:

> The following extract from a note accompanying a copy of this pamphlet for republication is so respectable a testimony of its value that the printer hopes the distinguished writer will excuse its present appearance. It proceeds from a character equally eminent in the councils of America and conversant in the affairs of France from a long and recent residence at the court of Versailles in the diplomatic department; and at the same time that it does justice to the writings of Mr. Paine, it reflects honor on the source from which it flows by directing the mind to a contemplation of that republican firmness and democratic simplicity which endear their possessor to every friend of the "Rights of Man."

Young Smith then identified the writer of the note not by Jefferson's own name but only as the "Secretary of State," thus giving the sentiments that Jefferson expressed some official sanction. There was no indication that Beckley had been involved in the first place. Jefferson now appeared to be the sole American sponsor of the publication, this during an unusually difficult time he was having with Vice President John Adams.[6]

Jefferson's words about "political heresies which have sprung up amongst us" riled the pro-English, anti-French Federalists, especially Adams, who had just finished writing a longwinded anti-French series, *Discourses on Davila*. Adams thought the Secretary's remark was specifically directed against him, which in fact it could well have been. In any case, despite Jefferson's attempt to apologize, for which he was roundly criticized in the pro-French republican press, the line between Federalists and Republicans, respectively their pro-English and pro-French views, was now set. A series of eleven essays appeared in the *Columbian Centinel* (and widely reprinted), under the signature of Publicola—who was none other than Adams' son, John Quincy—only to be answered by republican critics, who charged Adams with favoring monarchy and aristocracy. Everyone thought that Publicola was John Adams the elder, so to many it appeared to be a political battle between the Vice President and the Secretary of State.

In any case, the affair basically destroyed Jefferson's relationship with Adams for the next twenty years.[7] Jefferson was clearly upset, but still convinced he was right. He wrote to Paine that there was a "sect" of men in America who were "preaching up and panting after an English constitution of king, lords, and commons, and whose heads are itching for crowns, coronets, and miters," and that Paine's pamphlet had "checked" their advance. The "people [were now] confirmed in their good old faith."[8]

Worse still, the matter was a political embarrassment to George Washington. In July of 1791 Paine sent the President fifty complimentary copies of his work, but Washington acknowledged them only after more than ten months had passed, on May 6, 1792, to Paine's frustration and displeasure. The President gave Paine a feeble apology. "To my friends and those who know my occupations, I am sure no apology is necessary for keeping their letters so much longer unanswered than my inclination would lead me to do. I shall therefore offer no excuse for not having sooner acknowledged the receipt of your letter of the 21st of June."[9] After all, Paine had dedicated the Rights of Man to George Washington "in defense of those principles of freedom which your exemplary virtue hath so eminently contributed to establish. That the *Rights of Man* may become as universal as your benevolence can wish, and that you may enjoy the happiness of seeing the New World regenerate the Old." (*RM* 33)

But Paine was unaware of the political flap in America. He was convinced that the sentiment he was expressing in the first part of the *Rights of Man* in fact coincided with Washington's feelings, especially with its primary focus on Burke's famous attack on the Revolution as undermining centuries of French history and tradition. Here, he focused almost exclusively on political issues: the nature and causes of the Revolution in France, the origins and nature of human rights, and the form of government that best protected those rights.

Part One was an immediate commercial success. Sales were brisk, outpacing the sluggish sales of Burke's *Reflections*. At one point, Paine estimated that between 400,000 and 500,000 copies had been sold. As with *Common Sense*, however, Paine realized no profits from this work. He turned his receipts over to the Constitutional Society.[10] The book won him many admirers. His friends in America—Jefferson, Madison, and Edmund Randolph (the latter had served in the Constitutional Convention as a delegate from Virginia and was now the first Attorney General of the United States)—all lobbied Washington to appoint Paine head of the United States Post Office. The Postmaster General, Samuel Osgood, had unexpectedly resigned, and the Republican members of the cabinet saw an opportunity to undercut the authority of one of their Federalist rivals, Alexander Hamilton, then the Secretary of Treasury. Since the post office was then part of the Department of the Treasury, "Postmaster General Paine" sounded sweet to Republican ears. But apparently the public embarrassment caused by Jefferson's unauthorized preface to the American edition of the *Rights of Man* was enough to make Washington consider Paine's candidacy for the post office, or anything else for that matter, impolitic.

The work also had its immediate detractors. A typical aristocratic reaction was made by the Earl of Mornington, who later told British Interior Minister Lord Grenville, "I wonder you did not hang that scoundrel Paine for his blackguard libel on king, lords, and commons. I suppose the extreme scurrility of the pamphlet, or the villainy of those who wish to disperse it amongst the common people, has carried through so many editions. For it appears to me to have no merit whatever; but it may do mischief in ale-houses in England, and still more in whiskey-houses in Ireland. I think it by far the most treasonable book that ever went unpunished within my knowledge; so, pray, hang the fellow, if you can catch him."[11] Such an assessment, to Paine, was praise and commendation.

Paine still had many admirers and sympathizers in France, England, and America. A new constitution was being formed in France and a new government brought into being, and there had been very little bloodshed. Many believed that the Glorious Revolution in England was being repeated in France on a scale which was taking

France into the modern world far ahead of England. In reality, the Revolution was not progressing well at all. There were bitter debates over various sections of the proposed constitution, especially the place of Catholic worship and clergy, and an anti-republican backlash in the countryside was beginning to make itself felt in terrorist attacks, murder, and pillaging.

Paine had returned to London on March 7, but almost immediately decided to go back to France the very next month, this time for three months, with three goals: to find a French publisher for the *Rights of Man*, which he did by May; to try to sell his bridge design; and to participate in French affairs as they happened. He initially lived by himself in conditions that his old nemesis Gouverneur Morris called "wretched."[12] By this time, Paine knew many of the leading revolutionaries. He soon accepted an invitation from Lafayette to stay at his house, and he also spent a great deal of time with the great French *philosophe*, the Marquis de Condorcet, discussing whether the Assembly ought to pressure the king to abdicate so that France could be declared a republic.[13]

Paine arrived in April in time to attend the funeral of Honoré de Mirabeau, a radical aristocrat who, though in his early years a wastrel, wrote several tracts against the ancien régime. He tried, even after 1789, to convince the king and queen to moderate their views and establish a constitutional monarchy, but to no avail. By 1791, Mirabeau was the unofficial leader of the National Assembly, now called the Constituent Assembly, as its focus changed to write a new constitution for France. And in 1791, at age forty-two, he was dead. The length of his funeral cortège was over ten miles long, and over 100,000 people, including Danton and Robespierre, accompanied this beloved man on his last journey.

Robespierre, then a member of the Constituent Assembly and later a leader of the Terror, at this time advocated the abolition of the death penalty: "Capital punishment is but base assassination," he declared, "punishing one crime by another, murder with murder. Since judges are not infallible they have no right to pronounce irreparable sentences."[14] Paine sympathized with this view, only to see it soon radically transformed into Robespierre's acceptance of the legal murder that he so strongly now decried. Two soon-to-be victims of public execution, whose fate was likely sealed in June 1791, were the king and the queen. Disguised as a valet and governess, they had attempted to flee Paris to join the counter-revolutionary Austrian army threatening France. At news of their escape, Lafayette burst into the sleeping Paine's room, shouting, "The birds have flown away!"[15] Paine replied that he hoped they would not be found. He preferred to see the throne remain empty and a republic established peacefully. The French had other ideas. Captured at Varennes after riding several days under an assumed name ("Durand"), Louis XVI returned to Paris under heavy guard. On hearing the developments, Paine visited his friend, Thomas Christie, who was then living at the Palais Royal. The two of them went to the Tuileries to find out what was happening. Paine had commented to Christie about "the absurdity of monarchical governments; here will be a whole nation disturbed by the folly of one man."[16]

A story about the king's return to Paris, which may well be apocryphal, has it that an officer of the National Guard ordered everyone in the waiting crowd to put on their cockades, the red, white, and blue hats symbolizing freedom and equality. Paine had apparently lost his and there was a shout to hang him "à la lanterne, à la lanterne," meaning any nearby lamppost. But Paine was saved at the last minute when someone explained to the mob who he was.

After the king's flight, most people, including Paine, perceived Louis XVI as a duplicitous sort not to be trusted. Therefore, in July, Condorcet, and probably three others founded the Republican Society and used its newspaper, *Le Républicain, ou le Défenseur du gouvernement représentatif,* to attack monarchy in general and to agitate for the establishment of a French republic. The others were most likely Duchâtelet, Jacques-Pierre Brissot de Warville, the editor of the revolutionary newspaper, *Le Patriote français,* and Nicolas de Bonneville, who, along with Condorcet in 1791, had founded the Social Circle. At the time, the four of them were on the cutting edge of revolutionary republican thought in France. (On the extreme, of course, was Marat, calling for execution of the king, Lafayette, and just about everyone else.) Bonneville, answering for himself and his colleagues in his own newspaper, *La Bouche de Fer,* called for "No more kings! No dictator! Assemble the people in the face of the sun;

proclaim that the law alone shall be sovereign, the law, the law alone, and made for all!"[18]

All five were convinced that France must have a republic without a king rather than merely a republic with the king as a titular or even with suspended powers. Brissot had started his career as a lawyer and wrote on penal reform. Known by French police for harboring radical ideas, he had briefly served time in the Bastille for sedition. English speaking, he had traveled to America and England. He and Paine easily communicated their ideas to one another with Paine writing for his newspaper, *Le Patriote français*. A friend to the American cause, Brissot, like Paine, advocated an end to slavery and the slave trade by founding a Society of the Friends of the Blacks (Société des Amis des Noirs). While Brissot never supported the total redistribution of land, he was reputedly the author of a phrase later made famous by Proudhon: "Property is theft." Although he believed that revolutionary ideas would spread throughout Europe through the conduit of France's revolutionary army, Brissot was a leader of the Girondin, or moderate faction.

Nicolas de Bonneville had lived at times with Brissot in England in the mid-1780s, and even translated a history of Europe into French. Along with Brissot, he visited several Masonic lodges, which may have served as the origin of several of his spiritualist ideas, usually permeated with images of the sun, of a society of harmony, unity, and peace. His relationship with Paine was strengthened after 1797, when Paine lived with him and his family for five years.

When Paine heard that *Le Républicain* was to begin publication, he wrote to Condorcet, Bonneville, and Lanthenas, asking to join the venture. His letter was a plea, a kind of judicial petition, to convince them to let him participate.

> Being the citizen of a land [America] that recognizes no majesty but that of the people, no government except that of its own representatives, and no sovereignty except that of the laws, I tender you my services in helping forward the success of those principles which honor a nation and contribute to the advancement of the entire world; and I tender them not only because my country is bound to yours by the ties of friendship and grati-

tude, but because I venerate the moral and political character of those who have taken part in the present enterprise and feel proud of being their associate.

Paine explained honestly that he was unable to use any language other than English so that his potential services were quite limited, but he was anxious to join the cause. He promised to sign his pieces "Common Sense" since he thought that was the most identifiable designation he possessed. No one would think someone else had written his articles with that signature.

Paine loved the idea that the name of the publication carried the word "republican," because that meant that it was totally dedicated to "the interests of the state." His hope was that the ideas of the French Revolution with its emphasis on republican principles would spread to all the major nations of the world, including "Spain, Russia, Germany, Turkey, and the whole of Asia. That I may live to see the freedom of these lands is my ardent desire," he wrote. When those and all other nations ended the scandalous business of hereditary succession, "the fallacy of the right of certain individuals, either now born or about to be born, to the possession of human beings as their property," then he would be satisfied. He then added a rather curious note. Even if a man should "in some future period return to life," he could never relinquish his rights. By the same token, it was just as cruel and unjust for a man to rob his children of their rights by claiming he ruled by hereditary succession. Monarchy and hereditary rights must therefore end and in their place the representative republic and the *Rights of Man* triumphantly emerge. With that, he hoped that he had demonstrated "that I am a sound republican."[19]

Paine was taken on immediately as a member. A manifesto proclaiming their position (and the position of the new Republican Society) was soon prepared for wide distribution. "A Republican Manifesto" called for the end of monarchy in France, and on July 1, along with Achille Duchâtelet, a revolutionary leader and friend and, like Condorcet, a marquis, Paine posted it on poles and buildings throughout Paris. Duchâtelet, who had served with French forces in America during the Revolution there, was well known as the grandson of Voltaire's mistress, Emilie du Chastellet. The poster declared:

[The king's] flight is equivalent to abdication; for, in abandoning his throne, he has abandoned his office; the brevity of the period during which he was absent counts for nothing; in the present case it is the attempt to escape that counts for everything.

The king had broken his oath of office and had secretly conspired to undermine France, just the opposite of what he was entrusted to do. From this standpoint, "he is no longer invested with authority. He has no claim on our allegiance. There is no distinction between him and other individuals; to us he is simply Louis Capet."[20] He had lost his identity as a monarch (his "person" of the king) and was but a man. Besides, "we have always been the miserable victims of monarchical oppression, sometimes being ruined by our own devotion to royalty, sometimes crushed to earth by its tyranny. Now that treason is added to the long series of cruelties and crimes which France has had to endure at the hands of kings, the long catalogue of their awful offenses is finished; there are no more crimes left for them to commit, therefore their claim to rule is a thing of the past." The "Manifesto" appeared the next day in Brissot's paper, *Le Patriote français*. This amounted to one of the first calls for a republic in France.

During the trial of Louis XVI and in a later letter, Paine claimed he had been the one who actually drafted the manifesto. The Republican Society, he said in 1793, opposed the restoration of the monarchy after Louis was returned from Varennes. With that in mind, he himself "traced out in the English language certain propositions, which were translated with some trifling alterations, and signed by Achille Duchâtelet . . . the law requiring the signature of a citizen at the bottom of each printed paper."[21]

Whether Paine acted as the principal writer or not was immaterial. In fact, the manifesto's demand for the end of the monarchy and the creation of a republic was far from universally accepted. In the Assembly, there were those who denied republican government. Jean Paul Marat was calling for the king's head in his journal, *L'Ami du peuple* [The Friend of the People], the suspension of the authority of the all monarchs, the seizure of all executive power, including the running of the ministries, and the establishment of a dictatorship. At the same time, the monarchist Malouet tore Paine's poster right off the door of the Assembly and demanded the immediate prosecution of Paine and Duchâtelet. While the members were clearly appalled that anyone or any one group would demand the end of the monarchy, they had not seen the last of the Republican Society. Its new journal immediately began to outline in greater detail the radical views of its founders. Paine wrote several essays for *Le Républicain*, which were translated by Condorcet's wife, Sophie de Condorcet. Unfortunately, the paper lasted but four issues.[22]

Paine and Condorcet now collaborated on an essay, "Answer to Four Questions on the Legislative and Executive Powers," which, while it did not appear in print for a year, represented their views in the spring and summer of 1791. Using the new American government as their primary model, the two writers demonstrated how a democratic republic could be properly structured. The most radical idea that they expressed, and one in which Paine was later to pay heavily for in England when he advocated it in the *Rights of Man*, Part Two, was the radical idea of a national convention. Conservatives who wished only for slow, incremental changes in government over long periods of time specifically abjured the idea of conventions, because they appealed directly to the people for ideas about democratizing government. In their "Answer," Paine and Condorcet explicitly hoped for "a convention of the representatives of the various nations of Europe, which would adopt measures for the general welfare. The felicity which liberty insures us is transformed into virtue when we communicate its enjoyment to others."[23]

Their views did not go without a response. Abbé Emmanuel Joseph Sieyès, the author of the famous 1789 pamphlet, "What Is the Third Estate?," which vigorously assailed noble and clerical privileges, answered their attacks on monarchy in *Le Moniteur*, the leading newspaper in Paris. Sieyès had served in the Estates General as a member of the third estate when Louis XVI finally called it into session in 1789, and he had helped write the Declaration of *Rights of Man* and Citizen as well as the Constitution of 1791. At the time of his response, he appeared to be a moderate who favored monarchy and the new constitution. He seemed to believe in an independent executive, possibly a king. Paine responded in the same newspaper on

July 8, 1791 with a vitriolic, anti-monarchical tract advocating a republican "government founded upon the principles of the Declaration of Rights; principles to which several parts of the French Constitution arise in contradiction." In this response, which was also printed in *Le Républicain*, Paine argued that there could never be a republic so long as there was a king. Now, Paine was not the personal enemy of any king. He wanted "to see them all in the happy and honorable state of private individuals; but I am the avowed, open, and intrepid enemy of what is called monarchy. . . . [And] it is against all the hell of monarchy that I have declared war."

Historians have long asked whether Paine and Sieyès undertook this seemingly adversarial exchange as a ploy. [24] There is some evidence that Condorcet acted as an intermediary between the two writers, highlighting and bringing into focus the great divisions between belief in monarchy and representative government. Sieyès, who soon became a spokesman for the Jacobins and voted for the execution of the king, in reality did not favor the monarchy. He really wanted Paine's arguments to be more powerful than his own: he hoped his readers, in short, would become convinced republicans. In 1796, Joseph Lakanal, who had served four years earlier with Paine, Condorcet, and Mary Wollstonecraft on the Committee of Public Instruction, reported in his journal that the Paine-Sieyès debate was totally orchestrated in order to hasten the establishment of a republic in France: the three (Paine, Condorcet, and Sieyès), he said, were "the first founders of the republic in France."[25] Lakanal apparently relied on the word of Condorcet.

Five days after responding to Sieyès, along with Etienne Dumont (who had thought "The Republican Manifesto" was too radical) and Lord Daer, Paine once again returned to London. One of Paine's traveling companions, Daer (Basil William Douglas), was a young Scottish radical nobleman who hoped to inculcate revolution in his home country. He joined two radical associations, the London Corresponding Society and the Society of the Friends of the People in Scotland, but soon died at the quite young age of thirty-one in 1794. The Genevan Dumont, a close friend and collaborator of Mirabeau, had written many of Mirabeau's speeches and after his death published a memoir of him. He later translated Jeremy

Bentham's work into French. Paine did not impress Dumont, who later recalled how much Paine's "unbelievable egotism" disgusted him.

> He was mad with vanity. . . . He was more vain than the
> French. He thought his book, the *Rights of Man*, would replace
> all the books in the world, and he said he had the power to
> destroy all the libraries, with no hesitation, because of all the
> errors contained in them, whereas the *Rights of Man* had set off
> a new chain of ideas and principles. He knew by heart all his
> own writings, and nothing else. . . . My curiosity about this
> famous writer was fully satisfied on this voyage, and I never saw
> him again.[26]

The three men arrived in London in time to commemorate the second anniversary of the fall of the Bastille, a celebration arranged by the Revolution Society, which was specifically created to memorialize the 1688 Glorious Revolution ending the growing absolutism of the Stuart kings. The celebration was to take place at the Crown and Anchor Tavern, a local gathering place for political radicals. A thousand people were to be in attendance. Paine, however, was suffering from exhaustion from his journey, and his doctor advised him to stay in bed, which he did.

In the meantime, the Earl of Gower, the British Minister in Paris, had warned authorities of Paine's arrival. In England, Paine "piously intends, if possible, to make confusions," Gower reported to the Interior Minister, Lord Grenville, "from thence, he makes it no secret, he is to go to Ireland for the same charitable purpose."[27]

By August, Paine was well enough to spend time with the Society for Constitutional Information (SCI). Liberal reform activist Christopher Wyvill had formed this organization in 1780, literally as a means to spread information and ideas having to do with parliamentary reform.[28] In time, other societies modeled after it were established in various English towns, principally Sheffield and Manchester. They were often in contact with one another, exchanging information and ideas. Just six months later, this format of communication became the model for the more radical association the

London Corresponding Society, under the leadership of the shoe-maker-turned-radical Thomas Hardy.

In the summer of 1791, the chairman of the SCI was John Horne Tooke, who was now, along with Paine, one of the most radical writers in England. Horne Tooke had at one time been an Anglican minister but was soon totally engaged in political radicalism. In the 1760s, he supported John Wilkes (though he became disenchanted with him in 1771) and became a great partisan of the American desire for separation from Britain. In fact, after what he considered the "murders" by the British at Concord and Lexington, Horne Tooke illegally raised money for the Americans and was incarcerated for it.

Because the government was increasingly suspicious of the activities of the SCI, its ideas of parliamentary reform in general and of Paine and Horne Tooke in particular, the proprietor of the Crown and Anchor, where the SCI usually met, declined to allow them to meet in his tavern to celebrate the second anniversary of the French government's August 4, 1789 decrees ending feudalism and the monarchy. The radicals repaired to the Thatched House Tavern, a more ideologically compatible establishment, where they ate, sang, and drank toasts to the French Revolution and hoped for the same in England.

In August, Burke's "Appeal from the New to the Old Whigs" answered the *Rights of Man*. It did not mention Paine by name but had only veiled references to him and his work. Burke repeated much of what he had said in the *Reflections*. He condemned the Revolution in France and reiterated his support of the good old cause of 1688, the principles of the Old Whigs, on the prescriptive grounds of historical precedent and continuity. That same month, an unfavorable biography, *Oldys' Life of Thomas Paine*, appeared both in England and America.[29] Largely underwritten by the British government, the work was exhaustively researched and written by George Chalmers, a cultivated gentleman who worked in the Board of Trade and had published works on English commerce, Shakespeare, and Defoe. It was from Chalmers' exhaustive research into Paine's first thirty-seven years that historians have acquired the facts (though some of them spurious) about Paine's early failures and frustrations.[30]

On August 20, Paine, who evidently was already working on Part Two of the *Rights of Man*, addressed the SCI. He appealed for help for the impoverished souls of England through revolutionary action. "As Englishmen we also rejoice, because we are *immediately* interested in the French Revolution," he proclaimed. And he took yet another swipe at Burke's notion of historical continuity and prescription: "We live to improve, or we live in vain; and therefore we admit of no maxims of government or policy on the mere score of antiquity, or other men's authority, the old Whigs or the new [an obvious reference to Burke's response]. . . . Beneath the feudal system all Europe has long groaned, and from it England is not yet free." Paine also mentioned that certain *"unnamed* and *skulking* persons"* had barred the SCI from meeting at the Crown and Anchor.[31]

In a few short years, the government made its own efforts to undermine English radical activities. The next year, for example, an organization led by John Reeves, the Association for the Preservation of Liberty and Property Against Republicans and Levellers, was approved and partially funded by the government. Its agents infiltrated the SCI, the London Corresponding Society, and other radical groups to collect information and arrest activists. Reeves, Chief Justice of Newfoundland, had been a legal historian and held the official position of Receiver of the Public Offices, which financially controlled the police operations in London. Soon, because of the publication of Part Two of the *Rights of Man*, Paine himself would be declared an outlaw and forbidden to return to his native land or face arrest and possibly execution.[32]

All this was in the future. Now Paine wanted to reply to Burke's "Appeal," this time in ways which were definitive. He moved to Marylebone Street to live with his long-time friend, poet and writer, Clio Rickman, whom he had known in Lewes and who now was a successful, middle-class, very overweight London bookseller. Rickman always enjoyed Paine's company, and was throughout his life an unswerving supporter of Painite ideology, risking life and limb (not to say reputation and business) by printing and selling his work. He even named one of his sons after Paine: Thomas Paine Rickman.

Paine spent his time at the Rickmans' during most of the autumn of 1791, writing the second part of the *Rights of Man* and visiting friends, especially Godwin, Wollstonecraft, Horne Tooke, several American diplomats, and scientist, political radical, and Unitarian minister Joseph Priestley. On November 4, Paine attended the meeting of the Revolution Society, where the life of Richard Price was celebrated and memorialized (Price had died seven months earlier). There, at a meeting chaired by Paine's old friend, Thomas Walker, Paine toasted Price's life and accomplishments, calling for world revolution and proclaiming, "God save the *Rights of Man!*" The old-regime nations, especially England, were wondering what to do to protect their interests against these very same republican ideas. British troops, long freed from their American commitment, had by now returned to England to protect the monarchy from republican assaults. Indeed, moves were afoot in Frederick the Great's Prussia and Leopold's Austria to create a broad coalition, if other monarchies joined them, to restore the French monarchy. By late fall 1791, Paine finished working on his most important work to date: Part Two of the *Rights of Man*.

Part Three

Social Responsibility
and Illuminist Spirituality

12 · "The most determined champion of republican principles"

With the exception of 1776, 1792 was perhaps the most successful, most pleasant year of Paine's career in journalism. He lived with Clio Rickman, with whom he got along quite well. George Romney painted his portrait, from which William Sharp later made an engraving. This engraving (the portrait is now lost) shows Paine at the peak of his physical health and his intellectual power. At fifty-five his hair, unruly as ever, was greying. Age lines appear around his eyes and jaw. The firm mouth is caught in a taut, sardonic half-smile. His nose, known for its length and hook at the end, in this portrait is well proportioned unlike one painted twelve years later by John Wesley Jarvis, which shows him looking much older than his sixty-seven years and with an extremely large nose. In the Romney painting, he is dressed for the occasion and probably washed, though Paine did not necessarily hold that cleanliness was next to godliness. This was a portrait of a man of enormous success and enduring fame.

In this year, Paine was made a citizen of France and elected to its National Convention, where he worked on a new constitution, France's second in as many years. In England, he was to be found guilty in absentia of seditious libel for writing and publishing the *Rights of Man*, the second part of which was his most radical work to date. Paine had largely ignored the unrelentingly hostile 1791 biography by George Chalmers, who had been paid by the Pitt ministry to denounce him.

In this period Paine enjoyed great popularity, especially among the working class people, the members of the SCI, and the new, even more radical organization of laborers and artisans, the London Corresponding Society. Paine was leaving England for good at a time when there was a growing reaction against liberal reform movements (like the SCI and LSC) and writings (like those of Thomas Paine). In addition, the government fought against working class demands for better wages and conditions. Paine and radicals like him, Joseph Priestley for one, had been blamed for the unrest caused by the reform movement in England. In 1791, the Church and King Riots, sponsored and led by the government, had injured a great deal of property and many people, Priestley especially. His laboratory and house in Birmingham were burned to the ground, and, fearing for his own life, he fled to London, where he remained for the next three years, finally giving up entirely on England and emigrating to America in 1794. He died in Northumberland, Pennsylvania, ten years later.

Paine's name during the summer and fall of 1791 appeared in the English press almost every day. Burke had referred to Paine and his *Rights of Man* only in passing in his "An Appeal from the New to the Old Whigs." Paine was still intent on carrying forward his argument, and besides everyone knew he was working on a second part, and many were anxious to see it, including the government which pursued him after its appearance. The authorities thought Paine was more dangerous than just an ordinary radical writer and thinker for at least three reasons. First, the English regarded him by now as a foreigner, and by virtue of that status clearly disloyal to the crown. This development had a curious ironic twist when the French government during the Reign of Terror recognized only Paine's English background and considered him a potential spy in its midst. But despite his French citizenship, Paine always considered himself an American, although at times he referred to himself as a citizen of the world (notably in *RM* 228). He had, after all, spent his adult life as a writer out of England, indeed fighting against his native country for the American cause, and he continued his vituperative assaults on British institutions. Only now he was doing so from England's traditional enemy, France, at a time when menacing events were unfolding and tearing away at the heart of British traditions and institutions.

Second, Paine was not an advocate of change in one nation at a time. He had supported the separation of America from England, but at that time he had not directly called for the overthrow of the British crown. In responding to Burke's condemnation of the French Revolution, however, Paine now called for world revolution. The rights of man were not spatially and temporally specific: they were the inheritance of all people everywhere. "A nation has at all times an inherent indefeasible right to abolish any form of Government it finds inconvenient," he had written in the *Rights of Man*, "and establish such as accords with its interest, disposition, and happiness." (*RM* 143) Finally, Paine's anti-clericalism, his support of the disestablishment of church and state, frightened many of those who would have normally supported his anti-monarchical, anti-aristocratic position. It was because of these three factors that the Earl of Mornington in July of 1791 had written to Interior Minister Grenville demanding the government indict Paine for libeling the king, lords, and commons. Once Paine published Part Two of the *Rights of Man* the following February, the government soon placed both him (in absentia) and his book on trial for seditious libel.

Paine completed the second part of his great work in the fall of 1791. He found, through a recommendation of Thomas Christie, a printer by the name of Thomas Chapman, who not only wanted to print Part Two but also a new edition of Part One. Paine agreed, but when Chapman wanted to purchase the rights to the *Rights of Man* for a thousand pounds, Paine refused. "I would never put it in the power of any printer or publisher to suppress or alter a work of mine, by making him master of the copy, or give to him the right of selling it to any minister, or to any other person, or to treat as a mere matter of traffic, that which I intended should operate as a principle," he wrote. After this refusal, despite the fact that Chapman had almost the entire book in print, Paine had to find another printer, and in fact the work was distributed jointly by Chapman and J.S. Jordan, who had printed the first part in 1791. He wrote to Jordan that neither he (Jordan) nor Johnson (another printer of the pamphlet) would suffer any consequences for anything illegal in the pamphlet: "I will, as soon as I am made acquainted with [the sanction of any kind of authority], appear and answer for the work personally."[1]

Paine had hoped that the second part would appear before the opening of the January session of Parliament. But due to Chapman's refusal to continue the printing, the work's appearance was delayed. In the meantime, William Pitt, knowing full well what the latest blast would be from Thomas Paine, tried to undercut Paine by proposing a tax reduction and other fiscal ideas that Paine was suggesting in his second part of the *Rights of Man*. It was apparent Pitt wanted to be perceived as a reformer. Paine was well aware of this: he wrote in an appendix that his and Pitt's proposals for tax reductions were so similar that "either the Author had taken the hint from Mr. Pitt, or Mr. Pitt from the Author."

How did Pitt know what Paine was going to say before the appearance of his work? It seems that George Chalmers, whose nefarious biography of Paine had been subsidized by the crown and had already appeared, worked in the royal postal service. The printer of this book was none other than Thomas Chapman, who had given Chalmers easy access to the printing studio, "where he would have the opportunity of seeing what was going on." (*RM* 275-78) Chalmers simply read what Paine had written in advance of publication and reported it to Pitt. Leaving publication in the hands of his friends in London, Paine left for Paris, where since the Revolution, his official reception had been quite different from his experiences in London.

Many French intellectuals knew who Paine was by the time the first part of the *Rights of Man* was published in 1791. A French version of *Common Sense*, entitled *Affaires de l'Angleterre et de l'Amérique*, had appeared shortly after its American debut in 1776, although for a while many people in France thought its author was John Adams. The translation did not include the anti-monarchical portions of the pamphlet or Paine's argument that the Bible did not admit monarchy. After all, France was still very much a monarchy in 1776, and Paine had stated in *Common Sense* that the scriptures had condemned monarchy as one of the sins of the Jews. (*CS* 73) Now, in 1791, a new and complete translation of *Common Sense* was published and cheered in the newspaper, *Le Moniteur*. Paine, the newspaper editorialized, was "the most determined champion of republican principles."[2] With the publication of the second part of the *Rights of Man* on February 16, 1792, Paine's most progressive tract to date, not only every revolutionary leader, but every radical became instantly familiar with the name of Thomas Paine.

The first part of the *Rights of Man* responded directly to Burke's condemnation of the French Revolution.[3] Paine's goal was to defend the cause of individual rights and liberty, which he hoped was inevitably spreading throughout Europe, including to somnolent old England. Everyone would soon reawaken to claim their natural rights. In this, "the age of Revolutions, in which everything may be looked for," the people would lash out against tyranny wherever it festered. Now, one year later, Burke's presence is barely noticeable in Paine's second installment. Although Paine demanded in his preface to know why Burke refused to respond directly to Paine's answer to Burke's *Reflections*, he had no intention of engaging in a political dialogue with him. He amusingly argued only that Burke was indeed right when he had claimed in his *Reflections* that "the age of chivalry is gone." Never known for his own chivalry, Paine said that Burke's refusal to respond to Paine's criticisms of the British monarchy and his celebration of the revolutionary events in France proved that Burke was rude and inconsiderate. Paine decided "to take the public for my guide (and the world know I am not a flatterer) that what they do not think worthwhile to read, is not worth mine to answer." (*RM* 155)

In any case, Paine chose to ignore Burke and instead turned to other more important, indeed critical matters. These went beyond the political to the social sphere of life, specifically, to the need for social services for those who lacked the means to provide the basic necessities for themselves: the less fortunate in society, which included the poor, the elderly, the young, the newly married. In the first part of the *Rights of Man*, Paine had already indicated a change in his thinking. There, rather than focus solely on individual rights and liberties, he added a new twist: the idea that individuals were part of a larger community, the Nation (which he invariably capitalized), which embodied something he referred to as "the general will." These ideas were firmly based in the writings of the great Genevan social and political theorist, Jean-Jacques Rousseau, who, in his 1762

The Social Contract, discussed in detail communitarian, rather than purely individual or political, concerns. The change in Paine's thinking was as profound and radical as it was significant. It represented a shift to a faith in the sovereignty of the people, the nation, or as Rousseau articulated it, the General Will, a corporate political will that went beyond the will of the atomized individual.

The origins of Paine's emphasis on communal and national rights and social responsibility are not entirely clear. The evidence is just too sketchy to determine for certain whether he was directly or indirectly influenced by Jean-Jacques Rousseau. Paine did cite Rousseau's work in the *Rights of Man*, just as, for example, he had cited Adam Smith's *Wealth of Nations* in Part One. Moreover, he was familiar with the works of Rousseau, because just a few months after the appearance of the second part, Paine published "An Essay for the Use of New Republicans," in which he referred approvingly to Rousseau's condemnation of kings. Besides, in France, Rousseau's ideas were always discussed. Everyone used his vocabulary and everyone talked about him. "In a sense, it is true, the whole generation of 1789 was Rousseauist," historian Alfred Cobban observes.[4] Paine's association with French writers and thinkers like Nicolas de Bonneville and the Marquis de Condorcet invited discussions not only about Rousseau but about the people's collective responsibilities.

Rousseau's concern, like Paine's, was to define the limits of authority: who to obey and to what extent.[5] Unlike Locke, who argued that the people had certain inalienable natural rights and liberties that they must act upon when tyranny threatened their political independence, Rousseau refused to identify human beings as atomized, isolated individuals. They had communal, even national, obligations: social actions, care, nurturance, all must be a part of one's life. For Rousseau it was important for the people to attach their will to society's needs, desires, and direction of the nation to be truly free. This concept, Rousseau called the General Will. Citizens would know that their individual, competitive selves were part of a larger, almost organic whole, like "cells in the human body," as historian Carol Blum puts it."[6] Good citizens were good when their interests and desires merged with the state, the nation itself, and became one. For Rousseau, the General Will was primarily an ethical concept, a goal of goodness and virtue for the nation to achieve. For Paine, the General Will was a political ideal. He reflected this notion in a statement, which used the very term "general will."

> The greatest forces that can be brought into the field of revolutions are reason and common interest. Where these can have the opportunity of acting, opposition dies with fear, or crumbles away by conviction. It is a great standing which they have now universally obtained; and we may hereafter hope to see revolutions, or changes in governments, produced with the same quiet operation by which any measure, determinable by reason and discussion, is accomplished. When a nation changes its opinion and habits of thinking, it is no longer to be governed as before; but it would not only be wrong, but bad policy, to attempt by force what ought to be accomplished by reason. Rebellion consists in forcibly opposing the general will of a nation, whether by a party or by a government. There ought, therefore, to be in every nation a method of occasionally ascertaining the state of public opinion with respect to government. (*RM* 265)

The weighing of public opinion could be done by gauging the General Will. This was a decisive moment in Paine's thinking as he moved to the communitarian, national ideals implicit in the work of Jean-Jacques Rousseau. Those ideals Paine now incorporated in the second part of the *Rights of Man*, and they reappeared a few years later in his last great work, *Agrarian Justice*.

Paine dedicated Part Two to his old friend and comrade, the Marquis de Lafayette, then serving the French nation as commander-in-chief of the Army of the Center, whose forces were embroiled in combat against the Austrians and Prussians. He promised Lafayette that if a spring campaign was likely, "I will come and join you. Should the campaign commence," he went on, "I hope it will terminate in the extinction of German despotism, and in establishing the freedom of all Germany." (*RM* 151-52) Since nations knew their true interests, they must act on those interests, he told Lafayette, and not wait for some distant time in the future. In essence, Paine advocated nothing short of world revolution, or what he called "the prospect of a general revolution in governments." (*RM* 266)

He continued in this vein: "The iron is becoming hot all over Europe. The insulted German and the enslaved Spaniard, the Russ and the Pole are beginning to think. The present age will hereafter merit to be called the age of reason, and the present generation will appear to the future as the Adam of a new world." (*RM* 268) This, Paine's first use of the term "age of reason," gave credence to his view that the nations of the world were in fact moving quickly into a new era of politics. But revolution had to be first, and it had to take place in every nation. Paine even projected, perhaps having Miranda in mind, "the independence of South America." (*RM* 269) After all, the nations which first experienced revolution and were now free had a duty to bring the rights of man to all people throughout the world, in effect "rescue the world from bondage." (*RM* 267) This call for world revolution was echoed by the French National Convention just a few months later, when it declared that "the French nation will extend its fellowship and assistance to all people who wish to enjoy liberty."[7]

Paine's emphasis on the nation, on the corporate nature of human beings, rather than on their individuality, ran throughout the *Rights of Man*, Part Two. In fact, he had been moving in this direction as early as 1789 when he defined nation in very Rousseauist terms as having a collective, or corporate, personality. "A Nation," he wrote, "is only a great individual, and that which is good or bad character for an individual is good or bad character for a Nation."[8] In the second part of the *Rights of Man*, his language was full of the influence of Rousseau. Paine argued that the nation was not simply a unit of many parts with separate functions. It was not merely a body comparable to the human body. It was, more particularly, "like a body contained within a circle, having a common center, in which every radius meets." (*RM* 181) It was not a mechanical, but an organic, Benthamite whole.

Throughout the work, Paine emphasized this idea. "The nation itself . . . possesses a perpetual stamina as well of body as of mind." "The first thing is a nation has a right to establish a constitution." "A nation can have no interest in being wrong." "Government is nothing more than a national association." "It is only by each nation reforming its own [government] that the whole can be improved, and the full benefits of reformation enjoyed." "Long experience . . . has shown that reforms of this kind are not those which old governments wish to promote, and therefore it is to nations, and not to such governments, that these matters present themselves." (*RM* 182, 198, 217, 266) The reform that these nations might expect to experience in the future would come about through revolutionary action. Once reformed, they would then try to form even larger collectives. They would form "connections and conventions, and when a few are thus confederated, the progress will be rapid, till despotism and corrupt government be totally expelled at least out of two quarters of the world." (*RM* 270) The entire globe would be united in one strong, historic republic.

A strong strain of apocalyptic thinking runs through Paine's call for world transformation and unification. Historians who have studied the period have often detected how, in times of crisis, writers will begin to have millennial expectations on a purely secular, rather than theological, level. Instead of longing for the return or coming of the messiah to reign over a thousand-year period of peace, harmony, and security, these secular millennialists argued that the future (often the very near future) held a transformation of life so radical that a new age of humanity would soon arrive. During this time of change, all corrupt political and social institutions would be overturned and all people at long last truly free.

Paine, too, was affected by these emotions. He often used imagery of evil followed by good, dark turned into light, winter followed by springtime to express his millennial longings, which reflected his belief in the presence of the divine in all things, a presence which he sometimes referred to as Providence with a female personality. He had already done this in his American revolutionary writings. In the *Rights of Man*, he mused that Providence did not say that the people could only choose between an elective or hereditary monarchy, "as if she had left to man no other choice with respect to government than between two evils." (*RM* 173) Today, the world moved beyond monarchy. It experienced "a morning of reason rising upon man on the subject of government, that has not appeared before." "From a small spark, kindled in America, a flame has arisen, not to be extinguished."[9] (*RM* 208, 210) In his most famous, most oft-quoted passage in the *Rights of Man*, he offered his readers a magnificent sign that the political winter had turned the corner:

> It is now towards the middle of February. Were I to take a turn
> in the country, the trees would present a leafless winterly
> appearance. As people are apt to pluck twigs as they walk along,
> I perhaps might do the same, and by chance might observe, that
> a single bud on that twig had begun to swell. I should reason
> very unnaturally, or rather not reason at all, to suppose this was
> the only bud in England which had this appearance. Instead of
> deciding thus, I should instantly conclude, that the same appear-
> ance was beginning, or about to begin, everywhere; and though
> the vegetable sleep will continue longer on some trees and plants
> than on others, and though some of them may not blossom for
> two or three years, all will be in leaf in the summer, except for
> those which are rotten. What pace the political summer may
> keep with the natural, no human foresight can determine. It is,
> however, not difficult to perceive that the spring has begun.
> (*RM* 272-73)

Monarchy and aristocracy (the very essence of all that was satanic)
would not last another seven years in the enlightened countries of
Europe. (*RM* 156)

Paine's ideas in this period were not always consistently
Rousseauist. He sometimes parted company with the Genevan, who
rejected the idea of representation. The sovereignty of the people, as
expressed through the General Will, could never be divided, and no
person could ever represent the wishes and desires of another person.
"Sovereignty," wrote Rousseau, "is indivisible for the same reason that
it is inalienable, for either the will is general, or it is not. It is the will
of either the people as a whole or of only a part."[10] He believed that
only in a direct democracy did the General Will operate without corruption, but Paine here disagreed, because he believed in representation. For him, the highest development of democracy was not when
all the people directly decided the laws of their community in town
meetings. The highest form of government was through representative government, which Paine believed would soon prevail throughout Europe. Nations "will become acquainted, and the animosities
and prejudices fomented by the intrigue and artifice of courts, will
cease." (*RM* 268) God was on the side of the just, and the just were

those who brought progress to the world through revolutionary transformation and the republic.

Monarchy, "the popery of government," was the embodiment of the Antichrist, which had crushed for centuries the rights and liberties of the people. (*RM* 184) Monarchy had come into the world through evil actions—through war and plundering—by "ruffian torturing ruffian." From the wicked deeds of "banditti of robbers" (a phrase quite close to one he had used in *Common Sense* to describe William the Conqueror's men) came the practice of kings of extracting revenue from their subject people, and when they saw how easy this was, they maintained the practice, calling it the law of the land. (*RM* 168)

This was why it must take an apocalyptic blast of enlightenment and revolution to change the world. As America had demonstrated, he wrote in the *Rights of Man*, "the sun needs no inscription to distinguish him [liberty] from darkness," an image he had also used in *Common Sense*.[11] America had acted not merely for herself: "She made a stand, not for herself only, but for the world," and now that revolutions have occurred in some places, "it is natural to expect that other revolutions will follow." The result will be "universal peace, civilization, and commerce . . . the happy lot of man." There is nothing that anyone could do to stop this chain of events, for God has ordained it. Monarchy has for centuries been the cause of war, "human wretchedness," "human butchery." Evil human will had replaced God's will: "This certainly is not the condition that Heaven intended for man." This state of affairs would soon end because "government founded on a moral theory, on a system of universal peace, and on the indefeasible hereditary Rights of Man is now revolving from west to east by a stronger impulse than the government of the sword revolved from east to west. It interests not particular individuals, but nations, in its progress, and promises a new era to the human race." (*RM* 159, 161, 162)

New constitutional political structures were being tested, first in America, now in France. It was an age of political experimentation, patterned on Paine's own scientific and engineering experiments with his iron bridge design and his other attempts at invention. The Americans had created a new form of government, which should act as a model for the world. America, a land of such great mixture and diversity, might have appeared to be an unlikely place for people being able to work together. This harmony was the creation of the republic, the only political organization in which "the representative element" checked the excesses of direct democracy, with its tendency to fall into chaos and anarchism. The republic was "no other than government established and conducted for the interest of the public, as well individually as collectively."

> Simple democracy was society governing itself without the aid of secondary means. By ingrafting representation upon democracy, we arrive at a system of government capable of embracing and confederating all the various interests and every extent of territory and population; and that also with advantages as much superior to hereditary government, as the republic of letters is to hereditary literature. It is on this system that the American government is founded. It is representation ingrafted upon democracy. (*RM* 178, 180)

Pure and simple, this was the image of good government in the classical republican tradition, now fixed in a Rousseauist demand for social responsibility and welfare.

The classical-republican tradition, with its origins in the thought of Aristotle, presumed that each of the three known positive forms of government, namely monarchy, aristocracy, and democracy, tended to degenerate into its negative form. By finding a balance between them in the same political structure with a system of representation, the tyranny of monarchy, the oligarchy of aristocracy, and the anarchy of democracy could all be overcome. Then the interests inherent in each of these negative forms would be arrested and government would work to achieve the common good, the public interest, the very meaning, as Paine pointed out, of the original term *res publica*, "the public thing" or good. (*RM* 178) The Americans had succeeded in doing just that, by installing the monarchical principle in an indirectly elected president, which was checked by an "aristocratic," indirectly elected Senate and a democratic directly elected House of Representatives. This, he argued, should stand as a model for the world.

Paine indicated how this fusion of interests worked when, "by the simple operation of constructing government on the principles of society and the rights of man, every difficulty retires, and all the parts are brought into cordial unison." It was an utopic dream come true: "There, the poor are not oppressed, the rich are not privileged. Industry is not mortified by the splendid extravagance of a court rioting at its expense. Their taxes are few, because their government is just; and as there is nothing to render them wretched, there is nothing to engender riots and tumults." Even if other nations rejected the American model, they must now experiment with their own ideas of the new era. For "revolutions create genius and talents," making every man "a proprietor in government." Indeed, he concluded, as Archimedes said of mechanical power, the people could now say about reason and liberty: " 'Had we,' said he, 'a place to stand upon, we might raise the world.' " (*RM* 167, 176, 188, 159) The republic was the world-historical event of the present.

Raising the world to this new level of political development was only half of Paine's argument in this, the second part of the *Rights of Man*, and it was at this point that despite the radicalism of his secular millennialist politics, he moved even further when he argued that social progress was just as critical as political transformations. "I speak an open and disinterested language, dictated by no passion but that of humanity," he wrote: "Independence is my happiness, and I view things as they are, without regard to place or person; my country is the world, and my religion is to do good." (*RM* 228) True transformation now shifted from politics to society, a significant and meaningful moment in the evolution of Paine's thought in particular and in social criticism generally. The focus was no longer on political rights and liberties as they affected the individual. It was, rather, on government's responsibility to provide a minimum level of social benefits for citizens who were incapable of caring for themselves.[12]

It was here more than anywhere else in this work that Paine de-emphasized Lockean theories of individual rights and liberties to focus on a Rousseauist (and modern) conception of community and communal responsibility.[13] A great deal of this responsibility, once again, centered on the financial stability of the republic, especially one without a horrific indebtedness. The state must reflect the needs of the people and respond to these needs by doing two things: reducing the taxes, which played most heavily on the poor, especially the working poor, and providing the necessary social services, which would be designed to help those who were unable to receive places in court, pensions from the crown, and other benefits from the king. For the first, "public money . . . was not the product of riches only, but of the hard earnings of labor and poverty. It is drawn even from the bitterness of want and misery. Not a beggar passes, or perishes in the streets, whose mite is not in that mass." (*RM* 237)

His solutions have a significantly contemporary ring to them, as the national debt of the United States in the mid-1990s reached over four trillion dollars. Reducing size of the government workforce and the pay of government officials (what Burke in the 1770s had favored as "economical reform") were two ways to reduce government spending. Paine even included deducting a certain amount of money from officials' salaries when they did not show up for work. As for the first, however, he urged not the reduction, but the increase in spending on social services, and here, for the eighteenth century, he cut a new swath in the arena of social welfare. How to provide relief for the poor was a problem he worried about seriously. He had witnessed poverty in England, America, and France, and he all too often himself felt poverty's sting. Although he could not foresee the rise of the modern social welfare state, in the *Rights of Man*, Part Two, Paine laid out several programs which he thought would alleviate the condition of the poor as well as those who were simply not in a position to help themselves, namely the elderly, young children, and newlyweds.

His first recommendation was to abolish all taxes that the poor were required by law to pay, and then to take the amount they had been paying, double it, and return it to them. Just who were these poor? Paine counted two classes of poor, large families with children and the elderly. First, every child for the first fourteen years of life should receive a governmental benefit of four pounds per year so their parents could send them to school. In this way, the poor would have income, and ignorance would be abolished. Second, for the elderly, Paine had two plans, one for those who reached age fifty, another for those at sixty. All persons between fifty and sixty (on the assumption they were still working and receiving an income) were to receive six pounds per year. After a person reached sixty and retired, payments increased to ten pounds per year. In addition, Paine proposed a system of public education, something he was soon to work with Condorcet on in France in the Committee of Public Instruction.[14] Subsidies from the government should go to the localities for local instruction to pay the teachers. At the same time, the government would give each family ten shillings per child per year "for the expense of schooling." He also thought it important to provide some assistance to newlyweds, who should receive a grant of twenty shillings at the moment they were married, and to new mothers, who should also receive twenty shillings for each child.

Finally, for those who died long distances from family and friends, the government should provide a payment to make certain they had a proper funeral. Paine also proposed that the government erect "employment buildings," that is, public employment facilities, to insure full employment for every able-bodied person in need of work. (*RM* 246) Here he verged on the socialist (but not communist) ideal that Marx himself would make famous more than fifty years. Payment was to be based on one's work:

> The only condition to be, that for so much, or so many hours work, each person shall receive so many meals of wholesome food, and a warm lodging, at least as good as a barrack. That a certain portion of what each person's work shall be worth shall be reserved, and given to him, or her, on their going away; and that each person shall stay as long, or as short time, to come as often as he choose, on these conditions. (*RM* 247)

For Paine, "this support . . . is not the nature of a charity, but of a right." (*RM* 245, 243) It is a form of social security for the working poor, an extraordinary idea for an eighteenth century mind.

But then the *Rights of Man*, Part Two, was in sum a remarkable document. Not only must the republic be established with its requisite institutional safeguards—its checks and balances and political rights and liberties: it must also include the economic rights and social responsibilities that made it possible for all citizens to enjoy the minimal necessities of life. While it is impossible to say whether its proposals directly or even indirectly influenced the development of what in the twentieth century is known as the social welfare state, it is certain that the *Rights of Man* was one of the first expressions of why government must care for its less fortunate citizens. Paine thought that they deserved no less because in the final analysis all people were the children of God. In the concluding passages of the work he revealed that in part he was motivated by his own religious principles.

Twice, he declared that "every religion is good, that teaches man to be good." (*RM* 260, 270) Being "good" necessarily meant serving God by working for the well-being of one's fellow human beings because the greatest offense to "the great Father of all," he wrote, was when "we seek to torment and render each other miserable." Paine was convinced that his proposals were godly, that he was in fact acting as God's agent on earth, chosen to perform the tasks he had undertaken and the efforts he made to educate and enlighten his audience.

> For my own part, I am fully satisfied that what I am now doing, with an endeavor to conciliate mankind, to render their condition happy, to unite nations that have hitherto been enemies, and to extirpate the horrid practice of war, and break the chains of slavery and oppression, is acceptable in his sight, and being the best service I can perform, I act it cheerfully. (*RM* 271)

Historian John Pocock has written that "perhaps the achievement of the *Rights of Man* was to employ its author's genius for invective, derision, and the creation of a mass public in the foundation of a subculture of disrespect."[15] And yet, this assessment looks only at Paine as a subversive and misses his role as a prophet, something he thought he was: a man absolutely certain that he was right because he fought for the cause he believed was just and, ultimately, good.

In the spring of 1792, Paine immediately ran into some serious problems. Peter Whiteside, who had helped Paine obtain his English patent for his bridge and who was a close associate of Robert

Morris (now having severe financial difficulties), declared bankrupt-cy. A creditor by the name of Mark Gregory learned from Whiteside that Paine had an outstanding debt to Whiteside of some two hundred pounds. Gregory demanded payment from Paine, and when he refused to or did not pay, Gregory had the authorities arrest Paine at the London Tavern during an April 13th banquet sponsored by the Society for Constitutional Information. Sent off to prison in King's Head, Paine was released an hour later with the help of Joseph Johnson and another bookseller, although not before the London newspapers were full of stories about the "republican debtor."[16]

The following week he attended another meeting of the SCI, this time without any scandal. He then set off to visit his aunt in Bromley (Kent), where according to his friend John Hall, he wanted to write a "funeral oration" for Burke, who in fact would not die for another five years.[17] While in Kent, he lived with the same William Sharp, who in June made the engraving of Paine from the Romney portrait.

The British government under William Pitt, in the mean-time, was quite distressed about the events in France and aware that any unrest in England was potentially very dangerous. Discontent among some artisans and sailors along with the publication of the *Rights of Man*, Part Two, was enough for the authorities to act. While Paine was in Kent, Pitt went after Paine's publisher, J. S. Jordan. By the time Paine returned to London on May 14, Jordan was already scheduled to appear in the Court of the King's Bench to answer charges of seditious libel. As Paine prepared a defense for Jordan with a lawyer named Bonney, and agreed to cover all legal fees, Jordan engaged his own counsel and betrayed his friend. Jordan, probably frightened for his life, decided it was a simpler matter to plead guilty and pay the fine. In addition, however, he turned all of his files over to the court.

On May 21, Paine was summoned to appear before the same court. That same day the king issued a royal proclamation against all seditious writings printed in England.[18] Was it directed against Paine? In fact it was, as Pitt admitted in an answer to a question from Charles James Fox in Parliament, although neither Paine nor his book were mentioned in the decree. Pitt told Fox just four days after

Paine's summons that Paine's writings "struck at hereditary nobility
. . . the destruction of monarchy and religion and the total subversion
of the established form of government."[19] The decree itself was as
broad as it was vague:

> Whereas diverse wicked and seditious writings have been print-
> ed, published, and industriously dispersed, tending to excite
> tumult and disorder, by endeavoring to raise groundless jeal-
> ousies and discontents in the minds of our faithful and loving
> subjects, respecting the laws and happy constitution of govern-
> ment, civil and religious, established in this kingdom, and
> endeavoring to vilify and bring into contempt the wise and
> wholesome provisions made at the time of the glorious revolu-
> tion. . . .
>
> We therefore being resolved as far as in us lies to repress the
> wicked and seditious practices aforesaid and to deter all persons
> from following so pernicious an example have thought fit, by the
> advice of our privy council, to issue this our royal proclamation
> solemnly warning all our loving subjects, as they tender their
> own happiness, and that of their posterity to guard against all
> such attempts which aim at the subversion of all regular govern-
> ment within this kingdom and which are inconsistent with the
> peace and order of society; and earnestly exhorting them at all
> times and to the utmost of their power to avoid and discourage
> all proceedings tending to produce riots and tumults; and we do
> strictly charge and command all our magistrates in and through-
> out the kingdom of Great Britain that they do make diligent
> inquiry in order to discover the authors and printers of such
> wicked and seditious writings aforesaid, and all others who shall
> disperse the same.[20]

Pitt's political enemy in the Commons, Charles James Fox (by now,
a longtime friend of Paine) denounced the proclamation, demanding
the ministry to mention the specific name of any author and the title
of a work under suspicion of libel.

Fox was answered by Henry Dundas, the Interior Minister
(he had replaced Grenville, when the latter became Foreign
Minister), who argued that the name of a book was not so important.
It was rather the *ideas* in the book that were the catalyst for London

radicalism. Paine responded to both Dundas and Attorney General Archibald Macdonald. He told Macdonald that despite rumors that he was in hiding, in fact he intended to defend his book should a trial take place. He claimed that Burke was ultimately behind the prosecution because he knew he had lost the debate with Paine. And besides, Burke, as everyone knew, was receiving 1,500 pounds per year as a government pensioner.[21]

In a long, open letter to Dundas, claiming that he had written only in a "spirit of benignity" and a strong "inculcation of moral principles," he ended with the words, "Not your obedient humble servant, But the contrary, Thomas Paine."[22] Dundas was not moved by any of this. He wrote Grenville, saying "I saw the advertisements sometime ago for the sale of the cheap editions of Mr. Payne's [sic] book and immediately took the proper steps upon it."[23]

The crown's case against Paine was set for June 8, and he actually appeared in court that day, only to find his trial was postponed until December 18. Despite that, he continued to write various government officials vituperative and sarcastic letters. He had Horne Tooke present a letter to Surrey County Lord Lieutenant, Onslow Cranley, who had praised the royal proclamation as an attempt to save England's "happy constitution," and the freeholders of Surrey. Accompanying the letter was a small gift from Paine: one hundred copies of the *Rights of Man* and one thousand copies of his letter to Dundas. He wanted Cranley and the others to be accurate in their accusations against him. He closed by sending them his "sincere wishes for their happiness, and for that of the nation in general," and he was undoubtedly serious in his sentiments.[24] Hearing that Horne Tooke was not permitted to read the letter (though it was printed in the newspapers), Paine wrote a follow-up letter to Cranley four days later on June 21:

> [It is] no wonder that you should be against reforms, against the freedom of the press, and the right of investigation. To you, and to others of your description, these are dreadful things; but you should also consider, that the motives which prompt you to act, ought, by reflection, to compel you to be *silent*.[25]

A similar letter went off to the Sheriff and freeholders of Sussex County on June 30—just as full of vituperation and venom. Because Sussex included the town of Lewes, where Paine had once lived, he demanded that the officials trot out all the criminal records to see whether Paine's name appeared on any of them. "Many of you will recollect, while I resided among you, there was not a man more firm and open in supporting the principles of liberty than myself, and I still pursue, and ever will, the same path."[26]

During the late summer, Paine readied himself for a return to Paris not to escape prosecution but because on August 26, the French National Assembly, on a motion by Marguerite-Elie Guadet, a leader of the Girondins who would later be outlawed for his criticisms of Robespierre and Marat, declared Paine a citizen of France. (Guadet was eventually hunted down and brought back to Paris to the guillotine.) The Assembly also chose other foreigners to carry French citizenship, such as Priestley, a Prussian baron-turned-journalist Jean-Baptiste (Anacharsis) Clootz, George Washington, and Welshman David Williams, author of the 1789 *Letters on Political Liberty*, who, like Price and Priestley, was a Dissenter. In addition, Alexander Hamilton and James Madison were named. Guadet's proposal was unequivocal in granting full, not honorary, citizenship to these men. It stated that "the National Assembly, in considering these men, by their writings and their courage, who have served the cause of liberty and prepared the emancipation of the people, cannot be treated as foreigners. . . . [The Assembly] decrees the honor of French citizenship to Dr. Joseph Priestley, to Thomas Payne" [the French spelling], and on the others.[27] One historian has argued that Paine and indeed all these men, including those originally from foreign countries who were executed during the Terror, now "were really French citizens," and not merely honorary ones.[28]

Almost immediately, Paine, Clootz, Williams, and several other foreigners were also elected to the new National Convention designed to write yet another constitution for France. Only Paine and Clootz actually took their seats. Although elected a delegate to the Convention from four constituencies, Paine took his seat as a member from Pas-de-Calais, which had been the first to elect him. He was especially moved to respond to Pas-de-Calais, because one of the electors, Achille Audibert, had traveled to London to tell him the splendid news. Paine wanted to remain in England to fight the prosecution of the *Rights of Man*, but Audibert told him he would be more useful in Paris constructing a democratic government. Besides, Audibert had with him a highly flattering and congratulatory letter from Hérault de Séchelles, the president of the Assembly: "Men of genius, the most capable for their wisdom and virtue, she [France] now calls to give to her people a government the most proper to insure their liberty and happiness."[29]

Like some of his more extremist revolutionary comrades, Marie-Jean Hérault de Séchelles later became a member of the ruling junta in the Reign of Terror. Born into a wealthy family, he became a leading attorney in the king's court, a favorite of Marie Antoinette until the Revolution, which he joined in 1789. A man wholly dedicated to making superficially good impressions, he stood for long hours in front of his mirror practicing gestures and training his voice. Along with Paine, Condorcet, and others, he helped draft the 1793 constitution, which never went into effect, because the Reign of Terror began before it could be implemented. With a shrug, he joined Robespierre, Louis Antoine de St. Just, and the others in the Terror's revolutionary tribunal. He did not see it to its end. He was executed as a supporter of Danton in April of 1794. He was the first of the twelve members of the Committee of Public Safety in the Terror to die.

Paine responded to Hérault's note with an equally adulatory address to the French people, published by Nicolas de Bonneville, a close friend and associate. Paine declared that the cause of France was now the cause of the world: "The scene that now opens itself to France extends far beyond the boundaries of her own dominions. Every nation is becoming her colleague, and every court is become her enemy." The brightness begun by America, now shining on France, was "a new ray of light . . . thrown over the world, and the Revolution will derive new strength by being universally understood."[30]

Paine left for Paris on September 13th with Audibert and John Frost, a lawyer and friend who had been a long-time member of the Society for Constitutional Information. On their way out, they were followed by government agents, who stopped them in Dover where the three were to stay the night and examined their luggage for letters, pamphlets, and other materials that might have contained treasonable works. According to one eyewitness account, a J. Mason, the agents kept them "an hour and five minutes in the room with the door locked a great part of the time." The officials even refused to let Frost go to "the necessary." When asked how much money he was carrying, Paine replied that he had about twenty-five guineas, and they let him keep it. Audibert apparently strenuously complained about the ill treatment and threatened to go to the English press with stories about the agents' actions. If the newspapers refused to print them, he then said he would, at his own expense, plaster the streets the London with posters condemning their actions and that of the crown. The agents confiscated a pamphlet that Paine had recently written attacking the king's proclamation declaring such works wicked and seditious.

Followed right up until they boarded their ship for France, Paine was once again subjected to a strict search of his belongings before he left for Calais. On the dock a huge crowd had gathered to "stare at Tom Paine as they called him," Mason continued. "He was hissed a great deal, and many ridiculous speeches were made relative to his trade (he has been a staymaker at Dover). The crowd increased very much: the wind being slack the packet was obliged to be towed out. I believe had we remained much longer they would have pelted him with stones from the beach." The crowd hurled the worst epithets at him with shouts of "down with Tom Paine," "death to the corsetmaker," and "down with the traitor."

This account was most likely accurate, although Mason, probably a government agent himself, was no friend to Paine. He concluded his testimony with the observation that "personally [Paine] is a very mean looking man." He added a comment on the relative sanity of the people of Calais for having voted Paine as their delegate to the Convention. "It is in my opinion a disgrace to them, rather than a merit, that a better representative cannot be found at home with having recourse to a foreigner like him. He is the very picture of a journeyman tailor who has been drunk and playing at nine-pins for the three first days of the week and is returning to his work on

Thursday."

Arriving in Calais a few days later, Paine was greeted by a far different spectacle than his last view of England. In France, "the people flocked to see him, and it was talked of saluting him with the guards as he passed the Place d'Armes." A young girl ran up to him and attached the tricolor cockade to his hat. From the pier they walked to city hall with crowds of people greeting him with along the way. At the Constitutional Society of Calais, an official welcome awaited Paine as a citizen of Calais and its representative in the National Convention. There under a bust of Mirabeau draped with flags uniting France, Britain, and America, Paine proudly accepted the honor of becoming a citizen of Calais. There were so many shouts of "long live the nation" and "long live Thomas Paine" that no one could hear the speeches given on his behalf.[31]

Just after his arrival in Calais, Paine hurled a blast at Dundas and the Pitt ministry. His response to those who had written of their undying support of the government against sedition appeared in a work entitled, "Letter Addressed to the Addressers on the Late Proclamation" (a copy of which the agents had confiscated from Paine at Dover). In this work, he again pleaded with all Englishmen to call a constitutional convention in order to construct a true republic without Parliament and the king. "A national convention thus formed, would bring together the sense and opinions of every part of the nation, fairly taken. The science of government, and the interest of the public, and of the several parts thereof, would then undergo an ample and rational discussion, freed from the language of parliamentary disguise."[32] His movements were noted by the English spy Captain George Munro who reported Paine's every move to Lord Gower, the British ambassador in Paris. "Tom Payne [sic] . . . who only arrived here last night is on his road to take his seat. I have heard nothing of Dr. Priestly [sic]. He has perhaps more sense than to come among such fools."[33] Paine was never to return to the country of his birth. A new man was born: Thomas Paine, *citoyen de France, délégué du Pas-de-Calais.*

13 · The Revolution Declines

I n 1792, the Revolution in France established itself as a highly complex phenomenon. Even in the late-twentieth century, the nature, content, and meaning of what went on in France during this period is constantly being reassessed.[1] The Revolution was changing, evolving. France was at war both with itself and with several foreign powers. Internally, the royalist enemies of the French republic attacked the government in Paris and in the countryside. Externally, the old regime nations of Europe believed they were threatened by the new ideas emanating from Paris.

France had declared war on Austria in April of 1792. Prussia soon entered the fray, followed by Holland and Spain, and was to be joined in early 1793 by Great Britain. A month and a half before Paine's arrival, on August 10, 1792, massive demonstrations, led mainly by the Girondins, contributed to the end of the monarchy and the creation of the first republic, precisely what Paine and Condorcet had advocated a year earlier in the summer of 1791. The mobs stormed the Tuileries Palace—formerly a medieval fort once belonging to the Comte d'Artois, brother of Louis XVI—where the king and queen were virtual prisoners. With this invasion, the monarchy, for all intents and purposes, collapsed. Louis, Marie Antoinette, and the rest of the family fled to the Assembly, and thereafter remained incarcerated in the Temple. The Assembly quickly called for the election of a convention to write a constitution for the new republic of France.

Paine found himself thrown into the stormy sea of Parisian politics as one of the delegates of the newly elected National

Convention. At first, he found it easy to communicate his ideas to the various factions and to people with very different ideologies. He was universally regarded as a leader in revolutionary activity, an intense laborer for human progress and liberty. Many French thought that he had played a portentous role in the American Revolution, and that he could repeat that role in France. He either knew well or was acquainted with just about all the important leaders in Paris: from moderates like Jacques-Pierre Brissot de Warville and (pre-extremist) Maximilien Robespierre, who thought that France would gradually evolve into a republic, to the most extreme radicals (the sans-culottes and enragés), who believed in the establishment of a people's republic through rioting and terror.[2]

When he arrived in Paris in the fall of 1792, Paine was especially close in his political ideas to several progressive thinkers, some of whom were, ironically, aristocrats and clerics. Here he was consistent in his thinking, not just his associations. His friends still included the Marquis de Lafayette, the Abbé Sieyès, and the Marquis de Condorcet. When the Revolution took a pivotal shift toward extremism, Paine was allied with the Girondins and Robespierre. He never drew close to the most militant and fanatical revolutionary leaders, like Jean Paul Marat, who advocated the summary liquidation of all "enemies" of the Revolution and the republic.

For now, Paine's political allegiances were with the Girondins, mainly lawyers, former aristocrats, and merchants, who made up the moderate republican faction until its collapse in June 1793. The name was ascribed to them, because initially most of the core of the leadership came from deputies sent from the Gironde region in southwestern France. Led by the journalist Brissot de Warville, they were originally known as Brissotins. Because so many of them spoke English and Paine never mastered the French language, he undoubtedly felt most comfortable with them. He was also quite sympathetic to their political principles. Also among them, along with Condorcet, were Bertrand de Barère, Jean-Marie and Jeanne-Manon (Madame) Roland de la Platière, and General Charles-François Dumouriez, who commanded the Army of the Republic on the northern and eastern fronts. Within a year, Barère joined forces with the radicalized Robespierre against the forces of moderation (including Paine). Dumouriez' defection to the Austrians in April 1793 as well as the Girondin inability to respond to the demands of the Paris working poor for tight economic controls contributed to their eventual downfall and to the Reign of Terror of 1793-94.

The Terror is the most confusing aspect of the entire Revolution, and its sweep and consequences are still debated among historians today. It was conducted by two organizations, the Committee of Public Safety, principally controlled by Robespierre, St. Just, and their allies, and the Committee for General Security, which had the authority to arrest anyone on mere suspicion of disloyalty to the republic. The goals of both committees were to combat counter-revolutionary threats to the regime, raise new armies to fight against France's enemies, and to regulate and stabilize the economy. Thousands of arrests were made, and thousands of people executed, although exact numbers are not known. Most of those guillotined hardly enjoyed due process: after a superficial trial before the Revolutionary Tribunal, which often included chaotic mob scenes, the condemned faced the guillotine the same day.

During the Terror, Paine joined forces with Georges-Jacques Danton, a lawyer who had first become known for his powerful revolutionary oratory, and Pierre Victurnien Vergniaud, also a lawyer, who had made his name in 1790 by successfully defending a group of peasants who had burned a castle. A leader of the Girondins, Vergniaud served a term as president of the Convention. Like Danton, Vergniaud supported the spread of revolutionary ideas by warfare against the major European ancien régime states, beginning with Austria and Prussia.

To the left of the Girondins were the Jacobins, so-called because they met in the Jacobin monastery, the Parisian name for the Dominicans. At first, the Jacobins and Girondins were united, but they split over the question of war against the old European authorities. The Girondins, who were in the majority, sought war, believing that the revolutionary principles they had achieved could be spread throughout the world. The Jacobins, which included Maximilien Robespierre, opposed war. Robespierre argued that no one liked the armed missionary (he soon changed his mind and became one himself).[3]   In 1792, the Jacobins comprised the radical wing of the Revolution and the Convention, representing the lower class and democratic sections of Paris, while the Girondins drew most of their power from the provinces. In the Convention, the Jacobins sat on the raised seats and were soon known as the Mountain. Their beliefs included a highly regulated economy, universal suffrage, public education, and the strict separation of church and state.

Between the Girondin and Jacobin factions lay the Plain, made up of the independent members of the Convention. The members of the Plain were leaderless most of the time, and unlike the Mountain, they sat on the lower benches in the Convention. Since they possessed a majority in that body, the Plain often controlled the voting until the Mountain took firm control through the Committee of Public Safety and instituted the Reign of Terror. The Plain did, however, have the last word, so to speak. It successfully ended the Terror in July 1794 with the overthrow and subsequent executions of Robespierre and St. Just.

In 1792, Paine had several journalist friends. Brissot de Warville was editor of *Le Patriote français*, a moderate, constitutionalist newspaper. Paine was a frequent contributor to these pages. Under the king, Brissot had been a police spy.[4] Paine's Girondin friend, François-Xavier Lanthenas, translated many of his works into French, and the two of them collaborated on inflammatory republican tracts. Paine was also a friend of Jean-Baptiste (Anacharsis) Clootz, who wrote favorably about Paine in *Le Patriote français* in the spring of 1792. Clootz, a strange personality, referred to himself as the Orator of the Human Race ("l'Orateur du genre humain"). In 1776, he had left Prussia for Paris in 1776 totally imbued with democratic and liberal ideals, which he claimed he had picked up from reading Diderot's great *Encyclopédie*. In 1790, he and a group of other foreigners styled themselves saviors of mankind, and he was elected to the National Assembly.

Changing his name to Anacharsis (it was more democratic-sounding, he thought, from a Greek perspective), he was best known for his advocacy of universalism. In August of 1792, just a few days after the slaughter of the king's Swiss guards, he paraded before the Assembly a huge crowd of people from different national groups, all

Thomas Paine, engraving by William Sharp
after a portrait in oil by George Romney, 1792.
(Courtesy of the Collection of The New-York Historical Society)

Published by R.Baldwin at the Rose in Pater Noster Row

John Locke (1632-1704).
(Courtesy of The Mansell Collection, London)

Augustus Henry, The Duke of Grafton (1735-1811).
(Williamson, *Thomas Paine: His Life, Work and Times*, 1973)

A Likely healthy Negro Wench, fit for any Service, to be fold : Enquire of the Printer.

THE Privateer Ship
Duke of Cumberland,
Capt. JAMES LILLY,

Mounting 16 Six-pounders, and is to carry 120 Men : Is now lying at the Watering-Place, and will proceed on her intended Cruize in a Week from the Date hereof : She is a compleat Ship and a prime failer. All Gentlemen Seamen and others, who intend making a Cruize, are defired to repair on board.

NOTICE IS HEREBY GIVEN,

THAT no Non-Subfcriber will for the future be admitted to the Dancing-Affembly, unlefs a Ticket be obtained from one of the Directors for his Admiffion, for which Application muft be made, at their Houfes, before

Privateer advertisement from the *New York Mercury,*
December 4, 1758, during the Seven Years War.
(Courtesy of the Collection of The New-York Historical Society)

Philadelphia in the late 18th century, by W. Birch, 1799.
(Courtesy of the Collection of The New-York Historical Society)

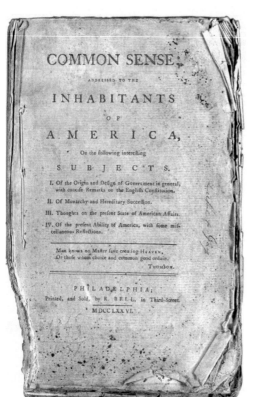

First edition of
Common Sense, 1776.
(Courtesy of The American
Philosophical Society)

Benjamin Franklin (1706-1790)
by Joseph Siffred Duplessis, 1778.
(Courtesy of The Fogg Museum,
Harvard University Art Museums)

Gouverneur Morris (1752-1816) and Robert Morris (1734-1806)
by Charles Willson Peale.
(Courtesy of The Pennsylvania Academy of Fine Arts, Philadelphia.
Bequest of Richard Ashhurst.)

The Marquis de Lafayette (1757-1834) during the American Revolution.
(Courtesy of the Collection of The New-York Historical Society)

George Washington (1732-1799)
by Charles Willson Peale.
(Courtesy of the Collection
of The New-York Historical Society)

John Adams (1735-1826).
(Courtesy of the Collection of
The New-York Historical Society)

Thomas Jefferson (1743-1826)
by Rembrandt Peale.
(Courtesy of the Collection
of The New-York Historical Society)

Bridge, modeled on Paine's design,
over the Wear River in Sutherland, England.
(Williamson, *Thomas Paine: His Life, Work and Times*)

Arrest of Louis XVI and Marie Antoinette at Varennes, June 1791.
(Courtesy of the Musée Carnavalet, Paris)

"A Democrat" with Paine's
Rights of Man in his pocket.
(Courtesy of The British Museum)

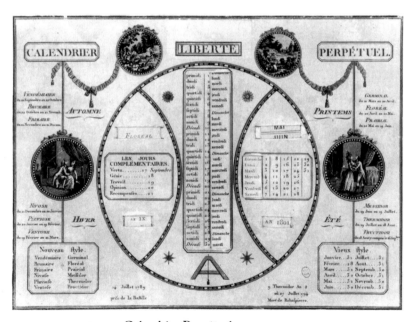

Calendrier Perpétuel,
designed by Philippe François Fabre D'Eglantine, 1755-1794.
(Courtesy of the Musée Carnavalet, Paris)

"The Rights of Man,
or Tommy Paine,
the little American tailor,
taking the measure of the crown
for a new pair of revolution breeches"
by James Gillray, 1791.
(Courtesy of The British Museum)

"Sedition, Levelling and Plundering," depicting a conspiring
Joseph Priestley (1733-1804) and Paine, by Isaac Cruikshank, 1792.
(Courtesy of The British Museum)

Last portrait of
Louis XVI by Ducreux, 1793.
(Courtesy of the Musée Carnavalet, Paris)

Execution of Louis XVI, January 21, 1793.
(Courtesy of the Musée Carnavalet, Paris)

Fashion Before Ease by James Gillray, 1793.
(Courtesy of The American Philosophical Society)

Georges Jacques Danton (1759- 1794)
on his way to execution, by Wille, 1794.
(Courtesy of the Musée Carnavalet, Paris)

"Cool Arguments!!!"
depicting defense counsel
Thomas Erskine (1750-1823)
by Isaac Cruikshank, 1794.
(Courtesy of The British Museum)

"Tom Paine's Nightly Pest," by James Gillray.
(Courtesy of The British Museum)

"Mad Tom's First Practical Essay on the Rights of Man,"
by Isaac Cruikshank, 1797.
(Courtesy of The British Museum)

"The Repeal of the Test Act" with Paine, in profile, standing on the right, Richard Price (1723-1791) above him on the pulpit with his hand held up, and Joseph Priestley on Price's right breathing fire and smoke. (Courtesy of The British Museum)

"Who Wants Me," depicting the radical Paine writing titles that allude to his works, by Isaac Cruikshank. (Courtesy of The American Philosophical Society)

Part 1, *Rights of Man*, 1792.
(Courtesy of The American
Philosophical Society)

Thomas Paine by John Wesley Jarvis, 1806.
(Courtesy of the Collection of The New-York Historical Society)

TOM PAINE'S HOUSE

Paine's New Rochelle cottage, c. 1812.
(Courtesy of the Collection of The New-York Historical Society)

293 Bleecker Street, New York,
Paine's residence,
Winter 1808-09,
photograph from 1903.
(Courtesy of the Collection
of The New-York Historical Society)

"Paine, Sin and the Devil,"
a letter from Satan to Paine
with an allusion to Joseph Priestley.
(Courtesy of The British Museum)

"The political champion turned resurrection man,"
depicting William Cobbett (1763?-1835) with Paine's bones.
(Courtesy of The British Museum)

dressed in their regional costumes. It made no political impact, though many people found it astoundingly silly. A few days later, his hired band demanded reimbursement for their services and for the costs of the costume rental. But he couldn't pay them.[5] Overall, Clootz favored the rapid spread of French republican ideas, especially to England, when the whole world would be united to France. England would simply become a section of the nation, "le département de la Tamise"—the department of the Thames.[6] Like Paine in 1792, Clootz was elected to the National Convention and, again like Paine, the following year consigned to the Luxembourg Prison.[7] Unlike Paine, however, he never made it out. He was executed on March 24, 1794.

Another journalist whom Paine respected was the young Nicolas de Bonneville. Paine was soon closely involved with Bonneville, who introduced him to Freemasonry and Theophilanthropy, which Paine wrote about extensively in later life. From 1797 until 1802, Paine lived with the Bonnevilles in Paris, and Marguerite, Nicolas' wife, and their sons eventually followed Paine to America.

Paine, of course, had many enemies as well as friends. His most fervent antagonist was Jean Paul Marat. Six years Paine's junior, trained as a physician, and author of several medical tracts in French and in English, Marat was one of the most radical ideologues of the Revolution. He abandoned medicine and turned to politics in 1789, creating his own political journal, *L'Ami du peuple*. This newspaper was his mouthpiece to unleash venomous hatred against anyone who held political power, especially aristocrats, including Lafayette (then the head of the National Guard), Mirabeau (then the unofficial head of the Assembly), and even the king himself. Because his attacks were so offensive, Marat was continually in hiding, finding security in the Paris sewers where he contracted a horrid skin disease that required him to take frequent warm baths. In the summer of 1792, he reemerged from hiding to take his ideological assaults public, and soon one of his targets was Thomas Paine, who had a reciprocal hatred for Marat. On reappearing in public, Marat called for the use of violence against his fellow French citizens.[8]

These calls in large part culminated by the end of the sum-

mer with the infamous massacres that took place ten days before
Paine arrived back in France in September. Huge mobs of sans-
culottes (those radicalized Parisian artisans, journeymen, and small
businessmen, who wore long pants to distinguish them from nobility
with their knee breeches) on September 2nd and 3rd crashed through
the barricades into jails all over France and murdered over 1,300 suspected royalist and reactionary prisoners.[9] Those killed represented
over one half of the people who were incarcerated in Paris at the time.
During the September Massacres, in some jails up to eighty percent
of the prisoners were butchered. Similar slaughters focusing mainly
on priests and royalists took place in prisons outside of Paris.

While Marat wanted Paine arrested and jailed, or at the very
least exiled, Robespierre at first would have none of it. Although
Robespierre had begun life in poverty, he studied law in Paris on a
scholarship. Generally a loner throughout life, due in part to his own
personal emphasis on austerity and rigidity, he did manage to have a
successful law career in his hometown of Arras. His portraits all show
him as a tall, unusually handsome man with a long, very straight nose
and an amiable, reassuring air. He had read a great deal of Rousseau's
writings and became convinced of Rousseau's ideas of democracy and
deism, but he was especially open to his emphasis on virtue, which
Robespierre interpreted as strict civic morality, a notion that soon
brought him the label the "Incorruptible."[10] Elected to the Estates
General in 1789, he became a member of the National (later the
Constituent) Assembly, promoting a democratic regime over monarchy. Joining the Jacobin Club early on, he was to become its leading
spokesman for change in the social mores and political structure of
France. Paine initially admired Robespierre, especially because of his
famous speech before the Assembly in 1791 decrying the death
penalty.[11] But Robespierre was soon swept up in the revolutionary
zeal of the Terror. He, along with St. Just and ten others, in the
spring of 1793 completed the downfall of the Girondins and other
moderate factions and eventually brought the Revolution and himself
to ruin.[12]

The Paris Commune, which was an offshoot of a civilian
authority established in that city during the Hundred Years War, was
soon controlled by Robespierre along with Marat, the radical atheist

Jacques René Hébert, and the extremist Pierre Gaspard Chaumette (the nominal leader of the Commune). The Paris Commune first dominated all of Paris, and then the provinces as it took the Revolution to the countryside by sending commissioners to all eighty-three *départements* into which France was now divided for administrative purposes and control. The Commune clamped down on a free press, sent to jail not only known supporters of monarchy but also some very ordinary, obscure people, and closed monasteries and convents.[13]

Chaumette, Hébert, and Marat headed the Cordeliers faction of the Jacobins, so-called because they had originally met in the former Franciscan monastery of Cordelier. Originally led by Danton and the journalist Camille Desmoulins in 1790, control of the Cordeliers was seized by the three radical extremists (Chaumette, Hébert, and Marat) just a year later. It had been Desmoulins's fiery out-of-doors speeches in July of 1789 that had significantly contributed to the uprising on the 14th of that month. When Jacobins joined with the Cordeliers, they formed the most radical, extremist faction of the Revolution, the Mountain. By June of 1793, the Mountain, in league with the Commune, controlled the Convention and within a very short period of time sent most of the Girondin leaders to prison or to their deaths.

As a result of the radicalization of the Cordeliers, historians have referred to them as Hébertists, which was not a name they themselves used. Chaumette and Hébert, both of whom despised royalty and religion in any form, argued for the creation of a democracy and a religion worshipping the goddess of Reason. Robespierre at first urged caution and moderation. Not until the trial of Louis XVI did he begin to lead the Revolution along its descent into Terror, replacing Hébert's religion of reason with his Cult of the Supreme Being, his faith in a Providence who watched over the Revolution.

This, then, was the situation when Thomas Paine arrived at White's Hotel d'Angleterre in Paris from Calais on September 19, 1792, at the peak of his journalistic career. Outlawed by one country, he was a national hero in two others, and now he sat in the French National Convention. He was there to do his honorable best, to help write a new and better constitution for France to overcome the weaknesses of the constitution of 1791.

Part of the problem was that France was not in control of its own destiny. First, it had been at war since spring with Austria and Prussia. Brissot and his Girondin allies had supported the war, first against Austria, which was soon joined by Prussia, then against Holland after the French republican armies tried and failed to seize that country. And second, civil war complicated matters as the provinces revolted against republican Paris. Earlier that year, in June, Lafayette and the National Guard had dispersed a mob that killed several people while attacking the Tuileries, the residence of the king and queen. It looked like a royalist attempt to regain control of government. At the same time, a rumor had spread that Marie-Antoinette had passed on French war plans to the Austrians (she had not).

In July, the English Duke of Brunswick, who commanded the Prussian troops, announced that if the king or queen were harmed, he would wreak vengeance on all who were guilty. France was now a nation in arms. At the same time, hundreds of Marseilles volunteers, who had arrived in Paris a month earlier singing the new revolutionary anthem, were massacred practically as they arrived. Within a week in August, after Parisian mobs had attacked the Tuileries, Louis was deposed, placed under arrest, and imprisoned.

The Jacobins were convinced that there were enemies inside and outside the country—nor were they wrong. Marat clearly had a hand in the September Massacres that year. Danton, then Minister of Justice, did not. Big and burly with a massive jaw, flashing eyes, and feral curls, Danton's oratory equalled the cadences of his former allies, soon to be enemies, Desmoulins and Marat. He had served on both the National Assembly and the Commune of Paris, though not as a leader of either. Thousands of people, however, responded to his support of the war against the old regime powers. For the Revolution to survive, he argued, it had to spread forcibly throughout Europe.

But the Revolution was becoming increasingly radicalized. Moderate forces were being driven out as the Convention, which came into being on September 21, 1792, officially declared royalty ended and France a republic with Danton's famous words just four days later: "The French Republic is one and indivisible." A year later, the government changed the calendar, but dated it from the day after the republic officially came into being (September 22), namely Year One of the Revolution, in the autumnal equinox. Thereafter, the twelve months had new names, devised by Fabre d'Eglantine, the French dramatist (he wrote a sequel to Molière's *Le Misanthrope*), who was guillotined in 1794. The new months, in order, were taken directly from nature: Vendémiaire (vintage); Brumaire (fog); Frimaire (sleet); Nivôse (snow); Pluviôse (rain); Ventôse (wind); Germinal (seed); Floréal (blossom); Prairial (pasture); Messidor (harvest); Thermidor or Fervidor (heat); Fructidor (fruit). Months were divided into three parts, known as decades, with the tenth day (décadi) set aside as a rest day. The remaining five days of the year were feast days known as Virtue, Genius, Labor, Reason, and Rewards. The new order of politics was fashioned to take into consideration the changed relationship that men had with nature, the universe, and the seasons.

Paine became a part of this new, confusing France on September 20 when he addressed the members of the National Assembly to thank them for conferring citizenship on him. He was heartily greeted. As John Frost noted in a letter to John Horne Tooke, the leader in London of the Society for Constitutional Information, Paine's speech, Frost wrote, "excited great curiosity among both men and women, and occasioned no small interruption." He then registered as a member of the new National Convention "with a great deal of nonchalance. . . . I have nothing more to add but that Mr. Paine is in good spirits, and indeed the flattering reception he has met with all through France could not fail of it. It is more than I describe. I believe he is rather fatigued with the kissing."[14]

Five days later, Paine addressed the citizens of France, thanking them for his citizenship, their faith in his abilities, and for electing him a member of the Convention. His tone was optimistic and uplifting. Using language that echoed his sentiments about America as he had expressed them nearly seventeen years earlier in *Common Sense*, he saw only positive achievements for France in the near future. "Convinced that the cause of France is the cause of all mankind ["the cause of America is in great measure the cause of all mankind," he had written in 1776], and that liberty cannot be purchased by a wish, I gladly share with you the dangers and honors necessary to success."

France had replaced America as a cause. It was now time to help free the people of that country. "It is the peculiar honor of France that she now raises the standard of liberty for all nations; and in fighting her own battles, contends for the rights of all mankind." As for himself, he was prepared to devote all his energy and intellect to help create a government in France dedicated to liberty and the rights of man. "Success is certain," he proclaimed, because Providence was on their side.

Paine however never fully saw, until it was too late, the terrible turn the Revolution would soon take. He might have been naive, or he might have been merely blind to the signs of political deterioration that began to occur around him. In his address, he urged the people of France to avoid squabbles and conflict among themselves. "Be calm," he advised, "let us punish by instructing, rather than by revenge. Let us begin a new era by a greatness of friendship, and hail the approach of union and success."[15] His advice ignored, revenge and terror took effect. In large measure, his optimism about the potential course of the Revolution had originally been shaped as a result of his longtime relationship with Lafayette.[16] But Lafayette was no longer in France. Disgraced by his part in the massacre in the Tuileries in the summer of 1792, the Marquis was removed from the command of the National Guard and sent to fight in the northeast against Austria. Constantly condemned by the Jacobins, especially Marat, who saw him as a royalist, Lafayette feared his own arrest. So he defected to the Austrians, who incarcerated him for the rest of the war as a revolutionary opposed to his king. Entering the Convention, into political office for the first time in his life, Paine perhaps could have used the guiding hand of a seasoned politician like Lafayette.

But now Paine was on his own. On October 11, the Convention appointed a committee to review plans on creating a constitution for the new republic, and Paine, along with Condorcet, Sieyès, Brissot, and several other key Girondins like Vergniaud, Armand Gensonné as well as Barère (now rapidly moving toward Robespierre) were chosen as members of the committee. Later Robespierre, Danton, and Collot d'Herbois (the Elector of Paris) joined its work. Jean Marie Collot d'Herbois, an actor and playwright, was at this moment one of the more moderate men of the

Revolution. In 1791, he had caused a stir among the more radical revolutionaries when he had supported a constitutional monarchy in his *Almanach du Père Gérard*. He later joined Robespierre and St. Just to become one of the twelve who ruled in the Reign of Terror. For now, however, his views mirrored those of the moderate Robespierre. Resenting this line-up, the Mountain resolved to avenge the slight, because they were certain that the committee was specifically designed to exclude them and to create a constitution that provided freedom only for moderates. Accordingly, they formed their own committee to work on an alternative document.

The tasks of the official Convention committee were divided between the members. Paine was responsible for preparing an initial draft, and Condorcet pulled the document together in its final version, which was modeled on the Pennsylvania Constitution of 1776. The constitution called for a unicameral legislature and a collective executive, both elected directly by the people. Having once favored the Pennsylvania Constitution and its single legislature, Paine had then changed his mind. Now, however, he again had second thoughts. As he explained it, a bicameral legislature could lead to the tyranny of the minority. If the two houses, for example, consisted of fifty members each, and one house voted unanimously for a measure, but it was defeated 26 to 24 in the other house, then a minority of one-fourth would have defeated the bill. Instead, if a single house were divided into two sections, each separately discussing the measure after hearing each other's side, they could vote on the measure together. In this way, "you gain all the advantages derived from separate debate without the evils which accompany the establishment of two chambers."[17] Along with the publication of the constitution was a document of nearly one hundred pages that outlined the circumstances under which the constitution might specifically be introduced in France. Disappointed with this final version, Paine thought a more universal document was being prepared. France, he thought, had a role to play in the world in leading other nations to democracy by convincing them of the "the reasons why the old system of monarchical government should be abolished." The constitution unfortunately "sacrificed too much to ceremony, and the impolitic fear of giving umbrage to foreign courts," as he told Danton.[18]

The new constitution was drafted, however, at a propitious moment. The government coupled its new framework with several autumn victories against old regime armies in the north and east, especially General Dumouriez' victories at Jemappes and Dieppe in the fall of 1792. Now Paine was beginning to think seriously about repeating the revolution in England. The situation in England for the moment was mixed. With the publication of the second part of the *Rights of Man* there, anti-Painite forces in London created a new association, the "Friends of the People," specifically designed to combat reform and revolution in England. The English ministry was certain that Paine, along with other expatriot Britons, wanted to stimulate the overthrow of the British monarchy. Despite the Pitt government's efforts to stifle radical activity, membership in the Society for Constitutional Information and the London Corresponding Society dramatically increased, if only temporarily. Thomas Hardy, the shoemaker president of the LCS, claimed he was signing up three hundred to four hundred new members each week. For Paine and his radical British friends in Paris, these events represented a major breakthrough for the revolutionary cause in England.

On October 20, 1792, Paine addressed the French Convention, congratulating it on ending the monarchy and creating a republic. His address appeared in Brissot's *Le Patriote français* as "An Essay for the Use of new Republicans in Their Opposition to Monarchy." In it, as he had in *Common Sense* nearly seventeen years earlier, Paine dehumanized and denatured kings, turning them into creatures that had to be disposed of. They were "monsters in the natural order, and what can we expect from monsters but miseries and crimes?" he asked. They were always ambitious in their desire to do whatever was necessary to hold onto to their power at the expense of their subjects. And their ministers were no better. Quoting Rousseau, Paine declared that aristocrats were "base marplots, ordinary rogues, mean intriguers" who could "do nothing but evil." What was worse is that the entire aristocratic system was based on heredity, which made its subjects no better than dumb animals. "Why, it is to treat our posterity as a herd of cattle who are entirely destitute of either rights or will," he exclaimed. Human beings would be far better off by simply following the law, which in the Rousseauist terms he was now accustomed to using meant "the expression of the general will," a theme Paine had used in the second part of the *Rights of Man*. Royalty had ended in France, because it had decayed to pure rotten- ness "under the Rays of the same Light."[19] Enlightenment and rev- olutionary activity were the only means to destroy the bestial, savage brutes that passed as kings and nobles.

As the most prominent, most popular exponent of liberty and democracy in Europe, Paine held court at White's Hotel from the autumn of 1792 until the spring of 1793. During this period the hotel, soon to be renamed the Hotel Philadelphie, was the headquar- ters of the British Club, home of several British and American ex- patriot or traveling radicals who gathered there to discuss the issues of the day, to plan revolutions all over Britain, Scotland, and Ireland, and to maintain ties with their native countries. The Club, formally known after January 5, 1793, as the Friends of the Rights of Man Associated at Paris, included (in addition to Paine) several British and American citizens living and working in Paris: Paine's friend and confidant, Thomas Christie, several members of the Society for Constitutional Information (like printer John Hurford Stone, the journalist, poet, and diarist Helen Maria Williams, and the banker Sir Robert Smyth). Stone, the titular president of the Club, was like Paine later to be incarcerated at the height of the Terror. He and Helen Maria Williams later fled France to the relative safety of Switzerland.

The Club also included the Connecticut writer and radical Joel Barlow, whom Paine had met in London in the spring of 1789 through John Trumbull, who had painted Paine's portrait in minia- ture for Jefferson in 1788, and Benjamin West.[20] Inspired by Paine, Barlow in his 1792 *Advice to the Privileged Orders* had also answered Burke's condemnation of the French Revolution. Arguing that gov- ernment did not represent only a particular class, but the people as individuals, he claimed that it must always be mindful of the people's welfare. His tract, *Vision of Columbus*, originally published in 1787, was printed in Paris in the summer of 1793.[21] Like Paine (though some months after him), Barlow was made a citizen of France and elected in January 1793 to the National Convention as a member from Savoy.

Also at White's was the Scot John Oswald, a habitué of Bonneville's Social Circle. Oswald died the following year, fighting with the French revolutionary armies in the north. He had once served in the British army in India, where he became a vegetarian. In 1791, he published a vegetarian pamphlet, *The Cry of Nature*, but his views within two years were consonant with the bloodthirsty regime of the Revolutionary Tribunal at the height of the Terror. Henry Redhead, who later added the last name "Yorke" to escape unnoticed from France during the Terror, watched Oswald one evening at White's Hotel, dining "on his roots", and at the same time "cooly" proposing that "the most effectual way of averting civil war . . . [was] to put to death every suspected man in France." Redhead reported that when Paine heard these remarks coming from a vegetarian, he remarked, " 'Oswald, you have lived so long without tasting flesh that you have now a most voracious appetite for blood.' "[22] A few years later, Redhead, now going by his adopted name of Yorke, was jailed in England for sedition. In 1802, he visited Paine in Paris for the last time just before Paine sailed to America. Other members of the Club included the Rev. William Jackson, a radical Irish clergyman, and Robert Madgett, a translator, first for the French Marine ministry, then later for the Committee of Public Safety.

One of Paine's visitors was a young Irishman, Lord Edward Fitzgerald, who was the son of the James Fitzgerald, the twentieth earl of Kildare and first Duke of Lancaster. From one of the most distinguished families in Ireland, young Fitzgerald had served in the army as well as the Irish House of Commons before becoming totally enthralled by the events in France after 1789. At age twenty-nine, he spent part of 1792 in France, and became so taken with the ideals of liberation that he later was named commander-in-chief of the United Irishmen, which had been founded the previous year by the young barrister Theobald Wolfe Tone, a Protestant and great Irish leader. Fitzgerald returned home with a young French wife, Pamela, who for years was thought to be the illegitimate daughter of Philippe-Egalité (formerly the Duc d'Orléans), but it has been recently shown that Orléans had adopted her from an English foundling home at age six and raised her in Paris. In any case, the very idea of the young, aristocratic Fitzgerald's marriage to a bastard certainly contributed to his growing reputation as a radical democrat.[23]

In October 1792, Fitzgerald was at White's, along with Paine, who was a strong supporter of Irish liberation from English control. Paine was, for one historian of Ireland, "the political philosopher of Ireland's coming revolution, the most prominent member of the group of Anglo-Irish exiles." On October 30, Fitzgerald told his mother, Lady Emily Mary Lennox, the daughter of the Duke of Richmond and the sister of Lady Holland, "I lodge with my friend Paine—we breakfast, dine, and sup together. The more I see of his interior, the more I like and respect him. I cannot express how kind he is to me; there is a simplicity of man, a goodness of heart, and a strength of mind in him, that I never knew a man before possess."[24]

Apparently, the two of them were conspiring on how to engage French financial support to fund an Irish rebellion. They, along with Achille Duchâtelet, arranged to speak about it with French Foreign Minister Pierre Lebrun. After all, the revolutionary regime had decreed on November 19, 1792 that it would offer assistance to any people anywhere seeking freedom. The Irish exiles in Paris took this promise literally and hoped for French support for an invasion of Ireland to separate it from the British empire.[25] Fitzgerald believed that 40,000 volunteers in Ireland with French funding in three months would liberate the nation. All of this was to no avail. Neither Paine nor Fitzgerald had adequate resources themselves or the substantial connections to either the French government or the Irish population to pull off a rebellion of any kind.

As it turned out, the French were not really interested in fomenting revolution elsewhere, as the Irish exiles soon found out when they attempted it in 1798.

At the same time, Edmond-Charles Genet, the very young French Minister to the court of Catherine the Great of Russia, returned to Paris and to White's where he fell in with Paine and his radical friends.[26] The red-headed Citizen Genet, as he preferred to be called, just twenty-eight years old, had already served as a diplomat in Berlin and Vienna as well as St. Petersburg. He was the younger brother of Madame Campan, the chief lady-in-waiting to

Marie-Antoinette. As a boy, he had played in the Queen's chambers in Versailles and in his father's office in the Bureau of Interpreters. At age sixteen, he became the head of that office, but soon moved into the world of diplomacy. An ardent supporter of the Revolution, he briefly served as the Minister to the Russian Empire for the new regime. Catherine the Great, however, outraged by Louis XVI and Marie-Antoinette's forced return to Paris from Varennes, expelled all French diplomats from St. Petersburg.

Genet left, but his ardor for revolutionary ideals was only heightened after his encounter with the radicals, especially Thomas Paine, at White's. Within a few months, the French government dispatched him to the United States as its ambassador. His orders were to try to raise an army and cut off the Spaniards in Spanish America. President Washington and the anti-French Federalists (especially Treasury Secretary Alexander Hamilton) were appalled by his activities. They thought this move by the French government to be highly provocative, especially after Genet was welcomed to America by huge throngs of pro-French Jeffersonians.

Despite the open disapproval of the American government, Genet stayed to raise an army, which was to be led by the Venezuelan adventurer and liberator Francisco del Miranda, to attack Spanish Florida. Genet was prevented from carrying out this plan when the Americans refused to allow French privateers to use American ports, despite the 1778 treaty between the Americans and French. Genet was now disgraced, but by the time President Washington demanded his recall, the Girondins had fallen from power. (The French government responded in kind by demanding that Washington recall Gouverneur Morris as the American Minister to France.) Had Genet returned to his homeland in 1794, he certainly would have faced the guillotine. Instead, he remained in America, with Washington's blessing, and married the daughter of New York Governor George Clinton.

On November 18, Paine, Fitzgerald, and at least seventy-five others, including Thomas Christie and possibly even William Wordsworth, attended a huge banquet at White's, sponsored by the Friends of the Rights of the People. The event, reported to Whitehall by Captain George Munro, now living at White's and still a spy for Lord Gower, the English ambassador in Paris, was specifically designed to celebrate General Dumouriez's November 6 victory over the Austrians in Belgium as well as other significant French victories in Valmy, Savoy, Nice, and Frankfort and on the Rhine.[27] The banquet attendees sang revolutionary songs like "Ça Ira" and the "Marseillaise," danced the "Carmagnolle," and sang an English version of the "Marseillaise" to a tune written most likely by Helen-Maria Williams. While at it, they gave thirteen toasts (symbolic of the thirteen freed states of America, apparently), one of which was to Thomas Paine and the royal prosecution of good books. Fitzgerald proposed to abolish all titles of nobility everywhere and even renounced his own, calling himself Citizen Edward Fitzgerald.

The Society, under Stone's presidency, decided to draft an address to the National Convention proclaiming British (or expatriot British, at least) solidarity with the armed victories of the new French republic against her old regime enemies. If Belgium could be free, why not Scotland? Wales? Ireland? England itself?[28] Everyone signed the address, except Paine, because he was a member of the Convention (hence one of those addressed). The document was then forwarded to the Convention. At the same time, the signers of the address collected one thousand pounds to purchase shoes for French soldiers.[29]   In addition, to show its solidarity with radicals in England, two members of the Society, John Frost (who had accompanied Paine to France along with Audibert) and Joel Barlow sent greetings to the Society for Constitutional Information in London.

In England, Richard Brinsley Sheridan, the famous dramatist (author of the well-known "The Rivals" and "The School for Scandal") and now a member of Parliament, defended the British supporters of the French Revolution against Burke, who was certain that the Paris banquet, the toasts, and the subsequent address condemned England to inevitable regicide and revolution. Later that same month, Fitzgerald was indicted by the Attorney General of England for attending the dinner at White's and for offering the toast to abolish hereditary titles. The authorities had Munro's report of the banquet. A short six years later, in 1798, when Wolfe Tone's Irish rebellion was betrayed, Fitzgerald, in the course of his arrest, was fatally wounded. He was thirty-five years old.

In one sense, this period closed an era for Thomas Paine. With the approach of the trial of Louis, a time of good feelings was truly coming to an end. The sense among the members of the British Club that there could be a united democratic Britain, Belgium, and France was certainly misguided and unrealistic. Even so, they tended to believe it was possible and continued to speak in these terms until it became clear that the Revolution was rapidly moving onto a new, uglier phase, heading toward its disintegration and terror.

In December, there were two omens that signaled the grim events to come: England began to plan to go to war against revolutionary France, and Paine was tried in England, in absentia, for having written and published the second part of the *Rights of Man*. First, on December 13, Parliament approved the "King's Speech," as it was known, that soon added England to the list of countries with which France was at war, although France issued a declaration of war officially against England only on February 1, 1793 after the British ministry demanded the recall of the French Minister to London, the Marquis de Chauvelin. (England responded to the French declaration on February 11 with its own declaration of war.)

Five days after the Convention's endorsement of the King's Speech came the long-awaited trial of Thomas Paine and his wicked, seditious, and malicious book. Just one month earlier, the Pitt ministry had unofficially formed an organization to investigate and infiltrate all suspected revolutionary groups in England. The organization sponsored demonstrations, riots, and witchhunts throughout England. Paine was burned in effigy in several towns and villages, and his books and other writings burned for real. Some of the gentry even inscribed the initials "T.P." on the hobnails on the soles of their boots so that when they walked, they crushed the name of Thomas Paine. In part, Reeves's Association helped in the investigations of Paine's most radical work to date and the subsequent trial, which began on December 18.

The very same Attorney General, Archibald Macdonald, to whom Paine had written the previous summer intended to declare Paine an outlaw and his works banned from England. He was successful. Paine was tried in absentia by a "special jury," which according to Rickman was "packed for all intents and purposes" to obtain the verdict the government wanted.[30] Still Paine enjoyed a spirited, though hopeless, defense by Thomas Erskine, a friend and attorney of the Prince of Wales and one of the most acclaimed lawyers of late-eighteenth century England. His fee and all the costs of Paine's defense were paid for by money raised by the SCI under Horne Tooke's leadership. Taking this case caused Erskine to lose the Prince of Wales as his client. Ironically, it was Erskine only a few years later who prosecuted Paine's *The Age of Reason* as an ungodly work of atheism.[31]

Meantime, Paine did not help his case at all. In November, he had written to Macdonald from France that he did not plan to attend his own trial. He considered his duties in France to be "of too much importance to permit me to trouble myself about your prosecution." What was worse, he insulted the king of England by referring to him as "Mr. Guelph," (an allusion to the Germanic origins of the Hanoverians), who surrounded himself with "profligate sons" (his ministers and advisors).[32] He was as impertinent as ever, telling Macdonald that he might as well "obtain a verdict against the Man in the Moon as against me." He attacked the entire English government as a "great, if not the greatest, perfection of fraud and corruption that ever took place since governments began."[33]

Erskine was unaware of the letter, so he was taken by surprise when Macdonald read it aloud in court. At that point, it became clear to Erskine that his case to defend Paine was lost. He brought forth his arguments anyway, in an arresting four-hour speech, based on his view of the laws of England and "the nature and extent of the liberty of the English press. The proposition which I meant to maintain as the basis of the liberty of the press, and without which it is an empty sound, is this: that every man, not intending to mislead, but seeking to enlighten others with what his own reason and conscience, however erroneously, have dictated to him as truth, may address himself to the universal reason of a whole nation, either upon the subject of governments in general, or upon that of our particular country."[34] Erskine concluded with a fable that was remembered long after the trial:

> Jupiter and a countryman were walking together, conversing
> with great freedom and familiarity upon the subject of heaven
> and earth. The countryman listened with attention and acquies-
> cence, while Jupiter strove only to convince him; but happening
> to hint a doubt, Jupiter turned hastily around and threatened
> him with his thunder. "Ah ha!" says the countryman, "now,
> Jupiter, I know that you are wrong; you are always wrong when
> you appeal to your thunder." This is the case with me. I can
> reason with the people of England, but I cannot fight against
> the thunder of authority.

Even before Macdonald had a chance to rebut Erskine's argument, the jury foreman came forward with a guilty verdict for Paine. Paine was now an outlaw. Should he ever set foot in England again, he could be imprisoned for life or even executed. For his part, Erskine was regarded as a national hero.

An observer reported that the crowd at the proceedings drew his "carriage home, he riding in triumph—his horses led by another party. Riots at Cambridge, Manchester, Bridport Dorset &c. &c. O England, how art thou fallen!"[35] At the same time, Paine's enemies reported the supposed death of the archtraitor Thomas Paine in France, and the government went after several booksellers who carried Paine's works. Sentences ranged from a few days in jail up to seven years in prison for printing and selling his work. Even newspaper owners were targeted for printing extracts of Paine's writings.

The first of the trials was that of the radical printer and dealer Thomas Spence on February 26, 1793. The government somehow botched his indictment, and he was acquitted. The ministry was not, however, to make the same mistake again. William Holland was sent to jail for a year and fined one hundred pounds for selling Paine's "Letter Addressed to the Addressers," Paine's defense of the *Rights of Man*, Part Two. H.D. Symonds went to prison for four years and was heavily fined for selling the *Rights of Man* and for publishing the same "Letter." The printer Fische Palmer received a seven year sentence of transportation for the same offence. Paine's friend, bookseller and printer Clio Rickman, escaped to France. Several years later the government was still hunting down Painite printers and booksellers.

Soon, all of Paine's works were proscribed, so that any publication with Thomas Paine's name on it led to serious trouble for the publisher. In 1797, for example, one Thomas Williams was indicted and convicted for printing a copy of *The Age of Reason*. His sentence was three years' imprisonment, later reduced to one. And as late as 1819, a full ten years after Paine's death, his longtime friend and publisher Richard Carlile was sentenced to three years in jail, and his wife to two, for selling proscribed Paine works.[36] In all, there were two dozen or so such trials, most of which were successful. The British government, fully aware of the dangers to its own authority and legitimacy by allowing such opposition texts to be printed, bought, and sold, cracked down brutally on radicals.

14 · The Two-Edged Sword of Liberty

t the end of 1792, yet another trial was in the offing, this time in France. Once that nation had become a republic and the monarchy abolished, the problem was what to do with Louis XVI. Could the king be tried at all? If so, who could legally try him? And what would the penalty be? The Girondins, by and large, did not want to bring him to trial, but the Mountain did. The Girondins formed a commission headed by Jean-Baptiste Mailhe to investigate what to do. In part, their spokesmen was Henri Morisson de la Bassetière, who argued that the constitution of 1791 had declared the body of the king to be inviolable, hence not subject to the law.[1]

Robespierre and the twenty-five year old Louis-Antoine de St. Just thought a trial a waste of time: Louis was guilty simply by virtue of being king. He was a festering abscess growing on a healthy republic of virtue. Like the sore, he had to be excised. All that was now needed was his execution. "Defenders of the king," St. Just demanded to know, "what do you want for him? If he is innocent, the people is guilty."[2] As St. Just spoke, crowds of sans-culottes, some with pikes, roamed the Convention, pounding them on the ground or applauding when they approved what was said, booing and hissing when they disagreed. The king's trial to them was a foregone conclusion. Like St. Just, they wanted to see him executed, because enemies of the revolution and the republic were everywhere: inside and outside France, and their focus was on the king, to restore him to full authority on the throne. He had to die. A full-scale war was now on: the enemies were even in the Convention, and soon they too would face the guillotine to preserve the Revolution's achievements.

The times demanded terror, and Robespierre and St. Just were there to supply it.

  Thomas Paine held a moderate position in the Convention. He definitely thought Louis should be tried not as a king but rather as a private person, as Louis Capet, a name Paine called him and which Robespierre and St. Just absolutely refused to use. Louis was the king and placing him on a commoner's level worked against their desire to see him dead. For Paine, however, having denied citizens their natural liberty and rights, Louis had to go before a public tribunal and defend himself. On November 20, a speech Paine wrote in English was translated and read before the Convention. Louis was a conspirator not only against France but all of Europe. His trial "can serve to prove to the world the flagitiousness of governments in general, and the necessity of revolutions."[3]

  Just days later, Jean-Marie Roland reported that an iron chest that Louis had with him in the Tuileries contained documents, which indisputably showed he had conspired even more to save his throne than any of the Girondins or Mountain fully realized. The chest was full of copies of documents he had sent to royal powers of Europe begging them to help restore his kingship. The first question was answered. Louis would be tried for treason, because he had entered into negotiations with the enemies of France, Austria and Prussia, and French emigrants to wage war against his own country. There were even letters from the once-celebrated and adored Mirabeau to Louis advising him how to restore his authority. The trial opened on December 11, 1792, as the Mountain demanded the death penalty. Robespierre called for the removal of Mirabeau's remains from the Pantheon and that all likenesses and busts of him destroyed. Danton, a friend of Paine's, did not wish to see the king executed. He wrote, however: "I am willing to try and save the king. . . . I warn you that although I may save his life I shall vote for his death; I am quite willing to save his head, but not to lose mine."[4] Barère and Marat wanted to see Louis dead. The Girondins, on the defensive now, weakly advocated that Louis simply be banished from France.

  Paine, convinced the king could and should be tried, supported the Girondin position for moral and practical reasons. No one hated kingship more than Paine, but Louis was no longer king. Paine quoted something he had heard repeated at the Jacobin Club once: "Make me a king today, and I shall be a robber tomorrow." What, however, if Louis had been a commoner? "I am inclined to believe that if Louis Capet had been born in obscure condition, had he lived within the circle of an amiable and respectable neighborhood, at liberty to practice the duties of domestic life, had he been thus situated, I cannot believe that he would have shown himself destitute of social virtues." Louis had demonstrated that he was a man who understood the ideals of liberty and rights. He had after all aided the Americans when they were at war against England, and for that reason alone deserved exile. "It is to France, I know, that the United States of America owe that support which enabled them to shake off the unjust and tyrannical yoke of Britain. The ardor and zeal which she displayed to provide both men and money, were the natural consequence of a thirst for liberty." Louis ought not be condemned to death. He should be banished to America: "Let then those United States be the safeguard and asylum of Louis Capet." Paine's high moral ground was peppered with practical politics as well. He feared that the spectacle of the king's execution would cause England to join forces with Austria and Prussia in a larger war against France. The Convention, he pleaded, ought not give "the tyrant of England" an excuse to invade France.[5]

Paine cited Robespierre's famous speech before the Assembly in 1791 calling for the end of capital punishment, but of course Robespierre was now demanding the death of the king. So the Convention was stuck between the moderate position of the Girondins and the radicalism of the Mountain. Some delegates decided to ask the nation to determine Louis' fate by a national referendum (though this effort was defeated by a vote of 424 to 287). Still defending the life of Louis, Paine once again argued for his exile, inflaming Marat against him more than ever. In a speech to the Convention on January 19, translated and read aloud by his friend and colleague Jean Henri Bancal des Issarts, Paine again pleaded for mercy and justice. Throughout the speech, Marat rose and angrily interrupted shouting curses, personally attacking Paine. "I deny the right of Thomas Paine to vote on such a subject," he screamed. "He is a Quaker, of course his religious views run counter to the infliction of capital punishment." Despite shouts from the members demanding that Bancal continue to read Paine's speech, Marat could not be stopped.

Soon Marat was joined by Jacques Alexis Thuriot de la Rozière, a delegate from the Marne, who claimed that Paine was not the author of the address. Marat approached Paine, who was standing next to Bancal, and asked him several questions, most likely in English, and then echoed Thuriot's charge. "I denounce the translator," he declared. "Such opinions are not Thomas Paine's. The translation is incorrect." Garran de Coulon then got up and said that he had read the text, and these words were those of Thomas Paine. Paine agreed. Of course, Louis was tried, found guilty, and the death penalty declared by a majority of one vote.[6]

The great French historian Albert Soboul commented once that all this was inevitable. "That the Convention deliberated under the menacing gaze of the galleries, there can be no doubt. What is more, by their applause, or their murmurs, they intervened in the debates."[7] Of course, Louis and his lawyers denied every accusation brought forward during the proceedings. He never questioned the evidence, however, and he never really said anything about the armoire de fer found in his apartment in the Tuileries. Although he was represented by counsel at the trial, Louis never defended himself at all. According to some observers, in his last months, he had entered a world of spirituality under the care of his chaplain, an Irish monk by the name of Henry Edgeworth de Firmont, and spent all his time tending to the emotional hardships of his family and meditating on his own.[8]

Two views of Louis have emerged over time. The first is that he refused to acknowledge the legitimacy of his trial. He was after all king, and though monarchy was ended, he did not have to cooperate with usurpers and thieves.[9] The second is that he knew that all struggle was futile, and he was doomed. Jules Michelet writes that by the time of his trial, Louis was "a man like so many others, he seemed like a bourgeois, living off his investments, a family man; he had a simple air about him, a bit near-sighted, his skin already pale from prison; he was sensing death."[10]

The trial of Louis XVI, horrifying for the king, was over.

Citizen Genet, on his way to becoming the French minister to the United States, wrote:

> This was the most forlorn spectacle I have ever witnessed. The room, poorly lit, was filled with paid ruffians of the [Mountain], and the muffled and vacillating light which shown on them gave their sinister faces the pallor of death. Everything was soiled with the blood of so many victims. These men greeted with curses and gestures each delegate, who refused to go along with the Mountain in the trials and threatened them with revenge that their desire for human blood demanded if they hesitated to pronounce a sentence of death....
> And to render this scene more hideous still, vendors never stopped passing out refreshments to this nest of vultures. . . . A great number of delegates opposed the death penalty and voted in favor of exile. I hesitate to say this but the unfortunate fate of the king was in the hands of the Girondins. . . . But the menacing attitude of the Mountain frightened them away from their real duty. Could they have counted on an appeal directly to the people? Or could they have hoped for a stay giving them time to send the prisoners to America? To that I do not know what to say.[11]

After the Convention refused, by a vote of 380 to 310, to stay his execution, the hapless Louis was beheaded on January 21, 1793 on the Place de la Révolution (formerly the Place de Louis XV, today the Place de la Concorde) before a massive crowd of twenty thousand people. On February 11, as Paine had predicted, England joined the other European nations and declared war on France, although ten days earlier the French government had already decreed that with the recall of their minister to London, Ambassador Chauvelin, France was in a state of war with the king of England.[12]

The antagonisms, which were supposed to decline after the execution of the king in January 1793, only increased in the months that followed. Louis' death marked the true decline of the Revolution into terror. From this point on, the Revolution was no longer about enlightenment, reason, and progress. It was about twisted principles and political duplicity. The success of Robespierre and the Mountain was practically a foregone conclusion in view of the absence of political leadership and the war that France, just after the king's execution, had entered into against England and the Netherlands. It was a war on two fronts: externally, it was the ongoing war against the nations that were appalled at the execution of a hereditary monarch. Internally, it was against the "enemies" of the Revolution. By the middle of March, the Convention had created a Revolutionary Tribunal and the first laws to ward off what it considered counter-revolutionary activity. It soon turned against just about anyone, including the moderate Girondins, many of the Mountain, several extremists known as the enragés, and even Thomas Paine.

One of Paine's political enemies in England had even predicted this turn of events as early as the previous fall. Writing to a friend, Lord Fortescue angrily wrote that "Tom Paine is just where he ought to be—a member of the Convention of cannibals. One would have thought it impossible that any society upon the face of the globe should have been fit for the reception of such a being until the late deeds of the National Convention have shown them to be most fully qualified. His vocation will not be complete, nor theirs either, till his head finds its way to the top of the pike, which will probably not be long first."[13] Just over a year later Paine was incarcerated in the Luxembourg prison. But in March, he was still a friend of many Girondin leaders, who retained some degree of authority.

These included Brissot, Jean-Marie Roland, though not his wife, Madame Roland, who held a low opinion of Paine. She thought he was totally self-absorbed and unfit to sit in the Convention. Writing her memoirs in the days before her execution, Madame Roland thought of Thomas Paine. "Of the number of people I received, included among the most notable was Paine. Declared a French citizen, as one of those famous foreigners whom the nation was bound to adopt, he was known by his writings, which were useful in the American Revolution, and he had tried to stimulate one in England. I will not allow myself to judge him absolutely, because he understood French without speaking it, and it was nearly the same in regard to my English. . . . The hardiness of his thoughts, the originality of his style, these strong truths . . . must have produced a great sensation. But Paine was better at sparking a revolution than creating a constitution. . . . For the cold discussion of a constitutional commission, I should think that [the Welshman] David Williams was intimately more suitable than he."[14]

Despite Roland's criticisms, Paine remained, because he thought he still had the task of finishing the constitution. The Girondins still possessed some power, and they named Paine to the Committee of Surveillance, which oversaw the condition of the prisoners in French jails. A great number of Englishmen were then living in Paris—some because they were politically radical and upheld the principles of the French revolution, others because they were there on business as representatives of their English or American companies. Then there were some like George Munro, the British spy, who had been transmitting reports on Paine's activities to the English ministry. He was arrested by French authorities after England declared war on France on February 11. Despite Paine's knowledge of what Munro was doing, he had him released and sent back to England.

A few weeks later, Paine was dining at White's one evening when a young British officer, a former aristocrat by the name of Captain John Grimstone who had apparently trundled out of London to avoid debtors' prison, began to argue with Paine about his association with the French government. He called him a traitor to his native country and eventually got so mad he struck Paine in the face. According to French law, striking a delegate of the National Convention was considered an attack on the entire French nation. He was arrested and faced execution. Paine, however, with the help of Barère, who served on the Committee of Public Safety, had him released, given a passport, and escorted from the country. Paine even paid the cost of his transportation.[15]

There were several other examples of Paine's desire to help his former countrymen. Paine was called to a prison by a jailor to meet a young merchant named Zachariah Wilkes. Wilkes was an associate of James Watt and Isaac Boulton, two great Birmingham entrepreneurs and major benefactors of Joseph Priestley and his chemistry experiments. Wilkes had been incarcerated for sending documents back home and was considered an agent of the English government. He did not know what to do, so the jailor suggested he send a letter to Thomas Paine to see if he could help him. Of course

Paine knew Priestley, and through Priestley was familiar with Watt and Boulton. Satisfying himself that Wilkes was telling the truth, he arranged to have him, like Munro and Grimstone, released and returned to England. Paine also helped an English banker, also a member of the British Club, Robert Smyth, who, along with his wife, had attended the banquet in November at White's. Although he constantly proclaimed his republican sympathies and even at one point renounced his title, Smyth was arrested. Paine, as a deputy in the Convention, successfully obtained his release, and a passport out of the country.[16] After Paine himself was imprisoned, the authorities allowed him for a short while to correspond with Lady Smyth. Her letters were always comforting to the horrified Paine.

Shortly after Smyth's release, a captain of the National Guard, who spoke perfect English, came to Paine's hotel one evening to speak on behalf of two young Englishmen who had been arrested and were in jail. Paine wrote a release for them. After discussing the Revolution with Paine and telling him that he owned a first edition of the *Rights of Man*, the captain told Paine he would be at his service whenever he should need it. On departing, he revealed that he "was no other than the public executioner Samson [sic], who guillotined the king, and all who were guillotined in Paris; and who lived in the same section, and in the same street with me."[17] Paine was referring to the public executioner Charles-Henri Sanson.

All this time, Paine, along with Condorcet and their committee colleagues, were crafting a new constitution for France. A plan with thirty-three proposals, written largely by Paine and translated by Condorcet, was submitted to the Convention on February 15. Although the Committee never implemented it, the plan indicated how far Paine's ideas had evolved. In it, he advocated unrestricted free expression and religious liberty, universal suffrage (though only for men) without property qualifications, the right of the people to veto directly the acts of the legislature (through referendum), free public education for everyone, and social aid to the poor. Moreover, he demanded that every person be allowed to serve in the government no matter his social or economic status. Even then, one generation could not bind future ones: "One generation has not the right to subject future generations to its laws."[18]   The Mountain denounced the plan, saying it was designed to install a new monarchy of ministers.

In March, Paine moved from White's Hotel, where he had constantly entertained visitors—especially the revolutionary leaders who spoke English—to part of a house where Madame de Pompadour once lived, in the Paris suburb of St. Denis. In 1793, it was still country, though it was less than ten kilometers from the Tuileries. For awhile, Paine resided there with two young Englishmen, William Johnson and William Choppin, whom he had met in England, and who were probably members of the British Club. There, he passed his time strolling about, writing, and meeting several friends like Joel Barlow and his wife Ruth, as well as Mary Wollstonecraft, when she visited Paris. His London friend, Clio Rickman, visited, since he too was now in exile. Rickman noticed how disillusioned Paine was becoming, and that he tended to drink a great deal to overcome his depression.

Several French associates also came to visit, among them Brissot and Bancal, who had read aloud Paine's defense of the king in the Convention. Condorcet and Bonneville also came out to see him, bring him news of the day, and hopefully cheer him up. The downstairs apartment of the house was occupied by his friend Thomas Christie and his wife. Paine, though despondent at times, enjoyed the tranquility of the house in the suburbs, which glaringly contrasted with the bustle of Paris. Living "a life of retirement and philosophical ease," he later recalled of his lodgings there.[19] They

> were the most agreeable . . . of any I ever had in Paris, except that they were too remote from the Convention, of which I was then a member. But this was recompensed by their being also remote from the alarms and confusion into which the interior of Paris was then often thrown. . . .
>
> The house, which was enclosed by a wall and gateway from the street, was a good deal like an old mansion farmhouse, and the courtyard was like a farmyard, stocked with fowls, ducks, turkeys, and geese; which, for amusement, we used to feed out of the parlor window on the ground floor. There were some hutches for rabbits, and a sty with two pigs.
>
> Beyond, was a garden of more than an acre of ground well laid

out, and stocked with excellent fruit trees. The orange, apricot, and greengage plum were the best I ever tasted; and it is the only place where I saw the wild cucumber. . . .

My apartments consisted of three rooms; the first for wood, water, etc., with an old fashioned closet chest, high enough to hang up clothes in; the next was the bedroom; and beyond it the sitting room, which looked into the garden through a glass door; and on the outside there was a small landing place railed in, and a flight of narrow stairs almost hidden by the vines that grew over it, by which I could descend into the garden, without going downstairs through the house.[20]

It was a pleasant situation for him. His friend Clio Rickman once told of a dinner Paine attended when, for over four hours, he kept the guests enthralled with his extraordinary memory. Paine recounted stories of "men and manners," told "numberless anecdotes of the American Indians, of the American war, of Franklin, Washington, and even of his Majesty, of whom he told several facts of humor and benevolence."[21]

The house provided an escape from the increasing chaos of Paris. Paine was aware that things were not going well for the revolution, but he was steadfast in his revolutionary zeal. He wrote to a friend in America in February, just one month after the king's execution, that "the first characters in Europe are in arms; some with the bayonet, some with the pen, and some with the two-edged sword of Declamation in favor of Liberty. The tyrants of the earth are leagued against France; but with little effect. . . . France can never fall; but by misapplying her own strength."[22] That is, of course, what France would eventually do: misapply its own strength by turning the sword, in this case the guillotine, on its own people.

Several questions must have lingered in Paine's mind. Had Burke been right? Would the destruction of institutions, which had lasted for ages, prove wrong? Would the Revolution deteriorate into tyranny? Despite Paine's disappointment over the death of the king, he was still relatively content with developments in his adopted France. However, he soon spotted signs of disintegration. General Charles François Dumouriez, despite his spectacular victory in Belgium, defected to the Austrians after the Convention moved to the left. He had actually ordered his troops to attack Paris. They refused, and he quit, only to spend the rest of his life in disgrace wandering around Europe, until he finally settled in England in 1804.

At the same time, inflation was growing spectacularly, and the Mountain advocated price controls, which the Girondins opposed. In March, in a herald of the downfall of the Girondins, disgruntled and poor Parisians, the extreme sans-culottes, known as the enragés and led by the infamous former priest Jacques Roux, protested rising food prices and demanded strict economic controls. They also demanded the overthrow of the Girondins. The result was that in early April the Convention established a powerful Committee of Public Safety consisting of nine members, who were supposed to act as a collective executive power over the nation. It was the beginning of the end of Brissot and his Girondin followers. Although not initially elected to the Committee, Robespierre waited patiently for his moment. Paine later wrote that he rarely went to the Convention at this point: "I found it impossible to join in their tremendous decrees, and useless and dangerous to oppose them."[23] Even worse, those advocating greater violence and bloodshed seemed to be taking greater control of events.

The day before the Committee was established, Marat, who was elected president of the Jacobin Club on April 5, addressed the nation: "Friends, we are betrayed. To arms! There is counter-revolution in the government and in the National Convention. There, in the citadel of our hopes, our criminal representatives pull the strings of the plot they have contrived with a horde of despots coming to cut our throats." He was in essence calling for the overthrow of the Convention itself, a new revolution with himself at the lead. Such a statement might have served as notice for the coming danger. No one picked it up, however, not even Paine.

On April 15, 1793, the Mountain declared war on the Girondins. The Commune of Paris presented the Convention with a petition naming twenty-two deputies of the Convention (including five on the committee working on the new constitution) as suspected counter-revolutionaries. These included several of Paine's friends and supporters like Brissot, Guadet, Vergniaud, Gensonné, and Lanthenas. While the Convention rejected the petition, it forecast the purges, which were to come soon. Paine wrote Jefferson on April 20 that "had this Revolution been conducted consistently with its principles, there was once a good prospect of extending liberty through the greatest part of Europe; but I now relinquish that hope. . . . I begin to contemplate returning home [to America]." He waited, however, for the final disposition of the constitution that was before the Convention.[24] His home in New Rochelle in fact had burned down, he told Jefferson. He had received this news from his caretaker.

Marat, still fuming over Paine's refusal to support the execution of the king, formally denounced Paine, but the Convention soundly rejected his request that the authorities arrest him. Paine wrote to Danton, who understood English, that he now despaired at seeing "the tumultuous misconduct with which the internal affairs of the present Revolution are conducted."[25] Danton, a Jacobin, but moderate in his thinking, was to be arrested himself in the spring of 1794, and then executed.

The list of those to be imprisoned grew day by day. Condorcet and Brissot were on it. Paine was not, thanks at one point to Danton, who had shouted in English for Paine not to enter the Convention. The Brissotins tried to take the offensive by acting first. They impeached Marat for the anti-Convention and anti-republican principles he had laid out in his April speech. At the same time, William Johnson, the young physician, who had been living with Paine in St. Denis and admired him greatly, attempted suicide. Although the attempt failed, Paine claimed that Johnson had wanted to kill himself, because, he said, he "came to France to enjoy liberty, but Marat has murdered it. I cannot endure the grievous spectacle of the triumph of imbecility and inhumanity over talent and virtue." Paine publicized the event in Brissot's newspaper, *Le Patriote français*.[26]

Since the wounds were so superficial, could it have been that Brissot and Paine orchestrated the affair to make Marat, their enemy, look even worse than he already did? A few days later Marat's trial began, where he claimed that in his April speech, he had not sought to denounce the Revolution or the Convention, but only Thomas Paine. The jury acquitted Marat, and Paine's standing fell even further in the eyes of his Jacobin enemies. The sans-culottes disgusted him, Marat in particular, who paraded around the city dressed as one. He was an unprepossessing figure: barely five feet tall, but with a loud voice. Along with his long trousers, Marat wore an open shirt, pistols stuck in his belt, and a dirty scarf wrapped around his head. The animosity between Marat and Paine could only end badly. Marat wanted Paine out of the Convention at best, dead if possible.

In the meantime, yet another political intrigue, that of General Francisco del Miranda, surfaced.[27] Miranda, a Venezuelan acquaintance of Paine's, had been inspired by American independence to seek the liberation of Latin America from Spain. Paine had known Miranda in America and England, and he was convinced that he had republican sympathies. History knows him as the "Precursor," which distinguished him from Simon Bolívar, who later carried on Miranda's struggle against Spain in Spanish America. Miranda fought by the side of the American rebels in 1781 in Pensacola, Florida when the Spanish government supported the new nation's struggle against England. After the war, he traveled throughout the United States and met Washington, Hamilton, Adams, and of course Thomas Paine. In defending Paine's *Rights of Man* against Burke, Miranda had apparently earned the disapproval of the defenders of church and king in England. In 1791, Paine once again met Miranda, this time when dining with bankers Turnbull and Forbes, whose agent in Paris was Paine's friend Thomas Christie.

During the revolution in France, Miranda took on a command in the French army under General Dumouriez. The Austrians soundly defeated their forces in Neerwinden in 1793 in a battle that was so fraught with cowardice that Dumouriez denounced Miranda, whose troops had fled, leaving Dumouriez unprotected. Miranda claimed, in turn, that Dumouriez was a traitor who was bent on marching on Paris and taking over the new republic for himself. Miranda was tried for treason. Paine and Joel Barlow testified on his behalf, primarily as character witnesses. Brissot and several Girondins also gave testimony, although the Mountain opposed him (most likely because he was supported so fervently by their rival Girondins). Thomas Christie told the court that Miranda was not a mere mercenary, but a man who sincerely wished to defend the common good. He said that Miranda had invested a large amount of money in Turnbull and Forbes and was ready to contribute to the economic well-being of France, which was then undergoing serious inflationary pressures and starvation. On the basis of such remarks, Miranda was acquitted.

Paine soon found that Miranda had accumulated his wealth in England when he conspired with the Pitt Administration to foment a revolution in the Nootka Sound (in the Pacific Northwest), which Spain and England both had claimed. Although the two countries negotiated a settlement to the disputed lands, Miranda argued for and won from Pitt a small fortune of 1,200 pounds sterling for his efforts. Later, when he was living in Paris, after Paine's release from prison in 1794, Miranda asked Paine to introduce him to the American minister, James Monroe. Despite the fact that Paine himself had once been a hired pen of Robert Morris and the French government, he thought Miranda's involvement with the conservative Pitt was a denial of liberal democratic principles. Accordingly, he "cautioned Mr. Monroe against him."[28] Miranda was later imprisoned in France on several occasions and finally departed in January of 1798. Paine never saw him again. Years later, in a power struggle, Bolívar turned Miranda over to the Spanish government, and he was exiled to Cádiz where he remained in a dungeon for the rest of his life.

Meantime, mobs of Parisians were constantly attacking the Convention, shouting insults and jeering from the gallery. On June 2, 1793, 80,000 people stormed the assembly, demanding purges and blood. Paine was appalled. It was clear to him that there was no real constituted government of France. The Committee expelled twenty-nine Girondins and two ministers from the Convention. Nearly eighty others left, revolted by this anarchic perversion of revolutionary principles. It was the end of Girondin rule—moderate rule— France had enjoyed in the years since 1789. Now a move was afoot to expel all foreigners from France. Paine, as a deputy, was exempt, but in danger. To make matters worse, his own constituency, Pas-de-Calais, voted no-confidence in him, and his friend Danton was replaced on the Committee of Public Safety by Robespierre. Paine returned to St. Denis to wait and drink, later admitting that because he was "borne down by public and private affliction, he had been driven to excesses in Paris" at this time.[29] By mid-July, Marat was dead, thanks to the knife of Charlotte Corday, who thought she could save the moderate revolution from what she considered the radical tyranny posed by Marat and his friends. She was too late.[30] The Revolution had already descended too deeply into the terror of mindless bloodletting.

The Convention, really the Committee of Public Safety, in April reorganized the constitution committee, adding to it St. Just and other more radical members. Hérault de Séchelles served on the committee, and in fact did most of the drafting, although at his trial the following April St. Just claimed that Hérault had done nothing, but sit there, silent and stupid. Like Paine, St. Just had been elected to the National Convention in 1792, as a deputy from l'Aisne. Loyal to Robespierre throughout the rise of the Mountain to absolute power and on into the Terror, he had written a statement about revolutionary dedication and self-sacrifice, which foreshadowed the writings of several Russian revolutionaries of the next century.

In 1869, two Russian nihilists, Mikhail Bakunin and Serge Nechaev, both devoted to the total destruction of the Russian imperial regime at all costs, drafted the most comprehensive and dehumanized definition of the revolutionary man. Among the essential points of the *Revolutionary Catechism* was the assertion that "the revolutionary is a lost man; he has no interests of his own, no cause of his own, no feelings, no habits, no belongings; he does not even have a name. Everything in him is absorbed by a single, exclusive interest, a single thought, a single passion—the revolution."[31] Some seventy-five years earlier, St. Just anticipated the catechism with his own words of the total absorption of a man into the cause:

> A revolutionary man is inflexible, but he is insensible, he is
> frugal; he is simple without advertising false modesty; he is
> the irreconcilable enemy of all lies, all indulgence, all affecta
> tion. As his aim is to see the Revolution triumph, he never
> criticizes it, but he condemns its enemies without enveloping
> them with the Revolution; he does not exaggerate it, but he
> enlightens it, and jealous of its purity, he watches himself

when he speaks of it, out of respect for it; he claims less to be
the equal of authority, which is the law, than the equal of
men, and above all of the unfortunate. . . .
The revolutionary man pursues the guilty and defends
innocence in the courtroom; he tells the truth in order that it
instruct, not for it to do damage; he knows that in order for the
Revolution to affirm itself, people must be as good as they used
to be wicked; his probity is not an intellectual finesse, but a
quality of the heart. Marat was kind at home, he threatened only
traitors. J.-J. Rousseau was a revolutionary and certainly was
not insolent: I conclude from this that a revolutionary man is a
hero of good sense and probity.[32]

In a few short months, Saint-Just condemned the guilty and the
innocent. Until then, he wanted to find public virtue and the
Supreme Being in the Revolution. But Paine's "Plan of a
Declaration," which had outlined thirty-three principles for the new
government, had contained no mention of God. Robespierre and St.
Just demanded that it include a statement that the Revolution was
under divine protection and guidance. They really meant that it was
under their guidance as they claimed divine sanction.

Accordingly, when the constitution was reported to the
Convention in June, it contained a preamble declaring that the constitution was presented to France "in the presence and under the
guidance of the Supreme Being." The Committee of Public Safety,
again more accurately Robespierre and St. Just, claimed that the new
rule of Virtue, and soon Terror, was ordained by God himself. But
this was not the Christian God of the Bible. Rather, it was God as
Reason, interpreted by the new believers in revolutionary terrorism.
The Cathedral of Notre Dame was transformed into the Temple of
Reason, and the clergy were forced to preach the new revolutionary
religion of the Goddess of Reason, Robespierre, and Terror. Helen
Maria Williams, who narrowly escaped the scaffold when she was
removed from the Luxembourg Prison to a convent/prison in
Charenton, drew a contemptuous picture of the new religion of lib-
erty, reason, and death.

The Goddess of Reason was a fine blooming damsel of the operahouse, and acted her part in this comedy also to the entire satisfaction of her new votaries. From her imperial throne, in which she was borne by four porters, she descended to the right hand of the president of the convention [Robespierre], and by a decree received the fraternal kiss as soon as the procureur of the commune, who attended as high priest or master of ceremonies, had announced her negative and positive character: first, that she was not like the objects of the ancient workshop, a cold and inanimate image; and next, that she was a masterpiece of nature, and that her sacred form had so inflamed every heart that only one universal cry was heard, "No more priests, and no other gods. . . ."

The most ludicrous masquerades presented themselves in every quarter. Pioneers and artillerymen led the march clothed in the surplices of the inferior clergy. The national guard were arrayed in the habits of the priests. The revolutionary citizens of the section were vested in garments still more costly. The revolutionary ladies and the priestesses of Reason had sanctified themselves with the dresses belonging to the Virgin and St. Frances and St. Bridget, and the revolutionary committee had reserved for their own decoration, with great prudence, all the garments of fine gold, embroidery and jewels, while the caps of the priests and the miters were placed on the heads of the horses employed in dragging these weighty spoils, which were to be presented to the convention. These offerings consisted of crosses, suns, vases, chandeliers, and chases, apostles, and saints in gold and silver, St. Anthony and his pig, St. Roche and his dog, and all the other saints registered in the calendar who were found to be of the same metallic worth.[33]

In the meantime, the twenty-two deputies, which the Communal Council of Paris had tried to indict in April, but which the Convention had subsequently refused to do, were now arraigned and soon condemned to death. Although the Convention adopted the new constitution and the *départements* ratified it, Robespierre thought he himself had no need for the constitution. He was the law. Accordingly, he suspended it until such time that harmony and peace returned to France, and he, St. Just, and the ten other members of the Committee ruled as the embodiment of the revolution. For the time being, the republic was dead.

To make matters worse for Paine, he once again ran into trouble with his old adversary, Gouverneur Morris, now the American Minister in France. Morris had detested Paine since the Silas Deane affair, and his antipathy toward him grew even deeper after he saw that for awhile Paine had regarded himself as the unofficial American ambassador to London. Paine was naïve about Morris' hatred for him. In fact, Morris fairly easily concealed it. His diary was, however, filled with highly unflattering references to Paine. In April 1791, he wrote, a friend of his referred to Paine "as being a little mad, which is not improbable." A few months later, he found Paine to be "inflated to the eyes and big with a litter of revolutions." In February of 1792, he wrote that Paine "seems to become very hour more drunk with self-conceit." He even predicted that Paine was soon to be "promoted to the pillory."[34] Although Paine might not have known how Morris felt personally about him, he was aware of his dislike for the revolution in France. This gave their rivalry a distinct ideological twist, since Morris had been a principal author of the American Constitution, having the greatest responsibility for its style.

The events in France had stunned Morris, just as they had earlier stunned Burke. His animosity toward France was so deep that some commentators have suggested that he did not believe in democracy at all. French historian Bernard Vincent writes that "in France, Morris's anti-republican ideas were a secret to no one. He had the king's ear, he abhorred the Revolution, and he was constantly in attendance in Parisian high society whose leisured morals coincided with his libertine tastes. He was quite the ladies' man, although he had lost a leg in 1780 after an accident. His passion for the good life and women were legendary and no one could ignore that he was the lover of the Comtesse de Flahaut nor that he shared those favors with Charles-Maurice de Talleyrand-Périgord and a British nobleman."[35] Talleyrand, a former bishop, now governmental official, and the father of Adéle de Flahaut's son, was well aware of Morris' visits to the Comtesse's blue room in the Louvre. The former administrator of Paris left for London in 1792, giving up warm conversations with the American Minister as well as the warm embraces of his young mistress.

Morris' personal goal as American Minister was to end the treaty between France and the United States and to establish a new, close relationship between England and America. In 1790, President Washington had sent him to London to test British feelings, and when war broke out between England and France in February of 1793, Washington became more convinced than ever, as did Morris, that America's future lay not with revolutionary France, but steady, old England. The Americans' first step was to declare neutrality in the war between France and England. Their second came in the form of the conclusion of the Jay Treaty in the fall of 1794. In between, Morris connived against Paine and the Revolution. When French warships seized forty-five American ships and sent them to Bordeaux, Morris did virtually nothing for them, hoping to increase the anger of American merchants against France. Paine, well aware of Morris' feelings toward France, asked Barère to obtain their release, and after Barère did so, he in turn asked Paine's help in obtaining supplies from America to help France avoid starvation. Instead of suggesting that Barère talk to Morris, Paine told Barère that he himself could do it. He claimed he was prepared to leave France to obtain flour from the United States. Jefferson, then Secretary of State, he told Barère, "is an ardent defender of the interests of France. Gouverneur Morris is badly disposed towards you. I believe he has expressed the wish to be recalled." Still, he warned Barère that he had better "have respect for Morris," given his position.[36] Morris naturally thought Paine wanted to replace him as Minister. He did not. It was clear, however, that after this incident the Minister's office would not interfere should Paine be arrested and jailed. At one point, Morris wrote to Robert Morris: "I suspected that Paine was intriguing against me, although he put on a face of attachment. Since that period, I am confirmed in the idea."[37]

In October, the Terror, having begun in June, now measurably increased its pace. Executions in the summer were few, around an average of three per week. By the fall, their numbers dramatically escalated. On October 10, the war with Europe continuing and the provinces in rebellion, on a proposal by St. Just, the Convention was suspended indefinitely and dictatorial power seized

by the Committee of Public Safety.   Now many Girondins were
openly condemned to prison and certain death.   Some 193 victims
were executed at the end of the year.   Some were royal and aristocratic, including Marie-Antoinette and the former Duc d'Orléans,
who had tried to resist arrest and certain death by changing his name
(though too late) to Philippe-Egalité.   Some 100 suspects a month
were taken before the Tribunal, although about half of them were still
being acquitted.   On October 3, the "ferocious" Jacobin Jean-
Baptiste-André Amar denounced the Girondins, including their
leader Brissot, as "agents of an English faction who have exercised a
fatal influence on the course of our revolution."   Amar's reasons were
that the Girondins had tried to save the life of the king and maintained close ties to the English enemy.   Brissot was condemned in
particular for his efforts to free black slaves.   Included in the indictment was the name Thomas Paine, also accused of voting against the
king's execution.   Declaimed André Amar, the deputy from l'Isère:

> At the same time the Englishman Thomas Paine, called by the
> faction [Girondin] to the honor of representing the French
> nation, dishonored himself by supporting the opinion of Brissot,
> and by promising us in his fable the dissatisfaction of the United
> States of America, our natural allies, which he did not blush to
> depict for us full of veneration and gratitude for the tyrant of
> France.[38]

Others thought of Paine as an Englishman and a danger to the security of the Revolution.   Robespierre, of all people, momentarily saved
him, arguing that for the time being only the original twenty-two
Girondins should be confined to prison.   By late winter, events began
to move rapidly, chaotically, bewilderingly.   The Terror was real.
People were paralyzed by the bloody scenes they witnessed around
them.   Any taint of political opposition meant the threat of execution.
     Paine's friend and editor, Brissot, was executed on October
31.   Vergniaud and the former Foreign Minister Lebrun soon followed.   Condorcet went into hiding and committed suicide in early
1794, as did Duchâtelet.   Even Roux, arrested earlier the previous
August, was imprisoned.   He died by his own hand in jail in January

of 1794. Barère and Sieyès survived. Paine always felt that the former had betrayed him in seeking his imprisonment. As for Sieyès, he was later to become a member of the Directory and a supporter of Bonaparte. For now, the focus was on arrest, imprisonment, death. The "archangel of the revolution," St. Just, desired to create a republic of terrible spartan virtue, and he brooked no dissent.

The Tribunal presided over the deaths of nearly one thousand suspects in the spring of 1794. By March, the extremist Hébertists (including Hébert himself and Desmoulins) and the moderate Dantonists (including Danton) fell under the blade of the guillotine, as did the calendar-maker Fabre d'Eglantine. Just before he was taken away, Danton told Paine, "What you have done for the good and liberty of your country, I have tried in vain to do for mine. I have been less fortunate, and no less guilty. . . . They are sending me to the scaffold. Well, my friend, I will go willingly."[39]

In November, Pierre Manuel, a former school teacher and now a member of the Convention, who, like Paine, had voted to preserve the life of the king, was executed. Manuel told the Tribunal that he agreed with Paine that the king should be exiled, not executed. This was enough for Barère, Robespierre, and St. Just. Paine and other foreign-born citizens represented a particular danger to the republic, especially in light of their past opposition to the king's death sentence, and now because of enemy victories over the French revolutionary army, especially the defeat of French forces at Toulon. Accordingly, on December 25, the increasingly radical Barère, moving ever closer to Robespierre and St. Just, publicly charged that all foreigners were by definition disloyal to France and the Revolution. Paine now stood accused of being a traitor simply for "being a foreigner, born in England."[40] This was the worst indictment possible, in view of England's war against the French republic. Paine later recalled his fears to his old American friend, Samuel Adams. "My friends were falling as fast as the guillotine could cut their heads off, and as I every day expected the same fate . . . I appeared to myself to be on my death-bed, for death was on every side of me."[41]

Johnson and Choppin had already left France, "highly pleased with their escape."[42] Paine did not. On December 27, the Committee of General Security and Surveillance of the National

Convention issued a warrant for the arrest of Anacharsis Clootz and Thomas Paine together:

> The Committee resolves that the named Thomas Paine and Anacharsis Clootz, formerly deputies of the National Convention, will be seized and imprisoned; that their papers will be examined and suspicious ones be brought under seal to the Committee of General Security.[43]

Three days later, while visiting at White's, Paine was hauled off to the Luxembourg Prison. Before Paine left, he asked only that a manuscript he had been working on be delivered to his friend, Joel Barlow, a request that the authorities granted. In all, the Terror would claim over 16,000, with more than 2,600 in Paris alone. Now, Paine too had reason to fear for his head—which might well be chopped off by his old admirer, the public executioner.

It is curious that at a moment when Paine's friends were either being jailed and executed or in hiding and killing themselves, he did not choose to leave. While it is impossible to say for certain why this was so, some speculation is possible. First, he knew he could not return to England. There, he was legally branded an outlaw and could face imprisonment or execution. Moreover, for the same reason, he knew that if he tried to leave France for America, he would need to leave on an official American ship to avoid being picked up at sea by the English fleet, and then taken to London. But, then again, he had enemies in America, too, who might like to have seen him turned over to British authorities. He could have tried to escape to Switzerland, as some of his acquaintances did. The president of the British Club, John Hurford Stone, and his mistress Helen Maria Williams did just that.

In the end, by his own actions—his sudden departure from White's to the country suburb of St. Denis, his refusal to go to the Convention anymore, his absorption in his theological interests (which became the first part of *The Age of Reason*)—all these contributed to his conscious or unconscious (it is not clear which) decision to refuse to have anything more to do with the Revolution. It was his misfortune to have returned for a short visit to White's on the night of the 27th, but with his arrest warrant issued, the authorities would have undoubtedly seized him sooner or later anyway. Paine seemed, at that moment, simply paralyzed by the events unfolding around him. In the end, he probably failed to leave because he just could not motivate himself to do so. The Revolution in America had experienced some terrible moments, too, and it was ultimately successful. His boundless optimism could have been telling him that even now, in the depths of Terror, the French Revolution could still be triumphant. But with his arrest, all hope had to have faded. He now faced the most arduous experience of his life.

15 · The Age of Reason

O riginally built for Marie de Medici in the early seventeenth
century, the Luxembourg was constructed on the site of a
palace once owned by the Duc de Piney-Luxembourg,
hence its name. The palace once held twenty-four paintings of the
life of Marie de Medici by the great Flemish artist, Peter Paul
Rubens. But this was all forgotten by the time Paine, Clootz, and up
to a thousand prisoners were sent there.

Paine remained in prison for just over ten months, from
December 28, 1793, to November 4, 1794. He never fully recovered
from the ordeal. His arrest warrant had been issued by the
Committee of General Security, on which neither Barère nor
Robespierre sat. For his part, Robespierre had at one time thought of
Paine as an American citizen, a fighter for republican causes, and
Barère had served with Paine on the Convention committee writing
the new constitution for France. But even so, there is no question
that had the Committee of Public Safety directly considered whether
he should be arrested, he still would have gone to jail. Paine always
blamed Robespierre for having "me seized in the night and imprisoned in the Luxembourg."[1]

Even worse, Robespierre wrote out Paine's order of execution
seven months after his arrest. Paine several times cited the order,
"signed in the handwriting of Robespierre," which read: "To demand
that a decree of accusation [death sentence] be passed against
Thomas Paine for the interests of America as well as of
France."[2] Convinced that Paine, a native Englishman (thus, now not
an American), was as much a danger to America as he was to France,

Robespierre believed that Paine deserved execution. Besides, he had sided with the Girondins, a danger to Robespierre himself, until they were defeated in the spring of 1793. Paine was therefore certain that "when Robespierre proposed bringing me to the tribunal, [it was] like sending me at once to the scaffold."

As for Barère, although he was not a member of the Committee of General Security, Paine knew he had signed his arrest warrant. Paine once noted that of the nine members of the committee that had been working on the new constitution for France, only he, Sieyès, and Barère had survived. The last of these had made it, he said, because he had "joined Robespierre" and betrayed Paine. Just after his own arrest in 1794, Barère "apologized to me for having signed the [arrest] warrant, by saying he felt himself in danger and was obliged to do it."[3] In effect, he sacrificed a colleague to save himself. Barère was transported to Guiana from where he escaped, only to remain in hiding for several years until he reemerged as a secret agent for Bonaparte. After Napoleon's final fall from power, Barère was banished during the restoration of the Bourbons, but again reappeared in the reign of Louis Philippe. He died in 1841 at age eighty-six.

Shortly after Paine's arrest, sixteen ex-patriot Americans living in Paris went to the Convention "in the name of our country . . . to reclaim our friend, our countryman, that he may sail with us for America where he will be received with open arms." Among this group were Joel Barlow, Paine's friend, as well as Peter Whiteside, with whom he had done business in London on his bridge, and Major William Jackson, who had gone to Paris with Paine and John Laurens in 1781. The group claimed that this "apostle of liberty," as they called him, ought not be imprisoned, for surely he was an American and nothing would give more heart to Englishmen in their war against republican France than if "this courageous and virtuous defender of liberty" remained in the Luxembourg. They pleaded for the Convention to release the man "whose courageous and energetic pen did so much to free the Americans, and whose intentions we have no doubt whatever were to render the same services to the French republic."

They were booed and hissed in the Convention, which was

still crowded with scores and scores of shouting sans-culottes, despite a polite, though firm, reply by the Convention's president, Marc Vadier. Vadier told them that he was delighted to see them, because the Americans had "sworn the destruction of kings and vowed an eternal hatred to tyrants and their instruments." While Paine was an Englishman and deserved his fate, Vadier promised to bring their petition before the Convention. He sent it to the Committee of Public Safety—where sat Robespierre, St. Just, Barère, and Jean-Nicolas Billaud-Varenne—and the Committee of General Security, led by Vadier himself, which had signed his fate in the first place. The response came from Billaud-Varenne, a lawyer by profession and a writer by conviction: their attempt to reclaim Thomas Paine "was only the act of individuals, without any authority from the American government."[4] More than any other person, Billaud-Varenne had in 1789 laid out the excuse for the Terror in his attack on the Catholic Church. "However painful an amputation may be, when a member is gangrened it must be sacrificed if we wish to save the body."[5] The real answer to the Americans' petition, unfortunately, was forthcoming in the stark terms of the more than ten months that Paine, now fifty-six years old, served in prison.

Conditions in the Luxembourg were neither the worst nor the best, considering the circumstances. In contrast, the Conciergerie, which today still stands next to the Palais de Justice, was abominable. It was the fortress to which the condemned were always sent before they learned of their impending trial, usually in the form of a notice referred to as "the evening paper." Soon afterwards, the prisoners appeared fleetingly before the Revolutionary Tribunal, which comprised their trial, an event immediately followed by their last ride in the cart to the scaffold on the Place de la Révolution. Helen Maria Williams described the Conciergerie as "that abode of horror, that anti-chamber of the tomb. I have seen those infectious cells where the prisoners breathed their contagion, where the walls are in some places stained with the blood of the massacres of September, and where a part of the spacious courtyard, round which the grated dungeons are built, remains unpaved since that period when the stones were taken up for the purpose of burying the dead."[6]

Life in the Luxembourg, more accurately a house of detention, was very different. At first, the place was relatively lax in terms of security: it was said to rank as one of the best brothels in Paris until the authorities decided that prisoners of the Republic ought not engage in the pleasures of the flesh. The population of the jail consisted of all classes of suspects and the condemned. Like most French prisons during this period, they were really more like hotels with guests even having to pay for rooms and meals.[7] So the wealthier a prisoner was, the better the conditions, because he could bring just about anything he wanted with him. After June 1794, the government began to crack down and instituted "the common mess" and took all of a prisoner's money over fifty francs. Thereafter "there was watery soup, stale herrings, bad bread, medicated wine."[8]

Paine later described in notably straightforward terms the conditions of his life in prison. In reading it, it seems that he did not live a particularly uncomfortable life. "The room in which I was lodged was on the ground floor, and one of a long range of rooms under a gallery, and the door of it opened outward and flat against the wall."[9] Paine was not the only foreigner in the prison. Clootz was there, and the two of them often discussed matters of politics and religion. In addition, Paine reported that General O'Hara, who had fought for the British against America in the war for independence, was also there. O'Hara was released several months before Paine.

The jailer at the Luxembourg, a man named Benoit, was a kind old gent of seventy, who received all of his charges "with humanity," but who was himself soon sent to the guillotine. Williams referred to the jailer as "le bon Benoit." His was "a name which many a wretch has blessed, for many a sorry soul his compassion and gentleness have softened. His heart was indeed ill-suited to his office, and often he incurred the displeasure of those savages by whom he was employed, and wished their victims to feel the full extent of their calamity, unmitigated by any detail of kindness, any attention to those little wants which this benevolent person was anxious to remove, or those few comforts which he had the power to bestow." Benoit had once served as the concierge of the Luxembourg before it was transformed into a prison. No wonder he was "ill-suited" to his job.[10]

Until the government's crackdown on prison life, Paine communicated with the outside world with letters to and from his friends and colleagues. One of his faithful correspondents was the wife of Sir Robert Smyth, his banker friend living in Paris. She comforted him, signing her letters "From a Little Corner in the World," and he replied as "the Castle in the Air." He later wrote her a poem in the same elementary rhyming style he had used twenty years earlier. The poem told of how his "castle of fancy" was beset by a storm and carried away.

> It pass'd over rivers, and valleys, and groves,
> The world it was all in my view;
> I thought of my friends, of their fates, of their loves,
> And often, full often of You.

The castle settled down to a place to which it was ineluctably attracted, "When whom should I meet in this charming retreat,/This corner of calmness, but You."[11]

On another occasion, he wrote her more verse, entitled "A New Covenant." Paine clearly had on his mind the manuscript on religion he had left with Joel Barlow as he was being taken to prison, because he related in this poem that he refused to accept the God which had, in scripture, chosen "the disobedient Jews."

> Their country often he laid waste,
> Their little ones he slew;
> But I have shown a better taste
> In choosing Y, O, U.[12]

What meaning can be determined by these missives to Lady Smyth? The last of Paine's two marriages had ended more than twenty years earlier. There was no indication in his writing or anything else that he ever again entered into an intimate relationship with a woman, until Lady Smyth. But there is no evidence that his feelings toward her were anything more than platonic. After all, he later lived with the Smyths for a time in 1796 while he was recovering from one of his bouts with illness. In ten years, there would be a fourth woman to enter his life, leading historians and commentators

to speculate about his amorous liaisons. But there can be no definitive conclusions about any of this.

Paine's correspondence was clearly a bit of a distraction for
him. Unfortunately, the Luxembourg was dangerously unhealthy, and
he soon fell ill. His illness may have saved him from the guillotine,
which took Clootz' life on March 24. Then just two months before
the fall of Robespierre on July 27, 1794 (9 Thérmidor), Paine contracted a very high fever, which, he said, "almost terminated my existence." (GW 2:699) Paine was ministered to by the prison's physician, Dr. Markoski, a Dr. Graham (another physician), and a Mr.
Bond, a surgeon. He often read aloud portions of *The Age of Reason*
to Bond, hoping that Bond would tell everyone that Thomas Paine,
should he be executed or die, never lost his faith or renounced his
ideas. When he was ill, the guards moved him to a larger cell with
three Belgian citizens, who also did what they could to take care of
him. One of these men was Joseph Vanheule, who was later released
and who eventually became the mayor of Bruges, where Paine visited
a few times. The other two were Michael Rubyns and Charles
Bastini, both from Louvain, but Paine (and history) never went into
any detail about who they were.[13] Paine never fully recovered from
his illness. Perhaps the authorities thought he would die naturally.
Or, perhaps, it was pure luck that saved him from summary death.
He knew at any moment he could be executed: "One hundred and
sixty-eight persons were taken out of the Luxembourg in one night,
and a hundred and sixty of them guillotined next day, of which I now
know I was to have been one." And in fact he believed that "there was
no time when I could think my life worth twenty-four hours, and my
mind was made up to meet my fate." Paine later depicted how he was
spared the scaffold.

> When persons by scores and by hundreds were to be taken out
> of the prison for the guillotine it was always done in the night,
> and those who performed that office had a private mark or sig-
> nal, by which they knew what rooms to go to, and what number
> to take. We, as I have stated, were four, and the door of our
> room was marked, unobserved by us, with that number in chalk;
> but it happened, if happening is a proper word, that the mark

was put on when the door was open, and flat against the wall, and thereby came on the inside when we shut it at night, and the destroying angel passed by it.[14]

An accident of fate that the door closed inward, with the mark of death on the inside so that it could not be seen when the prisoners were supposed to be taken to their deaths? Or a mistake by his jailers that they were either too busy or too stupid to notice, and they were spared?

In any case, the only official who could possibly have helped Paine was Gouverneur Morris, who was the only foreign diplomat to remain in Paris during the Terror. But Morris had no interest in seeing Paine leave prison alive. Morris received a communication from the French Foreign Minister, Chemin Deforgues, who explained that Paine was under the laws of France a citizen of England, and since he was originally born an Englishman, he was now suspected as a potential spy. Morris forwarded this letter to Paine, who on February 24, 1794 pleaded for help. While "you and I are not on terms of the best harmony, I apply to you as the Minister of America" to use his office to reclaim him.[15] Morris had no intention of doing so. To make matters worse, Morris had even told Deforgues that he agreed that Paine was English. Now, with Paine out of the way (giving credence to the idea that he might have been an English spy), Morris gave Deforgues the misleading impression that the Americans might send military assistance to France. Morris, a francophobe par excellence, had no intention of keeping that promise.

Morris had also been in contact with Thomas Jefferson about Paine. Jefferson, however, had resigned as Secretary of State on December 31, 1793, just four days after Paine's arrest, so he could do nothing. Edmund Randolph, the first Attorney General of the United States, had replaced him. Randolph, whose views about France were closer to Paine's than those of Morris and Hamilton, was never informed about Paine's plight.[16] In his duplicitous scheme against Paine, Morris first told Jefferson that Paine in prison "thinks that I ought to claim him as an American citizen; but considering his birth, his naturalization in this country [France], and the place he filled [as a deputy of the National Convention], I doubt much the right, and I am sure that the claim would be, for the present at least, inexpedient and ineffectual."[17]

Morris then told Jefferson he had informed French authorities that the Americans considered Paine to be an American citizen when he had not done this at all. "Mr. Paine wrote me a note desiring I would claim him as an American, *which I accordingly did*, though contrary to my judgment," he said. Morris had simply lied to Jefferson. Even so, as far as Morris was concerned, Paine must suffer the consequences of living in France and violating French law, "and he may see in the fate of the Brissotins [the Girondins], that to which he is exposed." In truth, if the Americans, Morris in particular, wanted to see Paine released, they could have done so quite easily, because the French government needed American support to continue its war against most of Europe. French Foreign Minister Deforgues (soon to see the axe himself), wrote to Morris: "Our only aim has been to maintain between the two nations the most perfect harmony."

Morris' main rationalization was that once Paine sat in the Convention, he became a French citizen, and was no longer an American. Even worse, he was impious and a blasphemer, two additional reasons to hate Paine. "Lest I should forget it, I must mention," he told Jefferson, "that Thomas Paine is in prison, where he amuses himself with publishing a pamphlet against Jesus Christ."[18] Morris' views of the man were obviously set in stone. The issue had always been a personal one for him. His preference was to see Paine liberated in only one way: headless and feet first. For the time being, Paine languished in the Luxembourg. What faith he had left was centered on his work on scripture, safely in the hands of his friend Barlow and, hopefully, close to publication.

The work that Paine turned over to Barlow as he was whisked off to prison was the first part of *The Age of Reason*. It had already been translated into French by François-Xavier Lanthenas and was well on its way to publication in France. Robespierre apparently accepted its premises, which agreed with his own emphasis on the centrality of a Supreme Being. Both Paine and Robespierre feared godlessness as much as they hated superstition.[19] In 1776, Paine had told John Adams that he wanted to write about religion, but had decided " 'it will be best to postpone it to the latter part of life.' " Adams had thought this aspiration was nothing more than "daring impudence."[20] That period finally arrived in 1793, when the leadership of France under Robespierre approved of Paine's ideas about God, creation, and the afterlife. Paine objected to organized religion, indeed to Christianity itself, and especially to Christianity's distortion of what appeared to Paine as simple, true facts about God and his creation.

Like Robespierre and Jefferson, Paine believed in a natural religion, generally denominated deism, but which in Paine's case went farther than any eighteenth-century deist might have gone. Deism was a theology, which posited a single deity, a "watchmaker God" who created the universe, but did not interfere in the operation of its laws. "I believe in one God," he told his readers, "and no more; and I hope for happiness beyond this life." (*AR* 50) The faith of a traditional Christian? No, far from it, because Paine, as a deist, believed that after God had created the universe, each generation of human beings became responsible for improving its own situation and the lives of all beings.

But Paine's deism went farther than this, because he was certain that God's divinity permeated everything on earth. While God did not (and would not) intervene in history, His very creation itself presupposed a godliness about nature and man. In effect, God's creative genius was a part of everything in the universe, but He did not intercede to guide the direction in which events might go. Anyone who claimed He did either misunderstood the nature of the universe or had some ulterior motive. This meant that organized religion—all churches in whatever forms they took throughout history—was wrong. We live in an age of reason, Paine wrote, and no longer one of superstition and priestcraft. It was time to undermine the remnants of these mysteries.[21] "All national institutions of churches, whether Jewish, Christian or Turkish, appear to me no other than human inventions, set up to terrify and enslave mankind, and monopolize power and profit." (*RM* 268) The very idea of revelation, of God speaking directly to people, was a fiction. It was literally impossible to verify any such occurrence independently, and to say that it happened simply defied reason.

Paine understood how people could believe in the miraculous events said to surround the life and death of Jesus. The propagators of the faith lived in a time of mythology and superstition, not reason. Thus, it was plausible for them to accept the idea that an extraordinary man was the son of God, that his mother was impregnated by a Holy Spirit, that he led a life of unusual virtue and saintliness, and that he rose from the dead after his interment. It was acceptable to Paine for people to believe this set of events, but they had no right to force their beliefs on anyone else. The story "has every mark of fraud and imposition stamped upon the face of it. . . . [I]t is impossible to conceive a story more derogatory to the Almighty, more inconsistent with His wisdom, more contradictory to His power, than this story is." (*RM* 54, 57)

Paine was at his acid best in attacking what he referred to as the religious "mythologists." No biblical story was safe. They were all targets of his fully developed contempt and wit. He was dealing with a work, the Bible, which he thought full of lies.

> Whenever we read the obscene stories, the voluptuous debaucheries, the cruel and torturous executions, the unrelenting vindictiveness, with which more than half the Bible is filled, it would be more consistent that we called it the word of a demon than the Word of God. It is a history of wickedness that has served to corrupt and brutalize mankind; and, for my part, I sincerely detest it as I detest everything that is cruel. (*AR* 60)

Old Testament prophets were poets who fabricated everything in their predictions. They were "useless and unnecessary." (*AR* 97) The Bible was full of stories made up by a few people who sought to spread what they understood to be the truths of their god to the world. Their truth, however, was based on miracles, which defied human reason and the known principles of science and mechanics. Take Jonah, for example: "The story of the whale swallowing Jonah, though a whale is large enough to do it, borders greatly on the marvelous but it would have approached nearer to the idea of a miracle if Jonah had swallowed the whale. . . . [I]s it more probable that a man should have swallowed a whale or told a lie?" (*AR* 91) Paine clearly did not oppose religion so much as the lies it promoted. Religion was a good thing. Twice in the *Rights of Man*, he had asserted that "every religion is good that teaches man to be good." (*RM* 260, 270) Most religions did this, but they did other things as well. They blinded people to the tasks before them: to make the world a better place to live, to help the downtrodden and poor, to end tyranny and spread democracy.

If God were as powerful as He was described by the traditional religionists, Paine wrote, there is no reason to believe that He created only one world with one kind of human creature. He was capable of creating "a plurality of worlds," each with its own history and traditions quite different from the world human beings could know because their vision was so limited. Such a thought made Christianity insignificant, even "ridiculous." It "scatters it in the mind like feathers in the air." (*AR* 85) God, having created one world, might well have tried His luck at creating other ones as well, on and on, ad infinitum, until multiple worlds, each with its own individual characteristics, existed throughout the universe. Certainly God had the power to undertake such a task, especially if He could perform miracles and speak to individual men. It was "solitary and strange" for God, "who had millions of worlds equally dependent on His protection, [to] quit the care of all the rest, and come to die in our world, because, they say, one man and one woman had eaten an apple?" And if there had been a multiplicity of creations, then Christ would have had to have gone on the road "in an endless succession of deaths, with scarcely a momentary interval of life." (*AR* 90)

Of all the parts of the Bible Paine attacked, he reserved his most venomous insults for the prophets, those few who claimed to speak directly for God after He directly sent them divine messages. Paine did not care whether they were Hebrew, Christian, or Moslem prophets. They were all either "perjurers" or at best poets, "who mixed poetry, anecdote, and devotion together— and those works still retain the air and style of poetry, though in translation." Really, they were "useless and unnecessary." They told fabulous stories, which no one ought to believe, because they defied God's "choicest gift, the gift of reason." (*AR* 51, 61, 97, 68)

What evidence, Paine the rationalist constantly asked, existed that God sent messages to individuals? None. The

Commandments of the Hebrew scriptures contained, for example, some very fine moral precepts, and human beings should follow them. But there was nothing particularly divine about how they were sent from God to mankind. "When Moses told the children of Israel that he received two tables of the commandments from the hands of God, they were not obliged to believe him, because they had no other authority for it than his telling them so; and I have no other authority for it than some historian telling me so." (*AR* 52) The same might be said for miracles, which have come down through history by the Hebrew and "Christian mythologists," the prophets, who believed in fables and superstition. Miracles defied nature, the natural order of the universe, and hence opposed reason. "We have never seen, in our time, nature go out of her course," he exclaimed, "but we have good reason to believe that millions of lies have been told in the same time; it is therefore at least millions to one that the reporter of the miracle tells a lie." (*AR* 55, 95) God did in fact figure in the world, but not through miracles.

Even the Quakers did not understand how spectacular God's creation was. It was a gloomy religion that hardly accounted for the wonders of nature.[22] After creation, God had given man that "gift of reason" to improve or destroy the world. He left it to men to figure out from there what to do with those wonders. "It is only by the exercise of reason that man can discover God," and from a study of his creation, through reason, human beings began to understand the arts and sciences. (*AR* 60, 50, 70) God was not like a man, and man not like God. A man could not make principles eternal and immutable. He could only discover them. God did not behave like men when they became angry or killed others. Man's duty was, however, to imitate God "in everything moral, scientific, and mechanical" (*AR* 84). As a creature of God, Paine believed that he was obliged to live the best life he possibly could.

Every human being, in fact, had a responsibility to avoid the myths of scripture. Their duty was to use their rational faculties to imitate "the moral goodness and beneficence of God, manifested in the creation toward all His creatures. That seeing, as we daily do, the goodness of God to all men, it is an example calling upon all men to practice the same toward each other." (*AR* 98) To do otherwise violated our moral duty. Thomas Paine was prepared to live according to these principles. He would do his utmost to influence others to do the same. That, at least, was his plan as he continued to endure the agony of prison.

There, Paine reassessed the revolutionary events which had taken place from 1789 to the time of his arrest. In fact, his life was becoming agonizingly frustrating, and it was not to get any better. The entire decade he spent in France after 1792 was fraught with disillusionment and disappointment. Revolution failed him, as it failed so many others. He thought that even America had totally abandoned him to his miserable fate. In his last months of incarceration, he began to target Washington as the primary cause of his continued imprisonment: as President of the United States, surely he could have used his power to convince the French government that Thomas Paine was an American citizen, a true patriot, and not a subversive Englishman. But Washington abstained either because he was unaware of Paine's predicament or for political and diplomatic reasons. The only American in Paris who could actually help him was someone he did not even know: the new American Minister, James Monroe, who arrived in August of 1794 to replace Gouverneur Morris. French authorities had expelled Morris in retaliation for the Americans' demand to have Genet, their Minister, recalled from the United States. Monroe, a Jeffersonian, was pro-French and a political enemy of Alexander Hamilton and John Jay, the two principal pro-British Federalists in the Washington cabinet.

Paine of course had more to be angry about and to fear than his imprisonment. His imprisonment symbolized the accuracy of Edmund Burke's old predictions, more accurate than Paine's had been. Revolution had declined into tyranny as the republic deteriorated into terror and as Napoleon rose to power, soon to be emperor. Paine had participated in the National Convention and the drafting of the Constitution of 1793; he forthrightly supported the reforms of his old friends, Brissot, Danton, and the Girondins; and now he himself suffered under the Terror. But even after St. Just and Robespierre's execution on July 28, 1794 (the day after they fell from power), Paine was not immediately freed. He suffered nearly another four months while his American friends in Paris worked tirelessly to have him released. The new French government ironically saw him as a subversive and a dangerous influence since he had participated in the revolutionary regime of the Convention.

Paine therefore remained in prison, terribly weakened by his fever, working on a revision of the *Rights of Man* and preparing the dedication to a new edition of *The Age of Reason*.[23] He wrote to the Convention, believing that with Robespierre and St. Just dead and gone, a petition to that body was now safe. He pleaded for his release, hoping that "your justice will restore me to the liberty of which I have been deprived."[24]

When Paine finally learned that a new American Minister to France had arrived, he immediately wrote to him even though he had not yet even learned who he was. "As I believe none of the public papers have announced your name right I am unable to address you by it, but a *new* minister from America is joy to me and will be so to every American in France," he said. He denounced Morris (now known to him as his "inveterate enemy," the same thing he had called Robespierre in his letter to the Convention) for leaving him to rot in jail. As a result, Morris "has permitted something of the national character of America to suffer."[25] In addition to writing to Monroe, Paine also asked Peter Whiteside to intervene directly for him with Monroe, but Whiteside soon came back with some grim news ten days later: "Mr. Monroe has told me that he has no order [meaning from the President, Mr. Washington] respecting you, but that he [Mr. Monroe] will do everything in his power to liberate you; but, from what I learn from the Americans lately arrived in Paris, you are not considered, either by their American Government, or by the individuals, as an American citizen." It was probably at this crucial juncture that Paine's distrust and hatred for Morris shifted to Washington. (*GW* 2:700) Paine again wrote Monroe, this time a long "memorial" (as he called it) recounting everything he had done since he had become a citizen of France, hoping this would convince Monroe that he had acted in the highest of political principles.[26] While waiting for Monroe's reply, a report began to circulate in London that Paine had been guillotined, giving rise to the famous (infamous?) "last dying words of Thomas Paine." Paine's enemies had once before circulated the rumor of his passing. At that time in

1792, after his effigy was burned throughout England, talk was adrift that he had actually been hanged in Ockham. Now, in 1794, he allegedly confessed his sins before he walked to the scaffold: "Ye numerous spectators gathered around, pray give ear to my last words; I am determined to speak the Truth in these my last moments, altho' I have written and spoken nothing but lies all my life."[27] A spurious falsehood, but one which Paine was now accustomed to hearing about himself.

Monroe replied to Paine on September 18 in a long letter that, although some considered Paine French, Monroe believed that he had never given up his American citizenship. Nor did the American people, who were deeply indebted to Paine for his service to his country. The President, too, understood this, and Monroe conveyed Washington's "wishes in seeking your safety." The new Minister promised to work for his release and hoped Paine could wait "with patience and fortitude." Several rounds of correspondence between Paine and Monroe then followed, but in fact he was not released until nearly two months later on November 4, 1794. In the meantime, his health, as he described it, was "suffering exceedingly." (*GW* 2:701-03) The lies about himself Paine could tolerate. His mental and physical suffering now greatly weighed on him as he became increasingly convinced that George Washington, despite his words, had abandoned him.

After three hundred fifteen days in the Luxembourg, the great American prisoner of the French Revolution moved in with the Monroes and stayed with them pretty consistently for the next eighteen months, until May of 1796. As in prison, Paine often became sick with fever, and the huge abscess in his side, which he had contracted in jail, was constantly raw and painful, a bitter reminder of his recent misery. Almost immediately, he was reinstated by a unanimous vote as a deputy in the National Convention on a motion by Antoine Thibaudeau. Paine's seat on the Convention, as he later described, had been taken by Joseph Lebon, "one of the vilest characters that ever existed, and who made the streets of Arras run with blood." While he was imprisoned, Lebon entered the Convention, and when Paine got out of prison, Lebon went to jail and was soon executed for his bloodthirsty actions. "He supplied my place all the way through."28   Now out of jail and reinstated by the Convention, Paine was offered a literary pension from the government, which he declined to accept. In addition, although the Convention owed him back pay for previous services, it is not known whether he ever received it.   He did, however, agree to rejoin the Convention, although he could not take his seat until the following spring, because he was so ill.

The Convention quickly passed a decree reconfirming the treaty the Americans and French had entered into in 1778. Monroe thought the treaty so important that he wrote to the Committee of Public Safety that the decree should personally be delivered to the American government by none other than Thomas Paine. Monroe was willing to send him not as an American, but because "Citizen Paine is a member of the Convention, I thought it better to submit this subject to your consideration."29 It is unclear why Monroe hoped that Paine would personally carry the decree to President Washington: perhaps because as a symbol of Paine's professional reinstatement in government, or perhaps (and more likely) because he wanted Paine out of his house. In any case, the Committee rejected the idea with no explanations given.

On December 3, the Convention began to write yet another French constitution, this time to be rid of the one that had sustained the control of the Mountain and the Reign of Terror. The new document was to be less radical than the one that Paine and Condorcet had worked on in 1793, with its one house legislature and elected executive council. For Paine's part, however, he wanted Convention members to focus on allowing all men (though not women), no matter their class, to vote. The committee of eleven, which was reviewing the proposals, appeared however to be moving away from the principle of universal suffrage. Paine was convinced that democracy should be open to all men, and not merely those who paid taxes (with the exception of soldiers), as the committee was suggesting. At one point during the deliberations over the new constitution, a mob reminiscent of the sans-culottes and enragés in 1793-94 broke into the Convention and frightened the deputies. It was never made clear what they wanted exactly, but the disturbance indicated that the Terror had not fully abated, and worked to convince them that all men were not yet ready to possess the right to vote.

In an effort to convince the Convention that voting should be universal, in July 1795, Paine printed his *Dissertation on the First Principles of Government*. Although originally addressed to the people of Holland just as they were rethinking their government, he decided to submit it to the Convention because of the decision the Convention was about to make. Despite his own suffering at the hands of a mob gone wild, Paine's belief in the fundamental morality of democracy remained unshaken. "The right of voting for representatives is the primary right by which other rights are protected. To take away this right is to reduce a man to slavery, for slavery consists in being subject to the will of another, and he that has not a vote in the election of representatives is in this case. The proposal therefore to disfranchise any class of men is as criminal as the proposal to take away property."[30] On July 7, despite his frail health, Paine asked to speak before the Convention on these very principles. Lanthenas made a motion to that effect, and the Convention unanimously approved it. This represented Paine's first address to the public since his release from prison. It was also his last.

Paine had nothing to win or lose. He had never entered the political world for personal gain, for power or wealth. He had never sent anyone to his death for harboring ideas with which he disagreed. Paine had acted only on the principles he knew best, the principles of the democratic republic. If the Convention passed a constitution for France that allowed only taxpayers to be citizens, then half the population would be disenfranchised. This represented a defeat of the revolutionary principles for which France had suffered. One of the Convention secretaries read his remarks:

> Citizens. The effects of a malignant fever with which I was afflicted during a rigorous confinement in the Luxembourg have thus long prevented me from attending at my post in the bosom of the Convention, and the magnitude of the subject now under discussion, and not other consideration on earth, could induce me now to repair to my station.
>
> A recurrence to the vicissitudes I have experienced, and the critical situations in which I have been placed in consequence of

the French Revolution, will throw upon what I now propose to submit to the Convention the most unequivocal proofs of my integrity, and the rectitude of those principles which have uniformly influenced my conduct. . . .

To deprive half the people in a nation of their rights as citizens is an easy matter in theory or on paper; but it is a most dangerous experiment, and rarely practicable in execution.

Paine's appeals were ignored. The new constitution was ratified on August 22 and became effective on September 23, 1795. French citizens voted indirectly: they chose electors who were required to own property (hence be among those who paid direct property taxes) or serve in the military. These electors in turn selected a two-tiered, bicameral legislature, a Council of Five Hundred, which was to propose legislation and then elect a Council of Ancients (or Elders), married men or widowers over forty years old, whose duty it was to review, accept, or reject the legislation from the Five Hundred. A Directory of five people, who were individually replaced one each year, was then to enforce the law.

Ironically for Paine, the new government was set up in the Luxembourg. Among the first order of business was the disinterment and transport of Condorcet's body from the former prison to the Pantheon. Thomas Paine was unimpressed. This was not an administration in which he had any faith. He thought it was hardly representative of the people and was in direct violation of the Declaration of Rights of Man and Citizen, the very thing the French had risked their lives and died for since 1789.[31] Paine, now a confirmed American citizen, would never again play a part in French government.

16 · "Some very ignorant and stupid pretenders"

The Paris that Paine encountered after his release from prison was quite different from the one he had seen before his arrest. With the fall of Robespierre and St. Just in July of 1794, it was now as if France's internal and external enemies had occupied the city. Signs of defeat and devastation were everywhere. Trash and garbage lined the streets, attracting more vermin and disease than ever before. Grain and bread were severely rationed as a result of drought and an extremely poor harvest, and prices were consequently higher than ever. "The hunger and cold were so extreme," according to historian Simon Schama, "that foraging animals—foxes and even wolves—began to appear on the perimeters of cities, looking for sustenance." Coal was scarce, and starvation and freezing temperatures plagued great sections of the countryside, especially along the Norman coast.

Nor did the Terror really end with the executions of Robespierre, St. Just, and their cohorts. Counter-revolutionary forces continued to operate with abandon in the Rhône Valley and other areas of Provence, killing thousands. Dead bodies were unceremoniously dumped into the rivers or left to rot in front of taverns and inns. "In many areas, Counter-Terrorists would gather together at an inn as if for a day's hunting, and go off in search of their quarry."[1] In Paris, conditions were no better. Mobs of people, reminiscent of the sans-culottes and enragés of 1793-94, roamed the streets and bullied the Convention deputies. Things looked about as bleak as possible. Paine's despair deepened as he witnessed members of the corrupt Directory squabbling endlessly and fighting with both Councils. These struggles worsened, and within three years led to an attempted royalist overthrow. Until then, Paine had religion on his mind, and in the summer of 1795 he completed the second part of *The Age of Reason*.

When Paine entrusted Barlow with the manuscript of *The Age of Reason* as he was carted of to prison in 1793, he had not intended it to be his last word on religion. Besides, he later claimed, he had written the first part of *The Age of Reason* without a Bible, quoting from memory all the passages cited in his pamphlet. (*AR* 168) Now, nearly eighteen months later, he had the Holy Scripture before him and he wanted to delve more deeply than before into his analysis, because he had found the scriptures "to be much worse books than I had conceived." (*AR* 103) If he had made any mistakes in his first work on the subject, he said, it was because he had not been hard enough on the Bible. In any case, he wanted to answer his critics, most of whom had already had an opportunity to attack his views.

Part Two of *The Age of Reason* was as harsh and discordant in tone as Part One. The main difference between the two was in the detailed, close exegesis of scripture that Paine undertook in the second part, exposing the contradictions and deep-rooted lies that he found in the Bible. Both parts were an extended rebuttal of religion, but in Part Two Paine provided an analysis and running commentary on almost every passage of the Bible. His goal was to reveal the mythologies, falsehoods, and superstitions of both the Old and New Testaments, of Judaism and Christianity, though he reserved his most caustic and uncharitable remarks for the latter. As in the first part, his goal was not to deny the existence of God, or even of an afterlife. It was to set the record straight about how some men had tried to shackle the minds and hearts of other men so that they were no longer free spirits to believe as they saw fit. His task was, as he saw it, to demonstrate that the Scriptures were neither true nor holy.

It has often been said that anything may be proved from the Bible, but before anything can be admitted as proved by the

Bible, the Bible itself must be proved to be true; for if the Bible be not true, or the truth of it be doubtful, it ceases to have authority, and cannot be admitted as proof of anything.

It has been the practice of all Christian commentators on the Bible, and of all Christian priests and preachers, to impose the Bible on the world as a mass of truth and as the Word of God; they have disputed and wrangled and anathematized each other about the supposeable meaning of particular parts and passages therein; one has said and insisted that such a passage meant such a thing; another that it meant directly the contrary; and a third that it meant neither one nor the other, but something different from both; and this they have called understanding the Bible.

It has happened that all the answers which I have seen to the former part of The Age of Reason have been written by priests; and these pious men, like their predecessors, contend and wrangle, and understand the Bible; each understand it differently, but each understands it best; and they have agreed in nothing but in telling their readers that Thomas Paine understands it not. (*AR* 103-04)

Paine was moving toward the spiritualism that would stay with him for about five years after 1797. For him, religious belief was a private affair. There was no room for intermediaries, who dictated to others what they should believe. Priests were such go-betweens, and they were placed in an even more powerful position when supported by kings and lords. Paine was a strict separationist, against an established state religion. A true democratic republic could only exist without the union of church and state, or without what Paine called "the otherwise mysterious connection of Church and State: the Church humane, and the State tyrannic." (*AR* 187) A person's spirituality had to come from within, and not by the force of another's command.

Paine's general distrust of government markedly increased during the Terror, after his middle-of-the-night arrest, his harrowing imprisonment, his illness. It was no wonder that he envisioned a conspiracy of church and government to defraud the citizenry. After all, Paine had observed in the *Rights of Man* that government had three sources, two of which were directly related to organized religion, and which undermined the people's interests: "First,

Superstition. Secondly, Power." The third was freedom, which involved "the common interest of society, and the common rights of man." (*RM* 69)

The Hebrew Scriptures mirrored these forces of superstition and power, to foist unsubstantiated beliefs on a gullible public. The scriptures were "written by some very ignorant and stupid pretenders to authorship several hundred years after the death of Moses."[2] (*AR* 107) No rational person could believe what they said. He cited several examples from both the Mosaic and post-Mosaic books, which he thought were preposterous. He called the books of Moses "spurious" and produced evidence of their contradictions. How was it possible for God's creation to be filled with so much murder and brigandery? The book of Ruth, for example, was "an idle, bungling story, foolishly told, nobody knows by whom, about a strolling country-girl, creeping slyly to bed with her cousin Boaz. Pretty stuff indeed, to be called the Word of God!" (*AR* 121) Although he did not make the parallel directly, his characterization of the people in these books were similar to his depictions of Robespierre himself, or Joseph Lebon, the murderous deputy who had replaced Paine from Calais, or the treatment by the English government of the people in the East Indies, or by any contemporary assassins of any name in the period. (Robespierre, for example, was "the enemy of every man of virtue and humanity;" Lebon was "one of the vilest characters that ever existed."[3]) These scriptures were "too horrid for humanity to read or for decency to hear." A person would soon have the wrong idea about the true nature of God. "Good heavens! It is quite another thing; it is a book of lies, wickedness and blasphemy; for what can be greater blasphemy than to ascribe the wickedness of man to the orders of the Almighty?" (*AR* 115)

If Hebrew scriptures were not bad enough, a reader could not but be impressed that the Christian Bible suffered from even worse diseases of the mind. Paine was intent on exposing the errors and flaws of its contents. "It is the duty incumbent on every true Deist, that he vindicate the moral justice of God against the calumnies of the Bible." (*AR* 109) So far as he was concerned, the Bible was full of unsubstantiated assertions, which could never be verified. "It is an easy thing to tell a lie, but it is difficult to support the lie after it is told," he wrote. (*AR* 162) And the lies in the Bible were told for the same reason that lies were told by government: to blind the people to truth, to what was happening around them. To go beyond the pure belief in God as the creator of man and the universe to those lies, which, for example, suggested not a single God, but three divine persons in a trinity, making no sense whatsoever. Paine's language was not merely direct: it was downright contemptuous and derisive.

> [W]hen, according to the Christian Trinitarian scheme, one part of God is represented by a dying man, and another part, called the Holy Ghost, by a dying pigeon, it is impossible that belief can attach itself to such wild conceits. (The book called the book of Matthew says—chap. iii, verse 16—that the Holy Ghost descended in the shape of a dove. It might as well have said a goose; the creatures are equally harmless, and the one is as much of a nonsensical lie as the other. The second of Acts, ver. 2, 3, says that it descended in a mighty rushing wind, in the shape of cloven tongues, perhaps it was cloven feet. Such absurd stuff is only fit for tales of witches and wizards.)
> It has been the scheme of the Christian Church, and of all the other invented systems of religion, to hold man in ignorance of the Creator, as it is of governments to hold man in ignorance of his rights. The systems of the one are as false as those of the other, and are calculated for mutual support.
> The study of theology, as it stands in Christian churches is the study of nothing; it is founded on nothing; it rests on no principles; it proceeds by no authorities; it has no data; it can demonstrate nothing; and it admits no conclusion. (*AR* 187)

Never one to allow a moment to pass without a blast of ridicule and sarcasm, Paine let loose on the fabulous stories the New Testament told. (Perhaps his illness only made him more irritable and impatient with what he considered pure nonsense.) The most hilarious example had to do with the immaculate conception, especially the story Mary told about her pregnancy. Such a belief in this foolishness denied reality of the natural world, of how creatures reproduce themselves. "Were any girl that is now with child to say, and even to swear it," he asked, "that she was gotten with child by a ghost, and that an angel told her so, would she be believed? Certainly she would not."

> Why, then, are we to believe the same thing of another girl, whom we never saw, told by nobody knows who, nor when, nor where? How strange and inconsistent it is, that the same circumstance that would weaken the belief even of a probable story should be given as a motive for believing this one, that has upon the face of it every token of absolute impossibility and imposture!

People died and were raised from the dead. Saints were killed, and then suddenly they were alive. "Strange, indeed, that an army of saints should return to life and nobody know who they were, nor who it was that saw them, and that not a word more should be said upon the subject, nor these saints have anything to tell us." (*AR* 160, 163) And what of Christ's alleged resuscitation from the dead? What could possibly explain such a story? His answer, as contemporary to the twentieth century as it was to the eighteenth, was that once a story was started, it was near impossible to stop. "It goes on a little and a little further till it becomes *a most certain truth*." This was the way with ghost stories. "Those who tell stories of this kind . . . have told us that when he arose he left his grave clothes behind him; but they have forgotten to provide other clothes for him to appear in afterward, or to tell us what he did with them when he ascended— whether he stripped them off, or went up clothes and all." (*AR* 170) No wonder Paine was accused of being an atheist.

But it was not atheism that moved Paine. It was, as always, his burning need to attack what he thought were outright lies and irrational belief. It was his desire to destroy, at least on paper, the overweening chains of the mind and the soul that the established Church had placed on so many human beings. No matter where it had raised its obnoxious, lying head, the Church could not continue to expect its believers to retain the blinding faith that it had subjected them to for centuries. If there was such a thing as God personally intervening in history, if all the tales and miracles of Holy Scripture were true, then where was God when the world, especially France, needed him during the Reign of Terror when so many innocent and good people were carted off to prison, and many to their deaths?

This assault on Christianity, indeed on organized religion generally, did not conflict with Paine's deist belief in God as creator. Throughout his work, Paine was consistent on this point. God had created the universe and everything in it, and it was the duty of all people everywhere to worship God and his creation in a spiritual way that was boundless. Indeed, God's works were beyond the capacity of men to understand fully. "We can know God only through His works," Paine wrote in the first part of *The Age of Reason*.

> We can have only a confused idea of His power, if we have not the means of comprehending something of its immensity. We can have no idea of His wisdom, but by knowing the order and manner in which it acts. The principles of science lead to this knowledge; for the Creator of man is the Creator of science, and it is through that medium that man can see God, as it were, face to face. (*AR* 187-88)

The after-life was no more difficult to comprehend, Paine said, "than that a worm should become a butterfly, and quit the dunghill for the atmosphere." (*AR* 179) This was not the God of the Jews. They had turned God into an assassin who killed His own people. Nor was this the God of the Christians; they had had the audacity to kill God Himself in order to destroy the religion of the Jews to found a new religion. What absurdities these notions were to Thomas Paine. They turned God into an imperfect creature, who, chameleon-like, constantly changed Himself into something that He was not. Paine's conclusion was straightforward: Hebrew Scripture and the Christian Testament were nothing, but forgeries. Human beings were the makers of their own destiny in God's creation. They could accomplish any goal for a good and moral cause that they themselves wished to achieve. All the people needed to know was that "great objects inspire great thoughts; great munificence excites great gratitude." (*AR* 188) With this concept in mind, a person could achieve a moral life, progress toward the good was inevitable, and the life of the human species enriched.

Paine's religious convictions have been the subject of debate for nearly two hundred years. Theodore Roosevelt referred to him as "the filthy little atheist."[4] In his own time, John Adams, with whom that "profligate and impious" Paine would soon have increasing conflict, was so put off by Paine's attack that he noted in his diary that "the Christian religion is above all the religion that ever prevailed or existed in ancient or modern times, the religion of wisdom, virtue, equity, and humanity. Let the blackguard Paine say what he will. It is resignation to God—it is goodness itself to man."[5] Paine responded to many of his contemporary detractors, especially Gilbert Wakefield in 1795 and Samuel Adams in 1803. The most significant of his replies was to none other than Thomas Erskine, who had unsuccessfully, but quite willingly and vigorously defended the *Rights of Man* during Paine's trial for sedition. Though a strong, articulate defender of Paine's political ideas, Erskine abhorred his theological views. In 1797, he agreed to prosecute a London publisher and bookseller, Thomas Williams, for selling *The Age of Reason*. Williams had been accused by the Proclamation Society for the Suppression of Vice and Immorality, a watchdog organization, which claimed to promote what was best for the people.

Paine's response was published as "A Letter to Mr. Erskine." Vintage Paine, it ridiculed and attacked Erskine ad hominem. According to Paine, Erskine had once told him that "were government to begin *de novo* in England, they never would establish such a damned absurdity as this is." Now Erskine had obviously changed his mind, because he had suppressed free expression in prosecuting Paine's publisher for his theological views. Erskine, "lawyer-like, undoes by one word what he says in the other," proclaimed Paine. The defense counsel wanted to read aloud passages from *The Age of Reason* to the jury to show that Paine's work was not blasphemous. The judge disallowed it. "Mr. Erskine then (Falstaff-like), having all the field to himself, and no enemy at hand, laid about him most heroically, and the jury found the defendant guilty."

Erskine had also sponsored a libel bill in Parliament, which would require indictment by a special or grand jury made up of either merchants or squires. Paine found the bill laughable: "Mr. Erskine vaunts himself upon the bill he brought into Parliament. . . . Mr. Erskine's bill is only vapor and smoke." Religion was a private affair between each person and God alone. No third party was needed.

"Anything that goes beyond this rule is an inquisition. Mr. Erskine talks of his moral education: Mr. Erskine is very little acquainted with theological subjects, if he does not know there is such a thing as a sincere and religious belief that the Bible is not the Word of God."

Paine again argued that the Bible was full of fabulous tales that have blinded people to the reality of truth, namely God's creation. The people's heads were filled with myths. "If the Bible be the Word of God, it needs not the wretched aid of prosecutions to support it, and you might with as much propriety make a law to protect the sunshine as to protect the Bible." Merchants and squires would be of no particular help in prosecuting someone who, like Williams or Paine himself, simply wanted to get out a message concerning their thinking on the subject of religion. Paine was particularly tormented by the idea that squires would be jurors in such a trial. What did they know about religion? "Tell them that God Almighty ordered a man to make a cake and bake it with a turd and eat it, and they will say it is one of Dean Swift's blackguard stories. Tell them it is in the Bible and they will lay a bowl of punch that it is not, and leave it to the parson to decide. Ask them also about theology and they will say they know of no such a one on the turf."

Paine neither wanted nor needed anyone, especially the likes of Thomas Erskine, to interpret for the world what he believed or what he had written. "The writings of Thomas Paine, even of Thomas Paine," wrote the author of *The Age of Reason*, "need no commentator to explain, compound, derange and rearrange their several parts, to render them intelligible; he can relate a fact, or write an essay, without forgetting in one page what he has written in another."[6] With this, so far as Paine was concerned, the issue of religion needed no other elaboration, until he concluded some years later that he ought to take on a rejoinder offered by Richard Watson, the bishop of Llandaff, entitled *An Apology for the Bible*. Paine thought of his response to the bishop as Part Three of *The Age of Reason*. It was, however, not printed in his lifetime. A New York magazine, *The Theophilanthropist*, only published it in the year following his death.

Watson had written a serious and sober response to *The Age of Reason*. He argued that Paine had misread the Bible and that he did not understand that Genesis was the oldest book in the world. In response, Paine provided practically a line-by-line, textual analysis of Genesis to show that it was drawn from several sources. He argued that much of the material in Genesis and Job both was originally derived from Persia, from the books of Zoroaster, the Persian lawgiver. Job was the work of "some of the Persian or Eastern magi." He cited sources, among them Eben-Ezra and Spinoza, who agreed that Moses could not have written the Pentateuch. In addition, Paine pointed to several highly contradictory passages in the text. Instead of the oldest book in the world, it "has been the last written book of the Bible, and . . . the cosmogony it contains has been manufactured." [7] With that, Paine did indeed put aside the matter of religion.[8]

Paine now turned his attention to the Jay Treaty. The British and Americans had signed the treaty on November 19, 1794, just two weeks after Paine's release from the Luxembourg. When the American government sent James Monroe to be the new Minister to France that year, it placed him in a very difficult position. He was the spokesman in Paris for American interests, which the French had long thought were tied to their own interests, just as the United States was concluding a major diplomatic breakthrough with England, the adversary of both America and France.

The Jay Treaty was designed to resolve several problems arising from violations of the Treaty of Paris of 1783, which ended the war between America and England. It was also supposed to regulate commercial and trade agreements between the two nations. In 1794, at the height of the English war against revolutionary France, Britain began to seize American ships trading with the French West Indies. The Americans were furious. President Washington sent the Chief Justice of the United States, John Jay, as envoy extraordinaire to London to work out the removal of British troops from the Northwest Territory, to settle the commercial problems the Americans had in the Indies, and to obtain a settlement on the British impressment of American seamen and the seizure of American ships. Jay was in part successful.[9] By the end of the year, Lord Grenville, the British Foreign Minister, and Jay had signed a treaty on behalf of the United States with Britain, which cleared the Northwest Territory of British troops and allowed settlers there to decide whether they would be British or American subjects. The treaty also provided for free trade between the two nations and allowed the Americans to have unrestricted passage on the Mississippi River. To the Americans' detriment, the United States' commercial operations with the West Indies, however, were severely restricted (the English still feared Americans would help the French there). And, perhaps worst of all, the British made no promises about ceasing their impressment of American seamen, something humiliating to the Washington Administration.

Many Americans despised the treaty, believing that Jay, under the influence of the pro-English Alexander Hamilton, the Secretary of the Treasury, had given up too much to America's former enemy. The treaty was denounced throughout the country, and Jay himself was burned in effigy in several cities. Hamilton was even spat upon and stoned when he defended it. After a stormy debate (which included a huge outcry by American citizens that the U.S. was still dominated by the British empire), the Senate ratified the treaty, and it went into effect in the spring of 1796.

To the French, the Jay Treaty was advantageous to the British. Monroe's position as ambassador to France was seriously compromised. It was difficult to explain America's reasons for signing the treaty, which he personally opposed. Paine shared Monroe's skepticism and openly opposed the treaty in a letter to the *Philadelphia Aurora* in which he suggested that the United States would be better off reaffirming its long-held ties to France. "So sublime and generous a manner of acting, which would not cost anything to France, would cement in a stronger way the ties between the two republics. The effect of such an event would confound and annihilate in an irrevocable manner all the partisans for the British in America," who Paine thought wanted to reestablish ties with the British crown.[10] Despite his disappointment with the French constitution of 1795, Paine still advocated a close Franco-American alliance and thus called for the renunciation by the Americans of the Jay Treaty. In the summer of 1796, without explanation, Washington suddenly recalled Monroe from Paris, no doubt due to his pro-French attitudes and his lukewarm support of the Jay Treaty.

In the month after his address on the treaty, in August of

1795, just after he completed the second part of *The Age of Reason*, Paine decided to leave Paris for awhile. He traveled by boat to Sèvres and then to Versailles, where he became violently ill. He returned to the Monroes, who found his condition to be so horrible that Monroe remarked to a friend that Paine "will not be able to hold out more than a month or two at the furthest." The Monroes had been practically out the door to spend several weeks with their daughter, who was living in St. Germain just at the moment Paine arrived, but with their house "guest" so sick, it now appeared not in their "power to do so."[11]

While Paine was convalescing, his attention once again turned to George Washington. Paine was still angry and deeply hurt by the action (or in this case, non-action) of the American President. He began to have doubts about the leadership of the United States, especially about the Federalists, who seemed to cast everything they did into the language and mode of operation of political party. Rather than having the interests of America as a whole in mind, they seemed to care only about their own prominence. Never once had any of them acknowledged Thomas Paine as an American citizen. They never seemed interested in his past efforts on behalf of the American cause. While living with the Monroes, Paine began to think how he could expose the President of the United States to the American public. Initially, Monroe successfully dissuaded him from publishing these ideas, suggesting that such a disclosure would embarrass the United States in France and do Paine no particular good.

To make matters worse, Paine was once again almost broke. The money he had received from Congress was mostly gone, and finances generally preyed on his mind. When first released from the Luxembourg, he told James Madison, he had to borrow 250 French crowns from Monroe.[12] Despite these dire circumstances, perhaps to divert himself from thinking about what he would like to print about Washington, Paine focused on the sorry state of British finances.

There has been some speculation that the Directory itself had funded the publication of what came to be known as *The Decline and Fall of the English System of Finance*, published in April of 1796. The basis of this speculation is that immediately on its appearance it not only appeared in French translation, but also in German (for consumption in the rest of Europe), and several hundred copies of the English version were spread all through the British Isles. Paine could not have paid for such a widespread publication by himself, and certainly Monroe would have had no hand in it. It looked suspiciously like the work of the French government. Perhaps once again, Paine was a hired pen, but as usual he was writing only what he firmly believed.

In his pamphet, Paine tried to show that the entire financial basis of England's economy was a disaster, clearly hoping that such information would stimulate revolution there. He argued that the national debt incurred by financing war after war after war would lead to national bankruptcy, which he actually predicted would occur in the very near future. With the savage ridicule and sarcasm for which he was known, Paine launched a full-blown attack on English financial operations. This system, he wrote, was so poor that even "the most stupid stock-jobber" ought to have seen how frail and fragile it was. It should "overpower the credulity of the most thoughtless Englishman," he said. (*DF* 2:671) The term "stockjobbers," when uttered by radicals, was a term of abuse, used specifically to decry the economic policies of the crown. Radicals employed it to attack the so-called "monied interest" of the king's court and ministry, which relied on that hated means of exchange, paper money. Therefore "every natural idiot can see" how the economy was being undermined. (*DF* 2:666) Indeed, Britain was on the verge of national economic disaster, "on the verge, nay even in the gulf of bankruptcy."[13] (*DF* 2:674)

Except for the Pitt Administration's intervention, Paine's predictions might well have come true. Pitt had served as George III's prime minister since the fall of the Portland administration in 1783. Although he followed a general liberal line (lower taxes, lower expenditures, reduction of the national debt), this thinking ended with the French Revolution when Pitt realized the threat to England's own stability posed by the revolutionary wars in Europe. In the fall of 1792, he sanctioned the formation of Reeves's anti-radical, subversive Association for the Preservation of Liberty and Property, and eventually suspended habeas corpus for all suspected radicals in

England. Several spectacular trials (including Paine's in absentia in the fall of 1793) led to the incarceration of several English radicals, although Thomas Hardy, head of the London Corresponding Society, was acquitted. After France declared war on England in 1793, Pitt immediately increased English military and naval forces, and consequently the debt itself. To say the least, he was hardly a favorite of the radical writers, and Paine took great exception to his economic and political policies.

Paine claimed that within twenty years the debt had to overrun the gold reserves, the result being a severe economic crisis. This was an "age of decrepitude in which death is every day to be expected, and life cannot continue long. But the death of credit, or that state that is called bankruptcy, is not always marked by those progressive stages of visible decline that marked the decline of natural life." (DF 2:664) After a run on the Bank of England in 1797, Pitt issued an order suspending cash payments of greater than one pound by the bank. Parliament did not reverse this policy until 1819. About the elimination of cash payments, Paine commented to Jefferson that "the Bank of England is now stopped. For my own part, I cannot see how it is possible the Bank of England should ever open again."[14]

It did open again, of course, once the financial situation stabilized. The fear in England in 1796 was national bankruptcy, and Paine understood this. He knew that insolvency affected individuals as well as governments. If "the quantity of bank notes payable on demand, which the bank has issued, is greater than the bank can pay off, the bank is insolvent; and when that insolvency is declared, it is bankruptcy." (DF 2:667) And when the official bank goes under, so will individuals, because "there are many thousand persons in London and in the country who are holders of bank notes." (DF 2:663) Paine was talking about the Bank of England as the official underwriter of British finance, of course, but his words could well apply to the United States and the savings and loan banking crisis of the 1980s, when literally hundreds of thousands of people found they held worthless promissory notes from bankrupt savings and loans.

Paine examined six wars that England had been engaged in since the end of the seventeenth century and showed how the debt grew at the end of each. He was very confident about the figures that he used to show England's growing and dangerous insolvency. He apparently obtained them from official publications by "Mr. Eden (now called Lord Auckland) and George Chalmers, secretary to the Board of Trade and Plantation, of which Jenkinson (now Lord Hawkesbury) is president." Chalmers, Paine's old enemy, had characterized him as a hired pen. Paine chose not to mention this fact. He fired arrows at Eden and Jenkinson, saying these "folks change their names so often that it is as difficult to know them as it is to know a thief." (*DF* 2:662) The only way in which England's indebtedness might have been forestalled, according to Paine, was if the kings had simply taxed their subjects to cover the costs of each war.

> Had the system begun an hundred years before, the amount of taxes at this time to pay the annual interest at four per cent (could we suppose such a system of insanity could have continued) would be two hundred and twenty millions annually.

Such an amount was absurd. England could not sustain such taxes, much less raise them. The result was that the debt "is the feather that breaks the horse's back." (*DF* 2:665) The burden just of paying the interest on the debt was destroying the people. One more small dose, one little feather of taxation more, was enough to break their backs. "Go, count the graces, thou idiot, and learn the folly of thy arithmetic!" (*DF* 2:666)

Convinced that he was right about the dangers to the English financial system, Paine wrote: "I have done an act of justice to those numerous citizens of neutral nations who have been imposed upon by that fraudulent system, and who have property at stake upon the event [forthcoming national bankruptcy]." (*DF* 2:674) Of course, he would not have minded economic disruptions throughout England leading to revolutionary changes in the British government. But this was not to be: England continued to prosecute the war against France without its economy collapsing and Paine was still an outlaw in his native land.

In the summer of 1796, Paine left the Monroes and went to Versailles to recuperate from surgery on his side. The abscess he had contracted in his prison days, almost two years before, was still haunting him. In Versailles, he stayed with the English banker, Sir Robert Smyth—a member of the British Club in 1792 and possibly a contributor of some of the ideas in Paine's *Decline and Fall* pamphlet—and his wife, to whom Paine had composed those blithely romantic love poems, "From the Castle in the Air, to the Little Corner of the World" and "The New Covenant." In August, Paine wrote to a French official requesting a safe passage for Smyth, who wished to travel to Hamburg.[15] Later, after he finally returned to America, Paine recommended to President Jefferson that he consider hiring Smyth's firm to help the Americans in their international trade affairs.[16]

Freed from the vow of silence Paine had given to Monroe, he now turned his attention to his current vexation, President Washington.

All through 1795, Paine had written, but published nothing about Washington. In September, Paine wrote to James Madison about the President. He told him that he had always expected to return to America, but that his illness prohibited his travel. "I owe this illness (from which I have not much prospect of recovering), partly to Robespierre, and partly to Mr. Washington." He then recounted for Madison's edification the entire history of how he had come to fall into prison and languish there with no help from Washington. "I have filled up the whole sheet with what you would not otherwise have been troubled with," he explained somewhat apologetically to Madison. "But I have long felt a wish to make somebody acquainted with the case, for I know that when men have done injustice, as I conceive Mr. Washington has done by me, that they are apt to do more to justify the first." Terribly embittered by what he took to be a personal affront by the President, Paine referred, somewhat sarcastically, to the President by his civilian title, "Mr. Washington."[17]

By the end of July 1796, Paine could wait no more. He sent off a widely published, open letter to George Washington, severely censuring him.[18] His attack was the first of many that Paine would launch against the Federalist party. His language was tough and strident. Paine had long been a staunch supporter of Washington. He stuck by him even when the Virginian was in danger of losing his post as the American commander-in-chief, and he had dedicated the *Rights of Man* to him.

But now Paine accused Washington of striving for personal aggrandizement and for the profit of his party. Neither the President nor the Federalists truly believed in the Constitution. They believed only in themselves, and their real goal was to rule America in perpetuity. Paine accused Washington of beginning his presidency "by encouraging and swallowing the grossest adulation, and you traveled America from one end to the other to put yourself in the way of receiving it." In cahoots with another impostor, John Adams, Washington schemed to turn America into a monarchy. Indeed, Paine compared Washington to James II, who was forced to flee the English throne in 1688 after he was accused of absolutism.

Paine said he understood what "Mr. Washington and his new fangled faction" were up to. (*GW* 2:700) Paine did not leave out John Jay and his damnable treaty in his attack: "this John was always the sycophant of everything in power, from Mr. Gérard in America to Grenville in England." (*GW*, 2:696) When the news was leaked to the press," every well-affected American blushed with shame." (*GW* 2:711) The United States would now supply both raw and finished materials to Britain on American ships. Because the ships were neutral, the goods would be regarded as neutral, too, meaning that in theory French warships could not interdict them. This agreement, Paine argued, was in direct violation of American agreements with France.

At the bottom of this criticism lay the connection between the Washington Administration and Paine's long stay in the Luxembourg Prison: "Could I have known to what degree of corruption and perfidy the administrative part of the Government of America had descended, I could have been at no loss to have understood the reservedness of Mr. Washington toward me, during my imprisonment in the Luxembourg. There are cases in which silence is a loud language." (*GW* 2:695-96) The Federalists had wanted to be rid of the republican Paine. They knew that Paine was opposed to their goal of taking over America, turning it into a monarchy with themselves at the helm, and then entering into a close relationship with Britain. How could they do this if they had allowed the journalist with the fiery pen to continue writing? They had said nothing, and let him rot in prison. "You folded your arms, forgot your friend, and became silent," he told Washington. (*GW* 2:707)

Paine ended his assault on Washington with a reassessment of Washington's military prowess. Earlier, in "Crisis Five," he had praised the general as a great military leader. Now, having felt the sting of being ignored, Paine wrote that Washington was overrated as a general. He had been a commander-in-chief in name only. In reality, the war was won in the north by Horatio Gates and in the south by Nathanael Greene. Washington had his own command, which did nothing. In fact, he almost lost the war. It was therefore "no wonder we see so much pusillanimity in the *President*, when we see so little enterprise in the General!"[19] (*GW* 2:719) In the end, it was French aid that had supplied the means for the Americans to defeat Britain, and it had been Paine who accompanied young John Laurens to France to secure the financial assistance and military materiel and supplies. And now, the United States, under the Washington Administration, was abandoning France (despite all that it did for the American cause) for renewed ties to Britain, as the Jay Treaty demonstrated. Paine, perplexed and angry, concluded his letter with a direct address to "Mr. Washington," just as he had referred to him earlier in his letter to Madison:

> And as to you, Sir, treacherous in private friendship (for so you have been to me, and that in the day of danger) and a hypocrite in public life, the world will be puzzled to decide whether you are an apostate or an imposter; whether you have abandoned good principles, or whether you ever had any. (*GW* 2:723)

Paine never considered that Washington's perspective, as the President of the United States, might well have directly conflicted with Paine's personal predicament. Washington had the great responsibility to insure that the interests of the new United States were always in focus, and not the interests of a single person. Old disputes and unresolved problems between England and the United States continued to exacerbate the relationship between those two nations. Washington's attempt to settle them, the President could argue, was made to benefit the United States and the United States alone, even if that meant entering into a new arrangement with England via the Jay Treaty. After all, he was the first President in an untried experiment, and he could not afford to fail.

But Paine, who always claimed himself to have been a citizen of America, despite his birth in England and his French citizenship, would have none of this nonsense. He had renounced the first, and as for the second, it had been, he said in error, only honorary. He had served in the Convention, which was not a government, but a body assembled to form a new constitutional structure for France and never intended to be part of an official body in that country. He was there only as a free spirit, a constitutionalist and a republican, desirous of spreading the word of liberty to Europe. France was the first on the list of countries, which would take hold of American values and principles. In addition, "no oath of allegiance or citizenship was required of the members who composed the Convention." (*GW* 2:697) In fact, there was nothing to swear allegiance to, since there was no constituted government, or at least no government that he recognized.

When Paine's letter to Washington was published in America in the fall of 1796, his enemies were both at once delighted and contemptuous: contemptuous, because they hated Paine and what he stood for, and yet the letter was another indication of Paine's outrageous convictions about democracy and constitutions. They were not surprised that the author of *The Age of Reason*, espousing what they thought was a heinous analysis of Christianity, had written such a scathing attack on the President of the United States and his Federalist allies.

The Federalists were also delighted. How convenient that Paine, who had been living with the Jeffersonian Monroe, had penned such unfounded, disrespectful invective. It placed a shadow over all republicans, particularly in a year (1796) when a presidential election was taking place. If John Adams won that election, then Federalism would be vindicated and secured. The President himself barely responded and certainly not in public. In a note to David Stuart in early 1797, he noted that William Cobbett, an English printer and commentator and a deep hater of Paine's ideas, had not only reprinted *Oldy's Life of Paine*, but attacked Paine's rebuke of

Washington. "Making allowance for the asperity of an Englishman [Cobbett] for some of his strong and coarse expression and a want of information of many official facts," Washington told Stuart, "it is not a bad thing."[20]   Having now released his pent-up anger at Washington, Paine had other issues to deal with and, as he had in the second part of the *Rights of Man*, he turned his attention to social and economic welfare.

17 · Justice, Agrarian Style

As Paine was predicting the economic collapse of England, he was also considering something the bishop of Llandaff had said in his reply to *The Age of Reason*. The bishop had suggested that mankind should praise God for the rich and the poor: indeed he had appended a sermon to his book attacking Paine's work, entitled "The Wisdom and Goodness of God, in having made both Rich and Poor."[1] As progressive as the *Rights of Man*, Part Two, was, Paine's last major work, *Agrarian Justice*, written in the winter of 1795-96 (though published only in 1797), was an even more radical statement about social justice and in some respects was a reply to the bishop's idea of what Paine considered to be an unjust god. At that same time, Paine had before him the activities of a social revolutionary by the name of François Noël (Gracchus) Babeuf, who attacked the Directory for its inability to take care of the poor of France.

Babeuf, a member of the petty bourgeoisie, had experienced a life of poverty, often working for members of the lower aristocracy. When the Revolution erupted in 1789, he became an instant supporter, and in 1794 at the moment of the Thermidorean reaction he was living in Paris. In his periodical, the *Journal de la liberté de la presse*, which he later called *Tribun de la peuple*, Babeuf argued that the French Revolution had made great strides in bringing about political freedom, but it had not gone far enough, because poverty and class inequality still existed throughout society. His ideas were rooted in the ideology of the sans-culottes, the revolutionary radical artisans and small businessmen of Paris, organized in the forty-eight Paris sections, who flourished especially in the years of the Terror.

The sans-culottes had emphasized the ideology of community, equality, and fraternity.[2]

Building on their ideals, Babeuf's solution to the social problem of inequality was a primitive form of communism, where land was equally distributed to all citizens of the nation, so that poverty would at last be ended. He believed in an agrarian law, which the Gracchi, two brothers in second century Rome, had wanted to implement to overcome the growing inequality in Roman life. He adopted the name "Gracchus" and began his agitation for land reform in France. On February 16 and March 3, 1794, the government, mainly St. Just, issued the Ventôse decrees, which moved in this direction. The decrees declared that land seized from suspects (and victims of the Terror) were now to be turned over to the landless. But those decrees had ceased with the fall of Robespierre and St. Just in July of that year. Babeuf, accused of radicalism, was imprisoned in 1795. On his release, he stepped up his activities, including the formation of a conspiracy (the *Conspiration des Egaux*, or Conspiracy of Equals) to bring into being his communist state. Recruiting artisans, peasants, and some members of the bourgeoisie, he organized his followers into cells and planned to seize control of the government by force. He differed from Marx some fifty years later in that his concern was agrarian—the inadequate equal distribution of goods throughout society—rather than industrial—the ownership of the means of production. In any case, his threat to the state was real insofar as the Directory was concerned. The plot revealed, he was arrested, tried, and executed in 1797. He was thirty-seven.

To a certain extent, Babeuf's ideas permeated Paine's thoughts about public welfare. A few people, such as the radical writer Thomas Spence, actually thought that Paine's ideas were too moderate.[3] Paine focused on social and economic improvement of the masses, but unlike Spence and Babeuf, he never advocated the abolition of private property or the redistribution of wealth. In no way was Paine a proto-Marxist. We cannot even say with any certitude that he somehow "anticipated" Marx, though he held some radical views about revolution and political equality. In fact, Thomas Paine was very much a man of his century. A creature of the Enlightenment, he believed in the capability of men and women to achieve just about anything rational they attempted, and if the human faculty of reason meant anything, it was a vehicle for improving the lives of the less fortunate, those who were unable to help themselves. In addition, Paine was constantly looking to the future, to a time when people would overcome their self-interest. Before the decline of the French Revolution into chaos, Paine often spoke of his vision of a universal republic, a league of nations united by the common purpose of providing the very best government possible for all people everywhere. At the end of the *Rights of Man*, for example, written while the Revolution was still in its relative infancy, he was optimistic that the time was not distant when all nations would join together for this purpose. First, America, France, and England would enter into an alliance of republics. Then the rest of Europe would follow suit. Following on the heels of this progress would be the liberation of South America "and the opening of those countries of immense extent and wealth to the general commerce of the world." (*RM* 232, 268, 267)

> As reforms, or revolutions, call them which you please, extend themselves among nations, those nations will form connections and conventions, and when a few are thus confederated, the progress will be rapid, till despotism and corrupt government be totally expelled. (*RM* 270)

Even Africa and parts of Asia would be drawn into the progressive nature of things. (*RM* 160)

Paine used the term "universal civilization," an ideal he held most of his journalistic career. He first addressed it in his letter to the Abbé Raynal in 1782, an essay, which places him in the category of visionaries like Woodrow Wilson and Franklin Roosevelt. Paine's ideas provide us with a bridge, so to speak, between the Enlightenment and the modern world, the world of people not like Marx, but like John Stuart Mill, who believed that the responsibility of a democratic republic was to provide its citizens with the basic things they needed for survival.

In one sense, Paine's ideas in *Agrarian Justice* were antiquated: his vision was rooted in a society still deeply linked to the land. It was, after all, "agrarian" justice that he advocated, not "social" justice. But his thinking was also very modern in the sense that what he proposed placed him in the category of twentieth-century writers who have argued that social change is possible; that the more fortunate people in society must do their share to insure the full participation of the less fortunate; that education can be made universal and good; that public assistance is a right, not a gift; that government must help resolve the problems of poverty and homelessness.[4] Poverty was not the result of some individual failing or some lack of "election," but of circumstances often beyond anyone's direct control. It was not the fault or the sin of the poor that they were poor. It was just the way things were, and government's duty was to work to ameliorate their condition.

The publication of *Agrarian Justice* effectively closed the age of reason for Paine. He never again wrote a pamphlet that developed a full argument on a particular subject. It did, however, open the way for social reform in the next two centuries. Paine had suffered enough to know that revolution was not the answer any more. It was no longer possible, as he had triumphantly stated in the *Rights of Man*, for change to take place through the kind of violence France had experienced. The Revolution had lost control, and too many innocent victims had suffered and died. The outcome may have been hard to imagine when he wrote the *Rights of Man*, but the Revolution had ended in a tyranny every bit as bad as, if not worse than, monarchy. In the end, Burke had been right, though Paine was unwilling to admit it. Paine now moved away from revolution and toward reform and social democracy. Because government itself was not the problem and poverty was, theoretically a monarchy could solve the problem just as easily as a republic could. But of course Paine did not go that far. The means to alleviate poverty lay within the system of private property, by which he meant landed property, as Babeuf had suggested. While Babeuf's ideas were correct, Paine thought his methods had failed him.

> He availed himself of the resentment caused by this flaw, and instead of seeking a remedy by legitimate and constitutional means, or proposing some measure useful to society, the conspir-

ators did their best to renew disorder and confusion, and constituted themselves personally into a Directory, which is formally destructive of election and representation. They were, in fine, extravagant enough to suppose that society, occupied with its domestic affairs, would blindly yield to them a directorship usurped by violence. (*AJ* 2:608)[5]

First, it is important to understand how only a few came to own most of the property. Here Paine followed John Locke concerning the origins of private property, but Paine went far beyond Locke's claims. In *The Second Treatise of Civil Government*, the work which influenced the Americans in 1776 concerning their break with England, Locke had assumed that God had given the earth to everyone to own in common. Paine echoed this thought: "The earth, in its natural uncultivated state was, and ever would have continued to be, the *common property of the human race.*" (*AJ* 2:613)

Locke had argued that because everyone in essence "owned" property—it was a gift from God—there were certain restrictions about its use and ownership. No one, for example, should take more than one needed. No one should take more property so that when crops grew on it, their wasteful spoilage occurred when no one consumed them. For Locke, however, once property became tied into a monied economy, it no longer really mattered how much property any single individual could (or should) accumulate. Gold and silver, as the means of exchange, transformed the land from its original condition to a commodity which men could gobble up. All they needed was the money for it.

Paine's views here sharply diverged from those of Locke.[6] Men who ruled over others had stolen the land and turned it into their property. They had never paid compensation to anyone for the land they appropriated. Here Paine again demonstrated his biting humor. "There could be no such thing as landed property originally. Man did not make the earth, and, though he had a natural right to *occupy* it, he had no right to *locate as his property* in perpetuity any part of it; neither did the Creator of the earth open a land-office, from whence the first title-deeds should issue." (*AJ* 2:611) To resolve this problem, there had to be some established mechanism so that those who owned property in some way reimbursed those less fortunate.

Paine approached the problem of poor people by formulating a legal fiction: those who owned property owed a debt to the poor. He thought of the owners of property as not really owners, but lessees. They occupied the land perhaps through inheritance, perhaps through sale, perhaps through thievery. In any case, there was no original deed, because the first person who took ownership had no "rights" to the property. He simply claimed it and seized it. Paine genuinely believed that poverty was the outcome of civilization. There was no such thing as poverty in a state of nature. In that pre-political condition, before civil society came into being, a person's life might have been threatened by wild animals, or even by other men. But he was not poor. He had plenty from the earth, and all he need-ed to do was to use it. This, too, differed from Locke, who had pre-sumed that even in a state of nature, a person might take control of a certain amount of property once he mixed his labor with it, that is, cultivated it and made things grow on it.[7]

In fact, Paine's views again display the heavy influence of Rousseau. In a tour de force, given Enlightenment ideas of progress, Rousseau had argued in his essays that civilization had essentially enslaved human beings. Civilization was irreversible, and the people could only try to deal with the problems that arose as a result of it.

> Astronomy was born of superstition, eloquence of ambition, hatred, flattery, lying; geometry of avarice; physics of vain curiosity; all of them, even moral philosophy, of human pride. Thus the sciences and the arts owe their birth to our vices; we would be less in doubt about their advantages, if they owed it to our virtues.

One of the most negative developments of civilization, said Rousseau, was the rise of private property, which created false dis-tinctions between people: "The first person who, having enclosed a plot of land, took it into his head to say *this is mine* and found people simple enough to believe him was the true founder of civil society. What crimes, wars, murders, what miseries and horrors would the human race have been spared, had someone pulled up the stakes or filled the ditch and cried out to his fellow men: `Do not listen to this imposter. You are lost if you forget that the fruits of the earth belong to all and the earth to no one!'"

It was impossible to undo centuries of historical development. Human beings could never destroy civil society and return to the state of nature. They had to build on what had already taken place, create the best (or most practical) form of government and work to overcome the inequalities that arose through time. In *On the Social Contract*, Rousseau explained that despite these difficulties, a human being in civil society had changed from a person who operated only according to instinct to one who understood the nature of justice. "His faculties are exercised and developed, his ideas are broadened, his feelings are ennobled, his entire soul is elevated to such a height that, if the abuse of this new condition did not often lower his status to beneath the level he left, he ought constantly to bless the happy moment that pulled him away from it forever and which transformed him from a stupid, limited animal into an intelligent being and a man."[8] The best form of government, Rousseau thought, was a small, democratic city-state, like his own native Geneva, where the General Will operated to fulfill the needs and desires of the people.

Paine, following Rousseau, also thought it was not possible to return to a natural state. Now that lands were cultivated and the arts and sciences practiced, all people could do was "to remedy the evils and preserve the benefits that have arisen to society by passing from the natural to that which is called the civilized state." The precept was "that the condition of every person born into the world, after a state of civilization commences, ought not be worse than if he had been born before that period." (*AJ* 2:610) What could the people do to ensure that this first principle was achieved? Paine suggested that if everyone who claimed to own property was no more than a lessee, then such people now had to pay a rent, not to any particular landlord, but to those who did not have any property at all. "Every proprietor, therefore, of cultivated lands, owes to the community a ground-rent (for I know of no better term to express the idea) for the land which he holds."[9] This rent was to be paid in the form of an inheritance tax of one-tenth the value of the land at the time it was transferred from the decedent to the beneficiary. The monies from this tax were to be used for social services for the poor: "It is from this ground-rent that the fund proposed in this plan is to issue." (*AJ* 2:611) In other words, Paine explicitly did not want to displace anyone. Ironically, like Burke, Paine accepted the idea of historical prescription here: time had given landowners the right to remain on their property. Only now they had to reimburse society as a whole for that right.

There was, after all, another right with which the right of property conflicted, namely the right of the "dispossessed" to have a decent standard of living. For Paine, "it is a right, and not a charity, that I am pleading for," an echo of his advocacy in the *Rights of Man* for social services and public assistance. (*AJ* 2:612, 618) His plan, an early form of welfare and social security, was that at the age of twenty-one, all persons, rich or poor, were to receive from the government a sum of fifteen pounds sterling to compensate them for the loss of their "natural inheritance, by the introduction of landed property."[10] In addition, a social security component to his plan presumably operated whether a person had worked or not. People at age fifty were to receive ten pounds per year for the rest of their lives. The source of the funding for these plans was the ground rent Paine had earlier advocated. Like social security in contemporary American society, it was totally free to those who were among the dispossessed, with the difference being that its funding would not have been the result of these individuals paying into a fund. Everyone, men and women alike, (Paine spoke of "the loss of his or her natural inheritance") received money from his fund, no matter their economic status. Paine did not want any "invidious distinctions" between people to cause even greater social turmoil between the classes. (*AJ* 2:613) It was clear, however, that a number of people did not need their allotment, and Paine naively hoped that these people would turn in their share to the common fund.

Paine owned no property in France, but he did have some in the United States. He was willing to start the plan in France, however, with a contribution of 100 pounds as a gift, much as he had helped jump-start the old Bank of North America. (*AJ* 2:621) He was never taken up on it.[11] *Agrarian Justice* displayed the continuing influence of Rousseau on Paine's thinking throughout 1790s. By the time he finished this, his last great pamphlet, he had emerged from Lockean liberalism to make a case practically for social democracy. He was convinced that if the proposals were adopted, they would radically change the social fabric of France:

> The plan here proposed will reach the whole. It will immediately relieve and take out of view three classes of wretchedness— the blind, the lame, and the aged poor; and it will furnish the rising generation with means to prevent their becoming poor; and it will do this without deranging or interfering with any national measures. (*AJ* 2:618)

He soon abandoned this Rousseauist communitarian thinking to adopt a new spirituality, which he acquired, it seems, while living with the Bonnevilles during his last years in Paris. Until that time, however, he tried to recover from the lingering aspects of the abscess in his side which continued to trouble him and to which he had even alluded in *Agrarian Justice* itself.

As the French were suing for peace with their adversaries, they arranged an exchange of prisoners with the Austrians. Some of Paine's friends from the Revolution now were able to return to Paris. Jean Henri Bancal des Issarts and Jean-Baptiste Drouet, two revolutionaries imprisoned by the Austrians, were exchanged for the daughter of Louis XVI. Lafayette, also imprisoned by the Austrians, came back to Paris in 1797, as republican as he had been eight years earlier when head of the National Guard. Never a Jacobin, he opposed a life consulship for Napoleon and then basically retired from public life. Paine again saw Theobald Wolfe Tone, the republican leader of the Irish rebellion of 1798, but the stubbornness of both these men apparently prevented a true friendship. Tone thought that Paine was "vain beyond all belief," but liked his social and political radicalism.[12] Paine got along quite well with Robert Fulton, who had moved in with Joel Barlow. They spent a good deal of time discussing the science of mechanics, especially Paine's old bridge design. Fulton was working on a submarine at the time, and Paine proposed that one way to move it around underwater was to tie it to a whale.[13] Paine was hardly serious about this suggestion, but Fulton surely found it (and Paine) amusing.

Paine continued to think about returning to America. He had thought he might return as early as 1795, but he was prevented from doing so by illness.[14] Two years later, he promised Col. John Fellows, who held the American copyright to *The Age of Reason*, that when he returned, he would come to talk to him. "It is my intention to return to America in the course of the present year," he told Fellows, who later managed the waterworks of New York City.[15] In the spring, he went to Havre-de-Grace to board a boat for the United States, but he never left. He later told Madison he had been concerned about England's intercepting neutral ships on the high seas and was afraid of being picked up and taken to an English prison (he was still after all an outlaw), maybe even to be executed. "[A]s I have lost all confidence in the American government, and had none in the Captain, I did not choose to expose myself to the hazard of being taken out of the vessel. It is no credit to the American government when a man who has acted towards that country as I have done, finds himself obliged to say this."[16]

French warships had also been picking up American vessels ever since the conclusion of the Jay Treaty. The French had taken self-interest to heart. The Treaty of Alliance of 1778, by which the French and Americans agreed not to harm neutral ships, was no longer applicable. By 1797, well over three hundred American vessels had been seized. Paine approved, because the Jay Treaty with England defamed the United States. "The neutral powers despise her for her meanness, and her desertion of a common interest," he told Jefferson. "England laughs at her imbecility, and France is enraged at her ingratitude, and sly treachery!"[17] Could the English retaliate and do the same with French ships? Paine thought they might.

In any case, in May 1797, Paine returned to Paris, only to find himself engaged in yet another controversy in French politics. The government had been experiencing severe internal dissension, not only between the two Councils and the Directory, but in the Directory itself. Paine's greatest worries were over the resurrection of the monarchy and the rehabilitation of the clergy. In the summer of

1797 he thought he saw both fears about to be realized. The elections that year had restored to government several men who wanted to establish a constitutional monarchy in France. Almost simultaneously, a conservative royalist deputy of the Council of Five Hundred, Camille Jordan, issued a report suggesting that some privileges of the clergy should now be restored along with the ringing of church bells. Paine, appalled by both of these spectacles, spewed out his venom against the return of a king to France, which he tied directly to the ringing of church bells. He had earlier expressed the fear of the coming together of church and state when writing the second part of *The Age of Reason*.

Paine's first salvo was against Jordan's support in the Council of Five Hundred for renewed rights for the Catholic clergy's privileges and the ringing of bells. Here he reiterated some of the points he had alluded to in *The Age of Reason*. Religion was "a private affair between every man and his maker," and government had no role in it. If government did try to intervene, either through its support of a particular religion or by giving certain privileges to the clergy, then it went beyond the bounds of its authority. Religion could be good, but since it "has been made into a trade, the practical part has been made to consist of ceremonies performed by men called priests; and the people have been amused with ceremonial shows, processions, and bells."

Here Paine once again recounted his own experience as a Quaker and the son of a Quaker, the people who truly eschewed ornate ceremony, showy procession, and loud tolling of the bells. The Quakers, despite their grimness, understood the precept that a truly religious people were a moral people, those who worked to better the lot of the less fortunate. "It is a want of feeling to talk of priests and bells while so many infants are perishing in the hospitals, and aged and infirm poor in the streets, from the want of necessaries. The abundance that France produces is sufficient for every want, if rightly applied; but priests and bells, like articles of luxury, ought to be the least articles of consideration." The Quakers cared for the poor and the education of their children. They had no need for the corruptions and extravagance that were found in Christian churches. Besides, and here his attack became more rancorous than usual, "as to bells, they are a public nuisance."

> If one profession is to have bells, and another has the right to
> use the instruments of the same kind, or any other noisy instru-
> ment, some may choose to meet at the sound of cannon, another
> at the beat of drum, another at the sound of trumpets, and so
> on, until the whole becomes a scene of general confusion. But if
> we permit ourselves to think of the state of the sick, and the
> many sleepless nights and days they undergo, we shall feel the
> impropriety of increasing their distress by the noise of bells, or
> any other noisy instruments.[18]

The danger here was not merely that the government might give in
to the demands for the clergy's restoration, but that the close tie
would return between the extinguished, now potentially revived,
monarchy and the established Catholic Church.

Fears of a royalist plot began to surface shortly after the dispute over church bells. In September, the royalists led by the president of the Five Hundred, Charles Pichegru, Director François de
Bartélemy, and others attempted to impeach three leading republican
members of the Directory, Paul Jean François Barras, Jean François
Reubell, and Louis Marie de la Reveillière-Lépeaux. Once they were
out of the way, the Luxembourg, then the seat of government, would
be seized and the French royalist emigrants, now financed by
England and massing on the Rhine, would attack Paris. Instead, an
armed struggle briefly ensued when Bonaparte dispatched General
Pierre François Charles Augereau to Paris the very next day to suppress the attempt. Paine soon wrote a commentary on the affair,
which he called not unexpectedly *The Eighteenth Fructidor*. The title
signified the new calendar date when the Directory was saved, if in
fact it was ever truly endangered.

Paine had absolutely no doubt that the threat was real. He
believed that Pichegru, who had led the impeachment of the
Directors, and the others on his side were in fact allied with Pitt, who
desperately wanted to see the Bourbon monarchy restored to power.
Paine envisioned the takeover of the Directory as part of Jordan's
scheme to reestablish the priesthood in France: "Pichegru occupied
himself about forming a national guard for the Councils—the suspi-

cious signal of war—Camille Jordan about priests and bells, and the emigrants, with whom he had associated during the two years he was in England." This was all too ominous for Paine to let pass without question. "The case reduced itself to a simple alternative—shall the republic be destroyed by the darksome maneuvers of a faction, or shall it be preserved by an exceptional act?" His answer was that the threat of monarchical government had to be counteracted, and indeed it was by Bonaparte "in an instant, without the stain of blood, and without involving the public in the least inconvenience."[19] Little did he know that constitutional government would soon give way to dictatorship, led by his present hero, Napoleon Bonaparte himself, on the eighteenth Brumaire.

This "plot" ended, Paine turned his attention to yet another scheme just unfolding, this time by the American government. An American delegation consisting of Charles Cotesworth Pinckney (the new ambassador to France), John Marshall, and Elbridge Gerry arrived in the winter of 1797-98 to try to stop French seizures of American ships. As a result of America's increasingly close ties to Britain, and especially the consummation of the Jay Treaty, which ratified those ties, France had unleashed hundreds of privateers against American shipping along the Atlantic coast, the Caribbean, and even on the high seas. The result was what came to be known in history as America's "quasi-war" against France. In an effort to settle the matter with the French, President Adams sent a delegation to Paris to speak with French Foreign Minister Charles Maurice de Talleyrand-Périgord.

Tallyrand was not much interested in meeting the Americans, who had already shown their dislike and distrust of the French. After all, the Washington Administration had recalled Monroe from Paris largely for his pro-French views and his distaste for the Jay Treaty. Then, in December of 1796, Adams replaced Monroe with Pinckney, and the French immediately refused to accept his credentials until they were satisfied that the Americans had not fully adopted the British interpretation of the law of the sea, especially regarding the seizure of neutral ships en route to an enemy country. In fact, at one point, French officials demanded the recall of Pinckney, who was then visiting in Amsterdam.

Because of their disgust over the warm relationship between the United States and Britain, the French withdrew their ambassador, Pierre August Adet, from the United States and did not replace him. With the signing of the Jay Treaty, the French were convinced that the Americans now aimed to assist the British in squelching the revolutionary armies of France. As far as the French were concerned, the alliance with the Americans originated in 1778 was dead. That treaty had been based on the principle of "free ships, free goods," which meant that in time of war a merchant ship from a neutral nation was guaranteed free and quiet passage so long as it was not carrying contraband military equipment to or from the enemy country.

The American delegation, now sent by President Adams, was instructed to work out these problems without antagonizing the French into a full-scale war with the United States. The American commissioners met with French officials, including Talleyrand, who later sent his own delegation to negotiate with them. This delegation, led by Madame de Villette (the landlady of Gerry and Marshall), consisted also of the famous XYZ, all agents of Talleyrand: Jean Conrad Hottinguer ("X"), a Swiss financier; a Monsieur Bellamy ("Y"), who was a banker with a Swiss background living in Hamburg; and Lucien Hauteval ("Z"), another Swiss. This group made several preliminary demands that had to be met even before negotiations with Talleyrand could take place, such as sizable loans from the United States and the payment of a bribe of some $250,000 (1,200,000 livres). This bribe, to which Pinckney allegedly sputtered, "No! No! Not a sixpence," was supposedly to stop the French from seizing American ships and torturing her sailors.

Paine soon became aware of what was known as the XYZ affair and warned Talleyrand that he had best receive the Americans "with a *civil signification* of reproach."[20] In addition, he had his own suggestion for a treaty of neutrality between the Americans and the French, which he hoped would lead to the beginning of world peace. It never developed into anything, though Paine thought he was once again playing an important role as an unofficial emissary of the United States to the Directory.[21] In fact, the French were a terrible annoyance to American shipping. They interdicted American merchant ships (300 vessels in 1797 alone), harassed, at times even tortured, American sailors, refused to allow American vessels into the French port of Bordeaux, and when their own French administrators owed money to the American shipping interests for goods shipped, the government often instructed those officials not to pay them. In addition, when Americans and French merchants entered into contracts concerning the shipments of goods, sometimes the French merchants simply declined to send the ordered materials.

The Federalists in America were delighted. These pro-English politicians liked nothing better than to see the relations between France and the United States deteriorate further. The American negotiators declined to submit to the French demands and left empty-handed. The United States, now without a navy, began war preparations by starting to build several sloops of war, raising an army, and creating the Marine Corps. Only Marshall returned home. Gerry, who was very much a republican and pro-French, remained in Paris to talk to Talleyrand and convince him to avoid war with the United States, while Pinckney took an ill daughter to southern France. Soon the French withdrew their demands. But it was too late. By then, the French had concluded the Treaty of Camp Formio with Austria, which allowed Napoleon to concentrate his forces against England without interference from the Americans. It was not until October of 1800 that the tensions between the United States and France relaxed sufficiently for the two countries to enter into the convention of Môrtefontaine at the site of Joseph Bonaparte's estate just north of Paris.[22]

Paine was now out of the picture. With Monroe gone, Pinckney had nothing to do with him, even if Paine wanted to act as the liaison between American and French officials. So he purposely stayed out of French affairs for a while. His journalist/publisher friend, Nicolas de Bonneville, invited him to stay with him and his family for a week or two in their home in Paris. Paine gladly accepted. Five years later, he was still there.

18 · Illuminism and Nicolas de Bonneville

L ife with the Bonnevilles was fairly easy. Paine had known Nicolas since the early days of the Revolution, and they had gotten along quite well, especially since Bonneville spoke excellent English. An inquisitive fellow, Bonneville was, like Paine, a radical journalist caught up in the heady moments of the French Revolution. He was also an Illuminist and spiritualist, a member of the "Illuminati," believing in the mind's capacity to understand reality beyond human reason: for the Illuminist, understanding came through the enlightened spirit of the mind. In 1792, Bonneville had published Lanthenas' French translation of Paine's *Rights of Man*. Now, in 1797, he published Paine's *Eighteenth Fructidor*, supporting the Directory's armed suppression of what it feared was a royalist plot to reestablish the Bourbon monarchy.

Living arrangements were more than satisfactory. Some years after Paine's death, Marguerite de Bonneville recalled: "Our house was at No. 4 Rue du Théâtre François. All the first floor was occupied as a printing office. The whole house was pretty well filled; and Mr. Bonneville gave up his study, which was not a large one, and a bed-chamber to Thomas Paine," who, according to Rickman, paid a small fee to the Bonnevilles for his room and board. Paine spent a good deal of time in the house, rising late, rarely leaving to go outside. He read many newspapers, some of which were in English, although he did understand written French, especially when it came to politics. Since Bonneville worked at home, Paine often left his small apartment to talk to him about the events of the day. Whenever he went out, he always walked, and rarely if ever took a coach. According to Marguerite, when Paine was in the house, he always seemed to be quite busy, either reading, writing, or engaging himself in some mechanical invention. Otherwise, he loved to entertain visitors: chat with them, sing to them, drink brandy with them. "Not a day escaped without his receiving many visits," she recounted. "Mr. Barlow, Mr. Fulton, Mr. [Robert] Smyth came very often to see him. Many travellers also called on him; and, often, having no other affair, talked to him only of his great reputation and their admiration of his works."[1] She said that he was gracious to all his callers, except when they began to bore him. Then he simply returned to his quarters, leaving them to their own thoughts.

In the evenings, he dined with his friends, again Barlow, Smyth, and Fulton. He spent time with General Tadeusz Kosciusko, the Polish liberator, and Thomas Holcroft, the English writer and liberal, as well as Constantin François Volney, a French deist and member of the Directory. He saw a good deal of the Marquis de Lafayette, but except for Volney and Lafayette he rarely saw many of his former French friends. One evening, he and friends dined at the home of Jean Lambert Tallien, a leader of the Directory. Also at the dinner was Louis Sebastien Mercier, the author of a work that was critical of several governmental officials, including Tallien, his host. On later being asked how this could be, Paine characteristically responded: French leaders could be jovial together and enjoy one another's company, but once they left their parties, they rushed off to report their conversations to the Committee for Public Safety.[2]

Many of Paine's French friends were dead, and his continued inability to master spoken French limited him to associating with Americans, British ex-patriots, Irishmen, and a few English-speaking French people. And his experience in the Luxembourg might well have soured his relationship with government officials. The only times he went to visit one of them was when someone, usually from America or Britain, needed his help with one of the agencies, and then he was delighted to intervene.

Having renewed these friendships, Paine also renewed his drinking, which by this time was well recognized by those who knew him well and even those who knew him a little. He apparently had taken up drinking as a serious avocation after his release from the Luxembourg—in part to allay the terror of his experience, in part, to try to feel better during his illness. At sixty, his day-to-day activities were now fairly routine: for example, "he never went out after dinner without first taking a nap, which was always two or three hours length. And, when he went out to a dinner . . . he often came home for the purpose of taking his accustomed sleep."[3]

Paine also enjoyed going to the Irish Coffee House on the Rue de Condé, where Irish nationalists met, drank, sang songs, and offered toasts to the liberation of Ireland. He knew English was spoken there, and besides, it gave him a chance to visit with American, Irish, and English ex-patriots who invariably passed on news to him of the British Isles and America. Paine was an honorary member of the Society of United Irishmen, which, according to historian Marianne Elliott, was "the most radical and most influential of all the British political clubs generated by the reform euphoria of the early 1790s." In 1797, he often ate at the Irish Coffee House with James Napper Tandy (who helped Wolfe Tone form the United Irishmen in 1791 and who popularized the "wearing of the green" as a symbol of Irish nationalism), Thomas Muir (who was a Scot), and other Irish exiles trying to free Ireland from British rule.

Intent on a successful "descent" onto Ireland, Napper Tandy, and Wolfe Tone in 1798 gathered together a small force and set out, but the French forces which were supposed to back them up failed to materialize, and the invasion was a disaster. The thirty-five year old Wolfe Tone was convicted of treason and sentenced to be executed when he committed suicide. Napper Tandy fled to Hamburg, where he was arrested and returned to Dublin. Sentenced to execution, he was reprieved and imprisoned. He died in 1803 at the age of forty-three.[4] Included in the group at the Irish Coffee House was the English Quaker physician, Dr. John Walker, who greatly admired Paine. Walker reputedly refused to join in a toast Tandy offered to the fall of the English monarchy not because he favored the monarchy, but because, as a Quaker, he opposed the practice of toasting and, as a teetotaler, he opposed alcohol. Paine, who could not let such a delicious moment pass without a biting comment, reputedly shot back, "Walker is a Quaker with all its follies, I am a Quaker without them."[5] Paine's longtime friend Joel Barlow apparently thought the Irish were beneath him and Paine, too, and never went to the Coffee House with Paine.

At this time, Paine became familiar with the theological works of the Reverend Elihu Palmer, a militant American deist, with whose writings he totally agreed and with whom he corresponded while in Paris. He would later write for his journal in America in 1804. Paine wrote to him just before his departure to the United States, saying that "some people can be reasoned into sense, and others must be shocked into it. Say a bold thing that will stagger them, and they will begin to think." He also told Palmer that he was coming to America with "the third part of *The Age of Reason* . . . which, if I mistake not, will make a stronger impression than anything I have yet published on the subject."[6] This "third part" was his response to the criticisms made by the bishop of Llandaff.

In 1797, Paine's attention was also directed toward revolution in England, which he thought could be stimulated by a French invasion. He set to work on a plan that became his obsession for the next five years: the "descent on England" to end the monarchy there forever. His first plan was published as "Observations on the Construction and Operation of Navies with a Plan for an Invasion of England and the Final Overthrow of the English Government," and he submitted it to the Directory. In January 1798, Paine again urged the French government to invade England. This time he was willing to risk whatever savings he had accumulated to influence French military policy toward England. He sent a note to the Council of Five Hundred, the legislative body of the Directory, along with one hundred French livres (a loan, he said) and "all the wishes of my heart for the success of the descent, and a voluntary offer of any service I can render to promote it." He also suggested that each French citizen do the same, but the Council of Five Hundred never did anything.[7] In addition to writing *The Eighteenth Fructidor*, Paine, in 1797-98, contributed several pieces on a future French invasion of England to *Le Bien informé*, Bonneville's newspaper, which he published in his house.[8]

Napoleon Bonaparte was the sole exception to French intransigence to discuss Paine's proposals on an invasion. As late as 1800, Paine was still recommending his ideas to Bonaparte, a professed admirer of Paine's, who once told him that he wanted to discuss Paine's ideas of using small gunboats, rather than large man-o'-wars, against England. Bonaparte also said that he respected the *Rights of Man* so much so that he slept with it under his pillow. He thought that a statue of gold in Paine's honor should be erected in every town in the universe, and he hoped Paine would some day visit him. Paine waited patiently for the day when the invasion of England would take place.[9]

So intent was Paine on destroying the English government that he even tried to engage Jefferson's interest in such an invasion.[10] This interest continued even after his return to America in 1802. He wanted the American government to take seriously his suggestion that several hundred small gunboats should be built for a frontal assault on England, and he even submitted a plan to that effect, but it was ignored.[11] His optimism about these small vessels seemed endless. If the U.S. would not consider using them against France, they were the "most effectual" means by which the United States could protect its shoreline.[12]

In addition, as a result of meeting Wolfe Tone, the Irish republican leader, he also began to suggest a renewed Irish rebellion against the British. His interest in liberating Ireland from Britain and freeing England from monarchy never seemed to stop. He wrote the leadership of the Directory in February of 1798, outlining his plan for an Irish invasion of England, and three years later he suggested in *Le Citoyen français* that Irish revolutionaries could launch an attack from America. Nothing ever developed from these suggestions. In September he discussed such an invasion with his friend Joel Barlow, who had just returned to Paris. Paine then wrote several pieces for *Le Bien informé* concerning the goals that Britain had during peace negotiations in Lille to cease the European war. He did not think the British were negotiating in a manner that would lead to a lasting peace.

In the meantime, the British secret service, active in Paris and other French cities from 1784 onward, was apparently not only aware of Paine's activities, but fearful that he might be successful.

Whitehall reported that should such an invasion take place, the monarchy overthrown, then England, Ireland, and Scotland would be separated into three republics. As for England, the report said, a new government was to be created, its leadership, called "the Directory in England," to include "Thomas Paine, John Horne Tooke, William Sharpe, John Thelwall, and the Marquis of Lansdowne."[13]

Paine's activities with the radicals at the Irish Coffee House and his ongoing association with Bonneville and his circle also alarmed the conservative Thermidoreans and made Paine a constant suspect of the government police. Many French liked Paine's ideas and loved what he wrote on their behalf, but they never really trusted him. He was, after all, often a renegade, an independent thinker and writer, and he had served in the National Convention, which by then was viewed with great suspicion. Napoleon continued to admire Thomas Paine but had several misgivings about him. Paine's association with Bonneville, whose newspaper was often at odds with the government, was possibly to blame. In March of 1798 the police interrogated Paine, because they figured he knew whether British agents were in Paris and, if so, where they might be. He did not know of any, or at least that was what he said. The police soon closed down *Le Bien informé*, which had published a spoof by Bonneville on Abbé Sieyès, who was then closely allied to Bonaparte. The Abbé had served on the Directory and had conspired with Napoleon to overthrow it in 1799. He was, with Bonaparte, one of the three original consuls in the new government.

Paine came to Bonneville's rescue with a kindly portrait of him in a letter to the Directory. He described Bonneville as an "honest and incorruptible" man," and "no one knew better than I the sincerity of his principles."[14] The paper was allowed to resume publication. But it was clear, even to the police, that the linkages between Paine and Bonneville were quite strong. Paine decided to disappear for a bit and spent some time in the fall of 1799 visiting a friend in Dièppe and then several months in Bruges with Jan Vanheule, whom he had known in the Luxembourg Prison. Vanheule told Paine he had heard that the French government had implemented his ideas about building gunboats to invade England.[15] After Bonaparte took absolute control of France, Paine recalled that "by an agreement between him and me, I was to accompany him, as the intention of the expedition was to give the people of England an opportunity of forming a government for themselves, and thereby bring peace." Paine was soon disappointed. Nearly two hundred fifty boats were now at the ready "when the expedition was abandoned for that of Egypt, to which the preparations had served as a feint."[16] But now, when he returned to Paris from Bruges, the police warned him that if he publicly criticized the government, they would deport him. To where he did not know, but he did not want to risk being sent to London.

Although Paine returned to military issues after his final move to the United States in 1802, it was through Bonneville's influence that he now moved away from the political sphere and toward Theophilanthropy and most likely Freemasonry.[17] For several years, France had been fully enmeshed in a series of radical changes in lifestyle, which followed on the heels of the vast political changes of the Revolution and the Terror. Religious ceremonies took on an earthy quality. A return to things natural, to nature herself, meant that ceremonies were regarded as festivals, or fêtes, where statues of Dame Nature became the centerpiece. Military parade grounds were transformed into great parks for festivals celebrating the new model of nature and light, where statues of Nature were erected. "From her fertile breasts (which she will press with her hands) will spurt an abundance of pure and healthful water of which shall drink, each in his turn, the eighty-six commissioners sent from the primary assemblies. . . . [A] single cup shall serve for all."[18] An enlightened populace had set off the spark of revolution, which in turn became an even greater flame that illuminated changes beyond the political to the cultural, and thus became the symbol of the new age of revolution, enlightenment, and reason. Spatially and temporally, life was transformed: parks and other venues for revolutionary fêtes replaced the Place de la Bastille and the Champ de Mars (the old military parade grounds and today the site of the Eiffel Tower). The new calendar broke symbolically with the past. Time, place, and all humanity were fully subsumed by nature and the seasons.

Paine was witness to this transformation of culture as well as to all the celebrations and festivals that took place in the 1790s. Sexual license, political innovation and speculation, utopian ideologies, all were part of the new world order. In this new world, the cafés of Paris, especially those around the Palais Royal, the home of the Duc d'Orléans, became focal points for new, revolutionary ideas and ideals. Duc Philippe himself, in the ardor of the moment (or maybe out of sheer terror), changed his name to Philippe-Egalité, and offered his residence to the revolutionaries. There and in other cafés, journalists, poets, writers, and others met and formed themselves into associations or "circles." They talked about the great issues of the day, conspired against the government, thought up new ideas for plays and poetry, or exchanged gossip.[19]

One of these groups was "le Cercle social," the Social Circle, which had been founded by Paine's friends and colleagues Nicolas de Bonneville and the Marquis de Condorcet. Bonneville, one of the most original journalists the Revolution produced, saw his publication "as a 'circle of light,' whose writers were to transform the world by constituting themselves as 'simultaneously a center of light and a body of resistance.' They were to be 'legislators of the universe,' preparing a 'vast plan of universal regeneration,' and opposing 'those pusillanimous beings whom the indifferent crowd call moderate people.' "[20] The ideas that Bonneville promulgated were not related only to revolutionary political action. Many of them originated in Illuminist, occult convictions, which gave them an aspect of the sensational and weird. Life, culture, and politics would all be led by those who possessed superior intelligence.

In one sense Bonneville looked back to Plato's vision of the appropriate leadership of the republic. Plato believed in rule by the single enlightened man, the philosopher king. In another sense, however, Bonneville's ideas about political leadership moved forward. They foreshadowed, for example, the Romantic movement in English and American literature of the next century as well as American Transcendentalism, which aspired to a heightened intellectual and spiritual vitality. Oddly enough, Bonneville's ideas were also an early (clearly non-communist) version of the Leninist notion of the dictatorship of the proletariat, the collective leadership that was supposedly to transform the world by those whose consciousness was raised above those of the masses. The "advance guard" of the proletariat knew that history moved in an ineluctable pattern and that it provided the spark that inaugurated the proletarian revolution.

But Bonneville did not advocate revolutionary violence. France had experienced too much of that already, with the Terror, the civil wars in the provinces, and the war with Europe. Still, Bonneville presumed a benevolent dictatorship, because these supremely intelligent leaders alone knew how to recognize "une lumière que vive . . . dans les sphères très-élèves de la maçonnerie" (a light that lives in the transported spheres of Masonry).[21] Freemasonry, with its emphasis on light and enlightenment, on Illuminist ideas, became a component of the ideology of the Social Circle.

Illuminism took its name from the way in which the sun radiated its light to distant circles.[22] Even the communist ideals in Gracchus Babeuf's attempt to overthrow the Directory in 1796 through his "Conspiracy of Equals" had a Bonneville connection through one of Bonneville's writers, Jean-François Varlet.[23] The hope was that the principles that underlay Freemasonry, magic, and the Revolution would mingle to improve humanity. Many of these ideas originated in the theories of Illuminism.

Illuminism originated in Bavaria, specifically in the ideas of Adam Weishaupt. Weishaupt founded the Order of Illuminati in the spring of 1776 at the University of Ingolstadt, where he was a professor of canon, or religious, law. Weishaupt thought a person could achieve a heightened state of awareness to the extent where it was possible to see beyond the simple reality of everyday life. Once a person reached that point, he joined the Illuminati. For the Illuminati, the relationship between God and man, between the divine and the secular, was so closely intertwined that they became one. Condemned by the Roman Catholic Church because it invited no priestly intervention or bishopric or popish intermediary, Illuminism was dissolved by the Bavarian government in 1785. In France, the situation was different. The clergy had lost its standing during the Revolution, and hence could not condemn the heresy. In these circumstances, the German-speaking Bonneville became an Illuminist under the influence of Johann Christian Bode, a follower of Weishaupt.

Into this picture stepped Thomas Paine. Bonneville most likely introduced Paine to the Social Circle and the principles of

Freemasonry and Theophilanthropism. For Bonneville, "man is God," and he was to "become angelic" as universal brotherhood spanned the world, ideas that fitted perfectly into Paine's universalism, which dated back to his 1782 letter to Abbé Raynal. In the poetry he wrote in 1793, Bonneville longed for the transformation of mankind:

> O Social Circle!
> Ever sweet hope of a general pact;
> Thy brotherhood of oppressed peoples
> Has sworn eternal, universal deliverance . . .
>   Free and pure as air, and in my republic,
>   All is brotherhood, German parenthood [Germanic purity] . . .
>   Sun of another world, in thy Majesty
> Become the divinity of another University . . .
>   I am burning. . . .[24]

Just as Paine wandered in the physical world, his intellectual development had clearly wandered from the classical republic and rights and liberties to these news ideas about spirituality. Now his intellectual development continued to evolve. Paine was still suffering from the effects of his imprisonment in the Luxembourg. He was profoundly disillusioned with the failure of the Revolution in France. Perhaps his submersion into spiritual causes was a direct reaction to his despondency. In many respects, his physical maladies paralleled his crisis of spirit. He was now a depressed and at times lonely man, often drinking.

In January of 1797, Paine and several other people founded a society known as the Theophilanthropists. They met in the suburb of St. Denis, and even established a library there. The idea was that this group of people could worship God according to the principles Paine had advocated in *The Age of Reason*. Theophilanthropism was a humanistic, deistic religion without superstition, mythology, or priesthood. It was one of the first ethical societies in the world. Paine never attended a religious service, not even a Quaker meeting, but now there was a community of believers, the Theophilanthropists, to which he could belong. As he came more and more under the influence of Bonneville, these tendencies became increasingly pronounced in his last years in Paris.

Paine described his association with the Theophilanthropists at the end of his letter to Erskine defending *The Age of Reason* against charges of sedition in England. He explained the word *Theophilanthropy* as a compound of "three Greek words, signifying God, Love, and Man." Simply put, the members of the group were lovers of God and man. General meetings, which excluded no one, were prepared in advance by a committee consisting of the "fathers" of the founding families. These general meetings took place at "general assemblies," which Paine called fêtes or festivals, like the festivals in honor of Dame Nature throughout Paris in the early 1790s. The members instructed each other in moral and spiritual matters. The group itself comprised a "circle," a ring of unbroken devotion to God. Remarkably spiritualist, Theophilanthropism looked to the spirit of humanity as the basis for a moral life on earth. Its beliefs were grounded in the affective spirituality of the Illuminati that Bonneville had brought from Germany to Paris. Theophilanthropism became the means for Paine to achieve a renewed spirit.

Two principles essentially underlay Theophilanthropism, and Paine expressed them in French: "les Théophilantropes croient à l'éxistence de Dieu, et a l'immortalité de l'âme" (the Theophilanthropists believe in the existence of God and the immortality of the soul).[25] Paine put the tenets of Theophilanthropism in a manual of some sixty pages, which were a distillation of the beliefs previously declared in *The Age of Reason.* He denied the divine origin of the Bible, most of its stories (particularly those pertaining to miracles), and the whole idea of the resurrection of the body after death. These were all superstitions, sustained by mythologies that the priests themselves promulgated. Their goal was to blind the believer into obeying the will of the clergy. For Paine, God was the creator of the universe and all things in it. He was responsible for everything, but only insofar as He served as creating force. He was not responsible for man's misconduct and errors. To study God is to study His works, and "the true Bible" is "the inimitable work of God."

Do we want to contemplate His power? We see it in the
immensity of the Creation. Do we want to contemplate His
wisdom? We see it in the unchangeable order by which the
incomprehensible WHOLE is governed. Do we want to contemplate His munificence? We see it in the abundance with
which He fills the earth. Do we want to contemplate His
mercy? We see it in His not withholding that abundance even
from the unthankful. In fine, do we want to know what GOD
is? Search not written or printed books, but the Scripture called
the creation.

This was Paine's Illuminist vision of the universe. God
dwelled within all his creation. The world was a godly place, made
so by a divine creator, but also one which could easily be ruined by
men, who were themselves created by God. Atheism was wrong and
in fact an untenable system of thought. Atheists, especially natural
philosophers, "stop short and employ the knowledge they acquire to
create doubts of [God's] existence. They labor with studied ingenu-
ity to ascribe everything they behold to innate properties of matter,
and jump over all the rest by saying that matter is eternal." A person
had to believe in God as Creator of the sun, stars, the earth, the universe itself. He alone was the root of all power, the spiritual power of
man and the universe, which God alone had created.

We profess, and we proclaim in peace, the pure, unmixed, comfortable and rational belief of a God as manifest to us in the
universe. We do this without any apprehension of that belief
being made a cause of persecution as other beliefs have been, or
of suffering persecution ourselves. To God, and not to man, are
all men to account for their belief. . . All the principles of science are of divine origin. . . . Those principles are eternal and
immutable. We see them in the unchangeable nature of the
Divinity. We see in them immortality, an immortality existing
after the material figures that express those properties are dissolved in dust. . . . [If we instruct others in these principles]
they will be led to see the hand of God in all these things.[26]

God surely was an indwelling spirit throughout all his creation everywhere. In a volume proposed by the Theophilanthropists for publi-

cation, no biblical scripture was included. Instead, they chose from the writings of the sixth century B.C., Greek poet Theognis, who wrote elegies admonishing his readers to be moderate, faithful, and dutiful and from the writings of Confucius and other Chinese poets. Their goal was to heighten the spirituality of all people, to bring them to harmony with themselves, their fellow human beings, the universe, and ultimately God. "They profess the immortality of the soul," Paine told Erskine, a soul that enjoyed life after death in a spiritual union with God, the Creator of the Universe.[27] For some unknown reason, they were not suppressed during the Revolution until 1800, when Napoleon permanently closed *Le Bien informé*.

After Paine returned to America, he set down his ideas about these matters in an essay on the origins of Freemasonry.[28] Bonneville printed the essay in French translation, but it did not appear in English until after Paine's death, when it was presented in a collection of his works edited by Marguerite de Bonneville. In this essay, Paine attributed the origins of Freemasonry to the rites of the Druids and their sun worship. "They paid worship to this great luminary, as the great visible agent of a great invisible cause, whom they styled `Time without limits.'" The sun, the illuminated symbol of man's consciousness, was the focal point of Masonry. The masons often had to hide their worship of the sun, because theirs is a "faith opposite to the faith of the gloomy Christian Church."[29]

Paine's association with Bonneville confirmed many of his beliefs about the nature of the universe, the place of God in it, the relationships of the sun, nature, and man's spiritual evolution in a time of spectacular, revolutionary transformation.

With Parisian authorities wondering anew about Paine's activities with Bonneville and British, Irish, and American radicals, he again began to think seriously of leaving France and returning to the United States. His relationship with the Bonnevilles had been a curious one. At first, a temporary guest, he wound up staying five years. Though younger than Paine, Bonneville reversed the role of mentor and became Paine's patron, publishing his work in his newspaper and leading him to the spirituality of Illuminism. In any case, Paine wrote very little his last two years in Paris. His last real work was a suggestion for the public improvements of roads, wells, and canals. Thereafter, his focus was almost solely on going home. In 1800, he again wrote that his "intention is to return to America as soon as I can cross the sea in safety."[30] Again, he told Jefferson that he would return to the United States, if he could be confident that some British vessel would not pick him up. He recounted how he had gone to Le Havre three years earlier, but "had no confidence in the captain of the *Dublin Packet*," the ship which was then sailing to America. So, for now, he just waited.

In this same letter, he mentioned that yet another new American commission led by Oliver Ellsworth, then Chief Justice of the United States, had arrived, with two others, to try to renew relations with France, which had fallen into total disarray as a result of the Jay Treaty and the XYZ Affair. "The commissioners," who in addition to Ellsworth consisted of Elbridge Gerry and John Marshall, "have been here about eight months, and three more useless mortals never came upon public business." His disgust with the Federalists, who were about to leave office as a result of Jefferson's narrow election in 1800, was increasing as he envisioned his return to America. The feeling was mutual. Paine's writings on religion, his open letter to Washington, and his criticism of the Adams Administration for recalling Monroe from Paris earned him the Federalists' enmity. "I know that the faction of John Adams abuses me pretty heartily. They are welcome. It does not disturb me, and they lose their labor."[31]

Paine was keeping in close contact with Jefferson, especially in regard to the possibility of returning to America. The President soon made him an extraordinary offer via an American diplomat, Beau Dawson, who was in France to sign a new treaty with the French: the right to return home on an official American military warship.

> You expressed a wish to get a passage to this country in a public vessel. Mr. Dawson is charged with orders to the captain of the Maryland to receive and accommodate you back if you can be ready to depart at such short warning. . . . I am in hopes you will find us returned generally to sentiments worthy of former times. In these it will be your glory to have steadily labored and

with as much effect as any man living. That you may long live to continue your useful labors and to reap the reward in the thankfulness of nations is my sincere prayer. Accept assurance of my high esteem and affectionate attachment.[32]

Paine was elated. "Your very friendly letter by Mr. Dawson gave me the real sensation of happy satisfaction, and what served to increase it was that he brought it to me himself before I knew of his arrival. I congratulate America on your election. . . . I thank you for the opportunity you give me of returning by the *Maryland*, but I shall wait the return of the vessel that brings Mr. Livingston."[33] He had decided not to return on the *Maryland*, because a Baltimore newspaper hostile to him had reported that the President had sent a naval warship to bring the renegade Paine back to America.[34] Paine did not want Jefferson to be placed in a bad light because of his association with Thomas Paine. He decided to wait a little longer. The ship that Robert Livingston, the new American Minister to Paris, was on however, was diverted to the Mediterranean, so his alternative plan for now would not work.

Paine's desire to avoid an embarrassment for Jefferson was also unsuccessful. He was so delighted that he had been offered transportation on a naval vessel that he indiscreetly placed Jefferson's letter in French newspapers. News of the offer by the new President of the United States was immediately picked up by the press and published in America, first by the republican (Anti-Federalist) Washington newspaper, the *National Intelligencer*. In less than a week, a Federalist paper in Philadelphia, the *Gazette of the United States*, printed an attack on Paine and on the editor of the *Philadelphia Aurora*, William Duane, a staunch republican and a friend of both Paine and Jefferson. Duane's rival paper printed the following notice (citing Duane's Irish ancestry):

TOM PAINE AND PAT DUANE

When the story arrived here that the President of the United States had written a very affectionate letter to that living opprobrium of humanity, TOM PAINE, the infamous scavenger of all the filth which could be raked from the dirty paths which have been hitherto trodden by all the revilers of Christianity, Duane, instead of attempting to refute this scandalous charge upon the President, admits that it may be true, and even endeavors to justify it.

This insult by the *Gazette* was soon followed by comment in other Federalist newspapers. In Boston, the *Mercury and New England Palladium* repeated some of Chalmers' worst lies about Paine: "What! Invite to the United States that lying, drunken, brutal infidel, who rejoiced in the opportunity of basking and wallowing in the confusion, devastation, bloodshed, rapine, and murder, in which his soul delights?"

Jefferson was not spared by the Federalist press, despite Paine's conscious decision not to take up his offer of traveling on a military vessel. The Philadelphia *Port Folio* launched into a virulent tirade against both men:

> If, during the present season of national abasement, infatuation, folly and vice, any portent could surprise, sober men would be utterly confounded by an article, current in all our papers, that the loathsome Thomas Paine, a drunken atheist, and the scavenger of faction, is invited to return in a national ship, to America, by the first magistrate of a free people! A measure, so enormously preposterous, we cannot yet believe has been adopted, and it would demand firmer nerves than those possessed by Mr. Jefferson to hazard such an insult to the moral sense of the nation.

The act of kindness shown him by President Jefferson only served to add to the rancor of the out-of-office Federalists, which hated the atheist Paine who had censured the beloved American Cincinnatus, George Washington.[35]

Paine was now more than ever anxious to return to America. He expressed his gratitude to the Bonnevilles for putting him up for so long and the wish to return the favor should they decide to leave France. Marguerite and her three sons did just that shortly after Paine's return. Nicolas was so seriously in trouble with the Napoleonic regime for his criticisms of the government that he could not leave. His paper was shut down after he compared Napoleon to Cromwell, and he eventually served time in jail for it.

Before leaving Paris, Paine also had an unexpected visitor. Henry Redhead Yorke, who had attended the November 1792 banquet at White's Hotel and who had subsequently been convicted of sedition in England seven years earlier, came to visit the aging radical. Thirty-five years younger than Paine, Yorke had returned to France for the first time since he was forced to flee for his life during the Terror. He had openly criticized the bloody Revolutionary Tribunal regime and had made "Yorke" his last name to escape notice when the government wanted to imprison him. He went looking for Paine, inquiring first at a bookseller's shop, only to find that his name "is now as odious in France as it is in England, perhaps more so." On mentioning Paine's name, the bookseller's wife and son raged down such a storm of abuse that Yorke "found it necessary to decamp without losing a moment of time."

From there, he went back to White's Hotel, thinking that Paine still resided there. He found that the establishment was now called the Hotel de Philadelphie, and Paine was not there. Yorke was sent to inquire at yet another bookseller's shop (obviously Bonneville's) on the Rue du Théâtre François. He was greeted at the door by "a jolly-looking woman" (no doubt Marguerite), who told Yorke that Mr. Paine was taking a nap, but she would rouse him. She showed Yorke into "a little dirty room, containing a small wooden table and two chairs. 'This,' said she, 'is Mr. Paine's room!' " Yorke was astounded.

> I never sat down in such a filthy apartment in the whole course of my life. The chimney hearth was a heap of dirt. There was not a speck of cleanliness to be seen. Three shelves were filled with pasteboard boxes, each labelled after the manner of a minister of foreign affairs: correspondance Américaine; Britannique; Française; Notices politiques; *Le citoyen Français*, Etc. In one corner of the room stood several huge bars of iron, curiously shaped, and two large trunks. Opposite the fireplace a board covered with pamphlets and journals, having more the appearance of a dresser in a scullery than a sideboard. Such was the wretched habitation of Thomas Paine, one of the founders of

American Independence, whose extraordinary genius must ever command attention, and whose writings have summoned to action the minds of the most enlightened politicians of Europe! How different this Apostle of Freedom from those gorgeous mansions tenanted by the founders of the French Republic!

At this point, Paine, arriving "in a long flannel gown," hardly remembered him.

Yorke assumed that Paine's poor memory was due to the deteriorated physical condition he was in during his final days in Paris. "I was forcibly struck by his altered appearance. Time seemed to have made dreadful ravages over his whole frame, and a settled melancholy was visible on his countenance," proof perhaps of his depression. When Paine finally recognized the much younger man, "a tear stole down his cheek," sentiment hardly being a characteristic of the man. Yorke claimed he spoke first. " 'Thus are we met once more, Mr. Paine,' I resumed, 'after a long separation of ten years, and after having been both of us severely weather-beaten.' 'Aye,' he replied, 'and who would have thought that we should meet at Paris.' " At dinner, Paine denounced the government of France, claiming it was not a republic, because the people were "'worse off than the slaves of Constantinople, for there, they expect to be bashaws in heaven by submitting to be slaves below. But here they believe neither in heaven nor hell, and yet are slaves by choice.'" Only one republic existed, and it was in America, where he hoped soon to be. "I have done with Europe, and its slavish politics."

Yorke had invited Paine and others to dinner so that a young Englishwoman of his acquaintance could meet Paine. He asked Paine not to talk about religious matters, because the young woman was a very devout Catholic. Paine captivated the guests with stories of his experiences in America and France, anecdotes about famous Americans he knew, and jokes about George III. "For above four hours he kept everyone in astonishment and admiration of his memory, his keen observation of men and manners, his numberless anecdotes of the American Indians, of the American War, of Franklin, of Washington, and even of his Majesty of whom he told several curious facts of humor and benevolence. When someone mentioned *The*

Age of Reason, however, Paine quickly moved into religious issues, despite the entreaties Yorke had made. Moses was a liar, Paine said. The movements of the stars showed that. Such talk, said Yorke, offended the ladies. "Nothing could stop him. In vain I attempted to change the subject by employing every artifice in my power and even by attacking with vehemence his political principles. He returned to the charge with unabated ardor. I called for a song, though I never heard him sing in my life. He struck up instantly one of his own composition, but the instant he had finished it, he resumed his favorite topic. Every time he took breath, he gained fresh strength."

Of course the ladies were appalled at his performance, and they stalked out of the room. When Yorke finally reminded Paine that he reneged on his promise, Paine simply retorted, " 'Oh! They'll come again. What a pity it is that people should be so prejudiced!' " When Yorke tried to argue that it was not prejudice but virtue that had moved the ladies, Paine quoted a long passage, from memory, from one of his works just on the subject of prejudice. Yorke was astounded at Paine's memory, asked him to repeat the passage, which Yorke took down in writing, and soon verified that it was a word-for-word quotation from Paine's *Letter to the Abbé Raynal* of 1782. Yorke was amazed by Paine's prodigious "power of retaining everything he has written in the course of his life."[36] Tired, ill, and growing old though Paine was, he never ceased to impress an audience.

In August, Clio Rickman came to help Paine get ready to sail for America. Rickman noticed that at that time Paine "did not drink spirits, and wine he took moderately; he even objected to any spirits being laid in as a part of his sea-stock."[37] On September 1, they set off for Le Havre. Paine was leaving France forever. Most of his friends there had already left or were dead. He was ready to return "home" to America. He arrived in Baltimore at the end of October 1802.

Part Four

Home in America

19 · Bitter Battles with Federalists

After Thomas Jefferson took the oath of office in the spring of 1801, life in America promised to be pleasant and easy for Paine in his last years. His return was something he had long desired, and he was delighted that Jefferson welcomed him back. The Federalist Adams administration, which was antagonistic to radical thinkers and writers, had ended, and America was now under the control of Jeffersonian Republicans. Paine was home to stay. This optimism did not last, however.

At first, Paine was welcomed to Baltimore, where he arrived at the end of October. Baltimore's *American Patriot* newspaper reported that Republicans "were the foremost to visit him, and with smiling friendly expressions, make him welcome in the city." Duane's *Philadelphia Aurora*, for which Paine would become a regular contributor in his last years, opined that Paine's arrival in Baltimore brought honor to that city. The report noted that "the writings of Mr. Paine on religious subjects were not even mentioned, and the right of private opinion was neither assailed, nor brought into question." Not brought into question until the Federalist press began its assault.

It was clear that the two main grievances that Paine's enemies held against him were his irreligion and his attack on George Washington. Almost immediately on his arrival, a Federalist Baltimore paper, misnamed the *Republican*, suggested that while a debt of gratitude was owed him for writing *Common Sense*, Paine had written it as "a hireling," which was certainly not true. The *Republican* noted that the crowds followed Paine to Fulton's Tavern, where after some brandy, he became lucid in conversation "and readily declared that Mr. Jefferson's invitations were the cause of his returning to this country." The paper thus directly linked the godless, inebriated radical Paine to the President of the United States. Paine was to go from Baltimore to Washington, the paper reported, and then "may visit the tomb of Washington."[1] One steadfast Federalist told Rufus King, U.S. Minister to Great Britain during the Adams Administration, that Paine would "do no harm—& perhaps some good. He was, I learn, civilly received by the President whom I suspect he will much embarrass."[2]

In response, some of his sympathetic republican editors attempted to downplay Paine's supposed atheism by suggesting that the citizens of America look first at what he accomplished for American freedom and the rights of man. But the swell of Federalist criticism was too great. These attacks on Paine and on his Jeffersonian friends only increased in scope and range with each passing day. When Paine was first released from prison, he had experienced a greater awareness of his own spirituality as he tried to adjust to freedom. But now, suffering increasing Federalist attacks, he found little solace or enjoyment in spiritual matters.

Paine quickly fell into a rather bitter frame of mind, which generally lasted to the end of his life. In these final years, Paine did not, however, lose his deeply felt commitment to liberalism and republican government. Nor did he lose his desire to help the poor and the downtrodden. His wanderings, no longer intercontinental, now became unhappy sojourns between New York and New Rochelle.

This assessment must not, however, be overstated. Paine did not spend this time as a grumpy old man, constantly barking out hatred and loathing of everyone and everything he once knew or loved. There were times when he was cheerful with his few remaining friends, as his old friend John Hall was to remark when the republican press welcomed him back. Still, he rarely achieved the elation that he undoubtedly felt the moment he reached Baltimore in the fall of 1802. Assaulted in the Federalist press, set upon by creditors, growing ever more ill with the abscess in his side, attacks of gout and fever, he gradually lost his sense of humor.

Perhaps worst of all, he now had a new responsibility of caring for Marguerite de Bonneville and her three sons, Benjamin, Thomas, and Louis (the eldest eventually returned to Paris to be with his father), a state of affairs that turned out very unsatisfactory and very unfortunate for old Thomas Paine. On Marguerite's arrival in Norfolk less than a month after Paine himself returned to America, he wrote to her that he gladly wanted to handle the expenses of their voyage, which came to twenty-two pounds, ten shillings. Paine was aware that she might not have any money and told her that any of his friends in Norfolk would lend her whatever she needed, and he would reimburse them. He hoped he could "depend on your economy in the use of it." He asked her to "embrace the poor boys for me and tell them they will soon see me at Bordentown," where he intended for them to stay until they finally settled in New Rochelle.[3] Paine always loved the company of friends and admirers and to be engaged in conversation and song. At first, he looked forward to their arrival.

Young, quite pretty, and thirty-one years Paine's junior, Marguerite was more than a mere tenant, but it did not take long for her to grow intolerant of the lonely, isolated life on Paine's New York farm. His relationship with Marguerite was far from intimate, despite the attempt by James Cheetham in his biography to state otherwise. Cheetham, originally an admirer of Paine, printed Paine's pieces in his newspaper until he and Paine had a falling out, and Cheetham's views turned reactionary. Cheetham claimed that Marguerite's second son—Thomas Paine Bonneville—"has the features, countenance, and temper of Paine." He argued that Paine seduced her from her husband, despite Nicolas's largesse in allowing Paine to live under his roof in Paris for five years. Cheetham's slanderous biography appeared immediately after Paine's death in 1809. Marguerite sued and won a judgment against him of $150.[4]

More than Chalmers or any of Paine's other enemies, Cheetham also contributed to the stories of Paine's excessive drinking habits. "He was daily drunk with his favorite brandy," he wrote, "and everybody saw or heard of his intoxication." While Paine was staying in New York after he left Washington, Cheetham said that "he fell over a high staircase in a paroxysm of intoxication." At the same time, Paine met several workers from England, Ireland, and Scotland to drink "grog in the taproom morning, noon, and night.

Admired and praised by them, he strutted about, or rather staggered about, showing himself to all and shaking hands with all. One day laborer would say, drink with me, Mr. Paine; another, drink with me, and he very condescendingly gratified them all."[5]

Paine continued to correspond regularly with President Jefferson, as he had from Paris. In fact, he visited the President after leaving Baltimore, shortly after his arrival in November. The two of them dined with Albert Gallatin, the Secretary of the Treasury, and Henry Dearborn, the Secretary of War. The republican press tried to play down these meetings, but the Federalists assailed them with an increasingly shrill voice. The *Gazette of the United States* wrote that "our stomachs . . . nauseate at the sight of their affectionate embraces, and we entertain no doubt that you, as well as we, have become impatient to get out of such impious company. . . . We leave them then to consummate their bliss." The *New York Evening Post* even ran a twenty-five verse poem, "Thomas Paine and the King," the latter meaning Jefferson, denouncing the cozy relationship:

> . . .The ship came into port,
> King Thomas he sent his coach and six,
> To bring Tom Paine to court.
> Dearborn before him ran,
> All on the point of a glittering spear
> Carrying the Rights of Man.
> Monsieur Gallatin from France,
> March'd on the right with a pas vite step,
> Carrying a flagon of Nantz. . . .

In the meantime, the Richmond *Recorder*, under the editorship of a Scot—the Federalist James Thomson Callender—set forth the rumor as fact that Jefferson had fathered several children by his slave, Sally Hemings, and that he brought Paine back to America to share the slavewoman.[6]

Paine's mind was, as usual, on politics, though he did not believe he would become engaged in politics the way he had once been. He was wrong. As the center of attention, he found the attacks both unwarranted and depressing. To be fair, his "Letters to the Citizens of the United States" were more about himself than

Jefferson or Jeffersonian policies. He wrote Clio Rickman, then in England, that "you can have no idea of the agitation which my arrival occasioned. From New Hampshire to Georgia (an extent of 1,500 miles), every newspaper was filled with applause or abuse."[7] Naturally Paine did not mind the applause, but the abuse got to him quite quickly. He was soon answering the attacks with his characteristic intensity and vigor. His style, however, was even more vicious and vituperative than before. Almost sixty-six years old, he was angry and out of patience with just about everything. When he visited Jefferson in the capital, the Federalist press once again geared up to attack him. In response, Paine wrote several pieces in 1802 and 1803, principally for the *National Intelligencer*, a Washington newspaper that served as mouthpiece for Jeffersonian Republicans. Its founder was Samuel Harrison Smith, the same printer whose publication of Jefferson's note in the preface to the American edition of the *Rights of Man* had embarrassed the then-Secretary of State.

Paine struck out at the Federalists practically from the moment of his arrival. He lived for a while at Lovell's Hotel in Washington, the new capital city, or "Federal City," as it was then called, which in many places was hardly more than a swamp between the congressmen's quarters and the new executive mansion. From there, he began his series of letters to inform his compatriots of the deceit and perfidy of the the Federalists. As far as Paine was concerned, the Federalists were intent on destroying the democratic basis of America. Paine had once admired Washington. He had initially gotten along with Adams, but their relationship was always cool. When Adams supported the Alien and Sedition Acts, Paine had lost all respect for him. Both presidents were guilty of unrepublican views: a virtual "Reign of Terror raged in America during the latter end of the Washington Administration, and the whole of that of Adams." [8] Paine was so angry that not only was his tone strident and shrill, but he often mixed metaphors, at once likening the first two presidents, especially John Adams, to various animals, then to mindless vegetables. Age appeared to be catching up with the wandering journalist, who once could turn a phrase with great style and character, but whose anger and bitterness now stymied him. He became so frustrated at one point that he called any Federalist "that undescribed and undescribable *nothing.*"

> Ask a man who calls himself a Federalist, what federalism is,
> and he cannot tell you. Ask him, what are its principles, and he
> has none to give. Federalism, then, with respect to government,
> is similar to atheism with respect to religion, a *nominal nothing*
> without principles.[9]

      In his first letter on the Federalists, Paine compared them to
a faction to indicate their selfishness and narrow-mindedness. They
were "scribbling and witless curs." Their "little barkings" indicated
that they represented "the cloven foot of faction," which "preach[es]
the language of ill-disguised mortification." These curs, rabid in
everything they did, were intent on undermining the very constitutional foundation of America.

> In every part of the Union, this faction is in the agonies of
> death, and in proportion as its fate approaches, gnashes its teeth
> and struggles. My arrival has struck it as with an hydrophobia,
> it is like the sight of water to canine madness.[10]

The presence of Thomas Paine had caused them to enter their death
throes. "Poor fellows, how they foam!"[11]
      In another letter, Paine first called Federalists "a nondescript
race," and then confused race with fungi: they had "started up with
the rapidity of a mushroom, and like a mushroom is withering on its
rootless stalk."[12] The end was at hand for the Federalists, especially
its leader, John Adams, who took the brunt of Paine's counterattack.
Like cannibals, they wanted to devour everything, including Thomas
Paine: "they cannot make up a bill of fare if I am not in it." Adams
was "a man of paradoxical heresies, and consequently of a bewildered
mind."
      At this point, Paine demonstrated the worst of his style: the
fanatical, inflamed use of personal vituperation. Adams' political
career was "to begin with hypocrisy, proceed with arrogance, and finish in contempt." He was gambling with high stakes, which amounted to
the very soul of the country, for his own success in taking over the nation.

I have had doubts of John Adams ever since the year 1776. . . . John was for independence because he expected to be made great by it; but it was not difficult to perceive, for the surliness of his temper makes him an awkward hypocrite, that his head was as full of kings, queens and knaves, as a pack of cards. But John has lost the deal.

Adams' "head was teeming with projects to overturn the liberties of America and the representative government." He was "l i k e a mole . . . grubbing his way to it under ground."[13] He lost the deal and also the game. He was defeated in 1800 by Jefferson, though barely, because the election was thrown into the House of Representatives. There had been three candidates, Jefferson, Adams, and Aaron Burr, and no one had a clear majority of electoral votes. The House of Representatives elected Jefferson on the thirty-sixth ballot, and, for Paine, the country was at last saved from these American monarchists.

      None of this stopped Paine from continuing to advise Jefferson, whether or not the President wanted his suggestions. Paine's thoughts briefly drifted from the Federalist press to a more serious issue, the disposition of the Louisiana Territory, which Spain had ceded to France and from which France, in turn, had excluded the Americans. On Christmas Day, 1802, at the suggestion of Dr. Michael Lieb, a congressman from Pennsylvania who lived at Lovell's, Paine wrote to Jefferson what he thought the United States should do to resolve the problems of American exclusion from New Orleans and navigation along the Mississippi. "Suppose then the government begin by making a proposal to France to repurchase the cession made to her by Spain, of Louisiana, provided it be with the consent of the people of Louisiana or a majority thereof." This was precisely the suggestion that Jefferson would adopt, not necessarily because it came from Paine but because it was clear that Napoleon simply needed the money to pursue his European goals. In fact, Paine knew this to be the case. He closed his letter with the thought that "the French treasury is not only empty, but the government has consumed by anticipation a great part of the next year's revenue. A monied proposal will, I believe, be attended to."[14] Jefferson replied the very next day. He wrote Paine that he indeed intended to try to purchase the Louisiana territory from France as soon as possible. Later, when Paine saw Dr. Lieb again, he told him what Jefferson had said. "I knew that, said he," Paine reported, somewhat stunned. "Why then, said I, did you not tell me so, because in that case I would not have sent the note. That is the reason, said he, I would not tell you because two opinions concurring on a case strengthen it."[15]

Paine had never forgotten his dream of building a bridge over the Schuylkill River. While still in the federal city, he had his models shipped from France, and tried to convince Congress to appropriate sufficient money to fund its construction. He was once again disappointed. He never received a reply from Congress. He showed his annoyance to Jefferson in January of 1803. "You have not only shown no disposition towards [the construction of the bridge], but have in some measure by a sort of shyness, as if you stood in fear of federal observation, precluded it. I am not the only one who makes observations of this kind."[16] An unkind cut perhaps, but the two men were no longer as close as they had been ten years before, although Paine still admired the President as a man of great principle. But Jefferson had no intention of using federal funds to undertake internal improvements. That was the responsibility of the states and private enterprise. The President later replied that he had delayed the discussion on the bridge because of the notoriety Paine's return had caused, and besides, pressing matters of state had kept his attention away from mechanical and mathematical projects such as this one. Although Paine was satisfied with the response, he was hurt. He did not give up, not yet anyway. He wrote a long essay on "The Construction of Iron Bridges," in a final attempt to get Congress to agree to build the span.[17] Once again he was sorely disappointed. Neither the President nor Congress did anything.

At the same time, Paine received a letter from his old Boston friend Samuel Adams, who was quite upset, as were so many Americans (including Benjamin Rush) about Paine's published views on religion. Adams told Paine that he was long an admirer of his views on American independence and the rights of man, but when I heard that you had turned your mind to a defense of infidelity, I felt myself much astonished and more grieved that you had attempted a measure so injurious to the feelings and so repugnant to the true interest of so great a part of the citizens of the United States. . . . Do you think that your pen or the pen of any other man can unchristianize the mass of our citizens, or have you hopes of converting a few of them to assist you in so bad a cause? We ought to think ourselves happy in the enjoyment of opinion without the danger of persecution by civil or ecclesiastical law.

Adams, like so many of Paine's detractors, misinterpreted Paine's beliefs, no doubt because he had neither the opportunity nor the inclination to read *The Age of Reason.* He even suggested that Paine's support of Thomas Jefferson made the President look bad when that support came from people whose "latent design [was] to promote the cause of infidelity."[18]

Although it took almost a month for Paine to receive the letter (the post office clerk misplaced it), he hurriedly replied in a long letter, which stated quite unequivocally, as he had done in his works on religion, that "I believe in God." He thanked Adams for recalling his work on behalf of the American cause of freedom, but was saddened that Adams did not understand what he had been trying to say when he condemned Christian mythology and fables. Throughout history, organized religion, in asserting revealed "truth," had achieved nothing but the division of man against man, blood against blood. "The case, my friend, is that the world has been overrun with fable and creeds of human invention, with sectaries of whole nations against all other nations, and sectaries of those sectaries in each of them against each other. Every sectary, except the Quakers, has been a persecutor." The sole truth in all of them seemed to be the one truth that all of Paine's detractors overlooked: a sincere, deep belief in God, the creator of the universe and everything in it. It was to Him and to Him alone that men must answer. "The key to heaven is not in the keeping of any sect nor ought the road to it be obstructed by any."[19]

The distortions, deliberate and otherwise, of Paine's religious thoughts continued for the rest of his life and beyond.

In February, Paine attended a dinner given in Washington for Jefferson. On this occasion, he wrote a long poem, a toast in fact, proclaiming Jefferson's greatness and at the same time using the moment to attack both his and Jefferson's Federalist enemies.

> I send you, Sir, a tale about some Feds,
> Who, in their wisdom, got to loggerheads.
> The case was this, they felt so flat and sunk,
> They took a glass together and got drunk.
> Such things, you know, are neither new nor rare,
> For some will harry themselves when in despair.
> It was the natal day of Washington,
> And they thought a famous day for fun;
> For with the learned world it is agreed,
> The better day the better deed.
> They talked away, and as the glass went round
> They grew, in point of wisdom, more profound;
> For at the bottom of the bottle lies
> That kind of sense we overlook when wise.
> Come here's a toast, cried one, with roar immense,
> May none know pleasure who love Common Sense.
> Bravo! cried some,—no, no! some others cried,
> But left it to the waiter to decide.
> I think, said he, the case would be more plain,
> To leave out Common Sense, and put in Paine.[20]

Having finished for the time being with his Federalist enemies, Paine left Washington and headed back to Bordentown. He stopped briefly once again in Baltimore. There he encountered a Swedenborgian minister, a believer in the New Jerusalem, a certain Reverend Hargrove, who told him that after having been missing for 4,000 years the key to the scriptures had at long last been found. "Then, said Paine in his own neat way, it must have been very rusty."[21]

Moving on to Philadelphia, Paine looked up his old friends. Some, including Rush, refused to meet him for the same reason Samuel Adams had written to him. Rush told James Cheetham that "his principles avowed in his *Age of Reason* were so offensive to me that I did not wish to renew my intercourse with him."[22] On the other hand, his friend Charles Willson Peale not only greeted him, but invited him to see his new museum. He even offered Paine a place in his museum for the bridge models. A few months later, Paine took Peale up on the offer and sent him the models with a note, thanking him for the opportunity to display his work. The note also indicated Paine's deep frustration and disappointment that his bridge never spanned the Schuylkill. "It would then have been an honor to the state," he bitterly lamented.[23]

By March 1803, Paine was in Bordentown, staying with his friends the Kirkbrides (the Bonnevilles were occupying his farmhouse there). His life was pleasant enough, meeting with old friends and discussing the issues of the day, often at a tavern called the Washington House. His habits were amusingly described by a contemporary, who was well aware of the negative opinion some had of Paine because of his published religious views:

> Mr. Paine was too much occupied in literary pursuits and writing to spend a great deal of his time here, but he generally paid several visits during the day. His drink was invariably brandy. In walking he was generally absorbed in deep thought, seldom noticed anyone as he passed, unless spoken to, and in going from his home to the tavern was frequently observed to cross the street several times. It is stated that several members of the church were turned from their faith by him, and on this account, and the general feeling of the community against him for his opinions on religious subjects, he was by the mass of the people held in odium, which feeling to some extent was extended to Col. Kirkbride.

The roadways were filled with anti-Paine posters and placards of the devil flying away with him, and the ministers of Trenton rudely denounced the faithless Thomas Paine.

But some welcomed Paine home. His former bridge mechanic, John Hall, noted his frame of mind. Paine, he said, "was well and appeared jollier than I had ever known him. He is full of whims and schemes and mechanical inventions, and is to build a place or shop to carry them into execution, and wants my help."

Paine, obviously happy at the moment, decided to put off for the time being his interests in mechanics when he traveled with Colonel Kirkbride to New York. Stopping in Trenton to pick up the stagecoach, the driver refused Paine a seat because of his known religious infidelity, and he was jeered rousingly by a crowd of angry bystanders. Not everyone was intent on insulting Paine, however. Once in New York, he visited his old friend and supporter James Monroe, whom Jefferson had reappointed American Minister to France. Paine asked Monroe to deliver letters to several of his friends who were still in Paris. Monroe, who naturally agreed, would soon begin the process that ended with the U.S. purchase of Louisiana. One of these letters was addressed to Clio Rickman, with whom Paine deeply wanted to remain in contact. Unfortunately, although Rickman was always an admirer of Paine, his attention was moving in other directions. Paine asked Rickman to send his regards to Colonel William Bosville, a wealthy benefactor of several radical organizations, whom Paine had known in Paris during the early years of the Revolution before the onset of the Terror. Though Paine thought him a good friend, Bosville disliked what he considered to be Paine's excessive consumption of alcoholic beverages.[24]

On March 18th, a lavish dinner was held in Paine's honor at the City Hotel in New York. Federalists were nowhere to be found. James Cheetham, one of its principal organizers, was still a great admirer of Paine. Several rallies in Paine's name were held in New York and then in White Plains, with toasts in his honor for the splendid work he did for America and rights and liberty everywhere. "Thomas Paine, the bold advocate of rational liberty—the people's friend!" they shouted.[25]

Returning to Bordentown, Paine continued his counterassault against the Federalists. In two additional letters, one in March, the other in April, Paine defended the policies of the Jefferson Administration. He claimed that the Federalists, in "opposition without a cause," attempted to push the Americans into a war with France over the Louisiana Territory. America was not a barbaric nation. It would be a simple matter to seize the territory, but far from civilized. "That New Orleans could be taken required no stretch of policy to plan nor spirit of enterprise to effect. . . . the dastardly sly-

ness of such an attack would have stained the fame of the United
States." Then, in a crack directed against Gouverneur Morris, now a
United States senator and who years before had lost his leg in a carriage accident, he said that the legless Morris could accomplish the
seizure of New Orleans. "Even Gouverneur, on such a march, dare
have shown a leg."

It was clear that Jefferson was determined to purchase
the Louisiana Territory, and on April 30, the United States paid
France a remarkably low $15 million (or around 13.5 cents an
acre) for it.[26] The question of war was made moot, but Paine did
not let up on his attack on John Adams and the Federalists during the
rest of the spring and summer. Even two years later, he would complain that all along Adams had wanted to go to war against France,
and this showed clearly that "the administration of John Adams was
a fraudulent and expensive imposition on the country."[27]

Paine was now worried whether the Federalists in Congress
could obstruct the President's attempt to purchase Louisiana (the
Senate had to ratify the treaty transferring the territory to the United
States). The Constitution contained no provision concerning the
purchase of new territory, although a broad reading of the document
could lead to the conclusion that such an action was one of the
implied powers of the President. Paine wrote to Senator John C.
Breckenridge of Kentucky, who favored the addition of Louisiana
and Mississippi to the United States. Breckenridge was a leader in
Congress for U.S. expansion westward, and became a spokesman for
the passage of the enabling legislation that brought about the
Louisiana Purchase. Paine asked him whether the Senate would have
to ratify the agreement to make the purchase, as if it were a treaty,
rather than an executive order by President Jefferson. Make this
"domestic policy," he urged Breckenridge, and avoid a Senate
wrestling match. "The only real ratification is the payment of the
money," he advised.[28]

Once the purchase agreement was completed, the question
arose of what to do with the inhabitants of Louisiana. Paine, and
Jefferson too for that matter, regarded them as very undemocratic with
their Spanish and French cultural roots and Roman Catholicism.
Inexperienced in the mechanics of democratic government, they

had to be taught how to rule themselves rather than be ruled by tyrants. Paine proposed to Jefferson that the Louisianans be given lessons in participatory democracy. "I take it for granted that the present inhabitants know little or nothing of election and representation as constituting government. . . . I should suppose that a *government provisoire* formed by Congress for three, five, or seven years would be the best mode of beginning. In the meantime they may be initiated into the practice by electing their municipal government, and after some experience they will be in train to elect their state government."[29]

At the end of August, Paine was in Stonington, Connecticut, to visit an old friend, Nathan Haley, and planned to stay there until "the wood cutting time comes on." He also planned to see to the education of young Thomas Paine Bonneville, who would soon be under the instructional care of the Unitarian minister there. From Stonington, Paine observed the events unfolding both in Europe and New England. As for the latter, he became intimately acquainted with the power that the Federalists had in Connecticut. They controlled it through the old constitution, which was originally granted by Charles II. It was appalling to Paine that Connecticut, unlike all other states in the union, had never written a new republican constitution. As a result, a bare majority in the Federalist upper house was so powerful that they stopped all legislation that had the appearance of Jeffersonian republicanism stamped on it, and they virtually appointed all judges to the state supreme court. Within a year, Paine would be writing on this subject in the Hartford *American Mercury*.[30]

For now, however, the national and international issues were on his mind. He continued his correspondence with the President about Louisiana, reiterating several of his earlier points to both Jefferson and Breckenridge. He was particularly heartened by the additional size that the country would take on with increased territory. He even recalled that at the very beginning of the American Revolution that it "contemplated . . . that Canada would, at some time or other, become a part of the United States." (There had even been a provision for that possibility in the Articles of Confederation.) Moreover, Paine noted, the Constitution itself accommodated the addition of territory (although not its purchase). "The cession makes no alteration in the Constitution; it only extends the principles of it over a larger territory, and this certainly is within the morality of the Constitution, and not contrary to, nor beyond, the expression or intention of any of its articles." Eventually, the arguments Paine set forth found supporters in Congress, and Louisiana became part of the United States in October, 1803, when the Senate finally ratified the treaty transferring Louisiana to the United States. On December 20, 1803, the American flag flew for the first time over New Orleans.

Meantime, Paine anxiously watched the events in Europe as France and England once again engaged in warfare. He was still hopeful that revolution would finally come to England, and if a new constitution were thereafter needed in that country, "it will throw a temptation in my way to make another passage cross the Atlantic to assist in forming a Constitution for England," Paine told Jefferson.[31] He was certain that Napoleon would invade England in November, which was less than two months away, and begin the process of turning that nation into a democratic republic.

Paine also wrote to Jefferson about religious matters, something which it seemed was constantly on his mind in his last years. This may have been because of the vehement criticism he was under for *The Age of Reason*, or it may well have been the obsession of an elderly man. He related to Jefferson an encounter he had with a group of Stonington Baptists, including three of their ministers, who were discussing the upcoming presidential election. Paine, of course, supported Jefferson's candidacy. One of the Baptists retorted that some people hated Jefferson because he was a deist, and said: " 'Well, a deist may be a good man and if he think it right it is right to him. ... For my own part, I had rather vote for a deist than for a blue skin Presbyterian.' " Paine wasn't so much shocked as he was dismayed by the man's obvious "hypocrisy." He answered that the goal was to keep the bigots out of office. They would work only to subvert everyone else's beliefs, " 'as the blue skins do.' "[32]

Paine also told Jefferson that he intended to move during the winter to his farm in New Rochelle and take with him some wood-cutters who would fell some trees on his property. He intended to earn "$3.50 per load. This will furnish me with ready money." He hoped to use the money in part to build a new house and a small workshop where he would do his "mechanical operations and make a collection, as the authors say, of my works."[33] While he was still in France, he had learned from his friend, General Lewis Morris, that his house in New Rochelle had burned down.

Paine soon divided his time between New Rochelle and New York City. When a small cottage on his land was expanded, he moved in, and Marguerite remained in Bordentown.

Paine had a rough autumn and winter in 1803-04. First, he heard news from Bordentown that two of his dearest friends had died. The deaths of Samuel Adams and Colonel Kirkbride in October deeply upset him. Later he hurt himself falling on the ice, and was forced to spend some time in bed. An attack of the gout had preceded the fall. It was bad enough that Paine could not write, but gout and the accident prevented him from carrying out his woodcutting scheme. Marguerite, although living in Bordentown, was no longer residing in Paine's house there (he had rented it). Paine wrote Mr. Hyer, her landlord, about his fall and his illness. "It was my intention to have cut a large quantity of wood for the New York market, and in that case you would have had the money directly, but this accident and the gout prevented me from doing anything." Hyer made arrangements to have part of the rent paid from other debts due Paine. He also told Hyer that because of his illness, he had to dictate a major newspaper piece, still hopeful that France might invade England.[34]

Since he could not care for himself, Paine spent part of the time while he was ill with the proprietor of a store in the village of New Rochelle.[35] He soon moved to the City Hotel in New York, where the banquet and celebration for him had been held one year earlier. He dined there with Dr. Nicolas Romaine, "the most learned physician in New York," and other famous politicians and citizens of the city. One of these eminent New Yorkers was John Pintard, a founder of the Tammany Society of New York, who today is regarded as one of the organizers of the modern Democratic Party. Paine had known him since the days of the American Revolution. When the first part of the *Rights of Man* was published in the United States in 1791, its editor was John Pintard who appended a poem to it:

> Rous'd by the reason of his manly page,
> Once more shall Paine a listening world engage;
> From reason's source a bold reform he brings,
> By raising up mankind he pulls down kings.

One evening at dinner, he told Paine that "I have read and re-read your *Age of Reason*. Any doubts which I before entertained of the truth of revelation have been removed by your logic. Yes, sir, your very arguments against Christianity have convinced me of its truth." Paine was delighted with someone who truly understood the nature of religion, who knew full well what it meant to be a religious man. "Well then," Paine told Pintard, "I may return to my couch tonight with the consolation that I have made at least one Christian."[36]

In New York, Paine met the Reverend Elihu Palmer, with whom he had corresponded from Paris. Paine knew and greatly admired Palmer's *Principles of Nature*, which was a veritable bible for the deistic societies. He had told Palmer at the time that it was an "excellent work:"

> I see you have thought deeply on the subject and expressed your
> thoughts in a strong and clear style. The hinting and intimating
> manner of writing that was formerly used on subjects of this
> kind produced skepticism, but no conviction. It is necessary to
> be bold. Some people can be reasoned into sense, and others
> must be shocked into it. Say a bold thing that will stagger
> them, and they will begin to think.[37]

The admiration was mutual. Palmer once wrote of Paine that he was "one of the first and best writers, and probably the most useful man that ever existed upon the face of the earth. His moral and political writings are equally excellent and the beneficial influence of the principles for which he contended will be felt through all the succeeding ages."[38] The two of them joined in the late winter of 1804 to form the Theistic Society, dedicated to deistic principles, and Paine contributed to Palmer's new journal, *The Prospect, or View of the Moral World*. Unfortunately, when Palmer died at the end of the year, the journal and the movement died with him. *The Prospect* itself folded in the spring of 1805.

Paine wrote seventeen pieces for the journal, beginning on February 18, 1804. They covered wide-ranging subjects, all from the same theological perspective he had developed in both parts of *The Age of Reason* and his response to Richard Watson, Bishop of Llandaff. Only now Paine raised his language to new heights of intolerance for opinions he claimed were false and for religious beliefs he thought were absurd. Once again, his chief target was the Bible: "The obscene and vulgar stories in the Bible are as repugnant to our ideas of the purity of a divine Being, as the horrid cruelties and murders it ascribes to Him are repugnant to our ideas of His justice. It is the reverence of the Deists for the attributes of the Deity that causes them to reject the Bible."

Nothing escaped Paine's blasts. He would more likely believe the testimony of an old maid having a child than the story of Mary's immaculate conception. Prove the existence of a Holy Ghost, he demanded. If Jesus were a God, how could he have died? A God did not die. If Adam disobeyed God by eating an apple, why didn't this all-powerful God simply start all over again. Why "impose on Himself the necessity of breeding from the old stock?" Paine pointed out the attacks long made by one religious group on another, each claiming to be the true religion, when in fact none of them were. "The Papists call the Protestant heretics, and the Protestants call the Papists idolaters. The minor sectaries have shown the same spirit of rancor, but as the civil law restrains them from blood, they content themselves with preaching damnation against each other." The fact was that they all worshipped the head of the Christian Church, someone once named Jesus, whereas the deists worship only God. Indeed, every person who claimed to believe in a God was a deist, "the first article of every man's creed."

> It is on this article, universally consented to by all mankind, that the Deist builds his church, and here he rests. Whenever we step aside from this article, by mixing it with articles of human invention, we wander into a labyrinth of uncertainty and fable, and become exposed to every kind of imposition by pretenders to revelation.

Even the puritanical Blue Laws of New England came under fire.

The sabbath day was set aside as a day of rest, but its enforcement was stupid because a person was forced "to sit still from sunrise to sunset on a sabbath day, which is hard work."

> One of the finest scenes and subjects of religious contemplation is to walk into the woods and fields, and survey the works of the God of the Creation. The wide expanse of heaven, the earth covered with verdure, the lofty forest, the waving corn, the magnificent roll of mighty rivers, and the murmuring melody of the cheerful brooks are scenes that inspire the mind with gratitude and delight.

But the gloomy Calvinist must not avail himself of such wonders. "Entombed within the walls of his dwelling he shuts from his view the Temple of Creation. The sun shines no joy to him. The gladdening voice of nature calls on him in vain. He is deaf, dumb, and blind to everything that God has made."[39] Even the dead did not escape Paine's malicious pen. He prepared an attack on the last rites given to Alexander Hamilton, who lay dying following his duel with Aaron Burr in 1804.

While Paine found New York agreeable, Marguerite de Bonneville, now quite lonely, found Bordentown to be excessively dull. She placed Paine in an exceedingly uncomfortable position by joining him in the city. His troubles with her now began to develop rapidly. He had taken a room in Wilburn's roominghouse, and so had Marguerite with her three sons. This situation complicated Paine's life no end: he had thought that with her in Bordentown and him in New York City (or at the very least New Rochelle), the two of them could live apart until her husband arrived. Paine now apparently told Wilburn he would not pay Marguerite's rent. When she incurred a bill for $35, Paine refused to pay it. Wilburn sued Paine, and although Paine won the suit, he paid the bill.[40]

Napoleon, however, refused to allow the renegade journalist, Nicolas de Bonneville, to leave France, so Paine was stuck. Marguerite's debts mounted, and Paine did his best, with varying degrees of success, to pay them and to convince her to live within his means. Paine soon grew depressed and more bitter than ever. He wrote his old friend in Paris, Fulwar Skipwith, the American consular officer there, bemoaning the fact that he had been abandoned. "I have not received a line from Paris . . . since I left it. We have now been nearly 80 days without news from Europe. What is Barlow about? I have not heard anything from him except that he is always coming." And then in a cry of despair, he demanded, "What is Bonneville about? Not a line has been received from him."[41] How Paine would have loved to have heard from Bonneville and have been able to pawn his young wife back off to him.

By the spring of 1804, Paine was back in New Rochelle (no doubt to escape Marguerite), where he set to work on a critique of the Connecticut constitution which appeared during the summer in a Hartford newspaper founded by Joel Barlow in 1784. Paine wrote that it was now time for Connecticut to call a convention to write a constitution deriving directly from the people, not from a non-existent monarch. (Connecticut was still under the charter granted by Charles II.) Even more critical for the moment was the fact that the old constitution had practically all supreme legislative and judicial power in a twelve-man upper chamber variously called a senate, council, or the Governor's assistants. Seven members of this upper house were united in insuring that their views, which were unanimously Federalist, won out on every single vote in state government, which included not only lawmaking, but all appointments to the state judiciary. In addition, the upper house was the state supreme court. Jeffersonians, led by Barlow and three other members of his Yale class of 1778, demanded that it was time for the people to ratify a new constitutional structure for their state, and Paine joined them in August 1804. Paine later wrote to his friend Elisha Babcock, the publisher of the Hartford *American Mercury*, that the people themselves should draft a new constitution, and not the legislature: "A law, enacted by a legislature, binds the citizens individually; but a constitution binds the legislature collectively."[42]

In the month previous to his article's appearance, Alexander Hamilton died from the result of a duel with Aaron Burr. Burr, though a Republican, had been accused of working against Jefferson in the election of 1800. Hamilton, a well-known Federalist activist, had fought for a more powerful central government at the 1787

Constitutional Convention and had served as Washington's Secretary of the Treasury. Paine was not overly concerned with the death of Hamilton or with his prior association with Washington. But he wrote a picayune attack on the funeral oration delivered by his old political adversary, Gouverneur Morris. He went after Morris' syntax as well as his facts and ideas. His tone was more sarcastic than ever. He attacked the Federalist notion of energetic government, for example, with the following words. "Gouverneur Morris and others of his description, who have *conceits* instead of *principles*, and *vanity* instead of *wisdom*, are very fond of this word *energy*, but they always mean the energy they are to *act themselves*, not that which they are to suffer." Their day, however, had passed. Jefferson was now President of the United States, and "it is thus the *representative system corrects wrongs and preserves rights.*"[43] This was the end of all the attempts by the Federalists to destroy American republicanism. After all, only two other notices of Hamilton's death, according to Paine, were printed: by the Reverend John Mitchell Mason, who had written a forty page pamphlet on Hamilton, and an editorial in Lang's *New York Gazette*, a Federalist newspaper.

"Nonsense from New York" was Paine's self-conscious satire, or rather burlesque, on the two publications. He could not have been more vicious in his ridicule on the message from the *Gazette:*

> The loss of gen. Hamilton <says this writer> cannot be considered by those who knew his extraordinary worth in any other light than as a *severe judgment upon the United States.* This being the case <as it happens not to be the case> it becomes everyone seriously to reflect on the *cause of the displeasure* and the only method for its removal. <*Now for it.*> The primary source, says he, of all the evils *appears to be the conduct of the citizens at the last presidential election.* From that moment discontent, division and confusion began to take place; and unless a speedy remedy be applied *more afflicting scenes may be expected.* Mr. Jefferson and Mr. Burr were elected, each having an equal number of votes.— <Burr was not voted for with the idea of his being president.> The public are now dreadfully convinced <*this is another severe judgment*> that the election of Mr. Burr was improper; and they have seen fall by his hand *their first citizen* and one of the most

enlightened and *honest* statesmen in the world.—Language fails
to express <that is, the writer has not wit enough to do it> the
extent of his *talents*, and of the *services* which he has rendered.

Paine attached to his letter some "remarks" from "Comus" (his old
pseudonym from the 1770s), in which he analyzed each phrase he
italicized, including his astonishment that the letter assumed that
God had decided to have Hamilton shot dead in a duel. The more
"afflicting scenes," he said, were those in which "the feds will certainly *shoot one another. This will be a severe judgment!* upon the republicans, for they will have—to bury them!!!" (All three exclamation
points were Comus'.) Comus then took on Mason's eulogy with the
same surly language, linking George III's madness to Mason's state of
mind. "The orator has certainly a crack in the brain," he announced,
"a touch of what they now call in England the 'King's Evil,' or he
would not rave thus."[44]

The fight in Connecticut was almost, but not quite, over.
There, republicans gathered in late August to request a new constitution
for their state in a declaration signed by five Connecticut supreme court
judges. The Federalist legislature summarily dismissed all five, including Judge William Judd, who died shortly thereafter. The Judge's pamphlet defending himself and his colleagues, appeared after his death.
On reading it, Paine responded in November with a short piece,
"Connecticut Has No Constitution," in the *National Intelligencer*. A
month later Babcock reprinted it the *American Mercury*. Although
unsigned, it clearly bears the mark of Paine's rhetorical style from an earlier era. Judge Judd, he said, "exposed his life in defense of our rights in
times which tried men's souls. . . . and human nature has surely sunk to
its lowest state, if the exertions of patriotism, which cost him his life, do
not arouse the spirit of liberty that slumbers in Connecticut."[45] Paine's
writing here directly paralleled *Common Sense* and the first "Crisis"
number. It was as if, but only for a moment, he returned to the powerful, non-abusive, and highminded style that his later work too
often lacked. In the end, the efforts of the republicans and Thomas
Paine were indirectly successful. Nine years after Paine's death, in
1818, a new constitution finally came into being in Connecticut.

20 · Final Days

Paine's life in New Rochelle was quite simple. He told Jefferson that "it is a pleasant and healthy situation commanding a prospect always green and agreeable as New Rochelle produces a great deal of grass and hay. The farm contains three hundred acres, about one hundred of which is meadowland, one hundred grazing and tillage land, and the remainder woodland."

He planned to build a second floor observatory "to live on in summer weather." He sent Jefferson a sketch of a plan for an arched roof with which he intended to replace the old roof.[1] As for furnishings, there were few. He said to his good friend and sometime literary agent, Colonel John Fellows (a former officer of the Continental Army during the Revolution and publisher of the first American edition of *The Age of Reason*, and now a constable in the city courts of New York), that he had "six chairs and a table, a straw-bed, a feather-bed," a few utensils, several animals, and not much else. "I live upon tea, milk, fruit pies, plain dumplings, and a piece of meat when I can get it."[2]

In addition to his concerns about his house, Paine was still very interested in his namesake and godson, Thomas Paine Bonneville, who had been attending school in Stonington. In 1805, Paine had asked his old friend, William Carver, whom he had known as a boy in Lewes, to take young Thomas to Connecticut, telling Carver that Thomas "shall not want for anything that is necessary if he be a good boy for he has no friend but me." Paine had wanted very much to take total charge of all the boys' education, but Marguerite disliked the idea of giving them up, or even of having young Thomas away at school in Stonington.

All along, Paine, who never tried to work the land himself, had entrusted his farm to a caretaker, Christopher Derrick. When Paine finally came home, he found that he no longer needed Derrick, but he kept him on to work off a debt of some $48 by constructing a stone fence. Paine also was stuck with a rather sizable debt that Derrick had built up at the local general store. But Derrick apparently was displeased with the arrangement, and after a Christmas of heavy drinking, he fired a gun at Paine. The bullet missed, but penetrated the wall just under the window where Paine was sitting, "making a hole large enough [for] a finger to go through. The muzzle must have been very near as the place is black with the powder, and the glass of the window is shattered to pieces." Paine apparently did not press charges against Derrick.[3]

Aside from the occasional potshot, both literal and literary, taken at him, it was a quiet life for Paine, especially with Marguerite in New York. But not for long: she soon followed him to New Rochelle and remained briefly. He finally had to send her back to New York with her son Benjamin. "Mrs. Bonneville was an encumbrance upon me all the while she was here, for she would not do anything, not even make an apple dumpling for her own children," he later told Fellows. Paine hoped she could find some useful employment but doubted the prospect. "It is certainly best that Mrs. Bonneville go into some family, as a teacher, for she has not the least talent of managing affairs for herself."[4] He sold about sixty-two acres of his farm for just over $4,000. The sale would give him some money to take care of Marguerite and the remaining boys, as he had promised at the end of 1802. He spent part of the money fixing up his New Rochelle farmhouse, including the new roof.

During the summer of 1804, Paine wrote a long address to the French who lived in Louisiana. They had written the United States Congress asking that their territory be granted statehood. At the same time, they wanted Congress to let them maintain their traffic in slaves. Paine compared this request to the degeneration of the Revolution in France. There, the leaders of the Revolution had achieved "power before they understood principles." The result was chaos, murder, and the Terror. "They earned liberty in words, but not in fact." Since they, the inhabitants of free Louisiana, had achieved freedom, it seemed wholly contradictory that they would now deprive another people of that freedom. "You are arriving at freedom by the easiest means that any people ever enjoyed it, without contest, without expense, and even without any contrivance of your own. And you already so far mistake principles that under the name of rights you ask for powers, powers to import and enslave Africans, and to govern a territory that we have purchased."[5] Should the French inhabitants of Louisiana pursue their demand, Paine predicted that they would face a massive, murderous slave revolt along the lines of the Santo Domingo revolt of 1791.

Although Paine often traveled into the city during the winter of 1804-05 to see Marguerite and Benjamin, his mind remained on Louisiana and slavery. He wrote to Jefferson from New York that he thought it proper for the United States to take in the fleeing slaves from Santo Domingo, who were still engaged in their revolt against France. "If a way can be found to bring about peace between France and Domingo through the mediation and under the guarantee of the United States, it would be beneficial to all parties." The U.S. would then be in good standing with all the countries of the Caribbean basin. "The United States is the only power that can undertake a measure of this kind." Otherwise the "endless slaughter on both sides" would continue.[6]

In addressing the issue of Louisiana, Paine was principally interested in the people of that territory, as opposed to its resources, as most others were. He told Jefferson that he had dined with Levi Lincoln, the Attorney General, and Senator Paine Wingate of New Hampshire, and had discussed the Louisianans' petition to Congress. Paine thought that this matter ought to be put quickly to rest. He did not think that the Louisianans were well prepared to settle it because their customs and habits were drawn from the French legal code. They could use their own language to engage in their affairs, Paine wrote, but not when it came to "government and legal jurisdiction." He was opposed to allowing the French of Louisiana to become "the legislators of the new settlers." In fact, he hoped that when the territory was eventually divided into states, that none of them would be named Louisiana. It was too French, and too associated with the deceased Bourbon king.

Paine was still bothered by the desire of the French to maintain slavery and the slave trade. Perhaps he never really understood French culture and language, and saw no good to its use in America. The French inhabitants must learn to be Americans, "under the same laws of Congress which Americans themselves are under." His solution was to send a bunch of Pennsylvanians, who understood what it meant to be American, to Louisiana. "The people of the eastern states are the best settlers of a new country," he claimed, and of all those on the eastern seaboard, those from Pennsylvania were the best citizens. What must be avoided at all costs was slavery. If the "poor Negroes" were brought in to cultivate the land, they would live in a state of "wretchedness" and "immorality." Paine learned from a ship captain who was recently in New Orleans that the Louisiana slave trade seemed to originate with ships from Liverpool, England. "Had I the command of the elements I would blast Liverpool with fire and brimstone. It is the Sodom and Gomorrah of brutality."[7]

By the spring of 1805, Paine was back in New Rochelle, again residing with Marguerite. He continued to cast his bitter lines at the Federalists. They in turn continued to attack Jefferson, especially since Paine backed Jefferson's proposal that a United States navy consisting primarily of small gunboats would be more effective in protecting the coastline than larger ships of the line. Paine also opposed the Federalists in their stronghold, New York City, where they continually lobbied the Jefferson Administration to fortify the New York harbor.[8] His support of a gunboat defense was well-known in America, producing this bit of anonymous doggerel, which appeared in 1807:

> TOM PAINE has exploded the old-fashion'd notion,
> That ships of the line are the lords of the ocean;
> And shown how a gunboat, with only one gun,
> In a clam can occasion a first-rate run:
> Nay, more, he has prov'd (to cut the thing shorter)
> The gunboat can blow the first-rate out of water!
> Then let nations be told, who great navies have arm'd,
> The Sovereign of Ships is a—gunboat becalmed![9]

Paine continued to rely on ad hominem insults rather than a close analysis of the issues involved. Federalists and their allies were always "blackguards" or "blackhearted" men, most likely hooked up with the English. In the course of intensified Federalist activities— probably a by-product of the campaign to regain the Presidency in the 1808 elections—the conservative press incited the aging rebel to paroxysms of rage, seemingly even worse than had his old adversaries, the "no-ability." The previous spring, Paine had viciously censured "a pettyfogging attorney," Mr. Hulbert, a Massachusetts state delegate, in a language that revealed his deepest resentments toward Federalists.[10] "When the poison-tooth of a rattlesnake is drawn, the bite and slaver of the reptile, like the slander and foam of Mr. Hulbert, become deprived of the power of injuring." The Federalists had lost in Massachusetts. The Republicans had extracted not only their venom but their teeth as well. "In this toothless condition, the rattle in its tail, like the rattle of the legislator of Sheffield, is heard without alarm."[11]

Paine next targeted a Virginian by the name of Thomas Turner. What is the nature of "a blackhearted man" but to throw "up mole-hills of dirt [and] blow them with its pestiferous breath into mountains." Paine did not know who Turner was, but he brought his attack on him together with his earlier condemnation of Hulbert. He guessed that Turner was "some petty-fogging attorney like that hyp-ocritical dabbler in dirt, *Hulbert*, of Sheffield."[12] They were "*two skunks who stink in concert.*" In June, Paine wrote his last letter to the citizens of the United States. It was a final charge against Federalism, a letter he inflated as "the most important of any I have published."[13] His tone was abusive and disparaging, again blasting Federalism as "a word without a meaning, [which] designates a fac-tion that has no principles." Federalists were all stupid, like the man condemned for being a liar who refused to change his ways because he was afraid his reputation would be ruined. Paine's main victim, as it had been in the earlier letters, was John Adams, "who was more the *dupe* of a party than the *leader* of it."[14] Paine still believed that Adams wanted to be president for life and then to pass the office on to his son, Quincy. Within just a few years, of course, John Quincy Adams would become President of the United States—but not for life.

Paine spent a few weeks with William Carver in New York, where he seemed to have misplaced some of his personal things. For a man who once had a terrific memory, he now seemed to be growing absent-minded. "I have left my penknife in the writing desk," he told his friend John Fellows. "It is a small French penknife that slides into the handle. I wish Carver would look behind the chest in the bedroom. I miss some papers that I suppose are fallen down there." He had returned to New Rochelle without them, and he was now awaiting young Thomas and Benjamin. Marguerite was in New York, and Louis had returned to Paris to be with his father. He expected the boys to bring his belongings along with some blankets for Marguerite and "my best blanket," which he had also left behind at Carver's. He also asked Fellows to pass some fatherly advice on to the boys when he saw them in New York: "Tell them that the better they behave the better it will be for them. I am now their only dependence, and they ought to know it."[15]

In the fall, 1805, Paine put the two boys in a boarding school in New Rochelle. Marguerite stayed in New York, finding a job, as Paine had thought appropriate. Lonelier than ever and seriously unable to take care of his basic needs, he decided to rent his little house and took a room at his neighbor's, Mrs. Bayeaux.

By this time Paine was reassessing the whole idea of constitution-making, focusing particularly on the New York and Pennsylvania constitutions. This was something that had bothered him since 1776, when he first suggested that England had no constitution. In the *Rights of Man* he made a remark that would become famous: "The American constitutions were to liberty, what a grammar is to language: they define its parts of speech, and practically construct them into syntax." (*RM* 95) Now, more than fifteen years later, he was still worrying about constitutions. His target in June 1806 was the New York document, which gave the executive the authority to grant charters (to corporations, for example), which he thought should be left to the people directly. This idea conflicted with the right of the people to engage in free elections: if a charter were granted, say to a bank, then a future legislature would be unable to repeal it, since the charter was empowered by the executive.

As for Pennsylvania, Paine hoped that a new constitution there would limit the legislature's authority to grant charters. Otherwise, the advantage would go to interests which sought incorporation through state charters. His attack focused on the lawyers. The then-current Pennsylvania constitution was only "for the emolument of lawyers." The more charters granted to corporations, the more work there would be for the legal profession. One way to overcome this problem was for one legislature to propose the charter and the next legislature to pass it, but only after an election. "It is the rapidity with which a self-interested speculation, or a fraud on the public property, can be carried through within the short space of one session, and before the people can be apprised of it, that renders it necessary that a precaution of this kind . . . should be made an article of the Constitution."[16]

In a few short years, in 1819, Supreme Court Chief Justice John Marshall would rule for the Court in *McCulloch v. Maryland* that the federal government possessed the power to grant such charters, even though this power was not specifically enumerated in the Constitution. Courts have argued ever since that the federal model is appropriate for states to follow, if they choose. In the long run, Paine lost this battle to the powerful nationalization of federal authority.

In 1807, Paine would again consider constitutional change, this time focusing on the judiciary. He raised an issue which is very much debated in our own time, namely the position of federal judges nominated by the President, confirmed by the Senate, then seated for life, so long as they manifest "good behavior." These judges are unaccountable to anyone because they never face reexamination or re-election, but they make policy decisions every bit as profound as legislators, who do face re-election. The Constitution designed the American federal judiciary to be independent of both the executive and legislative branches of government, the first time in history that such an arrangement had been made. Paine suggested that Congress should be able to remove judges by a majority vote of both houses, an act which could threaten the judiciary's autonomy. Still, his proposal merits reexamination as the twentieth century draws to a close.

The last years of Paine's life were generally years of aggravation, rejection, anxiety, and illness. This assessment must be tempered somewhat by the consideration that Paine was alone by choice. He was in danger of being a cantankerous old man. His counterattacks on the Federalists for their criticisms of Jefferson and his administration kept Paine on the Federalist "enemies list." In some respects, he must have enjoyed his notoriety. But the year 1806 was not very good to Paine, on two scores.

First, he was forced to sell his house in Bordentown. He had not lived there since 1803, and most of the people of Bordentown had never really appreciated him. After the appearance of *The Age of Reason*, many thought he was the devil incarnate. But he still had some friends in the town, and he enjoyed frequenting the Washington Tavern to carry on long conversations and drink some brandy. The town was the home of his dear friends the Kirkbrides, too, where he had probably spent more time than in his little Bordentown house. He sold the house in 1806 because he needed the money for himself and for the Bonnevilles. A friend, John Oliver, bought it for $300.

Paine's other major problem in 1806 was his worsening health. He was sick twice, once at Carver's and apparently in the summer. In August, he told Andrew Dean, who rented his farm in New Rochelle, he had been "struck with a fit of apoplexy that deprived me of all sense and motion. I had neither pulse nor breathing, and the people about me supposed me dead." He said he had felt very good during the day and so was surprised to become ill in the evening. He had had a bit of bread and butter for supper and was going up the stairs when the stroke hit him "as if I had been shot through the head." His subsequent fall left him so badly beaten up that two people had to help him get into and out of his bed. Coming so close to death, he found that he was not frightened, and perhaps most importantly, he did not feel the need to recant his religious convictions. "As to the people called Christians, they have no evidence that their religion is true. . . . It is education [that] makes all the difference." His letter then launched into a typical tirade against organized religion, especially Christianity. He added, however, that it had been three weeks since he was struck, and he was "now well enough to sit up some hours in the day, though not well enough to get up without help."[17]

Tired and alone, Paine was once again without money, despite the funds he had received from the sale of some of his farm land. Paine decided again to raise the old question of reimbursement for his services during the American Revolution. Twenty years earlier only Pennsylvania and New York had responded to his request for payment. He asked Jefferson to urge Congress to grant him a tract of land, which he could then sell. "I have been a volunteer to the world for thirty years without taking profits from anything I have published in America or in Europe."[18] Four months later, at the end of January 1806, he had heard nothing. He once again wrote an exceedingly long letter to Jefferson, this time offering himself as an envoy to France, along with Monroe, should the President wish to enter into negotiations with Bonaparte.[19] He was alone in America, he said, and desired to return to Europe. Jefferson declined his offer. Jefferson must have seen the obvious changes in his old friend, and wanted to distance himself from the aging curmudgeon.

What was worse, from the perspective of his angry state of mind, Paine read that an admirer of his, Isaac Hall, had gotten into trouble with the city of Philadelphia and its mayor, John Inskeep. Hall had wanted to take over the Vine Street Wharf. He had already agreed to a rent higher than anyone else and the city commissioners had approved his lease. But the mayor refused to allow him to do it, because, in the mayor's words, "Mr. Hall was one of Paine's disciples." Paine lashed into Inskeep in a letter published in the *Philadelphia Aurora*, saying he had never heard of anyone named Inskeep when he lived in Philadelphia, but he "must be some mushroom of modern growth that has started up on the soil which the generous services of Thomas Paine contributed to bless with freedom."[20] He then went on to review how he had written everything for the good of mankind with never a demand for remuneration for himself. It was a most gratuitously embarrassing letter.

In the summer of 1806, Paine wrote an essay on the causes of yellow fever, attributing the mosquito-borne disease to "effluvia that is fatal to life."[21] The disease had plagued New York in the summer and fall of 1803, and he had mentioned to Jefferson his theories about the illness. At that time, he had said that it was brought to the United States by ships from the West Indies. The proposal to prohibit them from docking in America from June until October might keep the disease out, he thought. "The disease may be in the cargo," he surmised, "especially that part which is barrelled up, and not in the persons on board, and when that cargo is opened on our wharfs, the hot steaming air in contact with the ground imbibes the infection. I can conceive that infected air can be barrelled up, not in a hogshead or rum, nor perhaps sucre, but in a barrel of coffee."[22] Paine was obviously quite wrong about the etiology of yellow fever, but he was logical in seeking its causes in air that people breathed.

Miserable, poor, and lonely, Paine finally decided to leave New Rochelle. He moved to New York, but not before one final demoralizing moment. He was denied an opportunity to vote in the New Rochelle elections. The election official, a man named Elisha Ward, a Federalist, claimed Paine was not an American citizen. "When the election . . . came on at New Rochelle last year for Members of Congress and Members of state assemblies," he recounted to Vice President George Clinton, "I tendered my tickets separately distinguishing which was which, as is the custom; each of which Ward refused, saying to me 'You are not an American Citizen.' Upon my beginning to remonstrate with him, he replied, 'Our minister at Paris, Gouverneur Morris, would not reclaim you as an American Citizen when you were imprisoned in the Luxembourg at Paris, and General Washington refused to do it.' "[23] So it was that Paine's Paris horrors and his old nemesis, Gouverneur Morris, came back once again to haunt him.

Paine had written to Clinton to engage his support, just as he had written James Madison, who as Secretary of State could supply direct information about Paine's nationality from the period when James Monroe was the American minister in Paris. He sued the election officials, but he lost the case, despite having several imminent figures come to his aid. Now it appeared that he could not even claim that he was a citizen of New York state. A new generation that was ignorant of *Common Sense* and the *Rights of Man* had come to power, and Paine was already on the way to being known only by his enemies' records. (It was not until July 1945, that New Rochelle restored Paine's citizenship.)

The Ward incident clearly left him agitated as he left New

Rochelle for the city, where he knew many people but had few friends. He often enjoyed the company of the mayor, DeWitt Clinton, who was George Clinton's nephew, among others, but he was frequently lonely and angry, especially when he was attacked in the press by his enemies, two of whom soon emerged in the persons of Carpenter and Cheetham.

In New York City, Paine lived for a while once again with William Carver. Carver was now doing some veterinary work, and he owned a shop. In July, Paine became quite ill again with apoplexy. Some people feared he was dying, but he recovered. Mrs. Elihu Palmer, the wife of the deist preacher who was a friend of Paine's and who died later that year in the yellow fever epidemic, came to care for him for some twelve weeks. Carver sent Paine a bill for twenty-two weeks' rent and the cost of housing Mrs. Palmer. When Paine refused to pay the $150, Carver complained that Paine was always filthy and drunk and insinuated that his relationship with Marguerite de Bonneville was more than platonic. He accused Paine of having fathered both sons who were still living with her. Carver apparently passed these remarks on to James Cheetham, thus providing the basis of that scurrilous biography. Later, when Marguerite sued Cheetham, the judge said that the biography had served religion well.[24]

Paine saw little of the Bonnevilles in 1806. He often seemed annoyed at Marguerite's incessant demands for money, but he appeared to treasure the boys, especially young Thomas. "I am glad to hear that Thomas is a good boy," he told Dean. "It will always give me pleasure to know that he goes on well." As the Bonnevilles were staying with Dean in New Rochelle, Paine told him that if Thomas needed anything, he should procure it for him and send Paine the bill. "You say that he begins to want a pair of trousers, shirt, and hat. You can take the horse and chair and take Thomas with you and go to the store and get him some strong stuff for a pair of trousers, hempen linen for two shirts, and a hat." Education of the young lad was still important, for Paine, who probably hoped Thomas would grow up to be just like his godfather. He quaintly admonished the child to behave himself: "He shall not want anything if he be a good boy and learn no bad words."[25] If Dean came to New York, Paine wanted him to bring Thomas with him. He obviously loved and missed the boy very much.

In the fall, Paine left Carver and moved in with the young up-and-coming artist John Wesley Jarvis, who painted Paine's portrait in November of 1806. The portrait shows Paine as an old man, although his hair remains brown. His nose is wider and longer than ever, and there is an expression of sadness around his mouth. His eyes lack the glimmer of the earlier Romney portrait. Here was a man deeply affected by prison, illness, fatigue, and bitterness. Paine's sense of humor, however, often appeared in the most unusual of circumstances. One day, he fell ill at Jarvis's house. He lay on the floor, in the midst of another stroke. Jarvis ran to his side. Paine looked up at him and said, "My corporeal functions have ceased. My intellect is clear. This is proof of immortality."[26]

Jarvis thought he sometimes drank too heavily, although he never accused him of being an alcoholic or a drunkard. The painter was nearly forty years younger than Paine, but the two got along quite well. He was as republican as Paine, but they differed, it appears, on religion. Paine wrote an essay on the biblical prophets' dreams, which was largely ignored in the press. Jarvis reportedly told him that if Paine wanted to be noticed, he should write his "recantation," as Voltaire had partially done at the end of his life. But Paine told him he would not do that, and besides, he felt just fine.[27]

The fact is that Paine was not just fine. He was often alone in these last years, increasingly ignored by his erstwhile friends. The Federalist press often used him as an example of anticlericalism and irreligion, which was an accurate view of course, but the accusations might well have kept his former friends away. In April 1807, he moved into two small rooms (one for sleeping, one for writing) in a house owned by Zakarias Hitt, a baker who was a Painite. There, he continued his attacks on the Federalists. He wrote so often for a republican newspaper, the *New York Public Advertiser*, that his relationship with that journal has long been disputed.[28] Most likely he served as one of its contributing editors because both his commentary and editorials appeared in it. He once noted that his enemies' attempts to make him a model of religious infidelity amounted to a "jesuitical trick . . . for I know of my own knowledge that the federal faction will *swear and lie and talk about religion.*"[29]   And at one point, he attacked John Marshall, the Chief Justice of the United States, a Federalist nominated by John Adams during the closing hours of his administration, and quickly approved by the Federalist-controlled Senate. When Paine was in France, he had denounced Marshall during the Adams Administration's XYZ Affair. This time the issue was not international affairs, but the disposition of Aaron Burr. Paine accused Marshall of being too lenient in Burr's appeal.[30]

Few came to see him, perhaps because no one wanted to, perhaps because the Hitt household was so far from downtown. He rarely heard from Barlow, Monroe, Rickman, or even Jefferson. He wrote to Barlow sadly, "You sometimes hear of me but I never hear of you." He wondered whether Fulton was having success with his experimental submarine, not knowing that he had given up on the submarines and was working on a steam-powered ship. What is Fulton up to, he asked Barlow: "Taming a whale to draw his submarine boat?" He asked Barlow to send him copies of the *National Intelligencer*, because he was lacking "authentic intelligence."[31] Paine wrote much in his last years, but most of it continued to be undistinguished attacks on Federalists. He was a man whose era had passed and whose friends had forgotten him.

Paine now targeted his pen against Federalist writer Stephen Carpenter (who sometimes wrote under the pseudonym of Cullen or McCullen). Carpenter was the editor of a journal called the *People's Friend*, a paper "continually filled in the first place with abuse and blackguardism against the national administration." Paine was convinced that Carpenter was an English spy, hooked into what Paine referred to as the "anglo-federal faction," which was intent on destroying confidence in the Republican Administration of Thomas Jefferson by making Americans believe that the French were about to invade and plunder New York. Paine's pieces appeared in a newspaper run by James Cheetham, the *American Citizen*, as well as in the *Philadelphia Aurora* and the *New York Public Advertiser*.[32] Accused of conspiring to overthrow the English government in 1798, Cheetham had come to New York, where he met Paine in 1803 and helped organize the 1803 dinner in his honor. Paine was certain that treasury official and friend of Burke, William Windham, was Carpenter's patron. Windham was also the patron of William Cobbett, who was at that time a severe Paine hater and supporter of the British government.[33] Carpenter, Paine wrote, had taken an essay of Paine's and falsified it, making Paine into a Tory, something that enraged Thomas Paine.

Aside from his attacks on Carpenter for being in the pay of the British ministry, some of Paine's pieces now focused on the question of fortifying New York harbor, an issue that split the Federalists, who wanted strong fortifications there, from the Republicans, who did not. In one of his first salvos, Paine directly attacked Rufus King, whom he named as most likely the writer of an invective against Jefferson for failing to strengthen the harbor's defenses. Paine pointed out that the citizens of Boston, Baltimore, Philadelphia, and Charleston had not requested federal help for their ports, and the only reason that New York had was the Federalists were not prominent there. Paine went on, sarcastically, to challenge Rufus King to announce in his paper that Paine had invited a couple of thousand French troops to plunder New York. If he dared do so, Paine promised to sue him "for LYING."[34] The Federalists in New York never bothered to raise the issue of fortification while Washington or Adams were president. To do so now only reinforced Paine's conviction that they were intent on undertaking a purely political battle with the Jeffersonian Republicans, to find a means to undermine American confidence in the President. They were obviously looking forward to the presidential election of 1808, now less than two years off.

Before having a serious and irreversible falling-out with Cheetham, Paine also published an essay in Cheetham's paper on a free press, which he of course supported. But Paine was wary of the press when it printed libel. He wrote that there was "a difference between error and licentiousness," although he offered no clear definition of either nor a direct solution to the problem.[35] Soon, it was all over between the two men, although the details of their split are not clear even today. It appears that Cheetham had once heavily edited Paine's prose to the extent that he changed Paine's meaning. Paine resented this so much that he soon published only in the *New York Public Advertiser*.

Another reason for their estrangement was Cheetham's changed political views. His *American Citizen* gradually became virulently anti-Jefferson, anti-Paine, and according to Paine, a Tory newspaper. Cheetham, having lost his admiration for Paine's ideas, began to gather material on Paine, particularly, sordid reports that he drank too much and neglected his personal hygiene and appearance. He told nefarious stories about Paine in his biography, saying he chose "to perform the offices of nature in his bed." He claimed that Paine was always intoxicated, even drinking with his black housekeeper, Betty. They would "both lie prostrate on the same floor, dead drunk, sprawling and swearing and threatening to fight, but incapable of approaching each other to combat. Nothing but inability prevented a battle."[36] Even before these stories appeared in print, Paine lashed out against Cheetham, calling his ideas "stupid." He said Cheetham himself spewed out "malignancy," was doing nothing but "libelling himself," was "an ugly tempered man," had "the vulgarity and forbiddingness of his countenance." Readers only "learned from absurdity" when they read Cheetham. When he wrote, he "vomited his spleen" and showed off his "abominable cowardice." Strong words from an angry old man. The examples of Paine's tongue-lashing seem unlimited, revealing more about Paine's state of mind and perhaps his lack of emotional well-being than Cheetham.[37]

Paine was especially tormented when Cheetham attacked him personally or misled the public about his published works. When Paine thought he had distorted a section of the *Rights of Man*, he concluded that "what is here given ought to cover James Cheetham with shame for the falsehood he has advanced. But as a man who has no sense of honor, no sense of shame, Mr. Cheetham will be able to read this with an unblushing front." As for the American Revolution, everything Cheetham wrote was just plain wrong. "James Cheetham talks of times and circumstances he knows nothing of, for he did not come here til several years after the war; yet in speaking of the revolution, he uses the words *we*, and *us*, and *our* revolution. It is common in England, in ridiculing self-conceited importance, to say, What a long tail *our* cat has got!"[38] He also denounced Cheetham's anti-French sentiments. Cheetham, he thought, had taken up where Carpenter had left off. A month after the closing of the *American Citizen* in August of 1807, Paine wrote: "Cheetham cannot live without quarreling, nor write without abuse."[39]

At one point, Cheetham even accused Paine of having no new ideas at all, deriving everything he said from John Locke, especially in *Common Sense* and the *Rights of Man*, in which he "followed Locke idea for idea." Paine's response appeared in the *New York Public Advertiser.*

> It may be so for what I know, for I never read Locke, nor ever had the work in my hand, and by what I have heard of it from Horne Tooke, I had no inducement to read it. It is a speculative, not a practical work, and the style of it is heavy and tedious, as all Locke's writings are.[40]

Paine sued Cheetham for slander, but Paine died before the suit could be litigated. He did not yet know how abusive Cheetham's biography would be. Supplemented by lies from Paine's former friend and landlord, William Carver, its invective surpassed even Chalmers' attack from 1791. It appeared in 1809, the year of Paine's death.

Throughout 1807 Paine was short of cash again, and he had to go begging. At one time he tried to sell his farm in New Rochelle and even thought he had made a deal on it, but the prospective purchaser died just as the contract was to be signed. Paine did not force the widow to consummate the purchase. Had he sold the farm, the purchase price would have been $10,000.[41] He applied once again to Congress for money on behalf of his services to the American cause. He never felt that the $3,000 he had received from Congress in October of 1785 was full compensation. Besides, that was long gone. In January of 1808, Paine wrote to the United States Senate: "The purpose of this address is to state a claim I feel myself entitled to make on the United States, leaving it to their representatives in Congress to decide on its worth and its merits." He then recounted the history of his appointment to join John Laurens to go to France to obtain loans and subsidies during the bleakest days of the Revolution. "As I never had a cent for this service, I feel myself entitled, as the country is now in a state of prosperity, to state the case to

Congress. . . ." He wrote *Common Sense*, he said, to awaken the Americans to the true nature of British tyranny and to stimulate them to separate from the empire. And he wrote the *Rights of Man* to warn others of the indignities of living under tyranny.

When the United States was unable to force the states to contribute money to the Revolutionary cause, Paine had been, he claimed, the first to suggest that a national legislature should have the authority to "make laws for the Union" as a whole. This was in fact a premonition of the powers bestowed upon the United States Congress in the American Constitution. After talking to George Clinton, now Vice President of the United States, Paine decided that if any compensation were due him, it should come directly from the individual states and not the country as a whole. New York had presented him with the farm in New Rochelle, and Pennsylvania had voted him five hundred pounds. No other states had come through, and none did now. The old Congress (of 1785) had given him only half of what he had asked for. "All the civilized world knows I have been of great service to the United States, and have generously given away talent that would have made me a fortune."[42] Within three weeks, Paine was writing virtually the same plea to the Committee of Claims of the House of Representatives. This time he argued that the salary he had received as Secretary to the Committee for Foreign Affairs was small at $800 per year. Even that had been "fretted down by the depreciation to less than a fifth of its nominal value."[43] He had lost the position because of the Silas Deane affair, which, he wrote, he had brought forth to the Congress so that they could see the real, despicable Deane.

As a result, he was without position or salary, even a depreciated one, and he thought Congress should now undo that injustice. Within another two weeks, Paine was writing a letter to the Speaker of the House, twice asking him whether there had been any action on his request to the committee. He seemed depressed in his second letter: "I know not who the Committee of Claims are, but if they are men of younger standing than 'the times that tried men's souls,' and, consequently, too young to know what the condition of the country was at the time I published *Common Sense* (for I do not believe independence would have been declared had it not been for the effect of that work), they are not capable of judging of the whole of the services of Thomas Paine."[44] Congress eventually rejected his request for further compensation.

Paine lived at the time, or as Conway puts it, was dying at the time, at 63 Partition Street in New York (he had moved out of his lodgings with Hitt, who had increased his rent by two dollars a week, and Paine was unable to pay it).[45] In July, he asked Jefferson to intervene on his behalf, but to no avail. Now he moved to a more comfortable place, the home of a Mrs. Ryder, who lived at 293 Bleecker Street; there he would be nearer to Marguerite and her sons. His final article was, appropriately, an attack on the Federalists, a short letter entitled "To the Federal Faction." After that he wrote nothing. In his final months, he met Willett Hicks, a Quaker watchmaker, whose cousin Elias founded in 1827 the Hicksite Quakers, a very liberal, antislavery faction, after the Society of Friends split. Shortly after drafting and signing his final will and testament on January 18, 1809, he fell ill again. He tried one more time with the Committee on Claims in February, but by the end of the month he was in bed with a high fever. Two weeks later, dropsy set in.[46]

At the end of April, he was well enough to move to a house on Grove Street with Marguerite, who took care of him along with a nurse, Mrs. Hedden, and his friend, a well-known physician, Dr. Nicholas Romaine, whose company Paine had enjoyed in New York. A Dr. Manly also came to see him, but he undoubtedly was Cheetham's spy because he passed on nasty pieces of information about Paine that Cheetham used in his biography. He told Cheetham, for example, that Paine had recanted before he died. He had not. The idea of a recantation may have been based on the appearance of Donald Fraser's "Paine's Recantation," which had appeared in New York when Paine still resided in France. It was a forgery that Fraser, a schoolmaster from Scotland, had designed to capitalize on the idea of selling several hundreds of copies of it to an unwary public. One of his last visitors was Kitty Nicholson Few, the daughter of Colonel Nicholson, with whom he had once corresponded from Paris. But he refused to see her, claiming that she had ignored him for too long. He then turned his head to the wall and said nothing. She left and sat out in the garden for awhile, weeping for her lost friend.[47]

Thomas Paine died peacefully at eight in the morning on June 8, 1809, in New York. He was seventy-two years old. The Federalist New York *Evening Post*, which once had so maligned him on his return to America, reported his death in simple terms, but concluded that "he had lived long, done some good, and much harm."[48]

Thomas Paine's body was transported from New York to New Rochelle in a cortege led by Marguerite de Bonneville, her son, Benjamin, Willett Hicks, and "two negroes." Perhaps a few others accompanied them. Paine had wanted to be buried in a Quaker cemetery and had asked Hicks to inquire at a local Quaker meeting-house whether this might be possible. The elders decided that it would be inappropriate. Paine's friends might wish to erect a statue or monument over his grave, and Quakers did not allow graven images. Instead, he was laid to rest in a quiet spot on his farm. Standing over the grave, Marguerite pronounced the final words.

> This interment was a scene to affect and wound any sensible heart. Contemplating who it was, what man it was, that we were committing to an obscure grave on an open and disregarded bit of land, I could not help feeling most acutely. Before the earth was thrown down upon the coffin, I, placing myself at the east end of the grave, said to my son Benjamin, "stand you there, at the other end, as a witness for grateful America." Looking around me, and beholding the small group of spectators, I exclaimed, as the earth was tumbled into the grave, "Oh, Mr. Paine, my son stands here as testimony of the gratitude of America, and I for France!"[49]

Shortly after Paine's death, Nicolas de Bonneville finally immigrated to America. He and Marguerite lived for awhile in New York until they decided to return to Paris, where they operated a bookshop together. After Nicolas died in 1828, Marguerite returned to the United States, in fact to St. Louis where her son, Benjamin, lived. Marguerite died in that city at age seventy-nine in 1846.

Paine's interment in New Rochelle was not the end to his wandering. Cobbett, a journalist who wrote under the name Peter Porcupine, in the 1790s had hated Paine's political and religious

ideas, especially *The Age of Reason* and *Letter to George Washington*.
But he converted to Painite economic ideas after reading *The Decline
and Fall of the English System of Finance,* which had appeared in 1796.
His admiration of Paine's ideas about political economy made him
decide that old Tom Paine rested in the wrong place. In his journal,
Cobbett's Weekly Political Register, he wrote that

> Paine lies in a little hole under the grass and weeds of an
> obscure farm in America. There, however, *he shall not lie, un-
> noticed, much longer.* He belongs to England. His fame is the
> property of England; and, if no other people will show, that they
> value that fame, the people of England will.[50]

In 1819, just before dawn one fall night, he, his son, and a friend
went to Paine's farm and disinterred the remains: they had decided
Paine's bones should have a proper burial in his native land.

At this point, the story is open to dispute. Cobbett never
publicly buried Paine's bones. Some historians claim that Cobbett
lost them overboard during his trip to England.[51] Others say that
Cobbett proudly displayed them in November 1819 in Liverpool.
The *Liverpool Mercury* quoted Cobbett as saying, "Great indeed must
that man have been, whose very bones attract such attention." In any
case, Cobbett vowed to celebrate Paine's life by variously erecting a
huge bronze statue of Paine, holding a grand dinner in his honor, and
selling gold rings containing Paine's hair. He did none of these
things. Instead, he probably kept the bones in a box in his house and
soon lost interest in them. After his death in 1835, Cobbett's son
auctioned off all of his father's worldly goods, but the auctioneer
refused to include the box which supposedly contained poor Paine's
bones.[52]

Cobbett's modern biographer, George Spater, believes that
they may have been buried on property owned by the Cobbett family.[53] On the other hand, in 1854, a Unitarian minister in England
claimed to own Paine's skull and his right hand, although he refused
to display them or speak much about them.[54] Indeed, there were
reports that various parts of Paine kept turning up throughout the rest
of the nineteenth century and into the twentieth. In the 1930s, a

woman in Brighton claimed that her family once owned Paine's jaw-bone.[55] The question of the final disposition of Thomas Paine will probably always remain open. Moncure Daniel Conway's remark is as relevant today as it was one hundred years ago: "As to his bones, no man knows the place of their rest to this day. His principles rest not."[56]

21 · Assessment

Thomas Paine, this apostle of freedom, combined the two virtues that the Greeks admired in human beings: a sharp intellect and a willingness to take action. Paine was a man who thought and wrote a great deal about the things that worried him and then did what he could to resolve them. He not only preached revolutionary change. He practiced it. After presenting his dazzling arguments for American separation from Britain, he served in the Continental Army and saw action along the Delaware in 1776 and 1777. Later he held an official position with the rebel government. He deeply desired American national unity, and did what he could, working with Robert Morris and others, to achieve that goal once the war with Britain ended. After 1789, he admired the revolutionary fervor that spread throughout Paris, leading to remarkable changes in that country. The calling of the National Assembly, its transformation into a Constituent Assembly to bring about a new constitution for France were precisely the things he had been thinking about since the success of the American model of change. But he did not stop at admiration. He directly participated in the National Convention in the effort to make the constitution of 1793.

Above all, Paine never lost sight of the final goals of political and social change. To the very end of his life, Thomas Paine argued that human beings were essentially good, that they possessed the potential to achieve justice, equality, and freedom everywhere, but that sometimes it was necessary to resort to violence and war to achieve those positive values.

When that violence was directed against his friends and colleagues, and ultimately himself, Paine condemned it as being misplaced, counterproductive, and contrary to the virtuous goals he thought could be achieved. He never put it better than when he claimed to "speak an open and disinterested language, dictated by no passion but that of humanity." His passion for his fellow human beings, for humanity, was his abiding, consuming concern. He only wanted to help the voiceless, the hopeless, the physically and spiritually impoverished, all those who were dominated not only by a tyrant who ruled their bodies, but also enslaved by the tyranny of superstition and falsehoods. "Independence is my happiness," he continued in that same passage in the *Rights of Man*. Paine's goal was to do all he could to work for human autonomy, universal independence. "My country is the world, and my religion is to do good."[1] (*RM* 228) He dedicated his life to the cause he favored, with no expectation of monetary reward. Only later, sick and poor, did he ask the government of the United States for compensation. But he did not ask to be paid. He asked for reimbursement of his expenses. That was all.

In many respects, a deeply religious devotion and respect for God's universe motivated Paine's pursuit of liberty and justice. His religious attitudes have caused consternation and perplexity among his readers. Did he believe in God? Was he an atheist? Most commentators have concluded that Paine, like Franklin and Jefferson, was a conventional eighteenth-century deist, who believed that God, having created the universe, left it to man to improve or destroy.[2] But Paine's worldview was far more complex because he saw God's handiwork in all of nature, including human nature. Those people who acted in the best interests of mankind—for liberty, justice, and equality—were truly human. They alone possessed that divine spark, which ignited their souls and motivated them to perform good deeds. On the contrary, those who acted for themselves alone were inhuman, denatured creatures, monsters who deserved the worst fate. Paine's religiosity was, if anything, pantheistic rather than solely deistic: he believed in a universal, ubiquitous God, who infused the world with his power and spirit, but human beings were sufficiently independent of him to make the world better or worse in their lifetime.[3]

Thomas Paine's work made an enormous difference. In America, he made it possible for the debate over American separation from Britain to become not only a privately discussed issue, but a public one. A straight line goes from the publication of *Common Sense* in January 1776 to the Declaration of Independence just six months later. Paine crystallized the thinking in France regarding the direction the Revolution there should take, although few listened to him. He was unable to stop the degeneration of the Revolution into Terror, to halt the Revolution from consuming not only itself, but almost him as well.

Thomas Paine was truly a singular American. While he at times claimed that his country was the world, that he was a man without a nation, the reality is that after July 4, 1776, he considered himself an American citizen. There were no true Americans until that date, he said, only Englishmen or English-Americans. They "were not called citizens till after the government was established," he told Monroe in 1794, "and not even then until they had taken the oath of allegiance."[4] He himself took the oath of allegiance to the United States on two occasions, once in 1776, again in 1777.[5]

Writing from France just after the Revolution there, he mentioned how much he missed "my much loved America. It is the country from whence all reformation must originally spring."[6] Clearly, the American spirit ran deeply in Thomas Paine, even when he had been gone for less than three years. This spirit stayed with Paine despite his becoming a French citizen in 1792 and serving in the National Convention. Writing from prison, he told James Monroe that he was not so certain of the meaning of the "honor." Embedded in this sentiment was Paine's distinction between "real" citizenship as opposed to a fake one with nationhood: "Certainly I had no more idea than [Washington] of vacating any part of my real Citizenship of America for a nominal one in France, especially at a time when *she did not know whether she would be a Nation or not.*" He told Monroe that he considered himself a true citizen of America. France did not yet have a consciousness of itself as a nation.

Did Paine write Monroe simply because he did not want to languish in prison? He never renounced the French citizenship that had been bestowed on him. He accepted the seat with great relish in the National Convention, and spoke there just as if he were a true patriot of France and the Revolution. But he in fact never once thought of himself as anything except an American: "I certainly then remained, even upon their own tactics, what I was before, a citizen of America." What Paine obviously meant, putting aside his predicament in prison, was that he wished to fulfill his job as well as he could, to help develop the new constitution for the nation, while remaining an American citizen. He was never a French national because he would never feel as if he fitted into that "circle with a common center." "I acted only as a friend invited among them as I supposed on honorable terms. I did not come to join myself to a government already formed, but to assist in forming one *de nouveau*, which was afterwards to be submitted to the people whether they would accept it or not, and this any foreigner might do."[7]

When Paine finally returned to America in 1802, he wrote that he was glad to be back. America, he said, "is the country of my heart." It was "the place of my political and literary birth. It was the American Revolution that made me an author, and forced into action the mind that had been dormant, and had no wish for public life."[8] Paine's national consciousness became a reality only after he came to America. Being English in England was second nature. He never really gave it much thought at all. Only when he arrived on American shores did he consider what it meant to be a "national" and attached to a particular country. But the other side to Paine's consciousness was his universalism, his judgment that he spoke on behalf of all people everywhere. In his 1782 *Letter to the Abbé Raynal*, for the first time, he pursued the idea that the goal of human progress was to move not toward the creation of a virtuous nation but to promote "universal society, whose mind rises above the atmosphere of local thoughts and considers mankind, of whatever nation or profession they may be, as the work of one Creator." The world needed "a system of extended civilization," and he considered himself to be "a universal citizen." Five years later he told the Marquis of Lansdowne that he was "a man who considers the world as his home." And in defending the life of Louis XVI, he told the National Convention that he considered himself to be "a citizen of the world."[9]

Thomas Paine was at once conscious of the contradictions that might have existed inherently in his American nationality and his internationalism. Emotionally, as he himself testified more than once, he was an American; but intellectually he was an internationalist. Writing from France just before the Revolution there, he remarked that "my heart and myself are 3,000 miles apart; and I had rather see my horse Button in his own stable, or eating the grass of Bordentown or Morrisania, than see all the pomp and show of Europe." These two—his Americanness and his internationalism— were compatible. He brought them together in a manner that allowed him at once to say that while his nationality was American, his mind was always on the whole world. Indeed, he could "defend the cause of humanity" as an American.[10] His remarkable life was punctuated by a national consciousness that was purely American after the break with England in 1776, and it would remain so until his death some thirty-three years later in 1809.

Since Thomas Paine's death nearly two hundred years ago, his life and work have been a source of inspiration for social and political reformers as well as a target of hatred and abomination for his detractors.[11] A generation ago, historian Dixon Wecter called him a "hero manqué," a "hero in reverse," because for too long people forgot the contributions he made selflessly on behalf of American independence and the spread of worldwide freedom. An old children's nursery rhyme, calling to mind Cobbett's ghoulish expedition, ran:

> Poor Tom Paine! there he lies:
> Nobody laughs and nobody cries.
> Where he has gone or how he fares
> Nobody knows and nobody cares.

Many of the stories about Paine's alcoholism and lack of personal hygiene derived from the scurrilous work of his early biographers, George Chalmers and James Cheetham, and the outrageous lies they perpetrated have never been fully overcome. For some time, several statues of him could not be erected because of the fear among various civic authorities that he was too dangerous to be memorialized. On the occasion of the one hundredth anniversary of the Declaration of Independence, the city of Philadelphia refused to allow a bust of Paine to be placed in Independence Hall. In 1933, a New York radio station first invited, then refused, to allow a City College professor to

THOMAS PAINE: Apostle of Freedom

give a short talk on Paine because the old radical was regarded as "a dangerous subject and not suitable for radio discussion." The station later relented. Of course the most dogged and oft-quoted critic of Paine was Theodore Roosevelt, in his 1888 biography of Gouverneur Morris. Roosevelt quoted Morris as characterizing Paine as that "filthy little atheist." When challenged nearly thirty years later, Roosevelt could not come up with the source of this quotation, although he claimed it appeared in Morris' Paris diary. It does not, and most likely Roosevelt picked it up from Chalmers' or Cheetham's biography, or perhaps Elkanah Watson's reminiscences of 1781 on Paine's first visit to France.[12]

Paine's works, used widely in college and university courses on American history and political thought, have now been republished in many modern editions.[13] Several municipalities in England and America, including Thetford, New Rochelle, and Morristown, have erected statues and monuments in his honor. English admirers have created a Thomas Paine Society to exchange ideas about his life and work and to publish new, recently-discovered documents. Throughout the nineteenth and twentieth centuries, he has often been cited in journals and magazines, and his disciples have held dinners and drunk toasts on his behalf. On the two hundred fiftieth anniversary of his birth in 1987, the Thomas Paine Society organized meetings in his honor throughout England and the United States, and the Thomas Paine National Historical Association commemorated the moment with a celebration in New Rochelle. In 1992, the United States Congress enacted a law, long overdue, to erect a monument to Thomas Paine in the District of Columbia.[14]

Commemorative and festive moments are, however, only part of his legacy: what is important is that Thomas Paine was an outspoken and articulate advocate for social and political change. His plain style of expression meant that his ideas were immediately accessible to a readership that consisted largely of working people: artisans, tradesmen, craftsmen, manufacturers, and laborers. Paine did not consciously write for the upper classes of society, although he intended them to read his work as well. He wanted everyone to understand his message, which was always ladened with ideas of freedom, equality, and democracy. Unlike Burke, he relied not on references from antiquity, but on common sense set forth in the ordinary language of the street.[15]

Thomas Paine assaulted rank and privilege. He demanded constitutional safeguards to protect those who were most vulnerable: the unemployed poor, the working poor, and the infirm. He favored universal suffrage so all citizens could participate in their government's decisions. He demanded an end to slavery in all its forms around the world: in America, in the Caribbean, and in India. He advocated a system of social welfare where individuals too crushed to help themselves had the support of their government, indeed of the entire society, to provide them with food, shelter, clothing, and education. Above all, he saw himself as speaking not merely as an American in his adopted country, but as a citizen of the world. As a result, his words have been inspirational to those in other nations who have read his works over the past two hundred years.[16] Peace, prosperity, happiness, and liberty could be achieved only if people worked together to realize them, he wrote. The problems Thomas Paine witnessed and for which he worked so tirelessly two hundred years ago tragically remain today.[17] Following the example of this apostle of freedom, the world must constantly renew his resolve to "begin the world over again" until such time as all people are free and safe from harm.

Notes

Chapter 1

1. Thomas Paine to John Inskeep, Mayor of the City of Philadelphia, February 1806, in *CW* 2:1480.

2. In chronological order, they are: Eric Foner, *Tom Paine and Revolutionary America*; Alfred Owen Aldridge, *Thomas Paine's American Ideology*; David A. Wilson, *Paine and Cobbett: The Transatlantic Connection*; Gregory Claeys, *The Political Thought of Thomas Paine*; Mark Philp, *Paine*; Jack Fruchtman, Jr., *Thomas Paine and the Religion of Nature*. Historical interest in Paine has dramatically increased over the past fifteen years, as the notes and bibliography here demonstrate. These works, each with their own individual virtues, are hardly biographical.

3. For two early important biographies, see Moncure Daniel Conway, *The Life of Thomas Paine*, 2 vols., and A. Owen Aldridge, *Man of Reason: The Life of Thomas Paine*. Conway's work was the first serious modern biography of Paine. It was, however, uncritical due to Conway's outright sympathy to Paine's Quakerism, deism, and philosophy of rights and liberty. Aldridge's work was the first objective scholarly biography of Thomas Paine.

4. Among contemporary studies of his life, the best is David Freeman Hawke, *Paine*, recently reprinted in a Norton edition. Other recent biographical studies include one in English by British journalist Audrey Williamson, *Thomas Paine: His Life, Work and Times* and two in French, one by historian Bernard Vincent, *Thomas Paine, ou la religion de la liberté*, and the other by journalist Jean Lessay, *L'Américain de la Convention: Thomas Paine, professeur de révolutions, député de Pas-du-Calais*.

5. J.G.A. Pocock, *Virtue, Commerce and History: Essays on Political Thought and History, Chiefly in the Eighteenth Century*, 276. Pocock reiterates this view in his "Political Thought in the English-speaking Atlantic, 1760-

1790. Part 1: The Imperial Crisis," in J.G.A. Pocock, ed., *The Varieties of British Political Thought, 1500-1800*, 279-80, 282. "Anti-Normanism" refers to the ancient myth of the English constitution, which held that when the Normans invaded from France they brought with them the outlines of a constitutional structure to ensure the balance of king, lords, and commons. The "New Model" army was the citizen armed force under Cromwell during the mid-seventeenth century English Civil War. A recent, quite different view is Samuel H. Beer, *To Make a Nation: The Rediscovery of Federalism*, 206-17.

6. For an analogous interpretation of Jefferson's political ideas, see Garrett Ward Sheldon, *The Political Philosophy of Thomas Jefferson*, esp. 16-18.

7. In light of new work recently produced by David V. Erdman, A. Owen Aldridge believes "Paine's French experience needs reinterpreting." See Aldridge, "John Oswald and the French Revolution," *The Eighteenth Century: Theory and Interpretation* 31 (Summer 1990):185. Erdman's work is *Commerce des Lumières: John Oswald and the British in Paris, 1790-1793*. For a reinterpretation of Paine's French experience, see Chapters 13, 17, and 18 below.

8. Most modern commentators seem satisfied to conclude that Paine was a deist. To argue that his beliefs were not only deistic but also pantheistic differs greatly from this conventional assessment.

9. Paine, "Essay on Cheetham," 22 August 1807, in the *New York Public Advertiser*, reprinted in Gilbert Vale, *The Life of Thomas Paine*, 165 and A. Owen Aldridge, "Thomas Paine and the *New York Public Advertiser*," *New-York Historical Society Quarterly* 37 (Oct. 1953):377. The original "Reply to Cheatham [sic]" may be found in the Richard Gimbel Collection of Thomas Paine Manuscripts deposited in the American Philosophical Society, Philadelphia.

10. Also called civic humanism, a heated academic controversy has raged in English and American scholarly circles for the past twenty-five years over whether the principal eighteenth century thinkers and writers in America and Britain were Lockean liberals or classical republicans (the latter with roots in Aristotle, Cicero, and Machiavelli as opposed to John Locke). There are several major players in the controversy. For starters, see J.G.A. Pocock, *The Machiavellian Moment: Florentine Political Thought and the Atlantic Republican Tradition* and Isaac Kramnick, *Republicanism and Bourgeois Radicalism: Political Ideology in Late-Eighteenth Century England and America*. An alternative historical framework has been provided by J.C.D. Clark, who argues for the reintegration of religion into the political theory of the era and against the economic reductionism of bourgeois ideology. For Clark's views on Paine, see his *English Society, 1688-1832*, 324-29.

11. On the mythology of the English ancient constitution, see J.G.A.

Pocock, *The Ancient Constitution and the Feudal Law: A Study of English Historical Thought in the Seventeenth Century, A Reissue with a Retrospective*, revised ed.

12. The eighteenth century concept of the republic is rooted in the writings of the political theorist Niccolo Machiavelli (1469-1527), known and maligned throughout history as the author of *The Prince*. Machiavelli was, however, as Pocock has firmly demonstrated, deeply republican in his thinking and preferences. His ideas originated in Aristotle and Cicero. See Pocock, *The Machiavellian Moment*, Chapters 6 and 7.

13. J.H. Plumb, *The Growth of Political Stability in England, 1675-1725*.

14. L.H. Butterfield, ed., *The Adams Papers. The Diary and Autobiography of John Adams*, 4 vols., 3:334.

15. Quoted in Ray B. Browne, "The Paine-Burke Controversy in Eighteenth-Century Irish Popular Songs," in Ray B. Browne, William John Roscelli, and Richard Loftus, eds., *The Celtic Cross: Studies in Irish Culture and Literature*, 84-85.

16. Quoted in Conway, *The Life of Thomas Paine*, 2:329-30. For recent assessments by three of his "fans," see A.J. Ayer, *Thomas Paine*; David Powell, *Tom Paine: The Greatest Exile*; and David Braff, "The Forgotten Founding Father: The Impact of Thomas Paine," *The Humanist* 47 (May/June 1987):21-23, 38. There is also the recently published doctoral dissertation of Walter Wöll, *Thomas Paine: Motives for Rebellion*, European University Studies Series XIV, Anglo-Saxon Language and Literature, Vol. 248. For earlier reassessments which helped stimulate the renewed interest in Paine in the twentieth century, see Harry Hayden Clark, "Toward a Reevaluation of Thomas Paine," *American Literature* 5 (May 1933):133-45; Robert P. Falk, "Thomas Paine and the Attitude of the Quakers to the American Revolution," *Pennsylvania Magazine of History and Biography* 63 (1939):302-10; Howard Penniman, "Thomas Paine— Democrat," *American Political Science Review* 37 (Apr. 1943):244-62; and John J. Meng, "The Constitutional Theories of Thomas Paine," *Review of Politics* 8 (July 1946):283-306.

Chapter 2

1. Paine to Mr. Secretary Dundas, 15 September 1792, in *CW* 2:466-69.

2. See the account in Thomas Bayly Howell, ed., *A Complete Collection of State Trials and Proceedings for High Treason and Other Crimes and Misdemeanors*, 33 vols., 24:535.

3. For a different view, see Caroline Robbins, "The Lifelong Education of

Thomas Paine (1737-1809): Some Reflections upon His Acquaintance among Books," *Proceedings of the American Philosophical Society* 127 (June 1983):135-42.

4. The forty pound requirement, which became law in 1430, was preserved in the great 1832 Reform bill, and not rescinded until 1867.

5. See Dorothy Marshall, *Industrial England, 1776-1851,* 57 and Paul Langford, *A Polite and Commercial People: England, 1727-1783,* 68-71.

6. [George Chalmers], *Life of Thomas Paine, the Author of Rights of Men, with a Defence of his Writings, by Francis Oldys, A.M. of the University of Pennsylvania,* 2. It is from Chalmers' biography that the stories of Paine's heavy drinking originated. Most of Chalmers' characterizations were unfair and inaccurate, though it is clear that Paine did like to take a drink, especially as he grew older and more despondent. According to Conway, Chalmers wrote into the title a pseudonym which he hoped readers would take for a learned clergyman (Chalmers did not have the A.M. degree). In addition, he called his biography a "defence" of Paine's work, which for Conway was "a trick which no doubt carried this elaborate libel into the hands of many 'Painites.'" See Conway, *The Life of Thomas Paine,* 1: xv.

7. The location of the farm is uncertain today.

8. Paine, "Forester No. 4," 8 May 1776, in *CW* 2:84.

9. Conway, *The Life of Thomas Paine,* 1:11, 13.

10. The ranks of craftsman, as they had been from the Medieval guilds, continued to be the learner (apprentice), the day laborer (journeyman), and the most experienced and chief executive (master craftsman).

11. See N.A.M. Rodger, *The Wooden World: Anatomy of the Georgian Navy,* 186 and James G. Lydon, *Pirates, Privateers, and Profits,* 194.

12. See Lydon, *Pirates, Privateers, and Profits,* 219 and Brian Lavery, *Nelson's Navy: The Ships, Men and Organisation, 1793-1815.*

13. The full story is to be found in Alyce Barry, "Thomas Paine: Privateersman," *Pennsylvania Magazine of History and Biography* 101 (Oct. 1977):451-61. I have used this invaluable article as the basis of this part of the narrative.

14. The captain's name was actually Edward Menzies.

15. See Rodger, *The Wooden World,* 125-26.

16. Barry, "Thomas Paine, Privateersman," 456-59.

17. Ludovic Fortolis, *Les Anglais en France: Des cochots de la terreur aux geôles de l'empire,* 20.

18. Thomas Clio Rickman, *The Life of Thomas Paine,* viii.

19. The Romney portrait has never been found. Only the Auguste Milière version of it and the William Sharp engraving based on it exist.

20. It is conceivable that beginning in middle age Paine suffered from what contemporary medical science identifies as Rosacea, a condition in which the nose tends to enlarge and redden and the cheeks near the nose turn crimson.

21. [Chalmers], *Oldys Life of Thomas Paine*, 8.

22. Quoted by Conway, *The Life of Thomas Paine*, 1:17, nt.1.

23. Paine, "Forgetfulness: From the Castle in the Air to the Little Corner of the World," addressed to Lady Smyth, 1794, in *CW* 2:1121-22.

24. Noted by Ernest A. Payne, "Thomas Paine: Preacher," Letter to the Editor, the *Times Literary Supplement* (31 May 1947):267, who claims that this proved that Paine was an itinerant preacher at this time.

25. Paine to Washington, August 1783, in *CW* 2:1222.

26. Williamson, *Thomas Paine*, 37-38.

27. See Foner, *Tom Paine and Revolutionary America*, 11-14.

28. Rickman called Chalmers' work "silly and contemptible." He also despised the work of yet another Paine biography, one which appeared the same year of Paine's death. This was James Cheetham's *The Life of Thomas Paine*. Cheetham was the first critic to spread stories of Paine's drunkenness. Rickman said that the work was full of "idle gossiping and gross misrepresentation." See Rickman, *Life of Thomas Paine*, 1.

29. Rickman, *The Life of Thomas Paine*, 12.

30. See A. Owen Aldridge, "The Poetry of Thomas Paine," in *Pennsylvania Magazine of History and Biography* 79 (Jan. 1951):82-84. Aldridge claims that in this poem, Paine wanted to "penetrate farther into the realm of imagination than he felt contemporary poets were venturing."

31. Paine, "The Death of General Wolfe," (originally written in 1759 at the death of General Wolfe), in the *Pennsylvania Magazine*, March 1775, in *CW* 2:1083.

32. Paine, "Farmer Short's Dog Porter: A Tale," in *Pennsylvania Magazine*, July 1775, in *CW* 2:1084-88.

Chapter 3

1. Paine, "Case of the Officers of Excise, with Remarks on the Qualifications of Officers, and on the Numerous Evils Arising to the Revenue, from the Insufficiency of the Present Salary: Humbly Addressed to the Members of Both Houses of Parliament," (1772, first printed in 1793), in *CW* 2:11-12.

2. See Paine to Oliver Goldsmith, 21 December 1772, in *CW* 2:1129-30.

3. Conway, *The Life of Thomas Paine*, 1:29. Conway was quoting from the Customs Board's minutes of that date.

4. Rickman, *The Life of Thomas Paine*, 15.

5. Cheetham, *The Life of Thomas Paine*, 226-27.

6. Rickman, *The Life of Thomas Paine*, 15.

7. Paine to Kitty Nicholson Few, 6 January 1789, in *CW* 2:1275.

8. Paine, "Reflections on Unhappy Marriages," *Pennsylvania Magazine*, December 1775, in *CW* 2:1119. Aldridge is certain Paine did not write this piece. See Aldridge, *Thomas Paine's American Ideology*, 287. Foner's dating of this essay is off by six months. For a review of research and criticism of recent scholarship on Paine, see A. Owen Aldridge, "Thomas Paine: A Survey of Research and Criticism since 1945," *British Studies Monitor* 5 (Winter 1975):3-27.

9. Paine to the Honorable Henry Laurens, 14 January 1779, in *CW* 2:1162. In addition to Franklin, Scott knew Dr. Samuel Johnson and Edward Gibbon, among others. For Franklin, see David Freeman Hawke, *Franklin* and A. Owen Aldridge, *Benjamin Franklin:Philosopher and Man*.

10. Franklin to Richard Bache, 30 September 1774, in Leonard W. Labaree, ed. (vols. 1-14), William B. Willcox, ed. (vols. 15-25), *The Papers of Benjamin Franklin*, 30 vols. to date, 21:325-26.

11. Paine to Franklin, 4 March 1775, in *CW* 2:1130-32.

12. Butterfield, ed., *The Diary and Autobiography of John Adams*, 3:334.

13. Forrest McDonald, *Novus Ordo Seclorum: The Intellectual Origins of the Constitution.*

14. See Bernard Bailyn, *The Ideological Origins of the American Revolution.*

15. Paine to Franklin, 4 March 1775, in *CW* 2:1130-32.

16. Foner, *Tom Paine and Revolutionary America*, 20-21.

17. Vincent, *Thomas Paine*, 42.

18. Aldridge, *Thomas Paine's American Ideology*, 28, Chapter 2 generally, and the Appendix. For the debate over Paine's use of names and ideas from classical antiquity generally, see Richard M. Gummere, "Thomas Paine: Was He Really Anticlassical?" *American Antiquarian Society Proceedings* 75 (Oct. 1965):253-69 and A. Owen Aldridge, "Thomas Paine and the Classics," *Eighteenth-Century Studies* 1 (June 1968):370-80. Kramnick and Foot's collection is to be found in *The Thomas Paine Reader*.

19. Atlanticus [Paine], "To the Public," in the *Pennsylvania Magazine*, January 1775.

20. [Paine], "The Magazine in America," in *Pennsylvania Magazine*, 24

January 1775, in *CW* 2:1109.

21. Paine to Franklin, 4 March 1775, in *CW* 2:1131. See also Paine to Laurens, 14 January 1779, in *CW* 2:1161.

22. See Paine, "Crisis Seven," 21 November 1778, *The American Crisis*, a series of papers written by Paine between 1776 and 1783, in *CW* 1:143-44. Hereafter these papers will be cited by number as published in the Foner edition. There are two exceptions, namely the two additional papers identified as part of the series, after Foner's collection was published. The two appeared in the *Pennsylvania Gazette* on June 13, 1778 and April 3, 1782, respectively, and were identified by A. Owen Aldridge in "Some Writings of Thomas Paine in Pennsylvania Newspapers," *American Historical Review* 56 (July, 1951):832-38.

23. "Esop" [Paine], "New Anecdotes of Alexander the Great," *Pennsylvania Magazine*, February 1775, in *CW* 2:1113-15.

24. "Esop" [Paine], "Cupid and Hymen," in *Pennsylvania Magazine*, March 1775, in *CW* 2:1115-18. Aldridge does not attribute this essay to Paine. Aldridge, *Thomas Paine's American Ideology*, 287-91.

25. [Paine], "A Dialogue Between General Wolfe and General Gage in a Wood near Boston," in *Pennsylvania Journal*, 4 January 1775, in *CW* 2:47-49. This was Paine's first piece in a publication other than the *Magazine*.

26. "Atlanticus" [Paine], "Reflections on the Life and Death of Lord Clive," in *Pennsylvania Magazine*, March 1775, in *CW* 2:23-27. Aldridge doubts Paine's authorship of this work. See Aldridge, *Thomas Paine's American Ideology*, 286-87.

27. [Paine], "Duelling," in *Pennsylvania Magazine*, May 1775, in *CW* 2:28-32.

28. "Vox Populi" [Paine], "Reflections on Titles," in *Pennsylvania Magazine*, May, 1775, in *CW* 2:33-34. Aldridge also doubts Paine's authorship of this piece (Aldridge, *Thomas Paine's American Ideology*, 287).

29. "Atlanticus" [Paine], "The Tale of the Monk and the Jew Versified," in the *Pennsylvania Magazine*, March 1775, though there is some question whether Paine was the author of this poem. See what may also be his poem, "Korath, Dathan, and Abiram" (based on the book of Numbers), which also appeared in 1775.

30. The official date of the beginning of the slave trade is now said to be 1441 when a Portuguese explorer gave twelve Africans to his prince in Lisbon. See Sylvia R. Frey, "Slavery and anti-slavery," in *The Blackwell Encyclopedia of the American Revolution*, Jack P. Greene and J. R. Pole, eds., 379-91, on which the following is largely based.

31. Billy G. Smith and Richard Wojtowicz, *Blacks Who Stole Themselves: Advertisements for Runaways in the "Pennsylvania Gazette," 1728-1790*, 5, 121, and generally for an eye-opening sampling of these advertisements.

32. Cheetham, *The Life of Thomas Paine*, 39.

33. "Justice and Humanity" [Paine], "African Slavery in America," in *Pennsylvania Journal*, March 1775, in *CW* 2:15-19. Aldridge sees no evidence that Paine wrote this piece. See Aldridge, *Thomas Paine's American Ideology*, 289-91. Conway thinks Paine wrote it.

34. "A Lover of Peace" [Paine], "A Serious Thought," in *Pennsylvania Journal*, 18 October 1775, in *CW* 2:20.

35. In August of 1775, a piece appeared in *Pennsylvania Magazine* concerning the emancipation of women. Some commentators have attributed it to Paine, others have not. The piece was "An Occasional Letter on the Female Sex," and it can be found in *CW* 2:34-38. See Frank Smith's definitive "The Authorship of 'An Occasional Letter on the Female Sex,'" *American Literature* 2 (Nov. 1930):277-80 and Aldridge, *Thomas Paine's American Ideology*, 288.

36. "Amicus" [Paine], untitled letter in the *Pennsylvania Magazine*, June 1775.

37. See generally Duncan J. MacLeod, *Slavery, Race and the American Revolution*; Ira Berlin and Ronald Hoffman, eds., *Slavery and Freedom in the Age of the American Revolution*; Donald L. Robinson, *Slavery in the Structure of American Politics, 1765-1820*.

38. [Paine], "The Dream Interpreted," *Pennsylvania Magazine*, May 1775, in *CW* 2:50-52. Aldridge denies Paine wrote this piece, Aldridge, *Thomas Paine's American Ideology*, 288.

39. "A Lover of Peace" [Paine], "Thoughts on Defensive War," July 1775, the *Pennsylvania Magazine*, in *CW* 2:52-53. This was Paine's response to the Quakers, who opposed an armed struggle against England and thus wound up on the side of the Tories, loyal to Britain.

40. "Atlanticus" [Paine], "Liberty Tree, A Song written early in the American Revolution," in the *Pennsylvania Magazine*, July 1775, in *CW* 2:1092. Aldridge recounts how Paine later revised this poem to apply to all revolutionary contexts by substituting, for example, the words "Of Kingcraft and Priestcraft are joining amain" for "King, Lords, and Commons are uniting amain," among other changes. Aldridge, "The Poetry of Thomas Paine," 85-86.

41. Paine with Captain Thomas Pryor, "Of Making Salt Petre," the *Pennsylvania Journal, and the Weekly Advertiser*, 22 November 1775. The notice said that Paine (he did not yet add the "e" to his last name) and Pryor had engaged in these experiments "to show the practicality of a plan, proposed by Mr. Pain, of forming a Salt-Petre Association for voluntarily supplying the public magazines with gunpowder."

42. Cited often, most recently in Conor Cruise O'Brien, *The Great Melody: A Thematic Biography of Edmund Burke*, 75.

43. "A Lover of Order" [Paine], "To the Members of the House of Assembly of Pennsylvania," in the *Pennsylvania Journal*, 22 November 1775. In this same issue, Paine demonstrated the results of his and Pryor's two experiments on saltpeter.

44. "A Continental Farmer" [Paine], "To the Members of the House of Assembly of Pennsylvania," in the *Pennsylvania Journal*, 6 December 1775.

45. Paine to Franklin, 16 May 1778, in *CW* 2:1150-51. Paine more than once used the image of the "country set on fire about my ears." See "Crisis Seven," 21 November 1778, in *CW* 1:143-44 and Paine to a Committee of the Continental Congress, October 1783, in *CW* 2:1227.

Chapter 4

1. See David Hackett Fischer, *Paul Revere's Ride*.

2. Paine to a Committee of the Continental Congress, October 1783, in *CW* 2:1227.

3. "Orrery" takes its name from a planetarium built in the early eighteenth century by John Rowley for Charles Boyle, the fourth Earl of Orrery.

4. On Rush, see David Freeman Hawke, *Benjamin Rush: Revolutionary Gadfly*; Donald J. D'Elia, *Benjamin Rush: Philosopher of the American Revolution*; and John M. Kloos, Jr., *A Sense of Deity: The Republican Spirituality of Benjamin Rush*. For Rittenhouse, see Edward Ford, *David Rittenhouse: Astronomer-Patriot, 1732-1796* and Brook Hindle, *David Rittenhouse*.

5. Benjamin Rush, *Autobiography*, George W. Corner, ed., 113. See also L.H. Butterfield, ed., *The Letters of Benjamin Rush*, 2 vols., 1:95-96 and 2:1008.

6. A. Owen Aldridge, "The Influence of New York Newspapers on Paine's *Common Sense*," *New-York Historical Society Quarterly* 60 (Jan. 1976):53-60.

7. Paine to Henry Laurens, 14 January 1779, in *CW* 2:1163. For the characterization of Paine as an Old Whig, classical republican, see Beer, *To Make a Nation*, 206-09. For the various editions of the pamphlet, see Richard Gimbel, *Thomas Paine: A Bibliographical Checklist of "Common Sense"*. See also Bernard Bailyn, "The Most Uncommon Pamphlet of the Revolution: *Common Sense*," *American Heritage* 25 (Dec. 1973):36-41, 91-93.

8. Examples include James T. Boulton, *The Language of Politics in the Age of Wilkes and Burke*; Seamus Deane, *The French Revolution and Enlightenment in England, 1789-1832*, 164-67; Evelyn J. Hinz, "The 'Reasonable' Style of Tom Paine," *Queen's Quarterly* 79 (Summer

1972):231-41; Olivia Smith, *The Politics of Language, 1791-1819*; Wilson, *Paine and Cobbett*, Bruce Woodcock, "Writing the Revolution: Aspects of Thomas Paine's Prose," *Prose Studies* 15 (Aug. 1992):171-86. See also Foner, *Tom Paine and Revolutionary America*.

9. Gimbel estimated that in 1960's terms, given the population of the United States, the book would have sold over 6.5 million copies. By today's standards the total would probably be closer to ten million, clearly a bestseller.

10. Locke is also known as one of the founders of English empiricism. Studies of his work abound. See John Dunn, *The Political Philosophy of John Locke*, Richard Ashcraft, *Revolutionary Politics and Locke's Two Treatises of Government*, and more recently, John W. Marshall, *Resistance, Responsibility and Religion: The Thought of John Locke*. Locke's first *Treatise* was a response to the patriarchalism of Richard Filmer. On the concept of the "thinking" revolutionary, see Ralph Lerner, *The Thinking Revolutionary: Principle and Practice in the New Republic* and his sequel, *Revolutions Revisited: Two Faces of the Politics of Enlightenment*.

11. For the view of Paine as "a natural democrat," see Stanley Elkins and Eric McKitrick, *The Age of Federalism: The Early American Republic, 1788-1800*, 322-29, esp. 324.

12. On the theological foundations of *Common Sense*, see Stephen Newman, "A Note on *Common Sense* and Christian Eschatology," *Political Theory* 6 (Feb. 1978):101-08

13. John Locke, *Second Treatise of Government* (1690), C.B. Macpherson, ed., 111, 113.

14. On Paine's notion of authority in *Common Sense* and the *Crisis* series, see Edward H. Davidson and William J. Scheick, "Authority in Paine's *Common Sense* and the *Crisis Papers*," *Studies in the Humanities* 18 (Dec. 1991):124-34.

15. Paine's ideas about bridge construction are a good illustration of his headstrong ways. Never having studied architecture or engineering, he forged ahead anyway to design what he thought was an improvement in iron bridges. See Chapter 8.

16. On imagery and metaphor in *Common Sense*, see Jack Fruchtman, Jr., "Nature and Revolution in Paine's *Common Sense*," *History of Political Thought* 10 (Autumn, 1989):421-38 and Fruchtman, *Thomas Paine and the Religion of Nature*, Chapter 2. See also Molly Anne Rothenberg, "Parasiting America: The Radical Function of 'Heterogeneity' in Thomas Paine's Early Writings," *Eighteenth-Century Studies* 25 (Spring 1992):331-51.

17. Winthrop D. Jordan, "Familial Politics: Thomas Paine and the Killing of the King," *Journal of American History* 60 (Sept. 1973): 294-308.

18. Ironically, even President Ronald Reagan, who didn't understand the breadth of Paine's radicalism, frequently quoted Paine throughout 1981-84. See Jack Fruchtman, Jr., "Reagan's Paine: Would Tom Recognize Himself?" the *Baltimore Sun*, 9 October 1984, and "God and Politics: Notes from the Age of Reason," the *Baltimore Sun*, 30 October 1984. For an earlier assessment, see Isaac Kramnick, "Tom Paine: Radical Democrat," *democracy* 1 (Jan. 1981):127-38, reprinted in Kramnick's *Republicanism and Bourgeois Radicalism*, 133-60 and Kramnick, "Tommy Paine and the Idea of America," in Paul Korshin, ed., *The American Revolution and Eighteenth-Century Culture*, 75-91.

19. Franklin to Charles Lee, 19 February 1776, in *The Papers of Benjamin Franklin*, 22:357.

20. "The Forester" [Paine], "Letter II," (10 April 1776), in *CW* 2:67. See also his account of the printing history in his letter to Henry Laurens, 14 January 1779, in *CW* 2:1162-63. In McCusker's terms, Bell's charge to Paine of 30 pounds would translate into almost $1,500 in 1991 dollars. On the other hand, a penny was worth about 19 cents in today's values. See John J. McCusker, "How Much is That in Real Money? A Historical Price as a Deflator of Money Values in the Economy of the United States," *American Antiquarian Society Proceedings* 101 (Oct. 1991) 292-373.

21. Quoted in Foner, *Tom Paine and Revolutionary America*, 86.

22. Lee to Washington, in *The Papers of Benjamin Franklin*, 22:357, nt.9.

23. Cooper to Franklin, 21 March 1776, in *The Papers of Benjamin Franklin*, 22:388.

24. Quoted in Lessay, *L'Américain de la Convention*, 72-73.

25. See Henry F. May, *The Enlightenment in America*. See also A. Owen Aldridge, "Paine and Dickinson," *Early American Literature* 11 (Fall 1976):125-38.

Chapter 5

1. Quoted by Alexander DeConde, *The Quasi-War: The Politics and Diplomacy of the Undeclared War with France 1797-1801*, 4.

2. Butterfield, ed., *The Diary and Autobiography of John Adams*, 3:330, 331, 333. Adams's pamphlet was entitled *Thoughts on Government: Applicable to the Present State of the American colonies. In a Letter from a Gentleman to His Friend* (1776).

3. Butterfield, ed., *The Diary and Autobiography of John Adams*, 3:333-34.

4. Rush, *Autobiography*, 114. See Foner, *Tom Paine and Revolutionary America*, 108-18.

5. Paine wrote that the Americans would know what to do because "common sense will tell us." (*Common Sense*, 105) Meantime, Isaac Kramnick tells us that "it is in the realm of common sense that the pamphlet bogs down." See editor's introduction, *Common Sense*, 45. (I am grateful to James R. Stoner, Jr., for alerting me to this observation.)

6. See Aldridge, *Thomas Paine's American Ideology*, 179-90. The full title of Chalmers' pamphlet was *Plain Truth; Addressed to the Inhabitants of America, Containing Remarks on a late Pamphlet entitled Common Sense.*

7. "The Forester" [Paine], "Letter II," 10 April 1776, in *CW* 2:69-70.

8. Quoted by Foner in his introduction to "The Forester Letters," in *CW* 2:60.

9. "The Forester" [Paine], "Letter I," 3 April 1776, in *CW* 2:62-65. The falsehood that Paine complained about was what he considered to be Cato's narrow version of freedom of the press. In his curmudgeonly approach, Paine was a kind of eighteenth century Patrick Buchanan, though with more grace and elegance of style than the modern-day commentator.

10. "The Forester" [Paine], "Letter II," in *CW* 2:66. The emphasis is in the original.

11. "The Forester" [Paine], "Letter I," in *CW* 2:64.

12. "The Forester" [Paine], "Letter II," in *CW* 2:73-74.

13. "The Forester" [Paine], "Letter III," 24 April 1776, in *CW* 2:79-80, 82.

14. "The Forester" [Paine], "Letter IV," 8 May 1776, in *CW* 2:85. For the conclusive argument of Paine's authorship of the *Four Letters*, see Aldridge, *Thomas Paine's American Ideology*, 219-21. I have focused on "Letter IV," which is reprinted in Michael Kammen, ed., *The Origins of the American Constitution: A Documentary History*, 3-8.

15. Pocock, *The Machiavellian Moment*, passim.

16. [Paine], *Four Letters on Interesting Subjects*, "Letter IV," in Kammen, *The Origins of the American Constitution*, 3.

17. "Common Sense" [Paine], "To the People of America," 3 April 1782, in the *Pennsylvania Gazette*.

18. [Paine], "Letter IV," *Four Letters*, in Kammen, *The Origins of the American Constitution*, 4-8.

19. On the translation of *Common Sense*, see Alexandre Pochard to Benjamin Franklin, 11 October 1776, in *The Papers of Benjamin Franklin*, 22:656.

20. Paine, "Remarks on Gouverneur Morris's Funeral Oration on General Hamilton," 7 August 1804, in *CW* 2:959. By this time, Paine was totally disillusioned with George Washington, because, as President, he had not acted swiftly or strongly enough to help free Paine from the Luxembourg Prison.

21. See Henry Steele Commager, *The Empire of Reason: How Europe Imagined and America Realized the Enlightenment.*

22. Paine to Henry Laurens, 14 January 1779, in *CW* 2:1164. For the relationship between *Common Sense* and the *Crisis* series, see Manfred Pütz and Jon-K Adams, *A Concordance to Thomas Paine's "Common Sense" and "The American Crisis."*

23. Paine, *Letter to the Abbé Raynal, on the Affairs of North America: in which the Mistakes in the Abbé's Account of the Revolution of America are Corrected and Cleared Up* (1782), in *CW* 2:226. Abbé Raynal, in his *Révolution d'Amérique*, had asserted that the war with Britain was not about rights and liberties but rather about taxation. Paine's *Letter* was written years before his imprisonment and subsequent disillusionment with Washington. A classic study of Paine's pamphlet is Darrel Abel, "The Significance of the Letter to the Abbé Raynal in the Progress of Thomas Paine's Thought," *Pennsylvania Magazine of History and Biography* 66 (Apr. 1942):176-90. Abel's study was roundly criticized by A. Owen Aldridge in "La Signification historique, diplomatique et littéraire de la lettre addressé à l'abbé Raynal de Thomas Paine," *Études Anglaises* 8 (1955):223-32.

24. Paine to Laurens, 14 January 1779, in *CW* 2:1164. Foner's 1945 edition of Paine's writings contain sixteen pieces in *The American Crisis*, but Aldridge's discovery of two additional ones in the *Pennsylvania Gazette* brings the total to eighteen. Paine called the last one Number Thirteen in honor of the thirteen colonies. (He labeled some "Crisis Extraordinary" so the series would be numbered correctly at the end.) I follow the numbering and designation system Foner used with the exception of the two most recently found. Paine used the term *The American Crisis* to distinguish his work from a series of papers that appeared in London in 1775-76 under the "Crisis" title. See the previously cited Aldridge, "Some Writings of Thomas Paine in Pennsylvania Newspapers" and his *Thomas Paine's American Ideology*, 240.

25. Paine, "Crisis One," 23 December 1776, in *CW* 1:50.

26. Paine relates this in his letter to Laurens of 14 January 1779, in *CW* 2:1164.

27. Cited in Foner's introduction to *The American Crisis*, in *CW* 1:49.

28. Paine, "Crisis One," in *CW* 1:53, 56.

29. Paine, "Crisis Two," 13 January 1777, in *CW* 1:69, 59, 61, 62. " 'The United States of America,' " he said in using the term for the first time, "will sound as pompously in the world or in history as 'the kingdom of Great Britain.' " (*CW* 1:59-60)

30. Butterfield, ed., *The Diary and Autobiography of John Adams*, 3:334.

31. Paine, "Crisis Seven," 21 November 1778, in *CW* 2:143-44. Yet another moment when Paine used the image of the "country set on fire about my ears."

32. On the Paine-Adams rivalry in later years, see Chapter 19.

33. Paine to Franklin, 20 June 1777, in *CW* 2:1132

34. Paine, "Crisis Three," 19 April 1777, in *CW* 2:90. According to Foner, the Quaker mistress of George III was Hannah Lightfoot. See the editor's note by Foner for the above.

35. Paine to Lee, 1 July 1777, in *CW* 2:1133-35. A brother of Arthur, Richard Henry Lee later opposed the new constitution as a threat to states' rights, and served in the Senate from Virginia. He was an important voice in favor of the Bill of Rights when it was introduced in the first Federal Congress.

36. Paine to Franklin, 9 July 1777, in *CW* 2:1135-36.

37. Paine, "Crisis Four," 12 September 1777, in *CW* 1:105.

38. Paine to Franklin, 16 May 1778, in *CW* 2:1143-51.

39. Paine to Lee, 30 October 1777, in *CW* 2:1138-40. For Paine's ideas about recruiting soldiers for the army, see his "A Plan for Recruiting the Army," June 1780, in *CW* 2:208-10.

40. Recounted by Aldridge, *Man of Reason*, 56-57 and Hawke, *Paine*, 71-72.

41. Paine, "Crisis Five," 21 March 1778, in *CW* 1:106, 107, 114, 125, 127-29.

42. Paine, "To the Citizens of the United States, Particularly to the Leaders of the Federal Faction," "Letter III," in the *National Intelligencer*, 29 November 1802, in *CW* 2:922.

43. Butterfield, ed., *The Diary and Autobiography of John Adams*, 4:5-6.

Chapter 6

1. Paine to Laurens, 11 April 1778, in *CW* 2:1140-42.

2. "Common Sense" [Paine], "To Governor Johnstone, one of the British Commissioners, on his late letters and offers to bribe certain eminent characters in America, and threatening afterwards to appeal to the public," in the *Pennsylvania Packet*, 28 July 1778, reprinted by the indefatigable A. Owen Aldridge, "The Poetry of Thomas Paine," *Pennsylvania Magazine of*

History and Biography 79 (Jan. 1955):87-88. The minister was William Pitt the Elder, whose son—also William Pitt—himself later became the king's prime minister in 1783, serving until 1801, but called from retirement in 1804.

3. Paine, "To the Public," 13 June 1778, in the *Pennsylvania Gazette*, one of the "Crisis" papers, which Aldridge located ("Some Writings of Thomas Paine in Pennsylvania Newspapers").

4. Paine to Franklin, 24 October 1778, in *CW* 2:1154.

5. Paine, "Crisis Six," 20 October 1778, in *CW* 1:138-39.

6. Paine to Franklin, 24 October 1778, in *CW* 2:1153-54.

7. Paine, "To the King of England," (printed in America as "An Address to Lord Howe"), 14 November 1778, in the *Pennsylvania Packet*. Aldridge, who reprinted the entire poem in "The Poetry of Thomas Paine," 90-92, finds no reason why the title of the poem changed in America, because it was clearly addressed to George III, not Howe. Aldridge believes that this poem was Paine's best (93).

8. Paine, "Crisis Seven," 21 November 1778, in *CW*, 1:145, 146, 153.

9. Paine, "A Serious Address to the People of Pennsylvania, On the Present Situation of Their Affairs," 1 December 1778, the *Pennsylvania Packet*, in *CW* 2:277-302 and in John J. Meng, "Thomas Paine, French Propagandist in the United States," *Records of the American Catholic Historical Society* 57 (Mar. 1946):10-21. There were three additional pieces on this subject on 5, 10, and 12 December of that year, and while Paine promised more, clearly the Deane affair interfered with his good intentions.

10. Lee to Vergennes, 29 February 1776, quoted in Conway, *The Life of Thomas Paine*, 1:121.

11. The Committee of Secret Correspondence: Certificate for Silas Deane, 2 March 1776, in *The Papers of Benjamin Franklin*, 22:369. The other two members of the Committee were John Dickinson of Delaware and Benjamin Harrison of Virginia.

12. For his instructions, see The Committee of Secret Correspondence: Instructions to Silas Deane, 2 or 3 March 1776, in *The Papers of Benjamin Franklin*, 22:369-74. Two different dates are given in this collection.

13. For the story behind this bogus company, which was a creation of Beaumarchais, see Brian N. Morton, " 'Roderigue Hortalez' to the Secret Committee: An Unpublished French Policy Statement of 1777," *The French Review* 50 (May 1977):875-90. The two million French livres would be worth over $20 million in 1991 dollars. See Mark Mayo Boatner III, "Money of the 18th Century," in *Encyclopedia of the American Revolution*, Bicentennial Edition, 713-16, where, he says, five livres were in rounded terms worth one dollar, and twenty-five livres were worth one British pound sterling. I wish to thank Elizabeth Nuxoll and Mary Gallagher of *The Papers of Robert Morris* for their invaluable help with these equivalents.

14. Meng, "Thomas Paine, French Propagandist," 3. The bill, in today's terms, would be worth about $85 million.

15. Willing, Morris, and Company was dissolved on December 31, 1777, according to Morris. See Morris to John and Francis Baring, 17 April 1783, in *The Papers of Robert Morris*, E. James Ferguson, ed., 7 vols. to date, 7:715. For the company's involvement in commercial affairs, see the editors' note, 7:550-51.

16. Paine directly replied to Morris in his "Reply to Gouverneur Morris," 2 March 1779, in the *Pennsylvania Packet*, in *CW* 2:162-64.

17. See Francis Wharton, ed., *The Revolutionary Diplomatic Correspondence of the United States*, 6 vols.; Foner's comment, in *CW* 1:197, nt.4; and Carl Van Doren, *The Secret History of the American Revolution*, 62-63, 145-175, passim.

18. Silas Deane to Robert Morris, 10 June 1781, in *The Papers of Robert Morris*, 1:135, 137.

19. Silas Deane, in the *Pennsylvania Packet*, 5 December 1778.

20. "Common Sense" [Paine], "To Silas Deane, Esq're," 15 December 1778, in the *Pennsylvania Packet*, in *CW* 2:103.

21. Quoted by "Common Sense" [Paine], "To the Public on Mr. Deane's Affair," which appeared successively in five installments, 31 December 1778—2, 5, 7, 9 January 1779, in the *Pennsylvania Packet*, in *CW* 2:119, 127.

22. "Common Sense" [Paine], "To the Public on Robert Morris's Address," 12 January 1779, in the *Pennsylvania Packet*, in *CW* 2:136-37.

23. "Common Sense" [Paine], "To the Public on Mr. Deane's Affair," 5 January 1779, in the *Pennsylvania Packet*, in *CW* 2:123(emphasis added).

24. Conway, *The Life of Thomas Paine*, 1:127.

25. Paine to the Congress of the United States, 8 January 1779, in *CW* 2:1159. For the rest of his life, Paine considered his position of Secretary of the Committee for Foreign Affairs as one of the most important in his professional career. In his works, most notably in both parts of the *Rights of Man*, he often identified himself as Secretary, although he elevated the position, calling it "Secretary for Foreign Affairs to Congress in the American War."

26. "Comus" [Paine], in the *Pennsylvania Packet*, 16 March 1779.

27. A. Owen Aldridge, "Thomas Paine and Comus," *Pennsylvania Magazine of History and Biography* 85 (Jan., 1961):71-72. I have relied on this essay for information about Paine as Comus.

28. Paine to the Continental Congress, 23 April 1779, in *CW* 2:1175.

29. Meng, "Thomas Paine, French Propagandist," 5. See also the correspondence in Jules A. Baignée and John J. Meng, "Philadelphia and the Revolution: French Diplomacy in the United States, 1778-1779," *Records of the American Catholic Historical Society* 57 (Mar. 1946):23-40 and John J. Meng, "French Diplomacy in Philadelphia, 1778-1779," *Catholic Historical Review* 24 (Apr. 1938):39-57. According to McCusker's formula, in 1991 dollars, Paine would be paid around $7,756 per year as contrasted with Cooper's $5,000 and Brackenridge's $4,432. Gérard obviously thought that Paine was worth a bit more than the other two men. See McCusker, "How Much is That in Real Money?" 312-32.

30. Gérard to Vergennes, 17 January 1779, *Despatches and Instructions of Conrad Alexandre Gérard, 1778-1780 with An Historical Introduction and Notes*, John J. Meng, ed., for the Institut Français de Washington, 481. The equivalent in 1991 dollars would be about $12,000 per year.

31. Paine, "Messrs. Deane, Jay, and Gérard," 14 September 1779, in the *Pennsylvania Packet*, in *CW* 2:184.

32. Paine to Laurens, 14 January 1779, in *CW* 2:1161.

33. The claim is asserted in Meng, "Thomas Paine, French Propagandist," 1-8. The quotation is from "A Serious Address to the People of Pennsylvania," reprinted in Meng, 17. Paine also wrote about lawyers in the same vein: "It would be happiness to society if none but honest men were suffered to be lawyers."

34. Paine to Laurens, 17 January 1779, in *CW* 2:1165, including the quotation from Gérard's letter to Congress of 14 January 1779.

35. Paine to Major-General Nathanael Greene, 31 January 1779, in *CW* 2:1166 and to His Excellency General Washington, 31 January 1779, in *CW* 2:1167.

36. See Paine to Franklin, 4 March 1779, in *CW* 2:1167-69.

37. Jared Sparks, *The Life of Gouverneur Morris, with Selections from His Correspondence and Miscellaneous Papers*, 3 vols., 1:202. See Max M. Mintz, *Gouverneur Morris and the American Revolution*, 121, 107-37.

38. In one of the great turnabouts in American history, Congress had a change of heart in 1842 and granted $37,000 to the descendants of Silas Deane.

39. See Foner, *Tom Paine and Revolutionary America*, Chapter 5.

40. Paine to Laurens, 14 September 1779, in *CW* 2:1178-79.

41. See Foner, *Tom Paine and Revolutionary America*, 145-82. See also C. Page Smith, "The Attack on Fort Wilson," *Pennsylvania Magazine of History and Biography* 128 (Apr., 1954):177-88 and John K. Alexander, "The Fort Wilson Incident of 1779: A Case Study of the Revolutionary

Crowd," *William and Mary Quarterly*, 3rd Series, 31 (Oct. 1974):589-612.

42. Quoted in Aldridge, *Man of Reason*, 80.

43. Paine, "Crisis Eight," March 1780, in *CW* 1:158.

44. Quoted by Foner in *CW* 1:165.

45. Paine to McClenaghan, May 1780, in *CW* 2:1184. Paine's donation, about $5,500 in 1991 dollars, was a substantial amount.

46. McCusker admonishes that "the result of such calculation is better considered hypothetical rather than definitive." See his "How Much is That in Real Money?" 313 and Table A-3, 333.

47. Paine, "Crisis Nine," 9 June 1780, in *CW* 2:169.

48. Paine, "Crisis Extraordinary," 4 October 1780, in *CW* 1:186-88. His reference to the lady Providence is to be found in a photocopy of a letter from Paine to Nathanael Greene, 17 October 1780, in the Richard Gimbel Collection of Thomas Paine Manuscripts deposited in the American Philosophical Society, Philadelphia.

49. Paine, *Public Good: Being an Examination in the Claim of Virginia to the Vacant Western Territory, and of the Right of the United States to the Same: to which is Added Proposals for Laying off a New State, to be Applied as a Fund for Carrying on the War, or Redeeming the National Debt* (December 1780), in *CW* 2:303-33.

50. Paine to Greene, 9 September 1780, in *CW* 2:1188.

51. Quoted by Foner, in *CW* 2:171.

Chapter 7

1. Franklin to the Comte de Vergennes, in *The Writings of Benjamin Franklin*, Albert Henry Smyth, ed., 10 vols., 8:210.

2. Paine to Hutchinson, 11 March 1781, in *CW*, 2:1191-96.

3. Winslow C. Watson, ed., *Men and Times of the Revolution, or Memoirs of Elkanah Watson*, Second Edition, 127-28.

4. Franklin to the Marquis de Lafayette, 14 May 1781, in *The Writings of Benjamin Franklin*, 8:251.

5. Washington to Rev. William Gordon, 8 March 1785, in *The Writings of George Washington*, 28:97. Washington was reminiscing. John Laurens accompanied General Greene in a 1782 mop-up operation after Cornwallis' surrender and was killed in a minor clash with the few remaining British forces. See Sarah Bertha Townsend, *An American Soldier: The Life of John Laurens*.

6. Paine to Samuel Huntington, 12 March 1781, in *The Writings of Benjamin Franklin*, 8:220.

7.The monetary equivalents would equal about $60 million in grants and $100 million in loans in 1991 dollars.

8. Franklin to Marquis de Lafayette, in *The Writings of Benjamin Franklin*, 8:250.

9. Paine to a Committee of the Continental Congress, [October 1783] in *CW* 2:1235. The livres were worth about $25 million in 1991 dollars.

10. Paine to Robert Morris, 24 January 1782, in *CW* 2:1205-06.

11. Paine to Robert Morris, 7 February 1782, in *The Papers of Robert Morris*, 4: 185. See also Morris' diary entry for that date in 4:178. The memorial has never been located.

12. Paine to Col. John Laurens, 4 October 1781, in *CW* 2:1199.

13. Paine to Washington, 30 November 1781, in *CW* 2:1203-04.

14. Paine to a Committee of the Continental Congress, October 1783, in *CW* 2:1236.

15. Paine to Morris, 26 November 1781, in *CW* 2:1202.

16. See "Agreement with Robert R. Livingston and George Washington," 10 February 1782, in *The Papers of Robert Morris*, 4:201. The $800 would be worth about $10,000 in 1991 dollars.

17. Paine to Morris, 20 February 1782, in *CW* 2:1206-08.

18. Paine, "Crisis Ten," 5 March 1782, in *CW* 1:193, 207.

19. See Robert Morris' diary entries for 8 and 10 April 1782 in *The Papers of Robert Morris*, 4:537-38, 552-53. See also Paine to Morris, 7 April 1782, 4:535.

20. Paine, "To the People of America," 3 April 1782, in the *Pennsylvania Gazette*.

21. Paine to Washington, 17 March 1782, in *CW* 2:1209. Paine also wrote to Morris the same day, in *CW* 1:1210.

22. Paine, "Crisis Eleven," 22 May 1872, in *CW* 1:214.

23. Paine, "A Supernumerary Crisis," 31 May 1872, in *CW* 1:218.

24. Paine to Washington, 7 September 1782, in *CW* 2:1213.

25. Paine to Morris, 6 September 1782, in *CW* 2:1211.

26. Paine, *Letter to the Abbé Raynal*, in *CW* 2:220-21, 232 (emphasis in the original), 214, 256.

27. Paine, "A Supernumerary Crisis," 9 December 1783, in *CW* 1:239. The $300 would be worth about $4,000 in 1991 dollars.

28. Paine, "Crisis Twelve," 29 October 1782, in *CW* 1:223, 229 (emphasis in the original).

29. Georgia dragged its feet for a while but eventually came around. Rhode Island had no intention of complying, and never did.

30. Editors, *The Papers of Robert Morris*, 7:78-79.

31. Paine to Morris, 20 November 1782, in *CW* 2:1214. See also his letters to Morris, 7 December 1782 and 23 January 1783, in *CW* 2:1216-17.

32. Editors, *The Papers of Robert Morris*, 7:80-85 generally. The quotation from Howell is to be found on 7:80, and the information about Sweden on 7:89-90, nt.9. Howell obviously had access to this information as a member of Congress himself.

33. "Sincerus" [Paine], Letter in the *Freeman's Journal: or, North-American Intelligencer*, 2 July 1783. For an indication of Paine's support of the states' paying the debts that Congress incurred, see also "Extract of a Letter" in the *Pennsylvania Gazette*, 9 July 1783. I wish to thank Mary Gallagher of *The Papers of Robert Morris* for identifying these letters.

34. Paine, "Crisis Thirteen," 19 April 1783, in *CW* 1:230.

35. See also Paine, *To the Citizens of the United States*, Letter II, 19 November 1802, in *CW* 2:914.

36. Paine, "Crisis Thirteen," in *CW* 1:234-35 (emphasis added).

37. Paine to his Excellency Elias Boudinot, President of Congress, 7 June 1783, in *CW* 2:1217-18.

38. Paine to a Committee of Peters, Clarke, Hawke in the United States Congress, 26 [20?] June 1783, in the Richard Gimbel Collection of Thomas Paine Manuscripts deposited in the American Philosophical Society, Philadelphia.

39. Even more difficult was the amending process under the Articles: it took unanimous consent of the states to change any part of the document. The Articles of Confederation and the American Constitution are to be found in numerous texts and editions. Above all, see Gordon S. Wood's still magisterial *The Creation of the American Republic, 1776-1787*.

40. Paine recounted this years later in "The Cause of Yellow Fever," 27 June 1806, in *CW* 2:1062-63.

41. Washington to Paine, 10 September 1783, in *The Writings of George Washington*, John C. Fitzpatrick, ed., 39 vols., 27:146-47.

42. Paine to Washington, 2 October 1783, in *CW* 2:1224-25.

43. Paine to a Committee of the Continental Congress, October 1783, in *CW* 2:1226-42.

44. Paine to Duane, 3 December 1783, in *CW* 2:1244.

45. Paine, "A Supernumerary Crisis: To the People of America," 9 December 1783, in *CW* 1:238.

46. Paine's original house burned to the ground while he was in Paris in 1792. The house built in its place, and the one which he occupied after he returned to the United States in 1802, is still standing there, as is a national monument and a statue of Paine.

47. States differed in these late years in the use of currency. Some used their own pounds, others the Continental dollar, created by Congress in 1775. To determine equivalent value, McCusker suggests the conversion of state pounds into the British pound sterling, and then from that point converting it to dollars. The farm would be worth around a quarter of a million dollars in 1991 terms.

48. Washington separately to Madison and to Henry, 12 June 1784, *The Writings of George Washington*, 27:420-22.

49. Conway, *The Life of Thomas Paine*, 1:209. It would be worth around $25,000 in 1991.

50. Paine to the Congress of the United States, 27 September 1785, in *CW* 2:1252. The equivalent amount in 1991 dollars would be about $50,000.

Chapter 8

1. Paine to Morris, 16 February 1784, in *CW* 2:1246-47.

2. Paine to Washington, 28 April 1784, in *CW* 2:1248-49.

3. Paine, "Hail Great Republic," in *CW*, 2:1095-96. See Garry Wills, *Cincinnatus: George Washington and the Enlightenment*.

4. The Anti-Federalists, who worked hard in 1787-89 to see that a bill of rights was added to the American Constitution, might have originated as a reaction to the founding of the Society of the Cincinnatus and the creation of the Tammany Society. They opposed the new Constitution because it was too powerful, too centralized, and far too oriented toward national unity. See Herbert Storing, *What the Antifederalists Were For*. After 1787, Paine was in England and France, so we do not know for certain where he would have stood in the Federalist/Anti-federalist debate. At this point, he was clearly moving in the direction of the Federalist position.

5. Often called the father of New York State because of his gubernatorial victories, Clinton was also an Anti-Federalist, opposing the new Constitution in 1787 because he thought it diminished the power of the states. He was no relation to Sir Henry Clinton, the supreme commander of British forces in America after 1778.

6. Paine to the Congress of the United States, 27 September 1785, in *CW* 2:1251-52. It was not unusual that the states still used the British pound sterling for currency, while the Federal Government used the Continental dollar. See McCusker, "How Much is That in Real Money?"

7. Paine to Sir George Staunton, Bart., Spring 1789, in *CW* 2:1045.

8. Paine to Franklin, 23 September 1785, in *CW* 2:1250-51.

9. Paine to Franklin, 31 December 1785, in *CW* 2:1025.

10. Conway, "The Hall Manuscripts," in *The Life of Thomas Paine*, 2:461, 472, 460.

11. Paine to John Hall, 22 September 1785, in *CW* 2:1257.

12. It is now questionable whether Paine actually invented the idea of a pierless bridge or whether the idea came from the French architect, Vincent de Montpetit, or the English architect, Abraham Darby.

13. Paine to George Clymer, Esq., 19 November 1786, in *CW* 2:1258.

14. Paine to Staunton, in *CW* 2:1044-45.

15. Conway, "The Hall Manuscripts," in *The Life of Thomas Paine*, 2:465, 467. The cost of construction in 1991 dollars would be between $1-2 million.

16. Paine, *Dissertations on Government; The Affairs of the Bank; and Paper Money*, 1786, in *CW* 2:372, 376, 378, 381, 383, 384.

17. See Paine's letter to McClenaghan, May 1780, in *CW* 2:1183-85. See Chapter 5.

18. See Robert Middlekauf, *The Glorious Cause: The American Revolution, 1763-1789*, 656.

19. Paine, *Dissertations on Government*, in *CW* 2:386, 397.

20. Paine to Henry Laurens, 11 April 1778, in *CW* 2:1142.

21. See Pocock, *The Machiavellian Moment*, Chapter 13.

22. See Bray Hammond, *Banks and Politics in America from the Revolution to the Civil War*.

23. Paine, "Addressed to the Opposers of the Bank," 7 March 1787, in the *Pennsylvania Gazette*, in *CW* 2:435. On Paine's conscience, see his letter to Thomas Fitzsimmons, 19 April 1785, in the *Pennsylvania Gazette*, reprinted in A. Owen Aldridge, "Why Did Thomas Paine Write on the Bank?" *American Philosophical Society Proceedings* 93 (Sept. 1949):311.

24. Paine, "Addressed to the Opposers of the Bank," in *CW* 2:435.

25. Historians have debated for decades the issue of why Paine wrote in favor of the bank. One could argue with some assurance that Paine probably wrote out of conviction and that he therefore really did approve of the bank. He had supported such an institution in 1780, a year before it was even established, and he believed that only a bank would give America a sound financial base. In addition to the Aldridge citation in note 21 above, see M.L. Bradbury, "Legal Privilege and the Bank of North America," *Pennsylvania Magazine of History and Biography* 96 (Apr. 1972):139-66; Foner, *Tom Paine and Revolutionary America*; and Janet Wilson, "The Bank of North America and Pennsylvania Politics, 1781-1787," *Pennsylvania Magazine of History and Biography* 66 (Jan 1942):3-28.

26. Paine, *Dissertations on Government*, in *CW* 2:405.

27. See Aldridge, "Why did Paine Write on the Bank?" 311-12. I have followed Aldridge's argument that Paine's position touched on both the political and economic consequences of destroying the bank. Aldridge, however, did not place Paine's position in the context of Lockean liberalism and classical republicanism.

28. Paine, "To the Printers," *Letters on the Bank*, 4 April 1786, in the *Pennsylvania Packet*, in *CW* 2:418. Paine quoted Smilie, who spoke before the Assembly in Philadelphia. (Paine's greeting "To the Printers" indicates it was a letter to the editor. Paine named two of these letters to the editor as "I" and "II" in his *Letters on the Bank*.)

29. Paine, "To the Printers," *Letters on the Bank*, 7 April 1786, in the *Pennsylvania Packet*, in *CW* 2:422.

30. Paine, "To the Public," "Letter III," 20 April 1786, in the *Pennsylvania Packet*, in *CW* 2:426-27.

31. Paine, *Dissertations on Government*, in *CW* 2:405, 411, 412. See also Paine's discussion in his letter to the *Pennsylvania Gazette*, 8 November 1786, in Aldridge, "Why Did Paine Write on the Bank?" 312-13.

32. Paine, "On the Advantages of a Public Bank," *Letters on the Bank*, 20 June 1786, in the *Pennsylvania Packet*, in *CW* 2:432.

33. Paine, *Dissertations on Government*, in *CW* 2:397, 398, 407, 404, 392.

34. Conway, "The Hall Manuscripts," in *The Life of Thomas Paine*, 2:466.

35. Paine, "On the Affairs of State," in the *Pennsylvania Gazette*, 20 September 1786. See Aldridge, "Why Did Paine Write on the Bank?" 312.

36. Paine to Hall, 22 September 1786, in *CW* 2:1257; Paine to Clymer, 19 November 1786, in *CW* 2:1258; Paine to Fitzsimmons, 19 November 1796, in *CW* 2:1260.

37. Paine to Franklin, 31 March 1787, in *CW* 2:1260.

38. Franklin to the Duke de la Rochefoucauld, 15 April 1787, in *The Writings of Benjamin Franklin*, 9:565-66. See also Franklin to Le Veillard, 15 April 1787, 9:562; to Comte d'Estaing, 15 April 1787, 9: 566-67; to the Marquis de Chastellux, 17 April 1787, 9:568.

39. Paine to Franklin, 22 June 1787, in *CW* 2:1263. Franklin was so certain that Perronet was dead, he wrote to Jefferson: "I am so sorry for the death of M. Perronet on account of Mr. Paine, who would have been pleased and instructed by conferring with that ingenious and skillful artist on the subject of his bridge,and it was my intention to introduce him Mr. Perronet's acquaintance." Franklin to Jefferson, 19 April 1787, in *The Writings of Benjamin Franklin*, 9:574.

40. Franklin to Jefferson, 19 April 1787, in *The Writings of Benjamin Franklin*, 9:574-75.

41. Paine to Franklin, 31 March 1787, in *CW* 2:1261.

42. Paine, "Addressed to the Opposers of the Bank," in *CW* 2:433.

Chapter 9

1. In a letter to George Clymer, for example, on 29 December 1787, Paine wrote: "I intend staying here until the Spring, and embarking for America in the April or May packet." See *CW* 2:1267

2. Paine to Franklin, 22 June 1787, in *CW* 2:1262.

3. Paine to Franklin, 22 June 1787, in *CW* 2:1262.

4. See his letter to the Royal Academy of Sciences, 21 July 1787, in *CW* 2:1263-64; to Sir George Staunton, Bart., spring of 1789, in *CW* 2:1041; to Clymer, 15 August 1787, in *CW* 2:1264.

5. Paine to Jefferson, 9 September 1788, in *CW* 2:1271.

6. Marie Jean Antoine Nicolas de Caritat, the Marquis de Condorcet, most likely committed suicide in prison in 1794 during the Terror, although there is some speculation he might have died of exhaustion.

7. Paine, *Prospects on the Rubicon*, in *CW* 2:632. See Simon Schama, *Patriots and Liberators: Revolution in the Netherlands, 1780-1813*.

8. Quoted by Aldridge, *Man of Reason*, 129. For Burke's support of the Americans, see his "Speech on American Taxation," 19 April 1774, in *The Writings and Speeches of Edmund Burke: Party, Parliament, and the American Crisis, 1766-1774*, Paul Langford, ed., 8 vols. to date, 2:406-63.

9. Paine recounted in the preface to the *Rights of Man* his correspondence with the secretary of the Archbishop, but did not identify him. It may have been the Abbé Morellet, whom he identified in an unpublished letter to Edmund Burke in 1788 (see the *Rights of Man*, 36-37).

10. Paine to Burke, August 1787, reprinted in A. Owen Aldridge, "Thomas Paine, Edmund Burke and Anglo-French Relations in 1787," *Studies in Burke and His Time* 12 (Spring 1971):1851-55. Aldridge's position that Paine's distinction between government and society was derived from Rousseau is inaccurate. Paine was articulating a well-known theory of John Locke. He did not encounter Rousseau's ideas until after 1789.

Aldridge repeated the error in his essay "*The Rights of Man* de Thomas Paine: Symbole du siècle des lumières et leur influence en France," in *Utopie et institutions au XVIIIe siècle: Le Pragmatisme des Lumières*, Pierre Francastel, ed., 283-84.

11. See Foner's assessment in *CW* 1:246, nt.2, where he claims that the letter from Jefferson to Paine has not been found, and Burke's response was to do nothing, though he never commented on the letter. Paine's letter to Burke, 7 August 1788, may be found in the Richard Gimbel Collection of Thomas Paine Manuscripts deposited in the American Philosophical Society, Philadelphia.

12. Paine to Jefferson, 19 February 1788, in *CW* 2:1268.

13. Paine to Clymer, 29 December 1787, in *CW* 2:1266.

14. Paine to Jefferson, Spring 1788, in *CW* 2:1298-99.

15. Jefferson to Paine, 23 December 1788, *The Papers of Thomas Jefferson*, Julian P. Boyd, ed., 25 vols. to date, 14:373.

16. Paine, "Crisis 12," 29 October 1782, in *CW* 1:229. See above, Chapter 7.

17. Paine to Jefferson, 9 September 1788, in *CW* 2:1271. Paine is allegedly quoting Lansdowne.

18. Paine to Jefferson, 16 February 1789, in *CW* 2:1283. Hawke corrects Foner's misdating of this letter. See Hawke, *Paine*, 433nt.

19. Gouverneur Morris, *A Diary of the French Revolution*, Beatrix Cary Davenport, ed., 2 vols., 1:516, 389.

20. Conway, *The Life of Thomas Paine*, 1:271.

21. Mintz, *Gouverneur Morris and the American Revolution*, 205-06.

22. Morris, *A Diary of the French Revolution*, 1:xli.

23. For a copy of the patent, see "Specification of Thomas Paine," in *CW* 2:1031-34. For the registration, see Paine to Jefferson, 9 September 1788, in *CW* 2:1268.

24. Paine to Jefferson, 9 September 1788, in *CW* 2:1269. A few months later, Paine wrote to Walker that "as a republican I think that the British constitution is a hodge-podge." Paine to Walker, 16 January 1789, in the Richard Gimbel Collection of Thomas Paine Manuscripts deposited in the American Philosophical Society, Philadelphia. See W.H.G. Armytage, "Thomas Paine and the Walkers: An Early Episode in Anglo-American Co-operation," *Pennsylvania History* 18 (Jan. 1951):16-30.

25. Paine to Kitty Nicholson Few, 6 January 1789, in *CW* 2:1274-77.

26. Paine to Walker, 26 February 1789, in *CW* 2:1278-81. Paine to Jefferson, in a letter over several weeks, 16, 26 February, 12 March 1789, in *CW* 2:1281-84 and Paine to Jefferson, 10 April 1789, in *CW* 2:1287-88.

27. Paine to Jefferson, 17 June 1789, in *CW* 2:1291; Paine to Jefferson, 13 July 1789, in *CW* 2:1294.

28. Paine to Jefferson, 15 September 1789, in *CW* 2:1295.

29. Jefferson to Paine, 11 July 1789, *The Papers of Thomas Jefferson*, 15:269. See Chapter 10 below.

30. Paine to Rush, 16 March 1790, in *CW* 2:1285. Foner dates this letter a year earlier and did not know to whom it was addressed. Hawke updates it and identifies the addressee as Dr. Benjamin Rush, the Philadelphia physician and political writer (see Hawke, *Paine*, 202).

31. Paine, "The Construction of Iron Bridges," 3 January 1803, in *CW* 2:1054-55.

32. See Georges Lefebvre, *The Great Fear of 1789: Rural Panic in Revolutionary France*, Joan White, trans.

33. See Jacques Revel, "Great Fear" and François Furet, "Night of August 4," in *A Critical Dictionary of the French Revolution*, 74-80, 107-113, respectively.

34. See Aldridge, *Man of Reason*, 125-26.

35. Alfred Cobban, ed., *The Debate on the French Revolution, 1789-1800*, second edition, 55.

36. The best book on the Paris context is the previously cited, Erdman, *Commerce des Lumières*. Christie's response, *Letters on the Revolution in France and the New Constitution Established by the National Assembly*, was as radical as Paine's though in a less lively style. It appeared in the spring of 1791.

37. Paine to [Rush], 16 March 1790, in *CW* 2:1285-86. Although this letter is printed in Foner's collection as addressed to "Anonymous," Hawke proved that Foner had misidentified the date and the recipient (Hawke, *Paine*, note on 434). See Paine to Jefferson, 10 April 1789, in *CW* 2:1288.

38. Paine to Washington, 1 May 1790, in *CW* 2:1303.

39. Paine to Washington, 31 May 1790, in *CW* 2:1304.

40. On Burke generally, see especially O'Brien, *The Great Melody* and Carl B. Cone, *Burke and the Nature of Politics*, 2 vols. A new biography on Burke by Fred P. Lock is forthcoming. See Lock's *Burke's Reflections on the Revolution in France*.

41. See Paine to Short, several letters in June 1790, in CW 2:1306-14 and the historical background provided by Harold W. Landin, "Some Letters of Thomas Paine and William Short on the Nootka Sound Crisis," *Journal of Modern History* 13 (Sept. 1941):367-74.

Chapter 10

1. See J. G. A. Pocock's edition of Edmund Burke, *Reflections on the Revolution in France* (1790), vii. I have used this edition for this study.

2. Edmund Burke, *Speech on Conciliation with the Colonies* (1775), introduction by Jeffrey Hart.

3. The theoretical and rhetorical differences are explored in R.R. Fennessy, *Burke, Paine, and the Rights of Man: A Difference of Political Opinion*; Tom Furniss, "Rhetoric in Revolution: the Role of Language in Paine's Critique of Burke," in Keith Hanley and Raman Selden, eds., *Revolution and English Romanticism: Politics and Rhetoric*, 23-48; and John Turner, "Burke, Paine, and the Nature of Language," in J.R. Watson, guest ed., *The Yearbook of English Studies: The French Revolution and English Literature and Art, Special Number*, 19:36-53. See also Francis Canavan, S.J., "The Relevance of the Burke-Paine Controversy to American Political Thought, *Review of Politics* 49 (Spring 1987):163-76; John C. Whale, "The Limits of Paine's Revolutionary Literalism," in Kelvin Everest, *Revolution in Writing: British Literary Responses to the French Revolution*, 121-37; and Whale, "Literal and Symbolic Representation: Burke, Paine, and the French Revolution," *History of European Ideas* 16 (Jan. 1993):343-49.

4. For some of the more fascinating assessments of Burke, see Tom Furniss, *Edmund Burke's Aesthetic Ideology: Language, Gender and Political Economy in Revolution* and Isaac Kramnick, *The Rage of Edmund Burke: The Conscience of an Ambivalent Conservative*.

5. Burke to the Earl of Charlemont (James Canfeild), 9 August 1789, in *The Correspondence of Edmund Burke*, Thomas W. Copeland, ed., 10 vols., 6:10.

6. Burke to Windham, 27 September 1789, in *The Correspondence of Edmund Burke*, 6:25.

7. Burke to Depont, November 1789, in *Correspondence*, 6:46 and the whole letter 39-50. For an analysis of Burke's claim that Marie Antoinette's chambers were "penetrated" by the mobs storming Versailles and she was forced to flee practically naked, see Tom Furniss, "Stripping the Queen: Edmund Burke's Magic Lantern Show," in Steven Blakemore, ed., *Burke and the French Revolution: Bicentennial Essays*, 69-96.

8. On Price, see D.O. Thomas, *The Honest Mind: The Thought and Work of Richard Price* and Martin Fitzpatrick, "Richard Price and the London Revolution Society," *Enlightenment and Dissent* 10 (1991):35-50. On Priestley, see Clarke Garrett, *Respectable Folly: Millenarians and the French Revolution in France and England*. For both, see Jack Fruchtman, Jr., *The Apocalyptic Politics of Richard Price and Joseph Priestley*.

9. Richard Price, *Discourse on the Love of Our Country, Delivered on*

November 4, 1789 at the Meeting House in the Old Jewry, to the Society for Commemorating the Revolution in Great Britain (1790), 39, 40.

10. Paine to Thomas Christie, 16 April 1790, in *CW* 2:1300. According to Thomas W. Copeland, this letter was addressed to Thomas Christie. See his *Our Eminent Friend Edmund Burke: Six Essays*, 176, nt.52. The Foner edition attributes the letter to Anonymous.

11. Cobban, ed., *The Debate on the French Revolution*, 158.

12. The question of how much information Burke had about France when he wrote the *Reflections* was a historical enigma until the publication of a previously unpublished letter from Paine to Burke. Burke was criticized for not having sufficient knowledge of the events in France to write anything about them by not only Paine but also by James Mackintosh, who later, like Paine, responded to Burke. Certainly, Burke had some information from his political acquaintances, including Sir George Staunton and William Windham and perhaps, unwittingly, Thomas Paine. See Boyd, *The Papers of Jefferson*, 15: 266-69 and J. T. Boulton, "An Unpublished Letter from Paine to Burke," *Durham University Journal* 43 (Mar. 1951):49-50, and Copeland, *Our Eminent Friend*, 146-77. A photocopy of the original may be found in the Richard Gimbel Collection of Thomas Paine Manuscripts deposited in the American Philosophical Society, Philadelphia.

13. Paine to Christie, 16 April 1790, in *CW* 2:1302. On the Paine-Burke relationship during this period, see Copeland, *Our Eminent Friend*, Chapter 5.

14. Burke, "Speech on Army Estimates," 9 February 1790, in O'Brien, *The Great Melody*, 397-98.

15. Pocock, editor's introduction, in Burke's *Reflections on the Revolution in France*, vii.

16. Burke, "Speech on Toleration Bill," 17 March 1773, in *The Writings and Speeches of Edmund Burke*, 2:389.

17. Burke, *Reflections*, 10, 78.

18. See Isaac Kramnick, *Bolingbroke and His Circle: The Politics of Nostalgia in the Age of Walpole.*

19. Burke, *Reflections*, 14, 66.

20. Pocock, editor's introduction, xxxii.

21. Burke, *Reflections*, 54, 75, 51, 69, 77, and 193. See also Burke, *Two Letters on a Regicide Peace* (1796), in *The Writings and Speeches of Edmund Burke: The Revolutionary War, 1794-1797; Ireland*, R.B. McDowell, ed., 9:187-296. On Burke's famous reference to "the swinish multitude," Pocock apologizes thus: "Burke may not have meant that *the* multitude— i.e., the poor—were swinish; only that there were always plenty of swine to be found" (see Pocock, editor's introduction, 223, nt.liv).

Chapter 11

1. A dozen years ago, Gayle Trusdel Pendleton demonstrated that the debate ranged far wider than it was ever thought, with over 4,000 responses literally creating a sub-culture of political debate. See her "Towards a Bibliography of the *Reflections* and *Rights of Man* Controversy," *Bulletin of Research in the Humanities* 85 (Spring 1982):65-103. Her appendix reproduces some 340 titles. For the wider responses, see Gregory Claeys, "Republicanism versus Commercial Society: Paine, Burke, and the French Revolution," *Society for the Study of Labour History Bulletin* 54 (Winter 1989):4-13.

2. Quoted in Browne, *The Celtic Cross*, 87-88. For Wollstonecraft, see Virginia Sapiro, *A Vindication of Political Virtue: The Political Theory of Mary Wollstonecraft*, 196-222, and for Mackintosh, see Lionel A. McKenzie, "The French Revolution and English Parliamentary Reform: James Mackintosh and the *Vindiciae Gallicae*," *Eighteenth-Century Studies* 14 (Spring 1981):264-82. For Paine's misrepresentation of what Burke actually said in the *Reflections*, see Strother B. Purdy, "A Note on the Burke-Paine Controversy," *American Literature* 39 (Nov. 1967):373-75.

3. Paine to Walker, 14 April 1790, in the Richard Gimbel Collection of Thomas Paine Manuscripts deposited in the American Philosophical Society, Philadelphia. The emphasis is in the original.

4. See Claeys, *Thomas Paine*; Fennessy, *Burke, Paine and the Rights of Man*; and Gary Kates, "From Liberalism to Radicalism: Tom Paine's Rights of Man," *Journal of the History of Ideas* 50 (Oct., 1989):569-87. Despite his radicalism, Paine, as a member of the National Convention in 1793, vehemently and openly opposed the execution of King Louis XVI, and this contributed to his own incarceration.

5. James Madison, "Federalist, Number 51," (1788) in Kammen, ed., *The Origins of the American Constitution*, 203.

6. For an account of the affair, see *The Papers of Thomas Jefferson*, 20:268-313, especially 270-89. For Jefferson's claim that he did not know Jonathan Bayard Smith, see his letter to George Washington, 8 May 1791, in Boyd, 20:291. For the unauthorized preface, see Boyd, 20:272.

7. For the context of this incident, see Elkins and McKitrick, *The Age of Federalism*, 236-40.

8. Paine to Jefferson, 19 July 1791 and 29 July 1791, in *The Papers of*

Thomas Jefferson, 20:308-09, 312-13.

9. See Paine to Washington, 21 July 1791, in *CW*, 2: 1318-20 and Washington to Paine, 6 May 1792, *The Writings of George Washington*, 21:120-21.

10. Paine, "Letters to the Citizens of the United States," Letter I, 15 November 1802, in the *National Intelligencer*, in *CW* 2:910.

11. Mornington to Grenville, 3 July 1791, in William Wyndham Grenville, Royal Historical Manuscripts Commission, Fourteenth Report, Appendix, Part V, *The Manuscripts of J.B. Fortescue, Esq., Preserved at Dropmore*, 10 vols., 2:120. Grenville served as Interior Minister (Home Secretary) from 1789 to 1791, and thereafter he was Foreign Minister until 1801.

12. Morris, "Entry for April 16, 1791," *A Diary of the French Revolution*, 2:163.

13. Condorcet, a famous mathematician and secretary of the French Academy, was a firm believer in the inevitable progress of all humanity. According to Keith M. Baker, Condorcet "embodied the convergence between the values and interests of organized science and those of the reforming state." See Keith M. Baker, "Condorcet," in *A Critical Dictionary of the French Revolution*, edited by François Furet and Mona Ozouf and translated by Arthur Goldhammer, 204, 204-12 generally. For Paine and Condorcet's parallel ideas and Paine's relations with other French "philosophes," see A. Owen Aldridge, "Condorcet et Paine: Leurs rapports intellectuels," *Revue de littérature comparée*, 32 (Jan. 1958):47-65 and Aldridge, "Thomas Paine and the idéologues," *Studies in Voltaire and the Eighteenth Century*, Transactions of the Fourth International Congress on the Enlightenment 151 (1976):109-17.

14. Quoted in Conway, *The Life of Thomas Paine*, 1:306.

15. Rickman, *Life of Thomas Paine*, 84.

16. Quoted by Conway, *The Life of Thomas Paine*, 1:307 from the *London Morning Chronicle*, 22 June 1791. On Christie, see Ann Thomson, "Thomas Christie, Paine et la révolution française," in Bernard Vincent, ed., *Thomas Paine, ou la république sans frontières*, 17-32.

17. This story appears in Chalmers' unflattering, hostile biography of Paine, and is repeated by virtually all Paine biographers. Some argue that Paine talked his way out of the crowd's wrath, others that Christie did, or that even a "badaud" (a fellow) came along and quieted the throng. For the latter, see Vincent, *Thomas Paine*, 208.

18. Cited in Conway, *The Life of Thomas Paine*, 1:307. According to her biographer, Thiérry Boissel, Sophie de Condorcet was also heavily involved in the formation of the Republican Society and just about everything else her husband did. See his *Sophie de Condorcet: Femme des* *lumières, 1764-1822.* See also Jean-Paul de Lagrave, "Thomas Paine et les Condorcet," in Bernard Vincent, ed., *Thomas Paine, ou la république sans frontières,* 57-64.

19. Paine to Messieurs Condorcet, Nicolas de Bonneville, and Lanthenas, June 1791, in *CW* 2:1315-18.

20. Thomas Paine, "A Republican Manifesto," 1 July 1791, in *CW* 2:517, 518.

21. Paine, "Reasons for Preserving the Life of Louis Capet," 15 January 1793, in *CW* 2:552.

22. For a contemporary facsimile edition, see Condorcet, *Le Républicain.*

23. [Paine and Condorcet], "Answer to Four Questions on the Legislative and Executive Powers," in *Chronique du mois,* June and July 1792, in *CW* 2:533.

24. Thomas Paine, "To the Abbé Sieyès," 16 July 1791, in *Le Républicain,* in *CW* 2:520. See R.C. De Prospo, "Paine and Sieyès," *Thought* 65 (June 1990):190-202.

25. Joseph Lakanal, *Journal des Patriotes de 1789,* 1er mars 1796, quoted by Vincent, *Thomas Paine,* 213. Nothing was produced by the members of the Committee of Public Instruction. Their work was interrupted by the onset of the Terror. See Sapiro, *A Vindication of Political Virtue,* 32 and Catherine Kintzler, *Condorcet: L'instruction publique et la naissance du citoyen.*

26. Etienne Dumont, *Souvenirs sur Mirabeau, et sur les deux premières assemblées legislatives,* 331-32. I appreciate the information on Lord Daer, which I received from John O'Neill of Hamilton College, Barry C. Noonan of the University of Wisconsin, Irwin Primer of Rutgers, Scott Veitch of Macquarie University School of Law, and Eric Walker of Florida State.

27. Gower to Grenville, 8 July 1791, in *The Manuscripts of J.B. Fortescue, Esq.,* 2:128.

28. Eugene Charlton Black, *The Association: British Extraparliamentary Political Organization, 1769-1793.*

29. See [Chalmers], *Life of Thomas Paine,* passim.

30. There were two editions. The first in 1791 did not mention Paine's drinking habits, mention of which appeared in the 1793 edition.

31. [Thomas Paine], "Address and Declaration at a Select Meeting of the Friends of Universal Peace and Liberty, Held at the Thatched House Tavern, St. James' Street, August 20, 1791," in *CW* 2:535-37. The "Address," when published, was signed by John Horne Tooke as SCI's chairman, but Paine wrote this tract.

32. See Chapter 13.

Chapter 12

1. Paine to Jordan, 16 February 1792, in *CW* 2:1324. See Ian Harris, "Burke and Paine: God, Nature and Politics," in *Public and Private Domaine: Essays in British History Presented to Sir Malcolm Cowling*, Michael Bentley, ed., 34-62, for a study of the metapolitics of the Burke-Paine controversy.

2. Cited in Aldridge, *Man of Reason*, 169. For the publication history of the *Rights of Man* in French translation, see Aldridge, "*The Rights of Man* de Thomas Paine," 277-87.

3. For a broad reading of the Burke-Paine controversy that goes beyond the texts, see Mark Philp, "The Role of America in the 'Debate on France' 1791-5: Thomas Paine's Insertion," *Utilitas* 5 (Nov. 1993):221-37 and Gregory Claeys, "The French Revolution Debate and British Political Thought," *History of Political Thought* XI (Spring 1990):59-80. Philp provides a careful argument against Kates' assessment that Paine moved from liberalism to radicalism in the period between the publication of the two parts of the *Rights of Man*.

4. For the citation, see the *Rights of Man*, 94 and Paine, "An Essay for the Use of New Republicans in their Opposition to Monarchy," 20 October 1792, in *Le Patriote français*, in *CW*, 2:543. Cobban, *Aspects of the French Revolution*, 152. See also Harry Hayden Clark, "Thomas Paine's Relation to Voltaire and Rousseau," *Revue anglo-américaine* (Apr. 1932):305-318 and (June 1932):393-405.

5. See A. Owen Aldridge, "Condorcet, Paine and Historical Method," in *Condorcet Studies*, Leonora Cohen Rosenfield, ed., 1:49-60. For a comparative study of the revolutionary and theological ideas of Paine and Blake, see David Bindman, " 'My own mind is my own church': Blake, Paine and the French Revolution," in Alison Yarrington and Kelvin Everest, eds., *Reflections of Revolution: Images of Romanticism*, 112-33.

6. Carol Blum, *Rousseau and the Republic of Virtue: The Language of Politics in the French Revolution*, 71-72. Blum shows how Rousseauist ideas permeated French revolutionary thought, literature, and drama, especially after Rousseau's death in 1778.

7. Cited in the original French in Vincent, *Thomas Paine*, 223.

8. Paine to Anonymous, [1789], in *CW* 2:1297. Foner has misdated this letter. Given its language, it was written later than 1789, probably as Paine was writing the second part of the *Rights of Man*.

9. For the view that Paine consciously turned the debate in 1792 away from France and onto America by focusing on his adopted land in Part Two of the *Rights of Man*, see Philp, "The Role of America in the 'Debate on France,' " passim.

10. Jean-Jacques Rousseau, *On the Social Contract, Or Principles of Political Right*, in *The Basic Writings*, Donald A. Cress, trans., 154.

11. See Paine, *Common Sense*, 82, where he wrote that "the sun never shined on a cause of greater worth. . . . 'Tis not the concern of a day, a year, or an age; posterity are virtually involved in the contest, and will be more or less affected, even to the end of time."

12. Burke has been confined to the preface only.

13. Paine was not alone in this radical shift from politics to society. Thomas Spence, for one, also considered these ideas. See Marcus Wood, "Thomas Spence and Modes of Subversion," *Enlightenment and Dissent* 10 (1991):51-77; H.T. Dickinson, *British Radicalism and the French Revolution: 1789-1815*; and Iain McCalman, *The Radical Underworld*. The classic Marxist interpretation remains that of E.P. Thompson, *The Making of the English Working Class*.

14. See Boissel, *Sophie de Condorcet*, 143-46.

15. Pocock, "Political Thought in the English-speaking Atlantic, 1760-1790. Part 2: Empire, Revolution and the End of Early Modernity," in *The Varieties of British Political Thought*, 307.

16. The story is recounted in Vincent, *Thomas Paine*, 230.

17. See Conway, "The Hall Manuscripts," in *The Life of Thomas Paine*, 2:472.

18. Quoted by Foner, editor's note, in *CW* 2:443. See Clive Emsley, "Repression, 'Terror,' and the Rule of Law in England During the Decade of the French Revolution," *English Historical Review* 100 (Oct. 1985):805-77 for discussion of Paine as a target of the proclamation and the general context of the times.

19. Quoted in Boyd, *Papers of Jefferson*, 20:270.

20. Cobban, ed., *Debate on the French Revolution*, 273-74.

21. See Paine to the Attorney General, n.d., in *CW* 2:443-45. The year before, Paine had accused Burke of being on a pension. (*RM* 119)

22. Paine to Mr. Secretary Dundas, 6 June 1792, in *CW* 2:446-57.

23. Dundas to Grenville, 2 September 1792, in *Manuscripts of J.B. Fortescue, Esq.*, 2:308.

24. Paine to Cranley, 17 June 1792, in *CW* 2:460.

25. Paine to Cranley, 21 June 1792, in *CW* 2:463.

26. Paine to the Sheriff of the County of Sussex, 30 June 1792, in *CW* 2:466.

27. Quoted in full in *Thomas Paine, Citoyen du monde*, textes reunis par Georges Kantin et la Ligue des Droits de l'Homme, 41. See this collection, which is in both French and English, for short essays on Paine's role during the Revolution.

28. John Goldworth Alger, *Englishmen in the French Revolution*, 171.

29. Séchelles to Paine, in Conway, "The Cobbett Papers," *The Life of Thomas Paine*, 2:439.

30. Paine, "Address to the People of France," 25 September 1792, in *CW* 2:538-40.

31. Mason to Burges, 13 September 1792, in *Manuscripts of J.B. Fortescue, Esq.*, 2:316-17. See also the detailed account in Fortolis, *Les Anglais en France*, 19-25.

32. Paine, *Letter Addressed to the Addressers on the Late Proclamation*, 1792, in *CW* 2:507. His letter to Dundas was dated 15 September 1792, in *CW* 2:466-69.

33. George Munro to Lord Gower, September 1792, in Oscar Browning, ed., *The Despatches of Earl Gower, English Ambassador at Paris from June 1790 to August 1792, To Which are Added The Despatches of Mr. Lindsay and Mr. Munro, and the Diary of Viscount Palmerston in France During July and August 1791*, 250. Munro used the French spelling of Paine's name ("Payne") and misspelled Priestley's ("Priestly").

Chapter 13

1. See, for example, François Furet, *Rethinking the French Revolution*, Elborg Forster, trans.; Mona Ozouf, *Festivals and the French Revolution*, Alan Sheridan, trans.; and Simon Schama's popular *Citizens: A Chronicle of the French Revolution*. These works stand in conflict with the more conventional interpretation of the period to be found in the *Annales* school of Albert Soboul and Georges Lefebvre.

2. See Furet and Ozouf, eds., *A Critical Dictionary of the French Revolution*, passim. For the changing nature of Robespierre's thought and activities in these years, Alfred Cobban's studies have retained their value and interest. See his two essays: "The Fundamental Ideas of Robespierre" and "The Political Ideas of Maximilien Robespierre during the Convention," in *Aspects of the French Revolution*, 136-91.

3. Cobban, *Aspects of the French Revolution*, 182.

4. Robert Darnton, "A Spy in Grub Street," in *The Literary Underground of* *the Old Regime*, 41-70.

5. See Helen-Maria Williams's account in her *Letters Containing a Sketch of the Politics of France from the Thirty-First of May 1793 till the 10th of Thermidor, Twenty-Eighth of July 1794 and of the Scenes which have Passed in the Prisons of Paris*, 3 vols., 2:21-22. On Williams, see Gary Kelly, *Women, Writing and Revolution 1790-1827*.

6. See Madeleine Rebérioux, "Anacharsis Cloots, The Other Citizen of the World," in *Thomas Paine, Citoyen du monde*, 31-40.

7. See R.R. Palmer, "Thomas Paine—Victim of the Rights of Man," *Pennsylvania Magazine of History and Biography* 46 (Apr. 1942):161-75. Some nineteen foreigners were elected to the convention at the same time. They included George Washington, James Madison, Alexander Hamilton, and Joseph Priestley.

8. See James H. Billington, *Fire in the Minds of Men: Origins of the Revolutionary Faith*, 34.

9. On the sans-culottes, see Albert Soboul, *The Sans-Culottes: The Popular Movement and Revolutionary Government, 1793-1794*, Rémy Inglis Hall, trans.; R.B. Rose, *The Making of the Sans-Culottes: Democratic Ideas and Institutions in Paris, 1798-1792*. Soboul's important study with its Marxist interpretation was first published in Paris in 1958.

10. Blum, *Rousseau and the Republic of Virtue*, passim.

11. See Paine, "Reasons for Preserving the Life of Louis Capet," 15 January 1793, in *CW* 2:555.

12. Originally published in 1941, the classic study in English remains R.R. Palmer, *Twelve Who Ruled: The Year of the Terror in the French Revolution*.

13. Blum, *Rousseau and the Republic of Virtue*, 170.

14. Quoted in Howell, "The Trial of Thomas Hardy for High Treason," *State Trials*, 24:535-36. For the context of these trials and the British environment generally during the Revolution, see the essays in Mark Philp, ed., *The French Revolution and British Popular Politics*, especially Philp's introduction, 1-17.

15. Paine, "Address to the People of France," 25 September 1792, in *CW* 2:537-40, and *Common Sense* 63.

16. See Lessay, *L'Américain de la Convention*, 146-47 for an elaboration of this view.

17. Paine, "Answer to Four Questions," (June-July 1792) in the *Chronique du mois*, translated by Condorcet, in *CW* 2:527. The *Chronique du mois* was the principal organ of the Social Circle of Bonneville and Condorcet.

18. Quoted by Vincent, *Thomas Paine*, 245.

19. Paine, "An Essay for the Use of New Republicans in Their Opposition to Monarchy," in Le Patriote français, 20 October 1792, in *CW* 2:541-47.

20. For the curious history of the Trumbull portrait, see Theodore Sizer, "Tom Paine's Portrait," *Yale University Library Gazette* 30 (Apr. 1956):139-42.

21. For names and activities of Americans like Barlow living and working in Paris, supporting the revolution, see Yvon Bizardel, *Les Américains à Paris pendant la révolution* and his list in *Bottin des Américains à Paris sous Louis XVI et pendant la révolution*. See also Bernard Vincent, "Les Américains sous la révolution: mythes et réalités," *Thomas Paine, ou la République sans frontières*, 87-103.

22. Henry Redhead Yorke, *France in Eighteen-Hundred and Two, Described in a Series of Letters*, J.A.C. Sykes, ed., 71.

23. For Oswald and the other British citizens in Paris, see Erdman, *Commerce des Lumières*, passim. For Fitzgerald and Tone, see Marianne Elliott: *Partners in Revolution: the United Irishmen and France*, 25-26, 54-56, passim and *Wolfe Tone*, and especially Ann Thomson, "Thomas Paine and the United Irishmen," *Etudes Irlandaises* 16 (June 1991):109-19.

24. Elliott, *Partners in Revolution*, 25, 59-60. The quotation from Fitzgerald is from Conway, *The Life of Thomas Paine*, 1:358.

25. Elliott, *Partners in Rebellion*, 51-61 and Erdman, *Commerce des Lumières*, 216-17, 223-43.

26. See Elkins and McKitrick, *The Age of Federalism*, 330-73.

27. Munro wrote Gower: "Should you therefore have occasion to write me you will address me at White's Hotel, No. 7 Passage des Petites Prêtres, Place des Victoires." He clearly meant Passage des Petits Pères, which was where White's was located (see Browning, ed., *Despatches of Earl Gower*, 260). On Wordsworth and Paine, see two essays by Gordon K. Thomas, " 'Glorious Revolution:' Wordsworth, Terror, and Paine," *Wordsworth Circle* 21 (Winter 1990):3-9 and " 'And When America was Free:' Thomas Paine and the English Romantics," *The Charles Lamb Bulletin*, New Series, 69 (Jan. 1990):164-77.

28. See Erdman, *Commerce des Lumières*, 231-33 and John Goldworth Alger, *Paris in 1789-94: Farewell Letters of Victims of the Guillotine*, 324-30. Alger describes the entire affair, and reprints the address to the Convention.

29. By McCusker's tables, this would equal just over $47,000 in 1991 dollars.

30. Quoted from Rickman's journal by Conway, *The Life of Thomas Paine*, 1:372.

31. The British government had warned Erskine that if he agreed to defend Paine, he would be fired, and in fact he was.

32. The Guelphs, direct predecessors of the Hanoverians, were a European dynasty whose origins lay deep in the ninth century.

33. Paine to the English Attorney-General, on the Prosecution Against the Second Part of *Rights of Man*, 11 November 1792, in *CW* 2:512.

34. Cobban, ed., *Debate on the French Revolution*, 299.

35. Quoted by Conway, *The Life of Thomas Paine*, 1:375; "The Hall Manuscripts," 2:472.

36. Carlile, like Rickman, was in fact one of Paine's earliest sympathetic biographers. See Richard Carlile, *The Life of Thomas Paine*. He served three years in jail and paid a 400 pound fine for printing Paine's *The Age of Reason* and other works in 1819. For Carlile, see Joel H. Wiener, *Radicalism and Freethought in Nineteenth-Century Britain: The Life of Richard Carlile*.

Chapter 14

1. See Mona Ozouf, "King's Trial," in *A Critical Dictionary of the French Revolution*, 95-106.

2. Quoted by Blum, *Rousseau and the Republic of Virtue*, 173, citing St. Just's famous speech of 27 December 1793 attacking the king.

3. Paine, "On the Propriety of Bringing Louis XVI to Trial," 20 November 1792, in *CW* 2:550.

4. Quoted in Conway, *The Life of Thomas Paine*, 1:377.

5. Paine, "Reasons for Preserving the Life of Louis Capet," in *CW* 2:551-55. See Jean Lessay, "Tom Paine: The Anti-Monarchist Who Tried to Save a King," *The Courier* 6 (June 1989):18.

6. The actual vote was 361 for death, 26 for death but with a plea for mercy, and 334 for banishment.

7. Quoted by Blum, *Rousseau and the Republic of Virtue*, 176.

8. On Henry Edgeworth de Firmont (Firmont was the estate near Edgeworthstown in County Longford, Ireland), see Alger, *Englishman in the French Revolution*, 134-38.

9. For day-to-day activities of the king and the royal family, see Schama, *Citizens*, 653-75 and François Furet, "Louis XVI," in *A Critical Dictionary of the French Revolution*, 242. Furet's account of Louis' responses to his accusers shows a much more placid man than does Schama. More generally, see David Jordan, *The King's Trial* and Michael Walzer, "The King's Trial and the Political Culture of the Revolution," in Colin Lucas, ed., *The French Revolution and the Creation of Modern Political Culture*, 2 vols.,

THOMAS PAINE: Apostle of Freedom

2:183-92.

10. Blum, *Rousseau and the Republic of Virtue*, 177.

11. Vincent, *Thomas Paine*, 259-60.

12. The 1786 commerce treaty between England and France stipulated "that the sending away an ambassador by either party, should be taken as an act of hostility by the other party. The declaration of war (February 1, 1793) by the Convention, of which I was then a member and know well the case, was made in exact conformity to this article in the treaty; for it was not a declaration of war against England, but a declaration that the French Republic is *in* war with England. . . . The declaration was made immediately on Chauvelin's return to France." (Paine, *The Eighteenth Fructidor*, 1797, in *CW* 2:609, nt.21.)

13. Conway, *The Life of Thomas Paine*, 2:17.

14. Madame Roland, *Mémoires de Madame Roland*, Nouvelle Edition, 2 vols., 2:13. Like Paine, Williams was granted French citizenship in September 1792.

15. Rickman, *The Life of Thomas Paine*, 47.

16. See Alger, *Paris in 1789-94*, 333-34.

17. Paine, "Forgetfulness" [unpublished, 1794], in *CW* 2:1124.

18. Paine, "Plan of a Declaration of the Natural, Civil and Political Rights of Man," 15 February 1793, in *CW* 2:560.

19. Rickman, *The Life of Thomas Paine*, 40.

20. Paine, "Forgetfulness," in *CW* 2:1123.

21. Rickman, *The Life of Thomas Paine*, 41.

22. Paine to Dr. James O'Fallon, 17 February 1793, in *CW* 2:1330.

23. Paine, "Forgetfulness," in *CW* 2:1124.

24. Paine to Jefferson, 20 April 1793, in *CW* 2:1331-32. He told Danton the same thing a few weeks later. See Paine to Danton, 6 May 1793, in *CW* 2:1337.

25. Paine to Danton, 6 May 1793, in *CW*, 2:1335.

26. Alger, *Paris in 1789-94*, 337-38.

27. See William Spence Robertson, *The Life of Miranda*, 2 vols. and A. Owen Aldridge, "Thomas Paine and Latin American Independence," in *Early American Literature: A Comparatist Approach*, 215-60.

28. Paine recounted the events some years later in "To a Gentleman in Philadelphia," 3 April 1806, in the *Philadelphia Aurora*, in *CW* 2:1480-82. Miranda's award of 1200 pounds would be worth approximately $50,000 in 1991 dollars.

29. Rickman, *The Life of Thomas Paine*, 4. Rickman claimed that when he was with Paine in France, "he did not drink spirits, and wine he took moderately; he even objected to any spirits being laid in as a part of his sea-stock."

30. Interest in Corday, whose full name was Marie-Anne-Charlotte Corday d'Armont and who was a direct descendant of Pierre Corneille, the seventeenth century playwright, has increased in France over the past decade. See Bernardine Melchior-Bonnet, *Charlotte Corday* and the catalogue produced in conjunction with an exhibit of Corday memorabilia in Rouen during the bicentennial of the French Revolution: *Charlotte Corday: Une Normande dans la Révolution.*

31. See Franco Venturi, *Roots of Revolution: A History of the Populist and Socialist Movements in Nineteenth Century Russia*, 365-66.

32. Quoted in Blum, *Rousseau and the Republic of Virtue*, 164-65.

33. Williams, *Letters Containing a Sketch*, 2:182, 185-86.

34. Morris, *A Diary of the French Revolution*, 2:163, 212-13, 370, 368.

35. Vincent, *Thomas Paine*, 281.

36. Paine to Citizen Barère, 5 September 1793, in *CW* 2:1332.

37. Williamson, *Thomas Paine*, 210.

38. Fortolis, *Les Anglais en France*, 60 and Conway, *Thomas Paine*, 2:94.

39. Charles-Aimé Dauban, *Les Prisons de Paris sous la révolution: d'après les relations des contemporains avec des notes et une introduction*, 246.

40. Paine to Samuel Adams, 6 March 1795, in *CW* 2:1376.

41. Paine to Samuel Adams, 1 January 1803, in *CW* 2:1436.

42. Alger, *Paris in 1789-94*, 338.

43. Cited in the original French in Vincent, *Thomas Paine*, 288.

Chapter 15

1. Paine, "Letters to the Citizens of the United States," "Letter III," 29 November 1802, in the *National Intelligencer*, in *CW* 2:919.

2. Paine cited the decree in the following: *The Age of Reason*, 102; a letter to Samuel Adams, 6 March 1795, in *CW* 2:1376; *A Letter to George Washington*, in *CW* 2:699; and "Letters to the Citizens of the United States," "Letter III," in *CW* 2:920.

3. Paine, "Letters to the Citizens of the United States," "Letter III," in *CW* 2:920.

4. Conway, *The Life of Thomas Paine*, 2:108, 114.

THOMAS PAINE: Apostle of Freedom

5. Quoted by Palmer, *Twelve Who Ruled*, 12. After the fall of Robespierre, Billaud-Varenne was exiled to French Guiana, and eventually emigrated to Haiti where he died in 1819.

6. Williams, *Letters Containing a Sketch*, 2:100. Williams also referred to the final notice of impending trials as "the evening paper." See *Letters*, 2:98.

7. Helen-Maria Williams reported that one of her friends imprisoned in the Hotel Talaru paid four francs per day. See her *Letters Containing a Sketch*, 2:122.

8. John Goldworth Alger, *Glimpses of the French Revolution: Myths, Ideals, and Realities*, 270-71.

9. Paine, "Letters to the Citizens of the United States," "Letter III," in *CW* 2:921.

10. Dauban, *Les Prisons de Paris*, 236, 235, 253, 234-69 generally. See Williams, *Letters Containing a Sketch*, 2:100-01 and the note on 133; 1:17-18.

11. Paine, "From the Castle in the Air, to the Little Corner of the World," (undated), in *CW* 2:1096-97.

12. Paine, "The New Covenant," (undated), in *CW* 2:1097-98.

13. Paine named these men in *The Age of Reason*, 102.

14. Paine, "Letters to the Citizens of the United States," "Letter III," in *CW* 2:921-22 (see Chapter 11 above). Dauban reported one hundred sixty-nine persons executed in that one night. See his *Les Prisons de Paris*, 254. The story of Paine's "miraculous" escape from the guillotine has been discredited by Alger, *Glimpses of the French Revolution*, 31-36. Prisoners, no matter who they were, were first taken to the Conciergerie to await "trial" before the Tribunal, and then usually summarily executed the same day, or the next, depending on how busy the guillotine was at any particular time. Despite this, Alger rightly concludes that "had Robespierre lived, Paine in all likelihood would have perished, for though he had been expelled from the Convention as a foreigner, which logically implied the restoration of his American citizenship, it is doubtful this would have protected him." Alger, *Glimpses*, 34.

15. Paine to Morris, 24 February 1794, in *CW* 2:1339.

16. Randolph had served as a delegate from Virginia to the Constitutional Convention in 1787 and had presented the Virginia Plan (of large states), on which the Constitution was eventually based. Despite his Federalist background, he was decidedly pro-French and had great difficulty as Secretary of State with Alexander Hamilton, the Secretary of the Treasury. In 1795, Charles Fauchet, the French minister to the United States, reported an alleged request for bribe money by Randolph, who was then dismissed by Washington. These accusations were false, but Randolph returned to the practice of law, and represented Aaron Burr in his 1807 trial for treason. Randolph died in 1813.

17. Conway, *The Life of Thomas Paine*, 2:109, 114, 115.

18. Morris to Jefferson, 21 January 1794 and Morris to Jefferson, 6 March 1794 (emphasis added) in *The Gouverneur Morris Papers*, deposited in the Library of Congress.

19. For the view that Paine wrote *The Age of Reason* as a direct assault on French revolutionary atheism, see John Keane, "Religion and Liberty: Tom Paine's Attack on Revolutionary Atheism," *Times Literary Supplement* (February 11, 1994):13-14.

20. Butterfield, ed., *The Diary and Autobiography of John Adams*, 3:333.

21. Paine had first characterized the times as an "Age of Reason" in the *Rights of Man*; indeed, his was the very first use of the term. "The present age will hereafter merit to be called the Age of reason, and the present generation will appear to the future as the Adam of a new world." *Rights of Man*, 268. For a comparison of Paine and William Blake concerning many of these ideas, see J.C.D. Clark, *The Language of Liberty, 1660-1832: Political Discourse and Social Dynamics in the Anglo-American World*, esp. 15, 38, 329-36, 286 and Robert N. Essick, "William Blake, Thomas Paine, and Biblical Revelation," *Studies in Romanticism*, 30 (Summer 1991):189-212.

22. The full quotation is worth repeating. "The religion that approaches the nearest of all others to true Deism, in the moral and benign part thereof, is that professed by the Quakers; but they have contracted themselves too much by leaving the works of God out of their system. Though I reverence their philanthropy, I cannot help smiling at the conceit that if the taste of a Quaker could have been consulted at the Creation what a silent and drab-colored Creation it would have been! Not a flower would have blossomed its gaieties, nor a bird been permitted to sing." (*The Age of Reason*, 84)

23. Paine would not write the second part of *The Age of Reason* until after his release. For an analysis of this work as a political treatise, see Edward H. Davidson and William J. Scheick, *Paine, Scripture, and Authority: "The Age of Reason" as Religious and Political Idea*, especially Chapter 4.

24. Paine to the National Convention, 7 August 1794, in *CW* 2:1341.

25. Paine to James Monroe, 17 August 1794, in *CW* 2:1341.

26. See Paine to Monroe, 10 September 1794, in *CW* 2:1345-54.

27. Conway, *The Life of Thomas Paine*, 2:152, nt.2.

28. Paine, "Letters to the Citizens of the United States," "Letter III," in *CW* 2:921.

29. Conway, *The Life of Thomas Paine*, 2:154.

30. Paine, *Dissertation on the First Principles of Government*, in *CW* 2:579. See also Paine's "The Constitution of 1795," a speech he wrote, but that Lanthenas delivered in French to the Convention on 7 July 1795, in *CW* 2:588-94.

31. Paine, "The Constitution of 1795," 7 July 1795, in *CW* 2:589-91.

Chapter 16

1. Schama, *Citizens*, 852.

2. Paine referred to Hebrew scripture consistently as "the Bible," whereas he calls the Christian part "the Testament."

3. For Robespierre, see Paine to the French National Convention, 7 August 1794, in *CW* 2:1339; for Lebon, see "Letters to the Citizens of the United States," "Letter III," 29 November 1802, in the *National Intelligencer*, in *CW* 2:921.

4. In commenting on Paine's request to Gouverneur Morris for assistance during his imprisonment in the Luxembourg, Roosevelt wrote, "Morris refused to interfere actively, judging rightly that Paine would be saved by his own insignificance and would serve his own interest best by keeping still. So the filthy little atheist had to stay in prison 'where he amused himself with publishing a pamphlet against Jesus Christ.'" Theodore Roosevelt, *Gouverneur Morris*, 288-89.

5. Butterfield, ed., *The Diary and Autobiography of John Adams*, 3:283, 234.

6. Paine, *Prosecution of "The Age of Reason"*, 1797, in *CW* 2:727, 742, 740, 744, 743, 732. For a fairly recent reinterpretation of this work, see Howard Prochaska, "Thomas Paine's *The Age of Reason* Revisited," *Journal of the History of Ideas* 44 (Oct.-Dec. 1972):561-76.

7. Paine, "Extracts from a Reply to the Bishop of Llandaff," (1810), in *The Theophilanthropist*, in *CW* 2:777, 771. This work, according to Paine, was to be the third part of *The Age of Reason*, but either he did not finish it or he was unable to find a publisher for it. It was finally published posthumously. See Paine to Elihu Palmer, 21 February 1802, in *CW* 2:1426. Paine more precisely dated this letter "February 21, 1802, since the Fable of Christ."

8. Until his letter to Samuel Adams in 1803, in *CW* 2:1434-38, when Paine defended his belief in deism and especially his belief in God.

9. John Jay, a leading American revolutionary, had written five of the *Federalist Papers* along with James Madison and Alexander Hamilton.

10. Paine, "Observations on the Jay Treaty," 2 July 1795, in the *Philadelphia Aurora*, in *CW* 2:570.

11. Monroe to Judge Joseph Jones, 15 September 1795, in Conway, *The Life of Thomas Paine*, 2:166.

12. Paine to Madison, 24 September 1795, in *CW*, 2:1378.

13. Paine may have had David Hume in mind. See David Hume, *Essays Moral, Political and Literary*, 355-61.

14. Paine to Jefferson, 1 April 1797, in *CW* 2:1388.

15. See Paine to Minister _____[?], 13 August 1796, in *CW* 2:1383-84. The recipient is not indicated.

16. Conway, *The Life of Thomas Paine*, 2:note on 240.

17. Paine to Madison, 24 September 1795, in *CW* 2:1378-81. For a different view of Paine's references to Washington, see Hawke, *Paine*, 320

18. Paine's letter was serially published in Philadelphia by Benjamin Franklin Bache in October and November in 1796. A pamphlet containing the complete series appeared in February the following year.

19. Paine's emphasis and mark.

20. Washington to Stuart, 8 January 1797, in *The Writings of George Washington*, 35:360

Chapter 17

1. Paine alluded to the sermon and its title in *Agrarian Justice*, in *CW* 1:609. For a recent assessment of this work, see John W. Seaman, "Thomas Paine: Ransom, Civil Peace, and the Natural Right to Welfare," *Political Theory* 16 (Feb. 1988):120-42.

2. Patrice Higonnet, "Sans-culottes," in *A Critical Dictionary of the French Revolution*, 393-99. By the decree of 21 May-27 June 1790, Paris was divided into forty-eight sections, principally for electoral purposes. On Paine's "moral economics," see William Christian, "The Moral Economics of Tom Paine," *Journal of the History of Ideas* 34 (July-Sept. 1973):367-80.

3. Spence was the author of *Pig's Meat*. More to the point, he answered Paine's *Agrarian Justice* with his own pamphlet of 1797, *The Rights of Infants, with Scriptures on Paine's Agrarian Justice*.

4. For the view that this work fitted more directly into themes of natural law, see Gregory Claeys, "Thomas Paine's *Agrarian Justice* (1796) and the Secularization of Natural Jurisprudence," *Society for the Study of Labour History Bulletin* 52 (Winter 1988):21-31.

5. The initial edition of *Agrarian Justice* did not include the reference to Babeuf. Paine added it for the second edition, which appeared in the spring of 1797. For earlier, but still sound assessments, see Joseph Dorfman, "The Economic Philosophy of Thomas Paine," *Political Science Quarterly* 53 (Sept. 1938):372-86 and James Eayrs, "The Political Ideas of the English Agrarians, 1775-1815," *Canadian Journal of Economics and Political Science* 18 (Aug. 1952):298-302.

6. And from Burke, too. See Tom Furniss, "Burke, Paine, and the Language of Assignats," in Watson, ed., *Yearbook of English Studies*, 19:54-70.

7. This is quite clearly a labor theory of value, something Marx would make use of in a highly sophisticated way, first in the 1844 manuscripts, and then later in *Capital*.

8. See Rousseau, "Discourse on the Sciences and the Arts" (1750), "Discourse on the Origins of Inequality" (1755), and *On the Social Contract* (1762), in *The Basic Political Writings*, 11, 60, 151.

9. Emphasis is in the original.

10. See the *Rights of Man*, 243. The fifteen pounds would be around $750 in 1991 dollars.

11. The gift would be worth about $4,700 in 1991 dollars. Williamson argues that Paine's plan anticipated the ideas of Henry George, who lived nearly one hundred years later at a time of growing class antagonisms in England in a new industrial world. See Williamson, *Thomas Paine*, 243. For a view entirely different from the one proposed here, see Richard Popkin, "*The Age of Reason* versus *The Age of Revelation*. Two Critics of Tom Paine: David Levi and Elias Boudinot," in J.A. Leo Lemay, *Deism, Masonry, and the Enlightenment*, 158-70.

12. Theobald Wolfe Tone, *The Life of Theobald Wolfe Tone edited by his Son*, 2 vols., 2:348. See Elliott, *Wolfe Tone*, passim.

13. See Lessay, *L'Américain de la Convention*, 208 and Hawke, *Paine*, 337.

14. Paine to Madison, 24 September 1795, in *CW* 2:1378.

15. Paine to Col. John Fellows, 20 January 1797, in *CW* 2:1384-85. Paine considered Fellows among his closest friends after he actually did return in 1802.

16. Paine to Madison, 27 April 1797, in *CW* 2:1394. See also two letters to Jefferson, 1 April 1797, in *CW* 2:1386-91 and 14 May 1797, in *CW* 2:1399-1400.

17. Paine to Jefferson, 1 April 1797, in *CW*, 2:1387.

18. Paine, "Worship and Church Bells, A Letter to Camille Jordan," 1797, in *CW* 2:757, 758, 760.

19. Paine, *The Eighteenth Fructidor: To the People of France and the French*

Armies, 1797, in *CW* 2:602, 605, 606.

20. Paine to Talleyrand, Year Six, in *CW* 2:1401. See Elkins and McKitrick, *The Age of Federalism*, 556-79 and DeConde, *The Quasi-War*, passim.

21. Paine printed his proposal in America in 1803. See his "Letter to the Citizens of the United States," 21 April 1803, "Letter VII," in the Trenton, New Jersey, *True-American*, in *CW* 2:940-45.

22. DeConde, *The Quasi-War*, 253-58. See also William C. Stinchcombe, *The XYZ Affair*.

Chapter 18

1. Conway, "The Cobbett Papers," *The Life of Thomas Paine*, 2:443-44. The Bonneville address today is 2, carrefour de l'Odéon. That rent was paid was attested to by Rickman, *The Life of Thomas Paine*, 55.

2. See Aldridge, *Man of Reason*, 266-67.

3. Conway, "The Cobbett Papers," in *The Life of Thomas Paine*, 2:444.

4. See Elliott, *Partners in Revolution*, 24-25, 59-60, and generally 165-240.

5. Aldridge, *Man of Reason*, 257 and Hawke, *Paine*, 336.

6. Paine to Elihu Palmer, 21 February 1802, in *CW* 2:1426.

7. Paine's 1797 "Observations" are reprinted by A. Owen Aldridge, "Thomas Paine's Plan for a Descent on England," *William and Mary Quarterly*, 3rd series, 14 (Jan. 1957):79-84. Paine to the Council of Five Hundred, 28 January 1798, in *CW* 2:1403. Paine's gift, clearly a token, would be worth about $250 in 1991 dollars.

8. Aldridge cites several articles and letters on a French invasion of England in *Le Bien informé* of 14 December, 1797, 15 December 1797, 29 January 1798, 18 March 1798, in "Thomas Paine's Plan for a Descent on England," 76-78.

9. That Bonaparte wished a statue of gold erected to Paine and that he slept every night with the *Rights of Man* under his pillow are attested to by Rickman, *Life of Thomas Paine*, note on 51 and Henry Redhead Yorke, Esq., *Letters from France, Describing the Manners and Customs of its Inhabitants: With Observations on the Arts, Manufactures, Public Institutions and buildings, Learned Societies, and the Mode of Traveling. Interspersed with Interesting Anecdotes of Celebrated Characters*, 2 vols., 2:367. Paine to Bonaparte, 1 October 1800, in *CW* 2:1413-16. Foner attributes this letter to Jefferson, but Hawke rightly concludes that this was in error. See Hawke, *Paine*, note on 452.

10. Paine to Jefferson, 1 October 1800, in *CW* 2:1413-16.

11. Paine, "To the People of England on the Invasion of England," 6 March 1804, in the *Philadelphia Aurora,* in *CW* 2:675-83.

12. See Paine, "Of Gun-Boats" and "Of the Comparative Powers and Expense of Ships of War, Gun-Boats, and Fortifications," in *CW* 2:1067-77. Both were printed in 1805 and 1807, respectively.

13. See *The Manuscripts of J.B. Fortescue, Esq., Preserved at Dropmore,* 4:69-70. For the activities of the British secret service in a period slightly before this statement, see Cobban, "British Secret Service in France, 1784-1792," *Aspects of the French Revolution,* 192-227. Cobban's view is that after 1792, the British were bolder than ever, sending their agents into Paris and other French cities to spy on the activities of French officials and foreigners like Paine who might be fomenting a revolution in England.

14. Vincent, *Thomas Paine,* 340, quoting from a letter in the French National Archives.

15. Williamson, *Thomas Paine,* 252.

16. Paine, "To the People of England on the Invasion of England," 6 March 1804, in the *Philadelphia Aurora,* in *CW* 2:680.

17. Gary Kates, *Le Cercle Social, the Girondins, and the French Revolution.*

18. Ernest F. Henderson, *Symbol and Satire in the French Revolution,* 357-58.

19. Billington, *Fire in the Minds of Men,* 25-33. I am indebted to this work for the information on Bonneville.

20. Billington, *Fire in the Minds of Men,* 35 (quoted from Bonneville's early Palais Royal journal, *Le Tribun du peuple*). See Wilson Carey McWilliams, "Civil Religion in the Age of Reason: Thomas Paine on Liberalism, Redemption, and Revolution," *Social Research* 54 (Autumn 1987):447-90.

21. Billington in *Fire in the Minds of Men,* 40-42. Billington also points out that the Social Circle was one of the first modern associations to advocate a feminist ideology and equality between the races.

22. Billington, *Fire in the Minds of Men,* 95 and more generally 86-105. For a larger context, see Margaret C. Jacob, *The Radical Enlightenment: Pantheists, Freemasons and Republicans.*

23. Billington, *Fire in the Minds of Men,* 43, 83-85. Billington notes that Babeuf's journal, *Le Tribun du peuple,* took its name from Bonneville's first effort in the newspaper business. For the suggestion that Paine may have believed in the coming of the millennium, see Jack Fruchtman, Jr., "The Revolutionary Millennialism of Thomas Paine," in *Studies in Eighteenth-Century Culture,* Vol. 13, 65-77. During the Directory, Babeuf sought to achieve a dictatorial republic and conspired to overthrow the government. He was guillotined in 1798.

24. Billington, *Fire in the Minds of Men*, 103.

25. Paine, *Prosecution of the Age of Reason*, 1797, in *CW* 2:745, 747.

26. Paine, "The Existence of God, A Discourse at the Society of Theophilanthropists, Paris," 1797, in *CW* 2:749-50, 755-56.

27. Paine, *Prosecution of The Age of Reason*, in *CW* 2:748.

28. It has long been questioned whether Paine was a member of the Masons. There is no definitive proof either way. There is no specific date known on which he joined nor a specific lodge to which he was attached. He did, however, have several friends who were masons in both America and France, from 1774 until his death. For the argument that he was not, see Vincent, *Thomas Paine*, 49-55.

29. Paine, "Origin of Freemasonry," 1805, in *CW* 2:833, 835. This essay was published posthumously by Marguerite de Bonneville.

30. Paine to Anonymous, 12 Thermidor, Year 8, in *CW* 2:1406.

31. Paine to Jefferson, 1 October 1800, in *CW* 2:1406, 1407, 1410.

32. Jefferson to Paine, 18 March 1801, in *The Writings of Thomas Jefferson*, Paul Leicester Ford, ed., 10 vols., 8:18-19.

33. Paine to Jefferson, 9 June 1801, in *CW* 2:1419.

34. Foner, editor's note, in *CW* 2:1419, nt.307.

35. Newspaper quotations are from Jerry W. Knudson, "The Rage Around Tom Paine: Newspaper Reaction to His Homecoming in 1802," *New-York Historical Society Quarterly* 53 (Jan. 1969):40-41.

36. Yorke, *Letters from France*, 2:337-67. The passage Paine quoted from memory in the *Letter to Abbé Raynal* may be found in *CW* 2:220.

37. Rickman, *Life of Thomas Paine*, 4.

Chapter 19

1. Knudson, "The Rage Around Tom Paine," 42-44.

2. William V. Murray to Rufus King, 12 November 1802, in *The Life and Correspondence of Rufus King*, edited by Charles R. King, 6 vols., 4:182.

3. Paine to Madame Bonneville, 15 November 1802, in *CW* 2:1430, 1431. Passage for Marguerite and her boys would cost about $1,000 in 1991 dollars.

4. About $1,650 in 1991 dollars.

5. Cheetham, *The Life of Thomas Paine*, 227, 233-34.

6. Knudson, "The Rage Around Tom Paine," 49-51.

7. Paine to Rickman, 8 March 1803, in *CW* 2:1439. On the evidence that Paine's letters to the citizens of the United States were more about himself, see Knudson, "The Rage Around Tom Paine," 54-55.

8. Paine, "Letter to the Citizens of the United States," "Letter III," 29 November 1802, in the *National Intelligencer*, in *CW* 2:918.

9. Paine, "Letter to the Citizens of the United States," "Letter VIII," 7 June 1805, in the *Philadelphia Aurora*, in *CW* 2:949.

10. Paine, "Letter to the Citizens of the United States," "Letter I," 15 November 1802, in the *National Intelligencer*, in *CW* 2:911.

11. Paine, "Letter to the Citizens of the United States," "Letter III," in *CW*, 2:919.

12. Paine, "Letter to the Citizens of the United States," "Letter II," 22 November 1802, in the *National Intelligencer*, in *CW* 2:912.

13. Paine, "Letter to the Citizens of the United States," "Letter III," in *CW* 2:920, 913, 915-16.

14. Paine to Jefferson, Christmas Day 1802, in *CW* 2:1431-32.

15. Paine recounted the story about Dr. Lieb in a long letter to Jefferson, 25 January 1805, in *CW* 2:1462-63.

16. Paine to Jefferson, 12 January 1803, in *CW* 2:1439.

17. Paine, "The Construction of Iron Bridges," in *CW* 2:1051-57.

18. Foner quoted the letter in full: Adams to Paine, 30 November 1802, in *CW* 2:1433.

19. Paine to Samuel Adams, 1 January 1803, in *CW* 2:1434-38.

20. Paine, "From Mr. Paine to Mr. Jefferson," 23 February 1803, in *CW* 2:1101.

21. Quoted by Rickman, *The Life of Thomas Paine*, 57.

22. Conway, *The Life of Thomas Paine*, 2:317-18.

23. Paine to Peale, 29 July 1803, in *CW* 2:1440.

24. Paine once admitted that just before he went to prison in 1793, he had indeed done some hard drinking.

25. Conway, *The Life of Thomas Paine*, 2:360, 325, 59-60, 329, and "The Hall Manuscripts," 2:472.

26. According to McCusker's formula, this amount would be about $200 million in 1991 dollars.

27. Paine, "Letter VIII," in *CW* 2:953.

28. Paine to Breckenridge, 2 August 1803, in *CW* 2:1444.

29. Paine to Jefferson, 2 August 1803, in *CW* 2:1441. Jefferson's views

were quite close to Paine's. See Sheldon, *The Political Philosophy of Thomas Jefferson*, 97-99.

30. Paine's concerns about Connecticut politics appeared in two letters to Elisha Babcock, who published the Hartford *American Mercury*. These letters are to be found in Richard Gimbel, "New Political Writings by Thomas Paine," *Yale University Library Gazette* 30 (Jan. 1956):97-100. See Chapter 20 below.

31. Paine to Jefferson, 23 September 1803, in *CW* 2:1447-51.

32. Paine to Jefferson, 25 January 1805, in *CW* 2:1459-60. Paine recounted the story after the election of 1804.

33. Paine to Jefferson, 23 September 1803, in *CW* 2:1449.

34. Paine to Mr. Hyer, 24 March 1804, in *CW* 2:1451-52. The piece was "To the People of England on the Invasion of England," 6 March 1804, in the *Philadelphia Aurora*, 2:675-83.

35. Conway, "The Cobbett Papers," in *The Life of Thomas Paine*, 2:447.

36. The descriptions of Romaine and Pintard are to be found in Conway, *The Life of Thomas Paine*, 2:331.

37. Paine to Palmer, 21 February 1802, in *CW* 2:1426.

38. Quoted by Foner, in *CW* 2:788.

39. Paine's *Prospect Papers* are to be found in *CW* 2:789-830. Paine signed these pieces with various pseudonyms (see the bibliography for a complete list).

40. This according to Vale, *The Life of Thomas Paine*, 147. The amount $35 would be the equivalent of about $400 in 1991 dollars.

41. Paine to Citizen Skipwith, 1 March 1804, in *CW* 2:1451.

42. Paine to Babcock, 27 August 1804, in Gimbel, "New Political Writings of Thomas Paine," 99. Babcock, at Paine's request, published a paragraph from this letter as "Extract of a letter from a gentleman to his friend in this city," dated August 27, 1804, in the *Mercury*. See also "A Friend to Constitutional Order," [Paine], "To the People of Connecticut on the Subject of a Constitution," 2 August 1804, in the Hartford *American Mercury*, reprinted in Gimbel, 100-02.

43. Paine, "Remarks on Gouverneur Morris's Funeral Oration on General Hamilton," 7 August 1804, in *CW* 2:960, 962.

44. "Comus" [Paine], "Nonsense from New York," 23 August 1804, in the *Philadelphia Aurora*, reprinted in Gimbel, "New Political Writings by Thomas Paine," 103-04. The reference to the "King's Evil" was clearly to the insanity of George III.

45. [Paine], "Connecticut Has No Constitution," 26 November 1804, in the *National Intelligencer*, reprinted 27 December 1804, the Hartford

American Mercury.

Chapter 20

1. Paine to Jefferson, 20 April 1805, in *CW* 2:1057-59.

2. Paine to John Fellows, 31 July 1805, in *CW* 2:1471.

3. Paine to William Carver, 16 January 1805, in *CW* 2:1455-56.

4. Paine to John Fellows, 31 July 1805, in *CW* 2:1471.

5. Paine, "To the French Inhabitants of Louisiana," 22 September 1804, in *CW* 2:963-68.

6. Paine to Jefferson, 1 January 1805, in *CW* 2:1453-55.

7. Paine to Jefferson, 25 January 1805, in *CW* 2:1456-64.

8. Paine, "On Gun-Boats" and "Of the Comparative Powers and Expense of Ships of War, Gun-Boats, and Fortifications," in *CW* 2:1067-77. See Chapter 18 above.

9. Printed on 25 September 1807 in the New York *Evening Post*, reprinted in Aldridge, "Thomas Paine's Plan for a Descent on England," 78, nt.11.

10. Paine, "Letter to the Citizens of the United States," "Letter VIII," in *CW* 2:951.

11. Paine, "To Mr. Hulbert, of Sheffield, One of the Mortified Federal Members of the Massachusetts Legislature," 12 March 1805, in the *Philadelphia Aurora*, in *CW* 2:975.

12. "A Spark from the Altar of '76" [Paine], "Another Callender—Thomas Turner of Virginia," 23 July 1805, Number I, in *The American Citizen*, in *CW* 2:983.

13. Paine to Elisha Babcock, 2 July 1805, in *CW* 2:1468.

14. Paine, "Letter To the Citizens of the United States," "Letter VIII," in *CW* 2:949, 955.

15. Paine to John Fellows, 22 April 1805, in *CW* 2:1467.

16. Paine, *Constitutions, Government, Charters* (June 1806), in *CW* 2:989, 991.

17. Paine to Andrew Dean, 15 August 1806, in *CW* 2:1483-85.

18. Paine to Jefferson, 30 September 1805, in *CW* 2:1473.

19. Paine to Jefferson, 30 January 1806, in *CW* 2:1473-79.

20. Paine to Inskeep, February 1806, in *CW* 2:1479-80, reprinted in the *Philadelphia Aurora*, 10 February 1806.

21. Paine, "The Cause of Yellow Fever, and the Means of Preventing It in Places Not yet Infected with It," 27 June 1806, in *CW* 2:1062.

22. Paine to Jefferson, 23 September 1803, in *CW* 2:1450-51.

23. Paine to Madison, 3 May 1807, in *CW* 2:1486-87. See also Paine to George Clinton, 4 May 1807, in *CW* 2:1487-88 and Paine to Barlow, 4 May 1807, in *CW* 2:1488-89.

24. For Carver's abusive attack on Paine, see Cheetham, *The Life of Thomas Paine*, 267-68. For Palmer, see two works by Kerry S. Walters, *Rational Infidels: The American Deists*, 192-230 and *The American Deists: Voices of Reason and Dissent in the Early Republic*, 240-77.

25. Paine to Andrew Dean, 15 August 1806, in *CW* 2:1483-85.

26. Conway, *The Life of Thomas Paine*, 2:375, nt.1.

27. Vale, *The Life of Thomas Paine*, 153.

28. A. Owen Aldridge, "Thomas Paine and the *New York Public Advertiser*," *New-York Historical Society Quarterly* 37 (Oct., 1953):361-82.

29. Paine, 22 April 1807, in the *New York Public Advertiser*, reprinted in Aldridge, "Thomas Paine and the *New York Public Advertiser*," 363.

30. Paine, "Of the Judiciary and Conduct of Chief Justice Marshall," 10 October 1807, in the *New York Public Advertiser*, cited in Aldridge, "Thomas Paine and the *New York Public Advertiser*," 382.

31. Paine to Barlow, 4 May 1807, in *CW* 2:1489.

32. See Paine, "Communication," 11 October 1806 and "The emissary Cullen otherwise Carpenter," 28 October 1806, both in the *American Citizen*, and Paine's extracts, 5 November 1806 and 19 November 1806, both in the *Philadelphia Aurora*, and Paine's letter, 8 April 1807, in the *New York Public Advertiser*, all cited and reprinted in Aldridge, "Thomas Paine and the *New York Public Advertiser*," 367-73.

33. Windham was the recipient of a September 1789 letter from Burke where he first expressed his skepticism about the French Revolution. See Chapter 10.

34. Paine, Letter, 13 November 1806, in the *American Citizen*, reprinted in Aldridge, "Thomas Paine and the *New York Public Advertiser*," 364-66.

35. Paine, "Liberty of the Press," 19 October 1806, in *The American Citizen*, in *CW* 2:1011.

36. Cheetham, *The Life of Thomas Paine*, 239, 241.

37. Paine, "Essay on Cheetham," 22 August 1807, in the *New York Public Advertiser*, reprinted in Aldridge, "Thomas Paine and the New York *Public Advertiser*," 376-78.

38. Paine, "Farewell Reprimand to James Cheetham," 5 September 1807, in the *New York Public Advertiser*, in Aldridge, "Thomas Paine and the

New York Public Advertiser," 379-82. In this essay, which was not his last, Paine added to his list of insults. Cheetham was, he said, "an idiot," and at one point Paine asked whether "the envy and malignity of his mind possessed him with a spirit of willful lying?" Paine continued his attacks on Cheetham in the *New York Public Advertiser* editions of 27 October 1807, 20 November 1807, 7 January 1808, and 25 August 1808, reprinted by Aldridge, 382.

39. Paine, "Cheetham and his Tory Paper," 25 September 1807, in *CW* 2:1017.

40. Vale, *Life of Thomas Paine,* 165.

41. The amount would have been about $120,000 in 1991 dollars.

42. Paine to the Honorable Senate of the United States, 21 January 1808, in *CW* 2:1489-92.

43. Paine to the Committee of Claims of the House of Representatives, 14 February 1808, in *CW* 2:1494.

44. Paine to the Honorable Speaker of the House of Representatives, 7 March 1808, in *CW* 2:1495.

45. Conway, *The Life of Thomas Paine,* 2:406.

46. Dropsy, or edema, is the abnormal retention of fluids in the body's tissues, affecting the arms and legs, and an indication of congestive heart failure. If the fluids move into the lungs, the result may be cardiac arrest.

47. See Conway, "The Cobbett Papers," in *The Life of Thomas Paine,* 2:429-59, 415.

48. Knudson, "The Rage Around Tom Paine," 61.

49. Conway, *The Life of Thomas Paine,* 2:418 and "The Cobbett Papers," 2:455.

50. Quoted in George Spater, *William Cobbett: The Poor Man's Friend,* 2 vols., 2:378. For a comparison of the views of Paine and Cobbett, see Ian Dyck, *William Cobbett and Rural Popular Culture,* 42-43 and Wilson, *Paine and Cobbett,* generally.

51. This is the view of Isaac Kramnick and Michael Foot. See the editor's introduction, *The Thomas Paine Reader,* 29.

52. Spater, *William Cobbett,* 576, nt.12 and 532 and Dyck, *Cobbett and Rural Popular Culture,* 44.

53. Spater, *William Cobbett,* 619, nt.6.

54. Conway, *The Life of Thomas Paine,* 2:427, nt.1.

55. David Powell quotes a letter in the London *Daily Telegraph* from a woman claiming that her mother used to play with Paine's jawbone before depositing it in a churchyard grave. See Powell, *Tom Paine,* 264. See also Leo A. Bressler, "Peter Porcupine and the Bones of Thomas Paine,"

Pennsylvania Magazine of History and Biography 82 (Apr. 1958):176-85.

56. Conway, *The Life of Thomas Paine*, 2:428.

Chapter 21

1. For the influence of secular, or civil, religion in Paine's own time as well as from the mid-nineteenth to the mid-twentieth centuries, see McWilliams, "Civil Religion in the Age of Reason," passim, and Susan Budd, "The Loss of Faith: Reasons for Unbelief among Members of the Secular Movement in England, 1850-1950," *Past and Present* 36 (Apr. 1967):106-25.

2. There are many statements of this. For the most recent, see Walters, *Rational Infidels*, 115-52.

3. For the full development of this view, see Fruchtman, *Thomas Paine and the Religion of Nature*.

4. Paine to James Monroe, 20 October 1794, in *CW* 2:1367.

5. Paine to Monroe, 10 September 1794, in *CW* 2:1353.

6. From a letter dated 16 March 1790, in Conway, *The Life of Thomas Paine*, 1:271.

7. Paine to Monroe, 18 August 1794, in *CW* 2:1342-43. See also Paine to Monroe, 10 September 1794, in *CW* 2:1345, 1353; 20 October 1794, in *CW* 2:1367.

8. Paine, "Letters to the Citizens of the United States," "Letter IV," in *CW* 2:926. This conclusion conflicts with Hawke's (see *Paine*, 310).

9. Paine, Letter to the Abbé Raynal, in *CW* 2:256; Paine to Lansdowne, 21 September 1787, in *CW* 2:1265; Paine, "Reasons for Preserving the Life of Louis Capet," in *CW* 2:552.

10. Paine to Few, 6 January 1789, in *CW* 2:1276 and Paine, *Prospects on the Rubicon*, 2:632. For Paine's impact, see Jack P. Greene, "Paine, America, and the Modernization of Political Consciousness," *Political Science Quarterly* 93 (Spring 1978):73-92 and Michael Durey, "Thomas Paine's Apostles: Radical Emigés and the Triumph of Jeffersonian Republicanism," *William and Mary Quarterly*, 3rd Series, 44 (Oct. 1987):661-88.

11. One of his most strident detractors (along with Chalmers, Cheetham, and Roosevelt) was William B. Reed, who wrote in 1843 that even Paine's *Common Sense* was not worth reading. See William B. Reed's review of "An Oration delivered at the celebration . . . of a birthday of Thomas Paine by John Alberger," *North American Review*, (Apr. 1843):9-51.

12. Dixon Wecter, "Hero in Reverse," *Virginia Quarterly Review* 18 (Spring 1942):243-59. For Watson, see Chapter 7, nt.2.

13. Among the most recent are the previously mentioned Kramnick and Foot edition, the reissue by Citadel Press of volume one of Philip Foner's 1945 edition of Paine's collected works, and a new edition by Gregory Claeys of the *Rights of Man*. In addition, a forthcoming collection of Paine's works by Eric Foner for the Library of America will include several essays and letters located after the Foner edition went to press nearly fifty years ago. See also *The Thomas Paine Collection at Thetford: An Analytical Catalogue.*

14. For earlier commemorative events, see Richard Gimbel, "The Resurgence of Thomas Paine," *Proceedings of the American Antiquarian Society* 69 (Oct. 21, 1959): 97-111 and Gimbel, "Thomas Paine Fights for Freedom in Three Worlds, The New, The Old, The Next," *Proceedings of the American Antiquarian Society* 70 (Oct. 19, 1960):397-492. For the 1992 law, see "An Act to Authorize Construction of a Monument in the District of Columbia or Its Environs to Honor Thomas Paine" (Government Printing Office, Superintendent of Documents, 1992). For Paine's enduring presence in American popular culture, see Tommy R. Thompson, "The Resurrection of Thomas Paine in American Popular Magazines," *The Midwest Quarterly* 33 (Fall 1991):75-92. The latest international conference devoted to Thomas Paine was held in England in February 1994.

15. Ronald Reagan, certainly one of the most conservative, reactionary Presidents in the twentieth century, took great pride in quoting Paine throughout 1984 at the beginning of his second term in office, one he called the "second American Revolution." Never hesitating to quote Paine's "we have it in our power to begin the world over again," there is some question of whether the President fully understood the radical thrust of Paine's statement.

16. For Paine's influence in countries other than America, Britain, and France, see Mark O. Kistler, "German-American Liberalism and Thomas Paine," *American Quarterly* 14 (Spring 1962):81-91; Asoke Mustafi, "Thomas Paine and Foreign Rule in India," *Calcutta Review* 158 (1962):204-06; A. Owen Aldridge, "Thomas Paine in Latin America," *Early American Literature* 3 (Winter 1968-69):139-47; Aldridge, "The Influence of Thomas Paine in the United States, France, Germany, and South America," in *Comparative Literature: Proceedings of the Second Congress of the International Comparative Literature Association*, Werner P. Friedrich, ed., two vols., 2:369-83; Peter C. Hogg, "Paine's *Rights of Man*, Swedenborgianism and Freedom of the Press in Sweden: A Publishing Enigma of 1792," *The British Library Journal* 19 (Spring 1993):34-43; John Keane, "Démocratie républicaine, nation, nationalisme: repenser les *Droits de l'Homme* de Thomas Paine," in Vincent, ed., *Thomas Paine ou la*

République sans frontiéres, 137-58.

17. See the most recent examples: "Man of Rights: Thomas Paine's Arguments for the French Revolution Were Alive with Meaning for his Time; David Caute Argues that They Remain Relevant," *New Statesman and Society* 2 (Jan. 7, 1989):12-14 and Bob Peterson, "Education: The Spirit of Thomas Paine," *In These Times* 18 (Feb. 21, 1994):30.

Bibliography

A Chronology of the Works of Thomas Paine

A number of scholars have disputed Paine's authorship of several pre-1776, unsigned works. These works are marked with an asterisk. A selection of Paine's major pieces of correspondence gives the name of the person to whom he wrote.

To Oliver Goldsmith, 21 December 1772.

"The Death of General Wolfe" [1759], March 1775, the *Pennsylvania Magazine: or American Monthly Museum.*

To Honorable Benjamin Franklin, Esq., 4 March 1775.

The Case of the Officers of Excise, 1772 (1793).

"The Magazine in America," January 1775, the *Pennsylvania Magazine.*

"Atlanticus" [Paine], "To the Public," January 1775, the *Pennsylvania Magazine.*

"The Snowdrop and the Critic," January 1775, the *Pennsylvania Magazine.*

"A Dialogue between General Wolfe and General Gage in a Wood Near Boston," January 1775, the *Pennsylvania Journal; and Weekly Advertiser.*

"Atlanticus" [Paine], "Useful and Entertaining Hints on the Internal Riches of the Colonies," February 1775, the *Pennsylvania Magazine.*

*"Esop" [Paine], "New Anecdotes of Alexander the Great," February 1775, the *Pennsylvania Magazine.*

*"Esop" [Paine], "Cupid and Hymen," March 1775, the *Pennsylvania Magazine.*

"Atlanticus" [Paine], "The Tale of the Monk and the Jew Versified," March 1775, the *Pennsylvania Magazine.*

"Old Bachelor" [Paine], "An Account of the Burning of Bachelor's Hall at Philadelphia, being Destroyed by Lightning, 1775," March 1775, the *Philadelphia Magazine.*

*"Justice and Humanity" [Paine], "African Slavery in America," March

1775, the *Pennsylvania Journal.*

*"Atlanticus" [Paine], "Reflections on the Life and Death of Lord Clive," March 1775, the *Pennsylvania Magazine.*

"O What a Pity!" April 1775, the *Pennsylvania Magazine.*

*[Paine], "The Dream Interpreted," May 1775, the *Pennsylvania Magazine.*

"Duelling," May 1775, the *Pennsylvania Magazine.*

*"Vox Populi" [Paine], "Reflections on Titles," May 1775, the *Pennsylvania Magazine.*

"Amicus" [Paine], Untitled Letter, June 1775, the *Pennsylvania Magazine.*

"Atlanticus" [Paine], "Liberty Tree," July 1775, the *Pennsylvania Magazine.*

"A Lover of Peace" [Paine], "Thoughts on Defensive War," July 1775, the *Pennsylvania Magazine.*

"Farmer Short's Dog Porter: A Tale," July 1775, the *Pennsylvania Magazine.*

To Honorable Benjamin Franklin, LL.D., 9 July 1777.

*[Paine], "An Occasional Letter on the Female Sex," August 1775, the *Pennsylvania Magazine.*

"Humanus" [Paine], "A Serious Thought," 18 October 1775, the *Pennsylvania Journal.*

"On the Making of Salt-Petre," 22 November 1775, the *Pennsylvania Journal.*

"A Lover of Order" [Paine], "To the Members of the House of Assembly of Pennsylvania," 22 November 1775, the *Pennsylvania Journal.*

"Epaminondas" [Paine], "Reflections on Unhappy Marriages," December 1775, *Pennsylvania Magazine.*

"A Continental Farmer" [Paine], "To the Members of the House of Assembly of Pennsylvania," 6 December 1775, the *Pennsylvania Journal.*

Common Sense, January 1776.

"Epistle to the Quakers," Appendix to *Common Sense*, 1776.

Letter to William Smith, 30 April 1776, in *Pennsylvania Evening Post.*

"The Forester" [Paine], "Letters," 3 April, 10 April, 24 April, 8 May 1776, in the *Pennsylvania Journal.*

[Paine], *Four Letters on Interesting Subjects*, Spring 1776.

"A Dialogue between the Ghost of General Montgomery just arrived from the Elysian Fields; and an American Delegate in a Wood near Philadelphia," Spring 1776.

The American Crisis: "Crisis I," 19 December 1776, the *Pennsylvania Journal*, published in pamphlet form on 23 December 1776.

"Crisis II," 13 January 1777.

"Crisis III," 19 April 1777.

"Crisis IV," 12 September 1777.

"Crisis V," 21 March 1778.

"To the People of America," 13 June 1778, the *Pennsylvania Gazette.*
"Crisis VI," 20 October 1778.
"Crisis VII," 21 November 1778.
"Crisis VIII," March 1780.
"Crisis IX," 9 June 1780.
"The Crisis Extraordinary," 4 October 1780.
"Crisis X," 5 March 1782.
"To the People of America," 3 April 1782, the *Pennsylvania Gazette.*
"Crisis XI," 22 May 1782.
"A Supernumerary Crisis," 31 May 1782.
"Crisis XII," 29 October 1782.
"Crisis XIII," 19 April 1783.
"A Supernumerary Crisis," 9 December 1783.
"To the People," 18 March 1777, the *Pennsylvania Packet.*
"Common Sense" [Paine], "Retreat Across the Delaware," 29 January 1777, the *Pennsylvania Journal.*
"Common Sense" [Paine], "Candid and Critical Remarks on a Letter Signed Ludlow [Benjamin Rush]," 21 May 1777, the *Pennsylvania Journal.*
To the Honorable Benjamin Franklin, Esq., 16 May 1778.
[Paine], "A Serious Address to the People of Pennsylvania on the Present Situation of their Affairs, 1 December, 5 December, 10 December, 12 December 1778, the *Pennsylvania Packet.*
"Common Sense" [Paine], "To Governor Johnstone, one of the British Commissioners, on his late letters and offers to bribe certain eminent characters in America, and threatening afterwards to appeal to the public," the *Pennsylvania Packet*, 28 July 1778.
To Henry Laurens, Spring, 1778.
"An Address to Lord Howe" (American edition), "Address to George III" (British edition), 14 November 1778, the *Pennsylvania Packet.*
"By the Goddess of Plain Truth, A Manifesto and Proclamation," 29 December 1778, the *Pennsylvania Packet.*
To the Honorable Henry Laurens, 14 January 1779.
On Silas Deane:
"To Silas Deane, Esq're," 15 December 1778, the *Pennsylvania Packet.*
"To the Public," 29 December 1778, the *Pennsylvania Packet.*
"To the Public on Mr. Deane's Affair," 31 December 1778, the *Pennsylvania Packet.*
"To the Public on Robert Morris's Address," 12 January 1779, the *Pennsylvania Packet.*
"To Mr. Deane," 16 January 1779, the *Pennsylvania Packet.*
"To Philalethes," 21 January 1779, the *Pennsylvania Packet.*
"To the People of America," 23 January 1779, the *Pennsylvania Packet.*
"On Philalethes," 26 January 1779, the *Pennsylvania Packet.*
Letter to the editor, 27 January 1779, the *Pennsylvania Packet.*

"To Silas Deane, Esquire," 16 February 1779, the *Pennsylvania Packet*.
"Reply to Gouverneur Morris," 2 March 1779, the *Pennsylvania Packet*.
"Comus" [Paine], in the *Pennsylvania Packet*, 16 March 1779.
"To Mr. Deane," 27 March 1779, the *Pennsylvania Packet*.
"To Mr. Deane," 13 April 1779, the *Pennsylvania Packet*.
"To Whitehead Humphreys," 16 July 1779, the *Pennsylvania Evening Post*.
"The Philadelphia Committee to Robert Morris," 24 July 1779, the *Pennsylvania Packet*.
"To the Public," 31 July 1779, the *Pennsylvania Packet*.
"To Mr. Dunlap," 10 August 1779, the *Pennsylvania Packet*.
"Messrs. Deane, Jay, and Gérard," 14 September 1779, the *Pennsylvania Packet*.
[Paine signed these pieces with his own name, or frequently "Common Sense," sometimes "T.P." or "C.S."]
"Common Sense" [Paine], "For the *Pennsylvania Packet*, Mr. Dunlap," 20 March 1779, the *Pennsylvania Packet*.
"Common Sense" [Paine], "Peace and the Newfoundland Fisheries," 30 June, 14 July, 21 July 1779, the *Pennsylvania Gazette*.
"Common Sense" [Paine], "To the Printer of the Pennsylvania Packet," 16 October 1779, the *Pennsylvania Packet*.
The American Philosophical Society, 14 February 1780, the General Assembly of Pennsylvania.
*[Paine], "Emancipation of Slaves," the Preamble to the Act Passed by the Pennsylvania Assembly, 1 March 1780.
To Blair McClenaghan, May 1780.
"A Plan for Recruiting the Army;" "Two Plans for Procuring the Supplies," June 1780, unpublished letters to Joseph Reed, President of the Supreme Executive Council of Pennsylvania.
Public Good, December 1780.
To His Excellency General Washington, 30 November 1781.
"A Friend to Rhode Island and the Union" [Paine], "Six Letters to Rhode Island," 21 December, 28 December 1782, 4 January, 11 January, 18 January, 1 February 1783, the *Providence Gazette*.
Letter to the Abbé Raynal, 1782.
To Robert Morris, Esq., 20 February 1782.
"To the Public," 13 March 1782, the *Freeman's Journal, or North-American Intelligencer*.
"Common Sense" [Paine], "To the People of America," 4 April 1782, the *Pennsylvania Packet*.
[Paine], 1 May 1782, the *Freeman's Journal*.
"Sincerus" [Paine], Letter, 2 July 1783, the *Freeman's Journal*.
"Extract from a Letter," 9 July 1783, the *Pennsylvania Gazette*.
"The Address of the Citizens of Philadelphia and of the Liberties thereof to His Excellency, the President, and the Congress of the United

States, 6 August 1783, the *Pennsylvania Gazette*.
"Hail Great Republic," 1783.
To His Excellency Benjamin Franklin, Esq., 31 December 1785.
Dissertations on Government, the Affairs of the Bank, and Paper Money, February 1786.
To His Excellency Benjamin Franklin, Esq., 2 June 1786.
"On the Advantages of a Public Bank," 20 June 1786, the *Pennsylvania Packet*.
"Letters on the Bank," 25 March, 28 March, 4 April, 7 April, 20 April 1786, the *Pennsylvania Packet*; 12 April, 20 September, 8 November 1786, the *Pennsylvania Gazette*. These letters were often signed "Common Sense" or with Paine's name.
"Common Sense" [Paine], "For the *Pennsylvania Packet*, and *Daily Advertiser*," 21 August 1786, the *Pennsylvania Packet*.
"Common Sense" [Paine], "On the Affairs of State," 20 September 1786, the *Pennsylvania Gazette*.
"Common Sense" [Paine], Untitled essay on Paper Money, 7 November 1786, the *Pennsylvania Packet*.
The Society for Political Inquiries, February 1787, Preamble to the rules and regulations of the Society.
"Common Sense" [Paine], "Addressed to the Opposers of the Bank," 7 March 1787, the *Pennsylvania Gazette*.
To Edmund Burke, August 1787.
Prospects on the Rubicon, 20 August 1787.
To Thomas Jefferson, May 1788.
To Thomas Jefferson, Spring 1788 (Foner has it as 9 September 1788).
To Edmund Burke, 7 August 1788.
"Specifications of Thomas Paine," 28 August 1788.
To Kitty Nicholson Few, 6 January 1789.
To Thomas Walker, 16 January 1789.
Letter, 9 February 1789, the *Federal Gazette*.
To Thomas Jefferson, 16 February 1789.
To Sir George Staunton, Bart., Spring 1789.
"At Tea," the *Federal Gazette*, 18 May 1789.
To George Washington, 15 October 1789.
To Edmund Burke, 17 January 1790.
To [Benjamin Rush], 16 March 1790. (Foner has it as 1789).
To William Short, several letters on the Nootka Sound, June 1790.
To Thomas Christie, 16 April 1790.
Rights of Man: Part One, February 1791.
To Condorcet, Nicolas de Bonneville, and Lanthenas, June 1791.
"A Republican Manifesto," a manifesto, 21 July 1791.
"To the Abbé Sieyès," 16 July 1791, *Le Moniteur*.
"Thoughts on the Establishment of a Mint in the United States," 17 November 1791, the *National Gazette*.

"Address and Declaration at a Select Meeting of the Friends of Universal Peace and Liberty," a manifesto, August 1791.
Rights of Man: Part Two, February 1792.
"To the Attorney-General," May 1792.
"To Mr. Secretary Dundas," 6 June 1792.
"Letters to Onslow Cranley," 17 June, 21 June 1792.
"To the Sheriff of the County of Sussex," 30 June 1792.
"Answer to Four Questions on the Legislative and Executive Powers," June, July 1792, the *Chronique du mois*.
"To Mr. Secretary Dundas," 15 September 1792.
Letter Addressed to the Addressers on the Late Proclamation, 1792.
[Paine], John Horne Tooke, "Address to the People of France," 25 September 1792.
"An Essay for the Use of New Republicans in their Opposition to Monarchy," 20 October 1792, *Le Patriote français*.
"To the English Attorney-General on the Prosecution Against the Second Part of *Rights of Man*," 11 November 1792.
"On the Propriety of Bringing Louis XVI to Trial," address to the National Convention, 20 November 1792.
"Plan of a Declaration of the Natural, Civil, and Political Rights of Man," with Condorcet, January 1793.
"Reasons for Preserving the Life of Louis Capet," address to the National Convention, 15 January 1793.
"Shall Louis XVI be Respited?" address to the National Convention, 19 January 1793.
"Observations on the Situation of the Powers Joined Against France," January 1793.
To Citizen Georges Jacques Danton, 6 May 1793.
"A Citizen of the United States of America" [Paine], "A Citizen of America to the Citizens of Europe," 28 July 1793.
To Citizen Barère, 5 September 1793.
"From the Castle in the Air to the Little Corner of the World," to Lady Smyth, 1794.
"The New Covenant, From the Castle in the Air to the Little Corner of the World," to Lady Smyth, 1794.
"Forgetfulness, From the Castle in the Air to the Little Corner of the World," to Lady Smyth, 1794.
To the French National Convention, 7 August 1794.
To James Monroe, 10 September 1794.
To James Monroe, 20 October 1794.
The Age of Reason, Part One, 1794.
The Age of Reason, Part Two, 1795.
Dissertations on First Principles of Government, July 1795.
"An American" [Paine], "Observations on Jay's Treaty," 2 July 1795, the *Philadelphia Aurora*.

"The Constitution of 1795," speech before the National Convention, 7 July 1795.

"Hail Great Republic," 1796, manuscript, New-York Historical Society. (see 1783)

"Contentment; Or, If You Please, Confession," 1796.

The Decline and Fall of the English System of Finance, April 1796.

Letter to George Washington, 30 July 1796.

"Epigram on George Washington," 1796.

Agrarian Justice, 1797.

*[Paine], "Epitaph on General Charles Lee," 1797.

Worship and Church Bells, a letter to Camille Jordan, 1797.

To Thomas Jefferson, 1 April 1797.

To Anonymous, 12 May 1797.

"The Recall of Monroe," 27 September 1797, letter to the editors of *Le Bien informé*.

The Eighteenth Fructidor, to the People of France and the French Armies, Fall 1797.

Letter to Mr. Erskine, with a "Precise History of the Theophilanthropists," September 1797.

Articles and Letters on a French "Descent" on England: 1797 letter to Jefferson, 14 December 1797, 15 December 1797, 15 January 1798, 29 January 1798, 18 March 1798, all in *Le Bien informé*; 11 October 1796, 6 March 1804, in the *Philadelphia Aurora*; 1 October 1800, unpublished.

To M. Tallyrand, 9 Vendemaire Year 6 (1797).

"The Existence of God," A Discourse at the Society of Theophilanthropists, Paris, 1797; 3 January 1801, *The Temple of Reason*.

To General Brune, 8 Brumaire, 8 Year (31 October 1799).

"To Sir Robert Smyth, What is Love?" 1800.

"Epigram on a Long-Nosed Friend," a poem, 1800.

To Thomas Jefferson, 1 October 1800.

To Thomas Jefferson, 25 June 1801.

To Madame Bonneville, 15 November 1802.

"An Essay on Dream," 1802, 1807.

"Letters to the Citizens of the United States and Particularly the Leaders of the Federal Faction," 15 November, 22 November, 29 November, 6 December 1802, 2 February 1803, the *National Intelligencer*; 14 May 1803, the *Philadelphia Aurora*; April 1803, the *Trenton True-American*; 7 June 1803, the *Philadelphia Aurora*.

To Samuel Adams, 1 January 1803.

"From Mr. Paine to Mr. Jefferson On the Occasion of a Toast Being Given at a Federal Dinner at Washington, of 'May They Never Know Pleasure Who Love Paine,' " 23 February 1803.

"The Construction of Iron Bridges," January, June 1803.

"Lines, Extempore, by Thomas Paine, July 1803."

To John C. Breckenridge, 2 August 1803.
To Thomas Jefferson, 23 September 1803.
To Elisha Babcock, 10 October 1803.
"To the People of England on the Invasion of England," 6 March 1804,
  the *Philadelphia Aurora.*
"A Friend to Constitutional Order" [Paine], "To the People of
  Connecticut," 2 August 1804, the *Hartford American Mercury.*
"Common Sense," [Paine], "Remarks on Gouverneur Morris' Funeral
  Oration on General Hamilton," 7 August 1804, the *Philadelphia
  Aurora.*
"Comus" [Paine], "Nonsense from New York," 23 August 1804, in the
  Philadelphia Aurora.
To Elisha Babcock, 27 August 1804.
"Common Sense" [Paine], "To the French Inhabitants of Louisiana," 22
  September 1804.
Anonymous [Paine], "Connecticut Has No Constitution," 26 November
  1804, the *National Intelligencer,* reprinted 27 December 1804, the
  Hartford American Mercury.
"Remarks on R. Hall's Sermon," 18 February 1804; "Of the Word
  'Religion' and Other Words of Uncertain Signification," 3 March
  1804; "Of Cain and Abel," 31 March 1804; "The Tower of Babel," 24
  March 1804; "Of the Old and New Testament," 31 March 1804; "Of
  the Religion of Deism Compared with the Christian Religion and the
  Superiority of the Former over the Latter," 30 June, 7 July 1804;
  "Hints Toward Forming a Society for Inquiring into the Truth or
  Falsehood of Ancient History So Far As History is Connected with
  Systems of Religion Ancient and Modern," 21 July 1804; "To Mr.
  Moore of New York, Commonly Called Bishop Moore," 4 August
  1804; "To John Mason, One of the Ministers of the Scotch
  Presbyterian Church of New York with Remarks on His Account of
  the Visit He Made to the Late Alexander Hamilton," 18 August 1804;
  "To the Members of the Society Styling Itself the Missionary Society,"
  1 September 1804; "Of the Books of the New Testament," 1
  September, 8 September 1804; "Biblical Anachronism;" "Religious
  Intelligence;" "Of the Sabbath-Day in Connecticut," 15 September
  1804; *The Prospect,* signing his pieces with his own name, or simply as
  T. P., "A Friend to the Indians," "An Enemy to Cant and Imposition,"
  "A True Deist," "A Member of the Deistical Church," "A Member of
  the Deistical Congregation," "Detector—P."
To Thomas Jefferson, 25 January 1805.
"To Mr. Hulbert of Sheffield, one of the Mortified Federal Members of
  the Massachusetts Legislature," 12 March 1805, the *Philadelphia
  Aurora.*
To Thomas Jefferson, 20 April 1805.
"Common Sense" [Paine], "Constitutions, Governments, and Charters," a
  pamphlet, June 1805.
"Remarks on English Affairs," 8 July 1805, the *Baltimore Evening
  Post.*

"A Spark from the Altar of '76" [Paine], "Another Callender—Thomas Turner of Virginia," 23 July, 24 July 1805, the *New York American Citizen*.

"Constitutional Reform: To the Citizens of Pennsylvania on the Proposal for Calling a Convention," August 1805, the *Philadelphia Aurora*.

To John Inskeep, Mayor of the City of Philadelphia, February 1806.

"The Cause of Yellow Fever and the Means of Preventing It in Places Not Yet Infected with It, Addressed to the Board of Health in America" 27 June 1806.

"Common Sense" [Paine], "A Challenge to the Federalists to Declare Their Principles," 17 October 1806.

"Liberty of the Press," 20 October 1806, the *New York American Citizen*.

"Letter on Fortification of New York Harbor," 13 November 1806, the *New York American Citizen*.

Paine's Responses to Carpenter: "Communication," 11 October 1806, in the *New York American Citizen*; "The emissary Cullen otherwise Carpenter," 28 October 1806, in the *New York American Citizen*; 5 November 1806, in the *Philadelphia Aurora*; and 19 November 1806, in the *Philadelphia Aurora*.

"Remarks on the Political and Military Affairs of Europe," 14 December 1806.

Examination of the Passages in the New Testament, Quoted from the Old and called Prophecies concerning Jesus Christ, 1807.

"Of the English Navy," January 1807.

"Common Sense" [Paine], "Of Gunboats," 11 March 1807.

"Three Letters to Morgan Lewis on His Prosecution of Thomas Farmar for One Hundred Dollars," April 1807, the *New York Public Advertiser* and the *Philadelphia Aurora*.

"Remarks, on a String of Resolutions offered by Mr. Hale, to the New York House of Representatives at Albany," 3 April 1807, the *New York Public Advertiser*.

"Remarks on Mr. Hale's String of Resolves Concluded," 4 April 1807, the *New York Public Advertiser*.

"On Gunboats," 22 April 1807, the *New York Public Advertiser*.

To James Madison, 3 May 1807.

To George Clinton, 4 May 1807.

"One Who Knows England" [Paine], "Of the Affairs of England," 1 June 1807, the *New York Public Advertiser*.

"Common Sense" [Paine], "Of the Comparative Powers and Expense of Ships of War, Gunboats, and Fortifications," 21 July 1807, the *New York Public Advertiser*.

"An Old Friend of 76" [Paine], on navies, 7 August 1807, the *New York Public Advertiser*.

"Common Sense" [Paine], "On the Question, Will There Be War?" 14 August 1807.

"To the People of New York," 18 August 1807, the *New York Public Advertiser*.

Paine's attacks on James Cheetham: 22 August 1807 5 September, 1807, 25 September 1807, 27 October 1807, 20 November 1807, 7 January 1808 25 August, 1808, all in the *New York Public Advertiser*.

"Of the Judiciary and the Conduct of Chief Justice Marshall," 10 October 1807, the *New York Public Advertiser*.

The Will of Thomas Paine, 18 January 1809.

Extracts from a Reply to the Bishop of Llandaff, posthumously published, 1810, *The Theophilanthropist*.

"Origins of Freemasonry," posthumously published, 1810.

"Predestination," posthumously published, 1820.

"Star in the East," undated poem.

*"The Strange Story of Korath, Dathan, and Abiram, Numbers, Chap. XVI, Accounted For," a poem, undated.

"On the British Constitution," a poem, undated.

*[Paine], "The Religion of the Sun," a poem, undated.

Manuscript Sources

The Richard Gimbel Collection of Thomas Paine Manuscripts, American Philosophical Society, Philadelphia.

The Gouverneur Morris Papers, Library of Congress, Washington, DC.

The Thomas Paine Collection at Thetford: An Analytical Catalogue. Norwich: Norfolk County Library, 1979.

Printed Individual and Collected Works of Thomas Paine

Aldridge, A. Owen. "Some Writings of Thomas Paine in Pennsylvania Newspapers." *American Historical Review* 56 (July 1951): 832-38.

_____ . "Thomas Paine and Comus." *Pennsylvania Magazine of History and Biography* 85 (Jan. 1961): 70-75.

_____ . "Thomas Paine, Edmund Burke and Anglo-French Relations in 1787." *Studies in Burke and His Time* 12 (Spring 1971): 1851-61.

_____ . "Thomas Paine and the *New York Public Advertiser*." *New-York Historical Society* Quarterly 37 (Oct. 1953): 361-82.

_____ . "Why Did Thomas Paine Write on the Bank?" *American Philosophical Society Proceedings* 93 (Sept. 1949): 309-15.

Boulton, J.T. "An Unpublished Letter from Paine to Burke." *Durham University Journal* 43 (Mar. 1951): 49-55.

Claeys, Gregory. *Rights of Man.* Indianapolis: Hackett, 1992.

Conway, Moncure Daniel, ed. *The Writings of Thomas Paine.* Four vols.

New York: G.P. Putnam's, 1894-96, rept. New York: AMS Press, 1967 and New York: Burt Franklin, 1969.

Foner, Eric, ed. *The Writings of Thomas Paine.* New York: Library of America, forthcoming in 1995.

Gimbel, Richard, ed. "New Political Writings of Thomas Paine." *Yale University Library Gazette* 30 (Jan. 1956): 94-107.

Kramnick, Isaac and Michael Foot, eds. *The Thomas Paine Reader.* Harmondsworth: Penguin, 1989.

Landin, Harold W. "Some Letters of Thomas Paine and William Short on the Nootka Sound Crisis." *Journal of Modern History* 13 (Sept. 1941): 357-74.

Meng, John J., ed. "Thomas Paine, French Propagandist in the United States." *Records of the American Catholic Historical Society* 57 (Mar. 1946): 1-25.

Paine, Thomas. *Common Sense* (1776), edited by Isaac Kramnick. Harmondsworth: Penguin, 1976.

_____ . *Rights of Man* (1791, 1792), edited by Henry Collins, and introduced by Eric Foner. Harmondsworth: Penguin, 1984.

_____ . *Rights of Man*, edited by Gregory Claeys. Indianapolis: Hackett, 1992.

_____ . *The Age of Reason* (1793, 1794), edited by Philip S. Foner. New York; Citadel Press, 1984.

_____ . *The Complete Writings of Thomas Paine.* Two vols., edited by Philip S. Foner. New York: Citadel Press, 1945. Volume One was reissued in paperback by Citadel in 1993.

Van der Weyde, William M., ed. *The Life and Works of Thomas Paine.* Patriot's Edition, ten vols. New Rochelle: Thomas Paine National Historical Association, 1925.

Printed Sources

Baisnée, Jules A. and John J. Meng, trans. "Philadelphia and the Revolution: French Diplomacy in the United States, 1778-1779." *Records of the American Catholic Historical Society* 57 (Mar. 1946): 23-40.

Browning, Oscar, ed. *The Despatches of Earl Gower, English Ambassador at Paris From June 1790 to August 1792, To Which are Added the Despatches of Mr. Lindsay and Mr. Munro, and the Diary of Viscount Palmerston in France During July and August 1791.* Cambridge: Cambridge University Press, 1885.

Burke, Edmund. *Reflections on the Revolution in France*, edited by J.G.A. Pocock. Indianapolis: Hackett, 1989.

_____ . *The Correspondence of Edmund Burke*, Thomas W. Copeland, ed. Ten vols. Cambridge: Cambridge University Press, 1958-78.

_____ . *Speech on Conciliation with the Colonies* (1775). Intro. by Jeffrey Hart. Chicago: Gateway, 1964.

_____ . *Writings and Speeches of Edmund Burke.* Paul Langford, gen. ed. Eight vols. to date. Oxford: Clarendon Press, 1981-92.

Butterfield, L.H., ed. *The Adams Papers. The Diary and Autobiography of John Adams.* Four vols. Cambridge, Mass.: The Belknap Press of Harvard University Press, 1961.

_____ . *The Letters of Benjamin Rush.* Two vols. Princeton: Princeton University Press for the American Philosophical Society, 1951.

Carlile, Richard. *The Life of Thomas Paine.* London, 1819.

[Chalmers, George]. *Life of Thomas Paine, the Author of Rights of Men, with a Defence of his Writings, by Francis Oldys, A.M. of the University of Pennsylvania.* London: J. Stockdale, 1791.

Charlotte Corday: Une Normande dans la Révolution. Rouen: Musées départmentales de la Seine-Maritimes, 1989.

Cheetham, James. *Life of Thomas Paine.* New York: Southwick and Pelsue, 1809.

Cobban, Alfred, ed. *The Debate on the French Revolution, 1789-1800.* Second edition. New York: Barnes and Noble, 1960.

Condorcet. *Le Républicain.* Paris: Edhis, 1989.

de Crèvecoeur, Henry St. John. *Letters from an American Farmer and Sketches of 18th-Century America,* Albert E. Stone, ed. Harmondsworth: Penguin, 1981.

Dumont, Etienne. *Souvenirs sur Mirabeau, et sur les deux premières assemblées legislatives.* Paris: C. Gosselin et H. Bossange, 1832.

Franklin, Benjamin. *The Papers of Benjamin Franklin,* Leonard W. Labaree, ed. (Vols 1-14), William B. Willcox, ed. (vols. 15-25). Thirty vols. to date. New Haven: Yale University Press, 1959- .

_____ . *The Writings of Benjamin Franklin,* Albert Henry Smyth, ed. Ten vols. New York: Macmillan Co., 1905-07.

Government of the United States. "An Act to Authorize Construction of a Monument in the District of Columbia or Its Environs to Honor Thomas Paine." Government Printing Office, Superintendent of Documents, 1992.

Grenville, William Wyndham. Royal Commission on Historical Manuscripts. *The Manuscripts of J. B. Fortescue, Esq., Preserved at Dropmore.* Ten vols. London: Printed For Her Majesty's Stationery Office by Eyre and Spottiswoode, Mackie and Co., and others, 1894.

Howell, Thomas Bayly, ed. *A Complete Collection of State Trials and Proceedings for High Treason and Other Crimes and Misdemeanors.* Thirty-three vols. London: R. Bagshaw, 1809-26.

Jefferson, Thomas. *The Papers of Thomas Jefferson,* Julian P. Boyd, ed. Twenty-five vols. to date. Princeton: Princeton University Press, 1950- .

_____ . *The Writings of Thomas Jefferson,* Paul Leicester Ford, ed. Ten vols. New York: G. P. Putnam's, 1892-99.

King, Charles R., ed. *The Life and Correspondence of Rufus King.* Six vols. New York: G. P. Putnam's, 1897; reprinted New York: Da Capo Press, 1971.

Kammen, Michael, ed. *The Origins of the American Constitution: A Documentary History.* Harmondsworth: Penguin, 1986.

Locke, John. *Second Treatise of Government,* edited by C.B. Macpherson. Indianapolis: Hackett, 1980.

Meng, John J., ed. *Despatches and Instructions of Conrad Alexandre Gérard, 1778-1780.* For the Institute Français de Washington. Baltimore: Johns Hopkins Press, 1939.

Morris, Gouverneur. *A Diary of the French Revolution, 1789-1793,* Beatrix Cary Davenport, ed. Two vols. Boston: Houghton Mifflin, 1939.

Morris, Robert. *The Papers of Robert Morris,* E. James Ferguson, ed. Seven vols. to date. Pittsburgh: University of Pittsburgh Press, 1973- .

Price, Richard. *Discourse on the Love of Our Country.* London, 1790.

Rickman, Thomas Clio. *The Life of Thomas Paine.* London: B.D. Cousins, 1819.

Roland, Madame. *Mémoires de Madame Roland.* Nouvelle Edition, accompagnée de Notes et d'Appendice, précedée d'une Notice biographique et ornée d'un beau portrait. Two vols. Paris: Chez Rapilly, 1823.

Rousseau, Jean-Jacques. *The Basic Political Writings.* Donald A. Cress, trans. Indianapolis: Hackett, 1987.

Rush, Benjamin. *Autobiography,* George W. Corner, ed. Princeton: Princeton University Press, 1948.

Sparks, Jared, ed. *The Life of Gouverneur Morris, with Selections from His Correspondence and Miscellaneous Papers.* Three vols. Boston: Grey and Bowen, 1832.

Tone, Theobald Wolfe. *The Life of Theobald Wolfe Tone, Edited by his Son.* Two vols. Washington: Printed by Gales and Seaton, 1826.

Washington, George. *The Writings of George Washington,* John C. Fitzpatrick, ed. Thirty-nine vols. Washington: Government Printing Office, 1931-44.

Watson, Winslow, C., ed. *Men and Times of the Revolution, or the Memoirs of Elkanah Watson.* Second Edition. New York: Dana and Co., 1856.

Wharton, Francis, ed. *The Revolutionary Diplomatic Correspondence of the United States.* Six vols. Washington: Government Printing Office, 1889.

Williams, Helen-Maria. *Letters Containing a Sketch of the Politics of France From the Thirty First of May 1793 till the 10th of Thermidor, Twenty-Eighth of July 1794 and of the Scenes Which Have Passed in the Prisons of Paris.* Three vols. London: G.G. and J. Robinson, 1795.

Yorke, Henry Redhead, Esq. *France in Eighteen-Hundred and Two, Described in a Series of Letters.* J.A.C. Sykes, ed. London: William

Heinemann, 1906.

_____ . *Letters from France, Describing the Manners and Customs of its Inhabitants: With Observations on the Arts, Manufactures, Public Institutions and Buildings, Learned Societies, and the Mode of Traveling. Interspersed with Interesting Anecdotes of Celebrated Characters.* Two vols. London: Sherwood, Neely, and Jones, 1814.

Books

Aldridge, A. Owen. *Benjamin Franklin: Philosopher and Man.* New York: J.B. Lippincott, 1965.

_____ . *Man of Reason: The Life of Thomas Paine.* Philadelphia: J.B. Lippincott Co., 1959.

_____ . *Thomas Paine's American Ideology.* Newark: University Press of Delaware, 1984.

Alger, John Goldworth. *Englishmen in the French Revolution.* London: Sampson, Low, Marston, Searle, and Rivington, 1889.

_____ . *Glimpses of the French Revolution: Myths, Ideals, and Realities.* London: Sampson, Low, and Marston, 1894.

_____ . *Paris in 1789-94: Farewell Letters of Victims of the Guillotine.* London: George Allen, 1902; rept. New York: AMS Press, 1970.

Ashcraft, Richard. *Revolutionary Politics and Locke's Two Treatises.* Princeton: Princeton University Press, 1986.

Ayer, A.J. *Thomas Paine.* London: Secker and Warburg, 1988.

Bailyn, Bernard. *The Ideological Origins of the American Revolution.* Cambridge, Mass.: Harvard University Press, 1967.

Beer, Samuel H. *To Make a Nation: The Rediscovery of Federalism.* Cambridge, Mass.: Belknap Press of Harvard University Press, 1993.

Berlin, Ira and Ronald Hoffman, eds. *Slavery and Freedom in the Age of the American Revolution.* Charlottesville: University Press of Virginia, 1983.

Billington, James H. *Fire in the Minds of Men: Origins of Revolutionary Faith.* New York: Basic Books, 1980.

Bizardel, Yvon. *Bottin des Américains à Paris sous Louis XVI et pendant la révolution.* Paris: Clavreuil, 1978.

_____ . *Les Américains à Paris pendant la révolution.* Paris: Calmann-Levy, 1972.

Black, Eugene Charlton. *The Association: British Extraparliamentary Political Organization, 1769-1793.* Cambridge, Mass.: Harvard University Press, 1963.

Blum, Carol. *Rousseau and the Republic of Virtue: The Language of Politics in the French Revolution.* Ithaca: Cornell University Press, 1982.

Boatner, III, Mark Mayo. *An Encyclopedia of the American Revolution.* Bicentennial Edition. New York: David McKay Co., 1974.

Boissel, Thiérry. *Sophie de Condorcet: Femme des lumières (1764-1822)*. Paris: Presses de la Renaissance, 1988.

Boulton, James T. *The Language of Politics in the Age of Wilkes and Burke*. Westport: Greenwood Press, 1963.

Claeys, Gregory. *The Political Thought of Thomas Paine*. Winchester: Unwin Hyman, 1989.

Clark, J.C.D. *English Society, 1688-1832*. Cambridge: Cambridge University Press, 1985.

_____ . *The Language of Liberty, 1660-1832: Political Discourse and Social Dynamics in the Anglo-American World*. Cambridge: Cambridge University Press, 1994.

Cobban, Alfred. *Aspects of the French Revolution*. New York: W.W. Norton, 1968.

Commager, Henry Steele. *The Empire of Reason: How Europe Imagined and America Realized the Enlightenment*. New York: Vintage, 1978.

Cone, Carl B. *Burke and the Nature of Politics*. Two vols. Lexington: University of Kentucky Press, 1957-1964.

Conway, Moncure Daniel. *The Life of Thomas Paine*. Two vols. New York: G. P. Putnam's, 1892.

Dauban, Charles-Aimé. *Les Prisons de Paris sous la révolution d'après les relations des contemporains avec des notes et une introduction*. Geneva: Slatkine-Megariotis Reprints, 1977; orig. printed Paris, 1870.

Davidson, Edward H. and William J. Scheick. *Paine, Scripture, and Authority: "The Age of Reason" as Religious and Political Idea*. Bethlehem: Lehigh University Press, 1994.

Deane, Seamus. *The French Revolution and Enlightenment in England, 1789-1832*. Cambridge, Mass.: Harvard University Press, 1988.

DeConde, Alexander. *The Quasi-War: The Politics and Diplomacy of the Undeclared War with France 1797-1801*. New York: Charles Scribner's Sons, 1966.

D'Elia, Donald J. *Benjamin Rush: Philosopher of the American Revolution*. Philadelphia: American Philosophical Society Transactions, 1974.

Dickinson, H.T. *British Radicalism and the French Revolution, 1789-1815*. Oxford: Blackwell, 1985.

Dunn, John. *The Political Philosophy of John Locke*. Cambridge: Cambridge University Press, 1969.

Dyck, Ian. *William Cobbett and Rural Popular Culture*. Cambridge: Cambridge University Press, 1992.

Elkins, Stanley and Eric McKitrick. *The Age of Federalism: The Early American Republic, 1787-1800*. New York: Oxford University Press, 1993.

Elliott, Marianne. *Wolfe Tone*. New Haven: Yale University Press, 1988.

_____ . *Partners in Revolution: The United Irishmen and France*. New Haven: Yale University Press, 1982.

Erdman, David V. *Commerce des Lumières: John Oswald and the British in*

Paris, 1790-1793. Columbia: University of Missouri Press, 1986.

Fennessey, R. R. *Burke, Paine, and the Rights of Man: A Difference of Political Opinion.* The Hague: Martinus Nijhoff, 1963.

Fischer, David Hackett. *Paul Revere's Ride.* New York: Oxford University Press, 1994.

Foner, Eric. *Tom Paine and Revolutionary America.* Oxford: Oxford University Press, 1976.

Ford, Edward. *David Rittenhouse: Astronomer-Patriot, 1732-1796.* Philadelphia: University of Pennsylvania Press, 1946.

Fortolis, Ludovic. *Les Anglais en France: Des cochots de la terreur aux geôles de l'empire.* Paris: Perrin, 1923.

Fruchtman, Jack, Jr. T*he Apocalyptic Politics of Richard Price and Joseph Priestley.* Philadelphia: American Philosophical Society Transactions, Vol. 73, Pt. 4, 1983.

_____ . *Thomas Paine and the Religion of Nature.* Baltimore: Johns Hopkins University Press, 1993.

Furet, François. *Rethinking the French Revolution.* Elborg Forster, trans. Cambridge: Cambridge University Press, 1981.

_____ and Mona Ozouf, *A Critical Dictionary of the French Revolution.* Arthur Goldhammer, trans. Cambridge, Mass.: Harvard University Press, 1989.

Furniss, Tom. *Edmund Burke's Aesthetic Ideology: Language, Gender and Political Economy in Revolution.* Cambridge: Cambridge University Press, 1993, 23-48.

Garrett, Clark. *Respectable Folly: Millenarians and the French Revolution in France and England.* Baltimore: Johns Hopkins University Press, 1975.

Gimbel, Richard. *Thomas Paine: A Bibliographical Checklist of "Common Sense."* New Haven: Yale University Press, 1956.

Hammond, Bray. *Banks and Politics in America from the Revolution to the Civil War.* Princeton: Princeton University Press, 1957.

Hawke, David Freeman. *Benjamin Rush: Revolutionary Gadfly.* Indianapolis: Bobbs-Merrill, 1971.

_____ . *Franklin.* New York: Harper and Row, 1976.

_____ . *Paine.* New York: Harper and Row, 1974; rept. Norton, 1992.

Henderson, Ernest F. *Symbol and Satire in the French Revolution.* New York: G. P. Putnam's, 1912.

Hindle, Brooke. *David Rittenhouse.* New York: Arno Press, 1980 [orig. publ. 1964].

Jacob, Margaret C. *The Radical Enlightenment: Pantheists, Freemasons and Republicans.* London: George Allen & Unwin, 1981.

Jordan, David. *The King's Trial.* Berkeley: University of California Press, 1979.

Kantin, Georges, ed. *Thomas Paine, Citoyen du monde.* Textes reunis par Georges Kantin et la Ligue du Droit de l'Homme. English trans. by

Simon Kantin. Paris: Editions Créaphis, 1990.

Kates, Gary. *Le Cercle Social, the Girondins, and the French Revolution.* Princeton: Princeton University Press, 1985.

Kelly, Larry, *Women Writing and Revolution, 1790-1827.* Oxford: Clarendon Press, 1993.

Kintzler, Catherine. *Condorcet: L'instruction publique et la naissance du citoyen.* Paris: Le Sycomore, 1984.

Kloos, John. M., Jr. *A Sense of Deity: The Republican Spirituality of Benjamin Rush.* Brooklyn: Carlson Publishers, 1991.

Kramnick, Isaac. *Bolingbroke and His Circle: The Politics of Nostalgia in the Age of Walpole.* Cambridge, Mass.: Harvard University Press, 1968.

————. The Rage of Edmund Burke: *The Conscience of an Ambivalent Conservative.* New York: Basic Books, 1977.

————. *Republicanism and Bourgeois Radicalism: Political Ideology in Late-Eighteenth Century England and America.* Ithaca: Cornell University Press, 1990.

Langford, Paul. *A Polite and Commercial People: England, 1727-1783.* Oxford: Clarendon Press, 1989.

Lavery, Brian. *Nelson's Navy: The Ships, Men and Organisation, 1793-1815.* Annapolis: Naval Institute Press, 1989.

Lefebvre, Georges. *The Great Fear: Rural Panic in Revolutionary France.* Joan White, trans. Princeton: Princeton University Press, 1973.

Lerner, Ralph. *Revolutions Revisited: Two Faces of the Politics of Enlightenment.* Chapel Hill: University of North Carolina Press, 1994.

————. *The Thinking Revolutionary: Principle and Practice in the New Republic.* Ithaca: Cornell University Press, 1987.

Lessay, Jean. *L'Américain de la Convention: Thomas Paine, Professeur de Révolutions, député de Pas-de-Calais.* Paris: Perrin, 1987.

Lock, F.P. *Burke's Reflections on the Revolution in France.* London: George Allen & Unwin, 1985.

Lydon, James G. *Pirates, Privateers, and Profits.* Upper Saddle River: The Gregg Press, 1970.

McCalman, Iain. *The Radical Underworld.* Cambridge: Cambridge University Press, 1988.

McDonald, Forrest. *Novus Ordo Seclorum: The Intellectual Origins of the Constitution.* Lawrence: University Press of Kansas, 1985.

MacLeod, Duncan J. *Slavery, Race and the American Revolution.* Cambridge: Cambridge University Press, 1974.

Marshall, Dorothy. *Industrial England, 1776-1851.* New York: Charles Scribner's Sons, 1973.

Marshall, John W. *Resistance, Responsibility and Religion: The Thought of John Locke.* Cambridge: Cambridge University Press, forthcoming.

May, Henry F. *The Enlightenment in America.* New York: Oxford University Press, 1976.

Melchior-Bonnet, Bernardine. *Charlotte Corday.* Paris: Tallandier, 1989.

Middlekauf, Robert. *The Glorious Cause: The American Revolution, 1763-1789*. New York and Oxford: Oxford University Press, 1982.

Mintz, Max M. *Gouverneur Morris and the American Revolution*. Norman: University of Oklahoma Press, 1970.

O'Brien, Conor Cruise. *The Great Melody: A Thematic Biography of Edmund Burke*. Chicago: University of Chicago Press, 1992.

Ozouf, Mona. *Festivals and the French Revolution*. Alan Sheridan, trans. Cambridge, Mass.: Harvard University Press, 1988.

Palmer, R.R. *Twelve Who Ruled: The Year of the Terror in the French Revolution*. New York: Atheneum, 1965.

Philp, Mark. *The French Revolution and British Popular Politics*. Cambridge: Cambridge University Press, 1991.

_____. *Paine*. Past Masters Series. Oxford: Oxford University Press, 1989.

Plumb, J.H. *The Growth of Political Stability in England, 1675-1725*. Harmondsworth: Penguin, 1967.

Pocock, J.G.A. *The Machiavellian Moment: Florentine Political Thought in the Atlantic Republican Tradition*. Princeton: Princeton University Press, 1975.

_____, ed. with the assistance of Gordon J. Schochet and Lois G. Schwoerer. *The Varieties of British Political Thought, 1500-1800*. Cambridge: Cambridge University Press, 1993.

_____. *Virtue, Commerce and History: Essays on Political Thought and History, Chiefly in the Eighteenth Century*. Cambridge: Cambridge University Press, 1985.

_____. *The Ancient Constitution and the Feudal Law: A Study of English Historical Thought in the Seventeenth Century, A Reissue with a Retrospective*. Cambridge: Cambridge University Press, 1987.

Powell, David. *Tom Paine: The Greatest Exile*. New York: St. Martin's Press, 1985.

Pütz, Manfred and Jon-K Adams. *A Concordance to Thomas Paine's "Common Sense" and "The American Crisis."* New York: Garland Publishing, 1989.

Robertson, William Spence. *The Life of Miranda*. Two vols. Chapel Hill: University of North Carolina Press, 1929.

Robinson, Donald L. *Slavery in the Structure of American Politics,1765-1820*. New York: Harcourt Brace Jovanovich, 1971.

Rodger, N.A.M. *The Wooden World: Anatomy of the Georgian Navy*. Annapolis: Naval Institute Press, 1986.

Roosevelt, Theodore R. *The Life of Gouverneur Morris*. New York: Houghton-Mifflin Co., 1888.

Rose, R.B. *The Making of the Sans-Culottes: Democratic Ideas and Institutions in Paris, 1789-1792*. Manchester: Manchester University Press, 1983.

Sapiro, Virginia. *A Vindication of Political Virtue: The Political Theory of*

Mary Wollstonecraft. Chicago: University of Chicago Press, 1992.

Schama, Simon. *Citizens: A Chronicle of the French Revolution*. New York: Alfred A. Knopf, 1989.

_____ . *Patriots and Liberators: Revoltuion in the Netherlands, 1780-1813*. New York: Alfred A. Knopf, 1977.

Sheldon, Garrett Ward. *The Political Philosophy of Thomas Jefferson*. Baltimore: Johns Hopkins University Press, 1991.

Smith, Billy G. and Richard Wojtowicz. *Blacks Who Stole Themselves: Advertisements for Runaways in the "Pennsylvania Gazette," 1728-1790*. Philadelphia: University of Pennsylvania Press, 1989.

Smith, Olivia. *The Politics of Language, 1791-1819*. Oxford: Clarendon Press, 1984.

Soboul, Albert. *The Sans-Culottes: The Popular Movement and Revolutionary Government, 1793-1794*. Rémy Inglis Hall, trans. Princeton: Princeton University Press, 1980.

Spater, George. *William Cobbett: The Poor Man's Friend*. Two vols. Cambridge: Cambridge University Press, 1982.

Stinchcombe, William C. *The XYZ Affair*. Westport: Greenwood Press, 1980.

Storing, Herbert. *What the Antifederalists Were For*. Chicago: University of Chicago Press, 1981.

Thomas, D.O. *The Honest Mind: The Thought and Work of Richard Price*. Oxford: Clarendon Press, 1977.

Thompson, E.P. *The Making of the English Working Class*. New York: Vintage, 1963.

Townsend, Sara Bertha. *An American Soldier: The Life of John Laurens*. Raleigh: Edwards and Broughton, 1958.

Vale, Gilbert. *The Life of Thomas Paine*. New York: Privately printed, 1841.

Van Doren, Carl. *The Secret History of the American Revolution*. New York: Viking, 1941.

Venturi, Franco. *Roots of Revolution: A History of the Populist and Socialist Movements in Nineteenth Century Russia*. Francis Haskell, trans. New York: Universal Library, 1966.

Vincent, Bernard. *Thomas Paine, ou la religion de la liberté*. Paris: Aubier, 1987.

_____ , ed. *Thomas Paine, ou la république sans frontières*. Nancy: Presses Universitaires de Nancy, Ligue des Droits de l'Homme, 1993.

Walters, Kerry S. *The American Deists: Voices of Reason and Dissent in the Early Republic*. Lawrence: University Press of Kansas, 1992.

_____ . *Rational Infidels: The American Deists*. Durango, Colorado: Longwood Academics, 1992.

Wiener, Joel H. *Radicalism and Freethought in Nineteenth-Century Britain: The Life of Richard Carlile*. Westport: Greenwood Press, 1983.

Williamson, Audrey. *Thomas Paine: His Life, Work and Times*. London:

George Allen & Unwin, 1973.

Wills, Garry. *Cincinnatus: George Washington and the Enlightenment.* Garden City: Doubleday, 1984.

Wilson, *David A. Paine and Cobbett: The Transatlantic Connection.* Kingston and Montreal: McGill-Queen's University Press, 1988.

Wöll, Walter. *Thomas Paine: Motives for Rebellion.* European University Studies Series XIV, Anglo-Saxon Language and Literature, Vol. 248. Frankfurt Am Main: Peter Lang, 1992.

Wood, Gordon S. *The Creation of the American Republic, 1776–1787.* Chapel Hill: University of North Carolina Press, 1969.

_____. *The Radicalism of the American Revolution: How a Revolution Transformed a Monarchical Society into a Democratic One Unlike Any That Had Ever Existed.* New York: Alfred A. Knopf, 1992.

Journal Articles and Opinion Pieces

Abel, Darrel. "The Significance of the 'Letter to the Abbé Raynal' in the Progress of Thomas Paine's Thought." *Pennsylvania Magazine of History and Biography* 66 (Apr. 1942):176-90.

Aldridge, A. Owen. "Condorcet et Paine: Leurs rapports intellectuels." *Revue de littérature comparée* 32 (Jan. 1958):47-65.

_____. "Condorcet, Paine, and Historical Method." In Leonora Cohen Rosenfield, ed., *Condorcet Studies*, Vol. I. Atlantic Highlands: Humanities Press, 1984, 49-60.

_____. "John Oswald and the French Revolution." *The Eighteenth Century: Theory and Interpretation* 31 (Summer 1990):181-86.

_____. "La Signification historique, diplomatique et littéraire de la lettre addressé à l'abbé Raynal de Thomas Paine." *Etudes Anglaises* 8 (1955):223-32.

_____. "The Influence of New York Newspapers on Paine's *Common Sense*." *New-York Historical Society Quarterly* 60 (Jan. 1976):53-60.

_____. "The Influence of Thomas Paine in the United States, England, France, Germany, and South America." In Werner P. Friedrich, ed., *Comparative Literature: Proceedings of the Second Congress of the International Comparative Literature Association*, Two vols. Chapel Hill: University of North Carolina Press, 1959, 2:369-83.

_____. "Paine and Dickinson." *Early American Literature* 11 (Fall, 1976):125-38.

_____. "The Poetry of Thomas Paine." *Pennsylvania Magazine of History and Biography* 79 (Jan. 1951):81-99.

_____. "The *Rights of Man* de Thomas Paine: Symbole du siècle des lumières et leur influence en France." In Pierre Francastel, ed., *Utopie et institutions au XVIIIe siècle: Les Pragmatismes des Lumières.* Paris: Mouton, 1963, 77-87.

_____ . "Thomas Paine and the *idéologues.*" *Studies in Voltaire and the Eighteenth Century*, Transactions of the Fourth International Congress on the Enlightenment 151 (1976):109-17.

_____ . "Thomas Paine and Latin American Independence." In A. Owen Aldridge, ed., *Early American Literature: A Comparatist Approach.* Princeton: Princeton University Press, 1982, 215-60.

_____ . "Thomas Paine and the Classics." *Eighteenth-Century Studies* 1 (June 1968):370-80.

_____ . "Thomas Paine: A Survey of Research and Criticism Since 1945." *British Studies Monitor* 5 (Winter 1975):3-27.

_____ . "Thomas Paine in Latin America." *Early American Literature* 3 (Winter 1968-69):139-47.

_____ . "Thomas Paine's Plan for a Descent on England." *William and Mary Quarterly*, 3rd series, 14 (Jan. 1957):74-84.

Alexander, John K. "The Fort Wilson Incident of 1779: A Case Study of the Revolutionary Crowd." *William and Mary Quarterly*, 3rd Series, 31 (Oct. 1974):589-612.

Armytage, W.H.G. "Thomas Paine and the Walkers: An Early Episode in Anglo-American Co-operation." *Pennsylvania History* 18 (Jan. 1951):16-30.

Bailyn, Bernard. "The Most Uncommon Pamphlet of the Revolution: *Common Sense.*" *American Heritage* 25 (Dec. 1973):36-41, 91-93.

Barry, Alyce. "Thomas Paine: Privateersman." *Pennsylvania Magazine of History and Biography* 101 (Oct. 1977):451-61.

Bindman, David. " 'My own mind is my own church': Blake, Paine and the French Revolution." In Alison Yarrington and Kelvin Everest, eds. *Reflections of Revolution: Images of Romanticism.* London: Routledge, 1993, 112-33.

Bradbury, M.L. "Legal Privilege and the Bank of North America." *Pennsylvania Magazine of History and Biography* 96 (Apr. 1972):139-66.

Braff, David. "The Forgotten Founding Father: The Impact of Thomas Paine." *The Humanist* 47 (May/June 1987):21-23, 38.

Bressler, Leo A. "Peter Porcupine and the Bones of Thomas Paine." *Pennsylvania Magazine of History and Biography* 82 (Apr. 1958):176-85.

Browne, Ray B. "The Paine-Burke Controversy in Eighteenth-Century Irish Popular Songs." In Ray B. Browne, William John Roscelli, and Richard Loftus, eds. *The Celtic Cross: Studies in Irish Culture and Literature.* West Lafayette: Purdue University Press, 1964, 80-97.

Budd, Susan. "The Loss of Faith: Reasons for Unbelief among Members of the Secular Movement in England, 1850-1950." *Past and Present* 36 (Apr. 1967):106-25.

Canavan, S.J. "The Relevance of the Burke-Paine Controversy to American Political Thought." *Review of Politics* 49 (Spring 1987):163-76.

Caute, David. "Man of Rights: Thomas Paine's Arguments for the

French Revolution Were Alive with Meaning for His Time; David
Caute Argues that They Remain Relevant." *New Statesman and Society*
2 (Jan. 7, 1989):12-14.

Christian, William. "The Moral Economics of Tom Paine." *Journal of the
History of Ideas* 34 (July-Sept. 1973):367-80.

Claeys, Gregory. "The French Revolution Debate and British Political
Thought." *History of Political Thought* 11 (Spring 1990):59-80.

_____ . "Republicanism versus Commercial Society: Paine, Burke, and
the French Revolution." *Society for the Study of Labour History Bulletin*
54 (Winter 1989):4-13.

_____ . "Thomas Paine's *Agrarian Justice* (1796) and the Secularization
of Natural Jurisprudence." *Society for the Study of Labour History
Bulletin* 52 (Winter 1988):21-31.

Clark, Harry Hayden. "An Historical Interpretation of Thomas Paine's
Religion." *University of California Chronicle* 35 (1933):56-87.

_____ . "Thomas Paine's Relation to Voltaire and Rousseau." *Revue
anglo-américaine* (Apr. 1932):305-18 and (June 1932):393-405.

_____ . "Toward a Reevaluation of Thomas Paine." *American
Literature* 5 (May 1933):133-45.

Darnton, Robert. "A Spy in Grub Street." In *The Literary Underground of
the French Revolution*. Cambridge, Mass.: Harvard University Press,
1982, 41-70.

Davidson, Edward H. and William J. Scheick. "Authority in Paine's
Common Sense and the *Crisis Papers*." *Studies in the Humanities* 18
(Dec. 1991):124-34.

De Prospo, R. C. "Paine and Sieyès." *Thought* 65 (June 1990): 190-202.

Dorfman, Joseph. "The Economic Philosophy of Thomas Paine." *Political
Science Quarterly* 53 (Sept. 1938):372-86.

Durey, Michael. "Thomas Paine's Apostles: Radical Emigrés and the
Triumph of Jeffersonian Republicanism." *William and Mary Quarterly*,
3rd Series, (Oct. 1987):661-88.

Eayrs, James. "The Political Ideas of the English Agrarians, 1775-1815."
Canadian Journal of Economics and Political Science 18 (Aug. 1952):287-
302.

Emsley, Clive. "Repression, 'Terror,' and the Rule of Law in England
During the Decade of the French Revolution." *English Historical
Review* 100 (Oct. 1985):801-27.

Essick, Robert N. "William Blake, Thomas Paine, and Biblical
Revelation." *Studies in Romanticism* 30 (Summer 1991):189-212.

Falk, Robert B. "Thomas Paine and the Attitude of the Quakers to the
American Revolution." *Pennsylvania Magazine of History and
Biography* 63 (1939):302-10.

_____ . "Thomas Paine: Deist or Quaker?" *Pennsylvania Magazine of
History and Biography* 62 (1938):52-63.

Fitzpatrick, Martin. "Richard Price and the London Revolution Society."

Enlightenment and Dissent 10 (1991):35-50.

Fruchtman, Jack, Jr. "God and Politics: Notes from *The Age of Reason.*" In the *Baltimore Sun*, Oct. 30, 1984.

_____ . "Nature and Revolution in Paine's *Common Sense.*" *History of Political Thought* 10 (Autumn 1989):421-38.

_____ . "Reagan's Paine: Would Tom Recognize Himself?" In the *Baltimore Sun*, Oct. 9, 1984.

_____ . "The Revolutionary Millennialism of Thomas Paine." In O. M. Brack, Jr., ed., *Studies in Eighteenth-Century Culture*, Vol. 13 Madison: University of Wisconsin Press, 1984, 65-77.

Furniss, Tom. "Burke, Paine, and the Language of Assignats." In J.R. Watson, guest ed., *The Yearbook of English Studies: The French Revolution in English Literature and Art, Special Edition.* London: Modern Humanities Research Association, 1989, 19:54-70.

_____ . "Rhetoric in Revolution: The Role of Language in Paine's Critique of Burke." In Keith Hanley and Raman Selden, eds. *Revolution and English Romanticism: Politics and Rhetoric.* New York: St. Martin's Press, 1990.

_____ . "Stripping the Queen: Edmund Burke's Magic Lantern Show." In Steven Blakemore, ed., *Edmund Burke and the French Revolution: Bicentennial Essays.* Athens: University of Georgia Press, 1992, 69-96.

Gimbel, Richard. "The Resurgence of Thomas Paine." *Proceedings of the American Antiquarian Society* 69 (Oct. 21, 1959): 97-111.

_____ . "Thomas Paine Fights for Freedom in Three Worlds, The New, The Old, and The Next: Catalogue of An Exhibition Commemorating the One Hundredth Fiftieth Anniversary of His Death, Yale University Library, October 1959." *Proceedings of the American Antiquarian Society* 70 (Oct. 19, 1960):397-492.

Greene, Jack P. "Paine, America, and the 'Modernization' of Political Consciousness." *Political Science Quarterly* 93 (Spring 1978):73-92.

Gummere, Richard M. "Thomas Paine: Was He Really Anticlassical?" *American Antiquarian Society Proceedings* 75 (Oct. 1965):253-69.

Harris, Ian. "Paine and Burke: God, Nature and Politics." In Michael Bentley, ed., *Public and Private Domaine: Essays in British History Presented to Sir Malcolm Cowling.* Cambridge: Cambridge University Press, 1993, 34-62

Hinz, Evelyn J. "The 'Reasonable' Style of Tom Paine." *Queen's Quarterly* 79 (Summer, 1972):231-41.

Hogg, Peter C. "Paine's *Rights of Man*, Swedenborgianism and Freedom of the Press in Sweden: A Publishing Enigma of 1792." *The British Library Journal* 19 (Spring 1993):34-43.

Jordan, Winthrop D. "Familial Politics: Thomas Paine and the Killing of the King." *Journal of American History* 60 (Sept. 1973):294-308.

Kates, Gary. "From Liberalism to Radicalism: Tom Paine's *Rights of*

Man." *Journal of the History of Ideas* 50 (Oct. 1989):569-87.
Keane, John. "Démocratic républicaine, nation, nationalisme: repenser les *Droits de l'Homme* de Thomas Paine." Bernard Vincent, trans., in Bernard Vincent, ed., *Thomas Paine ou la République sans frontières.* Nancy: Presses Universitaires de Nancy, Ligue des droits de l'homme, 1993, 137-58.
————— . "Religion and Liberty: Tom Paine's Attack on Revolutionary Atheism." *Times Literary Supplement* (Feb. 11, 1994):13-14.
Kistler, Mark O. "German-American Liberalism and Thomas Paine." *American Quarterly* 14 (Spring 1962):81-91.
Kramnick, Isaac. "Tom Paine: Radical Democrat." *democracy,* 1 (Jan. 1981):127-38.
————— . "Tommy Paine and the Idea of America." In Paul Korshin, ed., *The American Revolution and Eighteenth-Century Culture.* New York: AMS Press, 1986, 75-91.
Knudson, Jerry W. "The Rage Around Tom Paine: Newspaper Reaction to His Homecoming in 1802." *New-York Historical Society Quarterly* 53 (Jan. 1969):34-63.
Lagrave, Jean de. "Thomas Paine et les Condorcet." In Bernard Vincent, ed., *Thomas Paine ou la République sans frontières.* Nancy: Presses Universitaires de Nancy, Ligue des Droits de l'Homme, 1993, 57-64.
Lessay, Jean. "Tom Paine: The Anti-Monarchist Who Tried to Save a King." *The Courier* 6 (June 1989):18.
McCusker, John J. "How Much is That in Real Money? A Historical Price Index for Use as a Deflator of Money Values in the Economy of the United States." *American Antiquarian Society Proceedings* 101 (October 1991):297-373.
McWilliams, Wilson Carey. "Civil Religion in the Age of Reason: Thomas Paine on Liberalism, Redemption, and Revolution." *Social Research* 54 (Autumn 1987):447-90.
Meng, John J. "The Constitutional Theories of Thomas Paine." *Review of Politics* 8 (July 1946):283-306.
————— . "French Diplomacy in Philadelphia, 1778-1779." *Catholic Historical Review* 24 (Apr. 1938):39-57.
Morton, Brian N. " 'Roderigue Hortalez' to the Secret Committee: an Unpublished French Policy Statement of 1777." *The French Review* 50 (May 1977):875-90.
Mustafi, Asoke. "Thomas Paine and Foreign Rule in India." *Calcutta Review* 158 (1962):204-06.
Newman, Stephen. "A Note on *Common Sense* and Christian Eschatology." *Political Theory* 6 (Feb. 1978):101-08.
Palmer, R.R. "Thomas Paine—Victim of the Rights of Man." *Pennsylvania Magazine of History and Biography* 46 (Apr. 1942):161-75.
Payne, Ernest A. "Thomas Paine: Preacher." Letter to the Editor, *Times Literary Supplement,* May 31, 1947:267.

Pendleton, Gayle Trusdel. "Towards a Bibliography of the *Reflections* and *Rights of Man* Controversy." *Bulletin of Research in the Humanities* 85 (Spring 1982):65-103.

Penniman, Howard. "Thomas Paine—Democrat." *American Political Science Review* 37 (Apr. 1943):244-62.

Peterson, Bob. "Education: The Spirit of Thomas Paine." *In These Times* 18 (Feb. 21, 1994):30.

Philp, Mark. "The Role of America in the 'Debate on France' 1791-95: Thomas Paine's Insertion." *Utilitas* 5 (Nov. 1993):221-37.

Popkin, Richard. "*The Age of Reason* versus *The Age of Revelation*. Two Critics of Tom Paine: David Levi and Elias Boudinot." In J.A. Leo Lemay, *Deism, Masonry, and the Enlightenment*. Newark: University of Delaware Press, 1987, 158-70.

Prochaska, Howard. "Thomas Paine's *The Age of Reason* Revisited." *Journal of the History of Ideas* 33 (Oct.-Dec. 1972):561-76.

Purdy, Strother B. "A Note on the Burke-Paine Controversy." *American Literature* 39 (Nov. 1969):373-75.

Rebérioux, Madeleine. "Anacharsis Cloots, The Other Citizen of the World." In Georges Kantin, ed., *Thomas Paine, Citoyen du monde*. Paris: Editions Créaphis, 1990:31-40.

Reed, William B. "Review of an Oration delivered at the Celebration . . . of the Birthday of Thomas Paine by John Alberger." *North American Review* (Apr. 1843):9-51.

Robbins, Caroline. "The Lifelong Education of Thomas Paine (1737-1809): Some Reflections upon His Acquaintance among Books." *Proceedings of the American Philosophical Society* 127 (June 1983):135-42.

Rothenberg, Molly Anne. "Parasiting America: The Radical Function of Homogeneity in Thomas Paine's Early Writings." *Eighteenth-Century Studies* 25 (Spring 1992):331-51.

Seaman, John W. "Thomas Paine: Ransom, Civil Peace, and the Natural Right to Welfare." *Political Theory* 16 (Feb. 1988):120-42.

Sizer, Theodore. "Tom Paine's Portrait." *Yale University Library Gazette* 30 (Apr. 1956):139-42.

Smith, C. Page. "The Attack on Fort Wilson." *Pennsylvania Magazine of History and Biography* 128 (Apr. 1954):177-88.

Smith, Frank. "The Authorship of 'An Occasional Letter on the Female Sex.'" *American Literature* 2 (Nov. 1930):277-80.

Thomas, Gordon K. "'And When America was Free:' Thomas Paine and the English Romantics." *The Charles Lamb Bulletin*, New Series, 69 (Jan. 1990):164-77.

_____ . "'Glorious Revolution:' Wordsworth, Terror, and Paine." *Wordsworth Circle* 21 (Winter 1990):3-9.

Thomson, Ann. "Thomas Paine and the United Irishmen." *Etudes Irlandaises* 16 (June 1991):109-19.

_____ . "Thomas Paine, Thomas Christie et la révolution française." In Bernard Vincent, ed., *Thomas Paine ou la République sans frontières*. Nancy: Presses Universitaires de Nancy, Ligue des Droits de l'Homme, 1993, 17-32.

Thompson, Tommy R. "The Resurrection of Thomas Paine in American Popular Magazines." *The Midwest Quarterly* 33 (Fall 1991):75-92.

Turner, John. "Burke, Paine, and the Nature of Language." In J. R. Watson, guest ed., *The Yearbook of English Studies: The French Revolution in English Literature and Art, Special Number*. London: Modern Humanities Research Association, 1989, 19:36-53.

Vincent, Bernard. "Les Américains à Paris sous la révolution: Mythes et réalités." In Bernard Vincent, ed., *Thomas Paine ou la République sans frontières*. Nancy: Presses Universitaires de Nancy, Ligue des Droits de l'Homme, 1993, 87-103.

Walzer, Michael. "The King's Trial and the Political Culture of the Revolution." In Colin Lucas, ed., *The French Revolution and the Creation of Modern Political Culture*, Two vols. Oxford: Pergamon Press, 1988, 2:183-92.

Wecter, Dixon. "Hero in Reverse." *Virginia Quarterly Review* 18 (Spring 1942):243-59.

Whale, John C. "The Limits of Paine's Literalism." In Kelvin Everest, ed., *Revolution in Writing: British Literary Responses to the French Revolution*. Buckingham: Open University Press, 1991, 121-37.

_____ . "Literal and Symbolic Representation: Burke, Paine, and the French Revolution." *History of European Ideas* 16 (Jan. 1993):343-49.

Wilson, Janet. "The Bank of North America and Pennsylvania Politics, 1781-1787." *Pennsylvania Magazine of History and Biography* 66 (Jan. 1942):3-28.

Wood, Marcus. "Thomas Spence and the Modes of Subversion." *Enlightenment and Dissent* 10 (1991):51-77.

Woodcock, Bruce. "Writing the Revolution: Aspects of Thomas Paine's Prose." *Prose Studies* 15 (Aug. 1992):171-86.

Chronology of the Life
of Thomas Paine

January 29, 1737	Thomas Paine born in Thetford, England, son of Joseph Pain and Frances Cocke.
1750	Apprentice in father's staymaker shop.
1753	Attempt to board privateer, stopped by father.
1756-63	Seven Years War between England and France (known as the French and Indian Wars in the American colonies).
1756	Paine serves on privateer *The King of Prussia*.
1757	Journeyman staymaker in London, attends scientific lectures.
1758	Journeyman staymaker in Dover.
April 1759	Master staymaker in Sandwich.
September 27, 1759	Marries Mary Lambert, moved to Margate.
1760	Accession of King George III.
	Death of Mary Lambert.
1761	Paine returns to Thetford to study for entrance examination of the Excise as a taxman.
December 1, 1762	Enters the Excise.
March 9, 1764	First Stamp Act introduced into Parliament.
August 8, 1764	Paine's first permanent excise position in Alford Out-Ride, Lincolnshire.
August 1765	Dismissed from the Excise Service for negligence.

1765	Master staymaker successively in Diss, Alford, and London.
March 22, 1765	First Stamp Act passed.
1765-67	Paine is schoolmaster in London and Kensington.
February 29, 1768	Reenters the Excise Service in Lewes.
March 5, 1770	Boston Massacre.
March 26, 1771	Paine marries Elizabeth Ollive of Lewes.
Winter 1772-73	Paine petitions Parliament for better conditions for excisemen in the *Case of the Officers of the Excise.*
1772	Paine in London and meets Benjamin Franklin and other scientists.
December 16, 1773	Boston Tea Party.
April 8, 1774	Paine dismissed from the Excise Service for the second time.
April 14, 1774	Bankruptcy of Paine's tobacco-grocery business, originally owned by father-in-law.
June 4, 1774	Separation of Paine from Elizabeth Ollive, Paine returns to London.
September 1774	Franklin letter of introduction for Paine to his son-in-law.
September 5, 1774	First Continental Congress convened in Philadelphia.
November 30, 1774	Paine arrives in America.
January 1775	Joins *Pennsylvania Magazine* as writer, then writer/editor.
January 4, 1775	"A Dialogue Between General Wolfe and General Gage in a Wood Near Boston."
February 1775	"Useful and Entertaining Hints."
March 1775	"Reflections on the Life and Death of Lord Clive."
March 1775	"Liberty Tree, A Song Written Early in the American Revolution."
March 1775	"The Death of General Wolfe," originally written in Lewes.
April 19, 1775	Battles of Lexington and Concord.
May 10, 1775	Second Continental Congress convenes.

June 1775	Battle of Bunker Hill, Boston.
June 15, 1775	George Washington named Commander-in-Chief of the Continental Army.
Autumn 1775	Paine resigns from the *Pennsylvania Magazine*.
January 10, 1776	*Common Sense*.
Spring 1776	"The Forester Papers" and "Four Letters on Interesting Subjects."
July 4, 1776	Declaration of Independence decreed by Continental Congress; Paine joins Continental Army as aide-de-camp to General Greene.
December 19, 1776	First paper in *American Crisis* series.
1777-83	Remainder of *Crisis* series in various newspapers appears.
April 1777	Paine appointed Secretary to the Committee for Foreign Affairs.
April 1778	American negotiations with France.
1778-79	Silas Deane Affair.
January 9, 1779	Paine resigns as Secretary to the Committee for Foreign Affairs.
April 1779	Paine clerks for Owen Biddle.
1779-80	Paine clerks for the Pennsylvania Assembly.
July 4, 1780	Paine is awarded honorary M.A. by the University of Pennsylvania.
December 30, 1780	*Public Good*.
January-August 1781	Paine's first voyage to France, with John Laurens, to secure French aid for the American cause.
March 2, 1781	Congress convenes for the first time under the Articles of Confederation.
October 1781	Cornwallis surrenders to Washington at Yorktown.
Feb. 1782-Dec. 1783	Agreement with George Washington, Robert Morris, and Robert Livingston to write for the American cause.
August 1782	*A Letter to Abbé Raynal*.
Winter 1782-83	*Six Letters to the Citizens of Rhode Island*.
September 3, 1783	Treaty of Paris between Britain and the United States.

April 1784	Paine given land in New Rochelle by state of New York for services to America during the war.
Summer/Fall 1784	Rewarded by Pennsylvania and Congress for services to America.
1785-87	Designs an iron bridge without piers.
1785-86	Controversy over the Bank of North America.
February 18, 1786	*Dissertations on Government, The Affairs of the Bank, and Paper Money.*
June 16, 1786	Death of Nathanael Greene.
April 26, 1787	Paine's second voyage to France, principally to sell his bridge design.
May 25, 1787	Constitutional Convention convenes in Philadelphia.
August 20, 1787	*Prospects on the Rubicon.*
August 30, 1787	Paine visits aging parents in England.
September 17, 1787	Draft of the new American Constitution finished.
December 1787	Paine visits Paris.
1787-88	*The Federalist Papers*, written by Madison, Hamilton, and Jay, appears in various New York newspapers.
June 1788	Paine returns to London.
June 21, 1788	American Constitution ratified with vote of New Hampshire.
Fall 1788	George Washington elected President of the United States, and the first federal government begins.
June 1789	Paine returns to Paris.
July 14, 1789	Royal Prison at the Bastille taken, beginning of the French Revolution.
July 20, 1789	Beginning of the "Great Fear" in France.
August 4, 1789	End of feudalism in France.
October 1789	Paine returns to London.
November 1789	Returns to Paris and stays until March 1790.
November 4, 1789	Richard Price delivers sermon, "A Discourse on the Love of Our Country" to the Revolution Society in London.

March 1790	Paine returns to London.
April 17, 1790	Death of Benjamin Franklin.
June 1790	Paine returns to Paris.
July 14, 1790	Federation Festival, Paris, to celebrate the first anniversary of the Revolution.
October 1790	Paine returns to London; United Irishmen formed.
November 1790	Burke's *Reflections on the Revolution in France*.
December 1790	Mary Wollstonecraft's *Vindication of the Rights of Men*.
February 22, 1791	Part One, *Rights of Man*. Paine returns to Paris.
March 7, 1791	Paine returns to London.
Early April 1791	Paine returns to Paris.
April 18, 1791	Failed attempt by Louis XVI and Marie Antoinette to escape.
April 19, 1791	Death of Richard Price.
May 7, 1791	James Mackintosh's *Vindiciae Gallicae*.
July 1791	Church and King Riots throughout England.
July 1, 1791	*A Republican Manifesto*; Paine helps found the Société Républicaine with Condorcet, Bonneville, Duchâtelet, and others.
July 13, 1791	Paine returns to London.
August 1791	"Address and Declaration of the Friends of Universal Peace and Liberty."
September 1791	Constitutional Monarchy is established in France.
December 15, 1791	Bill of Rights is ratified.
January 25, 1792	Formation of the London Corresponding Society.
February 1792	Gouverneur Morris is appointed American Minister to France.
February 16, 1792	Part Two, *Rights of Man*.
April 1792	War between France and Austria (soon joined by Prussia).
May 21, 1792	King's "Proclamation against Sedition, Subversion, and Riot."

June 8, 1792	Trial summons issued to Paine.
Summer 1792	*Letter Addressed to the Addressers on the Late Proclamation.*
July 17, 1792	Massacres in the Champ-de-Mars.
August 10, 1792	End of the French monarchy, beginning of the French republic.
August 26, 1792	French citizenship conferred on Paine and others.
September 1792	Austrian-Prussian invasion of France.
September 2-5, 1792	September Massacres.
September 6, 1792	Paine is elected to the French National Convention.
September 13, 1792	Paine returns to France to take seat in Convention, moves into White's Hotel de Philadelphie with other radicals, never returns to England.
September 21, 1792	French monarchy abolished; new French revolutionary calendar dates retroactively from this moment.
October 1792	Paine meets with Edward Fitzgerald to plan republican revolution in Ireland.
October 11, 1792	Paine appointed to help draft new constitution.
October 20, 1792	"An Essay for the Use of New Republicans in Their Opposition to Monarchy."
Fall 1792	Washington reelected President of the United States.
November 18, 1792	Banquet at White's Hotel sponsored by the Friends of the Rights of Man to celebrate the Revolution and call for revolutionary activity in England.
November 20, 1792	Formation in London of the anti-Painite Association for the Preservation of Liberty and Property.
December 18, 1792	Paine's trial in absentia in England and his conviction for seditious libel.
December 26, 1792	Beginning of Louis XVI's trial for treason.
January 1793	Arguments on behalf of the life of Louis XVI.
January 21, 1793	Execution of Louis XVI.
January 1793	Paine moves to St. Denis suburb of Paris.

February 1793	William Godwin's *Enquiry Concerning Political Justice.*
February 1, 1793	France, anticipating war with England, declares war first.
March 1793	Rise against reaction in the Vendée department of France.
March 1793	Desertion of General Dumouriez to the Austrians.
April 1793	Creation of the Committee for Public Safety.
April 1793	Jean Paul Marat and Jacques René Hébert lead campaign against food hoarding.
Spring 1793	French translation of *The Age of Reason* appears.
June 2, 1793	Convention suspends twenty-two Girondin deputies.
June 25, 1793	New French Constitution approved, then suspended.
July 13, 1793	Charlotte Corday murders Marat.
July 27, 1793	Robespierre elected to the Committee for Public Safety.
October 1793	Arrest and execution of Girondin leaders.
October 5, 1793	New revolutionary calendar begins.
October 16, 1793	Execution of Marie Antoinette.
October 31, 1793	Executions of Brissot, Gensonné, Vergniaud.
Fall 1793-Summer 94	Height of the Terror.
December 28, 1793	Paine incarcerated in the Luxembourg Prison.
January 27, 1794	Americans resident in Paris unsuccessfully plead for Paine's release.
1794	Part One, *The Age of Reason.*
March 1794	Suicide of Condorcet.
April 5, 1794	Execution of Danton.
May 1794	Treason trials in London, suspension of habeas corpus.
July 27, 1794	Fall of Robespierre and St. Just, the Terror ends.
July 28, 1794	Executions of Robespierre and Saint-Just.

September 1794	James Monroe succeeds Morris as the American Minister in Paris.
November 4, 1794	Paine is released from the Luxembourg Prison.
1794-96	Paine resides with the Monroes.
December 7, 1794	Reelected to the National Convention.
December 1794	Jay Treaty between the United States and England.
1795	Constitution of 1795 and creation of the Directory.
July 1795	*Dissertation on First Principles of Government.*
July 7, 1795	"The Constitution of 1795."
Fall 1795	Part Two, *The Age of Reason.*
Fall 1796	John Adams elected President of the United States.
April 8, 1796	*Decline and Fall of the English System of Finance.*
July 30, 1796	*Letter to George Washington.*
November 1796	Monroe is recalled to Washington and replaced by Charles Cotesworth Pinckney.
1797-1802	Paine resides with the Bonnevilles.
July 9, 1797	Death of Edmund Burke.
1797	*Agrarian Justice* (written 1795-96).
September 1797	Prosecution of *The Age of Reason.*
September 4, 1797	Napoleon's coup d'état.
October 1797	*The Eighteenth Fructidor.*
1797-98	XYZ Affair.
1798	Alien and Sedition Acts passed by Congress.
May-October 1798	Insurrections in Ireland.
July 1799	London Corresponding Society banned in England.
November 9, 1799	Napoleon becomes First Consul.
December 14, 1799	Death of Washington.
1800	*Compact Maritime*, published in English in Washington on February 11, 1801.

Fall 1800	Thomas Jefferson elected President of the United States.
1802-05	Series of "Letters To the Citizens of the United States."
September 2, 1802	Paine departs France for the United States.
November 1802	President Jefferson welcomes Paine at the new presidential mansion.
November 1802	Marguerite de Bonneville and three sons arrive to live with Paine.
February 1803	Paine returns to New York via Philadelphia and Bordentown.
March 1803	Banquets and festivities in Paine's honor in New York.
April 30, 1803	Louisiana Purchase agreement signed.
June 1803	"The Construction of Iron Bridges."
October 2, 1803	Death of Samuel Adams.
1804	*Prospect Papers.*
February 6, 1804	Death of Joseph Priestley in Northumberland, Pennsylvania.
1805	"Origin of Freemasonry," first published 1818.
August 1805	*On Constitutional Reform.*
January 1, 1806	Revolutionary Calendar abolished in France.
May 8,1806	Robert Morris dies in poverty.
1807	*Examination of the Passages in the New Testament.*
June 8, 1809	Paine dies, age 72, in New York City and is buried on his New Rochelle farm.
1810	Extracts from *Reply to the Bishop of Llandoff*, Part Three of *The Age of Reason*, published posthumously.
November 16, 1816	Death of Gouverneur Morris.
July 4, 1826	Deaths of Thomas Jefferson and John Adams.
July 4, 1831	Death of James Monroe.
May 20, 1834	Death of Lafayette.
June 28, 1836	Death of James Madison.

Index

ist: 2, 44, 84, 160; deism of: 325-29, 338-44, 440, 446 nt.8; as non-philosophical: 1-2; as preacher: as inventor: 97, 150, 152, 157, 162-63, 257, 425-27; memory: 387-89; Headstrong Club: 31-32 use of pseudonyms: 43-44, 414; as editor and writer of the *Pennsylvania Magazine*: 44-56; and the Pennsylvania Constitution of 1776: 93, 109-10, 120, 163, 176-77; names the United States of America: 94; as commissioner to Indian tribes in Easton: 94; as Secretary of the Committee for Foreign Affairs: 95-18; as clerk for Owen Biddle: 121-24; as clerk of the Pennsylvania Assembly: 124-28; awarded an honorary master's degree from the University of Pennsylvania: 125; rejection by the American Philosophical Society: 128; first visit to France: 131-36; public grants from New York and Pennsylvania: 154-55; admission to the American Philosophical Society: 157-58; controversy over the Bank of North America: 163-75; removal to France: 181-82; patent on his bridge granted: 193; joins Republican Society: 234-37; election to French National Convention: 247, 266-67; service on the Convention:

279-83, 299-300; member of the British Club: 283-88; London trial in absentia: 288-91; house burns in New Rochelle: 304; testifies for Miranda: 305; incarceration in the Luxembourg: 313-14; illness in the Luxembourg: 322-23; in prison after Terror: 329-31; release from prison: 331; return to the Convention: 331-32; prosecuted by Erskine: 342-43; residing with the Monroes: 331-46; residing with the Bonnevilles: 371-89; at the Irish Coffee House: 373-74; plans to invade England: 374-75, 376-77, 407; plans to invade Ireland: 375; admired by Napoleon: 375, 376; the Social Circle: 8-9, 378-83; returns to the United States: 384-87; in Baltimore: 393-94; worries over Louisiana: 399-400, 405-07, 417-19; on a constitution for Connecticut: 412, 414-15; life in New Rochelle: 417; residing with Carver: 421, 427; sells Bordentown house: 424; last illnesses: 424, 427, 434; seeks compensation from the United States: 425; denied voter registration in New York: 426; Mrs. Palmer: 427; residing with Jarvis: 428; residing with Hitt: 428; residing with Mrs. Ryder: 434; last will, death, and bur-

These are the times that try men's souls. The summer soldier and the sunshine patriot will, in this crisis, shrink from the service of their country; but he that stands it now deserves the love and thanks of man and woman. Tyranny, like hell, is not easily conquered; yet we have this consolation with us, that the harder the conflict, the more glorious the triumph. What we obtain too cheap, we esteem too lightly: it is dearness only that gives everything its value. Heaven knows how to put a proper price upon its goods; and it would be strange indeed if so celestial an article as Freedom should not be highly rated. Britain, with an army to enforce her tyranny, has declared that she has a right (not only to tax) but "to bind us in all cases whatsoever," and if being bound in that manner is not slavery, then is there no such a thing as slavery upon earth. Even the expression is impious; for so unlimited a power can only belong to God.

— Thomas Paine, *American Crisis,*
Number One, December 23, 1776

CANADA

NOVA SCOTIA

L. Ontario

NEW ENGLAND

Lake Erie

Boston

MASSACHUSETTS

PENNSYLVANIA

New York

MARYLAND

Philadelphia

Baltimore

VIRGINIA

Atl

Oc

GEORGIA

FLORIDA

GULF OF MEXICO

The
VOYAGES
of
THOMAS
PAINE